RESEARCH ADVANCES IN ALCOHOL AND DRUG PROBLEMS

Volume Three

ADVISORY PANEL

RESEARCH ADVANCES IN ALCOHOL AND DRUG PROBLEMS

Volume Three

Edited by

ROBERT J. GIBBINS

YEDY ISRAEL (*Executive Editor*)

HAROLD KALANT

ROBERT E. POPHAM

WOLFGANG SCHMIDT

REGINALD G. SMART

Addiction Research Foundation
and University of Toronto, Toronto

A WILEY MEDICAL PUBLICATION

JOHN WILEY & SONS, New York • London • Sydney • Toronto

Library of Congress Catalog Card Number: 73-18088

ISBN 0-471-29736-4

Printed in the United States of America

10 9 8 7 6 5 4 3 2 1

CONTRIBUTORS

JOHN C. BALL, *Department of Psychiatry, Temple University Medical Center, Philadelphia, Pennsylvania*

RUTH COOPERSTOCK, *Addiction Research Foundation, Toronto, Ontario, Canada*

EVERETT H. ELLINWOOD, JR., *Behavioral Neuropharmacology Section, Department of Psychiatry, Duke University Medical Center, Durham, North Carolina*

R. M. GILBERT, *Addiction Research Foundation, Toronto, Ontario, Canada*

HAROLD KALANT, *Addiction Research Foundation and University of Toronto, Toronto, Ontario, Canada*

ORIANA JOSSEAU KALANT, *Addiction Research Foundation, Toronto, Ontario, Canada*

GLORIA K. LITMAN, *Addiction Research Unit, Institute of Psychiatry, The Maudsley Hospital, London, England*

HERBERT MOSKOWITZ, *University of California at Los Angeles and California State University, Los Angeles, California*

E. MANSELL PATTISON, *Department of Psychiatry and Human Behavior, University of California, Irvine, California and Education Division, Orange County Department of Mental Health, California*

WILLIAM M. PETRIE, *National Institute of Mental Health, Rockville, Maryland*

M. A. H. RUSSELL, *Addiction Research Unit, Institute of Psychiatry, The Maudsley Hospital, London, England*

PEKKA SULKUNEN, *Finnish Foundation for Alcohol Studies and Institute of Sociology, University of Helsinki, Finland*

PREFACE

During the last decade most parts of the world have experienced a growing interest in problems associated with the nonmedical use of drugs—specifically drug dependence. In part, this heightened awareness has corresponded to a real growth in the extent, diversity, and social impact of the use of drugs in many societies. Public concern, both reflected in and enhanced by the mass media of communication, has led to greater demands on experts of all types for information about the causes and consequences of drug use and about methods of coping with the perceived problems.

As a result, the amount of research and writing on the subject of drug problems has increased greatly. Thus as many clinical and scientific papers on the amphetamines have appeared since 1965 as were published from 1929 to 1965. This explosive growth of the scientific and clinical literature is not unique to the area of drug research. There is, however, an added difficulty—this field is an interdisciplinary one. It is almost a platitude to point out that the field of drug problems spans the entire range of investigation in social, behavioral, basic biological, and clinical disciplines. This means that the person who wishes to keep well informed about drug problems faces the difficulty of an expanding literature multiplied manyfold.

It is therefore impossible for one individual to keep up to date with all the relevant literature pertaining to the diverse aspects of the "drug problem." There is a particularly acute need in this field for critical reviews that assess the current developments. There are already a number of annual review publications, which have a well-established place in the continuing education of scientists. In general, however, they confine their attention to individual disciplines, such as biochemistry, physiology, psychology, medicine, and other traditionally defined fields of study. Many researchers and practicing professionals have felt a need for a single publication that would review the many aspects contributing to our understanding of drug use and drug problems. The present series, beginning with this volume, is intended to fill such a need.

Although one volume is to be published annually, the series is not intended to be an "annual review" in the usual sense. The aim is not to cover all the work reported during the preceding year in relation to a fixed selection of themes or disciplines. Rather, it is to present each year a number of critically evaluative papers dealing with selected topics in which enough recent progress has been made to warrant a review, or in which debate or confusion are such as to require an analysis and clarification of concepts. Consequently it is anticipated that a different selection of topics will be covered each year. Each paper will discuss the work appearing during a period of several years, the length of the period being determined by the relevance and amount of the material. The frequency with which any one topic is reexamined in later years will depend on the rate of progress of research on that topic.

Because of the multidisciplinary nature of problems of drug use and dependence, the papers published in each volume will be drawn from several disciplines or areas of research. It is even conceivable that an entire volume might be devoted to a particular problem, with individual reviews and papers examining various aspects of it. The desirability of such an approach will undoubtedly be easier to assess as the series evolves.

The composition of the editorial board and the international advisory board reflects these objectives of the series. The editors are members of the senior scientific staff of the Addiction Research Foundation of Ontario. Their own areas of special interest include the fields of biochemistry, pharmacology, anthropology, experimental and clinical psychology, sociology, and jurisprudence. The members of the international advisory panel are well known in this field. Their interests range over the relevant disciplines, and, they represent seven countries in Europe, North and South America, and Australia. On the basis of their knowledge of the relevant fields, and their reading of the literature in various languages, they propose to the editors each year a list of the subjects that are most appropriate for review, as well as the names of investigators in different parts of the world who might be best qualified to write the reviews. Obviously no publication can guarantee that it will fill the needs of all its readers with respect to sorting out fact from conjecture, the important from the trivial, or the permanent from the transitory. Nevertheless, we hope that this series will provide a lead in the desired direction and will stimulate the type of interdisciplinary inquiry that is widely advocated but seldom practiced. To this end the editorial board and the advisory panel will be happy to consider suggestions submitted by readers for reviews on subjects that they would like to see covered in future issues of the series.

The Editors

(Preface to volume 1)
July 1973
Toronto, Canada

It is with deep regret that the Editors record the premature death of their friend and colleague, Robert J. Gibbins, at Kingston, Ontario, on March 17, 1976. Dr. Gibbins was one of the original members of the Research Division of the Addiction Research Foundation of Ontario. He made major research contributions in such varied fields as the epidemiology of alcoholism, experimental psychological studies of alcohol and barbiturate tolerance, street drug analysis, and field studies of "speed" users. He was the author of the first Brookside Monograph, *Chronic Alcoholism and Alcohol Addiction,* published in 1953.

Friends in numerous centers of addiction studies in Canada and the United States join in this expression of tribute to Robert Gibbins, for his qualities as a person, a colleague, and a pioneer in alcoholism research.

CONTENTS

RESEARCH ADVANCES IN ALCOHOL AND DRUG PROBLEMS

Volume Three

CHAPTER ONE

TOBACCO SMOKING AND NICOTINE DEPENDENCE

M. A. H. RUSSELL, *Addiction Research Unit, Institute of Psychiatry, The Maudsley Hospital, London, England*

He who has smoked will smoke—
Jean Cocteau: Opium (1930)

1. INTRODUCTION

"Cigarette-smoking is probably the most addictive and dependence-producing form of object-specific self-administered gratification known to man" (118). This simply means that, throughout history, no other single biologically unnecessary object has meant so much to so many people who, after so few initiating experiences, have needed to have it so often, so regularly, and for so many years, despite trying so hard to do without it; and for which there is no other adequate substitute. Stated plainly, tobacco smoking is a form of drug dependence different but no less strong than that of other addictive drugs (116, 117).

Most smokers would like to give up, but find they cannot (97, 117). Only 2% are able to limit themselves to occasional smoking; once or twice a week or less. The majority are regular, dependent smokers who seldom go more than an hour or two without smoking, and over 60% report that, when they have no cigarettes, they frequently feel a craving for one (97). The casual smoking of a few cigarettes during adolescence is almost inevitably followed by escalation to regular dependent smoking which then, in the majority, continues until middle age or beyond (97, 117). Cocteau's dictum, "He who has smoked will smoke," is as pertinent to tobacco smoking now as it was to the smoking of opium in his time.

In this chapter, evidence is presented for attributing to nicotine the central role in the generation of cigarette dependence. The absorption, metabolism, excretion, and pharmacologic effects of nicotine are considered, with the emphasis on aspects relevant to its dependence-producing potency. We suggest that cigarette-smoking is particularly addictive because it delivers nicotine to the brain in the form of a puff-by-puff series of high-nicotine boli. This chapter presents a selective view, rather than a comprehensive review.

2. THE ROLE OF NICOTINE IN SMOKING

Nicotine is the one alkaloid present in tobacco and tobacco smoke that is rapidly absorbed and distributed throughout the body, including the brain, in sufficient amounts to produce a striking array of pharmacologic effects both centrally and peripherally. It is, in other words, a powerful drug. Surprisingly, this is largely overlooked or paid but passing comment by many behavioral scientists and health educators who grapple with and continue to be frustrated by their inability to understand or deal with the smoking problem. The role of the psychosocial determinants is overemphasized. Books and conferences devoted to the subject barely mention nicotine (18, 96, 114, 150). The bulk of the enormous research effort expended on the smoking habit over the past decade has focused too narrowly on the psychosocial aspects, and the money spent on it has in consequence been largely wasted. The voices have been relatively few who attribute to nicotine the central role in the determination of smoking behavior (4, 80, 117).

Historical Evidence

Throughout its history, tobacco use has fluctuated between chewing, snuffing, and smoking, but no population has dispensed with one form of tobacco use without replacing it with another. The only time the British gave up smoking was in the eighteenth century, when they switched to snuffing for almost a hundred years. Rather than any other consituent of tobacco smoke, the common factor here is nicotine, which is absorbed through the lungs in the case of cigarette smoking, the buccal mucosa in the case of chewing tobacco, and the nasal mucosa in the case of snuffing.

Unlike most other addictive drugs, tobacco has never been used as a substance for ingestion. It has never been eaten like opium or cannabis, nor used as a beverage like alcohol and caffeine. This is doubtless because, with absorption via the gut into the portal system, most of the nicotine, in its first passage through the liver, would be metabolized to cotinine (see below), which is psychopharmacologically inert. With absorption through the lungs or the nasal and buccal mucosae, however, the liver is bypassed, allowing the nicotine to get to the brain and other parts of the body in the active form. Thus, historical evidence shows that tobacco has been used only in ways which enable nicotine to exert a pharmacologic effect.

Finally, few would suggest that cannabis and opium are smoked primarily for the flavor, the tar, or the psychological image they might provide. Smoking as a habit has never been practiced in the absence of a pharmacologically active alkaloid. It is, therefore, most unlikely that tobacco would be smoked were it not for the nicotine. There is no other plant substitute because no other plant contains nicotine.

Theoretical Background

Very few experimental studies have specifically examined the role of nicotine as a determinant or crucial reinforcer of smoking behavior. The evidence to date strongly supports a central role for nicotine, but this is not yet conclusive. To prove this, it would be necessary to show, on one hand, that cigarettes are unacceptable if they are nicotinefree, though identical to popular brands in every other way (tar yield, draw resistance, flavor, and burning characteristics, etc.); and on the other hand, that nicotine alone can substitute for tobacco. These ideal experiments have not been possible: (*a*) because it is difficult to remove nicotine from tobacco smoke without altering the other characteristics (tar and nicotine yields correlate >0.95, (121); and (*b*) because it is difficult to administer nicotine as efficiently as occurs with the inhalation of tobacco smoke. One way, thus far not achieved, would be to produce an aerosol with particles as small as in smoke to enable penetration into the lung alveoli. Another method is technically more feasible but ethically suspect; namely, pulsed injections of nicotine via an arterial cannula, having its tip as high as the aortic valve.

Because of these difficulties, experimenters have had to limit themselves to the more modest goal of seeking evidence of what might be called a "nicotine-titration effect." This postulates that each smoker will smoke to obtain a fairly constant, individually characteristic nicotine level sufficient to produce the particular pattern of pharmacologic effects that he desires or requires. It postulates some kind of interoceptive discriminative control of nicotine intake. Evidence for this has been sought by looking for changes in smoking patterns in response to: (*a*) variations in nicotine yield of cigarettes; (*b*) nicotine administration by injection, chewing gum, or aerosol; (*c*) altering nicotine excretion by inducing changes in urinary pH; (*d*) pharmacologic blockade of nicotine actions. The relative merits and defects of these approaches are discussed below. The changes in smoking pattern may also be assessed in a number of ways, such as: crude consumption of cigarettes, butt length, weight of tobacco burned, puff analysis (rate, volume, etc.), butt analysis for nicotine, blood COHb changes, and blood and urinary nicotine levels. Again, many of these measures have limitations, some of which will be discussed. Since many of the defects and limitations of these approaches would tend to mask rather than enhance the postulated effect, any positive findings are especially significant. Moreover, positive findings would seem to be even more meaningful, in that they would have had to overcome the masking effects of other processes such as well-established secondary reinforcement and the functional autonomy of a long-established habit.

Experimental Evidence

Turning to actual experiments, most smokers are simply not satisfied, and may even suffer withdrawal symptoms after "blind" substitution of low-nicotine cigarettes (52, 89). The study by Finnegan et al. (52) is especially interesting for a number of reasons, and, in one respect, it is unique. Since the experimental cigarettes were prepared by using a tobacco naturally low in nicotine in order to produce a low-nicotine cigarette (0.34 mg) and then adding nicotine to this tobacco to produce a cigarette with higher yield (1.96 mg; about average for cigarettes in 1945), it can be assumed that the tar yield and the draw resistance of the two brands were similar, and that the smokers' responses may be attributed solely to the difference in nicotine yield. The important findings have been abstracted and condensed in Table 1. It will be seen that the smokers who increased their consumption on switching to the low-nicotine cigarettes did not suffer withdrawal symptoms, but that the smokers who did not increase consumption suffered severe withdrawal symptoms which persisted throughout the month they were smoking the low-nicotine cigarettes. The authors did not do a statistical analysis, but there is little doubt that, when this is done, these differences in consumption will prove to be significant. This is strong evidence that half the smokers modified their smoking to regulate their nicotine intake, and that those who did not maintain their nicotine intake suffered withdrawal symptoms as a consequence. It is surprising that Jarvik (80), in his appraisal of this study, concluded that it showed that smokers "did not titrate the number of cigarettes smoked."

That the compensatory increase in consumption of low-nicotine cigarettes was relatively small in the study of Finnegan et al. (52) does not negate the titration hypothesis, for the number of cigarettes smoked is but one rather crude index of how much nicotine is taken in. Two independent studies (9, 56) have clearly shown that smokers unconsciously modify their puff-rate to regulate their nicotine intake. When smoking a high-nicotine cigarette they puff less frequently, and when smoking a low-nicotine

TABLE 1 EFFECT OF NICOTINE YIELD ON CIGARETTE CONSUMPTION

	Average Daily Cigarette Consumption per group			
Subject Group	Usual Brand	1.96 mg Nicotine	0.34 mg Nicotine	1.96 mg Nicotine
No withdrawal symptoms (n = 6)	26.9	26.6	30.9	26.8
Transient mild withdrawal symptoms (n = 6)	22.4	22.0	26.5	23.9
Transient moderate withdrawal symptoms (n = 3)	23.6	28.3	28.6	27.6
Severe withdrawal symptoms persisting for one month (n = 9)	25.0	24.7	24.6	24.9

Abstracted from Finnegan et al. (1945). The nicotine yield of the subjects' usual brand was not given but an average yield for cigarettes of that period would have been around 2.0 mg. The experimental cigarettes were made from tobacco naturally low in nicotine (i.e., 0.34-mg yield), but nicotine was added to this tobacco to provide the cigarettes with the higher yield (1.96 mg). The order of administration was as shown from left to right. The exact period on each brand was not clearly stated but was about four weeks on the usual and low nicotine brands and two weeks for each period on the 1.96 mg brand.

Withdrawal symptoms on switching to the low nicotine cigarettes were graded as follows: mild, vague lack of satisfaction initially; moderate, missed their usual brand but eventually adapted to the low nicotine cigarettes; severe, missed their usual brand even after one month and experienced irritability, poor concentration and/or hungerlike feelings.

cigarette they increase their puff-rate, thus compensating for the low-nicotine yield. That the higher puff-rate caused an increase in nicotine intake, into the mouth at least, was confirmed by the butt analysis for nicotine which was done in one of these studies (9).

Butt nicotine analysis is used as an index of the amount of nicotine drawn into the mouth. This is calculated on the basis of the fairly constant relationship between the amount of nicotine drawn through a filter and the amount deposited in it. Some error arises, as the proportion deposited varies also with the rate at which the smoke is sucked through the filter.

Frith's (56) and Ashton and Watson's (9) studies were done in an experimental room with observations made on the smoking of single cigarettes.

Turner et al. (142) have confirmed the titration effect in subjects smoking under natural conditions. There were changes in the number of cigarettes smoked per day and in the butt nicotine levels on switching to low-nicotine cigarettes, showing that the smokers compensated for a lower nicotine yield by smoking more cigarettes and puffing them harder.

The results of our own studies (121, 122) are shown in Tables 2 and 3. Our subjects were studied before and after a 5-h period spent smoking under natural conditions at work. We went to their place of work to collect the blood samples. It will be seen that there was a 38% decrease in consumption on switching from the usual to the high-nicotine brand ($p < 0.01$). The 17% increase in the number of low-nicotine cigarettes smoked was not statistically significant. This was probably because the low-nicotine brand chosen was too extreme. It would have been necessary to smoke five or more of them at the same time to obtain an adequate nicotine intake. Furthermore, they were aversive in having an excessively high draw resistance. Another defect of our study and that of Turner et al. (142) was that standard brands of cigarette were used, so that subjects were aware of the differences in nicotine yield.

A new departure in our study was the use of carbon monoxide (CO) absorption as an index of inhalation. CO is not absorbed buccally, so that any increase in carboxyhemoglobin (COHb) is proportional to the degree of inhalation. On switching to high-nicotine cigarettes, our subjects took so much less smoke into their lungs that their COHb levels actually decreased, instead of increasing as on their usual brand ($p < 0.01$). The COHb decrease on the low-nicotine cigarettes was attributable to their low CO yield. We were unable to obtain brands having different nicotine yields, but the same CO yield. Ashton and Telford (8) did obtain such cigarettes, and they found that the absorption of CO was inversely proportional to the nicotine yield. This strongly suggests that the smokers were titrating the amount of nicotine they inhaled.

To validate the nicotine-titration hypothesis, counting cigarettes and puffs and measuring butt nicotine and blood COHb are no more than substitutes for inferring blood nicotine levels. This most obvious index of nicotine intake has not been used before because of the technical problem of measuring nicotine in the blood. We have managed to overcome this, and Tables 2 and 3, and Figure 1 show the similarity of the average blood nicotine level after smoking medium and high-nicotine cigarettes. However, the means conceal a degree of individual variation that can be clearly seen in Table 3 and Figure 1. Smoking their usual brands some subjects increase their nicotine levels during the day, while others do not. Again, some individuals increase their level on switching to the high-nicotine brand, but others do not. The consistency of an individual's pattern in this respect must await

TABLE 2 RELATION OF NICOTINE YIELD TO CIGARETTE CONSUMPTION AND CARBON MONOXIDE AND NICOTINE INTAKE. (MEANS OF TEN SUBJECTS)

Brand of Cigarette	Mean Nicotine Yield (mg)	Mean Carbon Monoxide Yield (mg)	Mean number smoked in 5-hr test period	Weight smoked in 5-hr test period (gm)	Mean COHb change in 5-hr test period (%)	Plasma Nicotine after 5-hr test period (ng/ml)
Usual	1.34	17.2	10.7	6.0	+1.79	30.1
Low nicotine	0.14	5.0	12.5	6.5	−0.34	8.5
High nicotine	3.2	16.7	6.7	4.2	−1.04	29.2

Abstracted from Russell et al. (121, 122). The mean CO yields are derived from Russell et al. (123). The order of taking the high and low nicotine cigarettes was balanced within the group. The data for the usual brand are the means of two 5-hr test periods. COHb percent (%) is a unit of measure not a percent change.

TABLE 3 CIGARETTE CONSUMPTION AND BLOOD NICOTINE LEVELS OF SEDENTARY WORKERS BEFORE AND AFTER 5 HR OF SMOKING HIGH-NICOTINE, LOW-NICOTINE, AND USUAL CIGARETTES (122)

		Usual Cigarettes Smoked		Number of Cigarettes Smoked over 5 hr			Blood Nicotine (nmol/l)			
								Afternoon Levels 5 hr Later		
Case No.	Age and Sex	Nicotine Yield (mg)	No./Day	Usual[a] Brand	High Nicotine	Low Nicotine	Initial Midmorning Level (Mean ± S.E. of Mean)[b]	Usual Brand*	High Nicotine	Low Nicotine
1	25 M	1.2	25	11.0	8	9	181.9 ± 17.9	180.6	326.8	55.5
2	19 M	1.3	30	8.5	7	15	174.5 ± 17.9	258.9	243.5	77.1
3	20 F	1.3	17	5.0	4	8	135.6 ± 3.7	146.7	117.1	52.4
4	23 F	1.4	35	14.0	9	13	129.5 ± 15.4	129.5	200.4	40.1
5	22 F	1.3	30	17.5	5	17	101.7 ± 19.1	157.2	52.4	39.0
6	25 M	1.4	35	12.0	6	15	106.7 ± 7.4	258.9	80.1	71.0
7	63 M	1.6	18	10.5	7	14	231.2 ± 23.4	286.7	280.5	74.0
8	26 F	1.5	35	8.5	8	15	108.5 ± 9.9	123.3	160.3	43.2
9	48 F	1.2	25	7.5	5	10	236.7 ± 21.6	215.8	221.9	49.3
10	29 F	1.2	22	12.0	8	9	95.6 ± 10.5	98.6	114.1	24.7
Mean ± S.D.		1.34 ± 0.13	27.2 ± 6.86	10.7 ± 3.5	6.7 ± 1.6	12.5 ± 3.2	150.4 ± 54.3	185.6 ± 66.0	180.0 ± 90.0	52.4 ± 17.3

[a] Mean of values on two different days.
[b] Mean of levels on four different mornings after smokers smoked their usual brand in their usual way.
Conversion: SI to Traditional Units—Nicotine: 10 nmol/l = 1.62 ng/ml.

further study. The fall in nicotine levels after switching to the low-nicotine brand was very consistent, but the yield of this brand was unfortunately too low to test the titration hypothesis. To have obtained the same level on these cigarettes would have been impossible. The study will have to be repeated using low-nicotine cigarettes with a yield around 0.5 to 0.8 mg.

The midmorning plasma nicotine levels obtained on four different mornings after subjects had smoked their usual cigarettes were fairly consistent within subjects (note small standard errors in Table 3). There was, however, marked variation between smokers ($p < 0.001$), and the individual levels ranged from 96 to 237 nmol/liter. It is of interest that the nicotine level obtained by the individual smoker bore no relation to his usual cigarette consumption ($r = -0.33$ n.s.) or to the nicotine yield of the cigarettes he smoked ($r = -0.04$). This shows that both cigarette consumption and nicotine yield are poor indices of nicotine intake, even among regular smokers who all claim to inhale deeply.

There are two studies which have been interpreted by their authors and are usually cited as disproving the nicotine-titration hypothesis. While it must be admitted that they do not support it, it is possible to explain their failure to do so. In the first (145), a national sample of 1466 American cigarette smokers who had been interviewed in 1964 were reinterviewed in 1966. Analysis of the changes in tar yield (and hence nicotine yield with which it is correlated) and their daily consumption of cigarettes did not

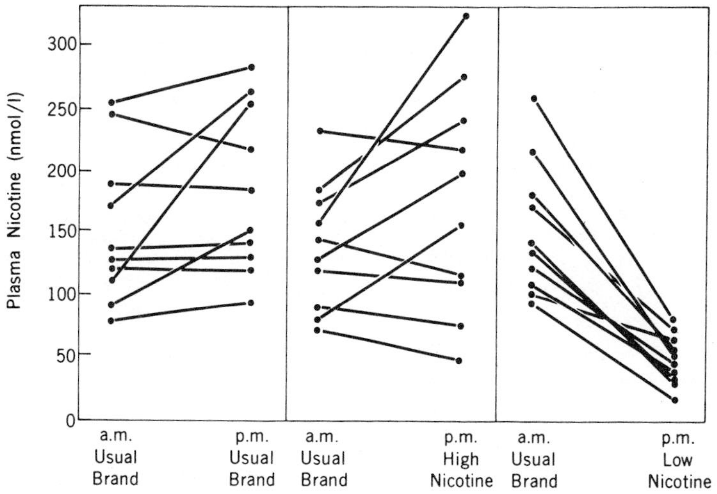

Fig. 1. Changes in plasma nicotine levels after five hours of smoking usual, high nicotine, and low nicotine cigarettes. Morning and afternoon levels on usual brand are means of two days' values. (Nicotine 10 nmol/1 = 1.62 ng/ml); (From Russell et al., ref (122).

reveal a relationship. In particular, there was no tendency for those who switched to cigarettes with a lower tar yield to increase consumption. It is possible that those smokers who switched to cigarettes with low nicotine yields were the ones with lower nicotine requirements. Also, they may have compensated in other ways, such as taking more puffs or inhaling more deeply.

The other study, by Goldfarb and Jarvik (63), is interesting. Eighteen subjects spent a week smoking cigarettes which had been cut to half the original length and another week smoking only the distal half of each cigarette which had a red line drawn around the halfway mark. Although the average number of these half-cigarettes smoked per day by the group as a whole was not significantly higher than on the control weeks with whole cigarettes, 12 of the subjects did increase the number of lined cigarettes smoked by an average of five per day, and the number of cut cigarettes by an average of seven per day, suggesting that these 12 subjects were trying to compensate. It is probable that further compensation was also achieved by deeper inhalation. It would be most interesting to repeat this experiment with measurement of blood nicotine levels.

Cherry and Forbes (31), found that on the basis of butt analysis of nicotine, a "majority" of smokers took in less nicotine when smoking a low-nicotine brand (0.77 mg) than on a brand delivering 1.35 mg nicotine. There were, however, a "minority" of smokers who titrated their nicotine and took in equal amounts of nicotine from both brands. Unfortunately, this important finding is vaguely reported, and many of the experimental details are not given.

On balance, the evidence from this class of experiment suggests that some smokers tend to modify their smoking pattern to regulate their nicotine intake. However, since tar and nicotine yields correlate by 0.95 or more, we cannot be sure that the smokers are titrating their nicotine intake, rather than their tar intake. The early study of Finnegan et al. (52) is the only one so far which has overcome this obstacle. Jarvik's group (64) attempted to do so by comparing the consumption (cigarettes per day) of lettuce leaf cigarettes with and without added nicotine (yields: 0, 1.26, and 2.25 mg nicotine/cigarette). The nasty taste of the lettuce smoke seems to have swamped all other effects, causing the subjects to smoke fewer experimental cigarettes than their usual brand, whatever the nicotine yield.

The first study of nicotine injections as a substitute for smoking was by Johnston (83). He injected smoking doses of nicotine hypodermically and intravenously into 35 volunteers. He reported that nonsmokers found it unpleasant, but "smokers almost invariably thought the sensation pleasant and, given an adequate dose, were disinclined to smoke for some time thereafter." The nicotine injections also relieved the withdrawal cravings of smokers deprived of tobacco. The nicotine administration was neither "blind" nor controlled, but this study was a landmark and there was no attempt at replication for over 20 years.

The next experiment of this type was the classic study of Lucchesi et al. (94). Five subjects spent at least nine 6-h sessions in an experimental ward. They were instructed to smoke as they felt inclined, and they were unaware that their smoking behavior was being monitored, believing that the object of the experiment was the recording of various physiologic measures such as heart rate. Throughout each session, they received a continuous intravenous saline infusion. When nicotine was added to the infusion in amounts up to 4 mg/hr, there was a 27% reduction in the number of cigarettes smoked from an average of 10 to 7.3 per session. This difference, though small, was highly significant ($p < 0.001$). When receiving nicotine intravenously, the subjects also took fewer puffs and discarded their cigarettes earlier. These findings have been used both to support and to reject the nicotine-titration hypothesis. It undoubtedly confirms that intravenous nicotine suppresses spontaneous smoking behavior, but the amount of suppression was small in relation to the dose of nicotine given. However, there may have been a reduction in the degree of inhalation which would have gone undetected. More important, though, is the fact that slow infusion is no substitute for inhaled smoking (see below). With inhaled cigarette smoking, nicotine is absorbed and circulated in a series of puff-by-puff boli of relatively high concentrations of nicotine. If this is what the cigarette smoker seeks, Lucchesi and his colleagues were not providing it intravenously.

We have recently sought to simulate cigarette smoking more closely by administering the nicotine intravenously as 10 rapid 100 μg doses given at a rate of 1/min to mimic 10 puffs of a cigarette. The effect of this on subjects' smoking behavior was minimal. Subjects continued to puff at their cigarettes while the injections were in progress. The analysis of this study is not yet completed. The result would seem to seriously challenge the role of nicotine as the main reinforcer of smoking. However, some pilot work we are presently undertaking suggests that blood nicotine levels are lower after intravenous injection than after smoking. Thus, 1.0 mg nicotine base intravenously will not produce as high a blood nicotine level as smoking a cigarette which yields 1.0 mg nicotine. This conflicts with the animal studies (4, 141) mentioned below, which show absorption of nicotine through the lungs to be less efficient than injection into the femoral vein or pulmonary artery. Injection into arm veins of humans possibly allows more time for bolus dispersion than in these animal studies.

It is remarkable that, besides the three studies described no other reference could be found in the literature to the effect of intravenous nicotine on smoking behavior. Jarvik (81) found that oral nicotine was only minimally effective at inhibiting smoking. Five tablets daily of nicotine tartrate, 10 mg, reduced the average daily cigarette consumption of 17 volunteers by only 8% ($p < 0.02$). This is not really surprising, since nicotine absorbed after ingestion does not bypass the liver and thus avoid first-pass metabolism to cotinine (see below).

We have examined the effect on smoking of nicotine chewing gum (120). The gum is buffered to an alkaline pH to enable buccal absorption of nicotine (50). Forty-three subjects chewed 10 nicotine (2 mg nicotine base) or placebo gums per day in a balanced cross-over design. The subjects were instructed to smoke as they felt inclined, but not to deliberately attempt to reduce their cigarette consumption. They were aware that the gum contained nicotine, but not that one of the gums was a placebo. The placebo gum was heavily spiced to make it as strong and irritating as the nicotine gum. There was a 31% reduction of cigarette consumption while on the placebo gum, compared to a 37% reduction while on the nicotine gum. Though significant ($p < 0.05$), this difference between the two gums is small. Blood nicotine studies have confirmed that nicotine is absorbed from this gum, but a gum containing 4 mg nicotine taken hourly is required to achieve blood levels approaching cigarette smoking. Even so, the absorption is slower and does not give the same peak levels or puff-by-puff boli obtained by cigarette smoking. Also, many smokers find the 4 mg gum too strong.

To simulate cigarette smoking more closely, we have also tried using a variety of nicotine aerosols. These have proved either too irritating or nicotine absorption has been inadequate, due mainly to the aerosol droplets being too large to penetrate to the small airways. Although physiologic effects similar to smoking have been reported with nicotine aerosols (44, 74), we have not found blood nicotine levels approaching those obtained after smoking.

Apart from the studies just discussed, which involve either varying the nicotine delivery in tobacco smoke or the administration of nicotine by routes other than tobacco smoke, two quite different approaches have been used to examine the nicotine-titration hypothesis. First, Schachter (125) has shown that smokers alter their cigarette consumption according to whether their urine is acid or alkaline. When smokers were given ammonium chloride to acidify their urine, this maximized the urinary excretion of nicotine, and they smoked more cigarettes, presumably to make up for this loss. Conversely, when the urine pH was raised by giving sodium bicarbonate, the subjects smoked less. The differences were not very great, but much variation in nicotine intake would have been missed, since crude cigarette consumption was the only smoking variable measured. The second novel approach was the use of a centrally acting nicotine antagonist, mecamylamine (134), which increased the number of cigarettes smoked by 30%. The number of puffs also increased. This suggests that more nicotine was needed to counteract the antagonist. Pentolinium, an antagonist with predominantly peripheral actions, had no effect on smoking behavior. Both these studies support the nicotine self-titration hypothesis.

Finally, evidence that nicotine can function as a primary reinforcer is provided by two studies which showed that monkeys (41) and rats (33) will self-inject nicotine for its own sake. Both of these studies have been reported with insufficient detail and descend almost to being anecdotal. This is unfortunate, since they are the only studies to be found in the literature of this classical and crucial type of evidence. Further study of this kind is urgently needed. Jarvik's group (62) has expended much time and effort training a few monkeys to smoke. This work has so far not revealed anything about smoking in humans which could not be done equally well with human subjects. It is not even certain that the monkeys were inhaling and absorbing appreciable amounts of nicotine. However, other researchers have shown that apes trained to smoke do absorb methylamphetamine, which has been added to the cigarettes (112). It is a pity that more of this effort has not been directed toward the study of intravenous self-administration of nicotine.

3. NICOTINE PHARMACOKINETICS

Nicotine is one of the few natural liquid alkaloids. It is colorless, volatile, and strongly alkaline. It turns brown on exposure to air and gives off a characteristic tobacco smell. It is readily soluble in water, alcohol, and ether and forms water-soluble salts. Under atmospheric pressure, it boils at 246°C. It is volatalized in the cone of burning tobacco, 800°C, and the free base is present in the smoke suspended on minute droplets of tar (0.3–1.0 μ) which are small enough to reach the small airways and lung alveoli. Nicotine has the empirical formula $C_{10}H_{14}N_2$. It is mainly levorotatory, and *l*-nicotine is much more potent than *d*-nicotine. Its molecular structure is that of a pyridine combined to a pyrrolidine ring (see Fig. 6).

Absorption of Nicotine

As the undissociated (free) base, nicotine is lipid-soluble and readily permeates cell membranes. As such, it is rapidly absorbed through the skin, the oral, buccal, and nasal mucosae, the gastrointestinal tract and the bladder, as well as through the lungs (138). An interesting case of nicotine absorption through the skin was described by Faulkner (49). A florist, using a nicotine insecticide spray accidentally got the seat of his trousers soaked with the spray, and within 15 min became critically ill with nicotine poisoning. He was admitted to hospital for 4 days and recovered; but his clothes had been tied up in a bag and not dried. When he dressed to leave, his trousers were still damp and 1 h later he was readmitted with exactly the same symptoms. A more recent example of cutaneous absorption is the account of nicotine intoxication in tobacco croppers who absorb it on hot days when they are sweating (59).

Though nicotine base is so rapidly absorbed into the body through virtually any route, this does not occur in the case of the nicotinium ion. The rate of absorption depends, therefore, on the proportion of nicotine present as free base. This, in turn, depends on the pH. It will be seen in Fig. 2 that at an acid pH very little nicotine is present as free base, whereas at pH 8, the proportion of free base is 52%. The absorption of nicotine is therefore pH dependent.

In a series of studies with cats, Travell (138) clearly demonstrated the pH dependence of nicotine absorption. Thus, application to the skin of a cat of nicotine in acid solution produced either no effect or moderate signs of toxicity, whereas the same dose in alkaline solution rapidly produced severe toxic effects and death in 17 out of 21 animals. Similarly, the instillation of buffered solutions of nicotine into the bladder of cats whose ureters had been ligated showed rapid absorption from alkaline solutions, but no effect occurred when lethal doses were given in acid solution. Thus it would seem

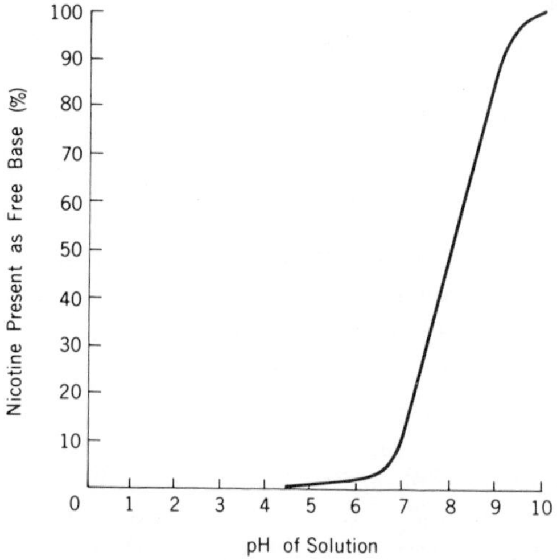

Fig. 2. Dissociation curve of nicotine in aqueous solution, expressed as per cent of undissociated (free) base. (From Travell, ref 138)

that when the urine is alkaline, it is not only the renal tubules, but the bladder too, which reabsorb nicotine excreted by the kidney (see below). The pH of a buffered solution affected even the toxicity of nicotine given by subcutaneous injection.

Travell also did experiments on gastric absorption. She ligated the stomachs of 55 cats at the cardia and the pylorus, preserving the blood supply along the greater and lesser curvatures. She reports her results as follows: "Nicotine injected into the ligated stomach at pH 8.6 in a dose of 20 mg/kg (at least twice the buffered subcutaneous fatal dose for cats) was fatal in 41 min, whereas 50 mg/kg injected at pH 1.2 caused no effects, even though the intragastric pH 24 h later had increased to 4.2." The role of gastric absorption could be important since there is some evidence (see below) that, after smoking, nicotine may be actively excreted in saliva and by related cells of the gastric mucosa. Though this would be reabsorbed in the intestine, gastric reabsorption as well might occur in smokers who were receiving alkalis for dyspeptic symptoms.

Travell did not study buccal absorption of nicotine, which is so relevant to the smoking and chewing of tobacco. However, Armitage and his colleagues have shown clearly how this too is pH-dependent (3, 6). When buffered solutions of radioactive nicotine were put into the mouths of cats, the carotid blood levels of nicotine increased more rapidly and reached much higher levels when the solution in the mouth was at pH 8 than when at pH 7 or pH 6 (Fig. 3). The peak concentration was four times higher at pH 8 than at pH 6, and the rate of increase differed eightfold. The fact that the difference is greater between pH 8 and pH 7 than it is between pH 7 and pH 6 is in keeping with the dissociation curve (Fig. 2), which rises more steeply above pH 7.

It is not only experimental solutions, however, that have pH ranges spanning the rise of the nicotine dissociation curve. The pH of different types of tobacco smoke have a similar range. The pH of air-cured tobaccos used mainly in pipes and cigars, but also in some brands of cigarette, is alkaline (about pH 8.5), whereas smoke from flue-cured tobaccos present in most brands of British cigarette produces a relatively acidic smoke (about pH 5.5). Buffering capacity of the smoke is another pertinent variable. From this, we would deduce that nicotine would be well absorbed through the buccal mucosa from the smoke of a cigar, but not from the smoke of a cigarette made of flue-cured tobacco. This is indeed the case (6).

Before it was possible to reliably measure nicotine levels in blood, Armitage and his colleagues developed a bioassay technique (2–4, 6). In a series of important studies, they used the effect of nicotine on the femoral arterial blood pressure of anesthetized cats as an index of nicotine dosage. They were thus able to show that 30 25-ml puffs of cigar smoke (pH 8.5)

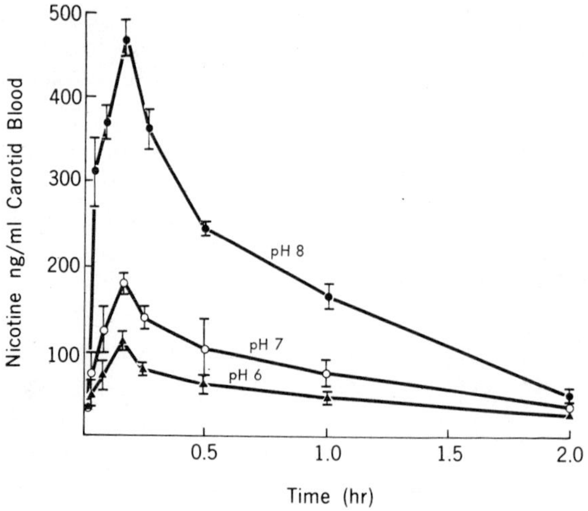

Fig. 3. Carotid blood levels of nicotine in ng/ml after the presence in the mouth for 10 minutes of solutions of nicotine buffered at three different pHs. Means ± SEM. (From Armitage and Turner, ref 6)

introduced into the mouth at 30-sec intervals over 15 min produced an increase in femoral blood pressure, whereas a similar amount of cigarette smoke (pH 5.4) had no effect (6). This difference occurred even though the cigarette smoke contained more nicotine than the cigar smoke. They were therefore able to clearly demonstrate the pH dependence of the buccal absorption of nicotine. However, the effect of buccal absorption of the 30 25-ml puffs of cigar smoke was small and slow to develop; whereas, in sharp contrast, a single 25-ml puff (whether of cigar or cigarette smoke) introduced into the lungs produced a far larger and almost instantaneous effect (4), showing that buccal absorption is very much slower and less efficient than absorption through the lungs with inhalation.

They also showed that the effect on the blood pressure of a 25-ml puff containing 170 μg nicotine, was equivalent to the effect of 120 μg nicotine base injected into the femoral vein (4). Thus, absorption through the lungs is very nearly as efficient as an intravenous injection; the slight difference is attributable to the greater tendency for inhaled nicotine to be retained and metabolized within the lungs. A study, using dogs (141), showed that only 6% of nicotine injected into the pulmonary artery is retained and metabolized in its first passage through the lungs, compared with 30% of the nicotine inhaled in cigarette smoke. Finally, Turner (140) showed, using cats, that higher blood nicotine levels were obtained after multiple bolus injections than after slow intravenous infusion of the same amount of nicotine given over the same period of time.

To return to human studies, Beckett and Triggs (12) have shown that buccal absorption of nicotine is pH-dependent. Buffered solutions of 1.0 mg nicotine base were kept in the mouth for 5 min. The amount absorbed was roughly as follows: 6% at pH 5.5, 15% at pH 6.5, 20% at pH 7.5, and 25% at pH 8.5. The pH of saliva shows diurnal variation and ranges from 5.6 to 7.6 (24). It increases very slightly after smoking and also changes before, during and just after a meal (138). It is possible that such fluctuations might affect buccal absorption of nicotine during smoking, as well as the salivary excretion and reabsorption of nicotine (see below).

The average amount of nicotine present in a standard 35-ml puff can be calculated by dividing the nicotine yield of the cigarette in question by the average number of puffs required to smoke the cigarette in the standardized way (one 2-sec puff/min). Thus, the puff nicotine content for current British cigarettes ranges from below 20 μg per puff to over 350 μg per puff for cigarettes, giving total yields of 0.14 mg and 3.4 mg nicotine, respectively. However, the puff nicotine content of the middle range of popular brands varies between 100 and 150 μg nicotine per puff or between 0.8 and 1.2 mg per cigarette. Further variation will arise from the wide differences in individual smoking patterns. Human experiments using cigarettes containing radioactively labeled nicotine show that a smoker absorbs over 95% of the nicotine from smoke which is inhaled (7). This conflicts with one study using dogs which found that only 26.6% of inhaled nicotine was abstracted (78) but agrees with all the earlier work (91). Possibly, dogs differ from humans in this respect.

Blood Nicotine Levels

The first reasonable attempt to measure blood nicotine levels after smoking was made in 1949 by Wolff et al. (149). They were puzzled by the fact that nicotine or nicotinelike substances were still present in the blood 10 hr after smoking, and that the levels were only a little higher after a period of 7 hr in which 20 cigarettes were smoked. The actual levels reported were higher than is shown by modern methods, and it is clear that they were measuring nicotine plus its metabolites. The time interval between the last cigarette and drawing the blood sample is not stated.

Schievelbein and Grundke (127) used a gas chromatographic method which enables nicotine to be distinguished from its metabolites. Nicotine levels after smoking one cigarette ranged from 5 to 64 ng/ml. The method was improved by Burrows et al. (28) and Isaac and Rand (79), and we have refined it further (51). One of the problems has been due to passive smoking by nonsmokers (119). In the past, calibration curves were constructed by adding nicotine to plasma from nonsmokers, despite the fact that this plasma showed gas chromatographic peaks identical to nicotine. Earlier workers (79) did not believe that these peaks in nonsmokers were actually due to nicotine, and plasma nicotine levels obtained in smokers were, therefore, "corrected" by subtracting the plasma "blank" values derived from nonsmokers. This would not have mattered had the levels in nonsmokers been constant, but plasma nicotine levels of nonsmokers vary from 0 to 6.8 ng/ml, according to the time spent recently in the vicinity of smokers (51).

The plasma nicotine levels we obtained with our gas chromatographic method in a small sample of smokers, just after smoking ranged from 15.5 to 38.4 ng/ml (Table 3). This accords well with other studies, using gas chromatography (79), cigarettes impregnated with ^{14}C–nicotine (7), and radioimmunoassay (29, 90). The distribution of blood nicotine between plasma and cells is in the ratio 1:0.8 (78). Figure 4 shows typical plasma nicotine profiles before and after smoking one cigarette in a smoker who inhales (usual consumption 30 per day) and a noninhaler (usual consumption 60 per day) following a period of 12 hr abstinence overnight. Both smokers had been instructed to smoke the cigarette in their own time in their usual way. This is similar to the profiles shown by Isaac and Rand (79), who found the plasma half-life of nicotine to be less than 30 min. The "rebounds" on the decay side of the curve are not errors and represent significant changes. These were also typical in Isaac and Rand's study, and are probably due to redistributions and metabolic recycling, which are discussed later. Indeed, there are often "bumps" in the ascent side of the curve, owing to the puff-by-puff intermittent bolus form of administration

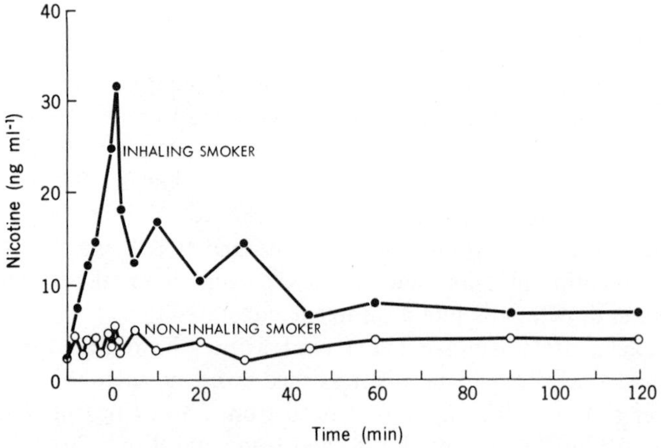

Fig. 4. Plasma nicotine concentrations in an inhaling smoker and a non-inhaling smoker during and after smoking one cigarette which was discarded at time = 0 min. (From Feyerabend, Levitt, and Russell, ref 51).

that characterizes inhaled cigarette smoking. This work was done on venous blood samples without rapid automated sampling. More refined continuously repeated sampling of arterial blood would enable the estimation of nicotine concentrations during and between boli. The arterial bolus concentrations may prove to be four or five times as great as the peak levels detected in our venous samples. It is in the effect on the brain of these boli of nicotine that the key to the pharmacologic rewards of nicotine no doubt lies.

Distribution of Nicotine in the Body

Apart from the dose, the distribution of nicotine depends very much on the route, the rate, and the mode (single vs. multiple-spaced doses) of administration. One hundred years ago, Lautenbach (92) demonstrated that a nicotine dose, which was lethal to dogs when given intravenously into the general circulation, had little effect when given into the portal venous system (mesenteric or splenic veins). This result is due to the rapid metabolism of most of the nicotine (see below) in its first passage through the portal system of the liver. This seems to explain why infants who swallow a cigarette containing 20–30 mg nicotine may show few effects, though this dose would be rapidly fatal if taken by other routes.

A study with mice using radioactively labeled nicotine showed maximum brain nicotine levels more than six times higher after intravenous injection than after intraperitoneal injection (131). The hepatic levels, on the other hand, were much higher after the peritoneal injection (Fig 5). Phenobarbitone pretreatment, known to increase the rate of metabolism of many drugs, enhanced liver metabolism of nicotine in vitro and in vivo. This pretreatment lowered brain nicotine levels obtained after intraperitoneal injection, but not the levels produced by intravenous nicotine. Phenobarbitone pretreatment also enabled animals to tolerate lethal doses of nicotine given intraperitoneally, but it did not alter the response to intravenous doses. All this tends to confirm that, because of first-pass metabolism in the liver, nicotine absorbed through the gut after ingestion has little pharmacologic effect compared with nicotine absorbed by routes such as the skin, nasal and buccal mucosae, lungs, and even the rectum, all of which allow the nicotine to be distributed in the general circulation before passage through the liver.

Stalhandske's work (Fig. 5) shows that intravenously injected nicotine is immediately taken up in the brain, reaching a maximum concentration within 1 min after injection. (The circulation rate in the mouse is obviously a lot quicker than in humans.) The brain level then falls rapidly with a half-life of about 5 min, and by 60 min it has fallen to only 1% of the maximum level.

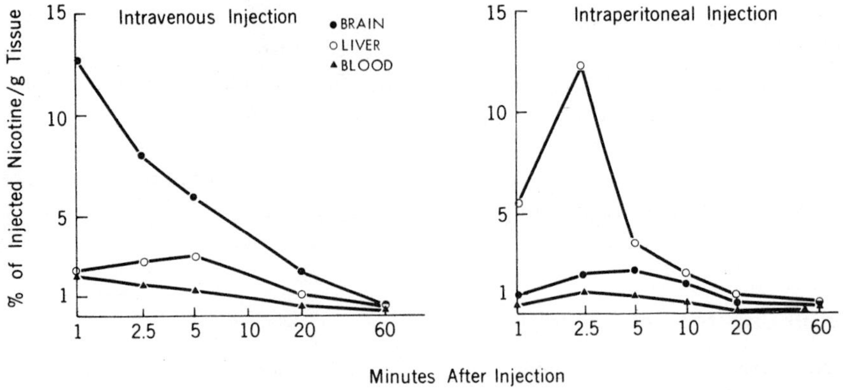

Figs. 5. (left) and 6. Nicotine concentrations in the brain, liver and blood of mice at various times after an intravenous or an intraperitoneal injection of ^{14}C-nicotine. Each value represents the average of at least three animals. (From Stalhandshake, ref 131).

The blood nicotine levels were also highest at 1 min after injection and fell steadily with a half-life as short as that of nicotine in the brain. The fact that this is so much shorter than the venous plasma half-life of nicotine in humans (20–30 min) may have something to do with the way the blood was collected. The animals were sacrificed by cervical dislocation and immediately bled by decapitation. The blood may, therefore, have been predominantly arterial, rather than venous. One minute after injection the ratio between nicotine levels in brain and blood was 5.6, and this remained relatively constant until 1 hr after injection, by which time it was reduced (Table 4).

After the intraperitoneal injections the brain nicotine level was not only very much lower than after an intravenous injection, but the contrast between the brain and blood levels was very much less (Figure 6 and Table 4). These findings seem to suggest two possibilities: a "bolus-uptake phenomenon" and a "differential retention". The large difference between brain and blood levels in Fig. 6 may have arisen because the brain level was derived from equilibration with an equally high bolus nicotine level. The intravenous nicotine bolus having passed within 1-min, the blood level would be very much lower, while the brain would be retaining nicotine taken up during the passage of the nicotine-filled bolus. As no high-concentration bolus would have passed through the brain after the intraperitoneal injection, the brain level would not be as high and the brain–blood difference not as great. The maintenance of a brain–blood difference suggests that the brain cells bind or retain nicotine against a gradient, and that the higher the brain level the greater the gradient (5.6 versus about 3.0 for post intravenous vs. intraperitoneal nicotine, respectively). How does one explain any brain–blood difference after the peritoneal injection? Active uptake by the brain against a concentration gradient is one possibility. The superior cervical ganglion has been shown to take up nicotine against a concentration gradient and to equilibrate at an intra/extracellular ratio of 6:1 ("resting uptake"). An additional uptake of 25% ("activation uptake") occurs on nicotine-induced depolarization of the cells (26, 27). These findings are in accord with Stalhandske's brain:blood ratios.

Stalhandske's findings (131) have been considered at some length because they provide some evidence for the bolus-uptake phenomenon which seems so crucial a difference between inhaled cigarette smoking as opposed to other forms of tobacco use such as snuffing, chewing, or noninhaled cigar and pipe smoking.

Earlier studies (128) of whole-body autoradiography of mice injected intravenously with ^{14}C-labeled nicotine clearly show the rapid uptake of nicotine by the brain, liver, kidneys, salivary glands, and cells in the fundus of the stomach. Five minutes after the injection, most of the injected nicotine is in these organs and tissues. Thirty minutes after the injection, most of the nicotine originally taken up by the brain has left it and has been taken up by other organs, specifically the liver, kidneys, salivary glands, and stomach. The radioactivity in the salivary glands is so concentrated that it suggests an active secretion of nicotine. It is surprising that the authors do not comment on this. The rapid clearance from the brain is not due to metabolism. The brain does not metabolize nicotine, and the small amounts of metabolites that occur in the brain are transported there from other organs. In contrast, by 30 min, most of the radioactivity in the liver and kidneys is due to metabolites rather than unchanged nicotine. The distribution of nicotine within the brain varies considerably. It is concentrated in the

TABLE 4 TIME COURSE OF BRAIN TO BLOOD LEVELS (131)

Minutes After Injection	Intravenous Injection		Intraperitoneal Injection	
	Controls	Pretreated[a]	Controls	Pretreated[a]
1	5.6	5.6	1.6	1.2
2.5	5.2	6.1	1.9	1.9
5	5.1	4.6	3.0	2.5
10	—	—	2.9	2.7
20	5.8	5.5	2.2	2.2
60	4.0	3.4	2.7	2.4

Each result represents the average of at least three animals.
[a] Phenobarbitone pretreatment.

gray matter more than the white matter, and particularly high levels occur in the cellular layers of the hippocampus. These findings have since been confirmed by similar studies in cats (139, 140).

Recirculation of Nicotine Within the Body

The fluctuations of blood nicotine levels that follow and distort the decay curve following the peak level obtained by smoking have been remarked upon. There are three nicotine recirculation processes that may contribute to these delayed elevations of blood nicotine.

Salivogastric Nicotine Recirculation

The concentration of radioactivity in the salivary glands and stomach following an injection of labeled nicotine described above prompted us (Russell and Feyerabend, in preparation) to measure the nicotine concentration in saliva following smoking. The levels we obtained were very high indeed, many times higher than is ever found in blood and of a similar order to concentrations which occur in urine. These levels are not simply due to nicotine deposited in the mouth during smoking, for they are also obtained after an intravenous injection of nicotine. It seems, therefore, that nicotine is actively secreted by salivary glands, and possibly also by related cells in the stomach. Depending on buccal pH fluctuations, some of the salivary nicotine would be reabsorbed through the buccal mucosa. The acid pH of the stomach would preclude gastric reabsorption under normal circumstances. Any nicotine from saliva and the stomach passing into the small intestine would be reabsorbed into the portal circulation, and most of it would then be metabolized in the liver. Thus, this salivogastric cycle might contribute slightly to delayed blood nicotine elevations by buccal absorption, but would contribute more to the rapid clearing of unchanged nicotine from circulation before returning it to the liver to be metabolized.

Nicotine-1′-N-Oxide Reduction

Nicotine-1′-*N*-oxide is one of the main metabolic forms in which nicotine is excreted in the urine of smokers (13). However, any nicotine-1′-*N*-oxide formed in the liver and passing via the bile into the intestine would be reduced back to nicotine by the N-oxide reductase system in the colon. This reduction is probably effected by the bowel flora or enzymes in the intestinal wall. However, any nicotine formed in this way, though absorbed, would be returned to the liver in the portal system, and mostly remetabolized. Nevertheless, some must escape into the general circulation, since nicotine-1′-*N*-oxide administered orally or rectally to humans results in the appearance of nicotine in the urine (82).

Urinary Bladder Reabsorption

It is well-known that the urinary excretion of nicotine is pH dependent (see below). Under alkaline conditions, the nicotine is undissociated and therefore reabsorbed through the renal tubules as rapidly as it filters through the glomeruli. This is not so much a recycling as a blocking off of renal excretion of nicotine. However, it has been mentioned earlier how the urinary bladder absorbs nicotine rapidly under alkaline conditions. Thus, a situation might occur in which a bladder has been half-filled with acid urine with a high nicotine concentration. Subsequent addition of alkaline urine could raise the average pH of the urine in the bladder sufficiently for the nicotine to be reabsorbed before the urine is voided. This type of recycling of nicotine would be an intermittent rather than continuous event.

Metabolism of Nicotine

Apart from unchanged nicotine, the two main basic metabolites of nicotine excreted in the urine of smokers are cotinine and nicotine-1′-*N*-oxide. These are formed by two alternative pathways of oxidative metabolism involving N-oxidation or alpha-carbon oxidation of the pyrrolidine ring (Fig 7). α-Carbon oxidation to cotinine was the first pathway of nicotine metabolism to be studied in detail (23), and it is probably the major pathway in most species, including humans. Conversion of nicotine to cotinine occurs in the liver, the kidneys, and in lung tissue (141), but not in the brain. It is a complex process involving a number of steps and two possible pathways; one via

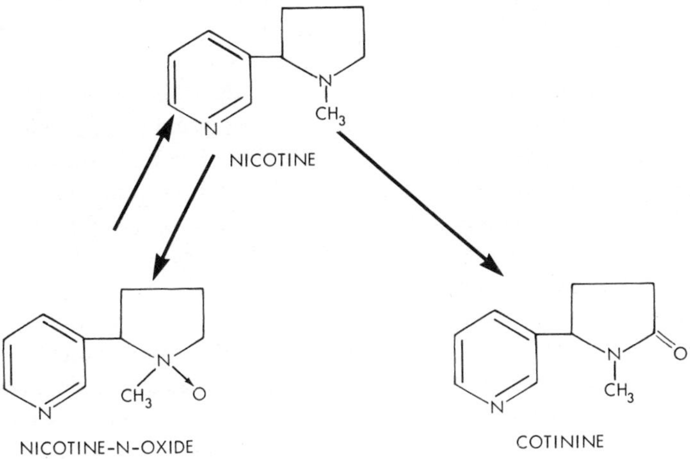

Fig. 7. Nicotine and its two main metabolites. The six-atom ring is the pyridine ring; the five-atom one is the pyrrolidine ring.

nicotine Δ 1′ (5′)-iminium ion (104). The iminium ion is of interest, as it is not physiologically active and may be a blocker of peripheral nicotine receptors. The conversion of nicotine to cotinine is inhibited by carbon monoxide (104), and COHb levels may exceed 12% in heavy smokers (121). The further metabolism of cotinine will not be covered here.

Oxidation at the pyrrolidine nitrogen atom has been recognized relatively recently as an important in vivo pathway of nicotine metabolism (17). Nicotine-1′-*N*-oxide is reduced to nicotine in the lower gastrointestinal tract, as already discussed above; but no reduction or other metabolism of the N-oxide occurs after intravenous injection (82). Under normal conditions of fluctuating urinary pH, the amount of nicotine-1′-*N*-oxide excreted in the urine of smokers is about half that of the cotinine excretion (13). It is of interest that the ratio of cotinine to the N-oxide in the urine is much higher in smokers with carcinoma of the bladder (mean ratio 6.8 compared with 2.2 for controls, $p < 0.001$). This could have implications regarding the etiology of bladder cancer (67).

Some time ago, it was shown that nonsmokers excreted in their urine as unchanged nicotine a higher proportion of a given dose of nicotine than did smokers (11). This suggested that the smokers were metabolizing the nicotine more rapidly, possibly due to enzyme induction as a consequence of their smoking. These studies have now been extended and comparisons made between males and females and between smokers and nonsmokers (14). Volunteers were given an intravenous injection of 3.07 mg nicotine hydrogen tartrate over 5–10 min (equivalent to 1 mg of nicotine base). Urine samples were collected over the next 24 hr and analyzed for nicotine and cotinine. The smokers had abstained from smoking for at least 36 hr before the injection, and all subjects had their urine acidified by ingesting ammonium chloride. The urinary recoveries of nicotine and cotinine are shown in Fig. 8. Female smokers excreted less nicotine but more cotinine than female nonsmokers, in keeping with the theory of an increased metabolism to cotinine as a result of enzyme induction from previous smoking. The results in the men are not so clear-cut. The male smokers seemed to fall into two groups. One group showed a high cotinine excretion, suggesting an increased metabolism to cotinine. The second group excreted less nicotine and cotinine than nonsmokers, which suggests that they were metabolizing nicotine more quickly than nonsmokers, but to some other substance rather than cotinine, possibly to nicotine-1′-*N*-oxide.

It is not relevant here to go further into all the complexities of nicotine metabolism. Those who are interested are referred as a starting point to an excellent recent review by Gorrod and Jenner (66). Finally, a number of reports are beginning to appear which show that smokers tend to have marginally more tolerance to various psychoactive drugs (19, 20, 135). This

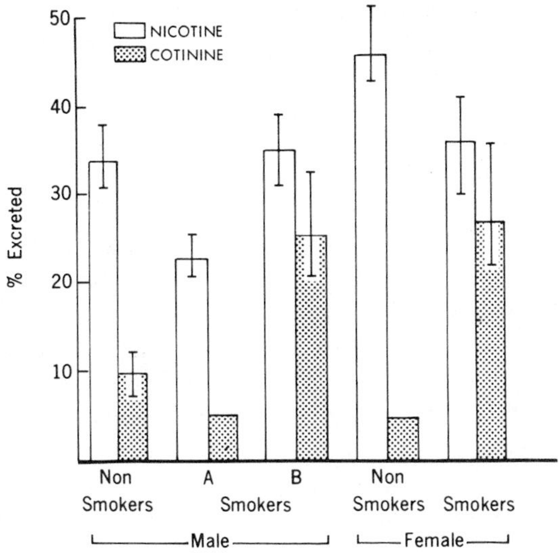

Fig. 8. Comparison of mean urinary (acidified urine) recoveries of nicotine and cotinine in male and female smokers and non-smokers after the intravenous administration of 3.07 mg (−)-nicotine hydrogen (+)-tartrate. A, low recovery group. B, high recovery group. (From Beckett et al., ref 13)

could be due to induction of enzymes by nicotine or other components of tobacco smoke, or indeed to the tendency for smokers to use more alcohol and drugs in general.

Excretion of Nicotine

Nicotine is present in sweat, saliva, and the milk of lactating women (110, 137), but the urine is by far the most important vehicle for the elimination from the body of nicotine and its metabolites. In the cat, 90% of the radioactivity of a given dose of labeled nicotine is excreted in the urine in 3 days, 77% in the first 24 hr (139, 140). As is the case with its absorption (see above), the excretion in the urine of unchanged nicotine is pH dependent. When the pH is low (5.5 or less), the nicotine is almost totally ionized and cannot be reabsorbed through the kidney tubules. Under these conditions, 30–40% of an intravenous dose, and, by inference, nicotine absorbed from smoking, is excreted in the urine as unchanged nicotine (Fig. 8). On the other hand, if the pH of the urine exceeds 8.0, most of the nicotine is reabsorbed not only through the renal tubules but from the bladder too (see above). Under normal conditions of fluctuating urinary pH, smokers excrete similar amounts of nicotine and cotinine in their urine and about half as much nicotine-1′-*N*-oxide (67). Of the two main metabolites, the excretion of cotinine is determined slightly by urinary pH, but also by the urine flow (15); whereas that of nicotine-1′-*N*-oxide is independent of urinary pH and volume (13).

4. PHARMACOLOGIC EFFECTS OF NICOTINE

Nicotine is one of the most powerful of all drugs. Two or three drops placed on the tongue would rapidly kill an adult, and the nicotine content of one cigar, about 60 mg, would be fatal to a human if injected intravenously. The actions of nicotine in the body are so complex and multitudinous that there are few other psychoactive drugs about which so much is known, though so little understood. Nicotine reaches and can have an effect on every organ in the body. This section will be limited to a brief and very selective account of those actions that seem most relevant to smoking, and especially those that may serve as a pharmacologic reward or motive underlying the habit. Several more detailed reviews, some by many authors, are available (46, 80, 102, 144).

The widespread and varied effects of smoking doses of nicotine seem to stem from its capacity to affect the actions and release of important neurochemical transmitters. There are two main types of nicotine action. First is its classical action as a cholinergic agonist, whereby, in small doses, it affects some cholinergic receptors causing depolarization and an acetylcholinelike stimulation. But the depolarization persists, and if the dose is sufficient to occupy all the receptors, a prolonged blockade ensues. The second type of nicotine action is an ability to cause the release of amine transmitters from nerve endings. Amines released by nicotine are noradrenaline, serotonin, and possibly dopamine. The two kinds of action occur wherever these receptors and transmitters are found, and nicotine therefore has effects throughout the nervous system. About the only receptors to escape a nicotine effect are muscarinic-type cholinergic receptors, and even these may be affected indirectly via an action on preganglionic fibres. Thus nicotine has effects on much of the synaptic transmission in the brain and spinal cord, in autonomic ganglia, at postganglionic autonomic effector sites, and at neuromuscular junctions.

Much of the complexity and paradox of nicotine effects result from the biphasic action, at cholinoceptive sites, as an agonist then blocker of acetylcholine (ACh). Confusion also arises from the fact that nicotine affects the balance of activity in a number of opposing systems centrally within the brain, as well as the balance between the sympathetic and parasympathetic systems peripherally. Thus, increase in the heart rate may arise from a blockade of parasympathetic activity, or from an increase in sympathetic activity. Compounded with this are variations in nicotine distribution and regional differences in the dose-effectiveness and the time-course of its actions on the opposing systems.

Effects on the Brain

Most of the evidence shows that the main effect of smoking doses of nicotine on the brain is to increase the level of arousal (4, 5, 25, 32, 43, 44, 68, 103, 105, 111). This stimulant effect is reflected in the EEG as desynchronization or attenuation of alpha activity. It has been shown in man and animals and is produced by smoking and nicotine administration. Unlike most other stimulant drugs, the arousal due to nicotine or tobacco smoking closely resembles normal arousal produced by stimulating situations. The cortical arousal is probably secondary to the effect of nicotine on the reticular activating system and the hippocampus. Nicotine also causes a release of ACh from the cortex. This too is secondary to effects in other areas, since ACh is not released when nicotine is applied directly to the cortex. The EEG arousal is short-lived, whereas the cortical ACh release is more prolonged, lasting an hour or more, suggesting that these two effects of nicotine are mediated by different processes (5). The EEG changes and the behavioral arousal that follow nicotine injections are blocked by mecamylamine, which shows that they are mediated by cholinergic mechanisms (43, 68). However, the response is extremely complex. Adrenergic mechanisms may also be involved, as may be other factors in tobacco smoke, possibly carbon monoxide (68).

The effect of nicotine on the brain is not one of straightforward stimulation. There may be an ensuing sedative action, especially with larger doses (5, 43). Moreover, for a given dose, part of the brain may be stimulated, while another part is depressed (65). Further complexity arises, since the effects of nicotine on the brain may be due to direct actions or secondary to the release of neurotransmitters. Apart from the release of ACh, which has been mentioned, smoking doses of nicotine affect noradrenaline (16, 70), 5-hydroxytryptamine (47), and probably dopamine also.

Finally, it has been suggested (35, 80, 117) that the dependence-producing potential possessed by some psychoactive drugs rests in their pharmacologic ability to directly or indirectly influence the hypothalamic reward system (106, 107). Activity in this system, it seems, is mediated by catecholamine release (132). Not only do smoking doses of nicotine release catecholamines in these areas (70), but nicotine actually influences hypothalamic electrical self-stimulating behavior (44).

Effects on the Cardiovascular System

As with the central nervous system, the cardiovascular effects of smoking doses of nicotine are predominantly stimulant, whether administered by injection, aerosol, or indeed by cigarette smoking. A meticulous study done many years ago (115) showed that smoking tobacco cigarettes caused a drop in skin temperature; an increase in the basal metabolic rate, the heart rate, and blood pressure; and a decrease in the amplitude of the T waves on the electrocardiogram. Similar effects were produced by intravenous injection of 2 mg of nicotine, but not after an injection of saline nor after smoking nicotinefree cigarettes. These effects have since been amply confirmed by later studies, which have also shown that both smoking and nicotine increase the cardiac output and stroke volume and reduce the cutaneous blood flow in the limbs (34, 53, 60, 74, 77, 85, 94, 109, 124). Smoking a single cigarette reduces blood-flow velocity in the fingers by an average of 42% (124). The cardiovascular effects, especially the heart rate and blood pressure, are most responsive after a period of abstinence from smoking. This suggests that most of the effect may simply be a relief of the abstinence, for smokers as a group do not have faster heart rates or higher blood pressures than nonsmokers.

It is not clear how much the cardiovascular effects of smoking are due to stimulation of the sympathetic nervous system, stimulation of chemoreceptors such as the carotid and aortic bodies (36), or the output of adrenaline from the adrenal medulla (53). The effect of smoking on the heart rate and blood pressure of humans lasts for as long as an hour (53, 60), whereas intravenous nicotine or the introduction of tobacco smoke into the lungs of anesthetized animals produces a very transient effect (2, 3, 78). The increase in blood pressure and cutaneous vascular resistance is not prevented by beta-adrenergic blockade, but the effect on heart rate is abolished (34).

Whatever the underlying mechanisms, the overall acute effect of smoking on the cardiovascular system is one of stimulation and activation, which may well be rewarding to the smoker, especially in situations of boredom or fatigue.

Effects on the Adrenals

It has long been accepted that, in situations of stress, adrenaline from the adrenal medulla is released into the blood stream and that its stimulant effect at numerous sites enhances physical and mental performance (2, 54) so as to help overcome the stress. This is just the kind of situation in which many smokers find it helpful to smoke, and smoking is an efficient way to increase the output of adrenaline. Frankenhauser and her colleagues (53,

54) have demonstrated this in a series of studies. The excretion of adrenaline in the urine was increased by an average of 38% during a 90-min period following the smoking of two cigarettes with a nicotine yield of 1.3 mg/cigarette. When two cigarettes with higher nicotine yields (2.3 mg/cigarette) were smoked, the urinary adrenaline was increased 83% over the no-smoking control condition. There were corresponding decreases in noradrenaline excretion of 12% and 17%, respectively.

There is also evidence that blood levels of adrenal cortical hormones are increased by smoking. One study showed an average increase in plasma 11-hydroxycorticosteroid level of 47% (range 27–77%) 1 hr after smoking, as compared with the slight expected diurnal morning fall under the no-smoking control condition. At 2 hr there was still a slight elevation, but the level was similar to the control condition at 3 hr after smoking (87). The release of both adrenaline and cortisone are two further nicotine effects that could be highly rewarding to the smoker.

Effects on Behavior and Learning

In keeping with the predominantly stimulant effect of smoking on the brain, the cardiovascular system, and the endocrine glands, nicotine seems to help rats to learn more rapidly and remember better how to avoid shocks, press a lever to obtain water, discriminate between visual stimuli, and learn a maze (20, 21, 42, 57, 58, 98, 99). However, this facilitation of learning and conditioning is biphasic, dose dependent, and varies between strains and species of rat. Thus smaller doses improve performance, while larger ones impair it. Medium doses produce initial depression followed by facilitation. The depressant action is potentiated by physostigmine, but not by neostigmine, suggesting that it is central rather than peripheral, and that it is mediated by the release of ACh (99). The stimulant effect may be mediated by different mechanisms—adrenergic, for example.

The effects could be explained by postulating that small doses of nicotine facilitate the behavior by releasing noradrenaline centrally, and that it requires larger doses to release ACh, which then depresses the response and swamps the noradrenaline action. This view is supported by Morrison's discovery that tolerance develops to the depressant effect of nicotine, allowing the stimulant effect to become manifest (101). It can be seen in Fig. 9 how spontaneous activity of rats is initially less just after daily injections of nicotine than after saline; but by the fourth day there is no difference, and on subsequent days, activity after nicotine steadily increases until it approaches the levels produced by amphetamine. Once acquired, this tolerance to the depressant action of nicotine was still apparent after 23 days without an intervening booster dose of nicotine. These findings have since been con-

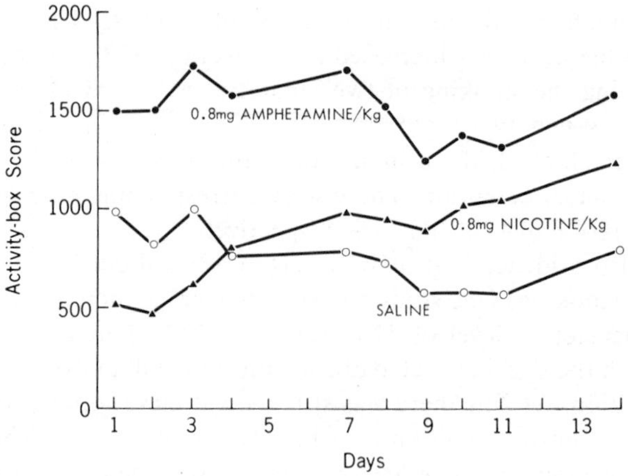

Fig. 9. Mean activity-box scores for groups of eight rats tested for 30 minutes during 10 trials. Animals were tested immediately after the injection of nicotine, (0.8 mg/kg), amphetamine (0.8 mg/kg) or saline (control). (From Morrison and Stephenson, ref 101)

firmed (133), with the tolerance still evident after 90 days. However, in this study, a metabolic component could have contributed substantially, since nicotine was given intraperitoneally, whereas Morrison gave it subcutaneously.

The suggestion has been made that nicotine's facilitatory effect on learning is mediated by adrenergic mechanisms, as opposed to the depressant effect of ACh release to which tolerance is acquired. The importance of adrenergic mechanisms is supported by the work of Orsingher, who found that the facilitation of learning was reversed by pretreatment with alpha-methyl-tyrosine, which is a specific inhibiter of catecholamine synthesis (108). Nicotine-induced theta-rhythm in the hippocampus (an EEG activity related to arousal and learning) and increase in hippocampal RNA levels may well be involved and are also blocked by alpha-methyl-tyrosine (40).

Rats who have been helped by nicotine to learn a difficult and stressful shock avoidance task more rapidly and to perform it more efficiently seem to depend on the continuation of nicotine to maintain their proficiency. When the nicotine is withdrawn, their ability to perform the task deteriorates progressively until they eventually do it no better than when they were novices (69). This is not simply a learning dissociation phenomenon whereby the animal is unable to remember what was learned under the influence of nicotine, for the disruption was relatively slight on the first day of withdrawal and deteriorated progressively.

Even if the nicotine is given after, rather than before, daily training sessions, subsequent performance is improved, suggesting that nicotine affects the consolidation process of imprinting the memory trace (48, 57, 58). This is supported by the possible involvement of hippocampal RNA in the process as discussed above.

The effects of nicotine and smoking on human performance and memory have not been so extensively studied. Compared with other psychoactive drugs, the effects of nicotine on human performance are less dramatic and very subtle. This lack of a prominent effect has, in some studies, been due to inadequate dosage. For example, one exhaustive study used only 0.1 mg nicotine in the form of a tablet that was sucked (146). Furthermore, when smokers are used as the experimental subjects, it is not possible to decide how much smoking actually enhances the performance or lack of smoking impairs it. It has, for instance, been shown that smokers are able to maintain initial levels of performance at prolonged monotonous reaction-time tasks, but that their performance becomes progressively poorer when they are deprived of smoking (54). However, these smokers were not compared with nonsmokers. In another study (72), during a prolonged 6-hr simulated driving task, deprived smokers made more tracking and vigilance errors than smokers who were allowed to smoke, but smokers who were allowed to smoke did not do better than nonsmokers. This suggests that smoking does not enhance performance, but that smokers are dependent on nicotine to perform as well as nonsmokers. Whether the smokers would have been able to perform as well without cigarettes before they had become dependent on them is another question.

The effects of smoking on less prolonged tests of reaction time and simulated driving have not produced consistent results (10, 38, 53). One study showed that smoking impaired verbal rote-learning during the performance, but improved subsequent recall, suggesting an effect on consolidation of memory in keeping with the animal work (1).

In summary, animal experiments suggest that nicotine affects the learning and performance of tasks in two ways: (*a*) a facilitatory effect that is obtained with small doses and is probably mediated by release of noradrenaline in the brain; (*b*) a depressant effect that requires larger doses and is apparently mediated by the release of ACh in the brain. Tolerance develops to the depressant action, after which the facilitatory effect becomes more evident. Animals become dependent on nicotine for the maintenance of an adequate performance. Similarly, human smokers show impairment of prolonged vigilance and reaction time tasks when they are not smoking, and seem to depend on smoking to maintain their performance. Smoking does not enable them to perform better than people who have never become dependent on smoking. Smoking may improve the memorization of new information.

The experimental data support the subjective experience that smoking helps smokers to think, concentrate, and cope with stresses. These are obviously highly rewarding effects, but they appear to be acquired symptoms of dependence, rather than a primarily rewarding effect.

Nicotine and Tranquilization

The use of cigarette smoking to reduce nervous tension and to provide relaxation are among the most common reasons people give to account for their smoking. This has been difficult to reconcile with the experimental evidence just discussed, which shows nicotine and smoking to be predominantly stimulant. It has been necessary to postulate that the sedative effect is obtained by taking larger doses. Though this accounts for the heavy smokers who use smoking like a tranquilizer, it does not explain the undoubted feeling of relaxation experienced by lighter smokers. There are, however, two quite different actions of nicotine that could account for the tranquilizing, rather than stimulant, effect experienced subjectively by many smokers. These are (*a*) a relaxing effect on skeletal muscle, and (*b*) an increase in the rate of habituation to unimportant stimuli.

A report that smoking caused a dramatic transient reduction in skeletal muscle tone in spastic patients (147) prompted Domino and his colleagues to explore this effect (44, 45). They showed that smoking a single cigarette produced a marked depression of the muscular contraction elicited by the patella reflex. This effect was dose related and was also produced by inhaling nicotine from an aerosol. It can be seen in Fig. 10 that the effect is maximal just after smoking and that it has largely disappeared 10 min after finishing the cigarette (i.e., at 25 min on the figure). This time-course is very similar to that of blood nicotine levels after smoking (Fig 4).

Isaac and Rand (78) also found a dose-related knee-jerk depression in dogs which lasted "some 10–30 min" and was obtained by intravenous nicotine and the introduction of tobacco smoke into the lungs. Isaac and Rand claimed that the knee-jerk depression did not show a time-course similar to the blood nicotine level. However, their method of blood nicotine analysis was crude, and they measured quantities as micrograms per milliliter whereas levels down to nanograms per milliliter are required for measuring nicotine intake in human smokers.

Domino (44) discusses the evidence suggesting that depression of the patella reflex is mediated by a stimulant action of nicotine on cholinergic receptors of the Renshaw cells in the spinal cord. This is a nice example of the way in which a stimulant action on an inhibitory interneuron can produce an overall depressant effect. The fact that smoking high-nicotine cigarettes had a greater effect than low-nicotine cigarettes does not challenge the self-titration hypothesis, since the subjects in this experiment

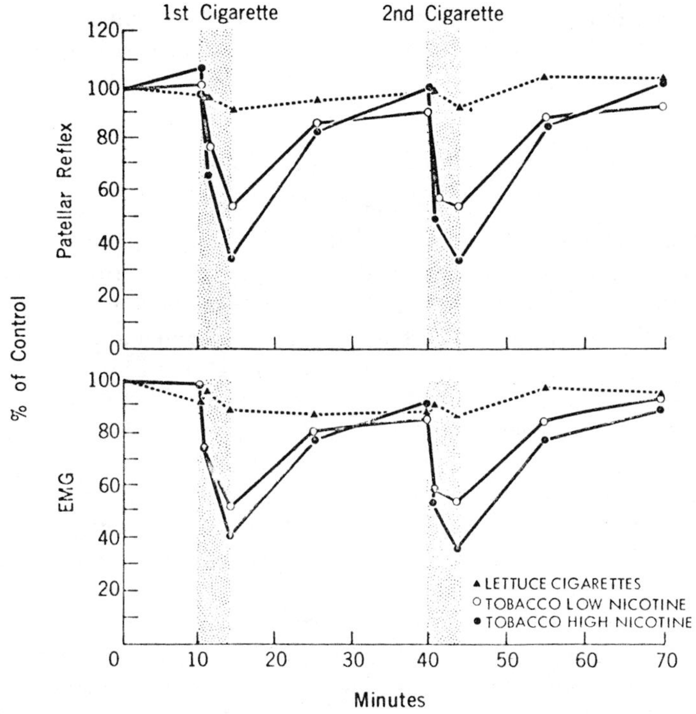

Fig. 10. Effects of smoking cigarettes of different nicotine content on the mean patellar reflex and electromyogram (EMG). *Above*: mean patellar reflex. The dotted line represents the mean amplitude of 22 subjects smoking lettuce cigarettes. The solid lines represent the mean amplitudes of subjects smoking low (19 subjects) and high (16 subjects) nicotine-containing cigarettes. *Below* EMG of the quadriceps femoris muscle for the same subjects. (From Domino and von Baumarten, ref 45)

were forced to inhale more deeply than usual. Indeed, some suffered unaccustomed dizziness.

It is clear from Domino's results that normal smoking may well reduce skeletal muscle tension. This provides one explanation for the relaxing effect experienced by so many smokers. Another possible explanation comes from the finding that smoking increases the rate of habituation of the orienting response to loud acoustic stimuli (55). Subjects grew accustomed and ceased to be startled by a repeated loud sound more rapidly after smoking a conventional cigarette than when they were deprived of cigarettes or had smoked a nicotinefree cigarette. The habituation point (absence of EEG desynchronization to the stimulus) was reached after an average of about 14 presentations when subjects were deprived of cigarettes or had smoked a nicotinefree cigarette, but after smoking two of their usual brand of tobacco cigarettes, the subjects habituated to the stimulus after only five presentations. This interesting study shows how smoking may help people to relax and startle less in situations where they are surrounded by noise and other excessive stimuli.

Effects on the Gastrointestinal Tract

There have been relatively few studies in this area, and the results have been conflicting and have shown much individual variation, possibly because scant attention has been paid to the degree of deprivation from smoking undergone by the subjects prior to testing. The effects observed have generally been attributed to stimulation of parasympathetic ganglia and cholinergic nerve endings leading to an overall increase in motility and secretory activity (144). However, central medullary mechanisms may also be involved, as is the case with the nausea and vomiting classically experienced by the novice who inhales too deeply before a tolerance is acquired.

In one detailed study (129), smoking was found to stimulate the secretion of saliva, inhibit hunger contractions of the stomach for up to an hour, to reduce gastric secretion, and delay the emptying time of the stomach in some subjects, and to generally increase the activity of the colon and the passage of stools. The inhibition of gastric secretion by smoking a single cigarette has been confirmed more recently (148). Pyloric competence is also impaired by one cigarette, and duodenogastric reflux was induced in 16 out of 22 subjects (113).

It is doubtful whether any of these effects are important to smoking motivation. However, transient constipation is not an uncommon withdrawal symptom, and the effect of smoking on reducing appetite and hunger contractions may be valued by those with a weight problem, or by those who are too busy to find the time to eat.

Effects on Body Weight and Metabolism

Gain in weight so commonly observed after giving up smoking is not only a result of increase in eating, but tends to occur even though calorie intake is reduced (93). Smokers seem to expend calories less efficiently than nonsmokers. One study showed that smokers weighed an average of 6.5 lb less, despite taking in 350 calories a day more than nonsmokers (93). Other studies have shown even larger weight differences between smokers and nonsmokers. The difference appears to increase with age, so that men over 40 years who had never smoked were on average 13 lbs (5.9 kg) heavier than smokers (37, 88). These differences are shown in Fig. 11. It can be seen that exsmokers also weigh less than nonsmokers. Gain in weight after giving up smoking is, in one sense, a return to normality, rather than a manifestation of oral substitution and weak control over eating.

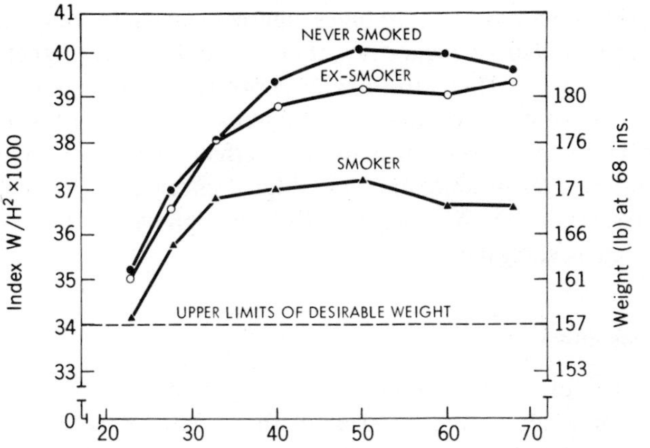

Fig. 11. Trends in obesity by age (yrs) and smoking habits in men. Weight/(Height)^2 (W/H^2) is used as an index of obesity. (From Khosla and Lower, ref 88)

Compared with overnight abstinence for 12 hr, stopping smoking for one month is accompanied by a decrease in oxygen consumption, serum protein-bound iodine, serum calcium, and changes in carbohydrate metabolism (61). It is well known that smoking or nicotine injections produce short-term increases in serum free fatty acids (FFA's) and triglycerides (86). It seems that the rise in body oxygen consumption induced by smoking or nicotine injections is mediated through the increased mobilization and consumption of FFA's, for the effect can be abolished if the lipolysis is inhibited with beta-pyridylcarbinol (76).

This metabolic effect of nicotine reduces the incidence of excessive body weight among smokers and provides an additional motive for smoking. An alarming increase in body weight is often a serious deterrent to giving up smoking.

Nicotine and Aggressiveness

Mood is difficult to measure objectively. One approach has been the use of self-rating mood scales. In one study of mood self-ratings before and after performing stressful and monotonous tasks, nonsmokers and deprived smokers showed an increase in feelings of aggressiveness, whereas smokers who were allowed to smoke showed no such increase. This suggests that smoking may have inhibited the development of aggressive feelings in this situation (73). Aggressiveness has also been studied using biting movements or jaw muscle myography as an index of aggression. In animals and humans, small doses of nicotine reduced aggressiveness as measured by these methods (75). Nicotine also reduces aggressiveness in rats (130). When smokers are deprived of cigarettes, they not only score higher on an aggression inventory but they also display more aggression on an "aggression machine," with which they administer "shocks" to other people (126).

The reduction of aggression is another effect of nicotine that may motivate smoking. Heavy smokers have high "chronic anger scores" (136), which suggests that they may have a similarly high need for an anger-reducing agent such as smoking.

Miscellaneous Effects

There are many other nicotine actions that have not been mentioned. No attempt has been made to document all of them. The focus has been on those actions that may possibly be rewarding to smokers. Three further effects are mentioned here that do not fall into any of the categories above. They are mentioned for their interest, rather than any reinforcing potential. The first is nicotine tremor, a well-documented finding which may impair performance of some fine motor tasks (53, 144). The second is the nicotine-induced output of vasopressin from the posterior pituitary gland, which is the basis of the antidiuretic effect of smoking. The third is the reduction of fetal breathing movements when the pregnant women smokes. This shows that there is a pharmacologic effect on the fetus, and the time-course suggests that this is a nicotine effect, rather than a carbon monoxide effect (95).

In summary, owing to its many actions, the overall effect of smoking doses of nicotine is extremely complex. A recent multiple-author book (46) has made considerable progress towards explaining the paradoxical dual action of nicotine, which stimulates and arouses, sedates and relaxes. Not only, does it seem, is this dependent on dose and individual constitution, but also on mood and situation. Thus, if we are angry or fearful, its effect is to calm and sedate; but if we are bored or fatigued, it will arouse and stimulate. It serves, therefore, as a means of maintaining mood homeostasis in situations of stress or languor.

5. SMOKING AND PHYSICAL DEPENDENCE

Physical versus Psychological Dependence

Dependence on smoking is often viewed less sympathetically because it is wrongly regarded as "merely psychological." Psychological dependence may be of two types. One, a pure psychological need for an object without the involvement of a pharmacologic effect, e.g., the dependence of an infant on its mother or betting to a compulsive gambler. The second type is the psychological need for, or dependence on, the pharmacologic effect of a drug, e.g., the tranquilizing effect of alcohol or the pleasurable effect of inhaling a cigarette. When these objects or effects are not available, intense distress and craving may be generated, but these kinds of withdrawal symptoms are regarded as psychological in the sense that this experience is similar whether it is the pharmacologic effect or the nonpharmacologic object that is being missed. Some conceptual difficulty arises here in that both types of psychological dependence, including the nonpharmacologic case, are mediated by changes in electrical activity in the brain and are in this sense "physical." This is not, however, the sense in which the term "physical dependence" is usually used. Two criteria are applied for labeling a dependence as physical: tolerance and a physical withdrawal syndrome. These phenomena involve adaptive changes at synapses that enable neural transmission to continue despite the blocking effect of the drug; i.e., tolerance. It is these same adaptive changes at synapses which are also responsible for the physical withdrawal syndrome. When the inhibitory effect of the drug is suddenly removed, there is a rebound overactivity at the synapses that produces the withdrawal syndrome. This rebound overactivity is very important because it is unpleasant and its relief or avoidance provides a powerful new acquired drive for continued drug taking. There is another less important type of tolerance that is not related to the withdrawal syndrome, nor does it produce any additional psychic drive. This is the development of an increased capacity to metabolize the drug due to induction of enzymes, usually in the liver.

Nicotine Tolerance

To return to smoking, it is quite clear that tolerance to nicotine occurs. Initial exposure gives rise to palpitations, dizziness, sweating, nausea, or vomiting. It is some time before the smoking pattern is such as to allow a high nicotine intake. Tolerance to the depressant effect of nicotine on spontaneous activity in rats has been shown to occur. It develops rapidly and lasts for as long as 90 days (101, 133). Tolerance to the depressant effect of nicotine on rearing activity in rats also develops, so that nicotine withdrawal then produces a rebound increase in the activity (84). The metabolic type of tolerance also occurs (131), and smokers metabolize nicotine more rapidly than nonsmokers (11).

Tobacco Withdrawal Syndrome

There is evidence of a clear-cut tobacco withdrawal syndrome. Apart from intense craving, tension, irritability, restlessness, depression, and difficulty with concentration (117), objective physical withdrawal effects have been demonstrated. These include a drop in pulse rate and blood pressure, gastrointestinal changes such as constipation, sleep disturbance (52, 89), impaired performance at simulated driving, and other vigilance and reaction-time tasks (54, 72), changes in the EEG and visual evoked potential (71, 79a, 143), and an increase in aggressiveness (73, 126). Finally the coping behavior of rats under stress is disrupted when nicotine injections are withdrawn (69, 100).

Nicotine Bolus Dependence

Historical evidence has shown that considerable satisfaction may be obtained from tobacco whether it is chewed, snuffed, or smoked in pipes or cigars, and that, over time, societies and individuals have been able to switch from one to another of these forms of tobacco use. These were the ways tobacco was used until the twentieth century. The tobacco was air-cured and produced an alkaline smoke from which nicotine is readily absorbed through the buccal mucosa without any need for inhalation into the lungs. The absorption of nicotine from all these routes (snuffing, chewing, noninhaled smoking) is very similar. There is a slow, steady increase to relatively low blood nicotine levels, and, in particular, no puff-by-puff nicotine peaks in the case of noninhaled smoking. The smoking of a whole pipe or cigar in this way provides but a single relatively nonintense pharmacologic reward or reinforcement. Historical testimony to the power of nicotine as a reinforcer even when it is slowly absorbed is provided by the rapid spread and extent of tobacco use before the twentieth century in the face of, at times, considerable penalties (117).

With cigarettes made from flue-cured tobaccos, the situation is altogether different. The acidity of the smoke makes buccal absorption negligible, so that to obtain a nicotine effect, it is necessary to inhale. The smoke is, at the same time, less irritating and therefore easier to inhale than the smoke from pipes or cigars or, indeed, cigarettes containing air-cured tobaccos. It has been discussed earlier how the rapid absorption through the lungs produces, with each inhaled puff, a bolus of blood containing a high concentration of nicotine, many times higher than the levels shown after mixing or those obtained by slower absorption of far larger quantities of nicotine. Equally rapid uptake by the brain ensures that it equilibrates with these bolus peaks so that the brain cells have higher nicotine levels than occur in the blood following dispersion of the boli. Furthermore, the high nicotine levels in these boli are in no way affected by acquired metabolic tolerance, which would tend to reduce the mixed blood levels, and hence the maximum levels obtained by slower buccal or nasal absorption. For some years, Armitage (3, 4) has emphasized the puff-by-puff finger-tip control which the inhaling cigarette smoker has over his nicotine intake. By altering the force and size of the puff, the proportion inhaled, the depth of inhalation and the time that smoke is held in the lungs, both the size of the bolus and the concentration of nicotine in it can be independently controlled.

The puff-by-puff bolus nicotine peaks provided by inhaled cigarette smoking not only produce higher brain nicotine levels and a more intense effect, but also substantially increase the number of reinforcements. Twenty cigarettes a day is 7300 a year, each puffed 7–10 times. Magnitude and number of reinforcements are important variables in the strengthening of operant behavior. The time interval between the response and the reinforcement is another important variable, and this too is maximized by inhaled cigarette smoking. Nicotine absorbed through the lungs reaches the brain more rapidly than after an intravenous injection. The arm-to-brain circulation time is around 13.5 sec, while the lung-to-brain time is only 7.5 sec.

It is suggested that it is the intermittent puff-by-puff high-nicotine bolus that reaches the brain within seconds of inhaling which makes cigarette smoking so highly addictive. Once this has been experienced, other forms of nicotine intake no longer suffice. Thus, addicted cigarette smokers who switch to cigars or a pipe almost inevitably continue to inhale (30, 39). It is likely that an addicted cigarette smoker would get more satisfaction and a higher level of nicotine in his brain after smoking and inhaling one of Jarvik's amputated cigarettes (63) than smoking but not inhaling a large cigar. It is not just nicotine which is so dependence-producing, but the inhalation-bolus form of intake which addicts the cigarette smoker.

6. CONCLUSION

There seems little doubt, in view of the evidence that has been presented, that pharmacologic factors play a dominant role in the maintenance of smoking and that most people smoke because they are dependent on nicotine. Furthermore, nicotine dependence is not always only psychological. Many cigarette smokers fulfil the criteria for physical dependence, namely tolerance and physical withdrawal effects. Finally, it is suggested that cigarette smokers are not simply dependent on nicotine so much as the inhalation-bolus form of intake, which makes cigarette smoking one of the *most* addictive of the addictive behaviors.

ACKNOWLEDGMENTS

I wish to thank Jean Crutch for secretarial assistance, and the Medical Research Council and Department of Health and Social Security for financial support. I am also grateful for helpful comments from A. K. Armitage, J. G. Edwards, M. E. Jarvik, P. Jenner, R. Kumar, M. Lader, the Editor, and an anonymous referee.

REFERENCES

1. Andersson, K., Effects of cigarette smoking on learning and retention. *Psychopharmacologia,* **41,** 1–5 (1975).
2. Armitage, A. K., Effects of nicotine and tobacco smoke on blood pressure and release of catecholamines from the adrenal glands, *Br. J. Pharmacol. Chemother.,* **25,** 515–526 (1965).
3. Armitage, A. K., in *Smoking Behavior: Motives and Incentives,* W. L. Dunn (Ed.), Winston, Washington, D.C., 1973, pp. 83–91.
4. Armitage, A. K., G. H. Hall, and C. F. Morrison, Pharmacological basis for the tobacco smoking habit, *Nature,* **217,** 331–334 (1968).
5. Armitage, A. K., G. H. Hall, and C. M. Sellers, Effects of nicotine on electrocortical activity and acetylcholine release from the cat cerebral cortex, *Br. J. Pharmacol.,* **35,** 152–160 (1969).
6. Armitage, A. K., and D. M. Turner, Absorption of nicotine in cigarette and cigar smoke through the oral mucosa, *Nature,* **226,** 1231–1232 (1970).
7. Armitage, A. K. et al. Absorption and metabolism of nicotine by man during cigarette smoking, *Br. J. Clin. Pharmacol.* **1** 180 P. (1974).
8. Ashton, H. and R. Telford, Blood carboxyhaemoglobin levels in smokers, *Br. Med. J.,* **4,** 740 (1973).
9. Ashton, H. and D. W. Watson, Puffing frequency and nicotine intake in cigarette smokers, *Br. Med. J.,* **3,** 679–681 (1970).
10. Ashton, H., R. D. Savage, R. Telford, and D. W. Watson, The effects of cigarette smoking on the response to stress in a driving simulator, *Br. J. Pharmacol.,* **45,** 546–556 (1972).
11. Beckett, A. H., and E. J. Triggs, Enzyme induction in man caused by smoking, *Nature,* **216,** 587 (1967).
12. Beckett, A. H., and E. J. Triggs, Buccal absorption of basic drugs and its application as an in vivo model of passive drug transfer through lipid membranes, *J. Pharm. Pharmacol.,* **19,** Suppl. 31S–41S (1967).
13. Beckett, A. H., J. W. Gorrod, and P. Jenner, The analysis of nicotine-1′-*N*-oxide in urine in the presence of nicotine and cotinine and its application to the study of in vivo nicotine metabolism in man, *J. Pharm. Pharmacol.,* **23,** 55–61S (1971).
14. Beckett, A. H., J. W. Gorrod, and P. Jenner, The effect of smoking on nicotine metabolism in vivo in man, *J. Pharm. Pharmacol.,* **23,** 62–67S (1971).
15. Beckett, A. H., J. W. Gorrod, and P. Jenner, A possible relation between pKa, and lipid solubility and the amounts excreted in urine of some tobacco alkaloids given to man, *J. Pharm. Pharmacol.,* **24,** 115–120 (1972).
16. Bhagat, B., Influence of chronic administration of nicotine on the turnover and metabolism of noradrenaline in the rat brain, *Psychopharmacologia,* **18,** 325 (1970).
17. Booth, J., and E. Boyland, The metabolism of nicotine into two optically active stereo-

isomers of nicotine-1′-*N*-oxide by animal tissues in vitro and by cigarette smokers, *Biochem. Pharmacol.*, **19,** 733–742 (1970).

18. Borgatta, E. F., and R. R. Evans, (Eds.) *Smoking, Health and Behavior,* Aldine, Chicago, 1968.
19. Boston Collaborative Drug Surveillance Program, Decreased clinical efficacy of propoxyphene in cigarette smokers, *Clin. Pharmacol. Ther.* **14,** 259–263 (1973).
20. Boston Collaborative Drug Surveillance Program, Clinical depression of the CNS due to diazepam and chlordiazepoxide in relation to cigarette smoking and age, *N. Engl. J. Med.*, **288,** 277–280 (1973).
21. Bovet, D., F. Bovet-Nitti, and A. Oliverio, Action of nicotine on spontaneous and acquired behavior in rats and mice, *Ann. N.Y. Acad. Sci.*, **142,** 261–267 (1967).
22. Bovet-Nitti, F., Facilitation of simultaneous visual discrimination by nicotine in four inbred strains of mice, *Psychopharmacologia,* **14,** 193–199 (1969).
23. Bowman, E. R., L. B. Turnbull, and H. McKennis, Metabolism of nicotine in the human and excretion of pyridine compounds by smokers, *J. Pharmacol. Exp. Ther.*, **127,** 92–95 (1959).
24. Brawley, R. E., Studies of the pH of normal resting saliva: Diurnal variation, *J. Dent. Res.*, **15,** 79–86 (1935).
25. Brown, B. B., Additional characteristic EEG differences between smokers and nonsmokers, in *Smoking Behavior: Motives and Incentives,* W. L. Dunn, (Ed.), Winston, Washington, D.C., 1973, pp. 67–81.
26. Brown, D. A., P. C. Hoffmann, and L. J. Roth, 3H-nicotine in cat superior cervical and nodose ganglia after close-arterial injection in vivo, *Br. J. Pharmacol.*, **35,** 406–417 (1969).
27. Brown, D. A., J. V. Halliwell, and C. N. Scholfield, Uptake of nicotine and extracellular space markers by isolated rat ganglia in relation to receptor activation, *Br. J. Pharmacol.*, **42,** 100–113 (1971).
28. Burrows, I. E., P. J. Corp, G. C. Jackson, and B. F. J. Page, The determination of nicotine in human blood by gas-liquid chromatography, *Analyst,* **96,** 81–84 (1971).
29. See ref. 67a.
30. Castleden, C. M., and P. V. Cole, Inhalation of tobacco smoke by pipe and cigar smokers, *Lancet,* **2,** 21–22 (1973).
31. Cherry, W. H., and W. F. Forbes, Canadian studies aimed toward a less harmful cigarette, *J. Nat. Cancer Inst.*, **48,** 1765–1773 (1972).
32. Cheshire, P. J., D. N. Kellett, and G. L. Willey, Effects of nicotine and arousal on the monkey EEG, *Experientia,* **29,** 71–73 (1973).
33. Clark, M. S. G., Self-administered nicotine solutions preferred to placebo by the rat. *Br. J. Pharmacol.*, **35,** 367 (1969).
34. Coffman, J. D., Effect of propranolol on blood pressure and skin blood flow during cigarette smoking, *J. Clin. Pharmacol.*, **9,** 39–44 (1969).
35. Collier, H. O. J., Humoral transmitters, supersensitivity, receptors and dependence. in *Scientific Basis of Drug Dependence,* H. Steinberg (Ed.), Churchill, London, 1969, pp. 49–66.
36. Comroe, J. H., The pharmacological actions of nicotine, *Ann. N.Y. Acad. Sci.*, **90,** 43–51 (1960).
37. Comstock, G. W., and R. W. Stone, Changes in body weight and subcutaneous fatness related to smoking habits, *Arch. Environ. Health,* **24,** 271–276 (1972).

38. Cotten, D. J., J. R. Thomas, and D. Stewart, Immediate affects of cigarette smoking on simple reaction time in college male smokers, *Percept. Motor Skills,* **33,** 336 (1971).

39. Cowie, J., R. W. Sillet, and K. P. Ball, Carbon-monoxide absorption by cigarette smokers who change to smoking cigars, *Lancet,* **1,** 1033–1035 (1973).

40. Daroqui, M. R., and O. A. Orsingher, Effect of alpha-methyl-tyrosine pretreatment on the drug-induced increase of hippocampal RNA, *Pharmacology,* **7,** 366–370 (1972).

41. Deneau, G. A., and R. Inoki, Nicotine self-administration in monkeys, *Ann. N.Y. Acad. Sci.,* **142,** 277–279 (1967).

42. Domino, E. F., Some behavioral actions of nicotine, in *Tobacco Alkaloids and Related Compounds,* U.S. von Euler, (Ed.), MacMillan, New York, 1965.

43. Domino, E. F., Electroencephalographic and behavioral arousal effects of small doses of nicotine: A neuropsychopharmacological study, *Ann. N.Y. Acad. Sci.,* **142,** 216–244 (1967).

44. Domino, E. F., Neuropsychopharmacology of nicotine and tobacco smoking, in *Smoking Behavior: Motives and Incentives,* W. L. Dunn, (Ed.). Winston, Washington, D.C., 1973, pp. 5–31.

45. Domino, E. F., and A. M. von Baumgarten, Tobacco, cigarette smoking and patella reflex depression, *Clin. Pharmacol. Ther.,* **10,** 72–79 (1969).

46. Dunn, W. L., *Smoking Behavior: Motives and Incentives,* Winston, Washington, D.C., 1973.

47. Essman, W. B., Nicotine-related neurochemical changes: Some implications for motivational mechanisms and differences, in *Smoking Behavior: Motives and Incentives,* W. L. Dunn, (Ed.), Winston, Washington, D.C., 1973, pp. 51–65.

48. Evangelista, A. M., R. C. Gattoni, and I. Izquierdo, Effect of amphetamine, nicotine and hexamethoninum on performance of a conditioned response during acquisition and retention trials, *Pharmacology,* **3,** 91–96 (1970).

49. Faulkner, J. M., Nicotine poisoning by absorption through the skin, *JAMA,* **100,** 1664–1665 (1933).

50. Fërno, O., et al., A substitute for tobacco smoking, *Psychopharmacologia,* **31,** 201–204 (1973).

51. Feyerabend, C., T. Levitt, and M. A. H. Russell, A rapid gas-liquid chromatographic estimation of nicotine in biological fluids, *J. Pharm. Pharmacol.,* **27,** 434–436 (1975).

52. Finnegan, J. K., P. S. Larson, and H. B. Haag, The role of nicotine in the cigarette habit, *Science,* **102,** 94–96 (1945).

53. Frankenhauser, M., A. L. Myrsten, and B. Post, Psychophysiological reactions to cigarette smoking, *Scand. J. Psychol.,* **11,** 237–245 (1970).

54. Frankenhauser, M., A. L. Myrsten, B. Post, and G. Johansson, Behavioral and physiological effects of cigarette smoking in a monotonous situation, *Psychopharmacologia,* **22,** 1–7 (1971).

55. Friedman, J., T. Horvath, and R. Meares, Tobacco smoking and a "stimulus barrier", *Nature,* **248,** 455–456 (1974).

56. Frith, C. D., The effect of varying the nicotine content of cigarettes on human smoking behavior, *Psychopharmacologia,* **19,** 188–192 (1971).

57. Garg, M., The effect of nicotine on two different types of learning, *Psychopharmacologia,* **15,** 408–414 (1969).

58. Garg, M., and H. C. Holland, Consolidation and maze learning: A further study of post-trial injections of a stimulant drug (nicotine), *Int. J. Neuropharmacol.,* **7,** 55–59 (1968).

59. Gehlbach, S. H., W. A. Williams, L. D. Perry, J. I. Freeman, J. J. Langone, L. V. Peta, and H. Van Vunakis, Nicotine absorption by workers harvesting green tobacco, *Lancet*, **1,** 478–480 (1975).

60. Gershon-Cohen, J., A. G. B. Borden, and M. B. Hermel, Thermography of extremities after smoking, *Br. J. Radiol.*, **42,** 189–191 (1969).

61. Glauser, S. C., E. M. Glauser, M. M. Reindenberg, B. F. Rusy, and R. J. Tallarida, Metabolic changes associated with the cessation of cigarette smoking, *Arch. Environ. Health*, **20,** 377–381 (1970).

62. Glick, S. D., B. Zimmerberg, and M. E. Jarvik, Titration of oral nicotine intake with smoking behavior in monkeys, *Nature*, **233,** 207–208 (1971).

63. Goldfarb, T. L., and M. E. Jarvik, Accommodation to restricted tobacco smoke intake in cigarette smokers, *Int. J. Addict.*, **7,** 559–565 (1972).

64. Goldfarb, T. L., M. E. Jarvik, and S. D. Glick, Cigarette nicotine content as a determinant of human smoking behavior, *Psychopharmacologia*, **17,** 89–93 (1970).

65. Goldstein, L., R. A. Beck, and D. L. Mundschenk, Effects of nicotine upon cortical and subcortical electrical activity of the rabbit brain: Quantitative analysis, *Ann. N.Y. Acad. Sci.*, **142,** 170–180 (1967).

66. Gorrod, J. W., and P. Jenner, The metabolism of tobacco alkaloids, in *Essays in Toxicology*, Vol. 6, Academic Press, New York, 1975, pp. 35–78.

67. Gorrod, J. W., P. Jenner, G. R. Keysell, and B. R. Mikhael, Oxidative metabolism of nicotine by cigarette smokers with cancer of the urinary bladder, *J. Nat. Cancer Inst.*, **52,** 1421–1424 (1974).

67a. Haines, C. F., D. K. Mahajan, D. Miljkovic, M. Miljković, and E. S. Vesell et al., Radioimmunoassay of plasma nicotine in habituated and naive smokers, *Clin. Pharmacol. Ther.*, **16,** 1083–1089 (1974).

68. Hall, G. H., Effects of nicotine and tobacco smoke on the electrical activity of the cerebral cortex and olfactory bulb, *Br. J. Pharmacol.*, **38,** 271–286 (1970).

69. Hall, G. H., and C. F. Morrison, New evidence for a relationship between tobacco smoking, nicotine dependence and stress, *Nature*, **243,** 199–201 (1973).

70. Hall, G. H., and D. M. Turner, Effects of nicotine on the release of 3H-noradrenaline from the hypothalamus, *Biochem. Pharmacol.*, **21,** 1829–1838 (1972).

71. Hall, R. A., M. Rappaport, H. K. Hopkins, and R. Griffin, Tobacco and evoked potential, *Science*, **180,** 212–214 (1973).

72. Heimstra, N. W., N. R. Bancroft, and A. R. DeKock, Effects of smoking upon sustained performance in a simulated driving task, *Ann. N.Y. Acad. Sci.*, **142,** 295–307 (1967).

73. Heimstra, N. W., The effects of smoking on mood change, in *Smoking Behavior: Motives and Incentives*, W. L. Dunn, (Ed.), Winston, Washington, D.C., 1973, pp. 197–207.

74. Herxheimer, A., R. L. Griffiths, B. Hamilton, and M. Wakefield, Circulatory effects of nicotine aerosol inhalations and cigarette smoking in man, *Lancet*, **2,** 754–755 (1967).

75. Hutchinson, R. R., and G. S. Emley, Effects of nicotine on avoidance, conditioned suppression and aggression response measures in animals and man, in *Smoking Behavior: Motives and Incentives*, W. L. Dunn, (Ed.), Winston, Washington, D.C., 1973, pp. 171–196.

76. Ilebekk, A., N. E. Miller, and O. D. Mjös, Effects of nicotine and inhalation of cigarette smoke on total body oxygen consumption in dogs, *Scand. J. Clin. Lab. Invest.*, **35,** 67–72 (1975).

77. Irving, D. W., and T. Yamamoto, Cigarette smoking and cardiac output, *Br. Heart J.*, **25,** 126–132 (1963).

78. Isaac, P. F., and M. J. Rand, Blood levels of nicotine and physiological effects after inhalation of tobacco smoke, *Eur. J. Pharmacol.*, **8,** 269–283 (1969).

79. Isaac, P. F., and M. J. Rand, Cigarette smoking and plasma levels of nicotine, *Nature*, **236,** 308–310 (1972).

79a. Itil, T. M., G. A. Ulett, W. Hsu, H. Klingenberg, and J. A. Ulett, The effects of smoking withdrawal on quantitatively analysed EEG, *Clin. Electroencephalography*, **2,** 44–51 (1971).

80. Jarvik, M. E., The role of nicotine in the smoking habit, in *Learning Mechanisms in Smoking*, W. A. Hunt, (Ed.), Aldine, Chicago, 1970, pp. 155–190.

81. Jarvik, M. E., S. D. Glick, and R. K. Nakamura, Inhibition of cigarette smoking by orally administered nicotine, *Clin. Pharmacol. Ther.*, **11,** 574–576 (1970).

82. Jenner, P., J. W. Gorrod, and A. H. Beckett, The absorption of nicotine-1′-*N*-oxide and its reduction in the gastro-intestinal tract in man, *Xenobiotica*, **3,** 341–349 (1973).

83. Johnston, L. M., Tobacco smoking and nicotine, *Lancet*, **2,** 742 (1942).

84. Keenan, A., and F. N. Johnson, Development of behavioral tolerance to nicotine in the rat, *Experientia*, **28,** 428–429 (1972).

85. Kerrigan, R., A. C. Jain, and J. T. Doyle, The circulatory response to smoking at rest and after exercise, *Am. J. Med. Sci.*, **255,** 113 (1968).

86. Kershbaum, A., and S. Bellet, Cigarette, cigar and pipe smoking: Some differences in biochemical effects, *Geriatrics*, **23,** 126–134 (1968).

87. Kershbaum, A., D. J. Pappajohn, S. Bellet, M. Hirabayashi, and H. Shafiiha, Effect of smoking and nicotine on adrenocortical secretion, *JAMA*, **203,** 275–278 (1968).

88. Khosla, T., and C. R. Lowe, Obesity and smoking habits, *Br. Med. J.*, **4,** 10–13 (1971).

89. Knapp, P. H., C. M. Bliss, and H. Wells, Addictive aspects of heavy cigarette smoking, *Am. J. Psychiat.*, **119,** 966–972 (1963).

90. Langone, J. J., H. B. Gjika, and H. Van Vunakis, Nicotine and its metabolites: Radioimmunoassays for nicotine and cotinine, *Biochemistry*, **12,** 5025–5030 (1973).

91. Larson, P. S., Absorption of nicotine under various conditions of tobacco use, *Ann. N.Y. Acad. Sci.*, **90,** 31–35 (1960).

92. Lautenbach, B. F., On a new function of the liver, *Philad. Med. Times*, **7,** 387–394 (1876–1877).

93. Lincoln, J. E., Weight gain after cessation of smoking, *JAMA*, **210,** 1765 (1969).

94. Lucchesi, B. R., C. R. Schuster, and G. S. Emley, The role of nicotine as a determinant of cigarette smoking frequency in man with observations of certain cardiovascular effects associated with the tobacco alkaloid, *Clin. Pharmacol. Ther.*, **8,** 789–796 (1967).

95. Manning, F., E. Wyn Pugh, and K. Boddy, Effect of cigarette smoking on fetal breathing movements in normal pregnancies, *Br. Med. J.*, **1,** 552–553 (1975).

96. Mausner, B., and E. S. Platt, *Smoking: A Behavioral Analysis*, Pergamon Press, New York, 1971.

97. McKennell, A. C., and R. K. Thomas, *Adults' and Adolescents' Smoking Habits and Attitudes*, Government Social Survey, Her Majesty's Stationery Office, London, 1967.

98. Morrison, C. F., Effects of nicotine on operant behavior in rats, *Int. J. Neuropharmacol.*, **6,** 229–240 (1967).

99. Morrison, C. F., The modification by physostigmine of some effects of nicotine on bar-pressing behavior of rats, *Br. J. Pharmacol. Chemother.*, **32,** 28–33 (1968).

100. Morrison, C. F., Effects of nicotine and its withdrawal on the performance of rats on signalled and unsignalled avoidance schedules, *Psychopharmacologia*, **38,** 25–35 (1974).

101. Morrison, C. F., and J. A. Stephenson, The occurrence of tolerance to a central depressant effect of nicotine, *Br. J. Pharmacol.*, **46,** 151–156 (1972).

102. Murphree, H. B., (Ed.), The effects of nicotine and smoking on the central nervous system, *Ann. N.Y. Acad. Sci.*, **142,** 1–333 (1967).

103. Murphree, H. B., C. C. Pfeiffer, and L. M. Price, Electroencephalographic changes in man following smoking, *Ann. N.Y. Acad. Sci.*, **142,** 245–260 (1967).

104. Murphy, P. J., Enzymatic oxidation of nicotine to nicotine Δ 1′(5′) iminium ion, *J. Biol. Chem.*, **248,** 2796–2800 (1973).

105. Nelson, J. M., K. Pelley, and L. Goldstein, Chronic nicotine treatment in rats: EEG amplitude and variability changes occuring within and between structures, *Res. Commun. Chem. Pathol. Pharmacol.*, **5,** 694–704 (1973).

106. Olds, J., R. P. Travis, and R. C. Schwing, Topographic organization of hypothalamic self-stimulation functions, *J. Comp. Physiol. Psychol.*, **53,** 23–32 (1960).

107. Olds, J., Hypothalamic substrates of reward, *Physiol. Rev.*, **42,** 554–604 (1962).

108. Orsingher, O. A., and S. Fulginiti, Effects of alpha-methyl tyrosine and adrenergic blocking agents on the facilitating action of amphetamine and nicotine on learning in rats, *Psychopharmacologia*, **19,** 231–240 (1971).

109. Pentecost, B., and J. Shillingford, The acute effects of smoking on myocardial performance in patients with coronary arterial disease, *Br. Heart J.*, **26,** 422–429 (1964).

110. Perlman, H. H., and A. M. Dannenberg, The excretion of nicotine in breast milk and urine from cigarette smoking, *JAMA*, **120,** 1003–1009 (1942).

111. Phillips, C., The EEG changes associated with smoking, *Psychophysiology*, **8,** 64–74 (1971).

112. Pieper, W. A., and J. M. Cole, Operant control of smoking in great apes, *Behav. Res. Meth. Instrum.*, **5,** 4–6 (1973).

113. Read, N. W., and P. Grech, Effect of cigarette smoking on competence of the pylorus: Preliminary study, *Br. Med. J.*, **3,** 313–316 (1973).

114. Richardson, R. G., (Ed.), *The Second World Conference on Smoking and Health*, Pitman Medical, London, 1971.

115. Roth, G. M., J. B. McDonald, and C. Sheard, The effect of smoking cigarettes, *JAMA*, **125,** 761–767 (1944).

116. Royal College of Physicians, *Third Report on Smoking and Health*, Pitmans, London, 1977. In preparation.

117. Russell, M. A. H., Cigarette smoking: Natural history of a dependence disorder, *Br. J. Med. Psychol.*, **44,** 1–16 (1971).

118. Russell, M. A. H., The smoking habit and its classification, *Practitioner*, **212,** 791–800 (1974).

119. Russell, M. A. H., and C. Feyerabend, Blood and urinary nicotine in nonsmokers, *Lancet*, **1,** 179–181 (1975).

120. Russell, M. A. H., C. Wilson, C. Feyerabend, and P. V. Cole, Effect of nicotine chewing gum on smoking behavior and as an aid to cigarette withdrawal. In preparation (1976).

121. Russell, M. A. H., C. Wilson, U. A. Patel, P. V. Cole, and C. Feyerabend, Comparison

of effect on tobacco consumption and carbon monoxide absorption of changing to high and low nicotine cigarettes, *Br. Med. J.*, **4,** 512–516 (1973).

122. Russell, M. A. H., C. Wilson, U. A. Patel, C. Feyerabend, and P. V. Cole, Plasma nicotine levels after smoking cigarettes with high, medium and low nicotine yields, *Br. Med. J.*, **2,** 414–416 (1975).

123. Russell, M. A. H., P. V. Cole, M. S. Idle, and L. Adams, Carbon monoxide yields of cigarettes and their relation to nicotine yield and type of filter, *Br. Med. J.*, **3,** 71–73 (1975).

124. Sarin, C. L., Effects of smoking on digital blood-flow velocity, *JAMA.*, **229,** 1327–1328 (1974).

125. Schachter, S., *Lecture given at Institute for Psychiatry*, London, March 18th, 1975.

126. Schechter, M. D., and M. J. Rand, Effect of acute deprivation of smoking on aggression and hostility, *Psychopharmacologia*, **35,** 19–28 (1974).

127. Schievelbein, H., and K. Grundke, Gas chromatographic method for the estimation of nicotine in blood and tissues, *Z. Anal. Chem.*, **237,** 1–8 (1968).

128. Schmiterlöw, C. G., E. Hansson, and G. Andersson, L. E. Applegren, and P. C. Hoffman, Distribution of nicotine in central nervous system, *Ann. N.Y. Acad. Sci.*, **142,** 2–14 (1967).

129. Schnedorf, J. G., and A. C. Ivy, The effect of tobacco smoking on the alimentary canal, *JAMA*, **112,** 898–903 (1939).

130. Silverman, A. P., Behavior of rats given a "smoking dose" of nicotine, *Anim. Behav.*, **19,** 67–74 (1971).

131. Stalhandske, T., Effects of increased liver metabolism of nicotine on its uptake, elimination and toxicity in mice, *Acta Physiol. Scand.*, **80,** 222–234 (1970).

132. Stein, L., and C. D. Wise, Release of hypothalamic norepinephrine by rewarding electrical stimulation or amphetamine in the unanaesthetised rat, *Fed. Proc.*, **26,** 651 (1967).

133. Stolerman, I. P., R. Fink, and M. E. Jarvik, Acute and chronic tolerance to nicotine measured by activity in rats, *Psychopharmacologia*, **30,** 329–342 (1973).

134. Stolerman, I. P., T. Goldfarb, R. Fink, and M. E. Jarvik, Influencing cigarette smoking with nicotine antagonists, *Psychopharmacologia*, **28,** 247–259 (1973).

135. Swett, C., Drowsiness due to chlorpromazine in relation to cigarette smoking, *Arch. Gen Psychiatr.*, **31,** 211–213 (1974).

136. Thomas, C. B., The relationship of smoking and habits of nervous tension, in *Smoking Behavior: Motives and Incentives*, W. L. Dunn, (Ed.), Winston, Washington, D.C. (1973), pp. 157–170.

137. Thompson, W. B., Nicotine in breast milk, *Am. J. Obst. Gynec.*, **26,** 662–667 (1933).

138. Travell, J., Absorption of nicotine from various sites, *Ann. N.Y. Acad. Sci.*, **90,** 13–30 (1960).

139. Turner, D. M., The metabolism of (^{14}C) nicotine in the cat, *Biochem. J.*, **115,** 889–896 (1969).

140. Turner, D. M., Metabolism of small multiple doses of (^{14}C) nicotine in the cat, *Br. J. Pharmacol. Chemother.*, **41,** 521–529 (1971).

141. Turner, D. M., A. K. Armitage, R. H. Briant, and C. T. Dollery, Metabolism of nicotine by the isolated perfused dog lung, *Xenobiotica*, **5,** 539–551 (1975).

142. Turner, J. A. M., R. W. Sillet, and K. P. Ball, Some effects of changing to low-tar and low-nicotine cigarettes, *Lancet*, **2,** 737–739 (1974).

143. Ulett, J. A., and T. M. Itil, Quantitative electroencephalogram in smoking and smoking deprivation, *Science*, **164**, 969–970 (1969).

144. Volle, R. L., and G. B. Koelle, in *The Pharmacological Basis of Therapeutics*, L. S. Goodman and A. Gilman (Eds.), Macmillan, New York, 1970, pp. 585–600.

145. Waingrow, S., and D. Horn, Relationship of number of cigarettes smoked to tar rating, *National Cancer Institute Monograph. No. 28*, 29–33 (1968).

146. Warwick, K. M., and H. J. Eysenck, Experimental studies of the behavioral effects of nicotine, *Pharmakosychiatr. Neuropsychopharmakol.*, **1**, 145–169 (1968).

147. Webster, D. D., The dynamic quantitation of spasticity with automated integrals of passive motion resistance, *Clin. Pharmacol. Ther.*, **5**, 900–908 (1964).

148. Wilkinson, A. R., and D. Johnston, Inhibitory effect of cigarette smoking on gastric secretion stimulated by pentagastrin in man, *Lancet*, **2**, 628–632 (1971).

149. Wolff, W. A., M. A. Hawkins, and W. E. Giles, Nicotine in blood in relation to smoking, *J. Pharmacol. Exp. Ther.*, **95**, 145–148 (1949).

150. Zagona, S. V. (Ed.), *Studies and Issues in Smoking Behavior*, University of Arizona Press, Tucson, Arizona, 1967.

CHAPTER TWO

CAFFEINE AS A DRUG OF ABUSE

R. M. GILBERT, *Addiction Research Foundation, 33 Russell Street Toronto, Canada*

Say, shall then
These less than coffee's self, these coffee-men,
These sons of nothing that can hardly make
Their broth for laughing, how the jest doth take,
Yet grin, and give for the vine's pure blood
A loathsome portion—not yet understood,
Syrup of soot, or essence of old shoes,
Dashed with diurnals or the book of news.

Anon, 1663. (Quoted in A. Gray, *Over the black coffee*, 1902.)
Also attributed to
Ben Jonson, 1573–1637.

1. INTRODUCTION

In their preface to the first volume of this series (141), the editors offered alternative criteria for the selection of topics to be included. An area would be covered if "enough recent progress had been made to warrant a review," or if "debate or confusion are such as to require an analysis and clarification of concepts." Caffeine as a topic meets neither criterion. Although the caffeine literature dated 1974 alone includes well over 100 items, there have been insufficient recent research advances in caffeine problems to justify a review. Furthermore, whatever debate and confusion exist with respect to caffeine will likely be resolved by empirical rather than by conceptual analysis.

This chapter is dedicated to the memory of Dr. Robert J. Gibbins, who was a kind man and a devoted scientist.

Nevertheless, there are some reasons for writing about caffeine at this time. The focus of public concern about drugs seems to be shifting away from the harm caused by psychotropic drugs that are used by comparatively few people, such as heroin, cocaine, and LSD, and towards the harm caused by drugs that many people use, such as alcohol, barbiturates, and the minor tranquilizers. Caffeine is almost certainly one of the four most widely used psychotropic drugs; the other three are alcohol, arecoline (a central nervous system stimulant that occurs in betel nuts), and nicotine. A substantial proportion of the adult population of North America and many other parts of the world may be physically dependent upon caffeine. Although it is apparently benign in normal use, there are worrisome suggestions that caffeine may be implicated in anxiety states and heart conditions, in genetic abnormalities, and in a host of other pathologies. Thus it seems appropriate to report on the extent of the use of this drug, and on the degree of its implication in disease. A further reason for reporting on caffeine is that caffeine use is a prominent but little researched human behavior, whose investigation may give us insights not only into the dynamics of drug taking, but also into what is sometimes grandly referred to as the human condition.

This paper will focus on the possibility that caffeine is a drug of abuse. The only available definition of drug abuse—"persistent or sporadic excessive drug use inconsistent with or unrelated to acceptable medical practice" (406)—is not entirely appropriate in the case of caffeine because there is no acceptable medical practice regarding caffeine beverage consumption. In elaborating their concept of a *drug problem,* the Kalants (208) have argued that there are two types: ". . . a *social problem* arises whenever the use of these substances by certain members of society puts them in conflict with the rest of society . . . an individual *medical problem* arises whenever the extent of the drug use is such as to produce injury to the health or mental well-being of the user" (p. 3). One kind of social problem exists only when use of the drug is proscribed. Clearly, caffeine does not present this kind of problem except among certain groups, including members of the Mormon and Seventh-Day Adventist churches. Another kind of social problem occurs as a by-product of a medical or behavioral problem. Drug-related disease may be a burden upon associates, who suffer the abuser's drug-caused disabilities, and upon the community at large, who may pay for medical treatment and other means of support. It is also possible that the benefits accruing to a society from its use of caffeine far outweigh such disadvantages. For the moment, consideration of the costs and benefits to society of caffeine or of any other psychotropic drug is largely a matter of speculation. The focus of concern about caffeine must necessarily be directed towards caffeine use as a medical or behavioral problem, and much of this paper consists of evaluation of the need for concern.

In considering whether or not caffeine is a drug of abuse, it is necessary to establish (*a*) that caffeine is a drug, (*b*) that a large amount of it is used by an appreciable number of people, and (*c*) that use of large amounts is associated with established pathologic conditions. There seems to be little doubt that caffeine is a "chemical agent that affects living processes" (116), and not much more doubt that caffeine is a "substance, other than those required for the maintenance of normal health (as opposed to the correction of a disease), which by its chemical nature alters the structure or function of a living organism" (208). Nevertheless, in order to stress the point that caffeine is a drug, the substantive part of this chapter begins with an overview of caffeine's pharmacology. At least two good, fairly recent reviews are available, by Truitt (388) and by Ritchie (325)*. While being reasonably comprehensive, the overview given here is decidedly superficial, partly because emphasis is given to material published since those two reviews were prepared, i.e., since 1969–1970, and partly because of the competence of the present reviewer. Certain areas that were given little attention in those reviews are given more attention here, notably the behavioral pharmacology of caffeine and the interactions between caffeine and other drugs. The overview will at least give readers an impression of the scope and status of research on caffeine's pharmacology in the early 1970s. It will provide ways into the current literature for those who wish to pursue particular matters in further detail. Above all, it will help to dispel any lingering doubts that caffeine is a drug. Readers who are bored by or otherwise disaffected by pharmacology would do well to skip the next eight sections.

A drug must be used before it is abused. Although there can be no doubt that caffeine is widely used, the actual extent of its use is not well established. Accordingly, the sections on pharmacology and related topics are followed by an attempt to portray the extent of caffeine use, with special emphases on the range of consumption and on the proportion of heavy users in the population. This section is the only part of the chapter that contains wholly original material. Readers familiar with the caffeine literature may well want to read Section 10 and no other. It provides a context for Section 11, in which recently available data on the incidence of pathologies associated with caffeine use are reviewed. A concluding section suggests that caffeine is a drug of abuse in many countries, in the sense that an ap-

* Since the preparation of this chapter, a fifth edition of Goodman and Gilman's compendium has appeared, dated 1975. Two associate editors have been added (A. G. Gilman and G. B. Koelle). Ritchie's chapter on the xanthines has been updated by the citation of 31 new references and the omission of 35 of the 63 cited in the fourth edition. The chapter has been shortened from 13 to 12 pages, but a brief new section on the xanthines and myocardial infarction has been included. The 31 new references include 25 not cited in the present chapter; most of them concern theophylline.

preciable portion of the population ingests a quantity of the drug sufficient to increase the risk of occurrence of many behavioral and medical disorders that are probably caused by caffeine.

2. DOSE LEVELS AND CONCENTRATIONS OF CAFFEINE

> Breakfast ought, in rigid training, to consist of plain biscuit (not bread), broiled beef steaks or mutton chops, under-done without any fat, and half a pint of bottled ale—the genuine Scots ale is the best. Should it be found too strong fare at the commencement, we permit instead of the ale, one small breakfast cup—not more—of good strong black tea or of coffee—weak tea or coffee is always bad for the nerves as well as the complexion.
>
> Advice on 'Beauty training for ladies'
> given in *The Family Oracle of Health*, 1824.

In attempting to make sense of the literature on caffeine, I was often helped by recourse to longer versions of Tables 1 and 2. These two tables briefly in-

TABLE 1 SELECTED CAFFEINE CONCENTRATIONS

Concentration (μg/ml)	Source, Equivalent or Use	Reference
0.8	Found in plasma of human newborn	187
1	Average level of exposure of most cells of many humans	218
5	Potentiated toxicity of carcinogen	98
6	Approximate peak plasma concentration 30 min. after a strong cup of coffee	249
8	Urine concentration when plasma concentration was probably close to 1 μg/ml	187
60	Enhanced cell killing by chlorambucil	25a
65	Approximate taste threshold in normal humans	168
144	Typical concentration in tea	149
360	Typical concentration in coffee	149
400	Minimum concentration causing muscle contraction	240
500	Minimum concentration causing chromosome breaks in human cells	288
650	Approximate taste threshold in non-PTC tasters	168
1170	Maximum concentration in coffee	149
1400	Caused stomach ulcers in rats	308
4000	Apparently nontoxic as sole drinking fluid for mice	109
15,000	Approximate solubility at room temperature	—
20,000	Highest concentration used in an experiment	37

TABLE 2 SELECTED CAFFEINE DOSES

Dose (mg/kg)	Route	Species	Source or Effect	Reference
0.4	Oral	Human	Typical cup of tea (27 mg)	149
1.1	Oral	Human	Typical cup of coffee (74 mg)	149
2.0	?	Human	Minimum toxic dose	307
2.5	Oral	Human	Strong cup of coffee (176 mg)	149
2.9	Oral	Human	Reduced fatigue effects	287
3.2	Oral	Human	Raised free fatty acid levels	85
3.6	Oral	Human	Raised fasting metabolic rate	261
4.3	Oral	Human	Raised ocular tension in glaucoma	158
5.0	i.p.	Mouse	Reduced aggression	392
6.3	Oral	Rat	Caused gastric ulcers in 4 days	308
7.0	i.v.	Human	Caused convulsions	307
10	Oral	Rat	Blocked absorption of ethanol	352
22	Oral	Rat	Blocked metabolism of other drugs	216
25	i.p.	Mouse	Doubled activity	368
26	Oral	Rat	Increased preference for ethanol	322
50	?	Mouse	Lowest daily dose producing embryotoxicity	274
57	i.v.	Human	Lowest recorded fatal dose	307
80	i.v.	Cat	Estimated LD_{50}	307
150	Oral	Rat	Estimated LD_{50}	42
325	Oral	Mouse	Nonfatal when given daily but reduced pregnancy rate	109

dicate the ranges of caffeine concentrations and doses that are encountered in the literature. (The comments beside the various levels are necessarily laconic, and they may be misleading without reference to the respective sources.)

Dose levels in Table 2 are given in terms of milligrams of the drug per kilogram of body weight, which is the usual mode of expression. Such rationalization is useful within a species, but it can be very misleading when applied between species. Drug effects, like most other effects (164, 165), tend not to be invariant with respect to body weight. An alternative basis for comparison is surface area. The basal metabolic rate of many species, including mouse, goose, and man, is close to 1000 kcal/m^2 of surface area per day (28). Peters (307) has indicated that the lethal doses of caffeine for rats, cats, and humans are the same when correction is made for surface area. The surface area of an animal in square meters is approximately 0.07

× (body weight in kg)$^{3/4}$. This relationship has given rise to the notion of metabolic weight (= body weight$^{3/4}$), which has been used by some authors (1, 264) in characterizing the dose levels used in their studies with animals: doses are described as being equivalent to so many cups of coffee or tea in humans. Dose equivalents based on metabolic weight are substantially lower than those based on body weight: 20 mg/kg in the rat is equivalent to about 23 cups of coffee (at 75 mg caffeine per cup) in a 70-kg man on a body-weight basis, but to only 8 cups of coffee when correction is made for differences in metabolic weight. Other authors, apparently oblivious of the inadequacy of conversions based on body weight, claim extraordinarily large beverage-intake equivalents for their animals (274, 379, 380, 419), and thereby perpetrate misleading impressions about the safety of caffeine when these seemingly large doses are found to be without effect.

3. BASIC PHARMACOLOGY OF CAFFEINE

> Coffee is supposed to owe its characters to a peculiar chemical principle called Caffein.*
>
> John Lindley, *An Introduction to the Natural System of Botany*, 1830.

Chemistry

Caffeine is a trimethylated xanthine (molecular weight 194.19), sharing two methyl groups with each of two pharmacologically active dimethylxanthines, theophylline (found in tea), and theobromine (found in cocoa). Xanthine is dioxypurine, and is thus structurally similar to the two purines, adenine and guanine, that constitute two of the four symbols of the genetic code. These compounds are configured in Fig. 1, together with paraxanthine and 1-methylxanthine, which have been reported to be metabolites of caffeine. Caffeine is not acidic, unlike the other methylxanthines. It will form true salts only with strong acids, but fairly stable double salts or complexes can be formed with the alkali salts of weak organic acids. One of these is formed by mixing caffeine and sodium benzoate to provide a source of caffeine that is often used therapeutically because it is more soluble in water

* There is a small puzzle concerning the spelling of caffeine. When first isolated from coffee by Runge in 1820, it was known as caffein, but by 1863 an "e" had been appended, in England at least, to provide what is now the conventional orthography on both sides of the Atlantic. In 1911, however, the *Journal of Pharmacology and Experimental Therapeutics* in the United States still appeared to prefer caffein (312). The caffeine in tea is sometimes called "theine" (never "thein"), which was the name given by Oudrey to caffeine when he isolated it from tea in 1827, supposing it to be a distinctly different compound.

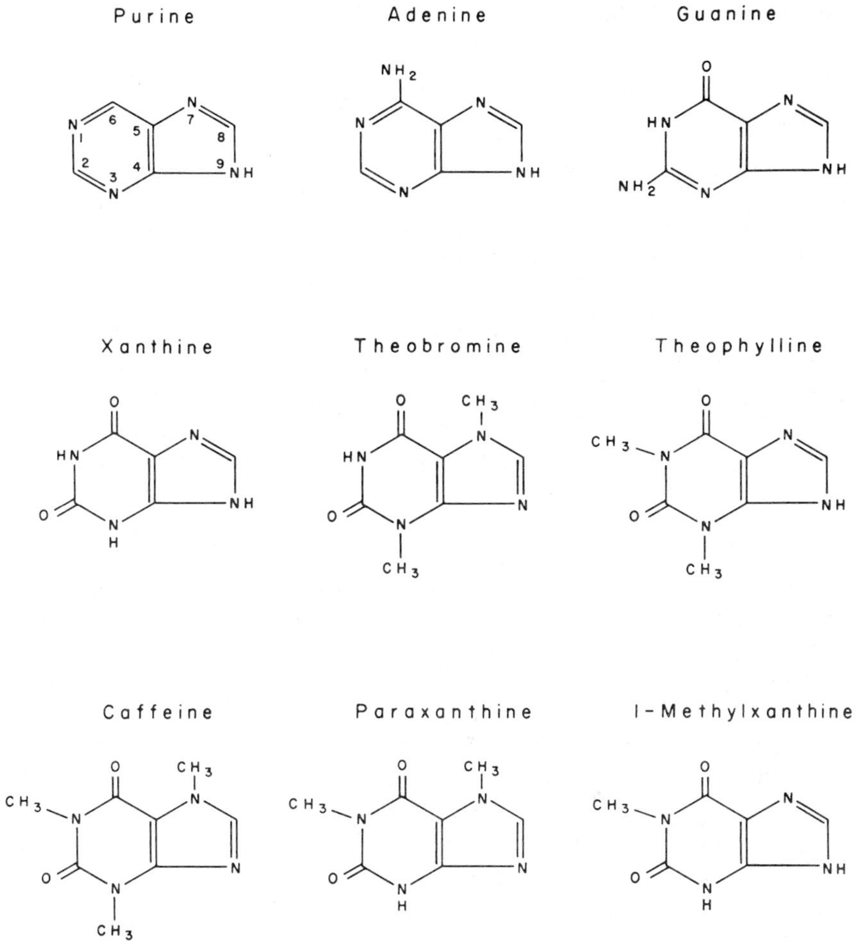

Fig. 1. Formulae of purine and eight purine derivatives, including adenine and guanine, which are involved in genetic coding, xanthine, and five methylxanthines of which three, caffeine, theobromine, and theophylline, occur in beverages, and two, paraxanthine and 1-methylxanthine are reported metabolites of caffeine in human urine.

than caffeine alone (> 40% as opposed to < 3% at 20°C, although caffeine's solubility in boiling water approaches that of caffeine sodium benzoate). Another therapeutic mixture is caffeine and citric acid (water solubility ≃25% at 20°C). As used, both mixtures provide close to 50% caffeine. A number of clinically used drugs form complexes with caffeine in near-body-temperature solutions (182, 183). It is possible that each member of such a complex affects the other member's bioavailability when both are present in an organism (32), thereby providing a basis for some of the drug interactions discussed in Section 8.

Sources

> Foreign drinks to be found in England are coffee, thé, and chocolate at coffee houses.
> John Locke, 1679. (Quoted in Peter King's *Life of John Locke, with extracts from his journals, correspondence, and commonplace books*, 1830.)

Caffeine is classed as an alkaloid, because it forms salts with acids, because of its physiologic action, and because it occurs in plants. The alkaloid has been found in the leaves of tea, guarana, and various members of the holly family, in kola nuts, coffee beans, and in cocoa beans. A small amount also occurs in the leaves of the coffee plant, and in the leaves and pods of the cocoa plant (358). With the possible exception of the leaves and seeds of the guarana plant, native to Brazil (69), tea leaves have the highest concentration of caffeine (1.8–4.1%), and they are used to provide the pure alkaloid, as well as for beverage purposes. Caffeine biosynthesis in tea occurs during formation of the tea shoot. It is probable that the systems involved in caffeine biosynthesis are closely associated with purine nucleotide and nucleic acid metabolism. Little is known, however, about the physiologic significance of caffeine formation or about the role of caffeine in plants (375). Caffeine can be synthesized artificially from dimethyl urea and malonic acid. Coffee beans contain between 1.0 and 2.1% caffeine (211, 252). However, as will be indicated later, when human caffeine consumption is being considered, coffee in beverage form usually contains more caffeine than tea in beverage form because a much greater weight of coffee is used to make a given quantity of beverage.

Absorption and Distribution

Caffeine is readily absorbed, either parenterally or from the gastrointestinal tract, and rapidly distributed throughout all tissues and organs as a function of water content. Caffeine injected into the carotid artery appears within the brain in 15 sec (284). Peak brain levels occur at about 5 min after intraperitoneal injection (341). Peak plasma levels may occur later after intramuscular injection (339), but there appear to be no good comparisons between absorption rates after administration via different routes. Oral, rectal, and subcutaneous routes have been reported to be almost equally toxic (307).

Caffeine administered orally appears in all tissues within 5 min, although, as with every drug, its rate of entering and leaving different organs varies (52). Peak blood plasma levels are reached at about 30 min after oral administration in man (249, 339). There may be considerable species differences; for example, in the pig, peak plasma levels are not reached until about 5 hr after oral administration (83). The circumstances of administration of caffeine can affect absorption. Caffeine in Coca-Cola has been found to be much more slowly absorbed than caffeine in tea or coffee (249), which appeared to be absorbed at about the same rate as a caffeine solution in water (339). The absorption of caffeine in Coca-Cola could have been delayed by its lower temperature, which may have reduced the rate of gastrointestinal blood flow. Other substances in Coca-Cola may help to retard absorption, especially sucrose, which constitutes 10% by weight of most soft drinks; gastric emptying of a caffeine meal has been shown to be delayed by glucose (66).

Absorption of theophylline from rat intestine is facilitated by weak (5%) and retarded by strong (20%) solutions of ethanol (229), but a similar effect of ethanol on caffeine absorption has not been reported. (Caffeine's effect on ethanol absorption is discussed in Section 8.)

Peak blood plasma levels after the ingestion of a strong cup of coffee or its equivalent (160 mg caffeine) by an average man appear to be in the order of 6 μg/ml (249, 332, 339), although lower values have been reported (20). Caffeine crosses the placenta (156, 187) and appears to accumulate in fetal brain tissue (136); it is secreted into maternal milk (363), and it enters gonadal tissue (156).

Metabolism and Elimination

Caffeine is almost entirely transformed in humans; only about 1% of the alkaloid is excreted via urine (20, 80). Some mammals transform less of the drug; for example, about 9% has been reported unchanged in the rat (217, 318), 3–6% in the mouse (51), and 3% in the squirrel monkey (50). The principal metabolites appearing in human urine have been reported to be methyluric acid and 1-methylxanthine (Fig. 1), accounting for 30 and 20%, respectively, of ingested caffeine (80). In other species, paraxanthine (Fig. 1) has been reported to be a major metabolite (50–52, 217), and a recent study identified 1,3,7-trimethyldihydrouric acid as the principal metabolite of caffeine appearing in mouse urine (318). Paraxanthine and theobromine (rather than 1-methylxanthine) have also been identified as the principal methylxanthine metabolites in human urine (345), and paraxanthine has been shown to be the main tissue metabolite (402). Clearly, further work is required to resolve these considerable discrepancies. One feature of such work should be determination of baseline methylxanthine levels, a feature that seems to be absent from reported studies of human caffeine metabolism. Because of prevalence of purine compounds in organisms and in their food, and because of the many opportunities for methylation and oxidation during metabolism, indigenous production and excretion of methylxanthines are to be expected.

Even though little caffeine may be excreted via human urine, considerable renal concentration may occur. One human mother had a urine concentration of 7.7 μg/ml at childbirth, when her plasma concentration was probably in the order of 1 μg/ml (187). There is some doubt as to whether caffeine is accumulated. An early study (20) showed accumulation through the day with repeated coffee drinking, but virtually complete disappearance overnight. More recently it has been reported that it may take about seven days to decaffeinate the blood of habitual coffee drinkers, and that caffeine metabolism and storage rates may differ between habitual and other users of caffeine (402); however, relevant data were not given in the report and a promised follow-up of this potentially important 1969 study has yet to appear. The half-life of theophylline has been found to be much shorter in smokers than nonsmokers (200). This could be because smokers typically drink much more coffee than nonsmokers (see Section 10), and because metabolism of all xanthines is more rapid among habitual users of any one. Alternatively, heavy smokers may metabolize most drugs more quickly, because metabolism of the wide variety of tobacco combustion products may induce a wide range of hepatic drug-metabolizing enzymes.

The plasma half-life of caffeine in man has been reported as ranging from 2.5 to 4.5 hr (20, 339), 12–22% being metabolized per hr. This rate is a little lower than that for the mouse (52), and considerably higher than those for the squirrel monkey (50) and the pig (83), for whom half-lives of 11 and 12 hr, respectively, have been reported. Aranda and colleagues (10b) have reported that the plasma half-life of theophylline in newborn is very much longer than in adult humans, and, informally, that the difference for caffeine is even greater. (See A. W. Burg, *Drug Metabol. Rev.*, **4,** 199–228, 1975.)

Basic Biochemical Mechanisms of Caffeine Action

There are at least three possible mechanisms of caffeine action—via direct action on nucleic acids, via inhibition of cyclic 3′,5′-nucleotide phosphodiesterase and a consequent increase in cyclic adenosine 3′,5′-monophosphate (cyclic AMP), and via release of calcium ions from intracellular pools. Two or more of the three mechanisms may have a common basis; alternatively, other, quite independent mechanisms may also exist, such as the one responsible for norepinephrine turnover.

Because of the similarity of caffeine to elements of the genetic code, it is not surprising that the compound is biologically active. However, because it is substituted at the 7-position, caffeine does not form a stable bond to deoxyribose at the 9-position, and it is therefore not incorporated into deoxyribonucleic acid (152). Theophylline, very small amounts of which occur in tea, is not substituted at the 7-position (Fig. 1), and thus it is possible that theophylline is incorporated into DNA. Of more consequence, a compound that may be a principal metabolite of caffeine in humans, 1-methylxanthine, is also not substituted at the 7-position (see Fig. 1), and thus may also be incorporated. In fact, the similarity of both theophylline and 1-methylxanthine to adenine and guanine is remarkable, especially in the vicinity of the 9–position. The differences in the 1-, 2-, and (in the case of adenine) the 6-positions, which are involved in base pairing, would ensure that, if theophylline or 1-methylxanthine were taken up by deoxyribose, accurate replication of the DNA strand would not occur, thus raising the possibility of a variety of kinds of mutagenesis. Alternatively, any of the xanthines, including caffeine, could affect cell reproduction by altering the normal base ratios in the DNA precursor pool, thus causing errors in base pairing (152). Caffeine may also intercalate between base pairs, causing what are known as frame-shift mutations (68, 209, 389). Caffeine does not appear to affect the rate of DNA or RNA synthesis (235). On the other hand, DNA has been found to block certain actions of caffeine, notably caffeine's inhibition of glucose metabolism by epididymal fat (7).

Production of cyclic AMP is an important step in the adrenalin-induced mobilization of blood-glucose from liver- and muscle-stored glycogen. This substance is also a secondary messenger, mediating many of the effects of a variety of hormones (374). Concentrations of cyclic AMP in postsynaptic nerve cells are closely associated with the process of synaptic transmission (257). Cyclic AMP levels are regulated, at least in part, by phosphodiesterase, and thus it might be expected that they would be raised by interference with the activity of this enzyme. Caffeine inhibition of phosphodiesterase activity has been observed in vitro and in vivo, but a pharmacologically active dose of caffeine (20 mg/kg in the rat) did not change the phosphodiesterase activity of cerebral cortex, only the anterior pituitary (393). Moreover, the evidence for caffeine-stimulated cyclic AMP elevation in neural tissue is indirect (135), and there is at least one example of brain cyclic AMP levels being lowered by caffeine (341).

Caffeine may play a more direct role in neuromuscular activity by affecting the availability of calcium ions, whose level is highly correlated with the contractile state of muscle fibers. Caffeine has been shown to raise Ca^{2+} levels in barnacle fibers (37), in mammalian smooth muscle (278), in heart muscle (279), and in skeletal muscle (385). The exact mechanisms are unclear. Action could be solely on the sarcoplasmic reticulum (386), by increasing the release of Ca^{2+} (198), and by reducing Ca^{2+} uptake (283). Calcium could also be released at the neuromuscular junction (285).

Carbohydrate and Lipid Metabolism

Caffeine is generally believed to raise blood sugar levels, an action that can be plausibly explained in terms of cyclic AMP accumulation (388). The evidence is inconsistent, however; recent studies show little or no effect (16, 85, 282) even in obese subjects, although one study (63, 64) indicated that significant elevation by caffeine may occur only in ill health. Caffeine in coffee appears to increase glucose tolerance in normal subjects (114), but to reduce it in diabetics (199, 338, 371); no plausible mechanism has been proposed for the difference. Caffeine has been shown to have an opposite effect from insulin on the metabolism of glucose by adipose tissue (7), i.e., caffeine inhibits glucose metabolism. Moreover, caffeine antagonizes the stimulatory effect of insulin. Thus, where insulin production is faulty, caffeine may be especially likely to raise blood glucose levels.

Plasma free-fatty-acid levels have been raised in normal human subjects by coffee and caffeine (16, 85, 314a), and in liver-diseased subjects by caffeine (286), although one study has shown that serum lipid and lipoprotein levels are correlated with usual coffee consumption only in patients with heart disease and not in normal subjects (242). The rise in fatty acid levels can be blocked by insulin (314a) and by nicotinic acid (30). In one study, no elevation was found to occur in obese patients, whether diabetic or nondiabetic (85). In another study, a significant elevation in free fatty acid levels did occur in obese subjects after caffeine administration, but it was much less than the increase in subjects of normal weight (282). However, because caffeine-induced lipolysis can be blocked by simultaneous food intake (371), the lack of an effect in obese patients should not be surprising. Alternatively, because lipolysis appears to occur at a higher basal rate in the adipose tissue of the obese (334), there may merely be less scope for caffeine-induced enhancement. The lipolytic effect of a given quantity of coffee appears to be greater in young subjects than in older normal subjects (16), perhaps indicating tolerance to caffeine among the older subjects. The possibility that caffeine may be atherogenic (29) has been discounted (16). The possibility that weight regulation may be effected by caffeine-induced lipolysis does not appear to have been raised, although in one recent paper (261), the authors claimed that the increased metabolism levels associated with caffeine use may aid weight reduction. (In a recent investigation, thrice daily administration of a tablet containing 25 mg of the nasal decongestant, phenylpropanolamine, 100 mg caffeine, and vitamins to obese patients was found to aid weight loss significantly when compared with similar administration of a placebo (161). It was concluded, without further analysis, that phenylpropanolamine was the effective ingredient.)

Tea may contain a substance that counteracts the lipolytic effect of caffeine. Tea drinking is negatively correlated with serum lipid levels in heart-disease patients (242). Moreover, the prevalence of atherosclerosis seems to be higher among coffee-drinking than among tea-drinking populations (414). Tea may even be beneficial. Rabbits fed an atherogenic diet developed less atherosclerosis and evidenced lower serum lipoprotein levels when tea, rather than water, was their sole drinking fluid (414). Theophylline was found to have no such effect.

Neurochemical Effects

Caffeine's effects on the nervous system are believed to be mediated by its inhibition of phosphodiesterase breakdown of cyclic AMP (325, 388). The evidence is not good, however. Although cyclic AMP is found in greater concentration in neural tissue than elsewhere, and appears to be involved in neural activity (257, 341, 374), and, although caffeine reduces phosphodiesterase activity in the anterior pituitary (393), there is in fact no report that caffeine actually increases cyclic AMP levels in the brain, and there are at least two reports to the contrary (53, 341). Notwithstanding the lack of evidence, cyclic AMP continues to be implicated in caffeine's effects (26, 223). One recent line of research involved the induction by caffeine of increased synthesis of adrenomedullary catecholamines in intact rats, but not in spinally transected rats (357), suggesting a possible modulation of adrenal tyrosine hydroxylase synthesis by cyclic AMP during normal or increased neural activity. In an informal study in humans, prior consumption of a caffeine beverage was found to be associated with an increase in norepinephrine excretion in stressed subjects, but not in unstressed subjects (70).* Other evidence on caffeine's effects on neurotransmitter mechanisms is reviewed in Section 8, where consideration is given to caffeine's interactions with drugs that directly affect neural transmission.

As mentioned earlier, caffeine's effects on neuromuscular transmission may occur as a consequence of its effects on calcium ion levels. In a test of this possibility, caffeine was found to increase end-plate transmitter storage, mobilization, and release in a way that could be mimicked by raising local calcium levels (408).

* This work is not consistent with Swedish studies of coffee's effects on catecholamine excretion. Two reports (129a, 238a) demonstrated coffee- or caffeine-induced elimination of both epinephrine and norepinephrine in unstressed humans. In both studies the change was proportionately less in the case of norepinephrine. In the latter study (129a) epinephrine but not norepinephrine excretion was also increased by false knowledge that caffeine-free coffee contained caffeine. The caffeine doses were 225 mg (238a) and 750 mg (129a), probably sufficiently higher than in Cobb's study (70) to account for the different results.

Other Biochemical Effects

Caffeine is a well-known diuretic. It is believed to be less potent in this respect than other methylxanthines (325), but recent evidence suggests that is may be more effective than theobromine (99). The diuretic effect may be due to increased renal blood flow, and also to a direct effect on the renal tubule (271). However, there are paradoxical cases of water retention that appear to be caused by caffeine (326). These could arise from synergism between the action of antidiuretic hormone and cyclic AMP (374). Other effects on the kidney include an increase in enzyme excretion rate and a potentiation of the renal effects of salicylates (316). Effects on hepatic drug-metabolizing enzymes are discussed in Section 8.

Caffeine has been shown in vitro to inhibit and reverse blood platelet aggregation induced by adenosine diphosphate (11). Its effects on normal blood clotting are not known, however. Via cyclic AMP, caffeine acts synergistically with the hormones ACTH and glucagon (374). There may be stimulation of the thyroid (409) and of melanocyte activity (233). Simultaneous administration of coffee has been found to increase vitamin B_{12} absorption in certain fasting patients (93), possibly via caffeine's stimulation of gastric secretion of hydrochloric acid and pepsin (see below).

Caffeine's biochemical effects have often been examined using concentrations of the drug that are higher than those encountered in the bodies of normal or even excessive drinkers of caffeine beverages. Although useful for elucidating possible mechanisms of caffeine action, the results of these studies should not necessarily be a guide to what actually goes on inside organisms when caffeine is administered. A similar consideration applies to the next section, where reference to dose levels and concentrations has also beem omitted. Dose levels and concentrations are of the essence in pharmacology, however, and any serious attempt to relate a particular experimental finding to normal practice must give special consideration to these if relevance is to be established.

4. EFFECTS OF CAFFEINE ON ORGAN SYSTEMS

Central Nervous System

A certain liquor which they call coffe*. . . . which will soon intoxicate the brain.

William Parry. *A new and large Discourse of the Travels of Sir Antonie Sherley*, 1601.

* This seems to have been the first use of the word coffee in the English language. The beverage itself was apparently not imbibed in England until 1650, when it may have been used in Oxford, or until 1652, when it was more certainly used in London. The tercentenary of the

Caffeine is often reported to be a powerful central nervous system stimulant (388), but very few studies seem to have been carried out on the drug's effects on the activity of the brain. Apart from objective sleep studies, which are reviewed in Section 7, there seem to have been only three recent investigations of human brain activity after caffeine administration. In one study, caffeine produced a negative shift in vertex EEG that is consistent with excitation (13). In a second one, brain activity was apparently depressed (372). The third study, investigating the effects of caffeine on the amplitude of vertex-averaged evoked potentials induced by stimuli of varying intensity, showed depression in most male but excitation in most female subjects (224). The authors suggested that the depression may be transient.

Two animal studies conducted in the Soviet Union concerned caffeine-induced structural changes in the brain (314) and the effects of caffeine on the activity of sensorimotor cortical units (12). Caffeine produced more marked changes in cortical than in subcortical neurons in the first of these studies. In the second, 20 mg/kg caffeine increased the percentage of spontaneously firing neurons in unanesthetized cats without having a significant effect on the mean firing rate. The same dose also reversed inhibition of spike activity in sensorimotor units caused by caudate nucleus stimulation—more so than an allegedly equivalent dose of amphetamine (1 mg/kg; according to Lader [232], 0.33 mg/kg amphetamine would be equivalent to 20 mg/kg caffeine in humans). Amphetamine was also selective in its counterinhibitory effect. When sensorimotor unit inhibition was caused by stimulation of the dorsomedial part of the caudate nucleus, or of other cortical structures, amphetamine was ineffective, whereas caffeine reversed inhibition, however caused. It was concluded that caffeine's stimulant effect is largely a matter of direct cortical excitation, but that amphetamine acts by disturbing the relationships between the cortex and the caudate nucleus (12).

When caffeine is described as a central nervous system stimulant, the supporting evidence that is provided is usually indirect and often behavioral in nature (388). The behavioral pharmacology of caffeine is discussed here in Section 6.

Smooth and Skeletal Muscle

> There are many points of difference in the action of [tea and coffee], taken in poisonous excess; but one common feature is very constant, viz. the production of muscular tremor.
>
> F. E. Anstie. *Stimulants and Narcotics*, 1864.

---

first London use was celebrated on March 25, 1952, by the unveiling of a plaque in the City of London (354). Tea had arrived in England a few years earlier, in 1644, according to the author of *Larousse Gastronomique*.

Generally, caffeine's effect is to relax visceral smooth muscle and to contract skeletal muscle. However, contrary findings regarding smooth muscle have been reported (198, 278), as well as a biphasic effect consisting of initial excitation and subsequent inhibition of contractile activity (373). Caffeine has been shown to cause inhibition of regular phasic contraction of smooth muscles in the upper part of the alimentary canal, but excitation of phasic contraction in the lower part (198). More specifically, instillation of caffeine sodium benzoate into the human stomach has been reported to produce a fall in the closure tension of the lower esophageal sphincter (65).* Skeletal fibers contract uniformly with application of caffeine, the tension being an increasing function of caffeine concentration, until the fibers snap if they are not allowed to shorten sufficiently (37); the actual contraction itself may be biphasic (269). Contracture in human skeletal muscle seems more easily reversible than in muscle of other species, following addition of relatively low concentrations of caffeine (269). Pretreatment of fibers with low concentrations of caffeine makes them less sensitive to challenge by higher concentrations (240). Although the effect of caffeine on skeletal muscle can be direct (37, 240, 385), the concentrations required (i.e., in excess of 400 μg/ml) are so much higher than likely plasma levels that caffeine's usual effects upon muscles can be presumed to be mediated by the nervous system.

Cardiovascular System

> Tea-sots are well-known to be affected by palpitation and irregularity of the heart.
>
> G. W. Balfour. *Encyclopaedia Britannica,* 1877.

Caffeine appears to have a variety of effects on the cardiovascular system. Direct effects upon cardiac muscle include an increase in the force of contraction and a change in the duration of the action potential (67), with an initial effect upon the relaxation phase alone (283). The twitch response is markedly potentiated (219). Longer exposure has resulted in habituation (62). Species differences have been found in the effects of caffeine on contraction, and the course of shortening in isolated heart muscle (39). Caffeine has been found to affect chronotropic action in preparations of dog and rat heart muscle (15). Certain direct effects of caffeine on isolated heart muscle have been inhibited by the simultaneous addition of a weak (4.5 g/liter) ethanol solution (117).

Some of the apparent anomalies between and within species can be re-

* Caffeine has also been shown to have no effect on esophageal sphincter tension (70b).

lated to procedures and to caffeine concentrations. Some arise also because of caffeine's effects on the vagal nerve, whose stimulation reduces heart rate, and upon blood vessels. Caffeine appears to cause peripheral vasodilation, except in the cerebrum, where a marked increase in vascular resistance occurs. The net effect may be to raise blood pressure because the reduced pressure that would ensue with vasodilation does not compensate for the increased output caused by caffeine's direct effects on the heart and on metabolism (325). Where the cardiovascular response to caffeine administration in a group of human subjects is assessed, some are likely to show increased blood pressure, some increased heart rate, some neither, and some perhaps both (273). Such differences may have their basis in part in habitual caffeine consumption, but no relevant data are available. In rats, a modest rise in blood pressure has been reported after chronic ingestion of coffee (700 μg/ml caffeine) as the sole drinking fluid; when crowded, a substantial coffee-induced rise occurred under the same conditions (176).

As well as the direct effects on heart, on the vagal nerve, and on blood vessels, caffeine and other methylxanthines have a variety of other effects that are relevant to cardiovascular action. These have been very briefly reviewed by Atuk and Westfall (15) and include increase in urinary catecholamine excretion after intravenous and oral administration to human subjects; release of norepinephrine from isolated heart after methylxanthine perfusion; effects on blood sugar and cardiac phosphorylase; chronotropic effects and their inhibition by beta-adrenergic blocking agents and by pretreatment with reserpine.

Respiration and Metabolic Rate

Caffeine increases blood flow through the lungs by relaxing arterial smooth muscle, and it increases air supply to the lungs by relaxing bronchiolar and alveolar smooth muscle. There is also a direct stimulant effect upon the medulla respiratory center (388). The total effect seems to be a small one, however, except where respiration is otherwise suppressed (31). Nevertheless, caffeine causes measurable increases in basal metabolic rate (261).

It might be supposed that an increase in metabolic rate would be accompanied by an increase in body temperature. Caffeine, however, has been found to have a short-term hypothermic effect in rats (33). This could arise because of heat loss through peripheral vasodilation. In one human subject, an increase in body temperature seemed to be associated with regular periods of high caffeine-beverage intake (323). The hyperthermia seemed to have been a direct effect of caffeine; it fell, along with pulse rate and blood pressure, when caffeine was withdrawn.

Circadian Rhythm

> I have measured out my life with coffee spoons.
>
> T. S. Eliot. *The Love Life of J. Alfred Prufrock*, 1911.

The effect of theophylline on deep-body temperature has been examined in the context of drug-induced changes in circadian rhythm (108). Administration of 75 mg/kg of the drug to rats living without information as to the time of day (i.e., without zeitgebers) produced shifts in the deep-body temperature rhythm. The direction of the displacement varied according to the position of the injection in relation to the daily peak temperature. When drug administration occurred shortly before or at the peak, the rhythm was delayed; i.e., subsequent peaks occurred at a later hour of the day. When the drug was given later, the rhythm was advanced. The maximum shift was a delay of 18 hr induced when injection occurred shortly before the peak. Injection of saline or a lower dose of theophylline had no effect on the temperature rhythm. Pentobarbital (40 mg/kg) produced delays, but not advances in the rhythm. Unpublished data of the same authors suggest that theophylline may cause shifts in circadian rhythm even when other zeitgebers (i.e., regular food, light) are available (108). Caffeine has not been investigated in this respect but, because of its similarity to theophylline, it is reasonable to suppose that it would have similar chronotypic properties. Some of the variation in response to caffeine may arise from interaction of the drug and its time of administration with circadian periodicity.

Gastrointestinal System

> The paralysing influence of narcotic doses of tea is further displayed by the production of a particularly obstinate kind of dyspepsia; while coffee disorders the action of the heart to a distressing degree.
>
> F. E. Anstie. *Stimulants and Narcotics*, 1864.

The effect of caffeine upon the smooth muscles of the alimentary canal has already been mentioned. In particular, caffeine's inhibition of the peristaltic activity of the stomach is believed to be responsible for a delaying effect on ethanol absorption (352). Caffeine also affects activity in the upper part of the tract by stimulating gastric juice in humans after oral (329) and intravenous (70a) administration and in rats (228) and cats (329). There is doubt as to whether this effect is mediated by the hormone gastrin, which maintains secretion in the presence of food (70a, 228). Other ingredients of coffee do elevate the plasma gastrin response in humans (34), and thus it seems that coffee may be a more potent cause of stomach acidity than caffeine alone, although an informal study has found that approximately 38 mg of caffeine and instant coffee containing 75 mg caffeine, both in solution and administered orally, had a similar elevating effect upon the level of gastric hydrochloric acid in human subjects (206). Also, caffeine and coffee have been found to cause ulcers in stressed rats with more or less equal facility (111). Caffeine may affect the action of the lower tract by inhibiting the synthesis of protein and RNA in the indigenous bacterium *Escherichia coli* (36), thus raising the possibility of the production of enteropathogenic strains of these bacteria and consequent intestinal upset.

5. REPRODUCTION AND TOXICITY

This section considers caffeine's effects on the reproduction of cells and organisms, and also the toxic effects of the drug.

Mutagenesis and Carcinogenesis

One of the April 1974 issues of the journal *Mutation Research* was entirely devoted to the subject of "Caffeine as an environmental mutagen and the problem of synergistic effects." In his introduction, Kihlman (218) reviewed data on the effects of caffeine on genetic material, noting that the alkaloid is an effective mutagen and a potentiator of mutagenic activity, but at concentrations considerably higher than those that result from beverage ingestion. He concluded that the mechanism of caffeine's broad range of effects remains obscure, although direct binding with DNA is probably implicated. An earlier estimate, made in the first report of mutagenic activity of caffeine in human cells (288), placed the amount of chromosome breakage arising from caffeine-beverage drinking in the neighborhood of the "natural mutation rate." A similar estimate has been made more recently by Goldstein and his colleagues (152, p. 659).

More than a quarter of the work published on caffeine during 1974 involved caffeine's mutagenic effects. In most cases, caffeine was being used merely as a tool in the elucidation of more general genetic phenomena. For example, caffeine has been shown to inhibit repair of DNA damaged by ultraviolet radiation, and it is used extensively to clarify the nature of the repair process (387). Caffeine, in concentrations similar to those found in beverages, has been found to protect mouse skin against cancers induced by ultraviolet light (418). At higher concentrations, it may inhibit the carcinogenic action of cigarette smoke condensate (330). The claims that caffeine's mutagenic activity may not be relevant to human beverage consumption seem to have been contradicted by a study in which caffeine at concentrations lower than those found in blood serum (i.e., < 5 $\mu g/ml$) was found to enhance the modification of DNA by a number of carcinogens (98). One of these was benzo(*a*)pyrene, an established carcinogen that probably occurs in roast coffee (230) and in the combustion products of cigarette-lighting materials (248). Another possible cocarcinogenic agent in coffee is chlorogenic acid, which constitutes about 13% of the roast bean, and which may, because it is a readily oxidized phenolic compound, catalyze formation of carcinogenic N-nitrosamines in the digestive tract (61).

Although there has yet to be experimental demonstration that caffeine is carcinogenic—indeed, caffeine has been shown to inhibit tumor formation under certain circumstances—there seems to be little doubt that caffeine is active with respect to genetic material at concentrations similar to those occurring in caffeine-beverage drinkers. Thus, a laboratory demonstration of caffeine-induced carcinoma would not be surprising. The only experimental test that may be relevant involved incorporation of instant-coffee powder in the food of 193 rats for periods of up to two years (419). Bladders only were examined (because coffee drinking has been implicated in cancers of the lower urinary tract more than at any other site—see Section 11), and no tumors were found, either in the coffee-drinking rats or in the 58 control animals. Rats and humans appear to metabolize caffeine in different ways; humans, in particular, but not rats, may eliminate via urine substantial quantities of the likely carcinogen 1-methylxanthine after caffeine administration (see Section 3, above). Thus the failure of chronic caffeine ingestion to produce bladder cancer in rats is not necessarily evidence against the implication of caffeine in urinary tract cancers in humans.

Teratogenesis

Teratogenesis is often merely another aspect of mutagenesis, but it is considered separately from carcinogenesis because it involves organisms, rather than individual cells. In a recent review of caffeine's teratogenic effects on animals, Mulvihill (274) concluded that because the lowest daily dose required to produce obvious embryotoxicity in mice is in the order of 50–100 mg/kg, there can be little teratogenic danger to humans, for whom 20 mg/kg per day would be very high caffeine beverage consumption. As indicated in Section 2 above, however, because a human weighs about three thousand times as much as a mouse, a dose of 75 mg/kg for the mouse would be equivalent to 10 mg/kg or about nine cups of coffee in man, when "metabolic weight" is considered. Thus, Mulvihill may be unduly sanguine in his extrapolation. Nevertheless, he seems to be right when he asserts that "no human malformation has been attributed to caffeine." The closest seems to be a recent German report implicating caffeine consumption in prematurity and in deaths of premature infants (254); a later version of the same study (255), however, seems to contradict even this implication, suggesting only that coffee (not tea or cola) consumption might lead to lower birth weights. Unfortunately, as in other studies, the actual levels of consumption were very poorly specified, and possible in utero effects of caffeine cannot be gainsaid on the basis of these data.

Caffeine-induced fetopathy could occur indirectly rather than because of the drug's direct action on genetic material. It appears that the fetopathic effect can be blocked by propranolol (132, 133), as discussed in Section 8 below, suggesting that this toxic effect of caffeine may arise from its induction of increased catecholamine levels in fetal circulation. The absence of a direct effect on germ cells may account for caffeine's failure to potentiate the fetopathic effect of known mutagens when administered to male mice prior to mating (109).*

Fertility

Various studies have shown that caffeine administered via injection (109) and via drinking water (109, 379) can reduce the fertility of male mice. The drinking-water studies involved caffeine concentrations of the order of 300 μg/ml, which approximate those of tea and coffee. A subsequent, cross-generational study involving lower caffeine concentrations produced no consistent effect on fertility, although offspring were underweight compared with controls (380). In another study, consumption of 200 μg/ml caffeine in water by 60 male Chinese hamsters for 60 days had no effect on fertility, embryonic mortality, or litter size, when compared with water-drinking controls (403). However, among the progeny of treated males, there was a remarkable skewing of the sex ratio in favor of females (61.4% as opposed to the usual 49.2%—$p < 0.025$). Caffeine-fed females produced normally distributed litters after mating with untreated males. The authors noted that

* In a brief to the U.S. Department of Health, Education, and Welfare (Jan. 1976) the Washington-based Center for Science in the Public Interest reviewed additional evidence, noted that "... if a company were proposing caffeine or coffee as a new food additive, it is unlikely that either would be approved," and urged that "DHEW should . . . immediately inform doctors and pregnant women that caffeine may cause birth defects or miscarriages and that women in the first three months of pregnancy should minimize their consumption of . . . caffeine." Among the new evidence was a finding by P. Weathersbee, reported in the Medical World News (Jan. 26, 1976), that 13 of 14 women found to be drinking 7 or more cups of coffee a day had experienced "problem pregnancies" including miscarriages and stillbirths. The brief did not cite a careful study in rats in which intraperitoneal injections at 6-hr invervals throughout pregnancy, amounting to 20, 40 or 80 mg/kg/day caffeine produced more resorptions, smaller litters, and lower fetal and placental weights in a dose-related manner than in controls given saline injections (141a). The lowest caffeine dose is equivalent to 4.8 mg/kg/day in a 55-kg pregnant woman on a metabolic weight basis, i.e., less than 4 average cups of coffee per day.

their data are consistent with earlier reports linking caffeine administration to an increased incidence of female offspring in fruit flies, and with an effect of caffeine on Y-bearing spermatozoa, but they offered no specific explanation for their interesting finding.*

Caffeine has been shown to reduce the fertility of roosters. Dietary inclusion of 0.1% caffeine for about 30 days caused a reversible cessation of spermatogenesis (18). Addition to pullets' food of a lower concentration (0.05%) increased embryonic mortality (19). Higher concentrations caused the laying of soft-shelled eggs and subsequent cessation of egg production (17). Caffeine (0.5–1.0%) in the food of immature male rats for 3–16 months caused marked bilateral testicular atrophy and aspermatogenesis, according to a preliminary report (129). The mean relative testicular weight of 18-week-old rats having had 0.5% caffeine for 13 weeks was 0.27%, as opposed to 0.74% for controls. Similar effects could result from starvation, and it is not clear whether the rats rejected caffeine-contaminated food because of its taste. If adult rats, who eat about 8% of their body weight of chow each day, were to have 1.0% caffeine added to their chow, they would be receiving a daily dose in the order of 800 mg/kg—a fatal dose—if they ate up all their food.

Caffeine may have a role to play in increasing fertility. Solutions of caffeine in the order of 2000 μg/ml have been found to increase the motility and longevity of ejaculated bovine (137) and human (167) spermatozoa. A much lower concentration (30 μg/ml) increased the motility, but not the survival of hamster sperm (268). As well as being used to buttress the view that cyclic AMP is involved in sperm activity (167, 268), these findings have raised the possibility that caffeine added to semen could improve fertility in patients whose specimens are of low motility (347). The effect of caffeine on sperm motility might also account for the remarkable sex-ratio shift in hamsters mentioned earlier. The effect on motility appears greater for sperms that are initially of lower motility (137, 347). Thus, the heavier, and possibly slower-swimming female sperms could be especially energized by caffeine, increasing the likelihood that they, rather than male sperms, would fertilize available ova.

Toxicity in Animals

A comprehensive review of caffeine toxicity by Peters (307) appeared in 1967. He reviewed data, primarily on caffeine's lethality, from a variety of species, including toads and rabbits, and from a variety of situations. Few reports have appeared since then; almost all seem to have involved rats or

* Unpublished work by the same group has extended this finding to other species. The University of Illinois has patented the procedure, which may be of great interest to stockbreeders.

mice. Some have shown little or no toxicity at what appear at first sight to be remarkably high levels of daily caffeine ingestion (370, 379), although if appropriate corrections are made (see Section 2 above), the levels seem more reasonable when compared with human caffeine consumption. In one recently reported study, rats were given 800 $\mu g/ml$ caffeine, in the form of caffeine solution or coffee, as their sole fluid for over six months; they received a daily caffeine dose of close to 60 mg/kg (370). The coffee-fed rats showed lower weight gain, but this can be attributed to their lower liquid consumption, which probably occurred because the coffee tasted more bitter than the caffeine solution. Peters reported that the maximum daily dose producing no deaths in rats is 110 mg/kg. He also noted that the minimum single oral dose that is lethal for rats is close to 192 mg/kg. The fatal intravenous dose appears to be considerably lower; the LD_{50} is close to 100 mg/kg for both rats and mice. Peters did not give data from intraperitoneal administrations, and thus it is not possible to make a comparison with the careful study by Muller and Vernikos-Danellis (272) of the influence of environmental temperature on caffeine's toxicity. They reported an LD_{50} of 275 mg/kg for mice at normal room temperature (20°C), but considerably lower lethal doses with even moderate departure; e.g., the LD_{50} was 180 mg/kg at 30°C. The room-temperature value is close to an LD_{50} of 300 mg/kg found for mice when caffeine was administered subcutaneously (170). In this last study, the LD_{50} was elevated to 340 mg/kg by increasing air pressure to 6 atmospheres, but the difference was not statistically significant. One recent study reported an LD_{50} of 195 mg/kg for the rat when caffeine was administered intraperitoneally (33). The LD_{50} for caffeine was found to be substantially reduced by two monoamine oxidase inhibitors, thereby adding to the list of drugs reported by Peters (307) to have this effect.

Peters also mentioned that the minimum toxic dose for both rats and mice lies between 25 and 50 mg/kg and that the median convulsant dose for mice is 85 mg/kg. No further details were given. An earlier study by Peters (305) had demonstrated that the susceptibility of rats to the toxic effects of a daily 185 mg/kg oral dose of caffeine was not affected by starvation unless food rations were reduced by more than 50%. Caffeine aggravated the effects of starvation, causing augmented weight loss in minimally fed rats and consequent cachexia. Many deaths also resulted from hemorrhage following automutilation. Other caffeine-specific toxic signs included diuresis, accompanied by glycosuria and slight alkalinuria, and hair loss.

Toxicity in Humans

Balzac in his early thirties wrote hour after hour and when he flagged and his head seemed to burst, he went to the coffee pot and brewed the strongest black

> coffee he could find, made from the beans of Bourbon, Martinique and Mocha. He was resorting to a slow course of coffee poisoning and it has been estimated that in his life he drank 50,000 cups of it. When dawn came he stopped writing and, imitating Napoleon, lay for an hour in a hot bath. (p. 111)
> He was nearing forty and he was exhausting himself. The fits of giddiness came oftener; his hair was greying, his lungs were weakened. He coughed, he said, like an old man, and excess of coffee gave him stomach cramps. (p. 199)
> V. S. Pritchett. *Balzac*, 1973.

Honoré de Balzac was the nineteenth century's most famous caffeinist, but his lifetime consumption of coffee may have been low when compared with that of many of today's coffee drinkers (see Section 10). Caffeinism* is rarely reported in the literature (159), but may nevertheless be a prevalent condition (323). Toxicity is generally an extension of caffeine's usual pharmacologic actions on the nervous, gastrointestinal, respiratory, cardiovascular, and other systems (388), and there is no characteristic cause of death, when it occurs (96). One recent report (5) claimed to be the first account of a human caffeine fatality. Apart from the fact that a different version of the same report had been published eight years earlier (297), there seem to be at least five other descriptions of human fatality in the literature. They are all mentioned in a case report on a five-year-old girl who had swallowed about 50 over-the-counter diuretic tablets, each containing 99 mg caffeine (96). The other fatalities included three iatrogenic mishaps, one apparent suicide by consumption of caffeine-containing tablets (5), and one from an unknown cause. The lowest fatal doses were 3.2 g, administered intravenously to a 35-year-old woman, and the 5.3 g self-administered orally by the 5-year-old girl (96), of which 2.3 g was found in the stomach. It could be reasonably concluded that the lowest oral dose that might be fatal to an adult is probably in the order of 5 g, a dose that is unlikely to be encountered through beverage consumption, although there is a recent report of an inmate in the Nevada State Prison who drank 50 cups of coffee a day, i.e., probably about 3.5 g caffeine per day, and suffered little more than "severe anxiety symptoms" (265).

6. BEHAVIORAL PHARMACOLOGY OF CAFFEINE

> Of all the studies on the effect of drugs those of coffee or its active agent, caffeine, are probably exceeded in number only by studies of alcohol.
>
> A. R. Gilliland and Dorothy Nelson,
> *The Journal of General Psychology*,
> Vol. 21, 1939.

* The term was originally "caffeism," first appearing in print in 1886 in the United States. In 1889, the influential U.S. *Century Dictionary* was to record the use of "caffeinism," but writers in Britain were still using caffeism into the twentieth century.

A brief review of caffeine's effects on human and animal behavior by Calhoun (57), published in 1971, provides a useful addendum to a masterly review of the drug's effects on human performance by Weiss and Laties (404) that was published in 1962. The present section will attempt to update these two sources and provide discussion of certain areas that were omitted in the earlier reviews.

Sleep and Wakefulness

This topic may not seem to qualify for inclusion as a behavioral effect of caffeine. However, as most assessments of sleep quantity and quality have relied on subjective reports, rather than objective measurement, there is at least one good reason for considering caffeine's effects on sleep as a behavioral problem. A series of careful studies by Goldstein and his associates has confirmed beyond doubt the popular assumptions that caffeine interferes with sleep and aids wakefulness (151, 153, 155, 157). These effects of caffeine apply most appropriately to light users of the drug (up to about 150 mg/day). A dose of 150 or 200 mg caffeine administered 1 hr before bedtime in a double-blind study prolonged wakefulness in 31 out of 74 light users, whereas lactose similarly administered disturbed only 4 of these subjects in this way (151). Only 8 out of 28 subjects that regularly drank five or more cups of coffee a day (i.e., more than about 400 mg caffeine per day) were so affected by the caffeine nightcap. Sleep quality was similarly affected. The behavioral nature of the study was evidenced in the discovery of a "reverse placebo" effect, whereby subjects knowingly receiving caffeine—in a separate part of the study—were less likely to suffer wakefulness than subjects who were in doubt. (Accurate knowledge about the nature of the administration also reduced the effectiveness of caffeine in a study of fatigue [130]. Clearly, this is an important effect that should be acknowledged when everyday effects of caffeine beverages are interpreted in terms of experimental findings.) In a subsequent study, 20 subjects were studied in detail (157). Administration of 300 mg caffeine or placebo for 10 consecutive nights revealed large intersubject differences in sleep quantity and quality. The major relationship to habitual consumption was that heavy users reported sounder sleep than usual on placebo nights (they had also abstained from caffeine for about 10 hr), suggesting that they suffered chronically from some degree of caffeine-induced insomnia. In another study (205), it was found that heavy drinkers of coffee or tea go to bed later than abstainers or moderate drinkers.

All of the findings mentioned above were essentially confirmed in a subsequent study by Goldstein and associates in which 239 young housewives completed a questionnaire about their coffee consumption and its effects (153). In the final investigation of the series (155), both abstainers and heavy drinkers of coffee were compared in their response to morning administration of 150 or 300 mg caffeine or a placebo (in lieu of their regular morning beverage). Heavy users were found to require caffeine in order to avoid morning tiredness and irritability. Abstainers, on the other hand, experienced dysphoric symptoms when caffeine was administered, including jitteriness, nervousness, and gastrointestinal upset. The differential effect of caffeine on the sleep of users and nonusers was confirmed in a subsequent double-blind study from another institution (76), although differences in detail were noticed. Dose–response relationships for caffeine (0–250 mg) and each of sleep quality and quantity were established in a study that did not distinguish between the different use patterns of the subjects (99).

Further evidence of deterioration of sleep by caffeine was provided by a study in which 250 mg caffeine or 100 mg pentobarbital, or both, were administered to hospitalized United States veterans who needed a night-time hypnotic (123). The results are difficult to interpret because of a discrepancy between table and text regarding sleep-onset time; nevertheless, it appears that caffeine affected sleep adversely and counteracted the hypnotic effect of the barbiturate. In addition to these various experimental studies, there are clinical reports of insomnia relieved by reducing consumption of coffee, tea, and cola drinks (159, 353).

The subjective evidence reviewed above is substantiated by data from the few studies that have provided objective measures of sleep quality and quantity. Where gross disturbances during sleep have been recorded, caffeine has been found to produce sizable increases in body movement (343, 364). The first study of the effect of caffeine on brain activity during sleep did not show a statistically significant effect of a night-time dose of 175 mg caffeine on the stage 1 EEG–REM sleep of young adults, although five of the seven subjects showed an increase in proportion of REM sleep that might be consistent with a reduction in sleep quality (160). Of the same seven subjects, six showed a decrease in REM sleep proportion when approximately 70 g ethanol (about 8 oz liquor) was administered. Only the first 300 min of sleep was analyzed. A more recent and more intensive study by Brĕzinová (45) showed a significant reduction in the proportion of REM sleep throughout the night after 300 mg caffeine in decaffeinated coffee had been administered to six late-middle-aged subjects, compared with sleep after decaffeinated coffee or no drink. However, when only the first 3 hr of sleep was analyzed, a nonsignificant *increase* in proportion of REM sleep was noticed. Thus, an effect of bedtime caffeine may be to increase REM sleep slightly early in the night and to reduce its later occurrence.

The same study (45) provided ample evidence for disturbance of sleep by caffeine. Latency to sleep onset increased from 18 to 66 min, on the average. Mean sleep duration fell from 475 to 350 min—a fact that in itself might account for the overall reduction in REM sleep, because REM sleep has been found to be disproportionately reduced by reductions in total sleep time (113). In particular, during the first 3 hr of sleep, there was a significant decrease in the amount of deep sleep (stages 3 and 4) after caffeine, and significant increases in the amounts of light sleep (stages 1 and 2) and wakefulness. Moreover, sleep quality after caffeine was reported by subjects to be significantly impaired when compared with the other two conditions. It is not clear to what extent subjects were aware of the drug conditions, and thus corroboration of Goldstein's earlier finding (151) of a "reverse placebo" effect is not possible from the data of Brězinová's otherwise extremely useful substantiation of caffeine's adverse effects on sleep.

Different aspects of the data from Brězinová's subjects have been compared with data from subjects sleeping without their usual night-time hypnotic (46). Caffeine administration and hypnotic withdrawal produced similar reductions in total sleep time, but in different ways. Caffeine produced longer periods of intervening wakefulness, without much effect on the duration of individual sleep stages. Hypnotic withdrawal caused briefer individual sleep stages, but it did not affect the duration of episodes of wakefulness. Clinicians could benefit considerably from an ability to recognize caffeine-induced insomnia as having characteristics that distinguish it from other kinds of sleeplessness.

Not all studies of the effects of caffeine on brain activity during sleep have yielded useful results. Another recent study (335) found little or no effect on sleep of 450 mg caffeine administered as Coca-Cola or in a sweet solution to 10 rather heavy (142–245 lb) male subjects. The various measures included computer-classified sleep stages, REM activity, sleep latency, awakening threshold, and computer-analyzed EEG measures. Unfortunately, caffeine was administered over a period of 10 hr prior to sleep onset, and it can be estimated that, thus distributed, the dose would have produced a sleep-time plasma-caffeine level of much less than half of an equal amount given just before retiring. Thus, the lack of an effect on sleep in this study need not be surprising.

A factor that should be taken into account in subsequent research into caffeine's effects on sleep is a possible chronotypic effect of the drug, as discussed in Section 4. If caffeine's effect in humans is the same as that found with theophylline in rats (108), administration of caffeine after the diurnal deep-body temperature peak, i.e., in the late evening, would advance the diurnal cycle, thus precipitating sleep. Administration shortly before or at the peak, i.e., during the afternoon or early evening, would delay the diurnal cycle, thus delaying sleep. Such effects might be more evident where familiar zeitgebers are absent, as in many experimental situations.

Activity, Work Output, and Fatigue

> Coffee soothes, eliminates the feeling of tiredness and exhaustion, makes mental work easier, dispels drowsiness. A larger dose can bring on nervous excitation, trembling, insomnia.
>
> Prosper Montagné. *Larousse Gastronomique*, 1938.

Simple activity studies have generally consisted of observation of rats or mice in running wheels or in "open field" environments. At injected doses up to about 25 mg/kg, caffeine has generally produced a dose-related increase in activity, but higher doses have decreased activity. Mouse activity seems to be increased by doses above 20 mg/kg (40, 110), but depression is almost invariably found at doses above 100 mg/kg. As well as being a function of the individual and of the species (231), the dose-response curve also varies with apparatus and previous experience (40, 57, 251). The change in work output can also be a function of the baseline rate; for caffeine, in common with other stimulants, has been found to exert a greater rate-increasing effect on behavior that starts initially at a low rate (40, 86, 392). One recent study involved observation of the effect of an oral dose of 20 mg/kg caffeine on rat performance in a swimming test (246). Caffeine increased initial swimming activity, but led to premature exhaustion and earlier drowning than among controls. The swimming test occurred 2 hr after drug administration, and all animals, even controls, were dead within 25 min of the beginning of the test. Thus, the exhaustion was probably genuine, rather than a biphasic effect of the drug. Accordingly, it seems that total work output may not necessarily be increased by caffeine; the drug may merely produce local changes in activity.

Comparable studies in humans have usually been directed toward studying caffeine's effect on fatigue. The conclusion of Weiss and Laties' earlier review (404), that caffeine "prolongs the amount of time during which an individual can perform physically exhausting work," is essentially unchallenged by more recent studies (57, 130, 287, 321, 405). Weiss and Laties expressed doubt as to whether work output or performance is actually elevated by caffeine, as opposed to being merely restored after degradation by fatigue. More recent work has tended to show an increase in the level of work output due to caffeine (130, 237, 277, 321, 405), although there have been exceptions (154), particularly when fine motor coordination is required (104), or there is simultaneous stress (121). Comparison between these studies is difficult because of the variety of situations, caffeine doses, and subjects. In particular, the subjects' experience with caffeine has rarely been taken into account. Where elevation or prolongation of performance has occurred, a dose of 200 mg (i.e., about 3 mg/kg) has generally been found sufficient; but higher doses have had no effect (154), and lower doses have produced significant increases (405). It is possible that very much higher doses would depress human activity, as it does animal activity, but such doses have not been employed.*

Complex Behavior

As might be expected from the previous paragraph, caffeine's effects on complex behavior, especially complex human behavior, are unclear. Where fine motor coordination or hand steadiness is required, caffeine often seems to cause deterioration in performance (104, 298), whereas an unequivocal effect on what might be described as intellectual activity has yet to be reported, except where fatigue is prevented (57, 121, 191, 298). Alertness or vigilance or attention, on the other hand, may be enhanced (21, 287, 321). One recent study, after some unnecessarily complex statistical manipulation, demonstrated an effect of 300 mg caffeine on performance at a paced memory task (263). Performance was improved when, and only when, subjects had caffeine and knew that they were getting it.

Attitude and Mood

> I leave John Caddle a silver teapot, to the end that he may drink tea therefrom to comfort him under the affliction of a slatternly wife.
>
> From the last will and testament of Dr. William Dunlop,
> who died near Montreal in June, 1848.

Caffeine has been shown to elevate mood or attitude at least as often as it has been shown to affect performance. The question arises as to whether the performance changes might depend on mood, or vice versa (57, 404). The answer must be complicated by quite contrary findings of caffeine-induced performance changes without favorable subjective reports (130), and of caffeine-induced augmentation of mood without corresponding changes in subjective measures of performance (154). Generally speaking, where mood

* No direct studies seem to have been carried out on the effect of caffeine on the performance of athletes, but because of pertinent suggestions from the experimental literature and familiar anecdotes about caffeine, there has been considerable controversy about its use as a doping agent. Williams (407) notes that the use of caffeine in conjunction with athletic competition was forbidden in Italy in the mid-1960s, but that its appearance as a doping agent on the list of the International Olympic Committee was successfully challenged in time for the 1972 competitions. The evidence reviewed above suggests that caffeine may possibly enhance gross motor activity in the short term, but that without further drug administration premature exhaustion could ensue. Tests with amphetamine drugs indicate that at best only very slight performance increments might be expected from these stimulants, and that toxic doses of caffeine may be required to produce similar enhancement (227). A recent, careful study found no significant effect of caffeine on the maximum endurance capacity of human females (303a).

changes have been assessed, insufficient attention has been given either to the immediate social setting or to the subjects' experience with the drug, both of which might have a profound influence on this kind of effect of caffeine. Knowledge about drug administration is such a factor. Swedish subjects, used to coffee, were much less likely to report fatigue when they were told correctly whether or not they were given caffeine (actually 750 mg!) than when they were told that caffeine-free coffee contained caffeine, or that regular coffee contained no caffeine (130). The same subjects were also more likely to report feeling tense and nervous when they knew, accurately, that they were getting caffeine than under any other condition (6). Thus knowledge about drug administration can change anticipated caffeine effects on mood in opposite ways. On the other hand, the subjects' actual test performance improved more after caffeine administration when they knew that caffeine was being administered. It seems increasingly clear, from data on sleep (151), performance (263), and mood (6, 130), that caffeine's effects on human behavior are determined strongly by knowledge about the drug.

One report, which may have some relation to attitude or mood but which I have been unable to pursue, claims that Russian therapy using caffeine has produced general improvement in the behavior of chronic deteriorated schizophrenics (361). On the other hand, there is also clinical evidence, discussed in Section 11, that chronically high levels of caffeine intake may be implicated in anxiety states (159). Curiously enough, a finding that caffeine increases the number of shocks received by rats during a punishment procedure was interpreted to mean that caffeine has an antianxiety effect (26); perhaps the assumption is that an untroubled rat would take its punishment "like a man."

Social Behavior

> There, amid the snows of the north, under an Eskimo's hospitable roof, for the first time I shared with them in that cheering, invigorating emblem of civilization—tea!
>
> C. F. Hall. *Arctic Researches and Life among the Esquimaux*, 1865.

Although caffeine seems to be an important component of many human social situations, its role in and its effect on human social behavior do not seem to have been investigated.* Social behavior was not referred to in

* Caffeine may have a role to play in social behavior that is at least as great as that of ethanol, especially in the social behavior of politicians, bureaucrats, and middle managers. Consumption of coffee at their various meetings may be exceeded only by that of former alcoholics undergoing group therapy. John Kenneth Galbraith wrote somewhat darkly in his novel *The Triumph*: "There is nothing over which history draws so dense a curtain as the effect of alcohol

either of the reviews that introduced this section, except for a reference to caffeine's stimulation of the sexual behavior of male rats (420). An injected dose of 10 or 20 mg/kg caffeine (the report is not clear) enhanced most aspects of sexual activity in rats that engaged in mating, but it had no effect on the participation rate. Another study (59) showed that 20 mg/kg caffeine increased the gregariousness of male rats when assessed in terms of body contact. The quality of the contacts was also different. Compared with those of the pairs of rats that received saline, the contacts were briefer but more intense, with fighting occurring occasionally among rats receiving caffeine, but not among control rats. Aggression has also been noted among female rats housed 10 to a cage when intubated with 185 mg/kg caffeine daily (306). Solitary rats given the same treatment were much more likely to engage in automutilation, especially when diet was impoverished or restricted. Often, they would injure themselves to the point of death from hemorrhagic shock. An earlier study (308) had reported occasional automutilation in rats after an intraperitoneal dose of 100 mg/kg. Because of the drug's ability to cause lethal automutilation in solitary animals, aggregation may actually lower the toxicity of a given high dose of caffeine (307), unlike the amphetamines, for which aggregation appears to markedly increase toxicity (138). Caffeine has, nevertheless, been shown to produce marked increases in the blood pressure of aggregated mice when compared with solitary mice (176).

Aggressive behavior has also been reported as a consequence of the chronic administration of moderately large doses of theophylline to rats (336, 337). Stereotyped behavior was observed after the theophylline administration, as it is with most other stimulants (333), but caffeine seems to be an exception (119, 223). No stereotyped behavior was observed in rats, even after subcutaneous administration of 150 mg/kg (119). However, a much lower dose (20 mg/kg) has been found to potentiate the stereotypy induced by *d*-amphetamine (223). The effect of caffeine on aggression may be species-specific. One report suggests that caffeine reduces aggression in cats (259), and another indicates that the drug has an antiaggressive effect on mice, the peak effect occurring with an intraperitoneal injection of 10 mg/kg (392).

---

on modern statecraft." The economist and statesman may very well have made a similar observation regarding caffeine, but I have been unable to find one. The current bible of middle managers and similar functionaries (*Management: Tasks, Responsibilities, Practices*, by P. F. Drucker) makes no mention of either kind of beverage. Coca-Cola and Pepsi-Cola are mentioned, but only as examples of companies engaging in diversification.

Eating and Drinking

> If a person wishes to be served with more tea or coffee, he should place his spoon in his saucer. If he has had sufficient, let it remain in the cup.
>
> Anon. *Our Deportment; or the Manners, Conduct, and Dress of the Most Refined Society*, 1883.

Because many of the effects of caffeine are similar to those of the amphetamines (232), it might also be expected that caffeine would reduce eating* and drinking. According to one source, it has been reported that caffeine has little effect on the food intake of rats except at toxic dose levels, although water consumption may be reduced by lower acute doses (226). Reduced body weight gain has been found in rats whose sole fluid for 6 mo was coffee, when compared with those that had only an equivalent caffeine solution (370), but, as indicated earlier, this could have been because the bitter taste of coffee reduced liquid intake. Taste could also have been important in an observation that incorporation of coffee or caffeine into the food of malnourished rats caused an increase in total fluid consumption and a marked shift in preference to a 10% ethanol solution over water (322). I have replicated this interesting finding, but not in a way that allows elucidation of the mechanism of the increase in total consumption or of the shift in preference (145). One problem with examining caffeine's effect on eating or drinking is that consummatory behavior may be stimulated by low doses of the drug in much the same way as other kinds of behavior are stimulated. An earlier finding of enhanced eating by rats after a subcutaneous administration of about 25 mg/kg may have arisen from such an action of caffeine (355).

Learning and Memory

Data on caffeine's effect on the rate of acquisition of new behavior are few, whether human (404) or animal (57) subjects are being considered. Part of the problem lies in the definition of learning (142), and part in the separation of caffeine's effects on attention, vigilance, activity, performance, and the like from its effects on anything that might be called learning. Thus, almost all of the animal studies that seem to provide evidence for an effect of caffeine on learning could be equally interpreted as evidencing performance or other changes (57). One exception may be a study reported by Pavlov (302), in which caffeine was found to reverse temporarily the effect of an inhibitory stimulus on conditioned salivation. A similar finding may

* According to the *Oxford English Dictionary*, the word coffee stems from the arabic word *qahwah* (pronounced *kahveh* in Turkish), a word that in turn is a derivative of the verb-root *qahiya*, meaning "to have no appetite."

have been made by Skinner and Heron (355), who noted that caffeine restored operant behavior during extinction. Another exception may be a study in which retroactive facilitation of learning, or facilitation of memory, was produced by giving rats a single 30 mg/kg injection of caffeine shortly after reaching criterion on a discrimination task, two days before the first retention test (296). A later study of the same phenomenon, but in mice (366), produced no evidence of retroactive facilitation by any dose in the range 10–80 mg/kg, but a tendency towards facilitation of subsequent performance when no prior training had been given. Retroactive facilitation of the conditioned avoidance behavior of rats was a feature of a recent Bulgarian study, throughout the dose range 2.5–25 mg/kg caffeine (331). In the same study, prior administration of 2.5 mg/kg caffeine significantly improved acquisition and retention of the avoidance behavior, but 10 mg/kg produced, if anything, a deterioration. Another recent study, however, found no facilitation of the discrimination performance of rats over the range 1–60 mg/kg (140). The rats had been unable to distinguish a tone from a tone and a light during 6 mo training, and subcutaneously administered caffeine did not help. Other drugs, including nicotine (0.05–2 mg/kg) and chlordiazepoxide (1–20 mg/kg), did improve performance.

The response to punishment may be regarded as an aspect of learning. A study was mentioned earlier in which caffeine appeared to reduce the suppressive effects of punishment (26). A similar effect was noted by Morrison (267) in the shock-suppressed, water-reinforced bar pressing of most rats receiving a caffeine dose of 15 mg/kg. In the same experiment, doses of 0.4–1.2 mg/kg amphetamine usually had the opposite effect, i.e., punished behavior was further suppressed: nicotine (0.1–0.4 mg/kg) also suppressed punished behavior. Thus caffeine's effect on punishment may be different from that of other stimulants, although clearly other data are needed. Since 1935, at least, the scientific literature seems to be devoid of reports on caffeine's effects on human learning and memory. The whole area is one in which "an analysis and clarification of concepts" (141) may be of value, but the confusion is not peculiar to caffeine.

Schedule-controlled Behavior

A favorite tool of behavioral pharmacologists is the reinforcement schedule, a device for explicit arrangement of the consequences of behavior. The use of reinforcement schedules in drug research is well established (see references 94 and 258 for excellent examples), but their application to caffeine problems has been infrequent. Reinforcement schedules can provide exquisite control over response rate, and are especially appropriate for analysis of interactions between drug effects and the rate of occurrence of behavior. I mentioned earlier that caffeine's effect on behavior can be a function of the baseline rate of the behavior. Caffeine's rate-increasing effect may be confined to low baseline rates, with higher rates, if anything, being suppressed by caffeine (86). In this same study, which involved squirrel monkeys receiving 1–30 mg/kg caffeine intraperitoneally, only the three lowest doses increased response rate under a schedule of positive reinforcement (fixed interval)—the highest dose suppressed rate under this schedule. All four doses produced an increase over similar baseline rates maintained by a continuous shock avoidance schedule, however, suggesting that caffeine's effects upon behavior may be schedule- or reinforcer-dependent, as well as rate-dependent. Mechner and Latranyi (258a) have shown quantitative differences in the rate-changing effects of caffeine, when compared with methamphetamine and methylphenidate, even between performances under different schedules of positive reinforcement. However, they found little evidence of rate-dependent effects.

Further complication comes from a study in which the bar-pressing rate of squirrel monkeys under a schedule of intermittent sweet-liquid reinforcement was varied by testing both in light and in the dark (362). Oral doses of approximately 1–4 mg/kg caffeine suppressed the lower rate in the dark more or less equally, but only the 1 and 2 mg/kg doses suppressed the higher rate in the light—the 4 mg/kg dose was without effect. Considering other evidence on arousal (70, 176), a greater effect of caffeine in this species might be expected in the light. Moreover, because the baseline rates in this study (362) were extremely low—in the order of 0.03 responses/sec—caffeine might, if anything, have been expected to exert a rate-enhancing effect, as occurred when low rates were investigated in other studies (86).

There are other indications that caffeine's effect on avoidance behavior may be a function of the schedule of presentation of the aversive events. The highest dose of caffeine (10 mg/kg) administered to golden hamsters in a study of discrete-trial shock avoidance suppressed avoidance behavior (60), and the same effect was found with all doses (12.5–50 mg/kg) in a similar study that involved rats bred for their emotionality (340). The other three strains of rats used in this last study, however, showed facilitation of avoidance behavior when given the two lowest doses (12.5 and 25.0 mg/kg). In a study that involved rhesus monkeys working under a continuous avoidance schedule (172), intramuscular injection of caffeine increased the rate of avoidance behavior in all three subjects at the four highest doses (20, 40, 60, and 80 mg/kg), and in one subject also at the lowest dose used (10 mg/kg). Thus, it seems that behavior maintained by a continuous avoidance procedure is peculiarly resistant to the rate-suppressive property of high doses of caffeine. In the last-discussed study, response rate was varied by making shock delivery specific to one level of light intensity and then varying ambient illumination, thus providing a stimulus generalization function. As well as increasing overall rates of responding, caffeine also flattened the generalization functions by causing a greater proportional increase in the lower response rates, possibly providing further evidence of the rate-dependent effect of caffeine.

Sensation and Perception

> Coffee (which makes the politician wise, and see
> through all things with his half-shut eyes)
> Sent up in vapours to the Baron's brain
> New strategems, the radiant lock to gain.
>
> Alexander Pope. *The Rape of the Lock*, 1712–1714.

In the above-mentioned study of stimulus generalization (172), caffeine appeared to reduce control by the varying stimuli in that the monkeys responded more similarly in the presence of different stimuli. This result was interpreted as a rate-dependent effect, but it could also have been an effect upon sensation or perception. Caffeine may make some or all external stimuli less distinctive. A comparison of the effects of various drugs, including caffeine, on the discriminative accuracy of pigeons, using a sophisticated, conditional discrimination procedure, yielded clear effects, some positive and some negative, with all drugs tested except caffeine (38). Even though the sole caffeine dose used was a possibly low 10 mg/kg, administered orally, the fact that the drug produced opposite effects in different birds argues against a specific effect of caffeine on visual discrimination. A study of rats' visual discrimination that might, from its title, be expected to yield information on the question of caffeine's effect on stimulus control, actually provided no useful information (296).

There is reasonably good evidence that caffeine increases sensitivity to extreme stimuli (i.e., painful subcutaneous electric shock) in rats in a dose-dependent manner (290), but this finding may have little relevance to the problem of caffeine's effect on control by more subtle cues. Moreover, it seems to be contradicted by a report that caffeine reduced sensitivity to aggravation of inflammation in rats' hind paws, i.e., caffeine was analgesic (351). More relevant to the question of whether or not caffeine changes sensitivity to subtle cues may be a study by Diamond and Cole (95) in which the visual intensity threshold in humans was found to be decreased by 1.5 and 3 grains (= 97.2 and 194.4 mg) of caffeine. Unfortunately, the procedure used did not allow examination of the possibility that caffeine merely made subjects more likely to report the presence of the light, independently of its intensity, and thus that caffeine had no effect on visual sensitivity.

There have been two studies of caffeine's effects on the flicker fusion threshold in human subjects. In one, an oral dose of 200 mg raised the threshold slightly in young adults (104). In the other study, the same dose administered to children (mean age 10 years) also raised the threshold, but an oral dose of 300 mg administered to young adults merely prevented the decline in threshold that occurs with repeated testing (131). Because of the sensitivity of this threshold to the luminance, wave length, and other characteristics of the stimulus source, one might suppose that, in increasing the threshold, caffeine was affecting the subject's sensation or perception of the intermittent stimuli. Alternatively, caffeine may have made the subjects more alert to the subtle perturbations that indicated flicker. Furthermore, neither study used controls involving an unflickering stimulus, and it is not possible to assess the effect of caffeine on the disposition to report flicker as opposed to constant light.

The blocking by caffeine of the normal decline in fusion threshold that occurs with repeated testing may have been merely an effect on alertness; meprobamate (400 and 600 mg, respectively) further reduced the threshold (131). On the other hand, caffeine (150 mg and 300 mg) administered orally to young male adults has been shown to slow the habituation to 20 loud individual auditory stimuli presented at intervals ranging from 45 to 80 sec, as assessed in terms of skin conductance responses (232). Increased alertness in this case might have been expected to reduce the "surprise" value of the stimuli and thus hasten habituation. Alertness was assessed on a subjective rating scale; caffeine at both doses caused slight but statistically significant increases. Spontaneous alternation in a T- or Y-maze is often taken to be evidence of habituation to stimulation in animal studies. Caffeine (about 33 mg/kg) has been reported to increase spontaneous alternation in rats (81), but, more recently, doses of 10 and 20 mg/kg were reported to reduce alternation in ferrets (195). The evidence regarding caffeine's effects on sensation and perception is obviously full of contradictions, and it is clear also that in human experimentation in this area, insufficient attention has been given to caffeine's effects on the behavior involved in reporting the various stimulus conditions.

Caffeine's effect on alertness or attention is a well-established experimental phenomenon, in the sense that caffeine appears to make human subjects more expeditious in their response to unpredictable events. An oral dose of 200 mg caffeine, administered in a double-blind counterbalanced procedure, was found to enhance the average performance of 24 young males at the control of an automobile driving simulator, as assessed in terms of four measures of alertness (321). Likewise, oral doses of 200 or 400 mg caffeine significantly reduced "response blocking" (i.e., lapses in attention) on a night-driving simulator when compared with a placebo (21). In both of these studies, a supplemental dose of caffeine administered 60 or 90 min later produced further increments in performance. Another study of alertness, attention, and vigilance produced results suggesting that, under some circumstances at least, caffeine has an effect only on the performance of extraverted subjects, and then only when these subjects would otherwise be exhibiting a decline in performance during continuous testing (213). Subjects who provided low scores on the extraversion scale of the Eysenck Personality Inventory showed no decrement in performance during a 144-min vigilance task, and no effect on performance when 200 mg caffeine was administered orally prior to the session. These results were interpreted as supporting a cortical arousal basis for the difference between introverts and extraverts, the former allegedly being insensitive to caffeine because of high baseline arousal levels. However, as caffeine appeared to have an effect only on deteriorated performance, and as only one of the two groups exhibited deteriorated performance, it is difficult to justify the claim that the two groups differed in their response to caffeine. Moreover, because there was no assessment of caffeine consumption prior to experimentation—an unpropitious omission in much human experimentation on caffeine—it is possible that a real difference in caffeine effect would not have been observed, even if the procedure had been capable of detecting one.

Other Stimulus Effects of Caffeine

Stimuli can function in three different ways with respect to behavior. They can have unconditioned (or apparently unconditioned) effects, as in the case of pupil constriction to a bright light or salivation to meat odor. They can function as discriminative stimuli, as in the case of a signal for food, or for shock, or a traffic light. They can also function as reinforcing stimuli, as in the case of food for a hungry animal, or more for a greedy man (384). The effects of caffeine discussed so far have all been of the first category; the unconditioned response to caffeine administration has been the focus of concern. Drugs, like other stimuli, may also exert discriminative control. This is evident from studies in which animal and human subjects were trained to distinguish between different drugs and even between different doses of the same drug (289). Because of this control, learning under one drug state may not be evident when tested under another drug state or in the absence of the drug. Caffeine, however, appears to be a drug that may not achieve discriminative control over behavior. After 60 sessions, rats were still not able to escape electric shock reliably by turning left or right in a T-maze, according to whether or not 50 mg/kg caffeine or a placebo had been administered intraperitoneally (289). By contrast, most shocks were escaped after 2 or 3 sessions when the drug was an anesthetic, and after 20 sessions when 0.5–5.0 mg/kg amphetamine was used. It remains possible that caffeine's unconditioned effects in the escape situation interfered with its ability to acquire discriminative stimulus control over behavior, a possibility that might be tested by examining control over behavior maintained by positive reinforcement.

Caffeine's effectiveness as a reinforcing stimulus is also in doubt. A drug is a reinforcer when its administration is a consequence of behavior and maintains behavior. The most convincing evidence of drug reinforcement occurs when an animal works hard for the opportunity to give itself a dose of the drug. For example, monkeys (196) and rats (310) will emit substantial amounts of behavior for the opportunity to self-administer a small dose of cocaine via an intravenous catheter. Caffeine has been classed as a drug that is intravenously self-administered by monkeys (309, 311), but the data that I have seen indicate only sporadic self-administration of the drug (91) or none at all (186, 413). It is possible, however, that, in one of these studies (186), the history of prior cocaine self-administration, which increases the response rates maintained by low doses of cocaine (100), may have blocked caffeine self-administration. Intravenous administration of caffeine by humans is rarely encountered. I could find only one report (27). This allegedly involved the intravenous injection of 3–10 g caffeine, although the actual dose cannot be believed because of its likely fatal effect. Reports of orally administered caffeine acting as a reinforcer of animal behavior are also lacking. On the other hand, caffeine is among the most widely self-administered of drugs used by humans, as will be indicated later in this chapter. Furthermore, it seems that people often seek out caffeine-containing beverages and preparations, rather than alternatives that do not contain caffeine (71, 75, 159). A genetic basis has been proposed for at least a part of the excessive caffeine-seeking behavior of some humans (152, pp. 481–482), but relevant data are few (79).

Individual Differences in Response to Caffeine

A characteristic of the caffeine literature, perhaps more than that of other drugs, is the wide variation in response that is reported, particularly with regard to the behavioral effects of caffeine. One of the problems with assessing this phenomenon in humans is the wide variation in normal caffeine consumption (see Section 10), which may interfere with the assessment because of tolerance, dependence or withdrawal phenomena (76, 155). On the other hand, a study specifically directed toward the description of individual differences in caffeine-induced wakefulness and caffeine absorption found wide inter- and intrasubject variation that could not be related to habitual caffeine consumption (157). The authors proposed that the individual differences "must reflect, for the most part, intrinsic differences in sensitivity of sites of action in the brain," although they did not indicate how such sensitivity might vary from day to day in the same subject.

Large and inexplicable differences have been found in animal studies where the question of habitual caffeine consumption does not arise. For example, a dose of 2.5 mg/kg was found to produce a substantial increase in the already high rate of a beagle dog's running on a treadmill, whereas a caffeine dose as high as 7.5 mg/kg had little or no effect on the lower running rate of another dog (231). The effect of caffeine on avoidance behavior has been alleged to have a genetic determination (340), but, as in the previous study, the differences in baseline performance could be the significant feature. In only one report have I found analysis of variation in response to caffeine in terms of other caffeine effects. Oral administration of about 350 mg caffeine to humans produced general elevation, but wide variation in the activity of the eyes as assessed by the electro-oculargram (273); the greatest effect occurred in those in whom caffeine caused substantial elevation in blood pressure, whereas when substantial elevation in pulse rate was observed, no elevation in EOG potentials occurred.

Some people claim hypersensitivity (171), and even allergy to caffeine, and, although there seems to be no known incidence of allergic response to caffeine (239)*, recruiters for caffeine studies often encounter potential subjects who decline on the grounds of sensitivity to the drug (e.g., 76, 153). As mentioned in Section 4, some of the variation in response could arise through interactions with circadian rhythms. If caffeine is found to have powerful chronotypic properties, care must be taken to administer the drug consistently with respect to circadian rhythm and to take account of possible phase shifts in the assessment of the effects of chronic administration.

7. ASPECTS OF THE CHRONIC ADMINISTRATION OF CAFFEINE

> We have seen several well-marked cases of coffee excess. . . . The sufferer is tremulous, and loses his self-command; he is subject to fits of agitation and depression; he loses colour and has a haggard appearance. The appetite falls

* One source claims that "it has recently been definitely determined that coffee is capable of producing allergic response . . . various symptoms of coffee allergy have been reported: severe migraine, gastroenteritis, and widespread hives." (69, P. 437). Chlorogenic acid was suggested as a possible allergen. No specific sources were cited, and I have found none in my survey of the caffeine literature. The first two symptoms may result from excessive caffeine consumption, which could also exacerbate a disposition to manifest hives. Evidence that coffee is a potential allergen has been provided recently by Ulett and Perry (390).

> off, and symptoms of gastric catarrh may be manifested. The heart also suffers; it palpitates or it intermits. As with other such agents, a renewed dose of the poison gives temporary relief, but at the cost of future misery. . . . [Tea produces] a strange and extreme degree of physical depression. . . . A grievous sinking may seize upon a sufferer. . . . The speech may become vague and weak. By miseries such as these, the best years of life may be spoilt.
>
> T. Clifford Allbut and Walter Dixon. In *A System of Medicine*, 1909.

Tolerance

Caffeine is generally thought of as a drug whose repeated administration produces very little change in responsiveness on the part of the recipient. Thus Truitt (388) claimed that tolerance is not an obvious feature of caffeine administration; Goldstein et al. (152) spoke of "a low degree of tolerance;" and Ritchie (325) reported that "little or no tolerance" develops to the effects of caffeine on the central nervous system, although "an appreciable degree of tolerance" may develop to certain effects, including the diuretic and vasodilatory actions. Caffeine was not mentioned in a recent survey of tolerance to nonopiate psychotropic drugs (207), and only passing reference to tolerance was made in Weiss and Laties' review of caffeine's effects on human behavior (404).

The evidence regarding caffeine tolerance is actually more uncertain than might be assumed from the above statements. The evidence for tolerance to the diuretic action in humans is good, although somewhat old (106). On the other hand, Peters (307) referred to unpublished data, indicating no development of tolerance to the diuretic effect in rats. An initial decline in food consumption did not persist, however, with daily caffeine administration. The evidence for tolerance to caffeine's vasodilatory action seems nonexistent, although a slight decrease in caffeine's blood-pressure elevating effect in humans has been noted with repeated administration of coffee (188). There is an indication that tolerance develops to caffeine's stimulation of salivary flow, at least when caffeine is administered in beverage form (411). Peters (307) reviewed other evidence on chronic caffeine consumption, including data on development of resistance to toxicity, and noted the problem of distinguishing genuine tolerance, or lack of it, from the general effects of repeated aspecific stress.

Regarding tolerance to central nervous system effects, there seems to have been only one study that involved nonhuman subjects (376). In this study of caffeine's effect on the activity of rats, it was concluded that tolerance develops very quickly, but the data do not readily support the conclusion. No trend was portrayed, and the comparison between chronic and acute caffeine effects involved a change in route of administration. Animal studies could play an important role in establishing whether or not there can be tolerance to any of caffeine's effects on behavior. Comparable human data could be generated only by finding known abstainers from caffeine and subjecting them to repeated caffeine administration, a procedure that might be difficult to implement.

Human studies of caffeine tolerance to date have generally compared effects on habitual users with those on nonusers. A stronger average effect of a given dose in nonusers, compared with that in users, provides some kind of evidence that users are exhibiting tolerance to the drug. However, as Goldstein (151) pointed out, in the first of a series of five studies of caffeine's effects, those who consume a lot of caffeine may be intrinsically less sensitive to the effects of the drug than those who consume only a little, a difference that itself might underlie differences in consumption. The second study (157) provides evidence of large individual differences, including large differences between repeated tests on the same subject, but these were not related to habitual levels of caffeine consumption. In the first study, Goldstein had found that caffeine caused less wakefulness in medical students who reported drinking five or more cups a day than in subjects who reported drinking less coffee (see Section 6). The third study (154) demonstrated that a 300-mg dose of caffeine affected mood, but not performance; that the effect on mood was stronger in medical students for whom sleep had been significantly delayed by caffeine in the second study, but that neither effect could be related to habitual levels of caffeine-beverage consumption. A later study by Colton and his associates (76) provided evidence that 150 mg caffeine caused a small but significant decrease in mean pulse rate when administered orally to noncoffee drinkers (≤ 1 cup/day), but not to coffee drinkers (> 1 cup/day). Again, the point made by Goldstein should be remembered—the noncoffee drinkers in Colton's study may have been avoiding coffee because they had observed that it lowered pulse rate, or because it produced some other effect, such as an increase in blood pressure. Clearly, the question of whether or not tolerance can occur to some or all of caffeine's effects is still very much open. Its investigation should not be confused by considerations of caffeine consumption prior to, or even during, experimentation. Nor should tolerance phenomena be confused with the phenomena of caffeine withdrawal, as could happen when habitual users are required to refrain from caffeine prior to an experimental session.

Dependence

Tea-faced—having a sallow or effeminate countenance like one addicted to tea-drinking.
Oxford English Dictionary, Vol. IX, 1912.

Tolerance and physical dependence often seem to occur together, as though they were "reflections of the same underlying biologic change" (152, p. 610). Tolerance without dependence has been reported, for example with LSD-25, but there seems to be no report of dependence without tolerance. Thus, it may be surprising to note that evidence of dependence upon caffeine is somewhat more substantial than evidence of tolerance. Dependence in this case means physical dependence, i.e., a condition typified by a characteristic withdrawal condition that arises on interruption of chronic administration of the drug, a condition that, in many instances, is opposite to the one produced by acute administration of the drug, and that can be reversed or ameliorated by administration of the drug or a similar compound.

The clearest evidence of physical dependence on caffeine comes from the last of the series of five studies by Goldstein and his colleagues (155). Californian women, some nonusers, some habitually drinking five or more cups of coffee a day, were given, in a blind, balanced fashion, a placebo or 150 mg or 300 mg caffeine in decaffeinated coffee powder. The sample was to be prepared and consumed after breakfast, subjects having been instructed to abstain from caffeine beverages since the previous evening. Self-ratings of mood according to 11 variables were made before drinking the sample, and at 30-min intervals thereafter for 2 hr. The coffee-drinking group exhibited a characteristic withdrawal syndrome that was relieved by caffeine, but continued when they received the placebo. Prior to receiving the sample, the users felt significantly less alert, less content and relaxed, less active and energetic, more sleepy and drowsy, and more irritable than did the nonusers. Two hours later, after the placebo had been administered, virtually the same differences existed; users now also reported being more jittery and nervous than the nonusers. Users were also more likely to report having a headache. Caffeine appeared to abolish all of the symptoms in users, but to create a different set in nonusers. Most effects were both time-related and dose-related.

The caffeine-withdrawal headache had been described before. Dreisbach and Pfeiffer (101) persuaded their subjects to abstain from caffeine for an unspecified period, then to consume supplementary caffeine in capsule form for a week, so that approximately 775 mg/day was ingested, and then to abstain again. Most subjects reported moderate to severe headache on the day of withdrawal. In many subjects, the headache was as severe as they had ever experienced. Normally migrainous subjects reported a quite different kind of headache following caffeine withdrawal. The withdrawal headache of all subjects responded to acetylsalicylic acid, but the most effective treatment was caffeine.

Many clinical reports of caffeine withdrawal have not detailed headache as a conspicuous feature. In one (323), caffeine intake was restricted in a patient who had been drinking more than 15 cups of apparently strong coffee daily. No withdrawal symptoms were reported, although the signs of caffeinism abated. However, withdrawal from caffeine may not have been complete; the patient's nicotine intake could have prevented withdrawal (although there is no evidence concerning the possibility of cross-tolerance or cross-dependence between caffeine and nicotine); the habitual use of phenobarbital could have had some effect. Headache was not mentioned in a report on abrupt withdrawal after a history of a chronically high level of caffeine consumption (326), withdrawal that was effective in relieving edema. Nor was it mentioned in connection with two of the three instances of caffeine withdrawal that Greden (159) reported. Caffeine-withdrawal headache may have been a feature of other investigations, however. For example, a recent study of stimulant effects in Czech medical students (396) indicated that 100 mg caffeine prior to an 80-min theoretical lecture on clinical pharmacology prevented the development of headache during the lecture.

One problem with recognizing headache as a symptom of caffeine-withdrawal is the possibility that headache may be a feature of occasional interruptions of caffeine use, and thus may not be recognized as specific to the withdrawal state. Greden's third patient suffered severe, recurrent tension headaches before being instructed to avoid caffeine. These occurred mainly at weekends between bouts of excessive caffeine consumption at his office (159). Another problem is that headache may be a response to caffeine administration, as well as to caffeine withdrawal (169). Graeber (158) reported that 300 mg caffeine can raise the intraocular pressure in glaucoma patients by a considerable amount when the glaucoma is unregulated, i.e., if pressure has not already been reduced by therapeutic intervention of some kind. This effect might cause headache in untreated glaucoma. Headaches could also occur as a direct consequence of caffeine-caused increases in blood pressure, or in tension in the neck and scalp. When caffeine-induced headache seems apparent, the temporal relations between caffeine consumption and appearance of headache should be monitored carefully, so that it is clear that the headache does not result from temporary withdrawal or from a caffeine "hangover" (which may amount to the same thing).

There is one experimental study of the effects of caffeine withdrawal on human performance. Horst and her colleagues (188) found that motor performance on two tasks was impaired for one week after daily administration of about 250 mg of caffeine was discontinued. Performance at one of these tasks had been impaired during caffeine administration, but performance at the other seems to have been improved by caffeine.

Caffeine withdrawal in animals has not been formally investigated. However, substantially decreased activity has often been observed after cessation of chronic caffeine administration. For example, Boyd and colleagues (42) administered 190 mg/kg caffeine orally via intragastric cannula to female rats five days a week for 100 days and found that locomotor activity after withdrawal was half of prewithdrawal levels, which did not differ from those of control animals. The depression lasted one week and was accompanied by a fall in colonic temperature and an increase in the protein and glucose content of the urine. One problem with interpreting a postcaffeine decline in activity is the possibility that mere fatigue has caused the depression, fatigue from chronic caffeine-induced excessive activity. In Boyd's study, however, the daily dose was sufficiently high that caffeine was not having a hyperkinetic effect (42); depression ensued, nevertheless. In one of my studies (143), adulteration of drinking water by caffeine for one day only, providing about 20 mg/kg of the drug, raised the running wheel activity of rats only slightly during the day of caffeine administration, but depressed it substantially on the following day, when no caffeine was administered. In this sense, the aftereffects of caffeine administration were more profound than the effects of the drug itself.

Although a withdrawal syndrome and its remedy by the drug are the defining conditions of physical dependence, there are two other indicators that may provide supportive evidence of dependence. One is systematic selection of the drug when similar but nonpotent alternatives are available. Although such selection could occur for other reasons, e.g., taste, it is possible that physical dependence is an underlying cause, as in a situation recently uncovered at the Women's Hospital in Sydney, Australia (75). A group of pregnant women was divided according to whether they took an analgesic preparation infrequently or daily, first thing in the morning. All 29 of the daily users were taking an analgesic compound that contained caffeine. Only 20 of the 34 infrequent users employed a caffeine-compounded analgesic.* Comparable evidence has come from a study involving rats (394), in which it was found that animals used to drinking a 500 μg/ml caffeine solution as their sole fluid preferred that solution over water and a mocha

* A Scotswoman suffering from analgesic nephropathy was reported to have consumed 20 Askit powders daily (275a). Each of these analgesic preparations contains 110 mg caffeine. The daily total intake of caffeine was therefore more than the equivalent of 27 average cups of coffee, as will be indicated in Section 10.

solution, whereas rats used to drinking either a 170 or a 340 μg/ml caffeine solution indicated no such preference. The second indication of caffeine dependence is difficulty in effecting withdrawal. It was difficult for the habitual users among the pregnant women in the Australian study to switch to a caffeinefree analgesic. Similarly, Furlong (134) has reported that it was extremely difficult to encourage caffeine abstention among his psychiatric patients, more than half of whom were drinking five or more cups of caffeine-containing beverages a day.

Although one can claim that there is a caffeine-withdrawal syndrome with somewhat greater confidence than one can claim that tolerance occurs to many of caffeine's effects, there is still much scope for defining the nature and the extent of the caffeine-withdrawal phenomenon.*

8. INTERACTIONS WITH OTHER DRUGS

Ethanol

> In addition to alcohol, the Bohemians used coffee. They drank vast quantities of this stimulant, were preoccupied with coffee, and suffered coffee as well as alcohol hangovers. Respectable citizens of that era were as horrified by the Bohemian coffee cult as today's respectable citizens are horrified by marijuana smoking. Eminent scientists . . . echoed this horror.
>
> Edward Brecher and associates. *Licit and Illicit Drugs*, 1972.

Ethanol and caffeine are the most widely consumed drugs in North America, and thus there is special reason for considering how these two drugs interact in their effects and how the consumption of one may be related to the consumption of the other. The fact that the interaction between the two drugs is complex has been noted at least since the early experiments of Pilcher (312). There is still considerable doubt as to whether caffeine, a stimulant, generally antagonizes the action of ethanol, a depressant. Studies of caffeine's effects on ethanol-deteriorated human performance were reviewed briefly by Calhoun (57), who echoed the conclusions of both Forney and Hughes (122) and Nash (277) that there is no clear effect, and certainly no good evidence for the caffeine–ethanol antagonism that had been sug-

* Aranda and colleagues at the Montreal Children's Hospital have recently found caffeine administration to be an effective treatment of apnea in preterm neonates. Doses of up to 30 mg/kg/day have been used (10a), equivalent on a body-weight basis to more than 2000 mg caffeine a day for a 70 kg adult. An intriguing hypothesis is that apnea in preterm newborn who are not breastfed may be a result of withdrawal from chronic caffeine administration in utero. The probable slow clearance of caffeine in utero (10b) adds fuel to this hypothesis, in that the possibility of caffeine dependence is enhanced.

gested by earlier studies. Indeed, Forney and Hughes (121) had found a tendency towards further deterioration of certain kinds of ethanol-impaired performance in most tests. It may be surprising that there are no more recent studies of caffeine–ethanol interactions in humans.

Studies of animal behavior in this area have produced mixed results, ranging from further deterioration by caffeine of ethanol-impaired performance (4, 194) to enhancement by caffeine of ethanol-stimulated locomotor activity (397). This last study illustrates the complexity of the interaction between the two drugs, even with respect to such a simple measure as gross activity. Caffeine at 25 or 50 mg/kg intraperitoneally further increased mouse activity when 1 or 2 g/kg ethanol intraperitoneally was also administered. These caffeine doses had no effect when the ethanol dose was 3 g/kg, and they abolished the increase in activity caused by 4 g/kg ethanol. A larger caffeine dose (100 mg/kg), which itself depressed activity, also antagonized the activity-increasing effect of all four doses of ethanol, although not completely in the case of the 2 g/kg dose. The only other recent study of possible caffeine–ethanol antagonism with respect to behavior demonstrated no effect of 100 mg/kg caffeine on the ability of rats to use ethanol as a discriminative cue (344). An approximately equivalent dose of *d*-amphetamine sulfate (i.e., 4 mg/kg—see ref. 232) did reduce ethanol's cue function. Indirect evidence of caffeine–ethanol antagonism may come from the work of Collier and his colleagues on the "quasi-abstinence syndrome" (see below). Theophylline was found to potentiate head-twitching during ethanol withdrawal in mice, at a dose that ordinarily does not increase head-twitching (73), and it is likely that caffeine would do the same. Such an effect, however, might be quite nonspecific to ethanol. Any stress could potentiate caffeine's effect on behavior that happens also to be characteristic of a withdrawal condition.

The available evidence does not permit a conclusion about the interaction between caffeine and ethanol, and certainly not about the possible restorative effect of coffee during alcohol intoxication. Noting that caffeine may sometimes elevate mood (154) and promote wakefulness (151), the net effect of coffee after drinking an excessive amount of alcohol may be to produce not the familiar sleepy, and therefore manageable, drunk but a dangerous, confident being called a "wide-awake drunk."

There is evidence that caffeine taken before ethanol may reduce blood-ethanol levels in rats by relaxing gastric musculature, and thus slowing the passage of ethanol into the small intestine, where most ethanol is normally absorbed (352). This effect occurred with an oral dose as low as 10 mg/kg. Apart from this effect on stomach emptying, ethanol absorption does not appear to be affected by caffeine (4, 352). Moreover, a study of the effect of approximately 250 mg caffeine on the metabolism of ethanol ingested 1 hr earlier by human subjects yielded no evidence of an effect (303).

The data on gastric motility raise the possibility of advising the would-be alcohol drinker to relax his stomach by drinking coffee before a binge, thereby reducing the peak blood-ethanol level, and thus the peak level of intoxication achieved with a given ethanol dose. Unfortunately, because inebriation would set in more slowly, drinking might go on for longer, the net effect being to raise consumption and cause more prolonged incapacitation. Moreover, there is evidence that rats given caffeine in their diet will drink much more of a 10% ethanol solution than they would otherwise, if they are also undernourished (322). I have replicated this finding under somewhat different conditions (145), but not in such a way as to indicate whether caffeine's effect is due to a pharmacologic or to another kind of mechanism. Taste could be an important variable, although its involvement would have to be specific to the dietary deficiency. Alternatively, a more recondite mechanism could be involved, such as regulation of vitamin A plasma levels. Lack of this vitamin may distinguish diets that allow the caffeine effect on ethanol consumption from those that do not. Ethanol promotes release of vitamin A from the liver (236); it also competes with vitamin A for alcohol dehydrogenase. Caffeine, via its effects on liver activity (216, 264), may enhance one or another of these processes. Thus caffeine may make it easier for rats to control vitamin A levels by means of their alcohol consumption. There is evidence that rats can remedy vitamin A deficiencies by dietary selection (324).

In conclusion, for the moment, no comfort can be given to the alcohol drinker who wishes to improve his condition by resort to coffee or to other caffeine-containing beverages. The interactions between ethanol and caffeine remain obscure to a degree that is especially surprising in view of the apparent frequency of consumption of both drugs in North America and in other places.

Barbiturates

This class of drugs also has wide use. According to the report of the Le Dain Commission (77, p. 640), Canadian adults consumed an average of more than 40 hypnotic doses each during 1972. Thus, it is likely that many people, on occasion, have appreciable blood levels of both caffeine and barbiturate. Nonetheless, data on barbiturate–caffeine interactions are even fewer than those on ethanol–caffeine interactions. In the one study of human performance that has appeared in the last 15 years, 200 mg caffeine administered orally was found to antagonize the depressive effects of both amobarbital and neopentylallylbarbituric acid, at 200 and 400 mg, in terms of measures of reaction time, fine motor coordination, and intellectual and perceptual function (103). Caffeine also restored barbiturate-elevated pulse rate and barbiturate-depressed blood pressure. Self-ratings of mood and activation were reversed by caffeine, particularly with regard to excitation, but not alertness. The only other study involving humans assessed the effect of 250 mg of caffeine on the hypnotic effects of 100 mg of pentobarbital, both administered orally to medical and surgical patients (123). Separately, this caffeine dose delayed sleep onset and reduced sleeping time and sleep quality. The barbiturate dose had the opposite effect. Together the drugs were no different from the lactose placebo. Both of these two studies suggest a much clearer antagonism by caffeine than in the case of ethanol. The second report raises the possibility that some patients resort to higher barbiturate doses than would otherwise be necessary, in order to counteract the effects of habitual caffeine-beverage consumption.

Barbiturates may also stimulate behavior, as do most depressant drugs at low doses (320). In a recent study (399), caffeine (10 mg/kg) and pentobarbital (8–32 mg/kg) produced significant increases in the activity of aggregated mice. When the two higher doses of pentobarbital (16 and 32 mg/kg) were given together with caffeine, an additive effect appeared. Thus far, the results paralleled those of an earlier study by the same author on the interaction between caffeine and ethanol (397). However, because higher doses of caffeine and barbiturate were not used, evidence of possible antagonism between the two drugs with respect to activity must await further investigation.

Opiates

As in the case of ethanol and the barbiturates, opiate activity has been both enhanced and inhibited by caffeine, according to whether the opiate has had a stimulating or a depressing effect. Thus, two stimulant actions of apomorphine, the induction of stereotyped behavior in guinea pigs and rotation in unilateral nigrostriatal lesioned rats, have both been enhanced by caffeine (135, 223). A depressant effect on human respiration by codeine or morphine was reversed by 62.5 mg caffeine administered intramuscularly (31). Caffeine has also been found to produce slight antagonism of the reinforcing effects of codeine (186). Theophylline has been observed to antagonize intestinal stimulatory effects of morphine (163); caffeine was not investigated.

Intracerebral or intravenous administration of cyclic AMP has been found to antagonize morphine analgesia in both tolerant and nontolerant mice (184), and to accelerate the development of tolerance to and physical dependence on morphine (185). Thus, it might be supposed that drugs such as caffeine and theophylline, which are believed to elevate cyclic AMP levels (see Section 3), would have similar effects. Theophylline (100 mg/kg) was observed to have a similar analgesia-antagonizing effect in one of these studies (184), but a study of possible antagonism by caffeine yielded the opposite result. Caffeine (10 mg/kg) increased the analgesic potency of morphine (32 mg/kg) in rats and delayed the development of tolerance (253). Moreover, previously induced tolerance was "temporarily arrested," and the disappearance of tolerance was accelerated by caffeine. In the same report (253), it was noted that the 16:5 ratio of doses did not inhibit the development of physical dependence on morphine in Japanese monkeys, but the design was such that acceleration of dependence development would not have been observed. (One authoritative reviewer [378] asserted, incorrectly, that caffeine did inhibit the development of dependence in this study.) Regarding xanthine effects on the severity of physical dependence, it has been reported that 100 mg/kg theophylline (74), and an unspecified dose of caffeine (124), accentuate withdrawal signs in rats that are already opiate-dependent, as well as producing a "quasi-abstinence syndrome" in nondependent rats. Caffeine's involvement, if any, in opiate dependence remains an open question that needs careful investigation involving a range of dose levels.

Other Analgesics

Caffeine is often included as an ingredient of prescription and nonprescription analgesics, perhaps to compensate for a sedative effect that might accompany analgesia, but perhaps too because caffeine may have its own analgesic properties, especially with respect to headaches (see Section 7). Thus interactions between caffeine and drugs such as acetylsalicylic acid (ASA), phenacetin, and paracetamol are of some interest. Inhibition of absorption, such as has been found with paracetamol by Siegers (351), probably occurs because of caffeine's effect on stomach motility, observed by the same author with respect to ethanol (352). Seigers found that caffeine reduced the analgesic effect of paracetamol in rats at the lowest dose used (10 mg/kg, orally), but that higher doses of caffeine had no effect. Two laboratories have reported that oral doses of caffeine have no effect on the absorption and metabolism of phenacetin by rats (356, 382)—both used 30 mg/kg. (The possible discrepancy between these data and the data on absorption of ethanol and paracetamol may be worth examining.) Regarding ASA, it is possible that caffeine could inhibit analgesia in the same way as it inhibits the analgesic action of paracetamol (351). Recent attention has focused on the renal effects of ASA–caffeine combinations. After reporting that 50 mg/kg caffeine administered orally to rats potentiated the production of renal enzymes by ASA, Raab (316) concluded that caffeine might be implicated in the nephrotoxic effects that are observed after prolonged ingestion of commonly available analgesic preparations.

Effects of Caffeine on Hepatic Drug-metabolizing Enzymes

As well as modifying the absorption of another drug, caffeine may also change the drug's effectiveness by modifying its rate of metabolism and, thus, its disappearance from the body. The main site of metabolism is the liver, into which caffeine readily permeates. Two recent studies have demonstrated that caffeine may alter the activity of drug-metabolizing microsomal enzymes in the liver. In the first, oral administration of 30 mg/kg caffeine to rats for three days significantly increased the ability of appropriate liver fractions to metabolize various compounds in vitro (264). This effect was blocked by prior administration of known inhibitors of protein synthesis. Oral administration of caffeine as coffee or tea had an effect similar to that of caffeine. In the second study, daily administration of lower caffeine doses was observed for a longer period (216). Rates of change differed according to the enzymatic function, the general effect being an initial increase and a subsequent decrease; in particular, N-demethylating activity was only 38% of control values at the end of eight weeks. In the second experiment of the same study (216), animals given caffeine for six weeks were found to have a reduced hepatic response to a phenobarbital challenge. In the third experiment, levels of two liver enzymes were determined directly after a phenobarbital challenge that followed chronic administration of caffeine, revealing induction of one (cytochrome P_{450}) and suppression of the other (cytochrome b_5) when compared with controls. These effects of caffeine on the drug-metabolizing system have not yet been related to drug interactions as expressed in behavior or physiologic change, and clearly there is scope for experimentation in this area. Apparent idiosyncratic responses to certain drugs used clinically may very well be linked to the effects of chronic caffeine administration on the liver's ability to carry out drug metabolism.

Interactions of Caffeine with Drugs That Affect Neural Transmission

All drugs affect neural transmission in one way or another, but some are known to have specific effects on synaptic or neuroeffector junction sites. One line of research has involved the interaction between caffeine and L-dopa, a precursor of the adrenergic neurotransmitter norepinephrine. In a study by Strömberg and Waldeck (367), 25 mg/kg caffeine was found not to alter the depressant action of medium doses of L-dopa in mice, but to potentiate the hyperkinetic effect of higher doses. In a second study (368), the same authors found that pretreatment with 100 mg/kg of the peripheral dopa decarboxylase inhibitor MK 486 allowed 25 mg/kg caffeine to interact with a medium dose of L-dopa (125 mg/kg) to produce hyperactivity. In both studies, increased brain levels of dopamine were associated with caffeine–dopa-induced hyperactivity. In the second study, the dopa precursor tyrosine was administered in labeled form, and it was noted that the disappearance of brain dopamine and norepinephrine was not significantly changed by caffeine. From these and other data, it was concluded that caffeine's effect was due partly to increased dopamine levels, and partly to sensitization of the dopamine receptor. These actions could also underlie caffeine's ability to reverse puromycin suppression of memory in mice (118), which was interpreted as occurring due to an increase in norepinephrine turnover and release. Chronic administration of L-dopa is the treatment of choice in the management of Parkinson's disease and postencephalic parkinsonism. Caffeine may alter the therapeutic response to L-dopa, and thus the wide individual variation in response to this treatment (105) may be related to habitual levels of caffeine-beverage consumption. Indeed, one report concludes that caffeine itself may be of value in the treatment of parkinsonism, alone or as an adjuvant to L-dopa (223).

Related research has concerned the involvement of cholinergic transmission in caffeine's effect upon locomotor activity. Waldeck (398) found that a threshold dose of the anticholinergic drug atropine enhanced the stimulatory effect of caffeine in mice. Conversely, the acetylcholine esterase inhibitor, eserine, decreased locomotor activity. (Eserine has also been observed to inhibit caffeine-induced contractures in frog sartorius muscles [292].) There has also been an attempt to investigate possible interactions between adrenergic and cholinergic systems. Waldeck found that the activity-reducing effect of reserpine, which depletes norepinephrine from adrenergic terminals, could be reversed by treatment with both ET495, a dopamine agonist, and chloridine, a norepinephrine agonist, and that this reversal could be potentiated by caffeine (398, 399). Noting other evidence that atropine-stimulated activity can be inhibited with prior treatment by a tyrosine hydroxylase inhibitor, but not by a dopamine hydroxylase inhibitor, Waldeck concluded that the involvement of the cholinergic system in caffeine-stimulated activity also requires the cooperation of the catecholaminergic transmission system.

Notwithstanding the above evidence, Estler (110) has concluded that sympathetic activity is not an essential component of the stimulatory action of caffeine in mice. He found that blockade of the α- and β-receptors by phenoxybenzamine and propranolol, respectively, had no effect on the increased motility induced by 40 mg/kg caffeine. On the other hand, the brain serotonin depletor, *p*-chlorophenylalanine, did reduce caffeine's excitatory activity. Estler's finding is consistent with an earlier observation that monoamine oxidase inhibitors, including pargyline, iproniazid, tranylcypramine, and phenylisopropylhydrazine substantially increase the toxicity of caffeine (33). These drugs all prevent the disappearance of serotonin. Also, in the same study, it was observed that *p*-chlorophenylalanine was particularly effective in reducing the pharmacologic consequences of the caffeine–pargyline interaction. However, caffeine's action may be to increase serotonin metabolism. In one study, an increase in urinary excretion of 5-hydroxyindoleacetic acid, a serotonin metabolite, was found after oral administration of caffeine solutions to humans (90). The monoamine oxidase inhibitors also prevent disappearance of other presumed neurotransmitters that may be involved in caffeine's action. Interactions between caffeine and MAO inhibitors are of relevance to the clinical use of these drugs; they are sometimes used as antidepressants and, more rarely, in cases of cardiovascular hypotension. As in the case of L-dopa, individual variation in response may be based in part on variation in habitual caffeine-beverage consumption.

Although caffeine obviously interacts powerfully with many of the drugs that alter neural transmission, the precise nature of caffeine's effects remains unclear, as does the nature of neural transmission.

Miscellaneous Drug Interactions

> Fine Tea Coffee Chocolat Cocoa Nutts Vermachelly Sago and all other Drugges Sold by Page Hockett at ye Great Mogul at Brownlow Street end in Drury lane.
>
> Wording on an eighteenth century London merchant's trade card.

Peters (307) reviewed some of caffeine's interactions during his discussion of factors affecting caffeine toxicity. He reported that neither phenacetin nor ASA potentiates caffeine toxicity, but that potentiation may occur with the antitubercular drug, isoniazid, and also with the once widely used antianxiety agent meprobamate. Interactions between caffeine and currently popular antianxiety agents, including chlordiazepoxide and diazepam, do not appear to have been investigated. Domino (97) reported that caffeine has been shown to counteract chlordiazeproxide-induced depression in animal experiments, but he gave no reference.

Prevention of caffeine's fetopathic effect in mice has been achieved with prior administration of the adrenergic blocking agent, propranolol, leading to the suggestion that caffeine-induced fetal anomalies could arise as a consequence of the elevated levels of catecholamines that caffeine may cause in fetal circulation (132, 133). The caffeine dose used in these studies was 200 mg/kg, intraperitoneally, which is of the same order as the lethal dose (272, 307), although no deaths were reported. No evidence was presented regarding an increase in catecholamine levels, but the authors cited other studies to the effect that caffeine causes catecholamine release into circulation, that catecholamines cross the placenta, and that they induce developmental anomalies.

Another interaction between caffeine and a commonly used drug is that between caffeine and insulin. Insulin's function, whether produced endogenously or administered, is to control the production of glucose by muscle and fat. Insulin administration, therefore, tends to lower blood-glucose levels. Caffeine, as discussed in Section 3, may have the opposite effect. Antagonism by caffeine (100 mg/kg) of insulin-stimulated glucose metabolism in vitro has been reported (7), raising the possibility that caffeine ingestion may interfere with blood-glucose regulation by insulin in diabetes. Conversely, diabetics may ingest caffeine-containing beverages in order to correct hypoglycemia produced by excessive insulin administration. A similar basis for caffeine-beverage consumption might exist in other groups who are subject to wide fluctuations in blood sugar, including, for example, Canadian Inuit and other native peoples, whose insulin response to carbohydrate ingestion is delayed unless protein has been previously ingested (342).* Another condition of diabetes is an increased level of plasma free fatty acids. Caffeine may elevate blood-fat levels even more, thus raising the possibility of ketonemia. Caffeine's effect on free-fatty-acid levels may be antagonized by insulin (314a) and also by the vitamin, niacin (30), of which both coffee and tea happen to be good sources.

In summary, caffeine has been found to interact with a number of other drugs, sometimes synergistically, sometimes antagonistically, sometimes exhibiting both effects with one and the same drug, depending on the dose levels. There is sufficient evidence to suggest that response to many clinically used drugs may be determined by habitual caffeine consumption, although directly relevant data on this topic are nonexistent. There is also evidence of interaction between caffeine and recognized drugs of abuse. In all, the possible implication of caffeine is such as to deserve recognition of its effects when the clinical or recreational use of other drugs is contemplated.

* In the summer of 1975 Diane Beckett studied caffeine-beverage consumption among the native peoples of the James Bay area. Her unpublished report indicates that per capita tea consumption in this population is among the highest in the world. Individual consumption in excess of the equivalent of 20 average-sized cups a day did not appear to be unusual.

9. THE TASTE OF CAFFEINE

. . . base, black, thick, nasty bitter stinking, nauseous Puddle water

Anon. *The Women's Petition against Coffee*, 1674.

A feature of many blind and double-blind studies involving human subjects is the addition of controlled amounts of caffeine or no caffeine at all to decaffeinated coffee. This procedure was used, for example, in the studies by Goldstein and his colleagues (151, 154, 155, 157), by Fröberg et al. (130), and by Colton et al. (76), with a statement in each case that the presence of caffeine could not be detected. In one case (130), the subjects were quizzed after the experiment as to caffeine content and they did not respond accurately. Such ignorance could be surprising in view of a finding reported by Hall and her colleagues (168) that the caffeine in coffee is above the taste concentration threshold for a majority of the North American population (see Table 1, above). They demonstrated that individuals with an inherited inability to taste phenylthiocarbamide (about 30% of the population [152, p. 471]) find caffeine much less bitter than do normal subjects. Thus, it might be supposed that more than two-thirds of the subjects in the studies of caffeine effects would have been able to taste the caffeine if it were not masked by substances in coffee. One of Hall's colleagues, Bartoshuk (25), has argued that although intensities of tastes might be suppressed by mixtures, the individual components of mixtures can still be recognized. Thus, the possibility of detection remains. Hall and her colleagues raised the intriguing possibility that the taste sensitivity to caffeine might predict sensitivity to the pharmacologic effects of caffeine as a stimulant.

This matter would not be worth raising if it were not for the findings, mentioned in Section 6, that performance (263), and reports on sleep quality (151) and mood (6, 130), may be affected both by the administration of caffeine and by the information that is given about the administration. The findings described by Hall and associates caution against too easy acceptance of inability to distinguish oral caffeine from placebo, and raise the possibility of substantial individual differences in taste response to caffeine.

10. CAFFEINE CONSUMPTION

A realistic clinical perspective of caffeinism is difficult to formulate. Prevalence and incidence figures are simply not known. Average coffee and tea drinking patterns are not even known.

John Greden. *American Journal of Psychiatry*, Vol. 131, 1974.

Caffeine is consumed as a constituent of most popular nonalcoholic beverages, including coffee, tea, maté, yaupon, guarana, cocoa, chocolate drinks, and colas. Only the last are required by law to contain caffeine—not more than 200 parts per million in Canada (200 $\mu g/ml$, or about 5.7 mg per ounce) and not more than about 5 mg per ounce in the United States. Caffeine is a component of foods that contain coffee or chocolate. It is also the main or an ancillary ingredient of many prescription and nonprescription drugs, including analgesics, common cold remedies, antacids, and patent stimulants. It is possible that an individual's caffeine consumption from nonbeverage sources is quite high.* For example, a person taking five Excedrin tablets per day (65 mg caffeine per tablet) and two doses of Bromo-Seltzer (32.5 mg per capful) would be ingesting 390 mg caffeine per day from these sources alone, an amount that is possibly equivalent to more than five cups of coffee, as will be indicated later. I have not been able to find useful consumption figures for caffeine-containing substances other than coffee and tea. Indications are that caffeine ingestion from other sources, with the possible exception of cola drinks, occurs at a low level on the average, when compared with that from coffee and tea. Hence, estimates of caffeine ingestion to be presented here are based on coffee and tea consumption alone. It must always be remembered that these estimates will, accordingly, be on the low side, and that, in individual cases, quite a false picture of caffeine consumption can be gained if only tea and coffee consumption are taken into account.

Coffee Consumption

> Soluble coffee, more commonly known as instant coffee, was the invention of a Mr. G. Washington, an Englishman living in Guatemala. While waiting for his wife one day to join him in the garden for coffee, he noticed on the spout of the silver coffee pot, the fine powder, which seemed to be the condensation of the coffee vapour. This intrigued him and led to his discovery of soluble coffee. In 1906 he started experiments and put his product on the market in 1909. Since that time many varieties of instant coffee have appeared on the market with great commercial success.†
>
> Prosper Montagné. *Larousse Gastronomique*, 1938.

Beverage consumption can be estimated from total sales of raw tea and coffee, and also from surveys of drinking practices. Estimates of average

* In tropical Africa, where wild coffee used to be abundant, infusions of berry or leaf were never prepared, but chewing the raw bean was a general custom. According to nineteenth-century explorers, many African peoples cultivated coffee trees intensively for this purpose (174).

† Expresso coffee (in Italy) and the vacuum pack also made their first appearance at the beginning of the twentieth century. It was, as well, an important period for tea technology. Both tea bags and iced tea were introduced in 1904, the latter now accounting for 70% of tea consumption in the United States, according to one source (319).

consumption by the two methods are surprisingly consistent. The consistency is remarkable because of the many ways of transforming a given weight of coffee bean or tea leaf into an acceptable beverage, and also because surveys of alcohol beverage consumption have yielded results that are quite discrepant from estimates of consumption from sales (304).

Coffee is imported into Canada and the United States largely in the form of the unroasted, or green, bean. Canadian disappearance (i.e., net consumption) of green bean or equivalent in 1970 was close to 90.7 million kilograms (295), or approximately 5.19 kg per capita, if children under 10 years of age are excluded. Each kilogram of green coffee contains approximately 1.1% or 11 g caffeine (211, 252, 295). If it is assumed that the average cup of instant coffee contains 65 mg, and the average cup of regular coffee contains 100 mg (see Table 10 below), and it is noted that Canadians drink approximately equal numbers of cups of instant and regular coffee (294), the estimated number of cups consumed per day in 1970 based on green bean disappearance is 1.90 per capita. According to a drinking survey conducted for the Pan-American Coffee Bureau (294), the average consumption among Canadians over 9 years of age in 1970 was 1.99 cups per day. A corresponding calculation for the United States, based on a green bean disappearance of 7.58 kg per head in 1972 among nonmilitary residents aged 10 years or older, together with the observation that only about 30% of the coffee cups consumed in that country were prepared from instant coffee, yields a daily consumption of 2.55 cups of coffee. Survey data gained for the Pan-American Coffee Bureau indicate a 1972 mean consumption of 2.35 cups per day by the same population. The discrepancy in both cases is less than 10%, which may be compared with discrepancies of the order of 50% that were found for alcoholic beverages by Pernanen (304). The fact that the survey estimate exceeds the green bean estimate in the Canadian case, but falls short of it in the case of the United States, could mean that Canadian coffee is generally weaker than assumed, whereas American coffee is stronger, or that Canadians are unduly enthusiastic about reporting coffee consumption whereas Americans are more reticent, or that systematic errors were made in sampling, or indeed many other factors. Reticence in reporting consumption is a characteristic not only of alcohol drinkers (304), but also of excessive eaters. A recent survey of eating habits in Canada reported that fat people in all age groups eat less than thin people (281), which, of course, is most improbable. Presumably such anomalies will occur with the reporting of caffeine consumption, if caffeine consumption becomes something to worry about.

Table 3 is presented by way of comparing consumption of coffee in Canada and the United States with consumption in other countries during 1972, based on data given in the Pan-American Coffee Bureau's compen-

TABLE 3 PER CAPITA CONSUMPTION OF GREEN COFFEE BEAN IN CERTAIN COUNTRIES DURING 1972 (295)

	Green Bean Consumption (kg per Capita)	Ratio to Canadian Consumption
Sweden	13.5	3.29
Denmark	12.6	3.08
Finland	12.0	2.93
Norway	10.3	2.52
Netherlands	9.3	2.28
Belgium	7.3	1.78
U.S.A.	6.3	1.53
Switzerland	6.2	1.51
France	5.1	1.24
West Germany	4.9	1.20
Austria	4.1	1.01
Canada	4.1	1.00
Italy	3.4	0.82
New Zealand	2.5	0.61
Cyprus	2.4	0.58
Portugal	2.3	0.56
United Kingdom	2.2	0.54
Spain	2.2	0.53
Australia	1.9	0.46
Israel	1.8	0.43
Hong Kong	1.7	0.41
Jordan[a]	1.3	0.31
Czechoslovakia	1.1	0.27
Sudan[a]	0.7	0.17
Japan	0.5	0.11
Iraq	0.1	0.02

[a] Based on 1971 gross consumption and population estimates, rather than those for 1972.

dium of statistics (295).* The per capita figures are based on total national populations. No attempt is made in the table to convert green bean

* According to a recent article by Penny Lernoux in the U.S. magazine *The Nation* (August 2, 1975), coffee is the world's second most valuable commodity, after oil, and perhaps the most important in terms of employment. The article provides fascinating insights into the politics of what may be considered by some people to be just one aspect of the world market in psychotropic drugs. The point of the article, however, is that United States and Canadian success in preventing reasonable increases in the price of coffee is keeping millions of Latin Americans and West Africans in penury: ". . . because [coffee] buys so little, it is a bitter brew, the taste of poverty and human suffering."

consumption into cups per day because the split between instant and regular coffee is not known in most cases. However, dividing kilograms of green bean consumed per year by 2.5 probably gives a rough approximation to cups drunk per day; thus, Swedes over nine years old are estimated to have drunk an average of 5.4 cups each per day during 1972. It was noted earlier that physical dependence on caffeine among Californian women was associated with the drinking of five or more cups a day (155). On this basis, it might be supposed that the average Swedish adult is dependent on caffeine. It is possible that French adults used to be in the same state. In a 1952 paper from the University of Paris (313), it was asserted (without citing a source, however) that most people drank 10–15 cups of coffee a day, and, moreover, that each cup typically contained 180 mg caffeine, an amount in excess of anything we have found in a cup of coffee (see Table 10 below).

Frequency Distribution of Coffee Consumption

If the abuse prevalence of caffeine is to be estimated, it is necessary to have some idea of the incidence of excessive use of caffeine-containing beverages. Only two surveys known to me have yielded data that allow inferences about the frequency distribution of coffee drinking in an entire population. The first involved a representative sample of 1894 Ontario residents aged 15 years and over, interviewed on behalf of the Addiction Research Foundation about their drinking habits of all kinds during the spring of 1969. The survey is described in more detail by de Lint, Schmidt, and Pernanen (89), and some of its alcohol consumption data were reported in Volume 1 of this series (304). Jupiter and I have recently analyzed these data for caffeine-beverage consumption (148). Some of the analysis is presented in Table 4 (score sheets from 11 of the subjects could not be used). Also presented in this table are data from a "Psychotropic Drug Study," funded by the U.S. National Institute of Mental Health, as reported by Brecher and his associates (44). Here, a representative sample of the population aged 18 years and over was interviewed during fall 1970 or spring 1972. It can be seen that, in both cases, approximately one-fifth of the sample reported drinking five or more cups per day. The Ontario distribution may seem closer to the distribution in the United States than might have been expected from data given in the previous section. This reflects the fact that mean consumption by Ontario residents over 14 years is closer to the United States mean than to the Canadian mean (see Table 5 below). In Canada, as in the United States, more coffee is drunk as you go from east to west (and more tea as you go from west to east). The South reports the least coffee drinking in the United States (295). It is not known whether the

TABLE 4 FREQUENCY DISTRIBUTIONS OF COFFEE CONSUMPTION IN ONTARIO, CANADA (148), AND IN THE U.S.A. (44)

	Ontario Survey (N = 1883) Percent Who, on Previous Day, Drank		U.S. Survey (N = 2552) Percentage Drinking	
Cups/Day	This Amount	More Than This Amount	This Amount	More Than This Amount
0	24.1	75.8	18	82
<1			6	75
1	17.2	58.7	30	45
2	17.2	41.5		
3	12.4	29.1	24	21
4	10.1	19.0		
5	6.5	12.5	12	9
6	4.7	7.8		
7	3.3	4.5	9	—
8	1.6	2.9		
9	0.9	2.0		
10–14	1.8	0.2		
>14	0.2	—		

Note: Ontario respondents were asked about their previous day's beverage consumption, whereas members of the U.S. sample seem to have been asked about their usual beverage consumption. Thus it is not so easy to identify abstainers in the Ontario survey data.

North would report the most in Canada; its residents have not yet been surveyed.

The consistency between the distributions revealed by the two surveys is remarkable, especially in view of differences between methods of ascertaining consumption. Other surveys have generally produced discrepant data, probably because of large differences in sample selection. Furthermore, usually only a few points on the distribution scale have been sampled. Thus, of 180 Czech medical students, as many as 29% reported drinking no coffee (395). On the other hand, only 9% of 10,774 U.S. male veterans reported abstention from coffee, whereas 24% said that they drank six or more cups per day (192). More than 50% of a group of 72 United States male military personnel reported drinking five or more cups of coffee per day (401). In California, 111,000 health checkup examinees were asked about their coffee consumption—19.5% of females and 21.4% of males reported drinking seven or more cups per day; the proportions were highest among 40–49 year-olds, 24.9 and 25.6%, respectively (220).

Other Coffee Drinking Features

> Coffee, in the Middle East, is one of the first necessities of life. One of the commitments which a Turk takes on, it is said (or, at any rate, used to take on in the past), towards the woman he marries, is the promise that she shall never go short of coffee.
>
> Prosper Montagné, *Larousse Gastronomique*, 1938.

Three of the studies mentioned above have provided data on average consumption according to age, sex, and time of day. These data are compared in Table 5. There are two obvious similarities and two obvious dif-

TABLE 5 COFFEE CONSUMPTION IN CUPS PER DAY ACCORDING TO THREE SURVEYS ARRANGED BY VARIOUS CHARACTERISTICS

		Pan-American Coffee Bureau		Ontario Drinking Survey
		U.S.A. 1972 (295)	Canada 1970 (294)	1969 (148)
Age	10–14	0.12	0.26	—
	15–19	0.55	0.98	0.92
	20–24	1.48	2.33 (20–29)	1.99
	25–29	2.47		2.83
	30–34	3.51 (30–39)	2.92 (30–39)	3.07
	35–39			3.23
	40–44	3.72 (40–49)	2.60 (40–49)	3.34
	45–49			3.10
	50–54	3.35 (50–59)	2.45 (50–69)	3.21
	55–59			2.78
	60–64	2.85 (60–69)		2.44
	65–69			2.21
	70–74	2.49 (70 up)	1.62 (70 up)	1.80
	75 up			1.61
Sex	Female	2.23	1.85	2.49
	Male	2.48	2.14	2.71
Time	Breakfast	1.00	0.69	0.78
	Other meals	0.59	0.48	0.58
	Between meals	0.76	0.82	1.23
Overall mean (whole sample)		2.35	1.99	2.59
Overall mean (>14 years only)		2.57	2.16	2.59

ferences between the Canadian samples and the sample taken in the United States. In both countries, men drink more coffee than women, with most coffee being drunk at about age 40. Both Canadian samples, however, indicate more coffee drinking among younger age groups and less among older groups when compared with the United States sample. Also, the United States sample differs from the Canadian samples in that a considerably higher proportion of the daily consumption in the United States occurs at breakfast and a considerably lower proportion between meals.

The greater coffee consumption by men in the United States may not occur in all age groups and in all regions. Analysis of data gained from 1992 men and 2500 women aged 35–69 years who were participants in the continuing study of the population of Framingham, Mass., revealed that mean usual consumption reported by the women was 3.00 cups per day, whereas the men reported a mean of 2.84 cups per day (87). Moreover, consumption by women exceeded consumption by men in all age groups, except 60–64 years, the biggest difference occurring at age 35–39 years (3.38 vs. 2.96 cups per day). Also, more women than men reported drinking seven or more cups per day in all age groups except 60–69 years, the biggest difference occurring at age 45–49 years (10.3% vs. 8.1%). On the other hand, slightly more women than men reported abstaining from coffee in all age groups except 45–54 years; the overall abstention rate was about 9%.

The Coffee Bureau surveys also provide data on trends in consumption levels. In both cases, gross per capita consumption fell during the five years before the respective surveys, whether measured as green bean disappearance or as total cups drunk per day, although consumption of instant coffee rose during the same period in both countries.* The decline in total consumption occurred in all age groups, except perhaps the very oldest, and thus the trends do not reflect merely the increase in the proportion of teenagers that occurred in both populations during the late 1960s.

Tea Consumption

I did send for a cup of tee† (a China drink) of which I had never drunk before.

Samuel Pepys. *Diary*, September 25, 1660.

* Although coffee consumption seems to be declining, caffeine consumption could be increasing. Sivetz (354a) reports that an increasing proportion of the cheaper Robusta bean is being used in blends of ground coffee. Instant coffee is now sometines 100% Robusta. The Robusta bean contains about twice as much caffeine as the more commonly used Arabica variety (2.2% vs 1.1%). Robusta comes chiefly from Africa, mainly Angola, and Indonesia. Arabica comes mainly from Brazil, whose crops have been increasingly erratic.

† This is almost the first word in English. It derives from the Chinese word *t'cha*, of which the first written record dates from A.D. 350. A phonetically closer derivative persists in the British colloquial "char," which arrived later via Malay, Hindu, and the colonization of the Indian subcontinent.

Tea drinking is not a conspicuous feature of the North American scene, particularly the United States scene, and there is understandably less enthusiasm about collecting data concerning tea consumption. Moreover, as will be indicated later, although the caffeine content ranges of prepared tea and coffee overlap, it is likely that the typical cup of tea, as drunk in Ontario, at least, contains not much more than one-third of the caffeine present in the typical cup of coffee, as drunk. Thus, from the point of view of this article, tea consumption may be of less significance than coffee consumption. Nevertheless, it should be remembered that tea consumption in certain countries is considerable, and caffeine ingested via tea can, in some individuals, even in North America, provide a high level of caffeine intake by any standards. Table 6 allows international comparisons. For those countries for which both kinds of information are available (see Table 3), there is a rank correlation of -0.42 ($p < 0.05$), indicating that coffee

TABLE 6 ANNUAL PER CAPITA APPARENT CONSUMPTION OF TEA LEAF IN SELECTED COUNTRIES DURING THE PERIOD 1970–1972 (197)

	Tea leaf consumption (kg per Capita)	Ratio to Canadian Consumption
Ireland	4.0	4.28
United Kingdom	3.8	4.03
New Zealand	2.7	2.83
Iraq	2.1	2.23
Australia	2.1	2.12
Hong Kong	1.6	1.69
Ceylon	1.5	1.61
Jordan	1.1	1.18
Sudan	1.1	1.14
Japan	1.0	1.09
Canada	0.9	1.00
Netherlands	0.6	0.67
Denmark	0.4	0.39
U.S.A.	0.3	0.36
Sweden	0.2	0.26
Switzerland	0.2	0.26
West Germany	0.2	0.16
Czechoslovakia	0.1	0.11
France	0.1	0.07
Italy	0.1	0.05

TABLE 7 FREQUENCY DISTRIBUTION OF TEA CONSUMPTION IN ONTARIO, CANADA (148), AND THE UNITED STATES (44)

	Ontario survey (N = 1883) Percent Who, on Previous Day, Drank		U.S. Survey (N = 2552) Percent Usually Drinking	
Cups/Day	This Amount	More Than This Amount	This Amount	More Than This Amount
0	42.4 (0 and <1)	57.6	48	52
<1			22	30
1	14.7	43.0	21 (1–2)	9
2	13.2	29.8		
3	8.6	21.2	6 (3–4)	3
4	7.6	13.6		
5	4.4	9.2	2 (5–6)	1
6	3.8	5.4		
7	1.6	3.8	1 (7 to >14)	—
8	1.1	2.7		
9	0.8	1.9		
10–14	1.5	0.4		
>14	0.4	—		

Note: See Note to Table 4.

consumption is likely to be low in a country in which much tea is consumed, and vice versa. Loose black tea typically contains about 2.7% caffeine. Because green coffee beans contain only about 1.1% caffeine, the Swedish coffee consumption of 13.5 kg per capita represents about 1.4 times as much caffeine per head as the Irish tea consumption of 4.0 kg per capita. Because coffee as prepared may contain considerably more caffeine than does tea as prepared (see Table 10), it is possible that the Irish drink at least as many cups of tea a day as the Swedes drink cups of coffee.* Unfortunately, I have not been able to discover how many cups of each beverage are drunk by the Irish and the Swedes.

* A necrology of Eamon de Valera (1883–1975), erstwhile Premier and President of the Republic of Ireland, noted that in the late 1930s he had started an obviously unsuccessful movement to ban the use of tea, on the grounds that it was a foreign influence preventing the full flowering of Irish aspiration. Indigenous milk and beer were promoted, although de Valera himself was a teetotaler. (The word "teetotal" has nothing to do with tea—it is merely a reduplicated variant of "total," coined during an English temperance rally in 1833.)

Frequency Distribution of Tea Consumption

If the coffee is poorer, the tea is better.

From an article in *Harper's* magazine, July 1932, entitled "The unbridled frontier: Canada and the United States."

As in the case of coffee, frequency distribution data for tea are available only for the United States (44) and for Ontario (148). These are presented in Table 7. It can be seen that, unlike in the coffee data, there is a considerable difference between the two distributions. Moreover, if you eliminate those drinking less than one cup of the respective beverage from each analysis, the coffee and tea distributions for the Ontario sample become remarkably similar (e.g., 25.2% of coffee drinkers drink more than four cups per day and 23.6% of tea drinkers drink more than four cups per day), whereas the U.S. distributions remain quite different (28% vs. 10% in the equivalent comparison). Thus, fewer cups of tea than coffee are drunk in Ontario because fewer people drink tea, but in the United States it appears that (even) fewer cups of tea are drunk, both because fewer people drink tea and because those that drink tea drink less of it. It is interesting to speculate as to the cause of this curious difference (Boston Tea Party, climate?), but its nature must remain obscure for the moment because information about other features of tea drinking in the United States is not available.*

* It is also interesting to speculate as to why tea is the caffeine-containing beverage of preference in Britain and in many of the countries that once composed the British Empire. Burnett has provided some useful clues, and much of what follows is derived from his two books (54, 55). Coffee appeared to be more popular than tea in England during the seventeenth century, but both were "so rare as to be beyond the wildest hopes of most." In 1685 coffee powder cost 3 shillings a pound, i.e., 5 or 6 times the price per pound of butter, whereas tea cost 10 to 20 times as much as coffee. By the mid-eighteenth century tea was beginning to compete with coffee, even though it remained more expensive. Inexplicably, its use pervaded all classes, unlike coffee, which remained a middle- and upper-class beverage, and it was at this time that tea-drinking began to take the blame for what many regard as the characteristic idleness of English working people. (Perhaps similar class-consciousness regarding tea had occurred in China. In 1570 T'ien Yihing had written "One drinks tea to forget the world's noise: it is not for those who eat rich food and dress in silk pyjamas.") Tea imports into Britain rose tenfold between 1740 and 1788. A careful survey of family income in 1797 revealed that laborers in southern England were spending one-twentieth of their annual family income on tea, the 40 shillings thus spent buying about 5 lb of the leaf. (The same amount would buy four times as much butter.) At the beginning of the nineteenth century, per capita consumption of tea leaf was about 20 times that of coffee bean, even though tea remained more expensive. Part of the high cost of tea was an extraordinary import duty, rising above 300% of the wholesale price during the early nineteenth century at a time when the rate of duty on coffee was in the order of 20%. Probably as a consequence of the differential taxation, coffee consumption had caught up with tea consumption by 1840, when average adult use of both was close to 2 lb per year. In the 1840s, advances in journalism and analytical chemistry led to full revelation of an

Other Tea Drinking Features

> The slavery of the tea and coffee and other slop-kettle. . . . Experience has taught me that these slops are injurious to health.
>
> William Cobbett. *Advice to young men*, 1829.

Data on average tea consumption according to age, sex, and time of day are available from the Ontario Drinking Survey only (148). Data on tea consumption according to age and time of day are presented in Figs. 2 and 3, respectively, together with this sample's coffee consumption, already given in Table 5.

In Fig. 2, an attempt has been made to indicate caffeine consumption. This was estimated for each member of the sample by summing the number of cups of coffee drunk and half the number of cups of tea, one cup of coffee or two cups of tea constituting a "caffeine unit" for this purpose. (Data will be presented below suggesting that the caffeine equivalent of one cup of coffee for this sample is probably closer to three cups of tea than to two, but this difference would not affect the presentation in Fig. 1 and in subsequent figures to a substantial degree.) It is clear from Fig. 1 that tea and coffee drinking are distributed quite differently according to age, and that the increase in tea consumption with age does not compensate for the fall in caffeine ingestion that is the result of declining coffee consumption.

It is interesting to speculate as to whether the apparent substitution of tea for coffee with age represents a real change in preference or a progressive change in Ontarians' use of these two beverages. If coffee had been replacing tea as the beverage of choice in recent years, it is quite possible that this change would be reflected among younger age groups only, with older people continuing to consume tea as the beverage of choice. Unfortunately for this hypothesis, it appears that tea consumption per capita over the

---

ancient practice that may have contributed to the relative demise of coffee in the previous century, namely the well-developed art of adulteration. Coffee sold as powder was easy to mimic. It invariably contained large proportions of alien substances including chicory, roasted corn, vegetable roots, dyes such as red ochre, and even, in one instance, baked horse liver. Although there was a thriving industry concerned with the production of "British tea"—namely, dried used leaves wetted with gum, redried and mixed with black lead, red ochre or other appropriate dyes—it remained relatively easy for the purchaser to identify the real thing. In the latter part of the nineteenth century, the duty on tea was progressively reduced (although it was still higher than that on coffee in 1890), and the tea-growing plantations in the Indian subcontinent became viable (although in 1870 more than 90% of Britain's tea still came from China). By the end of the century British adults were each using on the average more than 7 lb (3.2 kg) of the leaf per year, close to the present rate (Table 6). Annual per capita coffee consumption reached a peak of 4 lb. (1.8 kg) in 1880, a level that was not regained until about 1960. Since 1900 the costs of tea leaf, coffee bean, and butter in Britain have tended to be nearly equal.

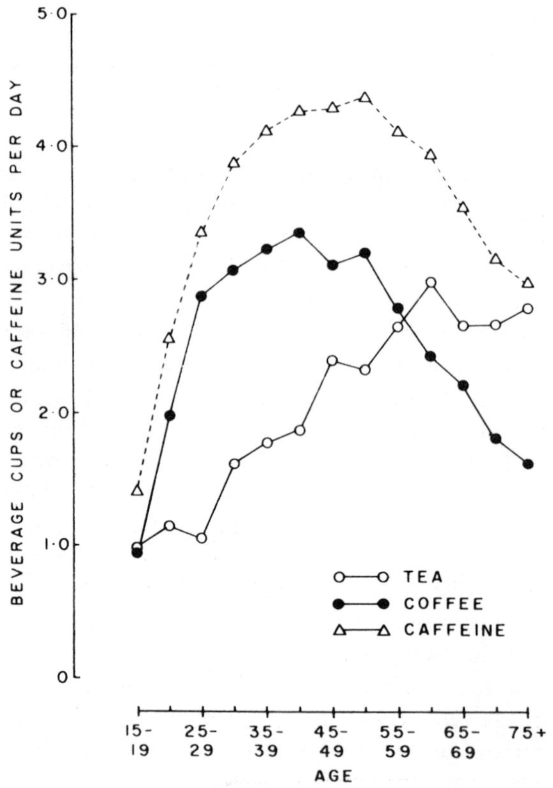

Fig. 2. Mean tea and mean coffee consumption reported for the day preceding the interview by 1883 Ontario adults, arranged according to 13 age groups (148). The estimation of caffeine consumption is explained in the text.

whole population has remained fairly constant, whereas coffee consumption has declined slightly. More tea is drunk by women than by men in Ontario, an average of 2.1 as opposed to 1.6 cups per day, according to our 1969 survey. Because the sex ratio changes in favor of women with advancing years, it is possible that the shift in apparent preference could reflect the change in sex ratio. However, as the female/male ratio in Ontario was 0.98 for the 25–44 age group and 1.20 for the 65–74 age group in 1969 (58), the 22.5% increase in sex ratio is unlikely to provide a sufficient explanation of the more than 50% decline in the ratio of coffee to tea consumption between these two age groups. Thus, for the moment it seems that the difference between age groups shown in Fig. 2 probably reflects a genuine change in beverage-drinking habits with advancing years. Aspects of a further possible basis for the difference—that coffee drinkers die at an earlier age than tea drinkers—are discussed in Section 11.

Figure 3 shows patterns of tea consumption by the Ontario sample according to time of day. Comparable coffee data are also presented (Table 5). Here the sample was split according to degree of consumption of each

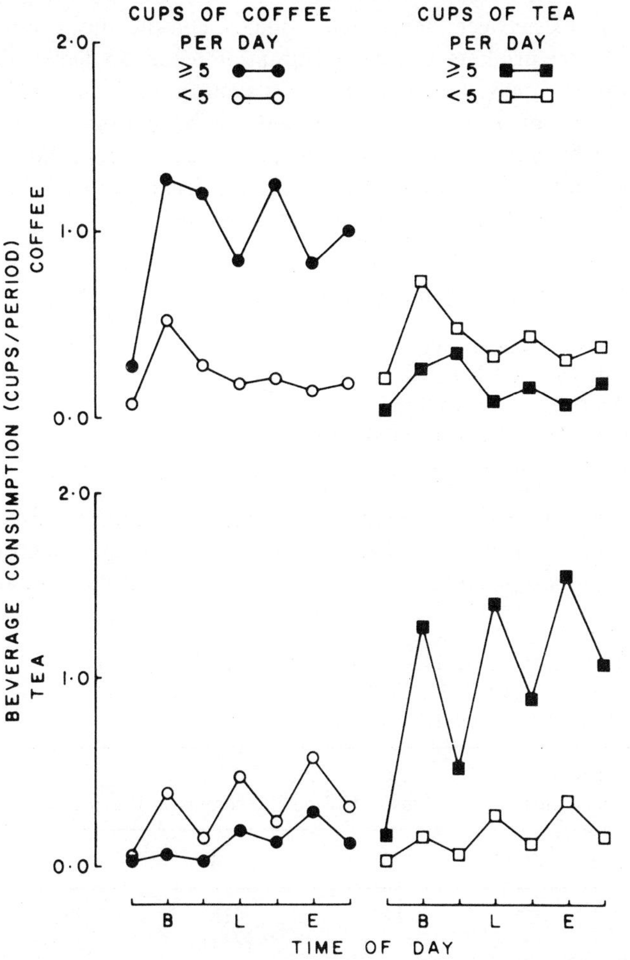

Fig. 3. Each panel represents mean consumption of tea or coffee reported for seven portions of the day preceding the interview by 1883 Ontario adults (148). The portions of the day are: before breakfast, at breakfast (B), between breakfast and lunch, at lunch (L), between lunch and the evening meal, at the evening meal (E), and after the evening meal. Within each panel data are arranged in terms of high consumers of the beverage given above the panel (filled points) and low consumers of that beverage (open points).

beverage; in the left-hand panels according to whether drinking more than four cups of coffee per day (N = 360) or less than five cups per day (N = 1523) was reported, and in the right-hand panels according to whether drinking more than four cups of tea per day (N = 252), or less than five cups per day (N = 1631) was reported. The upper two panels show that most coffee was drunk at breakfast, except by the high tea drinkers who drank most between breakfast and lunch. Also, except for breakfast, more coffee was drunk between meals than at meals, conspicuously so in the case of the high coffee drinkers. Coffee consumption tended to decline during the day. The lower panels show that most tea consumption occurred at meals and that more of this beverage tended to be consumed as the day progressed. It is notable that high drinkers of each beverage did not exhibit a different diurnal distribution of consumption from those that drank less; the high drinkers just drank more on each occasion.

Relation between Tea and Coffee Consumption

Molly, my sister and I fell out,
And what do you think it was all about,
She loved coffee and I loved tea,
And that was the reason we couldn't agree.

The Real Mother Goose, 1916.

It was shown earlier that a significant negative correlation exists between gross per capita consumption of tea and coffee by different countries. Table 8 shows that on an individual basis, the relationship between tea and coffee

TABLE 8 CONTINGENCY TABLE RELATING COFFEE AND TEA CONSUMPTION BY 1883 ONTARIO ADULTS (148)

Cups of Tea Consumed on Previous Day	Cups of Coffee Consumed on Previous Day		
	0	1–4	4
0	144	418	237
	(*192*)	(*454*)	(*153*)
1–4	182	540	110
	(*200*)	(*473*)	(*159*)
>4	127	112	13
	(*61*)	(*143*)	(*48*)

Note: Expected frequencies based on overall distributions are italicized in brackets below actual frequencies.

consumption is of a similar nature. The observed distribution of frequencies is significantly different from the distribution that would be expected if tea and coffee consumption were unrelated ($\chi^2 = 190.83$; $p < 0.01$), and the largest proportionate discrepancies between observed and expected frequencies occur in the four corner cells of the contingency table in a manner consistent with a negative correlation between consumption of the two beverages. It can be noted too that 41.2% of the sample reported drinking both beverages on the previous day, 34.8% drank only coffee, 16.4% drank only tea, and 7.6% reported drinking neither beverage on that day. True abstainers from coffee and tea would almost certainly comprise less than 7.6% of the population represented by this sample (see note to Table 4 above). In the survey conducted in the United States by the National Institute for Mental Health, it was found that 9% abstained from both beverages (44). It was also reported that 33% drank five or more cups of coffee or tea or both per day, and 25% drank six or more cups. Corresponding proportions for the Ontario Drinking Survey sample are: 44.4% drank five or more cups per day, and 32.0% drank six or more cups. It was noted in Section 7 that Goldstein and his associates found physical dependence on caffeine associated with the consumption of five or more cups of coffee a day. Again using the assumption that a typical cup of coffee has twice as much caffeine as a typical cup of tea, we estimated the proportion of Ontario adults drinking the caffeine equivalent of five or more cups of coffee. This was found to be 26.6%. Thus, it might be supposed that more than a quarter of Ontario's adult population is physically dependent on caffeine.

The only other available data on combined coffee and tea consumption come from a survey of 100 men and 119 women, who were patients in the general wards of the Alfred Hospital in Melbourne, Australia, a country whose tea consumption is considerably higher than Canada's (Table 6), and whose coffee consumption is considerably lower (Table 3). Drinking six or more cups of coffee and/or tea a day were 33% of men aged 15–49 years, 44% of women in this age group, 19% of men aged 50–80 years, and 32% of women in the same range (205). Given the preponderance of tea drunk in Australia, these data seem to be consistent with the Ontario finding that women drink more tea than men, but not with the observation that tea drinking in Ontario increases with age.

Coffee and Tea Consumption and Cigarette Smoking

It has often been reported that there is a high correlation between consumption of coffee and consumption of cigarettes. For example, in the study of over 10,000 male veterans in the United States referred to earlier (192), six or more cups of coffee per day were drunk by 42.9% of those smoking more than 30 cigarettes per day, with only 3.8% of heavy smokers drinking no coffee, but six or more cups of coffee per day were drunk by only 9.7% of nonsmokers, whereas 20.5% of this group drank no coffee. Other examples of a reported strong association between coffee drinking and cigarette smoking have come from the Framingham study (87), from the Kaiser–Permanente study (127), and from the Boston Collaborative Drug Surveillance Program (41). None of these reports provides data on the relationship between tea drinking and cigarette smoking. Two reports describe a significant positive correlation between coffee and tea drinking, on the one hand, and cigarette smoking on the other (82, 205), but, in both cases, coffee drinking could have been the sole contributor to the association. For example, in one of these studies (205), conducted in Australia, the correlation was significant only for 15–49-year-olds, who might have been expected to drink more coffee than 50–80-year-olds, for whom the correlation was not significant.

Figure 4 provides data from the Ontario Drinking Survey (148) that indi-

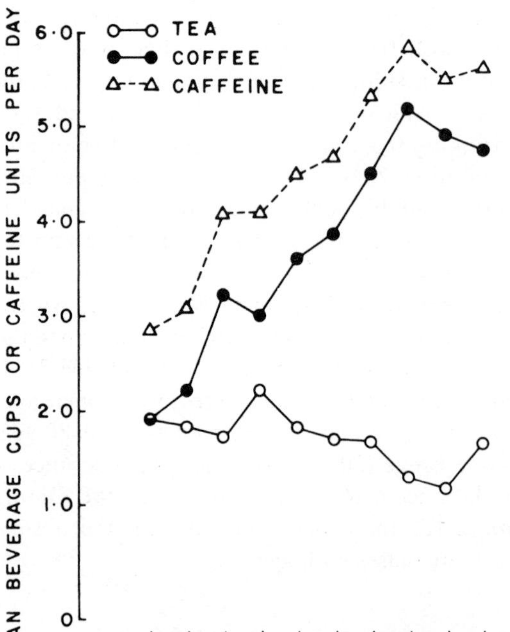

Fig. 4. Mean tea and mean coffee consumption reported for the day preceding the interview by 1883 Ontario adults, arranged according to 10 categories of reported usual cigarette consumption (148). The estimation of caffeine consumption is explained in the text.

cate a strong positive association between cigarette smoking and coffee drinking, but not tea drinking. In fact, a slight negative correlation between cigarette smoking and tea drinking is apparent. The difference is remarkable, in view of the apparent pharmacologic and functional similarity between tea and coffee. In looking for explanations of the difference, it may be useful to note the following: (*a*) Many more North Americans drink coffee than smoke cigarettes, especially female North Americans. In the various studies in the United States mentioned earlier in the previous paragraph, nonsmokers were found to comprise approximately 30% of males and 50% of females. (Because of sample selection factors, these are almost certainly low estimates—see, for example, the study by Wynder and associates [412], who reported 51% nonsmokers among 2910 adult United States males and 64% among 3248 adult United States females.) In Canada, in 1972, according to the Non-Medical Use of Drugs Directorate (92), 42.6% of males and 64.3% of females were nonsmokers, with Quebec alone having significantly lower proportions. Of the sample investigated in the Ontario Drinking Survey, 58.2% reported being nonsmokers (148). Abstainers from coffee likely comprise less than 25% of North Americans (see Table 4). Thus, the relationship between coffee drinking and cigarette smoking is far from perfect, as was also illustrated in the above analysis of the NRC veteran study (192). (*b*) The age distribution for cigarette smoking resembles that for coffee rather than that for tea. There were fewer Canadian nonsmokers aged 20–44 years in 1972, than below or above this range (92). (*c*) It is possible that the nicotine in tobacco contributes little to the relationship between cigarette smoking and coffee consumption, because nicotine in cigarettes may be metabolized too quickly to have a substantial physiologic effect (391),* and because nicotine's role in cigarette smoking is questionable for other reasons (146). (*d*) Except for breakfast, coffee drinking occurs mainly between meals, whereas tea drinking occurs mainly at meals, a difference that is exaggerated for heavy consumers of each beverage (see Fig. 3). It is possible that smoking and caffeine-beverage use are determined by similar environmental features, but for tea drinking, these features occur at meals rather than between meals (146).†

Because of the association between coffee drinking and cigarette smoking, it is possible that pathologies whose incidence appears to increase with coffee consumption may be determined more by smoking, especially if inci-

* But see Chapter 1 of this volume by M. A. H. Russell, who argues convincingly for dependence not simply on nicotine but on the "inhalation-bolus form of intake" that causes brief, extremely high brain levels of the drug.

† Two North American readers of an earlier draft suggested that cigarettes "taste right" with coffee but not with tea. I suspect that the taste is acquired, and that British and Irish smokers, for example, might feel differently.

dence does not also change with the consumption level of tea. This point will be considered in Section 11, when caffeine-related pathologies are discussed. The converse is also true, of course. Conditions attributed to smoking may be caused by caffeine-beverage consumption. For example, Ball and Turner (22) have claimed that, in Britain each year, about 26,000 people die of coronary heart-disease caused by smoking, without even considering the possible involvement of coffee drinking, which has also been implicated in heart disease (see Section 11). Recently, it has been proposed, with justification, that smoking may be beneficial in the prevention of cardiovascular disease (166). No such claim has ever been made for coffee drinking, although slight evidence for mutual protection between coffee drinking and smoking will be discussed in Section 11. Alcohol drinking may exert a similar protective effect (221).

Caffeine-Beverage and Alcoholic-Beverage Consumption

> This coffee-drink hath caused a great sobriety among all nations.
>
> James Howell. *Instructions for foreinne travell,* 1659.

Although coffee drinking and smoking are highly correlated, and also smoking and alcohol drinking (127, 166, 247, 383), attempts to demonstrate a relationship between coffee drinking and alcohol drinking have not yielded one (82, 87). (In the last of these reports, it was asserted that former heavy drinkers tend to drink a lot of tea and coffee, although no relevant data were presented. I have noticed myself that a lot of coffee drinking occurs at meetings of Alcoholics Anonymous.) Data from the Ontario Drinking Survey (148), presented in Fig. 5, possibly indicate why a relationship has not been found in the past. It appears from the left-hand panel of Fig. 5 that there is a positive correlation of coffee and alcohol consumption up to a consumption of about 40 ml alcohol per day, but that coffee consumption declines slightly with further increases in alcohol consumption. Tea consumption tended to decline with increasing alcohol consumption. The relation between estimated caffeine consumption and alcohol consumption is more obviously bitonic. The right-hand panel of Fig. 5 shows the reverse plot—that of alcohol consumption against caffeine-beverage or caffeine consumption. Here the bitonic nature of the relation between alcohol and coffee consumption remains. There is no support for a suggestion that alcohol consumption increases with coffee consumption. There is slight support, however, for the suggestion that alcohol consumption may increase with caffeine consumption.

A causal relationship between caffeine and alcohol consumption might be of the kind whereby high caffeine consumption earlier in the day produces

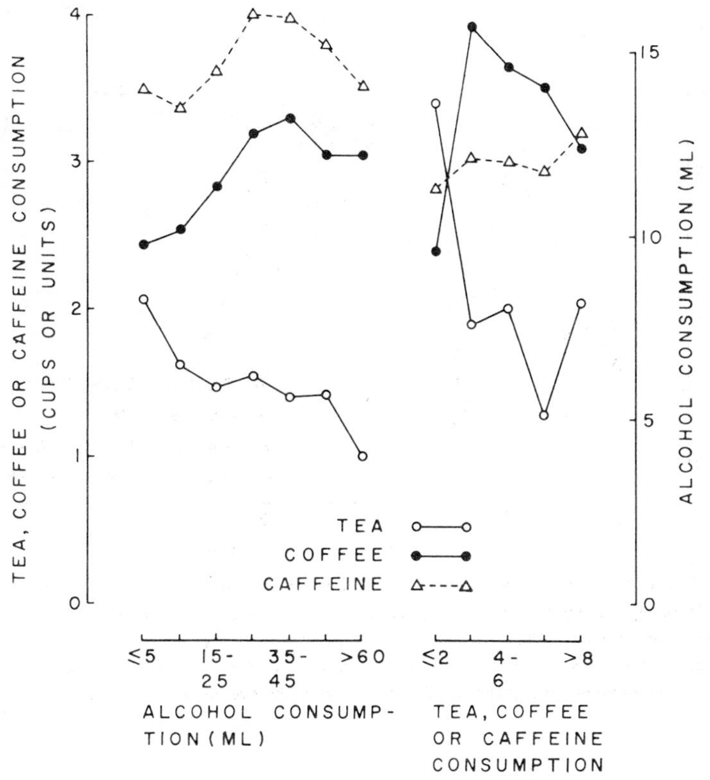

Fig. 5. The left-hand panel shows tea, coffee, and estimated caffeine consumption on one day reported by 1883 Ontario adults as a function of their reported alcohol consumption (in milliliters of pure alcohol) on the same day (148). Each point is based on data from more than 56 respondents. The right-hand panel is based on the same data; it shows alcohol consumption as a function of tea, coffee, and estimated caffeine consumption. Each point in the right-hand panel is based on data from more than 45 respondents. The estimation of caffeine consumption is explained in the text.

high alcohol consumption later in the day. More than 40% of all alcohol consumed by the Ontario Drinking Survey sample was drunk in the evening (148)—the proportion was even higher for heavy drinkers—and yet Fig. 3 indicates that considerable caffeine consumption was also occurring in the evening. Thus it is possible that the heavier drinkers of alcohol tended to consume their caffeine earlier in the day than moderate or lower drinkers of alcohol, who might nevertheless have been consuming similar amounts of caffeine. This possibility is explored in Fig. 6, where tea, coffee, and caffeine consumption by each of three groups of alcohol drinkers are shown for each of four periods of the day. There is only the slightest suggestion that

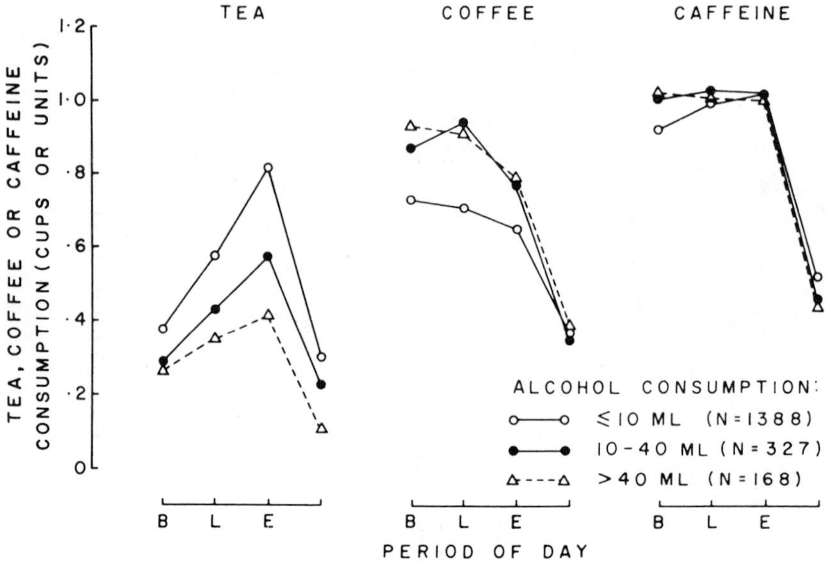

Fig. 6. Tea, coffee, and estimated caffeine consumption during four periods of one day by the Ontario Drinking Survey sample, segregated according to alcohol consumption (in milliliters of ethanol) on the same day (148). The estimation of caffeine consumption is explained in the text. The four periods of the day were: before breakfast and at breakfast (B), between breakfast and lunch and at lunch (L), between lunch and the evening meal and at the evening meal (E), and after the evening meal.

the heavier drinkers of alcohol drink their tea or coffee earlier in the day than the others. The slope of the line for heavy drinkers is more negative in each case, but the differences do not seem large enough to warrant further analysis.

The bitonic nature of the relation between coffee and alcohol consumption demonstrated in Fig. 5 may have prevented the appearance of a simple correlation in one of the two earlier studies (82). In the other study, mean alcohol consumption was given for various levels of coffee consumption, with no simple relationship being apparent (87). However, the unrepresentative nature of the sample (men aged 35–69) and the relatively high mean daily alcohol intake (≃23 ml/day), may have distorted the relationship.

The differences in relationships between alcohol drinking, on the one hand, and tea and coffee drinking, on the other, remain intriguing. A similar difference exists for cigarette smoking (see Fig. 3). It seems that common factors may cause cigarette smoking, alcohol drinking, and coffee drinking, but not tea drinking. The breakdown in the correlation between coffee drinking and alcohol drinking at a certain consumption level (see Fig. 5), may indicate merely that consumption of both becomes incompatible, because of the physical inability of the drinker to consume more than a certain amount of liquid.

Caffeine-Beverage Consumption and Total Liquid Intake

In searching for the reasons why some people drink a lot of coffee or tea (or indeed any other liquid), it may be useful to consider the possibility that the excessive coffee or tea drinking may be part of a disposition to engage in excessive behavior, a disposition that may be determined by particular environmental circumstances (147), or by other factors. Alcoholics, for example, have been shown to drink more than social drinkers of both alcoholic and other fluids during taste tests (250). Thiel and associates (381) reported that myocardial infarction patients drank more coffee than matched controls (36 as opposed to 28% drank more than eight cups per day) and more of all liquids (26 as opposed to 12% drank more than the equivalent of about 16 cups per day). Figure 7 shows the relation between

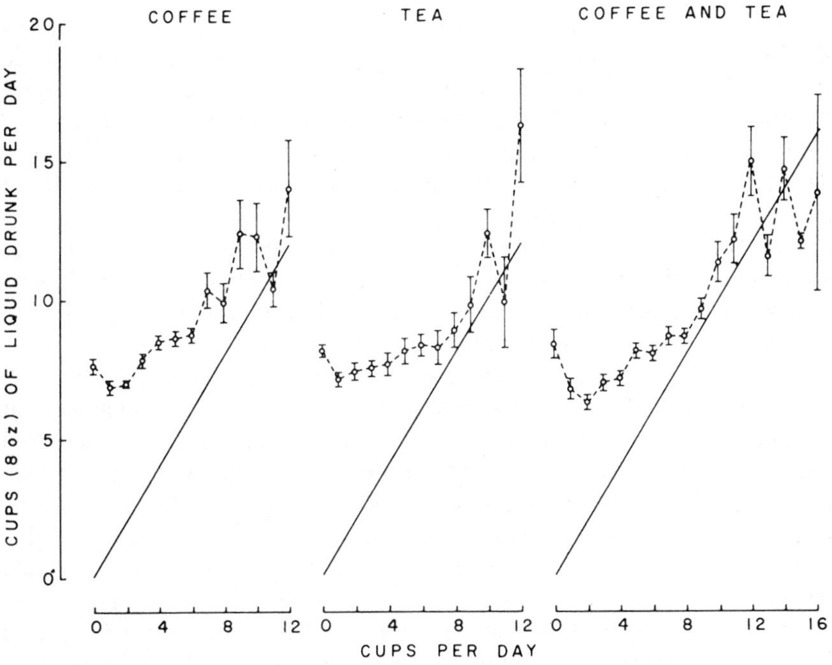

Fig. 7. Total liquid consumption reported by most respondents to the Ontario Drinking Survey as a function of their coffee, tea, and total coffee and tea consumption during the same day (148). Excluded are data from subjects drinking more than 12 cups of tea or coffee, and more than 16 cups of tea and coffee. Vertical lines from each mean represent standard errors. The solid sloping lines indicate what would be total consumption if coffee, or tea or coffee and tea, respectively, were the only fluids consumed.

coffee and tea consumption and mean total liquid consumption for most of the participants in the Ontario Drinking Survey (148). The figure indicates a tendency for total liquid consumption to rise with consumption of coffee and tea. However, the convergence of the lines.in each panel with increasing beverage consumption suggests that excessive coffee and tea drinkers in this sample were not also drinking excessive amounts of other fluids. In fact, people who drank more than approximately six cups of coffee and/or tea a day tended to drink little else. Thus the earlier indication (381) that excessive coffee drinking may be part of a pattern of excessive fluid consumption may be specific to myocardial infarction patients and, perhaps, their matched controls. Excessive beverage consumption among our survey respondents could, however, have been part of a generalized excessive behavior syndrome that included behaviors other than fluid consumption.

Cola Consumption

A few studies, including the Ontario Drinking Survey, have estimated soft drink consumption. Only one has distinguished between consumption of soft drinks that contain caffeine (i.e., colas) and consumption of those that do not. In this study (266), the respondents drank an average of less than a twentieth of a cup of cola per day. Their average age was in excess of 70 years, however, and their cola consumption cannot be regarded as typical. The total liquid volume of soft drinks consumed in the United States exceeds that of coffee and tea combined (360). The Ontario Drinking Survey (148) revealed a much lower soft drink consumption, but this may indicate only that most soft drinks are consumed by children under 15 years of age. Sales figures are not available that allow even a rough guess as to the proportion of soft drinks that are colas.

It appears that some individuals consume large amounts of cola. A magazine report of a study at Pennsylvania State University (71) noted that 57 drinkers of between 48 and 110 oz of cola a day had been uncovered among the student population. (As will be indicated below, this range may have a caffeine equivalent of approximately 2–5 cups of coffee or 6–14 cups of tea a day.) A matched sample averaged only 8 oz of cola per day. Some of the excessive drinkers reported "withdrawal-like" symptoms when cola drinking ceased; many claimed that it would be difficult to give up the habit; most complained of "behavioral difficulties." Unfortunately, I have not been able to trace the authors of this study, and thus to gain more information or even verification of the report.

Caffeine Content of Beverages

The real test of coffee is when it will float a four-bit piece.
Robert Gurd. *Johnny Chinook*, 1945.

The estimates of caffeine-beverage consumption given above have been based on cups or other volumetric measures, because this is the way in which the data were collected. When trying to relate these estimates to the distribution of caffeine consumption in a population, it is useful to have some idea of the amount of the beverage in a cup and of the caffeine concentration of the beverage. Unfortunately, no consumption survey has included procedures to provide this important information. Thus, one can only make intelligent guesses about caffeine consumption, guesses that take into account what is known about the caffeine content of caffeine-containing beverages.

Table 9 gives a sample of estimates of caffeine content that have appeared in the literature. Usually, these were given without source; although three of the reports in Table 9 describe laboratory determinations. Giving values for caffeine content seems to be a desirable feature of caffeine studies. Usually, these are based on somebody else's estimates; e.g., Truitt (388) uses the values from Wolman's laboratory (252, 410), and Greden (159) reports the values given by Truitt. An obvious feature of Table 9 is the range of reported values, for caffeine content per cup or serving, for cups or serving size, and for caffeine concentration. Clearly, reliance on the existing literature would be confusing for someone interested in discovering the range of caffeine consumption in the population. An additional problem is that even the laboratory estimates may not bear much relation to the doses that people give themselves in their homes, where, according to some surveys (294, 295), most coffee is drunk. Faced with these difficulties, we conducted a study of our own (149).

Randomly selected staff of the Addiction Research Foundation were invited to submit two samples of their usual home-prepared tea or coffee for analysis in our laboratory. One was to be from the first cup of beverage consumed on any day, the other was to be from any other cup. Samples were returned as drunk, complete with sugar, saccharin, milk, cream, lightener, and honey, as used,* together with a completed short questionnaire about methods of preparation, cup size, usual caffeine-beverage consumption, and personal data.

* In her extraordinary tome *The Book of Household Management* (1861), the 25-year-old Isabella Mary Beeton recommended "An excellent substitute for milk or cream in tea or coffee," the recipe for which called upon cooks to "allow one new-laid egg to every large breakfast-cupful", and to pour the beverage over the beaten egg very slowly so as not to distress it unduly (P. 880). Needless to say, we found not a trace of egg in our samples, new-laid or otherwise.

TABLE 9 SUMMARY OF LITERATURE ESTIMATES OF THE CAFFEINE CONTENT OF BEVERAGES

	Ground Coffee			Instant Coffee			Decaffeinated Coffee			Tea			Colas		
Reference No.	Stated mg/Cup	Stated Cup Size (ml)	Estimated Concen-tration (μg/ml)	Stated mg/Cup	Stated Cup Size (ml)	Estimated Concen-tration (μg/ml)	Stated mg/Cup	Stated Cup Size (ml)	Estimated Concen-tration (μg/ml)	Stated mg/Cup	Stated Cup Size (ml)	Estimated Concen-tration (μg/ml)	Stated mg/ Serving	Stated Serving Size (ml)	Estimated Concen-tration (μg/ml)
252[a]	88–119	250	352–476	55–62	250	220–248	13–35	250	52–140	43–110	250	172–440	—	—	—
410[a]	—	—	—	86–99	250	344–396	2–4	250	8–16	—	—	—	—	—	—
276	90–120	140	643–857	66–74	140	471–529	1–6	140	7–43	70	140	500	19	140	136
56[a]	100	155	645	30–75	155	194–483	2–6	155	13–39	—	—	—	25–37	280	89–132
5	100–150	225	444–667	—	—	—	—	—	—	30–50	225	133–222	—	—	40
260	96	140	686	—	—	—	—	—	—	19	140	136	—	—	—
313	170–190	—	—	—	—	—	—	—	—	—	—	—	—	—	—
319	90–125	140	643–893	60–80	140	429–571	30–75	140	214–536	30–70	140	214–500	30–45	335	90–134
388	100–150	—	—	-	—	—	—	—	—	100–150	—	—	35–55	335	104–164
Over-all Range Low	88	140	352	30	140	194	2	140	7	19	140	133	19	140	40
High	190	250	893	80	250	571	75	250	536	150	250	500	55	335	164

[a] Asterisked sources report laboratory determinations.

This table is taken from Gilbert *et al* (149) and is published with permission of the Canadian Medical Association.

Reports of the analysis for caffeine content are given in Table 10. Comparing Tables 9 and 10, it can be seen that for all types of beverage, the amount of caffeine found in a cup in our analysis of home-prepared coffee and tea tended to be lower and more variable than reported earlier. A better comparison is between caffeine concentrations, for concentration was determined exactly in our study, whereas cup size (and therefore caffeine content of a cup) was based on the questionnaire response. Caffeine concentrations were also generally lower in our study. At least four reasons can be given for our lower values: (*a*) Ontarians tend to make weaker beverages, both tea and coffee, than those prepared in the United States, where most other determinations occurred; (*b*) home-prepared beverages are generally lower in caffeine content than those prepared in laboratories, where manufacturers' instructions are usually followed; (*c*) the dilution of beverages by cream and other additives lowers caffeine concentration by a significant amount; and (*d*) our respondents, knowing that caffeine content would be determined, make weaker beverages than normal.*

If our determinations of caffeine content can be accepted as providing a better estimate of what people drink than has been available before, at least two conclusions may be drawn. The first is that the difference between the caffeine content of manufactured beverages (i.e., colas) and home-prepared beverages may be smaller than previously supposed. We did not analyze colas ourselves, but we solicited manufacturers' reports of the caffeine content of 10 varieties available in Toronto. The reported caffeine content per 10 imperial fl oz serving ranged from a low of 21.0 mg to a high of 45.4 mg, the most popular brands probably being Coca-Cola (38.0 mg) and Pepsi-Cola (31.0 mg) or Diet-Pepsi (28.0 mg). Both mean and median of the 10 values are close to 35 mg. In the absence of specific information about sales, it seems reasonable to take this value as the typical caffeine content of a cola serving, remembering that particular servings may contain considerably more or less, according to the brand. The typical amount per serving is therefore in excess of the median amount found by us in a cup of tea, and nearly half of the median amount found in a cup of coffee. As colas appear to be drunk mostly by children, who weigh much less than adults,

* Another report on the caffeine content of beverages as consumed at home has just appeared in abstract form (3). This study, conducted in Britain, revealed narrower ranges (58–125 mg/cup for coffee; 51–87 mg/cup for tea) and higher mean values for both coffee and tea (92 and 70 mg/cup, respectively, compared with our values of 88 and 32 mg/cup) when compared with our study. In both analyses coffee contained more caffeine than tea, though with much overlap between ranges. The main difference is that the British seem to make much stronger tea than Canadians. A paper by A. W. Burg in the Jan 1975 issue of the *Tea & Coffee Trade Journal* reviewed 46 recent commercial analyses of the caffeine content of beverages and concluded that the industry should adopt as standards 85 mg per 150-ml cup for ground coffee, 60 mg/cup for instant coffee, 30 mg/cup for instant tea, and, tentatively, 50 mg/cup for other tea.

TABLE 10 RESULTS OF ADDICTION RESEARCH FOUNDATION ANALYSIS OF HOME-PREPARED BEVERAGE SAMPLES

	Coffee					
	Ground		Instant		All Coffee (Except Decaffeinated)	Tea
	Percolated	Drip or Filter	Regular	Decaffeinated		
No. of samples (Σ = 86)	11	14	21	3	46	37
Caffeine per cup (mg)						
Lowest	39	56	29	1	29	8
Median	74	112	66	1	74	27
Highest	168	176	117	2	176	91
Cup size (ml)						
Lowest	140	170	170	225	140	115
Median	200	225	225	255	225	225
Highest	285	255	285	255	285	300
Caffeine concentration (μg/ml)						
Lowest	195	218	102	2	102	43
Median	436	621	328	5	360	144
Highest	1170	753	559	8	1170	400

This table is taken from Gilbert *et al* (149) and is published with permission of the Canadian Medical Association.

the effective dose of caffeine from colas may in many cases exceed that from coffee.

A small chocolate bar contains about 25 mg of caffeine. Thus, a 60-lb (27-kg) child ingesting four colas and three chocolate bars per day would be self-administering approximately 8.0 mg/kg caffeine. A 165-lb (75 kg) man would have to drink more than eight cups of coffee (at 74 mg caffeine per cup) in order to achieve the same daily dose. A similar argument could concern the caffeine content of proprietary and other medicines. Thus, the headache remedy Excedrin, which contains 62.5 mg caffeine per tablet, may also have more caffeine in relation to coffee and tea than had been previously supposed.

The second conclusion concerns the daily caffeine intake that is associated with physical dependence. As mentioned earlier in Section 7, Goldstein and associates found that dependence was associated with the use of five or more cups of coffee a day (155). Earlier, Goldstein had suggested that an average cup of coffee contains 130 mg (151). Thus, from these figures, it might be supposed that dependence was associated with the ingestion of 650 mg of caffeine per day, or more. Now it seems that dependence might occur with lower amounts, in the order of 370 mg per day. Of course, it is possible that the Californian housewives investigated by Goldstein, or heavy coffee drinkers generally, may prepare stronger-than-usual caffeine doses for themselves. Within our own study, heavy coffee drinkers did not appear to drink stronger coffee than other coffee drinkers. The mean caffeine content of the sampled cups drunk by those who in their questionnaire responses reported drinking 0, 1, 2, 3, 4, 5, and > 5 cups on the previous day was, respectively, 155, 68, 76, 90, 115, 78, and 76 mg ($F = 2.55$; $p > 0.05$). There is a slight and indirect suggestion from some American data that caffeine content and consumption may be inversely correlated, at least on a regional basis. More cups per pound of regular or instant coffee are brewed in the West, where consumption is highest, than in the East, where consumption is lower (222). These differences may not imply caffeine-content differences; coffee richer in caffeine may be used in the West. Moreover, they say nothing about a possible relationship between caffeine content and individual consumption levels.

Our data yielded some interesting differences and similarities between beverages and between methods of preparation of the same beverage. Both methods of preparing ground coffee yielded significantly higher caffeine concentrations than appeared in the instant coffees (Mann-Whitney $U = 54$; $p < 0.01$—for both comparisons). However, although the median caffeine concentration of percolated coffee was closer to that of instant coffee than to that of filtered/dripped coffee, the difference between the two methods of preparation from ground coffee was not significant ($U = 62$;

$p > 0.05$). The differences between the three methods are in the order that might be expected from what happens during the various preparation processes. The one pass of water over ground beans during filter or drip preparation dissolves about 20% of the bean, including nearly all of the caffeine. Repeated passing, as in percolation, can dissolve as much as 30% of the bean. The extra bean in solution adds to the bitterness of the coffee, but not to its caffeine content. Thus, less coffee bean per cup of water may be used in the percolation method in order to avoid making the brew too bitter. Hence, less caffeine appears in the coffee, even though it may taste as strong as filtered coffee. The variation in number of passes in the percolation method may also account for the wider range evidenced with that method than with the others (see Table 10). Instant coffee has been hydrolyzed, with the insoluble fraction removed. The result is to allow about 48% of the bean to appear in the beverage, but only the same amount of caffeine. Less of the bean is used in order to keep bitterness low. Thus, less caffeine appears in the coffee. Professional coffee tasters claim that dissolving 22% of the bean makes the best coffee—the proportion dissolved with filter or drip methods of preparation (56). These methods also tend to produce the strongest coffee in terms of caffeine, and it is not clear whether professional coffee tasters are interested in taste or in caffeine. The retail coffee cost per cup of instant coffee was close to 1.5¢ in Canada in 1972, and close to 2.0¢ per cup for ground coffee. The progressive shift in preference for instant coffee could have many reasons, including convenience, cost, taste (or the lack of it), and a reduction in caffeine intake.*

The difference between the caffeine concentrations of instant coffee and tea in our data (Table 10) is highly significant ($U = 68$; $p < 0.001$). The

* In his monumental *London Labour and the London Poor* (1851) Henry Mayhew relates a description of how an 1840s street coffee-stall keeper made his profit: "I usually buy 10 ounces of coffee a night. That costs, when good, 1*s*. 0½*d*. With this I should make five gallons of coffee, such as I sell in the street, which would require 3 quarts of milk, at 3*d*. per quart, and 1½ lb. of sugar, at 3½*d*. per lb., there is some at 3*d*. This would come to 2*s*. 2¾*d*.; and allowing 1¼*d*. for a quarter of a peck of charcoal to keep the coffee hot, it would give 2*s*. 4*d*. for the cost of five gallons of coffee. This I should sell out at about 1½*d*. per pint; so that the five gallons would produce me 5*s*., or 2*s*. 8*d*. clear." (Vol. I, P. 185). Even with no adulteration of the coffee powder (see p. 113), such coffee would have contained only about 30 mg caffeine per 9-oz cup. The caffeine concentration of coffee as drunk may have increased since the last century, although little is known about coffee as it was prepared at home. Mrs. Beeton (op. cit.) complained that "The greatest and most common fault in English coffee is the too small quantity of the ingredient" (P. 874). She endorsed Count Rumford's observation that a little less than a quarter ounce of the bean was required for a good after-dinner cup of coffee, i.e., about 75 mg caffeine per 140-ml cup. Her own "simple" recipe involves the use of more than twice as much coffee—equivalent to about 160 mg caffeine per 140-ml cup, a concentration close to the highest found in our study (Table 10). For café-au-lait, Mrs. Beeton proposed even higher caffeine concentrations, but it is not known to what extent her advice was heeded.

median value of caffeine concentration for all but decaffeinated coffees was 2.5 times that for tea; the comparable ratio for the median caffeine content of cups of the respective beverages was 2.74. Thus, it is reasonable to say that coffee, as prepared, has two to three times as much caffeine per cup as tea, as prepared, although the ranges are such that overlap occurs. The wide ranges in caffeine concentration, about 10:1 between highest and lowest for both coffee and tea, caution against the use of caffeine-consumption estimates based on cups of beverage consumed.

Consumption in Relation to Personality Type and Disorder

> In our common parlance we [the Japanese] speak of the man "with no tea" in him, when he is insusceptible to the serio-comic interests of the personal drama. Again we stigmatise the untamed aesthete who, regardless of the mundane tragedy, runs riot in the springtide of emancipated emotions, as one with "too much tea" in him.
>
> Okakura Kakuzo. *The Book of Tea*, 1931.

Major sources of variation in caffeine-beverage consumption discussed so far include age and nationality. Sex may be a less important source; moreover, sex differences may be age-specific. There are some indications that consumption may also vary with personality type and disorder, as determined by personality tests and/or clinical diagnosis. Only data with respect to coffee and tea consumption combined or coffee consumption alone are available, which is unfortunate because of the light such correlations with personality type and disorder might cast upon the differences between patterns of tea and coffee consumption, and upon the possible implication of one but not the other beverage in the various pathologic conditions to be discussed in Section 11.

Two studies indicate that psychiatric patients diagnosed as schizophrenic may have a lower beverage consumption than usual. Crowley and his associates (82) found that their schizophrenic patients drank an average of less than four cups of coffee and/or tea a day, whereas the average for all kinds of psychiatric admissions was closer to five cups a day (the difference was not significant, however). Furlong, in an unpublished study (134), reported that the median daily coffee consumption of a group of his schizophrenic patients was two cups per day, whereas the median for nonpatients was three cups. These two studies differ markedly with respect to two other kinds of patients. Crowley found that patients diagnosed as neurotic or personality disordered drank more and less than average amounts, respectively, whereas Furlong found the opposite. There is an interesting but indirect suggestion that patients diagnosed as schizophrenic may drink more tea than usual. It appears that an earlier controversy regarding the appearance of 3,4-dimethoxyphenylethylamine (the "pink spot") in the urine of schizophrenics has been resolved by observations that tea but not coffee ingestion is the source of this urinary amine (359). Thus, reports of its relative specificity to schizophrenia may have been merely unwitting reports that schizophrenics drink more tea than usual. Schizophrenics, like heavy tea drinkers, also appear to drink relatively less alcohol and consume relatively fewer cigarettes.

Only two studies, to my knowledge, have demonstrated a significant relationship between consumption of a caffeine beverage and measures of personality. In one of these, the Eysenck (Maudsley) Personality Inventory was used to identify 10 each of "neurotic extraverts," "stable extraverts," "neurotic introverts," and "stable introverts," all of whom were female smokers (24). They reported drinking means of 4.0, 6.5, 2.7, and 4.6 cups of coffee per day, respectively. The difference between extraverts (5.3 cups/day) and introverts (3.7 cups/day) seems to support Eysenck's assertion that extraverts seek stimulants, including caffeine (112). However, Eysenck argued too that neurotics should be no different from stables with respect to coffee drinking, whereas among these 40 subjects, the difference between the 20 neurotics (3.4 cups/day) and the 20 stables (5.7 cups/day) was greater than the difference between the 20 extraverts and the 20 introverts.

The other study, unfortunately, involved an even more unusual population, i.e., male veteran alcoholic inpatients, for whom no actual consumption figures were given (270). Coffee consumption, as observed in the hospital, was reported to be negatively correlated with scores on both the *Hy* (Hysteria) and the *Pd* (Psychopathic deviate) scales of the MMPI, and also with scores on the A and P subscales of the Guildford-Zimmerman Temperament Survey. Accordingly, the high coffee-consuming alcoholic was described as "conventional, submissive, moralistic, though critical and demanding," and the low coffee-drinking alcoholic was characterized as "rebellious, unreliable, socially bold though with shallow loyalties." Scores on the *Pd* scale of the MMPI are positively correlated with incidence of alcoholism (243), and thus possibly with alcohol consumption. It was demonstrated earlier (see Fig. 5), that, beyond a certain point, alcohol consumption and coffee consumption may be inversely correlated. Thus, the inverse correlation of *Pd* scores and coffee consumption is not inconsistent with the data in Fig. 5. The data may be in conflict, however, with the data described in the previous paragraph. Reported coffee drinking was found to increase with extraversion (24). Because extraversion scores and *Pd* scores are positively correlated (112), the inverse correlation between coffee drinking and *Pd* scores could be a puzzle.

The picture is further confused by some Australian work on personality correlates of sleep habits (204). Scores on both *Pd* and *Hy* scales were positively correlated with medical students' reports of poor sleep, especially the *Hy* scores. If coffee drinking were a significant cause of the poor sleep, one would expect that *Pd* and *Hy* scores would be *positively* correlated with coffee consumption, i.e., in opposite direction from that found with the alcoholic sample discussed above. One resolution of this possible discrepancy might be that the poor sleepers among the Australian medical students actually drank less than normal, in order not to worsen a bad situation. Another resolution might be that high *Pd* and/or *Hy* scores are associated with high liquid intake, which happened to consist of alcohol in the case of the alcoholics and coffee in the case of the medical students. Yet further confusion is provided by an examination of the differences between smoking and nonsmoking students (365), in which it was found that beer drinking and smoking, but not coffee drinking, were positively correlated to *Pd* scores on the MMPI to a significant degree. The puzzle here is the strong association between smoking and coffee drinking, which was reported in the same study and has also been discussed above.

Clearly, much work needs to be done in this area if the many assertions that caffeine beverage consumption varies with personality type (23, 178, 225) are to be given substance. Unfortunately, the difficulty with such investigations is that they tend to spawn masses of inconsistent and uninterpretable data, a situation that for alcohol drinking is neatly portrayed by Keller's Law. "The investigation of any trait in alcoholics will show that they have either more or less of it" (214).

11. PATHOLOGIC EFFECTS OF CAFFEINE

> The evil effects of tea and coffee have been grossly exaggerated.
> H. M. Sinclair and D. F. Hollingsworth. *Hutchinson's Food and Principles of Nutrition*, 1969.

A number of potentially pathologic effects of caffeine were noted earlier in the chapter, during the discussion of caffeine's pharmacology. These included effects upon germ and other cells, on fetuses, on metabolism, on gastrointestinal and cardiovascular systems, on liver function, and on behavior. They also included the effects of caffeine's withdrawal, and possible interactions with drugs that are used for recreational and therapeutic purposes. Additional pathologies can be gleaned from newspaper reports. The clippings file of the *Toronto Daily Star*, for example, cites caffeine as a cause of baldness and an irritant of eczema.* This section will focus upon caffeine-

* According to the *Medical World News*, Feb. 9, 1976, 30% caffeine ointment is effective treatment for atopic dermatitis. The clinical investigator claimed that caffeine's ability to raise cyclic AMP levels in skin was responsible.

related pathologies that have been suggested or denied by clinical and epidemiologic studies appearing in the recent medical and scientific literature.

Heart Disease

> The clinical literature on psychological and physiological reactions to caffeine is extensive and confusing. Perhaps more contradictions can be cited than in the literature on any other pharmacologically active agent.
>
> T. Colton, R. E. Gosselin, R. P. Smith. *Clinical Pharmacology and Therapeutics*, Vol. 9, 1968.

There has been concern about the possibility deleterious effect of high caffeine-beverage consumption on the heart since at least 1864, when Dr. Anstie reported his study of 48 excessive consumers of coffee and tea (9, p. 249). Little relevant work was done for a century, until in 1958, Landis (234) reported that there was no evidence that caffeine should be contraindicated even in heart disease, although he noted that it may be of "doubtful positive therapeutic value" in angina pectoris or coronary thrombosis.

The first recent indication that caffeine might cause heart disease came in a report by Paul and associates in 1963 (300). During a prospective study of 1162 employees of the Western Electric Company at the Hawthorne Works in Chicago, it was found that the 54 employees who developed angina, or myocardial infarction, or who died suddenly, drank an average of 4.2 cups of coffee a day, whereas the remainder drank only 3.5 cups a day ($p < 0.025$). Subsequently, Paul and his colleagues (301) demonstrated that most of the apparent association between heart disease and coffee drinking could be explained in terms of the association between coffee drinking and smoking, with a suggestion in the multivariate analysis that high coffee drinking might even offer some protection against the effects of excessive smoking. In a different analysis of more cases from the same study (i.e., 157 out of 1718), Paul (299) noted a U-shaped relationship between coffee consumption and prevalence of coronary disease, whereby both low and high, but not moderate, consumption were associated with angina, myocardial infarction, and sudden death.

In the year after Paul's first report, Yudkin and Roddy (417) provided data that appeared to implicate excessive caffeine-beverage consumption in myocardial infarction among an English population. Tea and coffee were not distinguished in this report. In a later report on a different series of patients, Yudkin and Morland (416) noted that the 40 infarct patients consumed an average of 7.7 cups of tea and 0.8 cups of coffee a day, whereas the 58 control patients consumed 5.6 cups of tea and 1.4 cups of coffee each day. Thus, these data appear to implicate tea and not coffee consumption in myocardial infarction. Such a difference between tea and coffee had also been found in an earlier study by Brown (48), who had sought information from surviving relatives about the living habits of people who had died from coronary disease. Yudkin was concerned mainly with the role of dietary sucrose, and he presented statistical analysis that appeared to eliminate tea (or caffeine) as a possible cause of infarction. Later, Paul and his colleagues (301) reviewed some of their own data and found little evidence for a role of sugar intake.

A year after Yudkin's first report, in 1965, Little and associates (241) reported no significant difference in either tea or coffee consumption between surviving infarct patients and controls. However, because coffee drinking and not tea drinking was found to be associated with serum lipid and cholesterol elevation in heart patients and not controls (242), the authors subsequently concluded that coffee contains a substance that may be associated with susceptibility to coronary heart disease. A lack of correlation between heart disease and coffee or tea consumption was also reported by Howell and Wilson (190), who surveyed workers at British Atomic Energy establishments. A rather broad definition of heart disease was used in this study, to the extent that 12.8% of those surveyed were cases; thus, the results may not be readily comparable with those from studies in which myocardial infarction or a closely related diagnosis was used. A retrospective Finnish study used a relatively precise diagnosis of myocardial infarction and found significant differences between the coffee consumption of infarct patients and matched controls (212). Of the infarct patients, 66% drank more than five cups of coffee a day, and 16% drank more than 10 cups; these proportions for the controls were 39% and 6%, respectively. Infarct cases drank an average of 7.3 cups per day, whereas controls drank an average of 4.9 cups per day ($p < 0.01$), an amount in itself considerably in excess of the average consumption reported by heart disease cases in the Hawthorne study (300). Finns, it may be remembered from Section 10, consume nearly twice as much coffee per capita as United States residents.

These reports led the workers in the Boston Collaborative Drug Surveillance Program (BCDSP) to analyze their data on drug use by hospital patients for an association between coffee and tea drinking and a discharge diagnosis of acute myocardial infarction. Their newsmaking 1972 report (41) indicated that infarct patients drank significantly more coffee, but not tea, than matched controls. Tea consumption was lower among infarct patients, but not significantly so. No association was found with respect to other forms of heart disease. Cigarette smoking, although strongly correlated with coffee drinking, was ruled out as a factor in infarction. In fact, coffee drinking appeared to increase the risk of infarction less for heavy smokers than for nonsmokers. A subsequent study by the same group (202), also retrospective, corroborated the difference between coffee and tea drinking. In both studies, the infarct risk associated with drinking six or more cups of coffee a day was estimated to be more than twice that associated with drinking no coffee at all. The authors concluded that no causal relationship between coffee drinking and acute myocardial infarction could be presumed in the absence of appropriate epidemiologic data, i.e., data from prospective studies.

Data from two prospective studies have become available since 1972. The first was based on the computer files of the Kaiser–Permanente Medical Center in Oakland, Calif. (220). Search of over 250,000 records of multiphasic health examinations for the years 1964–1970 yielded 464 persons who subsequently suffered a first myocardial infarction, 464 risk controls who were matched for cardiovascular characteristics, and 464 ordinary controls who were matched merely for age, sex, skin color (?), and examination date. Each examination had included the question, "Have you usually, in the past year, drunk more than six cups of coffee per day?" Close to 20% of each group reported drinking more than six cups of coffee a day, with none of the percentages being significant from each other or from the percentage of 110,000 unselected examinees that reported drinking more than six cups per day. Again, a curious relationship with cigarette smoking was found. Compared with risk controls who were smokers, infarct victims who were smokers were less likely to have reported drinking more than six cups of coffee a day (28.9% vs. 36.8%), whereas the proportion of nonsmokers drinking more than six cups a day was the same for victims and risk controls (10.8%). Thus, smoking and coffee consumption appeared to be less well correlated among infarct victims than among risk controls, suggesting indirectly that those who engaged in both to excess were less likely to suffer an infarct. Because of the demonstrated lack of a correlation between infarction and coffee consumption in this study, it could be argued that the data suggest a protective effect of coffee drinking against the effects of cigarette smoking.

The second prospective study involved the population of Framingham, Mass., which has been under scrutiny since 1949. Analysis of the files revealed no association between daily coffee consumption of the men in the cohort at the time of the fourth biennial examination and subsequent incidence among these men of various kinds of heart disease (87). Coffee consumption was positively correlated with subsequent incidence of deaths from all causes, but this association did not survive correction for amount of cigarette smoking. The authors concluded that their data "provide no support for the hypothesis that coffee intake is either qualitatively or quantitatively related to the initial development of manifestations of atherosclerotic disease," but left open the question of "a possible effect of coffee intake on the course of existing cardiovascular disease."

These studies, and particularly the BCDSP reports, stimulated considerable correspondence in the medical literature, ranging from the helpful to the hapless, that continues apparently unabated at the time of writing (88, 201). Among the helpful was an analysis of questionary data collected from the male veteran twin panel maintained by the U.S. National Research Council (192). This report indicated that the classification of angina occurs more frequently among those drinking six or more cups of coffee a day than among those drinking less. Further analysis, however, showed that the positive relationship between coffee drinking and heart disease held only for heavy smokers: for moderate smokers (1–30 cigarettes per day) the relationship appeared to be negative. Thus these data contradict the suggestion in the BCDSP data that heavy smoking protects against the effects of heavy coffee drinking on heart disease, and also the suggestions in the data of Paul and his colleagues (301) and the data from the Kaiser–Permanente study (220) that heavy coffee drinking protects against the effects of heavy smoking. The NRC twin study seems to have been retrospective, although that is not entirely clear from the report. The twin-panel data are based on incidence of angina, which is a more embracing definition than that used in most, although not all, of the studies discussed here. Lack of a common classification of heart disease is one of many difficulties in comparing these studies. It is possible that some of the discrepancies between reports could be explained in terms of the different classifications used, but, although I searched for consistency in preparing this review, I could not find any.

Many correspondents were intrigued by the BCDSP findings of a possible beneficial effect of tea. One writer (348) suggested that caffeine forms indigestible complexes with the "tannin" that occurs in black tea but not in green tea and coffee, thus making the caffeine in black tea less available than in coffee. There are three problems with this assertion. Firstly, there is no evidence that the polyphenols known as tannin complex with caffeine. Secondly, black tea has only a little more tannin than coffee, and considerably *less* than green tea, according to Sinclair and Hollingsworth (354), although Martinek and Wolman (252) report green and black tea as having approximately equal amounts of tannin and about 10 times as much as coffee; it may depend on what you are looking for in the analysis. Thirdly, and most pertinently, there is evidence that caffeine in tea and coffee are equally well absorbed, and it appears that the caffeine in Coca-Cola, which contains no tannin, is absorbed much more slowly (249). Tea polyphenols could contribute to a possible difference between tea and coffee in a quite different way. They have been shown to potentiate barbiturate-induced sleeping time in mice (275), and thus they may antagonize caffeine, which has the opposite effect (123). Coffee polyphenols may be less effective as antagonists of caffeine.

Other writers on the difference between tea and coffee claimed that cream in coffee was the culprit (84), or hot milk (315), or just plain milk (349), or, with biblical support, the peculiarly noxious effect on intestinal microflora of coffee and milk combined (115). Yudkin (415) wrote reasserting a role for sugar, and for dietary change after infarction (but he did not remind readers of his own and other data that suggest a difference between the effects of tea and coffee on serum lipids [1, 242, 414]). Personality factors were implicated (23, 225). The fat in coffee beans was proposed as a culprit (262). The adenine (178) and even the theophylline (317) in tea were offered as possible antagonists of caffeine that are present in tea and absent in coffee. It was noted that coffee contains more cobalt than tea, but that the difference is small in relation to normal daily intake of the metal (189). The conclusion in the BCDSP report that caffeine is not the culprit was challenged by a reiteration of some of caffeine's known effects upon the cardiovascular system (15), and, indirectly, by the Executive Director of the Tea Council of the U.S.A., who reminded readers of *Lancet* that a cup of coffee usually contains much more caffeine than a cup of tea (8), a protest that was challenged by the editor of that journal with support from the BCDSP workers.

The correspondence on the BCDSP data included further support for coffee's pathologic effect in terms of significant correlations between deaths from heart disease and coffee consumption involving 16 countries (293) and 24 countries (280), with the second correlation being challenged because it should have involved only eight countries (35) and because Greece was included twice (43). What is really interesting about the second correlation (280) is the accompanying scattergram. It shows that, of the eight countries with the highest death rates from ischemic heart disease, five are among the seven countries with the highest coffee consumption (Sweden, Denmark, United States, Finland, and Norway [Table 3]), and three are among the five countries with the highest tea consumption (United Kingdom, Australia, and New Zealand [Table 6]). This observation encouraged me to reanalyze some of the data in an earlier report in which no correlation had been found between mortality from myocardial infarction and national consumption of either coffee or tea (49). It appeared that the negative correlation between tea and coffee consumption (see Section 10) might prevent either being correlated when there were high tea-consuming and high coffee-consuming countries in the same series. By ordering countries in terms of caffeine consumption—i.e., by summing coffee and tea consumption after correcting for the fact that tea leaves have about 2.5 times as much caffeine as coffee beans (211, 252)—a significant correlation was revealed. The rank correlation between national average caffeine consumption and deaths from ischemic heart disease among males aged 55–64 was 0.624 ($p < 0.01$; N = 16). The respective correlations for coffee and tea were 0.17 and 0.40—both nonsignificant. The correlation with caffeine consumption was considerably higher than that for cigarette smoking ($r = 0.52$).

The whole discussion about the harmful effects of coffee and the beneficial effects of tea has ignored contrary data from other countries. Even in the first BCDSP study itself (41), which used data from four countries, there is a clear indication that the effect of coffee on myocardial infarction was largely confined to the cases from the United States, which has by far the highest coffee consumption of the four countries: the proportion of heavy coffee drinkers among non-United States infarct cases (from Canada, Israel, and New Zealand) was actually lower than the proportion of heavy coffee drinkers among the United States controls; on the other hand, non-United States patients consuming moderate amounts of coffee were actually found to be at higher risk than United States patients, possibly because they also drank tea (the association with combined coffee and tea consumption was not reported). The most surprising omission from the discussion about coffee and tea, however, has been the lack of reference to the two English studies (48, 416) that appeared to implicate tea but not coffee in ischemic heart disease.

Another theme of the correspondence stimulated by the BCDSP reports, articulated in three different journals by the same group of authors (178–181), consisted of the apparently irrelevant hypothesis that caffeine may be consumed by some people because it is good for them, i.e., because it compensates for inherited "metabolic dysoxidoses." The hypothesis may not seem so far-fetched if it is noted, as did at least two correspondents (128, 173) that the BCDSP and most of the other reports of a positive correlation between caffeine-containing beverage consumption and heart disease have involved data from the small proportion of myocardial infarction victims who survive. One critic of the BCDSP reports suggested that as many as 82% of victims die before or within 3 days of hospital admission (256). It is possible that the fatalities drank less coffee or tea than survivors. Thus, coffee or tea drinking may indeed be beneficial. Evidence for a lack of association has come largely from prospective studies. Only one of these, the Framingham study (87), distinguished survivors from nonsurvivors, and then not with sufficient clarity to allow a statement to be made about the role of coffee drinking in survival from myocardial infarction. One retrospective English study that distinguished those that survived their first heart attack from those that did not found that more than 10 cups of tea had been consumed daily by 17.9% of the first-time fatalities and only 10.7% of the survivors of the first heart attack (48). The proportion of excessive tea drinkers among survivors was even lower than that for controls free from heart disease (11.2%), thus confounding an argument that high caffeine-beverage consumption provides protection from acute myocardial infarction.

Prospective studies may be criticized on the grounds that there can be considerable change in coffee consumption between the original determination of intake and the occurrence of infarction. Retrospective studies, on the other hand, usually achieve greater contiguity between an effect and its possible causes (203). The Framingham study (87), in which as much as 12 years elapsed between determination and occurrence, is peculiarly vulnerable to such criticism (201). The criticism was countered by the observation that there was little difference between the cohort males' mean consumption of 2.8 cups a day in 1955–1957 and their consumption of 2.6 cups a day in 1971–1973 (88). The Framingham male population was aged 35–69 in 1955–1957. The study's own data (87) and Fig. 2 above indicate that maximum coffee intake occurs in the 40–44 age group, with a substantial decline after age 50–54. Thus during the 12-year period it is likely, on a statistical basis, that there was a decline in consumption of coffee by cohort members aged 42 and over, and an increase and then a decline by the remainder. The net result should have been a substantial decline. Because only a slight overall decline was reported, it seems possible that some individuals exhibited uncharacteristic increases in consumption during the period, increases that may have been related to subsequent heart disease but that would have been ignored in the analysis for association.

To the outsider, there seems to be no field as subject to contrary statistical interpretation as epidemiology, save perhaps economics. The correspondence has included wounding criticisms of the various studies (175, 201, 203), and remarkably resilient replies (88, 222) that quite confuse the befuddled reader. One point seems to have been absent from all of the polemic. It is the arbitrary nature of the classifications of coffee consumption, particularly the highest levels of consumption. No distinction has been made between people who drink 6 or more cups of coffee a day and people who drink (say) 10 or more cups a day. According to the Ontario Drinking Survey 2.0% of Ontario adults drink the latter amount of coffee and the United States proportion is probably similar (see Table 4). In the United States about 0.5% of all adults die of myocardial infarction (280); another 0.1% suffer and recover (202). Thus there is still a lot of scope for the causation of myocardial infarction (incidence = 0.6%) by really heavy coffee consumption, i.e., 10 or more cups a day (prevalence = 2.0%). It could be argued that strong determination by really heavy consumption should also manifest itself as weaker determination by consumption that is merely heavy, and, accordingly, that lack of an association for lower levels of consumption is evidence against determination by the highest levels. This would possibly be true if caffeine were the sole cause of myocardial infarction. As it is quite clear that myocardial infarction probably has many causes (381), the contribution of moderate caffeine consumption may be swamped by the variation that can be attributed to other relevant factors.

An example of inappropriate categorization may be the lack of association with tea drinking found in the BCDSP studies (41, 202). No association was found when patients were categorized into those drinking 0, 1–4, and >4 cups of tea, respectively. In one of the English studies reporting an association with tea drinking, the controls drank an average of 5.6 cups a day (416). The infarction victims in this retrospective study had been drinking an average of 7.7 cups of tea a day. In the other study that reported an association with tea drinking rather than with coffee drinking, more than 11% of controls and considerably more cases drank 11 or more cups of tea a day (48). It is likely that the BCDSP studies were using inappropriate consumption categories for establishing an association with tea drinking. Another way in which only very high levels of coffee consumption could be important is through alcohol drinking, which, according to another Kaiser–Permanente study (221), may give protection against myocardial infarction. As reported in Fig. 4, alcohol consumption in Ontario increases with coffee consumption up until about three cups per day and then declines. Thus many of those drinking in the region of three cups of coffee per day may be protected by their alcohol consumption.* An association between myocardial infarction and tea or coffee consumption may be apparent only at higher levels than those considered in most of the studies discussed in this section. The variation in these studies may be attributed, in part at least, to the greater importance of other factors at lower levels of caffeine-beverage consumption.

Another point that has been largely absent from the discussion is recognition of the possible variation among cups of coffee and tea. Table 10 above shows 10-fold differences in caffeine concentration from one cup to another (149). The wide ranges that were uncovered make nonsense of most attempts to deny or defend a role for caffeine in terms of coffee or tea consumption, nonsense that is exaggerated by our observation that caffeine concentration appeared to be quite unrelated to consumption (see Section

* There is very good evidence to suggest that former drinkers of alcohol are much more likely to develop myocardial infarction or to die from heart disease than drinkers or those who have never drunk (215, P. 92). If former drinkers really do drink much more tea and coffee than the average, as if often asserted (87), the high incidence of heart disease in this group provides indirect evidence of a relation between caffeine consumption and myocardial infarction. Other interpretations are possible, of course, including the obvious one that the former drinkers tend to be in poor general health.

10). The wide ranges themselves could account for the inconclusive literature.

Also absent from the discussion is implication of caffeine-induced sleep disturbance as a basis for a possible deleterious effect of caffeine on cardiovascular function. According to Lown and his colleagues (244, 245), severe cardiac malfunction can be associated with REM sleep in certain people but, generally speaking, sleep is beneficial to the heart. In some patients, erratic heart function that is difficult to control with drugs loses all irregularity during sleep. Animals deprived of sleep show lower thresholds for cardiac abnormality. The observation of Goldstein and colleagues (157) that regular users of five or more cups of coffee a day may suffer chronic sleep disturbance was reported in Section 6. Thus heavy coffee (and, presumably, caffeine) users may not benefit fully from sleep's restorative action, and may indeed suffer from adverse effects of sleep deprivation on the heart. Moreover, the suggestion that caffeine increases the proportion of REM sleep (160), also discussed in Section 6, raises the possibility that caffeine may be especially toxic in those individuals for whom severe cardiac irregularity is associated with the REM sleep phase.

The only reasonable way to conclude this section is to be somewhat inconclusive regarding the role of caffeine in cardiopathology. The evidence remains as Paul (299) characterized it in 1968, too suggestive and intriguing for dismissal but inadequate to permit firm and positive statements as to etiologic significance. Among the intriguing suggestions discussed is even a possible protective effect of excessive caffeine consumption. Nevertheless, the balance of evidence appears to me to be moving towards implication of caffeine in heart disease, probably at intake levels higher than those considered in most studies so far (i.e., probably at the equivalent of about eight cups of coffee and upwards), but at levels consumed by an appreciable proportion of the middle-aged population of many countries.

Four things are clear to me after reviewing the voluminous recent literature on this topic. (*a*) There is presently no basis for distinguishing between tea and coffee in terms of possible effects on myocardial infarction, and therefore caffeine cannot be ruled out because one but not the other may be involved. (*b*) Subsequent attempts to relate caffeine consumption to heart disease should do just that, i.e., determine caffeine consumption with some precision rather than via cups of beverage. (*c*) Very high levels of caffeine consumption should be given special consideration. (*d*) Caffeine remains suspect even if only because of the drug's known pharmacologic effects, direct and indirect, upon the cardiovascular system, although further work is needed to demonstrate how the results of these laboratory studies could be related to caffeine's implication in some kinds of heart disease and not others. One further coincidence should be acknowledged, one that has been overlooked in the heat of the discussion. Per capita coffee consumption in the United States reached a peak in 1962 and has declined since then (295). The age-adjusted death rate from ischemic heart disease among United States residents aged 35–84 reached a peak one year later, in 1963, and has also declined ever since (400). Nevertheless, coronary heart disease remains the leading cause of death in the United States and in most other countries that have a high per capita caffeine-beverage consumption.

Peptic Ulcer

> A great deal too much against tea is said by wise people, and a great deal too much of tea is given to the sick by foolish people. When you see the natural and almost universal craving in English sick for their "tea", you cannot but feel that Nature knows what she is about. But a little tea or coffee restores them quite as much as a great deal; and a great deal of tea, and especially of coffee, impairs the little power of digestion they have.
>
> The views of Nurse Florence Nightingale on coffee and tea, as recorded by I. M. Beeton in *The Book of Household Management*, 1861.

Landis (234), in his 1958 overview of caffeine's effects, claimed that the sole contraindication for caffeine beverages is in cases of gastrointestinal pathology. He gave no basis for this assertion, but it is likely that he was relying on the experimental work of Roth and colleagues, published in the 1940s (328, 329), in which ulceration was provoked and aggravated in cats and guinea pigs but not dogs, and aggravated in man. Roth's 1964 review of the role of drugs in gastroduodenal ulcer concluded that "although caffeine has not been shown to produce peptic ulcer in man, the prolonged daily consumption of 10 to 15 cups a day may exert a contributory influence" (327).

The two available epidemiologic studies of the relation between coffee drinking and peptic ulcer are contradictory. One, based on the Kaiser–Permanente files, appeared not to implicate coffee drinking (127). The study found that smoking was clearly related to peptic ulcer history among 36,656 men and women, but that coffee drinking, although highly correlated with cigarette smoking, "was not appreciably related to a history of peptic ulcer in either smokers or non-smokers." Unfortunately no data were given, and readers cannot unravel this puzzling inconsistency for themselves. The only question asked was whether or not more than six cups of coffee a day were usually consumed. Thus the effect of higher levels of consumption, of the order implicated by Roth (327), would not have been revealed in this study.

The other study, also from California, suggests that peptic ulcer might be associated with much lower levels of coffee drinking (291). Of a population of over 11,000 men, those who, at college, drank two or more cups of coffee a day were 1.8 times more likely to develop an ulcer in later life (i.e., up to 50 years later) than those who usually drank no coffee. Smoking was also implicated, but only when it had occurred in conjunction with coffee drinking.

Unfortunately, I was able to find no data pertaining to a possible relationship between tea drinking and gastroduodenal pathology, in spite of numerous claims (115) that tea may exert a beneficial effect. It would be interesting, for example, to relate incidence of peptic ulcer to the per capita coffee and tea consumption of various countries. In the meantime, in the absence of a consistent body of data, no firm conclusion can be made about the role of caffeine in gastrointestinal pathology, although it should be noted that the experimental evidence relating caffeine and gastrointestinal ulcer provocation is reasonably good. As in the case of heart disease, any further attempt to relate the two should pay close attention to the actual consumption of caffeine.

Cancer

> Strong green tea is highly pernicious, and should never be partaken of too freely.
>
> I. M. Beeton. *The Book of Household Management*, 1861.

In view of the large amount of work on caffeine's mutagenic effects, the dearth of studies relating caffeine-beverage consumption to the incidence of cancer may be surprising. There are five studies available and, fortunately for reviewers, but unfortunately for caffeine users, there is considerable agreement among them.

The first study was reported in 1971 by Cole (72), who sampled residents of eastern Massachusetts who were newly diagnosed with histologically confirmed cancer of the lower urinary tract. He interviewed 468 victims, and compared their responses with those of matched controls. Incidence of this form of cancer (mostly of the bladder) was highly correlated with coffee consumption, and the correlation survived correction for age, cigarette smoking, and occupation. Cole found that the association with coffee drinking was most distinct in those age and sex groups in which occupation and cigarette smoking played the smallest role, i.e., the association increased with age and was stronger for women. After controlling for cigarette smoking it was found that women aged 60–74 who drank one or more cups of coffee a day were at least four times as likely to suffer cancer of the lower urinary tract as women of the same age who drank no coffee or less than one cup per day. However, for this group and for all others there was no consistent relationship with amount of coffee drunk in excess of one cup a day. The finding has been essentially replicated (353a).

Cole's report prompted researchers at the U.S. National Cancer Institute to reanalyze some of their data on the incidence of bladder cancer in New Orleans during 1958–1964 (102). The earlier report had shown merely that this kind of cancer was not associated with consumption of any particular type of coffee. The new analysis (126) involved actual consumption levels of the beverage. It provided overall confirmation of Cole's data, but there was one curious inconsistency. The risk for white women *declined* with increasing coffee consumption. Perhaps abstainers from coffee were drinking tea.

Cole's findings have also been partially confirmed in a study conducted by Bross and Tidings (47) in a hospital in western New York state. This study was a case-control (i.e., retrospective) study, like the two just discussed. It involved 480 patients with a diagnosis of bladder cancer and 2669 control patients. Relationships similar to those found by Cole were reported for men—including the lack of a relation between dose and incidence—but not for women. The difference between the two series of women arose largely because the proportion of women cancer victims drinking less than one cup of coffee a day was much higher in the age group 60–74 in western New York than in eastern Massachusetts (17.4% vs. 5.6%). This may be related to the finding that younger women (20–59 years) in New York reported drinking less than one cup of coffee a day much less frequently than women of comparable age in Massachusetts (9.4% vs. 22.9%). The data suggest that more women gave up coffee drinking in New York as they aged. Accordingly, many of the non-coffee-drinking women victims aged 60–74 in New York could have been former heavy coffee drinkers and could have suffered cancer as a result of their heavy coffee drinking. Thus, Bross and Tidings' data are possibly not so inconsistent with those of Cole as they appear at first sight. The various differences discussed above did not appear in the data from male respondents. It seems that regional differences in coffee drinking habits in the United States may be smaller for men than for women.

The fourth recent study involved relating the mortality rate for renal carcinoma in 16 countries to respective per capita coffee consumption (350). A significant correlation was found ($r = +0.79$ for 1964, $r = +0.75$ for 1965, $p < 0.002$ in both cases). The author seemed surprised by some anomalous countries: "for instance, although more than five to six times as much coffee was consumed in the U.S.A. as in Britain, the mortality experience in the former country was only marginally higher." If the relation had been made on the basis of caffeine rather than coffee consumption there might have been no surprise. Unfortunately, I did not have sufficient data available to recalculate the correlation on the basis of caffeine consumption. However, it can be noted from Tables 3 and 6 above that even though United States coffee consumption considerably exceeds coffee consumption in the United Kingdom, the reverse is the case for tea, and moreover, when the fact that bulk tea contains about 2.5 times as much caffeine per kilogram as green coffee is allowed for, the differences between the two countries appear even smaller.

The remaining study is the only one that provides contrary data (266). A survey by mailed questionnaire involved 364 bladder cancer sufferers of whom only data from 232 were used in the study. Consumption of both tea and coffee did not differ between victims and controls. The main difficulty with this study is that the average age on providing information about caffeine beverage consumption was in excess of 70 years, an age when consumption may be unusually low (Table 5 and Fig. 1) and not typical of consumption during the years in which cancer of the bladder might be provoked.

For the moment it must be concluded that, as far as cancers of the kidney and lower urinary tract are concerned, there may be a risk associated with drinking any but the smallest amounts of caffeine. The conclusion is consistent with experimental data (see Section 5) and with our knowledge of how caffeine or its metabolites might affect cell reproduction (see Section 3), but clearly more research of an epidemiologic nature is required; in particular, it would be useful to have prospective data.

Regarding other forms of cancer, few data are available. Takahashi (377) related the age-adjusted death rate from cancer of various parts of the digestive and urogenital systems to national average coffee consumption and found a significant correlation only with respect to cancer of the prostate gland ($r = +0.70$, $N = 20$, $p < 0.01$). Unfortunately, as in most other studies, tea consumption was not taken into account, and thus it is difficult to comment on the possible carcinogenic action of caffeine.

Disorders of Behavior and Mood

Although a relation between caffeine use and abnormal behavior has often been suspected (144), only recently has a proper clinical investigation been made. Greden (159) described three patients all with apparent symptoms of anxiety, including one or more of the following: "nervousness," irritability, agitation, headache, tachypnea, tremulousness, reflex hyperexcitability, and occasional muscle twitchings. Noting that these symptoms are common to anxiety and caffeinism, Greden treated his patients by reducing their coffee intake, which was in excess of seven cups per day in each case. The treatment worked and Greden concluded that assessment of anxiety and similar pathologies should always involve determination of caffeine intake.

Greden notes that medical concern about caffeinism has been periodic, and that although "coffee nerves" seems to be a well-known phenomenon, little attention is paid to caffeine consumption in current psychiatric practice. He suggests that "high-risk" patients (i.e., potential sufferers from caffeinism) might include those who do not seem to respond to hypnotics, those with recurrent headaches (possibly on account of a vicious consumption–withdrawal cycle), those with coronary and psychophysiologic symptoms, and hyperkinetic children.

Isolated reports of a similar nature have appeared in the past but Greden's is the first to place caffeine-withdrawal therapy in the context of the manifest similarities between anxiety and caffeinism. The only studies that have related caffeine-beverage consumption to behavior and mood disorders were discussed in Section 10. None is satisfactory, and it is possible that Greden's paper will stimulate better investigation, including studies of an epidemiologic nature. Particular attention might be paid to the possibly pathogenic effects on behavior and mood of caffeine-induced insomnia. Moderate and heavy coffee drinkers may suffer from chronic sleep disturbances as a result of their coffee intake (157). Special attention might also be paid to the diurnal pattern of caffeine intake. Abstinence from caffeine can have powerful effects upon mood and behavior (101, 143, 155). Temporary abstinence caused by inadvertent interruption of a regular supply of the drug could have contributed to a dysphoric condition. Because of a possible relation between caffeine and stress (70, 176), the possible pathologic effects of the drug in already stressed subjects might also be given special attention.

A curious postscript to Greden's report is provided by an unsigned editorial in the *British Medical Journal* entitled "Anxiety symptoms and coffee drinking" (10). The editorial summarized Greden's article and accordingly advised the British medical profession to enquire about the coffee-drinking habits of patients. Greden's article was about caffeine consumption, however, not just coffee drinking; he very carefully included reference to all sources of caffeine in his discussion of the pathologic effects of excessive caffeine consumption on behavior. Moreover, as indicated in Section 10, most caffeine is consumed in Britain in the form of tea rather than coffee. Thus the British medical profession may very well miss the point of Greden's argument, and be puzzled when reductions in coffee consumption have no effect on anxiety. The editorial is a fine example of what might be called antethnocentrism—the tendency to view one's own culture in terms of another. As such, it is an interesting departure from what may be a more common medical practice (150a).

Hyperactivity

Coffee is recommended against the contagion.

Gideon Harvey. *A Discourse of the Plague*, 1665.

One of Greden's suggested categories of "high-risk" cases comprises the problem children who are variously described as hyperkinetic, hyperactive, exhibiting a hyperkinetic impulse disorder, and manifesting a learning disability. Such children are sometimes described as suffering from "minimal brain dysfunction," although, as Sroufe and Stewart (369) have pointed out, the neurologic invocation is invariably gratuitous. I mentioned earlier, in Section 10, that children are likely to ingest considerable amounts of caffeine via cola drinks and chocolate products. Schnackenberg (346) has suggested that hyperkinetic children do, in fact, ingest larger than average amounts of caffeine but that, paradoxically, the caffeine consumption is caused by the hyperkinesis rather than vice versa. The paradox is partly that of the effects of stimulant drugs on hyperactivity. Drugs that normally stimulate have what often seems to be an opposite effect on hyperkinetic children, although the notion that stimulant drugs actually sedate hyperkinetic children is no longer given credence (369). Schnackenberg had been treating hyperactive symptoms in 11 seven- and eight-year-old children by regular administration of methylphenidate. Because annoying side effects developed in each case, he instituted a three-week medication holiday and then administered caffeine in the form of one cup of coffee at breakfast and another at lunch. Hyperkinetic symptoms were exaggerated during the medication holiday, but their intensity fell to methylphenidate levels when caffeine was introduced. Schnackenberg concluded that caffeine in coffee was as effective as methylphenidate, and, moreover, produced no annoying side effects. (Weiss and Laties [404], in their comparison of the effects of caffeine and amphetamines on human performance, had concluded that caffeine is more likely than amphetamines to produce annoying side effects when doses that enhance human performance are being administered.)

In a subsequent interview (120), Schnackenberg noted that he was now using caffeine with every hyperkinetic child presented to him, with continuing success in all but one of 17 new cases, and that caffeine in a 250-mg timed capsule was being used instead of coffee to avoid gastrointestinal upset. In support of his claim that excessive caffeine consumption in children might be the result of self-administration to correct for hyperkinesis, Schnackenberg noted that the disorder is "most heavily reported in countries where children are predominantly milk-drinkers and not coffee-drinkers" (346). He suggested that hyperkinesis is not a problem in Latin American countries where "children have drunk coffee for decades;

many drink five to ten cups a day—and it's much higher in caffeine than ours" (120).

Schnackenberg's report has elicited at least one letter of support (125), in which alternation between caffeine and a stimulant [sic] was recommended by the writer because he had found caffeine as coffee to be effective in hyperkinesis, but less effective than either thioridazine or dextroamphetamine. The report has also stimulated at least three formal studies of caffeine's efficacy in hyperkinesis (139, 162, 193). All three showed insignificant effects of caffeine when compared with a placebo; in one (162), caffeine actually caused behavior to deteriorate slightly. Methylphenidate (15–40 mg per day) reduced the incidence of hyperkinetic behavior in all three studies. The mean age of the children was higher in each case than in Schnackenberg's study, and in two of the studies (139, 162) it is possible that lower doses of caffeine were used. In only one study (139) was the children's habitual caffeine consumption taken into account. Thus there can be doubt as to whether Schnackenberg's finding has been contradicted, although there can be no doubt that, if caffeine is to be considered seriously as therapy in hyperkinesis, further research is required.

One should ask first, however, whether caffeine or any other drug should be used chronically in the management of problem children. Sroufe and Stewart claimed (in 1973) that more than 150,000 children with behavior or learning problems were being treated with stimulant drugs (369). After exemplary consideration of the pertinent issues they conclude that, although administration of stimulant drugs may provide short-term benefit from the point of view of management, such therapy may be detrimental in the long term because it lowers the motivation of parents and teachers to take other steps to help the child: "The basic flaw of drug treatment is that it cannot teach a child anything, and it is not yet established that drug treatment makes the child more accessible to other intervention techniques" (p. 411). A considerable irony of drug therapy is that, properly formulated, the "other intervention techniques" themselves will suppress hyperactivity. Allyon and his colleagues (2) have shown, quite convincingly, that appropriate reinforcement of academic performance will reduce the frequencies of certain behavior patterns to levels achieved with methylphenidate (including gross motor behavior, disruptive noise with objects, disturbing others, and blurting out). Moreover, "the academic gains produced by the behavioral program contrast dramatically with the lack of academic progress shown by these children under medication" (2, p. 143).

If caffeine should meet with approval in the management of problem children, it is possible that its use in this way would flourish, unrestrained by the legal restrictions on the use of amphetamine and methylphenidate that may presently limit the popularity of drug treatment in the regulation of unacceptable behavior. (According to Sroufe and Stewart, more than 5% of elementary school children in the United States are hyperactive or learning disabled, but less than a third of these received stimulant drug medication. According to a 1970 report by Canada's Commission on Emotional and Learning Disorders in Children [78], one child in 10 has a learning disability.) If caffeine were really as harmless as it is generally supposed to be, and as efficacious as Schnackenberg believes, the prospect that hundreds of thousands of children would be rendered vigilant, persistent, and manageable by frequent recourse to coffee would not be discouraging. Given that caffeine has been implicated, albeit with differing degrees of certainty, in a wide range of pathologic conditions, any proposal to increase caffeine use, especially among children, must be regarded as alarming.

Caffeine Dependence as a Problem

> A kind of chronic narcotism, the very existence of which is usually ignored, but which is in truth well marked and easy to identify, is that occasioned by habitual excess in tea and coffee.
>
> F. E. Anstie. *Stimulants and Narcotics*, 1864.

There seems to be no doubt that chronic caffeine administration causes physical dependence in the sense that characteristic dysphoric symptoms are reported when regular use of the drug is interrupted. Moreover, it seems equally likely that physical dependence on caffeine is a characteristic of a large proportion of the adult population of many countries, possibly a majority in some. However, there is little evidence that physical dependence is itself a problem or even that physical dependence contributes to the consumption of caffeine—or indeed any other drug. The Addiction Research Foundation of Ontario, in its preliminary brief to the Le Dain Commission of Inquiry into the Non-Medical Use of Drugs (77), argued that

> . . . dependence is not necessarily bad in itself,* either for the individual or for society. The question to be evaluated, therefore, is not whether dependence can occur, but whether dependence in any given case results in physical, psychological or social harm (p. 293).

Nonetheless, even if no harm arises from use of a drug, the possibility of dysphoria from inadvertent or unavoidable interruption of supply, even in the case of such a ubiquitous drug as caffeine, should be considered as an argument against condoning dependence. The caffeine-dependent individual

* This organization's attitude may be changing. The 1975 version of its *Employee's Handbook* describes procedures for dealing with employees "who may be suffering from the problem of chemical dependence."

is less able to adapt, at least temporarily, to certain environmental changes, namely those that preclude caffeine use, than one who is not so dependent. On the other hand, dysphoria may accompany withdrawal of any regular consequence of behavior, and each of us is unadaptive to the extent that we rely on familiar things.

Miscellaneous Pathologies

Caffeine has been directly implicated in few human fatalities; these were reviewed in Section 5. A West German epidemiologic study has implicated coffee drinking in perinatal mortality, but only among premature births (254), although a subsequent report (255) suggested that the association was merely with lower birth weights. Other pathologies that might, from experimental evidence or pharmacologic considerations, be associated in some way with caffeine consumption have received little or no clinical or epidemiologic investigation. These include diabetes, obesity, certain hepatic and renal malfunctions, and goiter, which were briefly discussed in Sections 3 and 4; male infertility, discussed in Section 5; insomnia, sleep disturbance, and self-aggression, discussed in Section 6; chronic headache and other withdrawal signs, discussed in Section 7; and alcoholism and the excessive consumption of other psychotropic drugs, as well as absorption and metabolism of drugs used clinically, discussed in Section 8.

A clear contraindication is the use of caffeine in glaucoma. As mentioned in Section 7, Graeber (158) has reported that 300 mg of caffeine can raise the intraocular pressure by a considerable amount when the glaucoma is unregulated, i.e., if pressure has not already been reduced by therapeutic intervention of some kind. This effect might cause headache in untreated glaucoma and thus provide a basis for caffeine-provoked headache as opposed to caffeine-withdrawal headache. A recent newspaper report suggests that marijuana may be used soon as the therapy of choice in glaucoma, on account of its specific action on intraocular fluid, thus raising the question of interaction between caffeine and another commonly used drug.

One pathologic condition, associated with caffeine-beverage consumption, but which could not have been predicted from pharmacologic considerations, is scalding. Apparently, one-quarter of all treated cases of scalding in Denmark involve coffee (14). Nearly 0.1% of the total population and more than 0.2% of children under six years are scalded by coffee in Denmark, scalded to the extent that hospital treatment is required. It seems that the cost of this treatment is 1.0% of the market value of the coffee that is consumed. (Costs of managing and treating other pathologies associated with caffeine-beverage consumption are not known. If a tax on caffeine or caffeine-containing substances were to be proposed, such information would constitute a useful part of the justification for the tax.) The incidence of scalding by coffee in other countries is not known. It is probably lower in Canada and the United States, partly because less coffee is consumed, and partly because coffee filters, whose upset causes more than half of Danish coffee scalds, are used less frequently in North America.*

12. IS CAFFEINE A DRUG OF ABUSE?

> But why must innocent Coffee be the object of your Spleen?
> Anon. *The Men's Answer to the Women's Petition against Coffee*, 1674.

Is caffeine used by an appreciable proportion of the population to a degree that health or well-being is jeopardized? Recent attempts to answer this question have ranged from a blanket denial of caffeine's effects, to a recognition that caffeine *can* be a dangerous drug but with an assertion that few people are actually affected.

An example of the first position is provided by Heyden's 1974 review of some of the evidence concerning the effects of coffee during good health and disease (177). He concluded: "The modern literature shows that coffee and caffeine are two stimulants that have no unwanted side-effects on the cardiovascular system, on metabolism of lipids, sugar, and uric acid, and on the gastrointestinal and urogenital apparatuses."

A similarly sanguine, but more cautious, view was expressed by Kannel and Dawber (210) in their 1973 editorial on coffee and coronary heart disease in the *New England Journal of Medicine*, where they lamented the possibility that coffee drinking may have to be added to the list of things that are illegal, immoral, fattening or hazardous to the heart (a list that includes "almost everything," they observed). Kannel and Dawber argued that the huge problems of encouraging physical activity, of modifying diet, and of reducing cigarette consumption should not be complicated further by the advocacy of "premature restrictions of other pleasurable habits unless there is equally good evidence that such a change is warranted."

Brecher and associates, on the other hand, in the influential *Consumer Reports* compendium on licit and illicit drug use (44), described some of caffeine's effects and concluded that caffeine can be a dangerous drug. They outlined what they called the "coffee paradox"—"the question of how a drug so fraught with *potential* hazard can be consumed in the United States

* The scene is changing, however. According to a sales manager of Canada's largest department store chain "The percolator is dead. Everyone seems to be changing over to the filter-drip method" *Toronto Star*, May 7, 1975, P. 1.

at the rate of more than a hundred billion doses a year without doing intolerable damage—and without arousing the kind of hostility, legal repression, and social condemnation aroused by the illicit drugs." The paradox was resolved with reference to the observation that caffeine-beverages are domesticated, i.e., "caffeine has been incorporated into [the North American] way of life in a manner that minimizes (but though it does not altogether eliminate) the hazards inherent in caffeine use." Brecher and his associates may have made a useful observation about the role of "domestication" in the severity of drug effects, but they may not have resolved the paradox. Caffeine may only *seem* not to be hazardous. If more were known about caffeine's effects, and if what is known were known more widely, the damage done by caffeine might very well appear to be intolerable.

In my view there is sufficient evidence presented in this chapter, particularly in Section 10, to suggest that there is considerable risk to the health of an adult of average weight who ingests upwards of 600 mg of caffeine a day, i.e., more than about 8 cups of coffee, or about 22 cups of tea, or about 15 of the 10-oz bottles of Coca-Cola, or about 9 of certain headache pills, or the equivalent in combination. Such an adult is possibly more likely than normal to develop certain kinds of heart disease, ulcers of the stomach and duodenum, and carcinomas, especially of the kidneys and urinary tract, because of the caffeine consumption. Such an adult may be more likely than normal to experience headaches, insomnia, difficulty in and dysphoria on waking, and a constellation of symptoms that may be indistinguishable from anxiety. The range of caffeine-beverage consumption that could be equivalent to 600 mg of caffeine a day is enormous. The caffeine content of a cup of coffee could be as high as 333 mg, according to the Addiction Research Foundation study (i.e., coffee of maximum caffeine concentration in maximum coffee-cup size—see Table 10). One such cup consumed daily by a person half the average weight would provide more caffeine per kilogram than 600 mg consumed by a person of average weight. The lowest caffeine content per cup of coffee could be 14 mg, according to the same study (149). A person twice the average weight would have to drink 84 such cups in order to exceed the caffeine consumption per kilogram of an average-weight person drinking eight typical cups of coffee. Because of this potential range—and a greater one exists for tea consumption—difficulty must be expected in establishing associations between caffeine-beverage consumption and pathologic conditions. Clearly, further epidemiologic and clinical work on the pathologic effects of caffeine must be concerned with caffeine consumption rather than caffeine-beverage consumption.

The other aspect of abuse is that sufficient people consume damaging amounts of the substance for concern about excessive consumption to be legitimate. The fact that water can be abused (107) makes water a substance of abuse, in a sense. It is probable that so few people consume water to excess that concern about water abuse is not justifiable. (Food abuse is another matter.) The best information available suggests that upwards of 3% of the adult population of North America consumes 600 mg or more caffeine per day, i.e., more than 5 million people in the United States and more than 500,000 in Canada. In certain other countries, notably the four Scandinavian countries, Belgium, and the Netherlands, the proportion is probably much higher.

It is instructive to compare this proportion with that of heavy alcohol drinkers among the whole population. Various interpretations of the term "heavy alcohol drinking" have been proposed. After reviewing them, Lelbach (238) concluded that, in heavy drinkers, reported average intake exceeds 80 g of ethanol per day, and the remainder of his article provides justification for an argument that this is the lowest level of chronic use that is associated with organic pathology. According to the Ontario Drinking Survey (89), less than 1.6% of adults report drinking an average of more than 80 g of ethanol per day. National average consumption for Canada and for the United States is similar to that for Ontario, and the frequency distribution of consumption is unlikely to be very different. Thus one might conclude that more people may be at risk in North America because of consumption of caffeine beverages than because of consumption of alcoholic beverages.

It follows that consideration should be given to restriction of caffeine-beverage consumption as a public health measure. This could be done by favoring tea over coffee, by encouraging consumption of coffee with lower caffeine content, and by forbidding soft-drink manufacturers to include caffeine in their products, rather than requiring its presence. If government makes a serious attempt to reduce caffeine intake, care should be taken to avoid unwanted by-products of such action. The place of caffeine beverages in society should be recognized. Caffeine should remain—to use Brecher's term—domesticated, in order to avoid the problems posed by widespread use of a drug that is "wild."

An important part of the consideration would be support for further research on caffeine. If such research failed to substantiate the claims that have been made concerning the adverse effects of caffeine, it would be comforting to know that the most popular psychotropic drug is indeed as benign as the high levels of its consumption might lead one to suppose.

ACKNOWLEDGMENTS

During the preparation of this chapter I have been indebted to Marilyn Schwieder and to Evelyn Wollis for valuable assistance of all kinds; to Tina Prietz and June Shepperd for their labor in preparing the final draft; to Henzel Jupiter and Lonnie Currin for help with data analysis and presentation; to many colleagues at the Addiction Research Foundation for cheerfully given replies to what were often very silly questions; to Mary Ann Linseman, Evalyn Segal, and many others for helpful comments on an earlier draft; and to the editors for their patience, encouragement, and attention to detail.

REFERENCES

1. Akinyanju, P. and J. Yudkin, Effect of coffee and tea on serum lipids in the rat, *Nature*, **214**, 426–427 (1967).
2. Allyon, T., D. Layman, and H. J. Kandel, A behavior-educational alternative to drug control of hyperactive children, *J. Appl. Behav. Anal.*, **8**, 137–146 (1975).
3. Al-Samarrae, W., M. C. F. Ma, and A. S. Truswell, Methylxanthine consumption from coffee and tea, *Proc. Nutr. Soc.*, **34**, 18A–19A (1975).
4. Alstott, R. L., Studies of the combined effects of caffeine and ethanol, Ph.D. Dissertation, Indiana University, 1971.
5. Alstott, R. L., A. J. Miller, and R. B. Forney, Report of a human fatality due to caffeine. *J. Forensic Sci.*, **18**, 135–137 (1973).
6. Ammon, H. P. T., L. A. Carlson, J. Fröberg, C.-G. Karlsson, and L. Levi, *Effects of Coffee and Caffeine on Sympathoadrenomedullary Activity, Blood Lipids, Psychological Ratings, and Performance*, Report No. 31 from the Laboratory for Clinical Stress Research, Karolinska Institute, Stockholm, Sweden (1973).
7. Anderson, J., G. Hollifield, and J. A. Owen, Jr., The effects of caffeine, deoxyribonucleic acid and insulin on the metabolism of glucose by adipose tissue in vitro, *Metabolism*, **15**, 30–38 (1966).
8. Anderson, J. M., Coffee drinking and acute myocardial infarction. *Lancet*, **1**, 314 (1973).
9. Anstie, F. E., *Stimulants and Narcotics, Their Mutual Relations: With Special Researches on the Action of Alcohol, Aether and Chloroform, on the Vital Organism*, Macmillan, London, 1864.
10. Anxiety symptoms and coffee drinking, *Br. Med. J.*, **1**, 296–297 (1975).

10a. Aranda, J. V., W. Gorman, H. Bergsteinsson, T. Gunn, Efficacy of caffeine in apnea in the premature neonate. Paper given at the Canadian Society for Clinical Investigation meeting in Quebec City, January 1976.

10b. Aranda, J. V., D. S. Sitar, W. D. Parsons, and A. H. Neims, Pharmacokinetic aspects of theophylline in premature newborns, *N. Engl. J. Med.*, (in press)

11. Ardlie, N. G., G. Glew, B. G. Schulze, and C. J. Schwartz, Inhibition and reversal of platelet aggregation by methyl xanthines, *Thromb. Diath. Haemorrh.*, **18,** 670–673 (1967).

12. Arushanyan, É. B., Y. A. Belozertsev, and K. G. Aivazov, Comparative effect of amphetamine and caffeine on spontaneous activity of sensomotor cortical units and their responses to stimulation of the caudate nucleus, *Bull. Exp. Biol. Med.*, **77,** 776–779 (1974).

13. Ashton, H., J. E. Millman, R. Telford, and J. W. Thompson, The effect of caffeine, nitrazepam and cigarette smoking on the contingent negative variation in man, *Electroencephalogr. Clin. Neurophysiol.*, **37,** 59–71 (1974).

14. Asmussen, C. and B. Sørensen, Scalding with coffee, *Dan. Med. Bull.*, **20,** 9 (1973).

15. Atuk, N. O. and T. C. Westfall, Coffee and myocardial infarction, *N. Engl. J. Med.*, **289,** 977 (1973).

16. Avogaro, P., C. Capri, M. Pais, and G. Cazzolato, Plasma and urine cortisol behavior and fat mobilization in man after coffee ingestion, *Isr. J. Med. Sci.*, **9,** 114–119 (1973).

17. Ax, R. L., D. J. Bray, and J. R. Lodge, Effects of dietary caffeine on fertility and embryonic loss in chickens, *Poult. Sci.*, **53,** 428–429 (1974).

18. Ax, R. L. and J. R. Lodge, Caffeine effects on rooster spermatogenesis, *J. Anim. Sci.*, **39,** 986 (1974).

19. Ax, R. L., J. R. Lodge, and D. J. Bray, Increased embryonic loss in chickens from 0.05 per cent dietary caffeine, *Poult. Sci.*, **53,** 830–831 (1974).

20. Axelrod, J. and J. Reichenthal, The fate of caffeine in man and a method for estimation in biological material, *J. Pharmacol. Exp. Ther.*, **107,** 519–523 (1953).

21. Baker, W. J. and G. C. Theologus, Effects of caffeine on visual monitoring, *J. Appl. Psychol.*, **56,** 422–427 (1972).

22. Ball, K. and R. Turner, Smoking and the heart—The basis for action, *Lancet*, **2,** 822–826 (1974).

23. Barnett, B., A. MacKay, and R. Zaslov, Coffee and myocardial infarction, *N. Engl. J. Med.*, **289,** 978 (1973).

24. Bartol, C. R., Extraversion and neuroticism and nicotine, caffeine, and drug intake, *Psych. Rep.*, **36,** 1007–1010 (1975).

25. Bartoshuk, L. M., Taste mixtures: Is mixture suppression related to compression? *Physiol. Behav.*, **14,** 643–649 (1975).

25a. Basu, T. K., N. P. Bishun, and D. C. Williams, Accentuation of the cell-killing effects of chlorambucil by phenobarbital, caffeine and vitamin A, *Cytobios*, 9, 115–119 (1974).

26. Beer, B., M. Chasin, D. E. Clody, J. R. Vogel, and Z. P. Horowitz, Cyclic adenosine monophosphate phosphodiesterase in brain: Effect on anxiety, *Science*, **176,** 428–430 (1972).

27. Bejerot, N., in *Abuse of Central Stimulants*, F. Sjöqvist and M. Tottie (Eds.), Raven Press, New York, 1969, p. 85.

28. Bell, G. H., J. N. Davidson, and H. Scarborough, *Textbook of Physiology and Biochemistry*, Livingston, Edinburgh, 1953.

29. Bellet, S., L. Roman, O. P. DeCastro, K. E. Kim, and A. Kershbaum, Effects of coffee ingestion on catecholamine release, *Metabolism*, **18,** 288–291 (1969).

30. Bellet, S., L. R. Roman, H. Sandberg, and J. B. Kostis, The effect of nicotinic acid on

the caffeine-induced serum free fatty acid increase, *J. Pharmacol. Exp. Ther.*, **175,** 348–351 (1970).

31. Bellville, J. W., L. A. Escarraga, S. L. Wallenstein, K. C. Wang, W. S. Howland, and R. W. Houde, Antagonism by caffeine of the respiratory effects of codeine and morphine, *J. Pharmacol. Exp. Ther.*, **136,** 38–42 (1962).
32. Bender, M. and J. A. Nelson, Interaction of theophylline and phenobarbital in solution, *J. Chem. Soc., Faraday Trans. I.*, **69,** 2074–2079 (1973).
33. Berkowitz, B. A., S. Spector, and W. Pool, The interaction of caffeine, theophylline, and theobromine with monoamine oxidase inhibitors, *Eur. J. Pharmacol.*, **16,** 315–321 (1971).
34. Berkowitz, J. M., J. E. Shields, I. H. Andersen, and M. Praissman, Plasma gastrin response to coffee, Sanka, caffeine and water, *Gastroenterology*, **66,** 666 (1974).
35. Bignall, J. C., Coffee drinking and ischaemic heart disease, *Lancet*, **1,** 548 (1973).
36. Bilinski, T., H. Baranowska, W. Prazm̊o, and A. Putrament, The inhibition by caffeine of the synthesis of RNA and protein in yeast and *E. coli*, *Mutat. Res.*, **21,** 24 (1973).
37. Bittar, E. E., H. Hift, H. Huddart, and E. Tong, Effects of caffeine on sodium transport, membrane potential, mechanical tension, and ultrastructure in barnacle muscle fibres, *J. Physiol.* (*Lond.*), **242,** 1–34 (1974).
38. Blough, D. S., Some effects of drugs on visual discrimination in the pigeon, *Ann. N.Y. Acad. Sci.*, **66,** 733–739 (1957).
39. Bodem, R. and E. H. Sonnenblick, Mechanical activity of mammalian heart muscle: Variable onset, species differences, and the effect of caffeine, *Am. J. Physiol.*, **228,** 250–261 (1975).
40. Boissier, J. R. and P. Simon, Influence de la caféine sur le comportement en situation libre de la souris, *Arch. Int. Pharmacodyn. Ther.*, **166,** 362–369 (1967).
41. Boston Collaborative Drug Surveillance Program, Coffee drinking and acute myocardial infarction, *Lancet*, **2,** 1278–1281 (1972).
42. Boyd, E. M., M. Dolman, L. M. Knight, and E. P. Sheppard, The chronic oral toxicity of caffeine, *Can. J. Physiol. Pharmacol.*, **43,** 995–1007 (1965).
43. Bradshaw, S., Coffee drinking and ischaemic heart disease, *Lancet*, **1,** 548 (1973).
44. Brecher, E. M. and the editors of Consumer Reports, *Licit and Illicit Drugs*, Little, Brown, Boston, 1972.
45. Brĕzinová, V., Effect of caffeine on sleep: EEG study in late middle age, *Br. J. Clin. Pharmacol.*, **1,** 203–208 (1974).
46. Brĕzinová, V., I. Oswald, and J. Loudon, Two types of insomnia: Too much waking or not enough sleep, *Br. J. Psychiat.*, **126,** 439–445 (1975).
47. Bross, I. D. and J. Tidings, Another look at coffee drinking and cancer of the urinary bladder, *Prev. Med.*, **2,** 445–451 (1973).
48. Brown, A., Coronary thrombosis: An environmental study, *Br. Med., J.*, **2,** 567–573 (1962).
49. Brummer, P., Coronary mortality and living standard, *Acta. Med. Scand.*, **186,** 61–63 (1969).
50. Burg, A. W., R. Burrows, and C. J. Kensler, Unusual metabolism of caffeine in the squirrel monkey, *Toxicol. Appl. Pharmacol.*, **28,** 162–166 (1974).

51. Burg, A. W. and M. E. Stein, Urinary excretion of caffeine and its metabolites in the mouse, *Biochem. Pharmacol.*, **21**, 909–922 (1972).

52. Burg, A. W. and E. Werner, Tissue distribution of caffeine and its metabolites in the mouse, *Biochem. Pharmacol.*, **21**, 923–936 (1972).

53. Burg, A. W. and E. Werner, Effect of orally administered caffeine and theophylline on tissue concentrations of 3′,5′ cyclic AMP and phosphodiesterase, *Fed. Proc.*, **34**, 332 (1975).

54. Burnett, J., *Plenty and Want: A Social History of Diet in England from 1815 to the Present Day*, Thomas Nelson, London, 1966.

55. Burnett, J., *A History of the Cost of Living*, Penguin Books, Harmondsworth, England, 1969.

56. Caffeine: Grounds for concern?, *Consumer Reports*, **36**, 34–35 (1971).

57. Calhoun, W. H., Central nervous system stimulants, in *Pharmacological and Biophysical Agents and Behavior*, E. Furchtgott (Ed.), Academic Press, New York, 1971, pp. 181–268.

58. *Canada Year Book*, Statistics Canada, Ottawa, 1972.

59. Cappell, H. and B. Latané, Effects of alcohol and caffeine on the social and emotional behavior of the rat, *Q. J. Stud. Alcohol*, **30**, 345–356 (1969).

60. Castellano, C., M. Sansone, P. Renzi, and L. Annecker, Central stimulant drugs on avoidance behavior in hamsters, *Pharmacol. Res. Commun.*, **5**, 287–293 (1973).

61. Challis, B. C. and C. D. Bartlett, Possible cocarcinogenic effects of coffee constituents, *Nature*, **254**, 532–533 (1975).

62. Chapman, R. A. and D. J. Miller, The effects of caffeine on the contraction of the frog heart, *J. Physiol. (Lond.)*, **242**, 589–613 (1974).

63. Cheraskin, E. and W. M. Ringsdorf, Jr., Blood-glucose levels after caffeine, *Lancet*, **2**, 689 (1968).

64. Cheraskin, E., W. M. Ringsdorf, Jr., A. T. S. H. Setyaadmadja, and R. A. Barrell, Effect of caffeine vs. placebo supplementation on blood-glucose concentration, *Lancet*, **1**, 1299–1300 (1967).

65. Christensen, J., Pharmacology of the esophagal motor function, *Ann. Rev. Pharmacol.*, **19**, 243–258 (1975).

66. Chvasta, T. E. and A. R. Cooke, Emptying and absorption of caffeine from the human stomach, *Gastroenterology*, **61**, 838–843 (1971).

67. Clark, A. and C. B. Olson, Effects of caffeine and isoprenaline on mammalian ventricular muscle, *Br. J. Pharmacol.*, **47**, 1–11 (1973).

68. Clarke, C. H. and M. J. Wade, Evidence that caffeine, 8-methoxypsoralen, and steroidal diamines are frameshift mutagens for *E. coli* K-12, *Mut. Res.*, **28**, 123–125 (1975).

69. Claus, E. P., V. E. Tyler, and L. R. Brady, *Pharmacognosy*, 6th Ed., Lee & Febiger, Philadelphia, 1970.

70. Cobb, S., Physiologic changes in men whose jobs were abolished, *J. Psychosom. Res.*, **18**, 245–258 (1974).

70a. Cohen, M. M., H. T. Debas, I. B. Holubitsky, and R. C. Harrison, Caffeine and pentagastrin stimulation of human gastric secretion, *Gastroenterology*, **61**, 440–444 (1971).

70b. Cohen, S. and G. H. Booth, Jr., Gastric acid secretion and lower-esophageal sphincter pressure in response to coffee and caffeine, *N. Engl. J. Med.* **293**, 897–899 (1975).

71. Cola—the real thing, *Psychology Today*, **7**, 92–93 (1974).

72. Cole, P., Coffee-drinking and cancer of the lower urinary tract, *Lancet*, **2**, 1335–1337 (1971).

73. Collier, H. O. J., The concept of quasi-abstinence effect and its use in the investigation of dependence mechanisms, *Pharmacology*, **11**, 58–61 (1974).

74. Collier, H. O. J., D. L. Francis, G. Henderson, and C. Schneider, Quasi morphine-abstinence syndrome, *Nature*, **249**, 471–473 (1974).

75. Collins, E. and G. Turner, A suggestion for reducing the incidence of habitual analgesic consumption, *Med. J. Aust.*, **1**, 863 (1973).

76. Colton, T., R. E. Gosselin, and R. P. Smith, The tolerance of coffee drinkers to caffeine, *Clin. Pharmacol. Ther.*, **9**, 31–39 (1968).

77. Commission of Inquiry into the Non-Medical Use of Drugs (G. Le Dain, Chairman), *Final Report to the Minister of National Health and Welfare*, Ottawa, Canada, 1973.

78. Commission on Emotional and Learning Disorders in Children (CELDIC), *One Million Children*, Toronto, Canada, 1970.

79. Conterio, F. and B. Chiarelli, Study of the inheritance of some daily habits, *Heredity*, **17**, 347–359 (1962).

80. Cornish, H. H. and A. A. Christman, A study of the metabolism of theobromine, theophylline, and caffeine in man, *J. Biol. Chem.*, **228**, 315–323 (1957).

81. Cox, T., The effects of caffeine, alcohol, and previous exposure to the test situation on spontaneous alteration, *Psychopharmacologia*, **17**, 83–88 (1970).

82. Crowley, T. J., D. Chesluk, S. Dilts, and R. Hart, Drug and alcohol abuse among psychiatric admissions—Multidrug clinical-toxicologic study, *Arch. Gen. Psychiatry*, **30**, 13–20 (1974).

83. Cunningham, H. M. Biological half-life of caffeine in pigs, *Can. J. Anim. Sci.*, **50**, 49–54 (1970).

84. Dalderup, L. M. Coffee drinking and acute myocardial infarction, *Lancet*, **1**, 104 (1973).

85. Daubresse, J. C., P. Franchimont, A. Luyckx, E. Demey-Ponsart, and P. Lefèbvre, Effects of coffee and caffeine on carbohydrate metabolism, free fatty acid, insulin, growth hormone and cortisol plasma levels in man, *Acta. Diabetol. Lat.*, **10**, 1069–1084 (1973).

86. Davis, T. R. A., C. J. Kensler, and P. B. Dews, Comparison of behavioral effects of nicotine, *d*-amphetamine, caffeine, and dimethylheptyl tetrahydrocannabinol in squirrel monkeys, *Psychopharmacologia*, **32**, 51–65 (1973).

87. Dawber, T. R., W. B. Kannel, and T. Gordon, Coffee and cardiovascular disease—Observations from the Framingham study, *N. Engl. J. Med.*, **291**, 871–874 (1974).

88. Dawber, T. R., W. B. Kannel, and T. Gordon, Statistics of coffee and myocardial infarction, *N. Engl. J. Med.*, **292**, 266 (1975).

89. de Lint, J., W. Schmidt, and K. Pernanen, The Ontario drinking survey: A preliminary report. Addiction Research Foundation, Substudy No. 1–10 and 4 and 37–70, 1970.

90. Degkwitz, R. and H. Sieroslawsky, Erhöhung der 5-hydroxyindolessigsäure-(HIES-)-Ausscheidung im Harn nach Coffein, Pervitin und Preludin, *Klin. Wochenschr.*, **41**, 902–905 (1963).

91. Deneau, G., T. Yanagita, and M. H. Seevers, Self-administration of psychoactive substances by the monkey, *Psychopharmacologia*, **16**, 30–48 (1969).

92. Department of National Health and Welfare, Smoking in Canada—1973, *Rx Bull.*, **5**, 101–106 (1974).

93. Desai, H. G., M. P. Zaveri, and F. P. Antia, Increased vitamin-B_{12} absorption after ingestion of coffee, *Gastroenterology*, **65,** 694–695 (1973).

94. Dews, P. B., The behavioral context of addiction, in *Bayer Symposium IV; Psychic Dependence,* L. Goldberg and F. Hoffmeister (Eds.), Springer-Verlag, New York, 1973, pp. 36–46.

95. Diamond, A. L. and R. E. Cole, Visual threshold as a function of test area and caffeine administration, *Psychon. Sci.*, **20,** 109–111 (1970).

96. Dimaio, V. J. M. and J. C. Garriott, Lethal caffeine poisoning in a child, *Forensic Sci.*, **3,** 275–278 (1974).

97. Domino, E. F., Antianxiety drugs, in *Drill's Pharmacology in Medicine, 4th Ed.*, J. DiPalma (Ed.), McGraw-Hill, New York, 1971, 489–498.

98. Donovan, P. J., and J. A. DiPaolo, Caffeine enhancement of chemical carcinogen-induced transformation of cultured Syrian hamster cells, *Cancer Res.*, **34,** 2720–2727 (1974).

99. Dorfman, L. J. and M. E. Jarvik, Comparative stimulant and diuretic actions of caffeine and theobromine in man, *Clin. Pharmacol. Ther.*, **11,** 869–872 (1970).

100. Downs, D. A. and J. H. Woods, Codeine- and cocaine-reinforced responding in rhesus monkeys: Effects of dose on response rates under a fixed-ratio schedule, *J. Pharmacol. Exp. Ther.*, **191,** 179–188 (1974).

101. Dreisbach, R. H. and C. Pfeiffer, Caffeine-withdrawal headache, *J. Lab. Clin. Med.*, **28,** 1212–1219 (1943).

102. Dunham, L. J., A. S. Rabson, H. L. Stewart, A. S. Frank, and J. L. Young, Jr., Rates, interview, and pathology study of cancer of the urinary bladder in New Orleans, Louisiana, *J. Natl. Cancer Inst.*, **41,** 683–709 (1968).

103. Dureman, E. I., Behavioral patterns of anti-barbituric action after 5-phenyl-2-imino-4-oxo-oxazolidine, amphetamine, and caffeine, *Clin. Pharmacol. Ther.*, **3,** 163–171 (1962).

104. Dureman, E. I., Differential patterning of behavioral effects from three types of stimulant drugs, *Clin. Pharmacol. Ther.*, **3,** 29–33 (1962).

105. Duvoisin, R. C. and M. D. Yahr, Drugs used in the treatment of parkinsonism, in *Drill's Pharmacology in Medicine, 4th Ed.*, J. DiPalma (Ed.), McGraw-Hill, New York, 1971, pp. 318–323.

106. Eddy, N. B. and A. W. Downs, Tolerance and cross-tolerance in the human subject to the diuretic effect of caffeine, theobromine, and theophylline, *J. Pharmacol. Exp. Ther.*, **33,** 167–174 (1928).

107. Edelstein, E. L., A case of water dependence, *Br. J. Addict.*, **68,** 367 (1973).

108. Ehret, C. F., V. R. Potter, and K. W. Dobra, Chronotypic action of theophylline and of pentobarbital as circadian zeitgebers in the rat, *Science*, **188,** 1212–1215 (1975).

109. Epstein, S. S., W. Bass, E. Arnold, and Y. Bishop, The failure of caffeine to induce mutagenic effects or to synergize the effects of known mutagens in mice, *Food Cosmet. Toxicol.*, **8,** 381–401 (1970).

110. Estler, C.-J., Effect of α- and β-adrenergic blocking agents and para-chlorophenylalanine on morphine- and caffeine-stimulated locomotor activity in mice, *Psychopharmacologia*, **28,** 261–268 (1973).

111. Evert, G., F. Niedobitek, and E. Schmid, Ulzerogene Kombinationseffekte von emotionellem Stress und Koffein bzw. Bohnenkaffee im Tierversuch, *Z. Gastroenterol.*, **9,** 94–100 (1971).

112. Eysenck, H. J., *Smoking, Health and Personality,* Weidenfeld and Nicholson, London, 1965.

113. Feinberg, I., Changes in sleep cycle patterns with age, *J. Psychiat. Res.,* **10,** 283–306 (1974).

114. Feinberg, L. J., H. Sandberg, O. DeCastro, and S. Bellet, Effects of coffee ingestion on oral glucose tolerance curves in normal human subjects, *Metabolism,* **17,** 916–922 (1968).

115. Filip, L., Salutary tea and abominable coffee, *N. Engl. J. Med.,* **290,** 347 (1974).

116. Fingl, E. and D. M. Woodbury, General principles, in *The Pharmacological Basis of Therapeutics,* L. S. Goodman and A. Gilman (Eds.), 4th Ed., Macmillan, New York, 1970, 1–35.

117. Fisher, V. J. and F. Kavaler, The action of ethanol upon the contractility of normal ventricular myocardium, in *Alcohol and Abnormal Protein Biosynthesis: Biochemical and Clinical,* M. A. Rothschild, O. Oratz, and S. S. Schreiber (Eds.), Pergamon Press, New York, 1975, pp. 187–202.

118. Flexner, J. B. and L. B. Flexner, Puromycin's suppression of memory in mice as affected by caffeine, *Pharmacol. Biochem. Behav.,* **3,** 13–17, (1975).

119. Fog, R., Stereotyped and non-stereotyped behaviour in rats induced by various stimulant drugs, *Psychopharmacologia,* **14,** 299–304 (1969).

120. For hyperkinesia, a coffee break, *Emerg. Med.,* **6,** 219–221 (1974).

121. Forney, R. B. and F. W. Hughes, Effect of caffeine and alcohol on performance under stress of audiofeedback, *Q. J. Stud. Alcohol,* **26,** 206–212 (1965).

122. Forney, R. B. and F. W. Hughes, *Combined Effects of Alcohol and Other Drugs.* Charles C Thomas, Springfield, Ill., 1968.

123. Forrest, W. H., J. W. Bellville, and B. W. Brown, Jr., The interaction of caffeine with pentobarbital as a night-time hypnotic, *Anesthesiology,* **36,** 37–41 (1972).

124. Francis, D. L., A. C. Roy, and H. O. J. Collier, Morphine abstinence and quasi-abstinence effects after phosphodiesterase inhibitors and naloxone, *Life Sci.,* **16,** 1901–1906 (1975).

125. Fras, I., Alternating caffeine and stimulants, *Am. J. Psychiatry,* **131,** 228–229 (1974).

126. Fraumeni, J. F. Jr., J. Scotto, and L. J. Dunham, Coffee drinking and bladder cancer, *Lancet,* **2,** 1204 (1971).

127. Friedman, G. D., A. B. Siegelaub, and C. C. Seltzer, Cigarettes, alcohol, coffee and peptic ulcer, *N. Engl. J. Med.,* **290,** 469–473 (1974).

128. Friedman, J. G., Coffee and myocardial infarction, *N. Engl. J. Med.,* **289,** 978 (1973).

129. Friedman L., M. A. Weinberger, and E. L. Peters, Testicular atrophy and aspermatogenesis in rats fed caffeine or theobromine in the presence or absence of sodium nitrite, *Fed. Proc.,* **34,** 228 (1975).

129a. Fröberg, J., L. A. Carlson, C.-G. Karlsson, L. Levi, and K. Seeman, Effects of coffee on catecholamine excretion and plasma lipids, in *Coffein und Andere Methylxanthine,* F. Heim and H. P. T. Ammon (Eds.) Schattauer Verlag, Stuttgart, 1969, 65–73.

130. Fröberg, J., C.-G. Karlsson, L. Levi, L. Linde, and K. Seeman, Test performance and subjective feelings as modified by caffeine-containing and caffeine-free coffee, in *Coffein und Andere Methylxanthine,* F. Heim and H. P. T. Ammon (Eds.),Schattauer Verlag, Stuttgart, 1969, 15–19.

131. Frühauf, A., K. Graupner, E. Kálmán, and U. Wilde, Die Flimmer-Verschmelzungs-Frequenz unter dem Einfluss verschiedener Pharmaka. 1. Coffeine und Meprobamat, *Psychopharmacologia*, **21,** 382–389 (1971).

132. Fujii, T. and H. Nishimura, Prevention of caffeine teratogenicity in mice by pretreatment with propranolol: Relation to time intervals between treatments, *Teratology*, **10,** 81 (1974).

133. Fujii, T. and H. Nishimura, Reduction in frequency of fetopathic effects of caffeine in mice by treatment with propranolol, *Teratology*, **10,** 149–152 (1974).

134. Furlong, F. W., *Possible Psychiatric Significance of Excessive Coffee Consumption*, Unpublished manuscript, Clarke Institute of Psychiatry, Toronto, 1974.

135. Fuxe, K. and U. Ungerstedt, Action of caffeine and theophyllamine on supersensitive dopamine receptors: Considerable enhancement of receptor response to treatment with dopa and dopamine receptor agonists, *Med. Biol.*, **52,** 48–54 (1974).

136. Galli, C., P. F. Spano, and K. Szyszka, Accumulation of caffeine and its metabolites in rat fetal brain and liver, *Pharmacol. Res. Commun.*, **7,** 217–221 (1975).

137. Garbers, D. L., N. L. First, J. J. Sullivan, and H. A. Lard, Stimulation and maintenance of ejaculated bovine spermatozoan respiration and motility by caffeine, *Biol. Reprod.*, **5,** 336–339 (1971).

138. Gardocki, J. F., M. E. Schuler, and L. Goldstein, Reconsideration of the central nervous system pharmacology of amphetamine. 1. Toxicity in grouped and isolated mice, *Toxicol. Appl. Pharmacol.*, **8,** 550–557 (1966).

139. Garfinkel, B. D., C. D. Webster, and L. Sloman, Methylphenidate and caffeine in the treatment of children with minimal brain dysfunction, *Am. J. Psychiatry*, **132,** 723–729 (1975).

140. Geller, I., R. Hartmann, and K. Blum, Effects of nicotine, nicotine monomethiodide, lobeline, chlordiazepoxide, meprobamate and caffeine on a discrimination task in laboratory rats, *Psychopharmacologia*, **20,** 355–365 (1971).

141. Gibbins, R. J., Y. Israel, H. Kalant, R. E. Popham, W. Schmidt, and R. G. Smart (Eds.), *Research Advances in Alcohol and Drug Problems*, Vol. I. Wiley, New York, 1974.

141a. Gilbert, E. F., and W. R. Pistey, Effect on the offspring of repeated caffeine administration to pregnant rats. *J. Reprod. Fert.* 34, 495–499 (1973).

142. Gilbert, R. M., Discrimination learning?, in *Animal Discrimination Learning*, R. M. Gilbert and N. S. Sutherland (Eds.), Academic Press, New York, 1969, pp. 455–489.

143. Gilbert, R. M., Tolerance to and withdrawal from caffeine in the rat, Addiction Research Foundation, Toronto, Substudy No. 562, 1973.

144. Gilbert, R. M., Caffeine beverages and their effects, *Addictions*, **21,** 68–80 (1974).

145. Gilbert, R. M., Dietary caffeine and alcohol consumption by rats, *J. Stud. Alcohol*, **37,** 11–18 (1976).

146. Gilbert, R. M., Drug abuse as excessive behaviour. *Canadian Psychological Review*, (in press).

147. Gilbert, R. M. Schedule-induced drug consumption, in *Contemporary Research in Behavioural Pharmacology*, D. E. Blackman and D. J. Sanger (Eds.), Plenum Press, London (in press).

148. Gilbert, R. M. and H. Jupiter, Caffeine-beverage consumption in Ontario, (in preparation).

149. Gilbert, R. M., J. A. Marshman, M. Schwieder, and R. Berg, Caffeine content of beverages as consumed, *Can. Med. Assoc. J.*, **114,** 205–208 (1976).

150. Gilliland, A. R. and D. Nelson, The effects of coffee on certain mental and physiological functions, *J. Gen. Psychol.*, **21,** 339–348 (1939).

150a. Glaser, F. B., Medical ethnocentrism and the treatment of addiction, *Int. J. Off. Ther. Comp. Criminol.*, **18,** 13–27 (1974).

151. Goldstein, A., Wakefulness caused by caffeine, *Arch. Pharmak. Exp. Pathol.*, **248,** 269–278 (1964).

152. Goldstein, A., L. Aronow, and S. M. Kalman, *Principles of Drug Action: The Basis of Pharmacology*, 2nd Ed., Wiley, New York, 1974.

153. Goldstein, A. and S. Kaizer, Psychotropic effects of caffeine in man. III. A questionnaire survey of coffee drinking and its effects on a group of housewives, *Clin. Pharmacol. Ther.*, **10,** 477–488 (1969).

154. Goldstein, A., S. Kaizer, and R. Warren, Psychotropic effects of caffeine in man. II. Alertness, psychomotor coordination, and mood, *J. Pharmacol. Exp. Ther.*, **150,** 146–151 (1965).

155. Goldstein, A., S. Kaizer, and O. Whitby, Psychotropic effects of caffeine in man. IV. Quantitative and qualitative differences associated with habituation to coffee, *Clin. Pharmacol. Ther.*, **10,** 489–497 (1969).

156. Goldstein, A. and R. Warren, Passage of caffeine into human gonadal and fetal tissue, *Biochem. Pharmacol.*, **11,** 166–168 (1962).

157. Goldstein, A., R. Warren, and S. Kaizer, Psychotropic effects of caffeine in man. I. Individual differences in sensitivity to caffeine-induced wakefulness, *J. Pharmacol. Exp. Ther.*, **149,** 156–159 (1965).

158. Graeber, W., Zur Wirkung des Koffeins auf den intraokularen Druck bei operativ oder konservativ eingestelltem Glaucoma chronicum simplex, *Klin. Monatsbl. Augenheilkd.*, **152,** 357–365 (1968).

159. Greden, J. F., Anxiety or caffeinism: a diagnostic dilemma, *Am. J. Psychiatry*, **131,** 1089–1092 (1974).

160. Gresham, S. C., W. B. Webb, and R. L. Williams, Alcohol and caffeine: Effect on inferred visual dreaming, *Science*, **140,** 1226–1227 (1963).

161. Griboff, S. I., R. Berman, and H. I. Silverman, A double-blind clinical evaluation of a phenylpropanolamine-caffeine-vitamin combination and a placebo in the treatment of exogenous obesity, *Curr. Therap. Res.*, **17,** 535–543 (1975).

162. Gross, M. D., Caffeine in the treatment of children with minimal brain dysfunction or hyperkinetic syndrome, *Psychosomatics*, **16,** 26–27 (1975).

163. Grubb, M. N. and T. F. Burks, Selective antagonism of the intestinal stimulatory effects of morphine by isoproterenol, prostaglandin E_1 and theophylline, *J. Pharmacol. Exp. Therap.*, **193,** 884–891 (1975).

164. Günter, B., Allometric ratios, invariant numbers and the theory of biological similarities, *Pflügers Arch.*, **331,** 283–293 (1972).

165. Günter, B. and E. Guerra, Biological similarities, *Acta Physiol. Lat. Am.*, **5,** 169–186 (1955).

166. Gyntelberg, F. and J. Meyer, Relationship between blood pressure and physical fitness, smoking and alcohol consumption, *Acta Med. Scand.*, **195,** 375–380 (1974).

167. Haesungcharern, A. and M. Chulavatnatol, Stimulation of human spermatozoal motility by caffeine, *Fertil. Steril.*, **24,** 662–665 (1973).

168. Hall, M. J., L. M. Bartoshuk, W. S. Cain, and J. C. Stevens, PTC taste blindness and the taste of caffeine, *Nature,* **253,** 442–443 (1975).

169. Harrie, J. R., Caffeine and headache, *J.A.M.A.*, **213,** 628 (1970).

170. Hart, J. L., Effects of hyperbaric conditions on the responses of animals to central nervous system stimulants and depressants, *Arch. Int. Pharmacodyn.*, **207,** 260–269 (1974).

171. Hayreh, S. S., Coffee drinking and acute myocardial infarction, *Lancet,* **1,** 45 (1973).

172. Hearst, E., Drug effects on stimulus generalization gradients in the monkey, *Psychopharmacologia,* **6,** 57–70 (1964).

173. Hedberg, S. E., Statistics of coffee and myocardial infarction, *N. Engl. J. Med.*, **292,** 265 (1975).

174. Hedrick, U. P. (Ed.), *Sturtevant's Edible Plants of the World* (*1919*), Dover Publications, New York, 1972.

175. Hennekens, C. H., M. E. Drolette, M. J. Jesse, and J. E. Davies, Statistics of coffee drinking and myocardial infarction, *N. Engl. J. Med.*, **292,** 265 (1975).

176. Henry, J. P. and J. C. Cassel, Psychosocial factors in essential hypertension: recent epidemiological and animal experimental evidence, *Am. J. Epidemiol.*, **90,** 171–200 (1969).

177. Heyden, S., Effetti del caffè in condizioni di salute e di malattia dal punto di vista medico, *Minerva Med.*, **65,** 163–170 (1974).

178. Hickey, R. J., R. C. Clelland, and D. E. Boyce, Coffee and myocardial infarction, *N. Engl. J. Med.*, **289,** 978–979 (1973).

179. Hickey, R. J., R. C. Clelland, D. E. Boyce, and E. J. Bowers, Coffee, tobacco, and cardiovascular disease: Self-selection problem, *J.A.M.A.*, **228,** 160 (1974).

180. Hickey, R. J., R. C. Clelland, D. E. Boyce, and E. J. Bowers, Smoking, health, and confusion, *J.A.M.A.*, **230,** 209–210 (1974).

181. Hickey, R. J., R. C. Clelland, E. B. Harner, and D. E. Boyce, Coffee drinking, smoking, pollution, and cardiovascular disease: A problem of self-selection, *Lancet,* **1,** 1003 (1973).

182. Higuchi, T. and J. L. Lach, Investigation of some complexes formed in solution by caffeine. IV. Interactions between caffeine and sulfathiazole, sulphadiazine, *p*-aminobenzoic acid, benzocaine, phenobarbital, and barbital, *J. Am. Pharm. Soc. Sci. Ed.*, **43,** 349–354 (1954).

183. Higuchi, T. and J. L. Lach, Investigation of complexes formed in solution by caffeine. VI. Comparison of complexing behaviors of methylated xanthines with *p*-aminobenzoic acid, salicylic acid, acetylsalicylic acid, and *p*-hydroxybenzoic acid, *J. Am. Pharm. Soc. Sci. Ed.*, **43,** 527–530 (1954).

184. Ho, I. K., H. H. Loh, and E. L. Way, Cyclic adenosine monophosphate antagonism of morphine analgesia, *J. Pharmacol. Exp. Ther.*, **185,** 336–346 (1973).

185. Ho, I. K., H. H. Loh, and E. L. Way, Effects of cyclic 3′,5′-adenosine monophosphate on morphine tolerance and physical dependence, *J. Pharmacol. Exp. Ther.*, **185,** 347–357 (1973).

186. Hoffmeister, F. and W. Wuttke, Self-administration of acetylsalicylic acid and combinations with codeine and caffeine in rhesus monkeys, *J. Pharmacol. Exp. Ther.*, **186,** 266–275 (1973).

187. Horning, M. G., D. J. Harvey, J. Nawlin, W. G. Stillwell, and R. M. Hill, The use of gas chromatography-mass spectrometry methods in perinatal pharmacology, *Adv. Biochem. Psychopharmacol.*, **7,** 113–124 (1973).

188. Horst, K., R. E. Buxton, and W. D. Robinson, The effect of the habitual use of coffee or decaffeinated coffee upon blood pressure and certain motor reactions of normal young men, *J. Pharmacol. Exp. Ther.*, **52,** 322–337 (1934).

189. Horwitz, C. and S. E. Van der Linden, Cadmium and cobalt in tea and coffee and their relationship to cardiovascular disease, *S. Afr. Med. J.*, **48,** 230–233 (1974).

190. Howell, R. W. and D. G. Wilson, Dietary sugar and ischaemic heart disease, *Br. Med. J.*, **3,** 145–148 (1969).

191. Hrbek, J., S. Komenda, J. Mačáková, and A. Široká, Acute effect of chlorprothixen (5 mg), caffeine (200 mg), and the combination of both drugs on verbal associations, *Act. Nerv. Super.* (*Praha*), **13,** 207–208 (1971).

192. Hrubec, Z., Coffee drinking and ischaemic heart disease, *Lancet*, **1,** 548 (1973).

193. Huestis, R. D., L. E. Arnold, and D. J. Smeltzer, Caffeine versus methylphenidate and *d*-amphetamine in minimal brain dysfunction: A double-blind comparison, *Am. J. Psychiatry*, **132,** 868–870 (1975).

194. Hughes, F. W. and R. B. Forney, Alcohol and caffeine in choice-discrimination tests in rats, *Proc. Soc. Exp. Biol. Med.*, **108,** 157–159 (1961).

195. Hughes, R. N. and A. M. Greig, Spontaneous alternation in ferrets following treatment with scopolamine, chlordiazepoxide, and caffeine, *Physiol. Psychol.*, **3,** 155–156 (1975).

196. Iglauer, C. and J. H. Woods, Concurrent performances: Reinforcement by different doses of intravenous cocaine in rhesus monkeys, *J. Exp. Anal. Behav.*, **22,** 179–196 (1974).

197. International Tea Committee, *Annual Bulletin of Statistics*, London, 1974.

198. Ito, Y., T. Osa, and H. Kuriyama, Topical differences of caffeine action on smooth muscle cells of the guinea pig alimentary canal, *Jpn. J. Physiol.*, **24,** 217–232 (1973).

199. Jankelson, O. M., S. B. Beaser, F. M. Howard, and J. Mayer, Effect of coffee on glucose tolerance and circulating insulin in men with maturity-onset diabetes, *Lancet*, **1,** 527–529 (1967).

200. Jenne, J., H. Nagasawa, R. McHugh, F. MacDonald, and E. Wyse, Decreased theophylline half-life in cigarette smokers, *Life Sci.*, **17,** 195–198 (1975).

201. Jick, H. and O. S. Miettinen, Statistics of coffee drinking and myocardial infarction, *N. Engl. J. Med.*, **292,** 265 (1975).

202. Jick, H., O. S. Miettinen, R. G. Neff, S. Shapiro, O. P. Heinonen, and D. Slone, Coffee and myocardial infarction, *N. Engl. J. Med.*, **289,** 63–67 (1973).

203. Jick, H., M. P. Vessey, D. Slone, S. Shapiro, O. P. Heinonen, and O. S. Miettinen, Coffee drinking and myocardial infarction, *J.A.M.A.*, **227,** 801–802 (1974).

204. Johns, M. W., D. W. Bruce, and J. P. Masterton, Psychological correlates of sleep habits reported by healthy young adults, *Br. J. Med. Psychol.*, **47,** 181–187 (1974).

205. Johns, M. W., The sleep habits and lifestyle of cigarette smokers, *Med. J. Aust.*, **2,** 808–811 (1974).

206. Johnson, R. B., D. M. McCance, and W. M. Lukash, Coffee—Treat or trick? *Am. Family Physician*, **11,** 101–104 (1975).

207. Kalant, H., A. E. LeBlanc, and R. J. Gibbins, Tolerance to, and dependence on, some non-opiate psychotropic drugs, *Pharmacol. Rev.*, **23,** 135–191 (1971).

208. Kalant, H. and O. J. Kalant, *Drugs, Society and Personal Choice,* General, Toronto, 1971.

209. Kan, L. S., P. N. Borer, and P. O. P. Ts'o, A pmr study of the interaction of a short ribosyl helix, $(A_2GCU_2)_2$, and caffeine, *Fed. Proc.,* **34,** 707 (1975).

210. Kannel, W. B. and T. R. Dawber, Coffee and coronary disease, *N. Engl. J. Med.,* **289,** 100–101 (1973).

211. Kaplan, E., J. H. Holmes, and N. Sapeika, Caffeine content of tea and coffee, *S. Afr. Med. J.,* **48,** 510–511 (1974).

212. Kasanen, A. and J. Forsström, Eating and smoking habits of patients with myocardial infarction, *Ann. Med. intern. Fenn.,* **55,** 7–11 (1966).

213. Keister, M. E., R. J. McLaughlin, Vigilance performance related to extraversion–introversion and caffeine, *J. Exp. Res. Personality,* **6,** 5–11 (1972).

214. Keller, M., The oddities of alcoholics, *Q. J. Stud. Alcohol,* **33,** 1147–1148 (1972).

215. Keller, M., *Alcohol and Health,* (Second special report to the U.S. Congress from the Secretary of Health, Education and Welfare), National Institute on Alcohol Abuse and Alcoholism, Rockville, Md., 1974.

216. Khanna, K. L. and H. H. Cornish, The effect of daily ingestion of caffeine on the microsomal enzymes of rat liver, *Food Cosmet. Toxicol.,* **11,** 11–17 (1973).

217. Khanna, K. L., G. S. Rao, and H. H. Cornish, Metabolism of caffeine–^{3}H in the rat, *Toxicol. Appl. Pharmacol.,* **23,** 720–730 (1972).

218. Kihlman, B. A., Effects of caffeine on the genetic material, *Mutat. Res.,* **26,** 53–71 (1974).

219. Kimoto, Y., M. Saito, and M. Goto, Effects of caffeine on the membrane potentials, membrane currents and contractility of the bullfrog atrium, *Jpn. J. Physiol.,* **24,** 531–542 (1974).

220. Klatsky, A. L., G. D. Friedman, and A. B. Siegelaub, Coffee drinking prior to acute myocardial infarction—Results from the Kaiser–Permanente epidemiologic study of myocardial infarction, *J.A.M.A.,* **226,** 540–543 (1973).

221. Klatsky, A. L., G. D. Friedman, and A. B. Siegelaub, Alcohol consumption before myocardial infarction—Results from the Kaiser–Permanente epidemiologic study of myocardial infarction, *Ann. Intern. Med.,* **81,** 294–301 (1974).

222. Klatsky, A. L., G. D. Friedman, and A. B. Siegelaub, Coffee drinking and myocardial infarction, *J.A.M.A.,* **227,** 802–803 (1974).

223. Klawans, H. L., H. Moses, III, and D. M. Beaulieu, The influence of caffeine on *d*-amphetamine- and apomorphine-induced stereotyped behavior, *Life Sci.,* **14,** 1493–1500 (1974).

224. Klein, R. H. and L. F. Salzman, Paradoxical effects of caffeine, *Percept. Mot. Skills,* **40,** 126 (1975).

225. Koning, J. H., Coffee and myocardial infarction, *N. Engl. J. Med.,* **298,** 977–978 (1973).

226. Kosman, M. E., and K. R. Unna, Effects of chronic administration of the amphetamines and other stimulants on behavior, *Clin. Pharmacol. Ther.,* **9,** 240–254 (1968).

227. Kourounakis, P., Pharmacological conditioning for sporting events: Theoretical considerations, hazards, and limitations, *Am. J. Pharmacy,* **144,** 151–158 (1972).

228. Kowalewski, K., Caffeine-induced gastric secretion in rats, *Proc. Soc. Exp. Biol. Med.,* **144,** 1013–1016 (1973).

229. Koysooko, R. and G. Levy, Effect of ethanol on intestinal absorption of theophylline, *J. Pharm. Sci.*, **63,** 829–834 (1974).

230. Kuratsune, M. and W. C. Hueper, Polycyclic aromatic hydrocarbons in coffee soots, *J. Natl. Cancer Inst.*, **20,** 37–51 (1958).

231. Kusanagi, C., S. Fujii, and S. Inada, Evaluation of doping drugs by treadmill exercise in dogs. 1. Caffeine, *Jpn. J. Vet. Sci.*, **36,** 81–92 (1974).

232. Lader, M., Comparison of amphetamine sulphate and caffeine citrate in man, *Psychopharmacologia*, **14,** 83–94 (1969).

233. Lande, S. and A. B. Lerner, The biochemistry of melanotropic activity, *Pharmacol. Rev.*, **19,** 1–20 (1967).

234. Landis, C., Physiological and psychological effects of the use of coffee, in *Problems of Addiction and Habituation*, P. H. Hoch and J. Zubin (Eds.), Grune & Stratton, New York, 1958, pp. 37–48.

235. Laux, D. C. and P. H. Klesius, Suppressive effects of caffeine on the immune response of the mouse to sheep erythrocytes, *Proc. Soc. Exp. Biol. Med.*, **144,** 633–638 (1973).

236. Lee, M. and S. P. Lucia, Effect of ethanol on the mobilization of vitamin A in the dog and in the rat, *Q. J. Stud. Alcohol*, **26,** 1–9, (1965).

237. Lehmann, H. E., P. Black, and T. A. Ban, The effect of psychostimulants on psychometric test performance with special reference to conflict avoidance behavior, *Curr. Ther. Res.*, **12,** 390–393 (1970).

238. Lelbach, W. K., Organic pathology related to volume and pattern of alcohol use, in *Research Advances in Alcohol and Drug Problems, Vol. I*, R. J. Gibbins, Y. Israel, H. Kalant, R. E. Popham, W. Schmidt, and R. J. Smart (Eds.), Wiley, New York, 1974, pp. 93–198.

238a. Levi, L., The effect of coffee on the function of the sympathoadrenomedullary system in man, *Acta Med. Scand.*, 181, 431–438 (1967).

239. Levine, R. R., *Pharmacology: Drug Actions and Reactions*, Little, Brown, Boston, 1973.

240. Lin, W. and E. E. Bittar, Some observations on caffeine-induced contracture of barnacle muscle fibres, *Life Sci.*, **15,** 1611–1619 (1974).

241. Little, J. A., H. M. Shanoff, A. Csima, S. E. Redmond, and R. Yano, Diet and serum-lipids in male survivors of myocardial infarction, *Lancet*, **1,** 933–935 (1965).

242. Little, J. A., H. M. Shanoff, A. Csima, and R. Yano, Coffee and serum lipids in coronary heart-disease, *Lancet*, **1,** 732–734 (1966).

243. Loper, R. G., M. L. Kammeier, and H. Hoffman, MMPI characteristics of college freshmen males who later became alcoholics, *J. Abnorm. Psychol.*, **82,** 159–162 (1973).

244. Lown, B., Talk given at the Toronto Academy of Medicine, April 14, 1975.

245. Lown, B., M. Tykocinski, A. Garfein, and P. Brooks, Sleep and ventricular premature beats, *Circulation*, **48,** 691–701 (1973).

246. Makoč, Z. and F. Vorel, Caffeine influence on physical performance of rats evaluated by swimming test, *Act. Nerv. Super.* (*Praha*), **16,** 1–5 (1974).

247. Maletzky, B. M. and J. Klotter, Smoking and alcoholism, *Am. J. Psychiatry*, **131,** 445–447 (1974).

248. Marienfeld, C. J., Cigarette lighting and lung cancer: A new perspective, *Perspect. Biol. Med.*, **18,** 44–57 (1974).

249. Marks, V. and J. F. Kelly, Absorption of caffeine from tea, coffee, and Coca-Cola, *Lancet*, **1**, 827 (1973).

250. Marlatt, G. A., B. Demming, and J. B. Reid, Loss of control drinking in alcoholics, *J. Abnorm. Psychol.*, **81**, 233–241 (1973).

251. Marriott, A. S., The effects of amphetamine, caffeine and methylphenidate on the locomotor activity of rats in an unfamiliar environment, *Int. J. Neuropharmacol.*, **7**, 487–491 (1968).

252. Martinek, R. G. and W. Wolman, Xanthines, tannins, and sodium in coffee, tea, and cocoa, *J.A.M.A.*, **158**, 1030–1031 (1955).

253. Matsuda, K., Experimental studies on the effective procedure to inhibit the development of tolerance to and dependence on morphine, *Arzneim.-Forsch.*, **20**, 1596–1604 (1970).

254. Mau, G. Nahrungs- und Genussmittelkonsum in der Schwangerschaft und seine Auswirkungen auf perinatale Sterblichkeit, Frühgeburtlichkeit und andere perinatale Faktoren, *Mschr. Kinderheilk*, **122**, 539–540 (1974).

255. Mau, G. and P. Netter, Kaffee- und Alkoholkonsum—Risikofaktoren in der Schwangerschaft, *Geburtsh. Frauenheilk.*, **34**, 1018–1022 (1974).

256. Maugh, III, T. H. Coffee and myocardial infarction, *Am. Heart J.*, **88**, 672–673 (1974).

257. McAfee, D. A., M. Schorderet, and P. Greengard, Adenosine 3′,5′-monophosphate in nervous tissue: Increase associated with synaptic transmission, *Science*, **171**, 1156–1158 (1971).

258. McMillan, D. E., Effects of narcotics and narcotic antagonists on operant behavior, in *Narcotic Antagonists* (*Advances in Biochemical Psychopharmacology, Vol. 8*), M. C. Brande, L. S. Harris, E. L. May, J. P. Smith, and J. E. Villareal (Eds.), Raven Press, New York, 1973, pp. 345–359.

258a. Mechner, F. and M. Latranyi, Behavioral effects of caffeine, methamphetamine, and methylphenidate in the rat, *J. Exp. Anal. Behav.*, **6**, 331–342 (1963).

259. Medek, A., J. Hrbek, J. Navrátil, and S. Komenda, The effect of chlorprothixene and caffeine on the conditioned alimentary motor reflexes in cats, *Act. Nerv. Super.* (*Praha*), **13**, 210–211 (1971).

260. Medvei, V. C., Some notes on the pharmacology of caffeine, *J. Int. Med. Res.*, **2**, 359–365 (1974).

261. Miller, D. S., M. J. Stock, and J. A. Stuart, Effects of caffeine and carnitine on the oxygen consumption of fed and fasted subjects, *Proc. Nutr. Soc.*, **33**, 28A–29A (1974).

262. Misirlioglu, Y. I., Coffee drinking and acute myocardial infarction, *Lancet*, **1**, 46 (1973).

263. Mitchell, V. E., S. Ross, and P. M. Hurst, Drugs and placebos: Effects of caffeine on cognitive performance, *Psychol. Rep.*, **35**, 875–883 (1974).

264. Mitoma, C., T. J. Sorich, II, and S. E. Neubauer, The effect of caffeine on drug metabolism, *Life Sci.*, **7**, 145–151 (1968).

265. Molde, D. A., Diagnosing caffeinism, *Am. J. Psychiatry*, **132**, 202 (1975).

266. Morgan, R. W. and M. G. Jain, Bladder cancer: Smoking, beverages and artificial sweeteners, *Can. Med. Assoc. J.*, **3**, 1067–1070 (1974).

267. Morrison, C. F., The effects of nicotine on punished behaviour, *Psychopharmacologia*, **14**, 221–232 (1969).

268. Morton, B. and T. S. K. Chang, The effect of fluid from the cauda epididymidis, serum components and caffeine upon the survival of diluted epididymal hamster spermatozoa, *J. Reprod. Fertil.*, **35**, 255–263 (1973).

269. Moulds, R. F. W. and M. A. Denborough, A study of the action of caffeine, halothane, potassium chloride and procaine on normal human skeletal muscle, *Clin. Exp. Pharmacol. Physiol.*, **1,** 197–209 (1974).

270. Mozdzierz, G. J., F. J. Macchitelli, and T. J. Lottman, Personality correlates of coffee consumption in an alcoholic population, *Psychol. Rep.*, **32,** 550 (1973).

271. Mudge, G. H., Diuretics and other agents employed in the mobilization of edema fluid, in *The Pharmacological Basis of Therapeutics,* 4th Ed., L. S. Goodman and A. Gilman (Eds.), Macmillan, New York, 1970, pp. 839–873.

272. Muller, P. J. and J. Vernikos-Danellis, Effect of environmental temperature on the toxicity of caffeine and dextroamphetamine in mice, *J. Pharmacol. Exp. Ther.*, **171,** 153–158 (1970).

273. Müller, W., E. Haase, K. Wedekind, and R. Niedlich, Das Verhalten des EOG nach Kaffeegenuss, *Klin. Mbl. Augenheilk.*, **162,** 379–383 (1973).

274. Mulvihill, J. J., Caffeine as teratogen and mutagen, *Teratology,* **8,** 69–72 (1973).

275. Murari, R., S. Natrajan, T. R. Seshadri, and A. S. Ramaswamy, Barbiturate induced sleeping time in mice by tea polyphenols, *Curr. Sci.*, **42,** 540–541 (1973).

275a. Murray, R. M., Dependence on analgesics in analgesic nephropathy, *Br. J. Addict.* **68,** 265–272 (1973).

276. Nagy, M., Caffeine content of beverages and chocolate, *J.A.M.A.*, **229,** 337 (1974).

277. Nash, H., Psychological effects and alcohol-antagonizing properties of caffeine, *Q. J. Stud. Alcohol,* **27,** 727–734 (1966).

278. Nasu, T., and N. Urakawa, Effect of caffeine on contractile activity and calcium movement in guinea pig taenia coli, *Jpn. J. Pharmacol.*, **24,** 543–550 (1974).

279. Nayler, W. G., Effect of inotropic agents on canine trabecular muscle rendered highly permeable to calcium, *Am. J. Physiol.*, **225,** 918–924 (1973).

280. Nichols, A. B., Coffee drinking and acute myocardial infarction, *Lancet,* **1,** 480–481 (1973).

281. *Nutrition: A National Priority,* Report by Nutrition Canada to the Department of National Health and Welfare, Information Canada, Ottawa, 1973.

282. Oberman, Z., A. Harell, M. Herzberg, E. Hoerer, H. Jaskolka, and L. Laurian, Changes in plasma cortisol, glucose and free fatty acids after caffeine ingestion in obese women, *Israel J. Med. Sci.*, **11,** 33–36 (1975).

283. Ohba, M., Effects of caffeine on tension development in dog papillary muscle under voltage clamp, *Jpn. J. Physiol.*, **23,** 47–58 (1973).

284. Oldendorf, W. H., Brain uptake of metabolites and drugs following carotid arterial injections, *Trans. Am. Neurol. Assoc.*, **96,** 46–48 (1971).

285. Onodera, K., Effect of caffeine on the neuromuscular junction of the frog, and its relation to external calcium concentration, *Jpn. J. Physiol.*, **23,** 587–597 (1963).

286. Ortmans, H., and K. Eisenberg, Einfluss von coffein auf die Blutlipidwerte bei Leberkranken, *Z. Ernaehrungswiss.*, **13,** 43–58, (1974).

287. Orzack, M. H., C. L. Taylor, and C. Kornetsky, A research report on the anti-fatigue effects of magnesium pemoline, *Psychopharmacologia,* **13,** 413–417 (1968).

288. Ostertag, W. E., E. Duisberg, and M. Stürmann, The mutagenic activity of caffeine in man, *Mutat. Res.*, **2,** 293–296 (1965).

289. Overton, D. A., State-dependent learning produced by addicting drugs, in *Opiate Addiction: Origins and Treatment,* S. Fisher and A. M. Freedman (Eds.), Winston, Washington, D.C., 1973, pp. 61–75.

290. Paalzow, G. and L. Paalzow, Effects of caffeine and theophylline on nociceptive stimulation in the rat, *Acta Pharmacol. Toxicol.*, **32,** 22–32 (1973).

291. Paffenbarger, R. S., Jr., A. L. Wing, and R. T. Hyde, Coffee, cigarettes and peptic ulcer, *N. Engl. J. Med.*, **290,** 1091 (1974).

292. Pagala, M. K. D. Inhibition of caffeine contractures by eserine, *Am. J. Physiol.*, **226,** 1209–1211 (1974).

293. Palotas, G., Coffee and myocardial infarction, *N. Engl. J. Med.*, **289,** 979 (1973).

294. Pan-American Coffee Bureau, *Coffee Drinking in Canada*, New York, 1971.

295. Pan-American Coffee Bureau, *Annual Coffee Statistics*, No. 36. New York, 1972.

296. Paré, W., The effect of caffeine and seconal on a visual discrimination task, *J. Comp. Physiol. Psychol.*, **54,** 506–509 (1961).

297. Parish, R. F., C. Frick, A. B. Richards, and R. B. Forney, Human caffeine fatality, *Toxicol. Appl. Pharmacol.*, **7,** 494 (1965).

298. Paroli, E., Psychopharmacological aspects of coffee and of caffeine, *Minerva Med.*, **63,** 3319–3323 (1972).

299. Paul, O., Stimulants and coronaries, *Postgrad. Med.*, **44,** 196–199 (1968).

300. Paul, O., M. H. Lepper, W. H. Phelan, G. W. Dupertuis, A. MacMillan, H. McKean, and H. Park, A longitudinal study of coronary heart disease, *Circulation*, **28,** 20–31 (1963).

301. Paul, O., A. MacMillan, H. McKean, and H. Park, Sucrose intake and coronary heart-disease, *Lancet*, **2,** 1049–1051 (1968).

302. Pavlov, I. P., *Lectures on Conditioned Reflexes, Vol. 1*, Trans. by W. H. Gantt, International Publishers, New York, 1928.

303. Pawan, G. L. S., Alcohol metabolism in man: Acute effects of physical exercise, caffeine, fructose, and glucose on the rate of ethanol metabolism, *Biochem. J.*, **106,** 19P (1968).

303a. Perkins, R. and M. H. Williams, Effect of caffeine on the maximum muscular endurance of females, *Med. Sci. Sports* **7,** 221–224 (1974).

304. Pernanen, K., Validity of survey data on alcohol use, in *Research Advances in Alcohol and Drug Problems, Vol. 1*, R. J. Gibbins, Y. Israel, H. Kalant, R. E. Popham, W. Schmidt, and R. J. Smart (Eds.), Wiley New York, 1974, 355–374.

305. Peters, J. M., Caffeine toxicity in starved rats, *Toxicol. Appl. Pharmacol.*, **9,** 390–397 (1966).

306. Peters, J. M., Caffeine-induced hemorrhagic automutilation, *Arch. Int. Pharmacodyn.*, **169,** 139–146 (1967).

307. Peters, J. M., Factors affecting caffeine toxicity: A review of the literature, *J. Clin. Pharmacol.*, **7,** 131–141 (1967).

308. Pfeiffer, C. J. and G. H. Gass, Caffeine-induced ulcerogenesis in the rat, *Can. J. Biochem. Physiol.*, **40,** 1473–1476 (1962).

309. Pickens, R. and R. A. Meisch, Behavioral aspects of drug dependence, *Minn. Med.*, **3,** 183–186 (1973).

310. Pickens, R. and T. Thompson, Cocaine-reinforced behavior in rats: Effects of reinforcement magnitude and fixed-ratio size, *J. Pharmacol. Exp. Ther.*, **161,** 122–129 (1968).

311. Pickens, R. and T. Thompson, Characteristics of stimulant drug reinforcement, in *Stimulus Properties of Drugs*, T. Thompson and R. Pickens (Eds.), Appleton-Century-Crofts, New York, 1971, pp. 177–192.

312. Pilcher, J. D., Alcohol and caffein: A study of antagonism and synergism, *J. Pharmacol. Exp. Ther.*, **3,** 267–298 (1911).

313. Polonovski, M., E. Donzelot, S. Briskas, and T. Doliopoulos, The comparative effects of coffee and soluble extracts of coffee on normal persons and on cardiacs, *Cardiologia,* **21,** 809–816 (1952).

314. Popopava, E. N., K. S. Rayevskiy, G. N. Krivitskaya, T. S. Matveyeva, and Y. P. Gorschechnikova, The structure of neurons and interneuronal links in the brain of rats under the influence of caffeine and phenamine, *Farmak. Toks.*, **34,** 515–520 (1971), [As described in W. H. Fitzpatrick (Ed.), *Soviet Research in Pharmacology and Toxicology 1963–1972,* U.S. Department of Health, Education and Welfare (DHEW Publication No. NIH 75-696), Washington, 1974.]

314.a Portugal-Alvarez, J., A. Zamarrón, J. Yangüela, C. Perezagua, and A. Velasco, Lipolysis induced by coffee and tobacco: Its modification by insulin, *J. Pharm. Pharmacol.*, **25,** 668–669 (1973).

315. Poston, R. N., Coffee drinking and acute myocardial infarction, *Lancet,* **1,** 45–46 (1973).

316. Raab, W. P., Renal enzyme excretion following ingestion of salicylates, increased by caffeine, *Helv. Med. Acta,* **35,** 290–295 (1969).

317. Rajapakse, D. A., Coffee drinking and acute myocardial infarction, *Lancet,* **1,** 313–314 (1973).

318. Rao, G. S., K. L. Khanna, and H. H. Cornish, Identification of two new metabolites of caffeine in the rat urine, *Experientia,* **29,** 953–955 (1973).

319. Ray, O. S., *Drugs, Society and Human Behavior,* Mosby, St. Louis, 1972.

320. Read, G. W., W. Cutting, and A. Furst, Comparison of excited phases after sedatives and tranquilizers, *Psychopharmacologia,* **1,** 346–350, (1960).

321. Regina, E. G., G. M. Smith, C. G. Keiper, and R. K. McKelvey, Effects of caffeine on alertness in simulated automobile driving, *J. Appl. Psychol.*, **59,** 483–489 (1974).

322. Register, U. D., S. R. Marsh, C. T. Thurston, B. J. Fields, M. C. Horning, M. G. Hardinge, and A. Sanchez, Influence of nutrients on intake of alcohol, *J. Am. Diet. Assoc.*, **61,** 159–162 (1972).

323. Reimann, H. A. Caffeinism: A cause of long-continued, low-grade fever, *J.A.M.A.*, **202,** 1105–1106 (1967).

324. Richter, C. P., Total self-regulatory functions in animals and human beings, *Harvey Lect.*, **38,** 36–103 (1943).

325. Ritchie, J. M., Central nervous stimulants. II. The xanthines, in *The Phamacological Basis of Therapeutics,* 4th ed., L. S. Goodman and A. Gilman (Eds.), Macmillan, New York, 1970, pp. 358–370.

326. Ross, B. D., Caffeine and fluid retention, *J.A.M.A.*, **218,** 596 (1971).

327. Roth, J. L. A., Role of drugs in production of gastroduodenal ulcer, *J.A.M.A.*, **187,** 418–422 (1964).

328. Roth, J. A. and A. C. Ivy, Caffeine and "peptic" ulcer, *Gastroenterology,* **7,** 576–582 (1946).

329. Roth, J. A., A. C. Ivy, and A. J. Atkinson, Caffeine and "peptic" ulcer: Relation of caffeine and caffeine-containing beverages to the pathogenesis, diagnosis and management of "peptic" ulcer, *J.A.M.A.*, **126,** 814–820 (1944).

330. Rothwell, K., Dose-related inhibition of chemical carcinogenesis in mouse skin by caffeine, *Nature,* **252,** 69–70 (1974).

331. Roussinov, K. S. and D. I. Yonkov, Comparative study of the influence of caffeine and theophylline on the learning and memory of albino rats, *Dokl Bolgarskoi Academii Nauk*, **27,** 1605–1608 (1974).

332. Routh, J. I., N. A. Shane, E. G. Arredondo, and W. D. Paul, Determination of caffeine in serum and urine, *Clin. Chem.*, **15,** 661–668 (1969).

333. Sahakian, B. J., T. W. Robbins, M. J. Morgan, and S. D. Iverson, The effects of psychomotor stimulants on stereotypy and locomotor activity in socially-deprived and control rats, *Brain Res.*, **84,** 195–205 (1975).

334. Salans, L. B., Cellularity of adipose tissue, in *Treatment and Management of Obesity*, G. A. Bray and J. E. Bethune (Eds.), Harper and Row, Hagerstown, Md., 1974, pp. 17–27.

335. Saletu, B., M. Allen, and T. M. Itil, The effect of Coca-Cola, caffeine, anti-depressants, and chlorpromazine on objective and subjective sleep parameters, *Pharmakopsychiat. Neuropsychopharmakol.*, **254,** 307–321 (1974).

336. Sakata, T. and H. Fuchimoto, Further aspects of aggressive behavior induced by sustained high dose of theophylline in rats, *Jpn. J. Pharmacol.*, **23,** 787–792 (1973).

337. Sakata, T. and H. Fuchimoto, Stereotyped and aggressive behavior induced by sustained high dose of theophylline in rats, *Jpn. J. Pharmacol.*, **23,** 781–785 (1973).

338. Sandberg, H., L. J. Feinberg, O. DeCastro, and S. Bellet, The effect of caffeine on glucose tolerance tests in diabetics, *J.A.M.A.*, **208,** 1482 (1969).

339. Sant'Ambrogio, G., P. Mognoni, and L. Ventrella, Plasma levels of caffeine after oral, intramuscular and intravenous administration, *Arch. Int. Pharmacodyn.*, **150,** 259–263 (1964).

340. Satinder, K. P., Genotype-dependent effects of *d*-amphetamine sulphate and caffeine on escape-avoidance behavior of rats, *J. Comp. Physiol. Psychol.*, **76,** 359–364 (1971).

341. Sattin, A., Increase in the content of adenosine 3′,5′-monophosphate in mouse forebrain during seizures and prevention of the increase by methylxanthines, *J. Neurochem.*, **18,** 1087–1096 (1971).

342. Schaefer, O., P. M. Crockford, and B. Romanowski, Normalization effect of preceding protein meals on "diabetic" oral glucose tolerance in Eskimos, *Can. Med. Assoc. J.*, **107,** 733–738 (1972).

343. Schaff, G., M. T. Schwertz, and G. Marbach, Influence de l'alcool et de la caféine sur la motilité spontanée, la fréquence cardiaque, la fréquence respiratoire, et al température rectale au cours du sommeil, *J. Physiol.* (*Paris*), **54,** 411–412 (1962).

344. Schechter, M. D., Effect of propranolol, *d*-amphetamine and caffeine on ethanol as a discriminative cue, *Eur. J. Pharmacol.*, **29,** 52–57 (1974).

345. Schmidt, G. and R. Schoyerer, Zum Nachweis von Coffein und sein Metaboliten im Harn, *Deut. Z. Gesamte Gerichtl. Med.*, **57,** 402–409 (1966).

346. Schnackenberg, R. C. Caffeine as a substitute for Schedule II stimulants in hyperkinetic children, *Am. J. Psychiatry*, **130,** 796–798 (1973).

347. Schoenfeld, C., R. D. Amelar, and L. Dubin, Stimulation of ejaculated human spermatozoa by caffeine, *Fertil. Steril.*, **26,** 158–161 (1975).

348. Seakins, J. W. T., Coffee drinking and ischaemic heart-disease, *Lancet*, **1,** 666 (1973).

349. Segall, J. J., Coffee drinking and acute myocardial infarction, *Lancet*, **1,** 46 (1973).

350. Shennan, D. H., Renal carcinoma and coffee consumption in 16 countries, *Br. J. Cancer*, **28,** 473–474 (1973).

351. Siegers, C. -P., Effects of caffeine on the absorption and analgesic efficacy of paracetamol in rats, *Pharmacology*, **10**, 19–27 (1973).

352. Siegers, C. -P., O. Strubelt, and G. Back, Inhibition by caffeine of ethanol absorption in rats, *Eur. J. Pharmacol.*, **20**, 181–187 (1972).

353. Silver, W., Insomnia, tachycardia, and cola drinks, *Pediatrics*, **47**, 635 (1971).

353a. Simon, D., S. Yen, and P. Cole, Coffee drinking and cancer of the lower urinary tract, *J. Natl. Canc. Inst.* **54**, 587–591 (1975).

354. Sinclair, H. M. and D. F. Hollingsworth, *Hutchinson's Food and the Principles of Nutrition*, 12th Ed., Edward Arnold, London, 1969.

354a. Sivetz, M., *Coffee: Origin and use*. Coffee Publications, Corvallis, Oregon, 1974.

355. Skinner, B. F. and W. T. Heron, Effects of caffeine and benzedrine upon conditioning and extinction, *Psychol. Rec.*, **1**, 340–346 (1937).

356. Smith, R. L. and J. A. Timbrell, Factors affecting the metabolism of phenacetin. II. Effect of aspirin, caffeine, codeine, ethanol and phenobarbital on the metabolism of [*acetyl*-^{14}C]-phenacetin in the rat, *Xenobiotica*, **4**, 503–508 (1974).

357. Snider, S. R. and B. Waldeck, Increased synthesis of adrenomedullary catecholamines induced by caffeine and theophylline, *Naunyn Schmiedebergs Arch. Pharmacol.*, **281**, 257–260 (1974).

358. Somorin, O., Caffeine distribution in *C. acuminata, T. cacao* and *C. arabica*, *J. Food Sci.*, **39**, 1055–1056 (1974).

359. Stapenau, J. R., C. R. Creveling, and J. Daly, The "pink spot", 3,4-dimethoxyphenylethylamine, common tea, and schizophrenia, *Am. J. Psychiatry*, **127**, 611–616 (1970).

360. State of California Office of Alcohol Program Management, *California Alcohol Data 1973*, Sacramento, 1974.

361. Stern, J. A. and D. G. McDonald, Physiological correlates of mental disease, *Ann. Rev. Psychol.*, **16**, 225–264 (1965).

362. Stinnette, M. J. and W. Isaac, Behavioral effects of *d*-amphetamine and caffeine in the squirrel monkey, *Eur. J. Pharmacol.*, **30**, 268–271 (1975).

363. Stowe, C. M. and G. L. Plaa, Extrarenal excretion of drugs and chemicals, *Ann. Rev. Pharmacol.*, **8**, 337–356 (1968).

364. Stradomsky, N., Untersuchungen über Schlafbewegungen nach coffeinhaltigem und coffeinfreiem Bohnenkaffee, *Med. Klin.*, **65**, 1372–1376 (1970).

365. Straits, B. C. and L. Sechrest, Further support of some findings about the characteristics of smokers and non-smokers, *J. Consult. Psychol.*, **27**, 282 (1963).

366. Stripling, J. S. and H. P. Alpern, Nicotine and caffeine: Disruption of long-term store of memory and proactive facilitation of learning in mice, *Psychopharmacologia*, **38**, 187–200 (1974).

367. Strömberg, U. and B. Waldeck, Behavioural and biochemical interaction between caffeine and L-dopa, *J. Pharm. Pharmacol.*, **25**, 302–308 (1973).

368. Strömberg, U. and B. Waldeck, Further studies on the behavioural and biochemical interaction between caffeine and L-dopa, *J. Neural Transm.*, **34**, 241–252 (1973).

369. Sroufe, L. A. and M. A. Stewart, Treating problem children with stimulant drugs, *N. Engl. J. Med.*, **289**, 407–413 (1973).

370. Strubelt, O., C. -P. Siegers, H. Breining, and J. Steffen, Tierexperimentelle Untersuch-

ungen zur chronischen Toxizität von Kaffee und Coffein, *Z. Ernährungswiss.*, **12,** 252–260 (1973).

371. Studlar, M., Über den Einfluss von Coffein auf den Fett- und Kohlenhydrat-stoffwechsel des Menschen, *Z. Ernährungswiss.*, **12,** 109–120 (1973).

372. Šulc, J., G. Brožek, and J. Cmíral, Neurophysiological effects of small doses of caffeine in man, *Act. Nerv. Super. (Praha)*, **16,** 217–218 (1974).

373. Sunano, S. and E. Miyazaki, Effects of caffeine on electrical and mechanical activities of guinea pig taenia coli, *Am. J. Physiol.* **225,** 335–339 (1973).

374. Sutherland, E. W., A. Robison, and R. W. Butcher, Some aspects of the biological role of adenosine 3′,5′-monophosphate (cyclic AMP), *Circulation*, **37,** 279–306 (1968).

375. Suzuki, T. and E. Takahashi, Biosynthesis of caffeine by tea-leaf extracts, *Biochem. J.*, **146,** 87–96 (1975).

376. Tainter, M. L., Effects of certain analeptic drugs on spontaneous running activity of the white rat, *J. Comp. Physiol. Psychol.*, **36,** 143–155 (1943).

377. Takahashi, E., Coffee consumption and mortality for prostate cancer, *Tohoku J. Exp. Med.*, **82,** 218–223 (1964).

378. Takemori, A. E., Biochemistry of drug dependence, *Ann. Rev. Biochem.*, **43,** 15–33 (1974).

379. Thayer, P. S. and C. J. Kensler, Genetic tests in mice of caffeine alone and in combination with mutagens, *Toxicol. Appl. Pharmacol.*, **25,** 157–168 (1973).

380. Thayer, P. S. and C. J. Kensler, Exposure of four generations of mice to caffeine in drinking water, *Toxicol. Appl. Pharmacol.*, **25,** 169–179 (1973).

381. Thiel, H. G., D. Parker, and T. A. Bruce, Stress factors and the risk of myocardial infarction, *J. Psychosom. Res.*, **17,** 43–57 (1973).

382. Thomas, B. H., W. Zeitz, and B. B. Coldwell, Effect of acetylsalicylic acid, caffeine, and codeine on metabolism of phenacetin in the rat, *Toxicol. Appl. Pharmacol.*, **30,** 210–220 (1974).

383. Thomas, C. B. The relationship of smoking and habits of nervous tension, in *Smoking Behavior: Motives and Incentives*, W. L. Dunn (Ed.), Winston, New York, 1973, pp. 157–170.

384. Thompson, T. and R. Pickens (Eds.), *Stimulus Properties of Drugs*, Appleton-Century-Crofts, New York, 1971.

385. Thorpe, W. R., Some effects of caffeine and quinidine on sarcoplasmic reticulum of skeletal and cardiac muscle, *Can. J. Physiol. Pharmacol.*, **51,** 499–503 (1973).

386. Thorpe, W. R. and P. Seeman, The site of action of caffeine and procaine in skeletal muscle, *J. Pharmacol. Exp. Ther.*, **179,** 324–330 (1971).

387. Trosko, J. E. and H. Y. Chu, Inhibition of repair of UV-damaged DNA by caffeine and mutation induction in Chinese hamster cells, *Chem. Biol. Interact.*, **6,** 317–332 (1973).

388. Truitt, E. B., Jr., The xanthines, in *Drill's Pharmacology in Medicine*, 4th Ed., J. R. DiPalma (Ed.), McGraw-Hill, New York, 1971, 533–556.

389. Ts'o, P. O. P., G. K. Helmkamp, and C. Sander, Interaction of nucleosides and related compounds with nucleic acids as indicated by the change of helix-coil transition temperature, *Proc. Natl. Acad. Sci. U.S.A.*, **48,** 686–697 (1962).

390. Ulett, G. A. and S. G. Perry, Cytotoxic testing and leucocyte increase as an index to food sensitivity. II. Coffee and tobacco, *Annals Allerg.*, **34,** 150–160 (1975).

391. U.S. Public Health Service, *The Health Consequences of Smoking*, No. 1696, Department of Health, Education and Welfare, Washington, 1964.

392. Valzelli, L. and S. Bernasconi, Behavioral and neurochemical effects of caffeine in normal and aggressive mice, *Pharmacol. Biochem. Behav.*, **1,** 251–254 (1973).

393. Vernikos-Danellis, J. and C. G. Harris, III, The effects of in vitro and in vivo caffeine, theophylline, and hydrocortisone on the phosphodiesterase activity of the pituitary, median eminence, heart, and cerebral cortex of the rat, *Proc. Soc. Exp. Biol. Med.*, **128,** 1016–1021 (1968).

394. Vitiello, M. V. and S. C. Woods, Caffeine: Preferential consumption by rats, *Pharmacol. Biochem. Behav.*, **3,** 147–149 (1975).

395. Vojtěchovský, M., A survey on consumption of psychotropic drugs among university students, *Act. Nerv. Super.* (*Praha*), **14,** 139–140 (1972).

396. Vojtěchovský, M. and V. Šafratová, Comparative study of caffeine with other stimulants in university students, *Act. Nerv. Super.* (*Praha*), **14,** 138–139 (1972).

397. Waldeck, B., Ethanol and caffeine: A complex interaction with respect to locomotor activity and central catecholamines, *Psychopharmacologia*, **36,** 209–220 (1974).

398. Waldeck, B., Modification of caffeine-induced locomotor stimulation by a cholinergic mechanism, *J. Neural Transm.*, **35,** 197–205 (1974).

399. Waldeck, B., On the interaction between caffeine and barbiturates with respect to locomotor activity and brain catecholamines, *Acta Pharmacol. Toxicol.*, **36,** 172–180 (1975).

400. Walker, W. J., Coronary mortality—What is going on? *J.A.M.A.*, **227,** 1045–1046 (1974).

401. Walker, W. J. and G. Gregoratos, Myocardial infarction in young men, *Am. J. Cardiol.*, **19,** 339–343 (1967).

402. Warren, R. N., Metabolism of xanthine alkaloids in man. *J. Chromatogr.*, **40,** 468–469 (1969).

403. Weathersbee, P. S., R. L. Ax, and J. R. Lodge, Caffeine-mediated changes of sex ratio in Chinese hamsters, *Cricetulus griseus*. *J. Reprod. Fertil.*, **43,** 141–143 (1975).

404. Weiss, B. and V. G. Laties, Enhancement of human performance by caffeine and the amphetamines, *Pharmacol. Rev.*, **14,** 1–36 (1962).

405. Wenzel, D. G. and C. O. Rutledge, Effects of centrally-acting drugs on human motor and psychomotor performance, *J. Pharm. Sci.*, **51,** 631–644 (1962).

406. WHO Expert Committee on Drug Dependence, *Sixteenth Report*, 1969.

407. Williams, M. H., *Drugs and Athletic Performance*, Charles C Thomas, Springfield, Ill., 1974.

408. Wilson, D. F., Effects of caffeine on neuromuscular transmission in the rat, *Am. J. Physiol.*, **225,** 862–865 (1973).

409. Wolff, J. and S. Varrone, The methyl xanthines—A new class of goitrogens, *Endocrinology*, **85,** 410–414 (1969).

410. Wolman, W., Instant and decaffeinated coffee, *J.A.M.A.*, **159,** 250 (1955).

411. Winsor, A. L. and E. I. Strongin, A study of the development of tolerance for caffeinated beverages, *J. Exp. Psychol.*, **16,** 725–734 (1933).

412. Wynder, E. L., L. S. Covey, and K. Mabuchi, Current smoking habits by selected background variables: Their effect on future disease trends, *Am. J. Epidemiol.*, **100,** 168–177 (1974).

413. Yanagita, T., K. Ando, S. Takahashi, and K. Ishida, Self-administration of barbiturates, alcohol (intragastric) and CNS stimulants (intravenous) in monkeys. Paper presented at the 31st meeting of the Committee on Problems of Drug Dependence, NAS-NRC, 1969.

414. Young, W., R. L. Hotovec, and A. G. Romero, Tea and atherosclerosis, *Nature*, **216,** 1015–1016 (1967).

415. Yudkin, J., Coffee drinking and acute myocardial infarction, *Lancet*, **1,** 211 (1973).

416. Yudkin, J. and J. Morland, Sugar intake and myocardial infarction, *Am. J. Clin. Nutr.*, **20,** 503–506 (1967).

417. Yudkin, J. and J. Roddy, Levels of dietary sucrose in patients with occlusive atherosclerotic disease, *Lancet*, **2,** 6–8 (1964).

418. Zajdela, F. and R. Latarjet, Effet inhibiteur de la caféine sur l'induction de cancers cutanés par les rayons ultraviolets chez la souris, *C. R. Acad. Sci. Paris*, **277,** 1073–1076 (1973).

419. Zeitlin, B. R., Coffee and bladder cancer, *Lancet*, **1,** 1066 (1972).

420. Zimbardo, P. G. and H. Barry III, Effect of caffeine and chlorpromazine on the sexual behavior of male rats, *Science*, **127,** 84–85 (1958).

CHAPTER THREE

PSYCHIATRIC SYNDROMES INDUCED BY NONMEDICAL USE OF DRUGS

EVERETT H. ELLINWOOD, Jr., *Behavioral Neuropharmacology Section, Department of Psychiatry, Duke University Medical Center, Durham, North Carolina*

AND

WILLIAM M. PETRIE, *National Institute of Mental Health, Rockville, Maryland*

1. INTRODUCTION

In the recent era of heavy nonmedical drug use, clinicians have observed a number of psychiatric states which they felt were related to the use of drugs. An awesome number of clinical and research efforts have been devoted to clarifying this relationship. Psychiatrists and psychologists have been asked to treat and to understand (often in that order) a wide variety of responses, which in turn have contributed to our basic notions concerning the evolution and emergence of pathologic behavior. In this review, we will select only reports we feel are critical and/or appropriate to our main perspective. Unfortunately, the main body of clinical reports often provides inadequate quantification of data. Secondly, the clinical syndromes evolve in "uncontrolled" natural environment. The nature of the data from most reports did not lend itself to the reviewer's objective of summarizing quantitative measures and isolating specific mechanisms or effects. The model presented in this report is nothing more than a perspective for viewing the broad range of psychiatric clinical material.

The drugs considered here will be those most directly associated with psychiatric disturbances: psychotomimetics, cannabis, solvents, anticholinergics, and stimulants. We have omitted drugs (barbiturates, narcotics, alcohol, caffeine) for which our approach has less relevance. Similarly, we will not attempt to cover the addiction syndromes. A concept we will emphasize repeatedly is that drug-associated psychiatric states are *not* the results of the actions of drugs so much as the reactions of individuals to drugs in drug-taking situations.

One major approach in this review is that chronic and acute amphetamine intoxication provides a model for examining the evolution of pathologic and particularly psychotic states, as well as certain basic psychopathologic principles. Viewing amphetamine intoxication as a model for psychiatric states associated with use of other drugs has certain advantages. First, amphetamine intoxication is the most clearly understood of all drug-induced conditions. Clinical and experimental evidence combine to give a reasonably complete and consistent picture of amphetamine intoxication. Secondly, in the evolution of amphetamine psychosis, we have the clearest descriptions we know of the phenomenological evolution of psychosis.

Evaluation of the contribution of drug use to the development of psychopathology is difficult for many reasons. Consistent and significant transformation of personality–drug reactions into psychiatric syndromes occurs primarily in the chronically intoxicated state. As with alcohol, the de novo occurrence of significant or lasting pathology from a single intoxication is rather rare. On the other hand, organic, genetic predispositions, and/or unstable personality may provide the basis for seemingly dramatic changes under the influence of any of a number of significant stressful disorganizing circumstances, including single or occasional drug use. In these cases, it is difficult to determine the precise contribution of drug use to the behavior in question. More recently, the highly emotional, political, and cultural milieu of drug use, only now subsiding, has tended to make matters more confusing.

Relative Contribution of Drug Effect and Preexisting Psychopathology

The controversy over the importance of drug effect versus preexisting psychopathology in the production of drug-related psychopathology appears frequently in the literature (66). Two examples illustrate the extremes between which the majority of clinical cases lie. The dextroamphetamine study of Griffith et al. (52) provides an example of the drug as the major effect. In this experiment, nine volunteer subjects for whom psychological prescreening revealed only sociopathic tendencies were given small, frequent doses of oral amphetamine. After only five days of supervised administration, eight of the nine subjects experienced a paranoid psychosis that rapidly abated with drug interruption. Griffith felt sleep deprivation, predrug personality, or drug idiosyncrasies (previously thought crucial in the origin of amphetamine paranoia) to be insufficient as an explanation for the psychosis. (Unfortunately, previous psychosis while on amphetamines may have contributed to a low threshold for effect.) We agree with Griffith that a psychosis appears "highly probable" in response to high-dose amphetamine administration if given long enough to any individual.

On the other end of the spectrum, Glass (48) reports the case of an 18-year-old male who had taken LSD on several occasions preceding hospitalization for self-mutilation. The patient presented with somatic delusions, bizarre, guilt-laden ideation, and antisocial behavior. Glass states that this individual's diagnosis before hospitalization would have been schizophrenia, and that this picture of chronic psychosis was largely unaffected by drug use.

Despite research evidence on both sides of this issue, most clinicians would have only moderate difficulty either evaluating or formulating a treatment plan for each of these cases. In our effort to answer questions by means of sophisticated statistical or experimental techniques, we must not overlook the instructive value of carefully documented case reports.

Assessment of Drug Effect

Of the myriad of conditions and mechanisms that may influence the action of a drug, only a few can be accurately evaluated at this time. Many pharmacologic variables, such as cumulative results of prolonged or repeated use, have been considered only recently as exerting distinct influences on the pattern of drug effects. The build-up of drugs in fatty tissue, as with Δ9THC (103), or the progressive depletion of neurotransmitters or enzyme induction, as with amphetamine (38, 85, 90a, 90b) are difficult to assess, yet they may contribute significantly to the clinical picture. Genetic variation in neuronal reaction to drugs, in metabolism of drugs, or in the metabolism of endogenous neurotransmitters producing sensitivity or resistance to drug effect, is suggested by a number of provocative leads, but there are few hard data that relate directly to reactivity in man. Such phenomena, if demonstrated, could help in further fractionating what is known as "predisposing personality strength or weakness."

Suggestibility has been a factor most often related to nondrug variables, yet there is material to indicate that drugs such as LSD, marijuana, and barbiturates physiologically alter aspects of consciousness to make subjects more amenable to set and setting influences (42). Therapeutic responses have been observed in patients exposed to positive sets, and a relative worsening has been seen in those exposed to negative sets. Drug-induced suggestibility may be one of the main reasons for the incorporation of tryptaminergic drugs, anticholinergics, and hashish in certain subcultural or religious settings. In contrast to both the therapeutic and value-loaded situations, a totally neutral setting might negate an important drug effect (42), which could account in part for differing in drug effects observed on experimental settings versus "natural settings."

In general, although the pharmacologic actions may be accurately assessed, factors such as cumulative effects, genetic and metabolic differences, and suggestibility make the measurement and prediction of drug effects difficult. However, it is generally agreed that, with increasing drug dosage, the pharmacologic effects become more marked and increasingly important, relative to both nonspecific factors and personality variables.

Difficulties in Assessment of Personality

Distinguishing between preexisting psychopathology and drug-induced mental illness, which is intrinsically difficult, is made even more so when studies do not consider possible methodological biases. Perhaps the most important difficulty is the operation of the selection bias in the drug-using population. Drug availability, peer group influences, and both sociocultural and psychiatric influences are factors in determining who uses drugs. As chronic drug abuse develops and psychopathology emerges, additional selection processes occur. Even volunteers for drug studies have been shown to rank considerably higher than nonvolunteer controls in psychiatric pathology (40). Thus, we should recognize that personality differences noted in persons experiencing drug-related pathology reflect the accumulation of drug effects and the drug experience in a person whose personality may have differed from that of nondrug users prior to initiation of drug use. Studies of this nature, then, are useful in understanding the interaction effects of drug use, given certain preexisting traits.

Unfortunately, instead of documenting particular personality characteristics, many studies have resorted to assigning diagnostic labels. Furthermore, diagnostic impressions have been documented to have a relatively low interrater reliability, even under standardized conditions (113). Compounding these difficulties is the large proportion of adolescents in the drug-using population. In this group, there are broad ranges of normal behavior, apathy, lack of goal directedness, sexual acting out, and irritability that may or may not be indicative of pathology and that may or may not be casually related to drug use (66).

Nevertheless, Keeler (71) has provided evidence suggesting that the effects desired by drug users, as well as the chronicity of drug use, are strongly related to personality factors. In addition, the interaction of unstable or fragile personalities in certain settings has often been observed to precipitate the clinical expression of previously latent psychiatric symptomatology (20, 33, 45, 50, 57, 88). On the other hand, Ellinwood was not able to distinguish his amphetamine psychotics from nonpsychotic amphetamine users on the basis of MMPI profiles, although independent clinical impression demonstrated a clear separation. In addition, Griffith's data (52) certainly indicate that a specific psychopathology is not essential for persons to experience psychotic states from amphetamines intoxication.

The assessment of developmental history as a predisposing personality descriptor has been approached by many authors (14, 23, 37, 50, 75). The absence of friends in childhood or in school has repeatly emerged as a correlate to the development of drug-associated illness. Asociality is said to be associated with poorer outcomes and more schizophreniclike states (34, 50, 75).

Although there are many built-in difficulties in assessing the role of personality characteristics in drug-associated psychiatric states, careful observation, scrupulous description of personality characteristics, and careful attention to sample selection will certainly help clarify this area of research.

Other Factors

Set and setting have profound effects on the outcome of drug experiences. In the early 1950s, Pennes (104) administered amytal, pervitin desoxyephedrine, mescaline, and LSD-25 to 55 schizophrenic patients. The variability in the responses surprised Pennes. Although his patients were schizophrenic, his observations were relevant to many drug-use situations. In general, he found it difficult to explain the effects of these very different drugs on a pharmacologic basis alone. Pennes felt that any explanation of the drug effects must consider the following: (*a*) the same drug produced a wide diversity of effects in different subjects; (*b*) different drugs sometimes produced the same effect in a given subject; (*c*) often opposite effects were seen with the same drug in different subjects; (*d*) intensification effects were nearly always exaggerations of the personality structure; (*e*) the subject's psychological reactions formed a part of the reaction, sometimes continuing after the "direct" drug action should have disappeared. Pennes thought that pharmacological mechanisms accounted for only a fraction of the drug effects. Evidence for set effects has come from several sources. Schachter and Singer (117) for example, have shown that in the absence of other cues, normal subjects, dependent upon the experimental setting and instruction variables, attributed the arousing effects of epinephrine to either euphoria or anger.

2. AMPHETAMINE PSYCHOSIS

Chronic amphetamine intoxication often results in a syndrome indistinguishable from paranoid schizophrenia. The syndrome is as reproducible as any psychiatric state resulting from drug use. Delusions of persecution, ideas of reference, visual and auditory hallucinations, changes in body image, hyperreactivity and excitation occur without clouding of consciousness (23, 33, 68).

Clinical

The fixed nature of many delusions, stereotypic compulsive behavior, and a clear sensorium distinguish the amphetamine psychosis from an acute, toxic psychosis.

The presence of primary delusions is of both diagnostic and theoretical importance in the amphetamine psychosis. Slater and Roth (122) describe the primary (or autochthonous) delusion as a *fundamental functional disturbance that can occur in the absence of a distortion of sensory perception, apperception, or intellectual grasp.* The disturbance is one of symbolic meaning; the experience, usually being an immediate one, appears de novo without precursor or explanation, and carries with it an intense sense of conviction. Whereas interpretative delusions occur in most psychoses, primary delusions are more characteristic for schizophrenia (122). In their pristine form, they appear fully developed and are immediately and firmly believed by the patient. In the beginning, they may lack clear, ideational content; and, as Slater and Roth (p. 212) note, trivial observations, such as three chairs in a row or the reflections of sunlight in the street, suddenly have some important significance to the patient, leaving him in a perplexed condition. Some have called this state a delusional mood or delusional awareness (64a). With the delusional awareness, the patient suddenly feels charged with knowledge of incredible importance. Often, there is an unshakable reality and significance that fixes the primary delusion.

The sequence in amphetamine psychosis, as in certain schizophrenias (18, 94), involves early euphoric, pleasant changes in perception, marked by a new and intense interest and significance. At this point, stereotyped behaviors are also reported to appear in the amphetamine-induced process. The perceptual distortions and hallucinations occur either concomitantly, or even long after the next phase of delusional mood (Ellinwood, unpublished observations).

The early amphetamine-induced perceptual and attitudinal changes may provide insight into the early phase of psychosis in general. This initial phase is not well understood or documented in schizophrenia, probably because of its more subtle and extended occurrence over time (18, 94). Changes in sensory input has have been postulated as central to the schizophrenic process (137). Most of the hallucinogenics that we will deal with in this review exert some manner of perceptual change, often dramatic distortions, but only in a few cases, even with repeated experiences does a psychotic breakdown occur. Contrast of the development of hallucinogenic with the amphetamine drug conditions may provide insight into the requisite nature of this psychosis-inducing process.

In amphetamine psychosis, the investment of significance occurs initially as an interest or curiosity not infrequently displayed by repetitious examining, sorting, cleaning, or hoarding. In speed subcultures, this obsessive–compulsivelike behavior has been well-recognized by observers and participants alike. A change in perceptual focus to an emphasis on fine details often occurs, which is reflected in the attentive manipulation or even dismantling of watches, television and radio parts, or small pebbles or beads. Analogous cognitive stereotypies develop as well. Sherlock Holmes, whose signs of cocaine use parallel those of amphetamine use, provides a literary example of "genius for minutiae" (55), an extraordinary ability for discovering and evaluating details in the solution of difficult crimes. His portrayed interest in puzzles and cryptograms, and his suspiciousness are consistent with the change in perceptual focus and attention accompanying stimulant use.

For the amphetamine abuser, the early evolution phase of the primary delusion is usually centered around a pleasurable suspiciousness, as well as the discovery of "true" meaning or significance in previously meaningless details or thoughts (Fig. 1), often with a synthesis of relationships and details into a cohesive pattern. An exorbitant amount of time and energy is devoted to these pursuits, and insights attain the flavor of revelation. One patient described this feeling: "Everything became relative to some truth; a light ray would prove unity; a light ray breaking up would prove why men break up. . . . I suddenly discovered how the world began." (35).

It is at this point that philosophical or detective thought patterns break down and a delusional system with ideas of reference emerges. Elaboration and rationalization strengthen the conviction of the delusional thought. The fixing of the delusions during intoxication often establishes the delusional thought pattern, which then persists long after amphetamine withdrawal. These patterns may be hidden and detected only by careful questioning; but, on readministration of amphetamine, they can return with their former power.

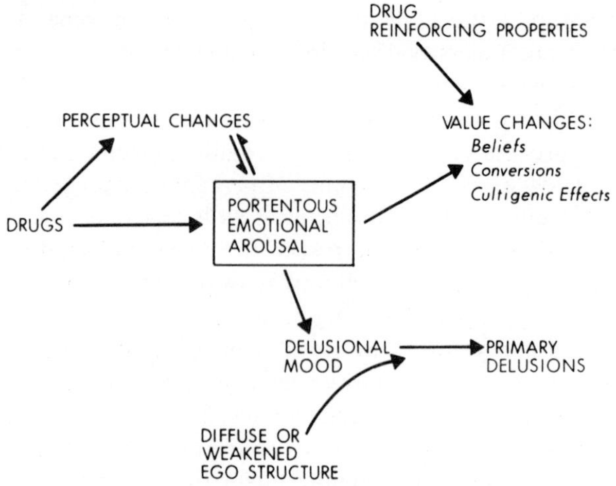

Fig. 1. Drug-induced delusions and value changes.

Subtypes of Amphetamine Reactions

Most amphetamine psychotic reactions in individuals without primordial psychotic tendencies reflect the evolution of psychotic symptomatology over a period of chronic amphetamine intoxication, with the symptoms becoming gradually more manifest. This is the only drug-induced psychopathology in which one clearly sees the development of a paranoid schizophreniclike syndrome with the relatively fixed primary delusions. The major alternative, but less frequent reaction, is the precipitation of a schizophrenic reaction or of delusional or psychotic symptomatology in a patient who has an underlying psychotic state. The well-known ability of amphetamine to enhance and precipitate psychotic symptomatology in borderline individuals has been used diagnostically for over 20 years (Sargant and Slater, 115). Simon and Taube first recognized the ability of methamphetamine to uncover previously hidden paranoid delusions (121). Lehmann (82) reported that, in more withdrawn schizophrenics, amphetamine is associated with aggravation of thought disturbances, delusions, excitement, and aggressive manifestations. Janowsky et al. (64), using acute psychotic individuals, demonstrated an activation of schizophrenic and, to a lesser extent, manic symptoms with the use of intravenous methylphenidate. The dramatic exacerbation of symptoms during the acute phase was not noted following clinical remission. The use of stimulants to precipitate psychosis, especially in borderline individuals, may provide us with a viewpoint for understanding psychotic reactions to other drugs as exaggerations or exacerbations of vulnerable aspects of the individual.

In their initial observation of amphetamine psychosis, Young and Scoville (142) ascribed the syndrome to release of latent paranoid traits. As mentioned previously, borderline, psychotic, and psychopathic individuals have a greater tendency to experiment with and to respond positively to the effects of amphetamine (61, 62); any tabulation of the personality structure of the individuals who develop psychosis needs to take into account this initial selection factor. A tabulation, extracted from reported studies of amphetamine psychosis (33), shows 70% had been diagnosed as sociopathic personality or schizophrenic. That a borderline or psychotic personality was not a prerequisite, however, for the development of amphetamine psychosis has been documented by the careful studies of Griffith et al. (52) and replicated by Angrist and Gershon (4) and Bell (9). Griffith et al. carefully excluded any borderline or psychotic individuals from a group of chronic amphetamine abusers, then reintoxicated the abusers with intravenous amphetamine in doses from 120 mg total given over one day, to 700 mg total infused over five days. Griffith's patients (as had those of Angrist and Gershon and/or Bell) all developed psychotic symptoms, indicating that in experienced amphetamine users, psychosis could be induced in a relatively short period of time. However, for ethical reasons, all these experimenters utilized experienced amphetamine abusers, who probably had previously experienced the amphetamine psychotic symptoms. Certainly, when an amphetamine abuser develops a psychosis on a dose of 80–150 g, in this case it is reasonable to assume that he has experienced an amphetamine psychosis previously, since the usual mean daily dose for a habit is most often above 150 mg per day. In our clinical experience, once the individual has developed the amphetamine psychosis, it is more readily triggered, even by small doses following a period of abstinence. Similar observations have been made by Kramer et al. (81), and Utena (135) has emphasized an increased potential for psychotic reaction to physical and psychological stress, as well as to subsequent exposure to amphetamine.

In animal studies, the reexposure to experimental conditions has caused the animals to reenter discrete aspects of the chronic amphetamine syndrome (e.g., restricted stereotypies) without any drug being given. Situations such as being placed in the experimental cage, or the entrance of the experimenter, have become conditioned stimuli, indicating the importance of conditioning in the drug response. Also, our observations in the amphetamine animal model have demonstrated that the chronic high-dose treatment leads to end-stage behaviors, after which lower doses can retrigger these same behaviors. Even in the nature of the emergence of the psychosis in the laboratory studies indicates a similar process. For example, Bell (9) has described the response of a patient with a history of amphetamine use who was given 120 mg intravenously in an interview setting: "Oh, not this again. I'm starting to get the wrong idea again about people. I feel they are all against me. All the questions in my mind—going through my mind. This is it, all over again." This presaged a short-lived psychosis of two days, which included auditory hallucinations and frankly paranoid delusions. What seems clear to us is that the patient apparently recognized the reprecipitation of her previously manifest delusional ideas in an early stage of the reintoxication, although later she became more overtly psychotic.

In considering the predisposing personality factors and the previous chronic experience with amphetamine, we most certainly do not wish to negate the dose level as a factor in contributing to the psychosis. Certainly, there is much animal data to indicate that there is a reasonable dose–response curve in the induction of abnormal behaviors. Furthermore, the amphetamine dosage is at a significantly higher level in abusers who developed psychosis than in those who do not (34). Thus, amphetamine in moderate to moderately high doses can trigger psychosis in borderline or prepsychotic individuals; chronic high dose amphetamine intoxication induces psychosis even in relatively stable individuals. Finally, it is not unreasonable to question whether other individuals with psychotic manifestations fall somewhere in between these two extreme positions.

Amphetamine Model

Our experience with the antecedent behaviors and attitudes that evolve into amphetamine psychosis has led us to postulate that perseverative, sustained pervasive attitudes and emotions are an integral step in the development of the eventual psychosis. From this portentous, emotionally aroused stage, one most frequently notes the evolution into a delusional mood represented in the hypothetical pathways in Figs. 1 and 2. With more intense delusional moods, one begins to note an increase in delusional experiences leading finally to fixation of delusions, and secondarily elaborating into a delusional system. Conditions leading to a loss of judgment of the observing ego directly influence the concrete expression of the delusional experience. At this point, sleep loss, sedatives, drugs or alcohol can sufficiently reduce critical thinking or judgment to the point that the individual begins to believe or act on the delusions he has previously thought through intensely but has considered to be half truths.

In fact, delusion-based homicide or other violent behaviors can occur at this stage (36). However, this period of previous cognitive elaboration in a

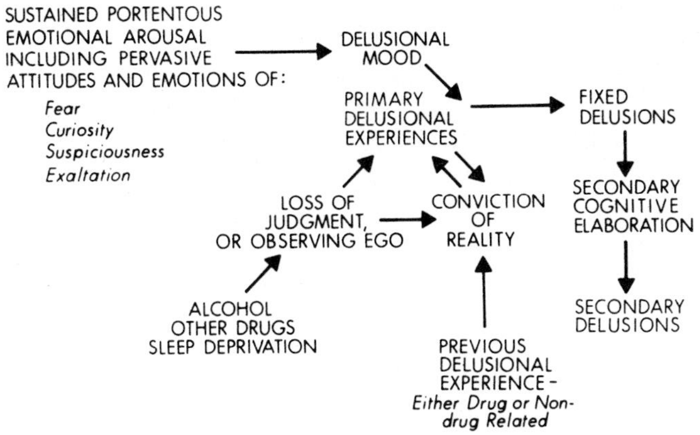

Fig. 2. Primary and secondary delusions induced by drugs.

setting of clear consciousness appears to be a necessary prerequisite; delirious or toxic or sedated states do not induce the more trenchant delusions. We also should mention that individuals who are "loners" and who do not have the support of or reality confrontation from other individuals frequently have difficulty in maintaining a perspective judgment about the delusions (36). This is probably one of the reasons that cohesive subcultural groups appear to have fewer reported instances of paranoid psychosis than individuals in a solitary pattern of amphetamine abuse.

Figure 1 depicts, however, that emotional arousal as an altered state of consciousness may set the stage for belief and value changes, conversions, etc., often within a subculture group (37). Of course, the reinforcing effects of the drug operating within the subcultural value system also enhance the cultigenic effects. More will be said about this later.

Perceptual changes (Fig. 1) are an important part of many psychotomimetic drug experiences. Chapman's (18) classical description of early perceptual change in schizophrenia bears many similarities to drug effects and temporal lobe epilepsy. Most of the schizophrenic patients who experienced this change reported that, for a time, everything around them looked fascinating, with objects standing out vividly in contrast to the background. These initial changes in mental function were experienced as pleasant, and a number of patients at this stage went through a transient period of mild elation. Coincident with this alteration in perception, these patients appeared to regard everything with new significance, and there was a general tendency for their interest to be turned to vague ruminations about meaning and essences, including more specific concerns with religion, psychology, philosophy, art, and literature. However, as the breakdown in visual perception progressed and as the other disturbances in perception and cognition developed, this early reaction changed to one of intense anxiety (18).

Thus, the perceptual changes may figure importantly in certain psychoses, e.g., those induced by sensory over- or underload. They may act by inducing a highly charged emotional arousal (Fig. 1), since they do not appear to be necessary for the induction of all psychotic states.

3. PROTOTYPIC RESPONSES TO ACUTE DRUG USE

One of the major emphases of this review is that individuals may show similar types of reaction to the diverse group of drugs under consideration, including such phenomena as depersonalization, anxiety–panic, depression, and emotional lability. Although there is a commonality of symptoms across drugs, there are certain differences in individual responses to each of these drugs which make particular reaction types more probable. Figure 3 lists the effects of these drugs in single recreational doses in "normal" individuals, and represents the drug effects as abstracted from various reports. The range of these drug effects includes such diverse phenomena as facilitation of concentration and focusing ability by the catecholaminergic drugs to states of clouded consciousness noted in the toxic psychosis induced by anticholinergic drugs and solvents.

Perhaps the main group of drug effects is associated with what has been called the altered state of consciousness (44, 90). These effects include

	TRYPTAMINERGIC	ANTICHOLINERGIC	CATECHOLAMINERGIC	CANNABIS	SOLVENTS
CAPACITY FOR INCREASED CONCENTRATION & FOCUS	O	—	+++	O	O
CLOUDING OF CONSCIOUSNESS	O	++++	O	O	+++
PASSIVITY	+++	+	—	++	+
SUGGESTIBILITY	++++	++	+	+++	++
EUPHORIA	+++	±	+++	++	+
DEPERSONALIZATION	+++	++	±	+	++
PERCEPTUAL CHANGES	++++	+	O	+	+
HALLUCINATIONS – formed, animated	+	+++	O	O	+
HALLUCINATIONS – ass'd with perceptual change	+++	+	O	O	+
FEELING OF SIGNIFICANCE, MEANING	++++	O	++	++	++
RUDIMENTARY DELUSIONS	++	+++	±	–	+
INTERPERSONAL WITHDRAWAL	+	++++	O	+	++

Fig. 3. Frequently observed drug effects of *moderate* dosage in recreational setting.

passivity, suggestibility, euphoria, feelings of significant or portentous meaning, and at times, depersonalization. Freedman (44) has included passivity as a major response to the psychotomimetic drugs, which contributes to the cultigenic as well as induced value changes. Suggestibility is an important constituent of all altered states of consciousness. Ludwig (90) relates numerous instances of suggestibility, as well as increased susceptibility and propensity of persons to uncritically accept and/or automatically respond to specific statements (i.e., commands or instructions of the leader, shaman, demagogue, hypnotist, or psychedelic guide) or nonspecific cues (i.e., cultural or group expectations, expectations for certain types of behavior or feelings). Hypersuggestibility, in Ludwig's view (90), also includes the tendency to misperceive or misinterpret various external stimuli or situations on the basis of inner fears or wishes. Fisher (42) has indicated that suggestibility is a specific or primary effect of psychedelic drugs, as well as having secondary causation. In our view, suggestibility is potentiated by, and mutually interacts with, the increased significance or meaning attributed to both internal and external perceptions and thoughts.

Catecholaminergic

These drugs include amphetamine isomers, cocaine, methylphenidate, and phenmetrazine hydrochloride. In moderate doses used infrequently, they have a stimulating effect on arousal mechanisms. Subjects report euphoria and talkativeness. Often, there is an enhanced focusing of attention and enthusiasm to perform simple repetitious tasks, especially where fatigue or boredom has intervened (53). At times, thinking is described as crystal clear, and there are feelings of cleverness and an invigorated aggressiveness. There is a feeling of increased physical well-being, often accompanied by hyperactivity. Anorexia and insomnia are also noted (32).

Tryptaminergic

These drugs, including LSD, psilocybin, mescaline, DMT, and certain methoxyamphetamines, produce signs of intoxication varying directly with the dosage used (Klee et al., 74). Somatic effects include dizziness, weakness, tremor, nausea, blurred vision, and paresthesias. Perceptually, there are alterations of shapes and colors, and difficulty in focusing vision. Psychic effects include changes in mood, tension, and time sense, with difficulty in expression. Dreamlike feelings and visual hallucinations are reported, with marked feelings of significance and portentousness (44). Depersonalization is frequent, especially with mescaline (60, 122). Concern with geometric configurations and various essential and all-inclusive "philosophical" problems is prominent. There is less attention to strictly rational processes, and the capacity to focus cognitively is impaired.

The passivity and suggestibility are induced with these drugs, in part explaining their historical use as adjuncts to religious experiences. Marked feelings of meaning and significance attached to percepts and thought can occur after single, moderate doses; this contrasts with the effects of acute amphetamine use. The hallucinations seen with these drugs are usually associated with the perceptual changes experienced. Delusions, if noted in association with these feelings, are often vague. The capacity for logical thought is somewhat impaired, and there is usually little secondary elaboration or rationalization of the delusional and portentous experiences unless "guided" by others. In summary, the net effect of tryptaminergic drugs, unlike that of amphetamine, is usually a moderate disorganization, with unusual perceptive and affective input associated with decreased cognitive ability to process these.

Anticholinergic

Recreational but toxic doses of anticholinergics produce impaired attention, concentration, and memory functions. Blurred vision, tachycardia, and pupillary dilation are noted, along with sleepiness and apprehensiveness. At higher doses, a toxic delirious state is noted, including confusion, stereotyped movements, euphoria or dysphoria, and hallucinations, usually of an animated, formed nature; the piperidyl benzylates (e.g., ditran) produce more hallucinations and euphoria (89). Depersonalization and terror are also noted with anticholinergic drugs. Scopolamine and similar drugs produce more psychic sedation and confusion.

The impairment of thinking, clouding of recent memory, and peripheral signs of parasympathetic blockade distinguish the effects of these drugs from other hallucinogens at the usual recreational dose level. The delusions seen with high doses are confused, rudimentary, and clearly part of the delirium (89). Although agitation and restlessness are reported, these are not drugs that promote activity of any kind. Feelings of significance are not as prominent; and, in contrast to amphetamine, there is a blurring of perceptual focus. Memory for the delirious psychotic state is poor.

Solvents

The effect of solvents should be classified with that of anesthetics. Both are general depressants whose first phase of action is characterized by excitation. In general, this stage of excitation is associated with euphoria and psychedelic effects, as well as occasional rudimentary delusions and hallucinations. As the intoxication proceeds, usually quite rapidly, the depressant effects predominate. Unequivocal neurologic signs, including EEG changes, nystagmus, and positive Romberg sign, are seen with intoxicating doses of the drug (47).

In keeping with the toxic effects of the solvents, thought processes and delusional content, when present, are very much disorganized. Likewise, rational thought is impaired. Bizarre or violent actions are more common than with any of the psychotomimetics (29). Memory for the toxic state is also poor.

Cannabis

The effects of the recreational dose range of cannabis are more difficult to assess than those of the other drugs mentioned. While there are some effects similar to those of depressants (drowsiness, decreased judgment, euphoria, exhilaration, and relaxation), there usually have been few subjective effects produced by moderate doses in naive subjects in neutral settings, especially when compared to more experienced users (138). This has been explained by many on the basis of social learning and acculturation of the drug. With higher doses there is clearly an alteration of time and space perception and dulling of attention, with fragmentation of thought. Psychotomimetic effects are also seen with these doses (65) and include hallucinations and feelings of insight and significance. Passivity and suggestibility are important effects of large doses of cannabis. Perceptual changes and depersonalization are less marked than with tryptaminergic drugs, and there is less cognitive disorganizing effect.

The relationships among many of these drug categories are unclear at best. Though the symptoms produced by high doses of THC resemble those of tryptaminergic drugs, the pharmacologic properties of the two are different, and there is no cross tolerance (62). Some amphetamine derivatives, e.g., methoxyamphetamines and MDA, exert both catecholaminergic and tryptaminergic effects and show cross tolerance with the tryptaminergic drugs. It is interesting that tryptaminergic drugs, and to a lesser extent cannabis, may produce marked changes in feelings of significance and emotional arousal, which are produced by amphetamines only after chronic administration. Perhaps because these changes develop rapidly with the former drugs, they do not attain the degree of integration that makes the amphetamine symptomatology more resilient and resistant to extinction.

4. ACUTE TOXIC HALLUCINATORY STATE

This state is noted with all the preceding drugs with sufficient dosages and is distinguished by the disorientation and clouding of consciousness, although rudimentary delusions and paranoia are seen. While personal material may appear as the drug dose increases, preexistent personality becomes less important. Usually this state lasts only as long as the drug is active pharmacologically, although persistent delirious states have been reported with PCP. With amphetamines, rudimentary delusions, hallucinations, and paranoia are noted with acute high doses (52, 68, 80).

Rudimentary delusions are defined for the purposes of this review as primitive stereotypical delusions, e.g., jealousy and elementary paranoid moods often noted in a confused, clouded consciousness, usually in a toxic delirium state, and not infrequently associated with formed hallucinations. The delusions, when induced in a state of impaired consciousness, tend to be vague, fluctuating, chaotic, and soon forgotten (122). A clearer and more acute consciousness is associated with more defined and more organized delusional experiences and consequent rationalization and systemization; it is from such states that residual delusional ideas and attitudes are maintained, often for a relatively long period of time (122). This condition is best typified by the delusions found in chronic amphetamine intoxication.

A toxic psychosis associated with cannabis has been extensively described by Tennant and Groesbeck (129). In 13 cases resulting from the intake of 5–30 grams of hashish, disorientation, delusions, anxiety, depersonalization, and confusion were seen within a few hours of intake and were resolved without residual effects within three days. (These patients were treated with chlorpromazine.) Keeler (70) and Talbott and Teague (126) also reported very similar cannabis-related, acute toxic syndromes after exposure to marijuana.

As presented earlier, anticholinergic and solvent abuse present a most typical picture of toxic psychosis. The clouding of consciousness is prominent; subjective and EEG changes are compatible with a true delirium (29, 46, 47). Perceptual distortions, hallucinations, and illusions are common. Delusions, frequently paranoid, have a disorganized, soon-forgotten quality.

At this point we might mention the group of drugs that includes ketamine and phencyclidine (PCP). They produce a toxic, delirious, dissociative state but do not fit neatly into the drug classes mentioned previously. The data on psychiatric sequelae are scanty, but prolonged psychotic reactions lasting a week or more have been reported (28). The neuropharmacologic basis of this state appears to be multidetermined (28) and difficult to assess.

5. INDIVIDUAL REACTION TYPES AND ACUTE DRUG EFFECTS

The concept of an individual reaction type implies that a given individual has a predilection to react to stress, hyperarousal states or drug-induced changes in a particular manner, but that the reaction can be influenced by aspects of the acute drug-taking situation, including the drug effect, the setting, the expectation, and the sociocultural background. There are common well-known psychiatric outcomes for which personality structure has a major influence. For example, an obsessive-compulsive individual who has a tendency to react to a variety of mind-altering drugs with anxiety–panic would have this effect potentiated in a chaotic and sensory-overloaded environment, especially if the individual had little sense or expectation of the drug effect. There is a plethora of clinical literature indicating that the reaction types to be discussed are reasonably common sequelae of severe stress, loss of boundaries, and high arousal where normally operating defense mechanisms no longer are capable of coping. Such conditions are noted in cases of sensory deprivation, battlefield stress, concentration camp experience, brainwashing or third-degree tactics; CNS insult also can induce similar reaction types (3, 44, 101, 109, 115, 141).

Depersonalization is another example of a reaction type that has been noted in cases of acute extreme stress; for example, there was an extremely high incidence of depersonalization among individuals in concentration camps (122). It is not infrequently reported in those who have narrowly escaped death or experienced similar circumstances. There is predilection in certain types of individuals to develop depersonalization; this includes mainly obsessive-compulsive individuals but also borderline or pseudoneurotic schizophrenics as well as schizophrenics (120). Thus, there is a spectrum of reaction types with an increased incidence in certain personality types, but with sufficient stress and the right conditions a given syndrome apparently can be induced in almost anyone. The end effects result from the interaction relationship of personality, expectation, setting, and sociocultural factors (Fig. 4).

Depersonalization

Depersonalization and derealization are reported most often with single dose use of psychotomimetics and marijuana; it has been suggested that these states are primitive defense mechanisms preserving psychic equilibrium (120). Depersonalization reactions are seen in acute schizophrenia, organic conditions including the epilepsies, stress reactions, electroconvulsive treatment, and general anesthesia as well as in normals. Depersonaliza-

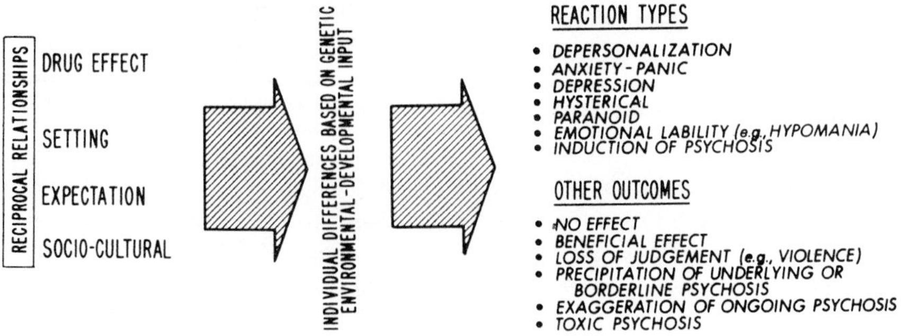

Fig. 4. Drug-induced reactions.

tion is a distortion of self-perception with concomitant loss of emotional tone. The feeling of one's own psychic or physical state, the relationship of one's self to the environment, or the relationship of the body to itself is profoundly disturbed. Derealization is a description of the distortion of the environment perceived during such a state. Depersonalization appears almost regularly as a primary drug effect with mescaline and was prominent in Hofman's (59) description of LSD intoxication. Ditman et al. (27), in comparing LSD casualties to LSD users who had not sought psychiatric care, felt that subjective descriptions of a depersonalized state during the drug experience (among other descriptions) were significant in differentiating these two groups.

A variety of hypotheses have been presented to explain the etiology of depersonalization. Because of its frequent association with epilepsy and organic conditions, the drug-induced state might be seen as the result of a triggering of an underlying subthreshold neuropathologic process. On the other hand, there is such a wide spectrum of depersonalization episodes precipitated by psychotomimetic drugs that a more common reaction type must be invoked. Once depersonalization has occurred, in our experience, there appears to be an increased probability for future occurrence with subsequent drug intake. In summary, depersonalization is a well-documented reaction type in both drug-using and nonusing populations.

Anxiety–Panic

Anxiety and panic states often occur when the drug user experiences an unpleasant loss of control of mental processes during intoxication. In this situation, the disorganized or affectively laden perceptual input may subjectively seem to overwhelm the ego's structuring capacity. For many, the mere experience of "boundlessness," hallucinations, or profoundly new and unusual experiences with LSD or marijuana may provoke anxiety and fear. Certainly the obsessive personality, accustomed to a structuring of experience, interpersonal control, and a relative isolation of affect, would be quite vulnerable to these reactions; for example, he may become disturbingly obsessed by bizarre material elicited with a drug (such as LSD in experimental conditions [115]). Anxious hysterical patients may make dramatic changes in either a positive or a negative direction (114).

Annis and Smart (5), in a sample of 6641 randomly selected students (grades 7–13) using marijuana or hashish, found that more than 20% reported "confusion, anxiety, or other unpleasant effects" at least once. Halikas and co-workers (54), in a survey of heavier users of marijuana, report that about half had had occasional occurrences of anxiety, fear, confusion, and bewilderment while acutely intoxicated. Tennant and Groesbeck (129) reported that 5 of 720 hashish users who came to medical attention reported short-term panic attacks.

Melges et al. (100) documented anxiety–panic attacks as differential responses to cannabis; they found the drug a euphoriant for normal volunteers while "acute" psychiatric patients usually reacted to the drug with temporal disintegration, depersonalization, or panic. A widely held impression is that THC effect varies not only with the character structure of the individual but with the affective measures in the personality as well. Ablon and Goodwin (1) found that unipolar depressives had a significantly greater number of anxiety–panic reactions under THC than did bipolar depressives, and the latter had a much greater number of such reactions than normal populations had. Six of their eight unipolar depressives suffered at least moderate anxiety and physiologic changes with THC in a double blind trial.

Panic reactions with LSD present similar, though generally more intense, complaints of dissociation, terror, confusion, or fear of going insane. Acute symptoms usually last 8–10 hr but may persist beyond the pharmacologic action of the drug. Like any anxiety reaction, once panic is induced, it may last long after the precipitating factors have abated. Fear of loss of control or of going insane is commonly seen. As anxiety and panic increase, these fears seem increasingly real. Consistent with the findings with THC, one study (73) indicated a striking correlation between the subjects' mean scores on the neuroticism and psychoticism scales on the predrug MMPI, and the extent of psychopathology exhibited after LSD.

Anxiety–panic states are seen only rarely with moderate doses of amphetamines, presumably because there is not the feeling of loss of control over the mind; rather there is enhanced function of rational processes. However, toxic doses may induce a severe panic state.

Depression

Depressive reactions to these drugs are rare, although they may occur along with anxiety and confusion in the postdrug period. Cohen (20) observed postdrug depression with LSD and postulated a letdown from the intense state and/or emergence of guilt and inability to integrate the new experience. Keeler reports a delusional depressive reaction to marijuana (70). The ability of hallucinogens and marijuana to amplify affects may worsen already existing mild or borderline depressive symptomatology. Similar, highly variable reactions to stimulants have been noted in depression (105).

Suicide during an acute drug episode has been a concern with many investigators. Suicides have been described with acute LSD since 1957 in both medical and nonmedical settings. Twelve unsuccessful suicide attempts have occurred as a result of LSD therapy (123), and there have been many more with unsupervised use. McGlothlin reported seven suicides in his follow-up of 284 subjects over 10 years. None, however, occurred during the acute LSD episode (96). There are rare reports of suicide attempts during acute marijuana use (98). The significance of suicides is not known since there is no comparison of drug-related suicide rates to those of an analogous population of psychotherapy subjects, psychiatric inpatients, or simply drug users or alcoholics.

Emotional Lability and Hypomania

Although emotional lability is commonly experienced in the drug state, hypomanic reactions are infrequently reported. Cohen (20) described an LSD reaction with manic features. Harding and Knight (56) reported four cases in which hypomanic symptoms predated an increased use of marijuana that resulted in modification of the hypomanic symptoms to a transient "schizophrenoform illness" that cleared after withdrawal of the marijuana. The ability of chronic amphetamine and cocaine use to produce manic symptomatology is well known (32), especially with intravenous administration (86).

Induction of Psychosis with a Single Drug Episode

In this category, we consider states that begin with a single administration of a drug, continue beyond the time of action of the drug, last as an acute psychotic state, and usually require hospitalization and treatment with antipsychotic medication. It is important in considering these reactions to appreciate the power of the placebo effect, however. Suicide attempts, paraplegia, migraine headaches, skin rashes, influenza, and acute psychotic episodes have been "precipitated" by injections of saline in double-blind studies (20).

There are a number of reports, best documented in therapeutic use of LSD, of a prolonged psychosis induced by the drug (20). Allentuck and Bowman (2a) reported that 6 of their 72 subjects given oral cannabis extract developed a psychosis within two to three weeks of the initial dose. There is a greater incidence of paranoid symptoms in the psychoses precipitated by acute drug use than in naturally occurring psychoses. Smart and Bateman (123), in their collected series of LSD reactions, report paranoia and overwhelming fear as the most typical symptoms. Tennant and Groesbeck (129) reported paranoia and hallucinations in 10 of their 13 acute marijuana psychoses.

Unlike the psychotic episodes from chronic drug use, these episodes are more difficult to explain from a learning model or even one of biological induction. Judgment of a pre-psychotic personality, seen so often in the literature, is rarely made before the fact. In both the Bellevue (99) and Los Angeles (134) studies, it was found that 30–50% of the prolonged psychoses developed after only one dose of LSD. The psychiatrist at Bellevue reported that prolonged LSD psychoses in 30 of their 52 patients cleared within 48 hr; 11 took up to 7 days; 6 required more time. They felt that 77% of the psychoses studies could not have been predicted from previous psychotic disturbance. Ungerleider, Fisher, and Fuller (132) reported that 39% of their patients with adverse reactions had had previous psychiatric treatment. Rosenthal (110) suggested that the ability of LSD to release overwhelming unconscious material in preschizophrenic subjects is the precipitating factor in psychosis. Hollister (60) has stated that LSD does not induce permanent psychosis but rather, it attracts emotionally disturbed people.

Bowers (13) described 12 drug-induced psychotic episodes; none of the patients had used psychotomimetics less than three times. These psychoses differed from nondrug psychosis in having more favorable prognostic signs that resembled those of "good premorbid" or "reactive" psychoses closely. Bowers' drug users scored higher than their nondrug psychotic controls on measures predicting favorable outcome. Moreover, the drug patients displayed lowered levels of 5-hydroxy-indoleacetic acid in the cerebrospinal fluid, compatible with that found in animals given LSD. This finding suggests a neurochemical basis for this psychotic state.

In considering the problem of the precipitation of a psychosis, it is important to consider its multidetermined nature. Bowers (13) discussed the emergence of psychosis determined by the form of the altered state (i.e., heightened awareness, perceptual changes, or memory changes), the content of the psychotic state, and the timing of the psychosis in terms of maturational developmental stages. He considered the crucial issue in a number of psychoses "associated with" childbirth, adolescent psychosexual development, heterosexual rejection, and marital crisis to be the ability of a personality to assimilate and integrate new cognitive and affective material. With this paradigm, psychosis could be considered a reaction-type consistent with the theme presented above.

The concept of a drug-induced psychosis, in a predisposed person, implies an accelerated development of overt psychosis. One can postulate that if it it is possible to change the course of a psychosis acutely, would this not be more probable over a longer period of time given conducive developmental, temporal, and psychological factors?

Other Reactions

The reaction types described above are the psychiatric sequelae most frequently noted in the literature. Two reaction types not emphasized are dissociative reactions (hysterical) and paranoid reactions. The very nature of the drug-induced state may contribute to this neglect, since paranoid and hysterical features are not uncommonly a part of the drug reaction itself. "Paranoid" became a term in the everyday parlance of the drug-using subculture and was seen as a frequent "normal" reaction while under the influence of drug, especially if the environment or influence of the drug was conducive. Similarly, drug-induced states have common features with the hysteria of high emotional states, including the ego-splitting, the increased suggestibility, and the adoption of beliefs. Many aspects of the flashback phenomenon, noted primarily during the 1960s, had elements of suggestibility, and, in our experience, the "flashback" was noted primarily in individuals prone to hysterical symptomatology. More precise diagnostic procedures in the future may delineate a clear role for these two categories in drug-induced reactions.

Loss of Judgment

Loss of judgment has been a frequently dangerous and, at times, fatal outcome of use of some of the drugs considered here. LSD has provided some of the more distressing situations in which a user, in acute intoxication, or in an acute panic state, has acted on his deranged thought or feeling and, in so doing, has become dangerous to either himself or others. Two components of these episodes appear relevant. The first is the loss of judgment or inhibition, similar to that seen in acute alcohol intoxication, in a person previously inclined to aggressive, violent behavior but in whom these drives are marginally held in check by normal controlling functions but lost with intoxication. Also, with solvents, LSD, and anticholinergics, the violent acts reportedly arise from a confused, irrational thought pattern—as often as not, premeditated (20). The second component would be the drugs' ability to provide the impetus or actual drive toward action or dangerous acts. Certainly this is the more controversial factor. Marijuana had a reputation in the 1930s as an inducer of such actions, and is still alluded to occasionally in the literature (11). In general, reports of gross loss of judgment with marijuana are rare.

A state of chronic amphetamine intoxication provides a clear example of an increase in this drive toward action, at times on the power and conviction of a delusional paranoid state. However, these addicts report crazy thoughts long before they act on them. Frequently an increase in dose, prolonged sleep deprivation, or the addition of another drug, causes them to lose the ability to appraise their delusion critically. Ellinwood (36) has reported premeditated acts of murder and assault in this state.

With LSD and solvent abuse there have been reports of death from stepping in front of cars, drowning, and from jumping out of windows (20). There have been numerous other cases cited in both experimental or unsupervised settings where it has been necessary to restrain the user to prevent violence (118). On the other hand, with tryptaminergic drugs and marijuana, the effects of euphoria, passivity or loss of will to act, and psychedelic effects, probably are deterrents to assertive action including violence.

Acute Reactions to Drugs in Schizophrenic Patients

Hospitalized schizophrenic patients have been used frequently as experimental subjects in the measurement of drug effects, with the assumption that nonschizophrenic individuals may react in similar ways. In view of the great variety of patients classified as schizophrenic, it is not surprising that their reactions have not been uniform. In chronic schizophrenic patients, LSD and mescaline have been found to exert a significantly less intense effect than in normals (22, 93, 125). Intensification of the psychotic symptomatology is more common in acute schizophrenics (17, 19, 57, 104). When precise criteria have been used, this distinction has been more marked. Hoch et al. (57) administered mescaline to four groups of schizophrenic patients: overt but not deteriorated, chronic deteriorated patients without affective blunting, chronic deteriorated patients with affective blunting, and borderline or schizoid patients. He found exaggeration of psychotic symptoms with both the overt nondeteriorated and the chronic deteriorated patients with preserved affects. However, in the deteriorated patients with affective blunting, there was almost none of the exaggeration of schizophrenic symptomatology seen in the other groups. The disorganization and exaggeration of symptoms was greatest in the borderline or schizoid group. Lindemann and Malamud (87) gave hashish to a small number of chronic schizophrenics and noted fewer time and perceptual changes but more withdrawal than in either normals or neurotics.

Precipitation of Schizophrenia

The precipitation of schizophrenia by a single drug episode supposes the development of signs of schizophrenia that formerly had been minimal or absent. Such a state has been characterized as "latent" schizophrenia, and has been used by many to explain the sudden drug-induced emergence of lasting schizophrenic symptoms. Sedman and Kenna (119) provided the only account in the literature of the presentation of an LSD challenge to latent or doubtful schizophrenics as well as to a control group. Prior to taking LSD, none of his patients had exhibited Schneiderian first rank symptoms of schizophrenia. Although there were significantly more post-drug acute pathologic response in the "latent schizophrenic" group, the number of patients reporting Schneiderian symptoms was not significantly different from that of the control group. There was no follow-up to determine if any of these patients ever developed symptoms of schizophrenia after the drug experiment. A major difficulty with any experiment of this nature is the often cloudy diagnosis of "latent schizophrenia" and its meaning, as well as the rather fine discrimination between pathologic and normal reactions to an acute dose of a psychotomimetic drug. Schizophrenia and its relation to drug use will be considered more fully in a later section.

Beneficial Effects

The production of beneficial psychological effects by a few or even single doses of psychotomimetic drugs poses a difficult problem to investigate. While positive effects are claimed for mescaline, psilocybin, marijuana and LSD, these are as imprecisely documented as the adverse effects. Psychotherapy with these agents, except in some experimental centers, has been abandoned. It was generally, however, the same structure-loosening quality of these drugs that was felt to produce positive results. Depending on the nature of the sample selected, 40–80% report a positive personality change after a period of a year or more (26, 96). These changes are usually: more understanding of self, more tolerance of others, less egocentricity, a less materialistic and aggressive orientation, and more appreciation of the arts and nature (96). In another study by McGlothlin et al. (96a), the subjective assessments of 58% of the subjects reporting long-lasting effects were not confirmed by predrug and postdrug psychological testing (AAS hypnotic-susceptibility test, Lulkerman sensation seeking scale, or Myers-Briggs type indicator). There was suggestive evidence of a decrease in stress anxiety as measured by galvanic skin responses, a tendency toward passivity, introspectiveness, and less defensiveness on the psychological measures. In general, people for whom control and structure are more important dislike the experience of these drugs, while those who choose a more unstructured, spontaneous, imaginative lifestyle respond to the drugs positively (96a).

Unger (131) pointed out how importantly variables other than the drug figure in the nature of the positive responses reported to psilocybin, LSD, and mescaline. Apparently, psychoanalytic patients reexperienced traumatic episodes of childhood, Jungian patients had "transcendental" experiences, and Harvard students grappled with age-old philosophical paradoxes.

In general, the positive responses depend on the same complex interaction of variables as do the adverse responses. At the Josiah Macy Conference on LSD Psychotherapy, upon hearing of the various results obtained with LSD, Charles Savage (116) expressed the following opinion:

> This meeting is most valuable because it allows us to see, all at once, results ranging from the nihilistic conclusions of some to the evangelical ones of others. Because the results are so much influenced by the personality aims and expectations of the therapists and by the setting, only such a meeting as this could provide us with such a variety of personalities and settings. It seems clear, first of all, that, where there is no therapeutic intent, there is no therapeutic result . . . I think that we can also say that, where the atmosphere is fear-ridden and skeptical, the results are generally not good . . . this is all of tremendous significance for so few drugs are dependent on the milieu and require such careful attention to it as does LSD.

6. PSYCHOSIS ASSOCIATED WITH CHRONIC DRUG USE

The syndromes associated with chronic drug use more closely follow our amphetamine model. Also, the progression from acute to chronic drug use invokes a greater operation of personality variables involved in the sustained drug use.

Historical Perspective

Bromides provide an older model of drug-induced psychosis, no more accurate but less heated by contemporary feelings and issues, which cloud the discussion of syndromes associated with current drugs. Although a simple toxic variety of bromide psychosis with delirium and with neurologic signs is possible, we will focus on "bromide schizophrenia" and hallucinosis. Levin (84) described a chronic intake of bromide that resulted in a transitory "schizophrenia" with paranoid symptomatology, at times indistinguishable from "ordinary schizophrenia." In 13 of his 74 collected cases of bromide psychoses, there were paranoid delusions, hallucinations, poor rapport, and ideas of reference. When the bromide was stopped, the symptoms cleared in a month to a year (84). Levin described most of these patients as having schizoid personalities with bromide bringing schizophrenia "out into the open." He also described bromide hallucinosis similar to that associated with hallucinogenic drug states. Levin saw these processes as a psychotic exaggeration, through organic means, of preexisting personality elements.

Wikler (140) makes a similar point about the psychoses accompanying abrupt withdrawal of barbiturates; along with disorientation, delusions, paranoia, and hallucinations, highly personal ideational changes may appear, which Wikler thought represented "release of repressed materials secondary to impairment of ego control." Kornetsky (79) reported that these psychoses were more apt to occur in individuals whose responses on Rorschach testing show evidence of marked constriction. Similarly Cohen (20) reported LSD psychosis to be more frequent in individuals with constricted or fragile personality structures.

The value of experimental data collected by giving drugs over time to individuals with stable, healthy personalities would not justify the risks these individuals might incur. We must rely on studies in the past or those done on selected populations, e.g., that by Griffith et al. (52). Well-planned follow-up studies of the psychoses occurring concomitantly with documented drug use history would help to clarify the issues. A five-to-ten-year follow-up on these patients would provide answers to questions on the development of psychosis; for instance, how commonly are extended psychotic reactions, associated with drugs, followed by recovery without residua? How frequently do drug-associated psychoses end in chronic schizophrenia? How many of these individuals are still difficult to assess? A study along these lines would provide data for issues which are, at this time, open to conjectures.

The amphetamine model allows for the somewhat different view that drug-induced arousal begins a process that may result in a permanent behavioral alteration. The permanence is noted even in animal studies; we find that cats with a history of chronic amphetamine intoxication, free of drug for a year, will reenter the amphetamine stereotypy when this is elicited by drug-associated external cues. Similarly, chronic amphetamine addicts may preserve an encapsulated delusional system for long periods (36).

Psychosis Associated with Hashish–Marihuana

Tennant and Groesbeck (129) described 112 psychotic reactions in servicemen who smoked hashish several times a day and abused other hallucinogens for at least three months. The individuals were using 25–200 g of hashish per month. Schizophrenic reactions occurred during the period of drug abuse, and, in each instance, premorbid histories indicated the presence of progressive psychiatric illness prior to their acute symptoms. They also described a state of chronic intoxication (5–6 g monthly), which they were able to follow continuously for 3–12 mo because the patients were returning for treatment of incidental medical complaints. All patients exhibited personality disturbances that had prompted psychiatric consultation during their period of heavy use. Symptoms during this chronic intoxication were dullness, lethargy, impairment of judgment and memory, and occasional confusional episodes. Nine of these patients were followed prospectively; symptoms were noted to appear with consistency at certain dose levels. On cessation of the hashish use, six of the nine were felt to have no residual impairment. Bernhardson and Gunne (11) reported 46 cases of psychosis in cannabis abusers. They divided these into episodic psychoses (N = 24); continuing paranoid delusions, motor restlessness, and hallucinations (all these in more than 60% of the cases); and a group of chronic psychoses which they diagnosed as primarily schizophrenic in nature (N = 20). They observed a consistent increase in abuse prior to the onset of psychosis and a relapse following renewed abuse. They interpreted the psychosis as drug-induced. These findings would be also consistent with Harding and Knight's (56) study in which psychiatric illness actually preceded and facilitated an increase in drug use.

Studies in Eastern countries, where dosages of marihuana or hashish are much greater than in the United States and the social backdrop of the drug is much different, indicated that cannabis produced a chronic psychosis resembling schizophrenia. Jones (65) thinks, on the basis of his experience, that this is schizophrenia with the addition of cannabis use. There is sketchy evidence from the Eastern literature of an acute psychosis, resulting from chronic cannabis use and lasting one to six weeks (95, 102).

The evidence indicates that those suffering from "cannabis psychosis" do not develop schizophrenic thoughts or delusions (95). The reports from Morocco emphasize an excited, confused manic state leading to violence (10, 25); this state sounds quite similar to the toxic delirious states ascribed by Tennant and Groesbeck (129) to high doses of hashish. McGlothlin (95) and Bernhardson and Gunne (11) have described similar episodic cannabis psychosis after repeated intoxication, which is also consistent with a toxic delirious state. The Indian Hemp Drugs Commission Report, 1893–1894 (107) concluded:

> It appears that excessive use of hemp drugs may, especially in cases where there is any weakness or hereditary predisposition, induce insanity. It has been shown that the effect of hemp drugs in this respect has hitherto been greatly exaggerated, but that they do sometimes produce insanity seems beyond question (p. 264).

There have been numerous anecdotal reports of psychosis with marijuana, usually in relation to a highly selective sample. Surveys by Tart (127). Halikas and co-workers (55), and Keeler and associates (72) reveal psychoticlike symptoms (not considered psychosis) during the intoxication phase, with milder effects persisting afterward. The Jamaican and Greek studies sponsored by NIDA have failed to document a cannabis psychosis in these populations with high dose chronic consumption patterns (91, 102). The NIDA study on chronic marijuana use in Jamaica (111) points to minimal or no differences between the smokers and the controls. Beaubrun and Knight (7) noted no changes in the incidence of mental illness, criminality, social change, abnormal thought, mood or behavior (N = 30). Bowman and Pihl (14a) reported a similar lack of differences in two studies comparing memory, concept formation, cognitive style, and perceptual functioning. They incidentally noted what they thought to be the development of considerable tolerance, very large dose producing minimal behavioral effects in their users. They also commented on a number of cultural artifacts that they identify with American use. For example, they noted that Jamaican users take marijuana to provide energy and to stimulate work, whereas in the United States the drug is considered a relaxant and one that might decrease work output.

Psychosis Associated with LSD and Other Psychotomimetics

Chronic LSD and other hallucinogens use occurs in spite of the fact that there is no known physiologic dependence, and daily use leads to rapid buildup of tolerance (96). These drugs cannot be used much more than twice a week without losing their original impact (96). Most authors note considerable predrug pathology in a significant section of the chronic hallucinogen users (26, 45, 132). However, during a psychotic episode, these patients can be differentiated in that they tend to have a more normal premorbid adjustment and have less chronic residual associated with their psychosis than schizophrenics (13). In Glass and Bowers' (49) cases of chronic psychosis precipitated by chronic drug use, LSD or other psychotomimetics were used on 50–250 occasions each. Ungerleider et al. (132) report a few cases in which LSD was used 100 times or more before psychiatric syndromes occurred. It is this kind of repetitive induction of altered consciousness that may be critically important in the chronic model. The psychotic picture in these reports is characterized by paranoid delusions, anxiety, depersonalization, and flattened affect. The course of these psychotic states typically lasts up to two to three months, and neuroleptics are usually prescribed (21, 133). Glass and Bowers' (49) four cases resembled chronic, undifferentiated schizophrenia. The authors, however, did not see this as simply a precipitation of an endogenous schizophrenia, but as an interaction between the subjects' personalities, the altered consciousness produced by the drug and the growth tasks of a particular maturational period. Leuner (83) reported three cases of "prolonged psychotic reaction" in 83 patients given an average of 27 LSD psychotherapy sessions.

Tucker et al. (130) compared Rorschach responses in a group of drug users (schizophrenic and nonschizophrenic) to a group of hospitalized controls. Drugs included primarily LSD, but also amphetamines, marijuana, and hallucinogens and were used on the average for one year or longer. The drug user showed a higher amount of "primitive drive material" on the Rorschach. Drug users with a longer history of drug use, moreover, demonstrated a higher incidence of disruptive thinking, boundary confusion, and slightly more idiosyncratic thinking. Only in these areas were differences noted. The overall thinking was not more disturbed than was the controls'. Another interesting aspect of this study was that the length of drug use seemed much more critical than the age at which it was initiated or the intensity with which drugs were used. (It is important to note here that there were no heavy users in this sample.)

Ungerleider et al. (133) compared 25 drug-using inpatients, of whom 10% were psychotic and 2% borderline psychotic, with a group of controls from a religious community who used LSD regularly as part of their religious practices. They were unable to identify any single factor that correlated with hospitalization or development of psychosis in their subjects (133). In summary, there apparently is a psychosis associated with chronic periodic use of hallucinogens, which may arise in part from repeated episodes of distortion and emotional hyperarousal affecting certain susceptible individuals. As in amphetamine abuse, it is a reasonable hypothesis that any individual subjected to this state over prolonged periods could develop psychotic symptoms. The paranoid quality of most of the psychoses reflects this change in arousal; and, as with amphetamines, the personality of the user becomes the substrate for the arousal whereby the arousal interacts over time with preexistent personality variables which become exaggerated and psychosis is gradually expressed.

7. CHRONIC DRUG USE AND SCHIZOPHRENIA

There are surprisingly few studies dealing clearly with schizophrenia and its relationship to chronic drug use. An important point to remember in examining this question is that many issues in schizophrenia are not well understood, especially in the area of precipitation, differentiation between reactive and process, and the interplay of psychological and biological forces. The mechanism by which the course of schizophrenia can be changed or precipitated by environmental or stress factors is still incompletely understood (8, 16). Breakey et al. (15) in a study evaluating the precipitation of endogenous schizophrenia in chronic drug abusers (amphetamines, marihuana, major hallucinogens), measured the evolution of symptoms in patients hospitalized for the first time for schizophrenia, schizophrenia with drug abuse, and in hospitalized controls (drug users and nonusers). They found that the first experience of schizophrenic symptoms and the first hospital admissions occurred nearly four years earlier in the drug users than in nonuser schizophrenic patients. The early hospital admission data also correlated positively with an increased estimated number of drugs used. Among the drug-using patients, schizophrenics had a pattern of greater drug use. Despite the relatively small sample used (N = 46) and the numerous uncontrolled variables involved, this is an impressive study indicating early precipitation of schizophrenia by drug use.

Klein and Davis (75) noted that many schizophrenics, unlike patients with drug-induced psychoses, have a history of early childhood asocial development, learning defects, poor peer relationships and emotional eccentricity. Glick and Winstead (50) corroborated these findings in 15 patients who were drug-abusing schizophrenics and 11 controls who were drug-abusing nonschizophrenics hospitalized with psychotic states. Their findings are consistent with Bowers' (13) "good premorbid" classification of drug abuse psychosis comparison to schizophrenic psychosis. Interestingly, schizophrenic drug users attributed their pathology to drug use, while the psychotics whose illness was diagnosed as drug reactions discounted any connection between their symptomatology and drug use.

8. NONPSYCHOTIC STATES

Amotivational Syndrome–Profound Value Changes

An "amotivational syndrome" or variant has been described as an end state of the chronic abuse of many drugs. West (139) described the picture with chronic marihuana use, about which much of the interest and debate has arisen. The "syndrome" ranges from social deterioration comparable to that seen in the chronic alcoholic to a much less tangible sense of loss of efficiency and desire to achieve, vaguely noted by the users. It consists of apathy, slowed mental processes, lack of interest and goals, flattened affects, irritability, confusion, and poor social judgment. The syndrome is at times nebulous and is certainly not specific to either marihuana or drug abuse. Motivation is difficult to measure and strongly shaped by cultural factors. Many reports have been weakened by subjective or unreliable categorization standards, especially when associated with unpopular beliefs and attitudes. The presence of value conflict along with the poorly understood biologic substrate of motivation, make evaluation of these reports of an amotivational syndrome difficult.

Kolansky and Moore (78) reported on 38 adolescent and 13 adult chronic, heavy marijuana users, who developed an amotivational syndrome. These cases generally improved with discontinuation of drug use, and there was a rough correlation between severity of symptoms and duration of marijuana use. Similar reports have come from many other sources. Tennant and Groesbeck's (129) chronic hashish users (N = 110) developed symptoms similar to those of dependence on depressant drugs, including apathy, lethargy, periods of confusion, and poor social judgment, and consistently became unable to function in their armed service capacities. All displayed a personality disturbance that had prompted psychiatric consultation during the period of heavy drug intake (smoking at least several times per day). Seventy of the 110 cases were prematurely discharged. In nine servicemen who were studied prospectively, they observed symptom development for three months, after which time voluntary abstinence cleared symptoms in two to four weeks in six of the cases; the remaining three experienced intermittent symptoms for extended periods, yet improved slowly. Jones (67) has experimentally observed heavy cannabis users and has noted symptoms similar to those associated with heavy use of sedatives or tranquilizers—CNS depression accompanied by loss of motivation and decreased performance. This continued heavy use, however, was followed by tolerance and a decrease in symptoms. Cohen (in Maugh 92), observing heavy users and controls, noted tolerance development but was unable to measure a change in motivation or mental function. Hochman and Brill (58) in a well-designed survey of chronic users (college students) noted no deterioration in function or adaptation, as compared to nonusers. While cannabis use is widespread, the heavy use described by Tennant and Groesbeck (129) and by Jones et al. (67) is more unusual. While there is provocative evidence for a marijuana-induced state of lethargy, confusion, and social withdrawal, the dimensions of the hypothesis are sufficiently broad that more data are required to draw conclusions, especially when the evidence is contrasted to the paucity of effects found in the stable, culture-sanctioned, chronic use mentioned in the Jamaican study (111).

Japanese investigators (128, 136) have reported a chronic, amphetamine-induced loss of initiative, emotional flattening and apathy, which persists for several months or years. The adynamia described by the Japanese is very similar to the frequent description of apathetic "spaced-out" conditions reported by previous high-dose amphetamine users in this country (32). Not infrequently the postamphetamine addict describes a rather emotionally colorless life in which there is little or no desire. The effects could result from psychological mechanisms as well as structural changes; for example, Escalante and Ellinwood (39) reported neuronal chromatolysis in areas of the brain stem subserving CNS activation. Furthermore, there is evidence of chronic central nervous system insult on the basis of cerebral vascular accidents as well as multiple petechial hemorrhages, found in amphetamine abuse cases coming to autopsy (51, 69, 112, 143). Evidence of residual psychological effects are also noted in MMPIs of chronic amphetamine abusers, which differ significantly from those of control addicts on the psychasthenic scale as well as the schizophrenic scale (34), indicating not only some degree of bizarre thinking, but also an emotional apathy. In summary, although there may be evidence for structural changes with chronic amphetamine intoxication, psychological mechanisms cannot be discounted as a basis for this response. Apathy and constriction are not unexpected responses to a chronic periodic overload of emotional stimulation, especially stressful arousal; for example, a picture quite similar to the amotivational syndrome is reported in other environmentally-induced states. The postconcentration-camp syndrome has been described (109) as "a tendency to withdraw, general apathy alternating with angry outbursts, feelings of helplessness, insecurity and lack of initiative and interest," a description quite similar to that of marijuana-induced amotivational states (77).

Depersonalization

Depersonalization has been occasionally described with chronic drug use. Glass and Bowers (49) describe it in three of their chronic LSD psychotics. Fink et al. (41) describe it in two of their three psychotics. It has often been reported to be associated with chronic marijuana use (70, 100, 126). The state itself may dominate the clinical picture; at times, it occurs continuously over a prolonged period, but more frequently, in discrete episodes. Although there are only a few isolated reports of chronic, primary depersonalization reactions precipitated by acute and/or chronic drug use, in our experience this is not a rare occurrence. The paucity of reported cases may reflect an overriding opinion that these cases are induced by dynamic interactions in hysterical personalities and that the drug is only incidental. We have seen several cases of chronic nuclear depersonalization in the relative absence of more severe pathology, for which the patient pinpoints the onset to a specific drug use episode (usually marijuana or a psychotomimetic). On two occasions, after an initial chronic depersonalization had abated, subsequent marijuana or psychotomimetic drug use retriggered the chronic state. In our sample of drug-induced depersonalization there has been a high incidence of minor electroencephalographic abnormalities (14 and 6 positive spikes and 6 per sec spike and wave). Alcohol or depressants may intensify the response; amphetamines, on the other hand, often ameliorate the syndrome; and, as in the depersonalization syndrome induced by other causes, amphetamine in moderate intravenous doses may produce a lasting favorable response (Davison, 24).

Depression

Depression is commonly noted after discontinuation of chronic stimulant use, but is otherwise seldom reported as a complication of chronic drug use. Some writers consider the amotivational syndrome a masked depression. While many case reports describe passivity, withdrawal, apathy and lethargy, we know of none describing the biologic concomitants of depression, and of none in which antidepressants are prescribed. However, depression is often a motivating factor in triggering drug and alcohol use. At least some of the suicides reported with chronic drug use are presumably due to a predrug depressive element in the personality. The depression secondary to the withdrawal of amphetamines is a well-known clinical entity. In general, this occurs 48–72 hours after drug withdrawal and generally clears within one to two weeks.

9. RESIDUAL EFFECTS

Chronic effects from drug use persisting long after drug use has stopped are termed residual effects. They appear to fall into three main categories.

Flashbacks

Flashbacks, the periodic return of drug-related imagery and feelings over extended periods of time after cessation of drug use, have been reported with all the hallucinogens and with marijuana. The most clinically important are the repeated intrusions of frightening images. Although the phenomenon was first described in persons receiving LSD therapeutically (31), it was not especially prevalent, as Cohen's 1960 paper (20) identified only a single instance of flashback in a survey of over 5000 people receiving LSD. With the development of a drug culture, however, flashbacks became more widespread, Horowitz (61) reporting an incidence of 1 in 20 in young California users. Robbins and associates (108) reported that 11 of their hospitalized drug abusers with psychosis experienced flashbacks. Keeler (71) reports flashbacks as being common with marijuana, at times necessitating psychiatric treatment. Annis and Smart (5) in their survey of high school marijuana users, reported that one in seven of their subjects had experienced a recurrence of the effects while abstaining. Fourteen percent of the subjects in McGlothlin and Arnold's 1971 follow-up study (96) reportedly experienced "uncontrolled LSD-like experiences without using drugs." These varied in nature from pleasant to extremely unpleasant. Those with at least 10 LSD exposures were twice as likely to experience flashbacks as those with fewer exposures, and those with serious psychiatric disorders were no more likely than others to experience the effects (96). Stanton and Bardoni (124), in their study of drug abuse in American armed forces in Vietnam, failed to corroborate McGlothlin and Arnold's correlation between the extent of drug use and flashbacks. They also found flashbacks in 5% of the amphetamine abusers, half of whom had not used LSD.

Chronic Brain Syndrome

Cases of residual brain damage have been reported, but so infrequently that they make systematic study almost impossible. Although the organic solvents have a reputation for causing brain damage, Glaser (47) found little evidence for this in his review of the literature. Knox and Nelson (76), however, described a case of permanent encephalopathy with cerebellar degeneration from 14 years of inhalation of toluene. The scattered reports of encephalopathy from other solvents in the medical literature are not surprising because of the wide variety of chemicals and combinations used in inhalation.

Acord and Barker (2) compared 15 hallucinogenic drug users with 15 controls on tests utilizing sections of the Indiana Psychology Battery, which they felt were sensitive to cerebral damage affecting higher level abstraction. The only impairment, according to these measures, was that drug users took more time to complete these tests. Blacker et al. (12) reported isolated EEG findings, including a nonspecific increase in abundance of delta, theta, alpha, and beta activity as well as changes in visual evoked potentials, in their 21 chronic volunteer LSD users.

McGlothlin and associates (97) studied 16 subjects (nonvolunteers) who had had 20 or more LSD exposures but most of whom had not had the drug within a year. Halstead's category test, sensitive to abstracting ability, was the only measure to show a significant difference between the experimental and control groups. On all other testing, including perceptual and motor, and other brain damage indices, there were no differences. They did not verify earlier studies suggesting perceptual and orientation problems. The authors attributed no causal relationship between the LSD use and the impairment of abstraction.

Chronic Psychosis

In the assessment of residual chronic psychosis or schizophrenia induced by drug use, it is important to consider that most psychiatrists do not perceive drugs as being able to produce this chronic deterioration. For this reason, these patients are generally diagnosed as chronic schizophrenics regardless of drug history. In fact, drug-induced psychoses, with the exception of those produced by amphetamine and marijuana which are not depicted as chronic schizophrenia, are rare. We have discussed the issue of precipitation of schizophrenia and the problems of diagnosis in an earlier section.

10. DRUG INTOXICATION AS AN ALTERED STATE OF CONSCIOUSNESS

We postulate that one of the primary mechanisms whereby the above drugs may be involved in personality change is through the production of a state of heightened emotional arousal. This may involve an intense emotional focus with feelings of meaning, portentousness, and significance. In the absence of intense emotional arousal, we propose that the probability of the development of a significant behavioral change is less (an hypothesis that should be experimentally testable). The emotional arousal effects have been reported as a component of the acute drug effects and are described throughout the literature, especially in subjective accounts.

A drug-induced state has many similarities to other altered states of consciousness, whether they are attained by meditation, sleep, stress, psychotherapy, brainwashing, religious experiences, powerful suggestive mechanisms, or exhaustion. Characteristics common to many of these states are alterations in thinking, disturbed time sense, loss of control, change in emotional expression, body image changes, perceptual distortions, hypersuggestibility, and changes in meaning and significance of experiences (90). Sargant (114) investigated the power of stress (including war and danger), drugs, religious conversion, and brainwashing in bringing about sudden attitudinal and behavioral change. He described a common process of being aroused to a high level of emotional intensity and interpreted that these were followed by "trans-marginal inhibition." During the period of emotional arousal new behavior or attitudes may be easily shaped or suggested, as Pavlov had noted with experimental animals. Sargant was first impressed by the importance of emotional arousal in amobarbital treatment of war neuroses. Similarly, he saw in certain emotionally arousing religious rituals, e.g., snake handling, the embodiment of the same principles in fixing attitudes and beliefs. Overwhelming fear is frequently utilized as the means to this arousal.

> William James (63) described similar mechanisms: Emotional occasions, especially violent ones, are extremely potent in precipitating mental rearrangements. The sudden and explosive ways in which love, jealousy, guilt, fear, remorse or anger can seize upon one are known to everybody. Hope, happiness, security, resolve, emotions characteristic of conversion, can be equally explosive. And emotions that come in this explosive way seldom leave things as they found them. (p. 198)

Drug-induced altered states of consciousness have been important in combining synergistically with rapid cultural and group changes. The role of drugs in the production of value and belief changes is very frequently important but not essential since the emotional arousal component can be induced by many means. In Fig. 5, we have depicted various groups that have utilized drugs in association with value changes. The avant-garde have frequently led the way in the use of amphetamines, narcotics, hallucinogens and marijuana (Ellinwood, 37). Their flexibility, dissatisfaction or search for new experiences is not necessarily associated with psychiatric pathology. Similarly, social maladaptation and inability to satisfyingly integrate into the major culture for whatever reason may draw relatively healthy per-

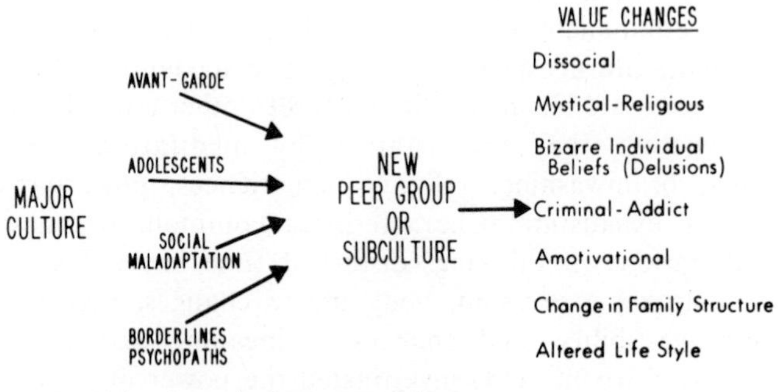

Fig. 5. Value change in the context of drug use.

sonalities into a drug-use, value-changing, subcultural matrix. Adolescents, sensitive to incongruities in major culture and parental values of ethics, may utilize the drug subcultural matrix in the service of rebellion or separation from parents. In the group of borderline personalities and psychopaths, there is also general evidence for difficulty in internalizing and sustaining cultural values. This may be correlated (106) with the evidence that psychopaths have significantly fewer spontaneous galvanic skin responses (43) and that they demonstrate poor conditioning performance in both avoidance and approach tasks (6). Similarly, borderline individuals have been described as having the inability to maintain satisfaction through interpersonal stimulation. These groups can attain arousal, stimulation, novelty or subculturally values significance by the use of drugs, especially with group support.

As the subculture or peer system develops, it may increasingly utilize drugs or other altered states of consciousness in the recruitment or strengthening of its ranks. Drugs may even become the symbol or rallying flag for the group's value change or orientation. In a culture oriented toward achievement, success, production and technical expertise, it is not surprising that the subculture has adopted views which include both caricatures (hustling, hard-driven narcotic addict) and antitheses of those of the major culture.

To evaluate the contribution of the various mind-altering states to the evolution of behavioral-value change, including the evolution of delusional beliefs, it is important to determine the order of events. Comparison of the process of various states of altered consciousness and their contribution to the evolution of delusions or other end-stage behaviors will help to determine the requisite factors in the ontogeny of psychosis. The close association of perceptual changes and feelings of significance, which occur in certain drug-induced states as well as in the functional psychoses, would appear to be a phenomenologically crucial step in psychosis formation. However, the feelings of portentousness and significance associated with the object world may actually precede the perceptual changes in the amphetamine-induced states. This suggests that, although portentousness or the exaggerated meaningfulness of percepts and thought may play a crucial role in the induction of either value changes or the more severe delusional mood, this feeling state may be induced either from alteration of the perceptual or information input (e.g., psychotomimetic drugs, sensory overload or underload) or by direct stimulation of the systems underlying these feelings with amphetamine. The next step, involving a shift from the normal emotional appraisal of external reality to the delusional mood, may involve both a loss of rational counterpointing judgment and a dramatic change in the attitudinal and emotional interpretation of the experience. The process of delusion formation is certainly influenced by the degree of conviction or sense of reality associated with these thoughts, but the nature of this process remains relatively unknown. The relationship between formation of an individual's bizarre beliefs (delusions) to the collective subcultural belief and value change is also fascinating but vaguely understood. Perhaps one of the few eventual positive results of the recent drug epidemic will be a more enlightened perspective on these processes and relationships.

11. SUMMARY

We have discussed an approach to the psychiatric syndromes associated with drug abuse, made from the perspective of amphetamine psychosis. We have attempted to apply experimental and clinical concepts from this more clearly documented area to other drug-related syndromes. We have argued that more precise clinical observation of the evolution of the psychosis enables a clinician to draw important conclusions about the nature of the delusion process (primary or secondary) and its relationship to drug use over time. Although each of the drug classes considered produces effects that bear an important relation to its pharmacologic action, the concept of individual reaction types places emphasis on the spectrum of individual variability in response to drug effects. In this manner, anxiety, panic, depersonalization, depression, mania or even psychosis could be viewed as an acute reaction by the individual to a drug. This tendency for a given reaction pattern may figure even more importantly with repeated drug experiences.

The psychoses associated with drugs such as LSD and marijuana have been difficult to classify and frequently bear an ambiguous relationship to schizophrenia. An emotional arousal and sense of portentousness or significance sustained by drugs over time figures importantly in psychosis formation. In nonpsychotic states, this arousal may lead to both behavioral and value change.

While there are few unifying concepts in the diverse material related to drug-induced psychiatric states, these concepts may have important implications for understanding the induction of functional psychiatric states and symptoms.

ACKNOWLEDGMENTS

The authors' research described in this review was supported by NIDA Grants DA 00057 and DA 01665-01.

REFERENCES

1. Ablon, S. I. and F. K. Goodwin, High frequency of dysphoric reactions to tetrahydrocannabinol among depressed patients, *Am. J. Psychiatry*, **131**, 448 (1974).
2. Acord, L. D. and D. D. Barker, Hallucinogenic drugs and cerebral deficit, *J. Nerv. Ment. Dis.*, **156**, 281 (1973).

2a. Allentuck, S. and K. Bowman, Psychiatric aspects of marijuana intoxication, *Am. J. Psychiatry*, **99**, 248 (1942).

3. Anderson, E. W., Abnormal mental states in survivors with special reference to collective hallucination, *J. Roy. Nav. Med. Serv.*, **28**, 361 (1942).
4. Angrist, B. M. and S. Gershon, The phenomenology of experimentally induced amphetamine psychosis—Preliminary observations, *Biol. Psychiatry*, **2**, 95 (1970).
5. Annis, H. M. and R. G. Smart, Adverse reactions and recurrences from marijuana use, *Br. J. Addict.* **68**, 315 (1973).
6. Arieti, S., Psychopathic personality: Some views on its psychopathology and psychodynamics, *Compr. Psychiatry*, **4**, 301 (1963).
7. Beaubrun, M. H. and F. Knight, Psychiatric assessment of thirty chronic users of cannabis and thirty matched controls, *Am. J. Psychiatry*, **130**, 309 (1973).
8. Beck, J. C. and K. Worthen, Precipitating stress, crisis theory and hospitalization in schizophrenia and depression, *Arch. Gen. Psychiatry*, **26**, 123 (1972).
9. Bell, D. S., The Experimental reproduction of amphetamine psychosis, *Arch. Gen. Psychiatry*, **29**, 35 (1973).
10. Benabud, A., Psychopathological aspects of the cannabis situation in Morocco: Statistical data for 1956, *Bull. Narc.*, **9**, 1 (1957).
11. Bernhardson, G. and L. Gunne, Forty-Six cases of psychosis in cannabis abusers, *Int. J. Addict.*, **7**, 9 (1972).
12. Blacker, K. H., R. T. Jones, G. C. Stone, and D. Pfefferbaum, Chronic users of LSD: The "acidheads," *Am. J. Psychiatry*, **125**, 97 (1968).
13. Bowers, M. B., Jr., Acute psychosis induced by psychotomimetic drug abuse, *Arch. Gen. Psychiatry*, **27**, 437 (1972).
14. Bowers, M. B., Jr., LSD-Related states as models of psychosis, in *Psychopathology and Psychopharmacology*, J. O. Cole, A. M. Freedman, and A. J. Friedhoff, (Eds.). The Johns Hopkins University Press, Baltimore, 1973.

14a. Bowman, M. and R. O. Pihl, Cannabis: Psychological effects of chronic heavy use, *Psychopharmacologia*, **29**, 159 (1973).

15. Breakey, W. R., H. Goodell, P. C. Lorena, and P. R. McHugh, Hallucinogenic drugs as precipitants of schizophrenia, *Psycho. Med.*, **4**, 255 (1974).
16. Brown, G. W. and J. L. T. Birley, Crises and life changes and the onset of schizophrenia, *J. Health Soc. Behav.*, **9**, 203 (1968).
17. Cattell, J. P., The influence of mescaline on psychodynamic material, *J. Nerv. Ment. Dis.*, **119**, 233 (1954).
18. Chapman, V., The early symptoms of schizophrenia, *Br. J. Psychiat.*, **112**, 225 (1966).
19. Cholden, L. S., A. Kurland, and C. Savage, Clinical reactions and tolerance to LSD in chronic schizophrenia, *J. Nerv. Ment. Dis.*, **122**, 211 (1955).
20. Cohen, S., Lysergic acid diethylamide: Side effects and complications, *J. Nerv. Ment. Dis.*, *130*, 30 (1960).

21. Cohen, S. and K. S. Ditman, Prolonged adverse reactions to lysergic acid diethylamide, *Arch. Gen. Psychiatry,* **8,** 475 (1963).

22. Condrau, G., Klinische Erfahrungen an GeistesKranken mit Lysergsaure Diathylamid (Clinical experiences in mental patients with lysergic acid diethylamide), *Acta Psychiat. Neurol. Scand.,* **24,** 9 (1949).

23. Connell, P. H., *Amphetamine Psychosis,* Chapman and Hall, London, 1958.

24. Davison, K., Episodic depersonalization, *Br. J. Psychiatry,* **110,** 505 (1964).

25. Defer, B. and M. L. Diehl, Les psychoses cannabiques aigues (apropos 560 observations), *Ann. Med. Psychol.* (*Paris*), **126,** 2260 (1968).

26. Ditman, K. S., M. Hayman, and J. Whittlesey, Nature and frequency of claims following LSD, *J. Nerv. Ment. Dis.,* **134,** 346 (1962).

27. Ditman, K. S., W. Tietz, B. S. Prince, E. Forgy, and T. Moss, Harmful aspects of the LSD experience, *J. Nerv. Ment. Dis.,* **145,** 464 (1968).

28. Domino, E. F., and E. Luby, Abnormal mental states induced by phencyclidine as a model of schizophrenia, in *Psychopathology and Psychopharmacology,* J. O. Cole, A. M. Freedman, and A. J. Friedhoff, (Eds.). The Johns Hopkins University Press, Baltimore, 1973.

29. Done, A. K., Inhalents, in *Drug Use in America: Problem in Perspective,* National Committee on Marijuana and Drug Abuse. U.S. Government Printing Office, Washington, 1972.

30. Doyle, A. C., *The Annotated Sherlock Holmes,* W. S. Baring-Gould (Ed.), Clarkson N. Potter, New York, 1967.

31. Eisner, B. G. and S. Cohen, Psychotherapy with lysergic acid diethylamide, *J. Nerv. Ment. Dis.,* **127,** 528 (1958).

32. Ellinwood, E. H., Amphetamine and stimulant drugs, in *Drug Use in America: Problem in Perspective,* National Committee on Marijuana and Drug Abuse, 2nd Report, U.S. Government Printing Office, Washington, 1973, p. 140.

33. Ellinwood, E. H., Amphetamine psychosis: A multidimensional process, *Semin. Psychiatry,* **1,** 208 (1969).

34. Ellinwood, E. H., Amphetamine psychosis. I. Description of the individuals and process, *J. Nerv. Ment. Dis.,* **144,** 273 (1967).

35. Ellinwood, E. H., Amphetamine psychosis. II. Theoretical implications, *Int. J. Neuropsychiatry,* **4,** 45 (1968).

36. Ellinwood, E. H., Assault and homicide associated with amphetamine abuse, *Am. J. Psychiatry,* **127,** 1170 (1971).

37. Ellinwood, E. H., The epidemiology of stimulant abuse, in *Drug Use: Epidemiological and Sociological Approaches,* E. Josephson and E. Carroll, (Eds.), Hemisphere, Washington, D.C., 1974, p. 303.

38. Escalante, O. and E. H. Ellinwood, Effects of chronic amphetamine intoxication on adrenergic and cholinergic structures in the central nervous system: Histochemical observations in cats and monkeys, in *Current Concepts on Amphetamine Abuse,* E. H. Ellinwood and S. Cohen (Eds.), U.S. Government Printing Office, Washington, 1972, p. 97.

39. Escalante, O. and E. H. Ellinwood, Central nervous system cytopathological changes in cat with chronic methedrine intoxication, *Brain Res.,* **21,** 555 (1970).

40. Esecover, H., S. Malitz, and B. Wilkens, Clinical profiles of paid normal subjects volunteering for hallucinogen drug studies, *Am. J. Psychiatry,* **117,** 910 (1961).

41. Fink, M., J. Simeon, W. Hague, and T. Itil, Prolonged adverse reactions to LSD in psychotic subjects, *Arch. Gen. Psychiatry*, **15,** 450 (1966).

42. Fisher, S., Non-specific factors as determinants of behavioral response to drugs, in *Clinical Handbook of Psychopharmacology*, A. DiMascio and R. I. Shader, (Eds.), Science House, New York, 1970.

43. Fox, R. and W. Lippert, Spontaneous GSR and anxiety levels in sociopathic delinquents, *J. Consult. Psychol.*, **27,** 368 (1963).

44. Freedman, D. X., On the use and abuse of LSD, *Arch. Gen. Psychiatry*, **18,** 330 (1968).

45. Frosch, W. A., E. S. Robbins, and M. Stern, Untoward reactions to lysergic acid diethylamide (LSD) resulting in hospitalization, *N. Engl. J. Med.*, **273,** 1235 (1965).

46. Gershon, S. and B. M. Angrist, Effects of alteration of cholinergic function on behavior, in *Psychopathology and Psychopharmacology*, J. O. Cole, A. M. Freedman, and A. J. Friedhoff (Eds.), p. 15. The Johns Hopkins University Press, Baltimore, 1973, p. 15.

47. Glaser, F. B., Inhalation psychosis and related states, *Arch. Gen. Psychiatry*, **14,** 315 (1966).

48. Glass, G. S., Psychedelic drugs, stress and the ego, *J. Nerv. Ment. Dis.*, **156,** 232 (1973).

49. Glass, G. S. and M. B. Bowers, Chronic psychosis associated with long-term psychomimetic drug abuse, *Arch. Gen. Psychiatry*, **23,** 97 (1970).

50. Glick, I. D. and D. K. Winstead, Childhood asociality in the differential diagnosis of schizophrenia with drug use vs. psychosis with drug intoxication, *Psychiatr. Q.*, **47,** 208 (1973).

51. Goodman, S. J. and D. P. Beker, Intracranial hemorrhage associated with amphetamine abuse, *J.A.M.A.*, **212,** 428 (1970).

52. Griffith, J. D., J. Cavanaugh, J. Held, and J. A. Oates, Dextroamphetamine: Evaluation of psychomimetic properties in man, *Arch. Gen. Psychiatry*, **26,** 97 (1972).

53. Grinspoon, L. and P. Hedblom, *The Speed Culture*, Harvard University Press, Cambridge, 1975, p. 70.

54. Halikas, J. A., D. W. Goodwin, and S. B. Guze, Marihuana effects: A survey of regular users, *J.A.M.A.*, **217,** 692 (1971).

55. Halikas, J. A., D. W. Goodwin, and S. B. Guze, Marihuana use and psychiatric illness, *Arch. Gen. Psychiatry*, **27,** 162 (1972).

56. Harding, T. and F. Knight, Marihuana—Modified mania, *Arch. Gen. Psychiatry*, **5,** 635 (1973).

57. Hoch, P. H., J. P. Cattell, and H. H. Pennes, Effects of mescaline and lysergic acid (*d*-LSD-25), *Am. J. Psychiatry*, **108,** 579 (1952).

58. Hochman, J. S. and N. Q. Brill, Chronic marihuana use and psychosocial adaptation, *Am. J. Psychiatry*, **130,** 132 (1973).

59. Hofman, A., Discovery of *d*-lysergic acid diethylamide—LSD, *Sandoz Excerpta*, **1** 1955.

60. Hollister, L. E., *Chemical Psychoses: LSD and Related Drugs*. Charles C Thomas, Springfield, Ill., 1968.

61. Horowitz, M. J., Flashbacks: Recurrent intrusive images after the use of LSD, *Am. J. Psychiatry*, **126,** 565 (1969).

62. Isbell, H., Effects of (−) Δ9-trans-tetrahydrocannabinol in man, *Psychopharmacologia*, **11,** 184 (1967).

63. James, W., *The Varieties of Religious Experience*, The Modern Library, New York, 1902.

64. Janowsky, D. S., M. K. El-Yousef, J. M. Davis, and H. J. Sekerke, Provocation of schizophrenic symptoms by intravenous administration of methylphenidate, *Arch. Gen. Psychiatry,* **28,** 185 (1973).

64a. Jaspers, K. *General Psychopathology,* 7th Ed., J. Hoenig and M. W. Hamilton (Trans.), Manchester University Press, London, 1963, pp. 58, 176, 274.

65. Jones, R. T., Drug Models of Schizophrenia, in *Psychopathology and Psychopharmacology,* J. O. Cole, A. M. Freedman, and A. J. Friedhoff (Eds.), The Johns Hopkins University Press, Baltimore, 1973.

66. Jones, R. T., Mental illness and drugs: Preexisting psychopathology and response to psychoactive Drugs, in *Drug Use in America: Problem in Perspective,* National Committee on Marijuana and Drug Abuse, 2nd Report: Technical papers, U.S. Government Printing Office, Washington, 1973.

67. Jones, R. T., N. Benowitz, and I. Feinberg, The 30 day trip: Brain–behavior–endocrine relationships during chronic tetrahydrocannabinol intoxication, Paper presented at the 8th Annual Winter Conference on Brain Research, Steamboat Springs, Colo., 1975.

68. Kalant, O. J., *The Amphetamines: Toxicity and Addiction, Brookside Monograph of the Addiction Research Foundation No. 5,* 2nd Ed. University of Toronto Press, Toronto, 1973.

69. Kane, E. J. F., M. K. Keeler, and C. B. Reifler, Neurological crisis following methamphetamine, *J.A.M.A.,* **210,** 556 (1969).

70. Keeler, M. H., Adverse reaction to marihuana, *Am. J. Psychiatry,* **124,** 674 (1967).

71. Keeler, M. H., Spontaneous recurrences of marijuana effect, *Am. J. Psychiatry,* **125,** 384 (1968).

72. Keeler, M. H., J. A. Ewing, and B. A. Rouse, Hallucinogenic effects of marihuana as currently used, *Am. J. Psychiatry,* **128,** 213 (1971).

73. Kerlinger, F. N. and E. J. Pedhazur, *Multiple Regression in Behavioral Research,* New York, Holt, Rinehart, and Winston (1973).

74. Klee, G. D., J. Bertine, W. Weintraub, and E. Callaway, The influence of varying dosage in the effects of lysergic acid diethylamide (LSD-25) in humans, *J. Nerv. Ment. Dis.,* **132,** 404 (1961).

75. Klein, D. F. and J. M. Davis, *Diagnosis and Drug Treatment of Psychiatric Disorders,* Williams & Wilkins, Baltimore, 1969.

76. Knox, J. W. and J. R. Nelson, Permanent encephalopathy from toluene inhalation, *N. Engl. J. Med.,* **275,** 1494 (1966).

77. Kolansky, H. and W. T. Moore, Toxic effects of chronic marihuana use, *J.A.M.A.,* **222,** 35 (1972).

78. Kolansky, H., and W. T. Moore, Effects of marihuana on adolescents and young adults, *J.A.M.A.,* **216,** 486 (1971).

79. Kornetsky, C. H., Effects of meprobamate, placebo and dextroamphetamine on reaction time and learning in man, *J. Pharmacol. Exp. Ther.,* **123,** 216 (1958).

80. Kramer, J. C., Introduction to amphetamine abuse, *J. Psychedelic Drugs,* **2,** 1 (1969).

81. Kramer, J. C., V. C. Fischman, and D. C. Littlefield, Amphetamine abuse-pattern and effects of higher doses taken intravenously, *J.A.M.A.,* **201** (1967).

82. Lehmann, H. E., Pharmacotherapy of schizophrenia, Paper Delivered to the American Psychopathological Association, Annual Conference, New York, 1964, p. 335.

83. Leuner, H., Present state of psycholytic therapy and its possibilities, in *2nd Interna-*

tional Conference on the Use of LSD in Psychotherapy and Alcoholism, Abramson, H. A., (Ed.), p. 101. Bobbs-Merrill, Indianapolis, 1967, p. 101.

84. Levin, M., Bromide psychoses: Four varieties, *Am. J. Psychiatry*, **104**, 798 (1948).

85. Lewander, T., Effect of chronic treatment with central stimulants on brain monamines and some behavioral and physiological functions in rats, guinea pigs and rabbits, in *Neuropsychopharmacology of Monamines and their Regulatory Enzymes*, E. Usden (Ed.), Raven Press, New York, 1974, p. 221.

86. Lewin, L., *Phantastica: Narcotic and Stimulant Drugs*, Dutton, New York, 1931, pp. 75–88.

87. Lindemann, E. and W. Malamud, Experimental analysis of the psychopathological effects of intoxicating drugs, *Am. J. Psychiatry*, **90**, 881 (1934).

88. Linton, H. B. and R. J. Langs, Empirical dimensions of LSD-25 reactions, *Arch. Gen. Psychiatry*, **10**, 469 (1964).

89. Longo, V. G., Behavioral and ectroencephalographic effects of atropine and related compounds, *Pharmacol. Rev.* **18**, 965, 1966.

90. Ludwig, A. M., Altered states of consciousness, *Arch. Gen. Psychiatry*, **15**, 225, 1966.

90a. Mandell, A. J. and S. Knapp, Cholinergic adaptation in the brain to chronic administration of amphetamine, in *Current Concepts on Amphetamine Abuse*, E. H. Ellinwood and S. Cohen (Eds.), National Institutes of Mental Health, Rockville, Md., 1972, p. 77.

90b. Mandell, A. J., D. S. Segal, R. T. Kuczenski, and S. Knapp, Etiological agent and defense in biological psychiatry, in *Psychopathology and Psychopharmacology*, J. O. Cole, A. M. Freedman, and A. J. Friedhoff, (Eds.). The Johns Hopkins University Press, Baltimore, 1973.

91. *Marihuana and Health*, Second Annual Report to Congress by the Secretary of Health, Education and Welfare, U.S. Government Printing Office, Washington 1972.

92. Maugh, T. H., Marijuana: Does it damage the brain? *Science*, **185**, 775, 1974.

93. Mayer-Gross, W., Experimental psychoses and other mental abnormalities produced by drugs, *Br. Med. J.*, **2**, 317 (1951).

94. McGhie, A. and J. Chapman, Disorders of attention and perception in early schizophrenia, *Br. J. Med. Psychol.*, **34**, 103 (1961).

95. McGlothin, W. H., The use of cannabis: East and West, in *Biochemical and Pharmacological Aspects of Dependence and Reports on Marihuana Research*, H. M. Praag, (Ed.), Haarlem, Netherlands, 1972, p. 167.

96. McGlothin, W. H. and D. O. Arnold, LSD revisited: A ten-year followup of medical LSD use, *Arch. Gen. Psychiatry*, **24**, 35, 1971.

96a. McGlothlin, W., S. Cohen, and M. S. McGlothlin, Long lasting effects of LSD on normals, *Arch. Gen. Psychiatry*, **17**, 521 (1967).

97. McGlothin, W. H., D. O. Arnold, and D. X. Friedman, Organicity measures following repeated LSD ingestion, *Arch. Gen. Psychiatry*, **21**, 704 (1969).

98. Mechoulam, R., *Marijuana Chemistry, Pharmacology, Metabolism and Clinical Effects*, Academic Press, New York, 1973.

99. Medical Society of the County of New York, Public Health Committee Subcommittee on Narcotics Addiction, *N.Y. Med.*, **22**, 241 (1966).

100. Melges, F. T., J. R. Tinklenberg, L. E. Hollister *et al.*, Temporal disintegration and depersonalization during marihuana intoxication, *Arch. Gen. Psychiatry*, **23**, 204 (1970).

101. Meltzer, M., Solitary confinement, in *Factors Used to Increase the Susceptibility of*

Individuals to Forceful Indoctrination, Group for the Advancement of Psychiatry, Symposium No. 3, Asbury Park, N.J., April 8, 1956.

102. Meyer, R. E., *Psychiatric Consequences of Marihuana Use: The States of the Evidence.* Academic Press, New York, in press.

103. Paton, W. D. M., Cannabis: Its problems, *Proc. R. Soc. Med.,* **66,** 718 (1973).

104. Pennes, H. H., Clinical reactions of schizophrenics to sodium amytal, pervitin hydrochloride, mescaline sulfate, and *d*-lysergic acid diethylamide—LSD-25, *J. Nerv. Ment. Dis.,* **119,** 95 (1954).

105. Post, R. M., Cocaine psychosis: A continuum model, *Am. J. Psychiatry,* **132,** 225 (1975).

106. Quay, H. C., Psychopathic personality as a pathological stimulation-seeking, *Am. J. Psychiatry,* **122,** 180 (1965).

107. *Report of the Indian Hemp Drugs Commission 1893–1894. Marijuana,* Waverly Press, Baltimore, 1969.

108. Robbins, E., W. A. Frosch, and M. Stern, Further observations of untoward reactions to LSD, *Am. J. Psychiatry,* **124,** 393 (1967).

109. Rosenman, S., The paradox of guilt in disaster victim populations, *Psychiat. Q.* Suppl. **30,** 181 (1966).

110. Rosenthal, S. H., Persistent hallucinogenic drugs, *Am. J. Psychiatry,* **121,** 238 (1964).

111. Rubin, V. and L. Comitas, *Ganja in Jamaica. A Medical Anthropological Study of Chronic Marihuana Use,* Mouton, The Hague, 1975.

112. Rumbaugh, C. L., R. T. Bergeron, C. H. Fang, and R. McCormick, Cerebral angiographic changes in the drug abuse patient, *Radiology,* **101,** 335 (1971).

113. Sanifer, M. G., A study of psychiatric diagnosis, *J. Nerv. Ment. Dis.,* **139,** 350 (1964).

114. Sargant, W., *Battle for the Mind,* Doubleday, Garden City, N.Y., 1957.

115. Sargant, W. and E. Slater, *An Introduction to Physical Methods of Treatment in Psychiatry,* Livingstone, Edinburgh, 1963.

116. Savage, C., Group interaction, in *The Use of LSD in Psychotherapy: Transactions of a Conference,* H. A. Abramson, (Ed.), p. 193. Josiah Macy, Jr., Foundation Publications, New York, 1960.

117. Schachter, S. and J. E. Singer, Cognitive, social, and physiological determination of emotional state, *Psychol. Rev.,* **69,** 379 (1962).

118. Schwartz, C. J., The complications of LSD: A review of the literature, *J. Nerv. Ment. Dis.,* **146,** 174 (1968).

119. Sedman, G. and J. C. Kenna, The use of LSD-25 as a diagnostic aid in doubtful cases of schizophrenia, *Br. J. Psychiatry,* **111,** 96 (1965).

120. Shorvon, H. J., The depersonalization syndrome, *Proc. R. Soc. Med.,* **34,** 779 (1946).

121. Simon, J. L. and H. Taube, A preliminary study of the use of methedrine in psychiatric diagnosis, *J. Nerv. Ment. Dis.,* **104,** 593 (1946).

122. Slater, E. and M. Roth, *Mayer-Gross Slater and Roth: Clinical Psychiatry,* 3rd Ed., Williams & Wilkins, Baltimore, 1969.

123. Smart, R. G. and K. Bateman, Unfavorable reactions to LSD: A review and analysis of the available case reports, *Can. Med. Assoc. J.,* **97,** 1214 (1967).

124. Stanton, M. D. and A. Bardoni, Drug flashbacks: Reported frequency in a military population, *Am. J. Psychiatry,* **129,** 751 (1972).

125. Stoll, W. A., Lysergsaure-Diethylamid, ein phantastikum aus der mutterkorngruppe (Diethyl amide of lysergic acid: An unusual derivative of ergot), *Schweizer Archiv für* Neurologie und Psychiatrie, **60,** 279 (1947).

126. Talbott, J. A. and J. W. Teague, Marihuana psychosis: Acute toxic psychosis associated with the use of cannabis derivatives, *J.A.M.A.*, **210,** 299 (1969).

127. Tart, C. T., Marijuana intoxication: Common experience, *Nature*, **226,** 701 (1970).

128. Tatetsu, S., Methylamphetamine psychosis, *Folia Psychiat. Neurol. Jap.*, Suppl. **7,** 337 (1963).

129. Tennant, F. S., Jr., and C. J. Groesbeck, Psychiatric effects of hashish, *Arch. Gen. Psychiatry*, **27,** 133 (1972).

130. Tucker, H. J., D. Quinlan, and M. Harrow, Chronic hallucinogenic drug use and thought disturbance, *Arch. Gen. Psychiatry*, **27,** 443 (1972).

131. Unger, S. M., Mescaline, LSD, psilocybin and personality change, *Psychiatry*, **26,** 111 (1963).

132. Ungerleider, J. T., D. D. Fisher, and M. Fuller, The dangers of LSD: Analysis of seven months experience in a university hospital's psychiatric service, *J.A.M.A.*, **197,** 389 (1966).

133. Ungerleider, J., T. Fisher and A. Caldwell, The "bad trip"—The etiology of adverse LSD reaction, *Am. J. Psychiatry*, **124,** 1483 (1968).

134. Ungerleider, J. T., D. D. Fisher, S. R. Goldsmith, M. Fuller, and E. Forgy, A statistical survey of adverse reactions to LSD in Los Angeles County, *Am. J. Psychiatry*, **125,** 352, (1968).

135. Utena, H., On relapse-liability, schizophrenia, amphetamine psychosis and animal model, in *Biological Mechanisms of Schizophrenia and Schizophrenia-Like Psychoses*, H. Mitsuda and T. Fukuda, (Eds.), Igaku Shoin, Tokyo, 1974, p. 285.

136. Utena, H., Behavioral abberations in methamphetamine intoxicated animals and chemical correlates in the brain, in *Progress in Brain Research, 21-B*, P. T. Tokizane and J. P. Schade, (Eds.), Elsevier, Amsterdam, 1966, p. 1902.

137. Weckowicz, T. E. and D. B. Blewett, Size constancy and abstract thinking in schizophrenic patients, *J. Ment. Sci.*, **105,** 909, (1959).

138. Weil, A. T., N. E. Zinberg, and J. M. Nelson, Clinical and psychological effects of marijuana in man, *Science*, **162,** 1234 (1968).

139. West, L. J. On the Marijuana Problem, in *Psychotomimetic Drugs*, D. Efron, (Ed.). Raven Press, New York, 1955.

140. Wikler, A., Mechanisms of action of drugs that modify personality function, *Am. J. Psychiatry*, **108,** 590 (1952).

141. Williams, G. W., Hypnosis in perspective, *Experimental Hypnosis*, L. M. LeCron (Ed.) Macmillan, New York, 1958, p. 4.

142. Young, D. and W. B. Scoville, Paranoid psychosis in narcolepsy and the possible danger of benzedrine treatment, *Med. Clin. North Am.* **22,** 637 (1938).

143. Zalis, E. G. and L. F. Parmley, Fatal amphetamine poisoning, *Arch. Intern. Med.* **112,** 822 (1963).

CHAPTER FOUR

DRINKING PATTERNS AND THE LEVEL OF ALCOHOL CONSUMPTION: AN INTERNATIONAL OVERVIEW

PEKKA SULKUNEN, *Finnish Foundation for Alcohol Studies and Department of Sociology, University of Helsinki, Finland*

1. INTRODUCTION

It is common knowledge that the level of alcohol consumption varies greatly from country to country and between different populations. This variation is related not only to demographic characteristics but also to cultural patterns, attitudes, and traditions. It has been almost as widely observed that the consumption levels are on the rise in most countries and populations at the present time, independently, one might be tempted to say, of the very same factors that seem to determine the variations in alcohol consumption cross-culturally.

The aim of this chapter is to describe the trends of growing consumption. Although I shall adopt some interpretative theoretical concepts for the purpose of organizing the diversity of statistical observations to be presented, I do not intend to offer an overall explanation of the trends. In my view, such explanations would, in principle, be vulnerable at the level of international comparisons because of the very great differences in social conditions that may be related to alcohol use and the diversity of cultural and historical traditions of drinking itself.

An explanation of the trends in a cross-national overview would presume that identical phenomena underlie the changes in the consumption level in all countries concerned. In fact, in what follows it will be suggested that, in a certain sense, this may really be the case. The increase in total alcohol consumption is perhaps, after all, a similar phenomenon even in some of the most contrasting conditions relating to the use of alcoholic beverages—but then this is a result, not an assumption.

Another difficulty in explanations of such general nature is that there are many kinds of possible causative factors that may affect the trends in alcohol consumption, even if these trends could be described in uniform supracultural terms. To name just a few, increasing general level of consumption, longer leisure hours, improved education, urbanization, and liberalization of the moral climate could be offered as explanatory factors for an increase in alcohol consumption. To assess the importance and interrelationships of such factors, a comprehensive theoretical system relating these phenomena to alcohol consumption is needed, but also detailed historical studies of alcohol consumption in each particular national situation will be necessary. This cannot be attempted here beyond the point of illustration.

Even with the modest aims of this paper, it is important that the descriptive concepts have *some* bearing on the possibility of finding causes for things, that is, for explaining them historically. In this respect, the basic point of departure of this presentation is that alcohol consumption is an aspect of general consumer behavior and as such can be seen as an object of economic analysis. In fact, there is a multitude of econometric studies about the elasticities of alcoholic beverages with respect to their price, consumers' income, and the prices of other commodities (25, 44). The values of such parameters of the econometric models can be of great practical significance as a device to be used in designing rational price policies, and they can be of interest from the standpoint of some theoretical approaches as well. However, for the interpretation of international consumption trends, the econometric approach is insufficient, although not useless, of course. In most cases it would be possible to develop a demand model with income and prices as independent variables and alcohol consumption as dependent variables. There are other aspects in alcohol consumption, however, which the statistical covariation in time or across a population of these variables would not reveal without further interpretation.

The most important of these is probably that consumers do not buy alcoholic beverages any more than other commodities merely because they can afford to, but because they have a need to do so. It is also likely that the quantities purchased depend on the particular uses to which the commodities are put. Also, the amounts in which certain commodities are used annually are related to the allocation of national productive resources and external trade capacity.

Considering the great historical and traditional differences in drinking cultures, it would therefore be unreasonable to expect that an econometric analysis could, in itself, explain the quantitative differences prevailing in the consumption of particular commodities between different periods or societies.

It is true, econometric studies can, in a certain way, be useful for the description of the different types of needs for which alcoholic beverages, among others, are being used. It is often concluded, on the basis of the elasticity values, that some commodities seem to belong to the group of luxury commodities, and some are rather like necessities, being insensitive to changes in incomes and prices. The problems of comparability due to methodologic differences and divergences in the data are usually great for international comparisons, for which reason this information could not be used in this overview, although the available number of studies is impressive (for a summary tabulation of the results from such studies, see ref. 44, Appendix 1–3).

Accepting, then, that alcohol consumption falls within the sphere of economic theory and that there are many kinds of concrete, historically determined causative factors that may affect the extent of alcohol use in different societies, in this paper we shall limit attention to only one, but important, aspect of the consumption trends—the uses of alcoholic beverages.

There are many commodities that can be put to different uses, not only as raw materials, but also in private consumption. Striking examples are various synthetic or natural fibers or, quite simply, water. There is no reason to assume a priori that alcohol must, in this respect, be an exception without qualification.

In classical economics, the varying property of commodities that satisfies needs is often termed their use value. In contrast to exchange value, which signifies the exchangeability of commodities in certain relatively constant quantitative terms convertible into money (prices), use value indicates the usability of commodities in their functions to satisfy certain specific human needs, of whatsoever kind or origin. It should be emphasized that, to have a use value, a commodity does not have to be in any sense "necessary" to human well-being, whether physical, psychological, or cultural. Nor do the needs have to be necessarily "natural" in any sense, but they can also be "artificially" created by vanity, advertising, and so forth. The essential requirement is only that consumption of the commodity yield sufficient satisfaction to its consumer for him to be willing to pay a certain sum of money for it.

The concept of use value is always necessarily present in any analysis of the consumption process. In a commodity economy, it does not alone determine the structure of private consumption, which is also affected, as a matter of course, by the relative prices of commodities and disposable income, as well as by economic and financial interests, and so on. Without it, however, the consumption of commodities by private persons and, especially, its historical and intercultural variation cannot be understood. At the same time, the concept of use value is a difficult one because of its very variability and the subjective elements that are often decisive in determining the usability of given commodities, including alcohol.

How, then, are we to decide what use values are important and what ones are not? What are the determining factors? It is often impossible to give any simple answer to these questions. It should be stressed, nevertheless, that use value is by no means solely a subjective concept. Although the same commodity can in many instances have several use values, of which one may be based on vanity and another on some essential need such as nourishment, it is often possible, however, to distinguish certain typical and dominant use values, which are determined by the technological stage of development of the society, the natural environment, traditions, etc. Uranium, for example, was all but useless until it was discovered how nuclear energy could be exploited, whether for purposes of war or of peace. Tar was highly useful as long as wooden ships were the most important means of navigation; but with the development of steel technology, its use value as an impregnating agent diminished greatly. The advances made in transport technology has had the effect that the use of fruits in the Nordic countries has changed from a luxury to a necessary part of the food economy. It is to be observed that the concept of use value can not be reduced to the physical properties of a commodity. The crucial element of a more or less extensive need always has a social origin.

Since the use values of consumers' goods also include elements of a subjective nature, their identification is exceptionally difficult. This applies especially to alcohol, the psychological effects and social implications of which are notoriously elusive. Certainly no absolutely accurate distinctions in this respect can be made. However, drinking patterns and the attitudes toward the use of alcohol, in many cases, reveal fundamental social and historical differences related to the use values of alcoholic beverages. In the following statistical analysis, therefore, drinking pattern is a central interpretative concept.

It should be noted, in this connection, that the concept of drinking patterns mainly signifies patterns that, in a sense, are typical or *average* in the social frame work concerned. Thus, this paper is not an account of *individual* differences in habitual behavior.

The study of use values in the light of socially typical drinking patterns does not spare us, however, from the problems of scanty research material. Drinking patterns have, to be sure, long been a central feature of alcohol studies. They have been brought into the discussion mainly to illuminate the drinking behavior of individuals, and the central parameters have been the frequency of drinking and the amounts ingested at a single sitting. In surveys designed to shed light on drinking patterns, these parameters are often combined as a so-called quantity–frequency index, with several socioeconomic and psychological background variables being set up to explain the variance. In some cases, we do not get to know very much through surveys of this kind about the persons who use alcohol, where and how they drink it, what they themselves think of it, how much money they spend on it, etc. As a social concept, drinking patterns usually refer to the assumption that society upholds certain norms to regulate alcohol consumption—mainly to determine whether it is proper to drink at all, whether it is proper to get drunk, or whether it is proper to drink often and in small quantities or less often but correspondingly large amounts at a time (for examples of this type of studies see refs. 4, 10, 13, 56a).

Investigations of this kind are of value, of course, when average or typical drinking patterns are being studied, if it is assumed that drinking is invariably oriented to intoxication. They rule out the possibility, however, that drinking can have other aspects too. For the purposes of culturally sensitive descriptions of drinking patterns, it is therefore necessary to go beyond the quantity–frequency index.

The most important of those aspects of drinking, which cannot be equated with intoxication (although it may not be unrelated to it), is the use of alcohol as a nutriment to supplement the caloric and liquid content of a meal. To illustrate the kind of distortions to which overlooking this aspect in international studies could lead, let us compare the alcohol conditions prevailing in Finland and Italy in the light of a few figures. In Italy in the early 1950s, the consumption of alcohol was about 10 liters per capita a year. According to Lolli et al. (32), approximately 80% of this total was drunk as a beverage with meals, which means that between meals roughly two liters a year were drunk by the average Italian. The total consumption of alcohol in Finland around the same period was only about 2.5 liters, but in this country alcohol is not customarily brought to the table with meals. Kuusi (23) reported, for instance, that about 9% of the drinks taken prior to the interview were motivated by "a meal, thirst, a chill, a cold in the head." Since the bulk of the wine drunk by Italians with their meals can scarcely be described as an intoxicant (32), and again, since the alcohol taken between meals can scarcely be considered to be primarily a nutriment, the conclusion is justified that the quantities of alcohol in terms of which it is easiest to compare Finns and Italians yield totals that are very much alike.

A similar observation applies to Poland, where the frequency of drunkenness (involving a blood alcohol concentration of over 0.1%) is more than double that reported for Italy, even though the Polish level of consumption is much lower than the Italian (59).

By confining our attention simply to examining the difference between Italian and Finnish alcohol conditions in the light of the norms and attitudes relating to drinking, we tend easily to confuse the food intake of one with the other's fun—and perhaps the other way around too.

The value of alcohol as a source of energy should not be underestimated. For example, according to OECD statistics, Italians obtain an average of about 6% of their total caloric intake from alcohol, assuming that wine contains 10 g/kg alcohol and that 1 g of alcohol amounts to 7.1 calories (42a). According to another estimate, the percentage may be as high as 25% for wide segments of the Italian population (4a). It is also interesting to note, in this context, that a joint WHO/FAO Expert Committee recently recommended that "energy derived from alcohol be included in the energy from foods in the estimate of national food supplies" (16a).

Besides the nutritional aspect, there are other use values attached to alcohol that have very little to do with the fact that this substance is most generally taken nowadays during periods of leisure for the enjoyment of its more or less agreeable intoxicating properties. Let us consider only, for example, the use of alcohol for medicinal purposes, which was quite common for example in the Nordic countries in the eighteenth century (11). Since, however, we shall give our attention mostly to societies where modern medical technology is at least known, if not applied in practice, and where, consequently, an all-purpose medicine like alcohol has very little use, we need not concern ourselves with this.

But there are many differences connected with the use of alcohol as an intoxicant that cannot be dealt with solely in terms of norms or attitudes toward drunkenness. The use of alcohol as a nondietary and nonmedicinal substance is likely to mean highly different things in various historical social situations. (I am not referring here to the fact that, to different groups of human beings, it naturally means different things, for even the mere description of the general historical picture is going to entail trouble enough.) For example, alcohol might be a rare luxury reserved for feasts; it might be nearly the only diversion during brief periods of leisure to break the monotony of constant hard work (53); it might be the workman's way of maintaining social relations with his friends (50); or it might be associated with seeking contacts of the opposite sex, or with religious rites or other ceremonies.

Provided only that we can perceive with sufficient clarity the existence of and differences in drinking patterns and use values shall we be able to add to our understanding of the circumstances that influence the general rise in the level of alcohol consumption.

By such means, the general features of alcohol consumption can be set forth in an international framework and on a historically specific level. I hope to be able to say something about these over and above the observation that the rate of consumption, as measured in terms of absolute alcohol, appears to be increasing generally nearly everywhere.

Three further limitations of the present analysis must be observed at the outset. The historical limits of the phenomenon of growth in alcohol consumption must first be noted, along with the phase covered by the present study. Table 1 shows that from the 1870s to World War II the trend in alcohol consumption was downward rather than upward in most of the industrialized world. The chief exceptions are the traditional wine-drinking nations, France and Italy, whose consumption has remained fairly constant. It can be said therefore that the decade of the 1940s marks a turning point in the evolution of alcohol consumption while being the driest period of the past century in the western world. It is possible and surely even probable that pressure existed in many countries, particularly the United States and Canada, as early as the 1920s and 1930s to raise the level of consumption, but such a rise was prevented to a certain extent by the great depression and war.

Secondly, although all the countries for which consumption statistics of sufficient reliability have been available are included in the quantitative study, the substantive results are applicable mainly to industrial countries—above all, the industrial countries of the West. This is due primarily to the fact that research data on the alcohol conditions prevailing in the developing world give only the bare statistics on consumption. It must also be observed that the changes in social conditions and way of living referred to in the foregoing as possible explanatory factors are either nonexistent in developing countries or, at least, are different in character from these phenomena as observed in advanced societies. It is for this reason that the developing countries included in the statistical survey serve mainly as objects of comparison, even though the data relating to them might have some intrinsic interest as well.

Thirdly, since the aim of the present study is expressly the description of the rising level of alcohol consumption in the international sphere, I do not intend to analyze on an empirical and theoretical basis the connection between the level of consumption and alcohol-related problems. It should be noted, nevertheless, that quite convincing evidence indicates that the prevalence of cirrhosis of the liver is closely connected with the consumption level. It would also appear that the general skew distribution of consumption affects this correlation to a fundamental extent (9, 28, 29, 48).

Leaving alcohol-related problems outside the bounds of this survey signifies a limitation essentially important here only insofar as they might, through restrictions imposed by political authorities or other social or economic mechanisms, have the effect of lowering the level of consumption or of restraining its rise. During the period following World War II,

TABLE 1 PER CAPITA CONSUMPTION OF 100% ALCOHOL IN LITERS IN SELECTED COUNTRIES (1871–1937) (17, 22, 49, 67)

Country	1871–1880	1881–1890	1891–1895	1896–1900	1901–1905	1906–1910	1919–1922	1925	1930	1936	1937
Austria	—	8.5	9.2	8.5	8.0	7.8	5.8	5.6	5.8	3.8	3.9
Belgium	10.3	10.2	11.4	11.7	11.3	10.6	9.0	9.4	10.8	8.1	—
Denmark	10.6	10.2	10.7	8.8	8.3	6.8	2.9	—	2.3[a]	2.2	2.3
Finland	2.8[b]	2.1[c]	1.8	2.1	1.7	1.6	—	—	0.5[d]	1.2	1.4
France	—	16.2	17.4	21.2	21.7	22.9	17.6	21.6	18.0	24.6	16.5
Germany	7.5	7.8	8.4	8.7	8.5	7.5	2.7	4.0	4.1	3.8	4.1
Hungary	—	8.0	6.6	6.5	7.5	7.6	5.7	3.0	3.4	3.3[e]	—
Italy	—	13.3	12.8	12.5	15.6	17.3	13.8	15.1	14.8	13.3	10.0
Netherlands	6.5	6.4	6.0	5.8	5.8	5.0	3.0	2.2[f]	2.4	1.3	1.4
Norway	3.5	2.4	2.8	2.8	2.7	2.4	2.0	2.1	2.3	2.0	2.1
Sweden	6.2	4.7	4.5	5.4	4.8	4.3	3.0	3.2	3.5	3.1	3.3
Switzerland	—	—	15.6	16.8	16.5	13.7	11.9	9.8[g]	11.9[h]	—	—
United Kingdom	12.3	10.4	11.0	11.6	10.9	9.7	6.3	5.9	5.2	4.6	4.7
Canada	10.8	9.2	8.1[i]	—	—	—	0.5[j]	0.6	0.9	0.6	0.7

[a] 1931; [b] 1876–1880; [c] 1886–1890; [d] 1932; [e] 1935; [f] 1926; [g] 1927; [h] 1929; [i] 1891–1893; [j] 1922.

mechanisms of this kind have not, however, to judge by the general evidence, had any marked effect, except, perhaps, in the case of France. Governments have sooner tended to relax the controls on the production, distribution, and consumption of alcoholic drinks and concentrated on the organization of treatment facilities for persons disabled by their addiction to alcohol (9, 37).

2. STATISTICAL GROUNDWORK

The material on which this article is based consists of data drawn mainly from international statistical publications. The statistics on consumption come mostly from publications issued by the Dutch alcohol producers' organization, Produktschap voor Gedistilleerde Dranken. They have been collected from this organization's annual statistical publication *Hoeveel Alkoholhoudende Dranken Worden er in de Wereld Gedronken*? dating from the years 1962–1970 (20). The statistics on the production and trade of alcoholic beverages have been drawn from several sources, the most important of which are the *U.N. Statistical Yearbook, the FAO Production Yearbook,* and the *FAO Trade Yearbook, The Growth of World Industry* (United Nations), and the *World Trade Annual* (United Nations) (16, 16b, 60–62).

These sources have been tapped for a statistical compilation called WAP (World Alcohol Project) Data, which covers the production, foreign trade, and consumption of beer, wine, and spirits, and the population in the countries from which data could be obtained.

Material of this nature naturally contains errors and defects. The most important of these are the difficulties stemming from the inexact reporting of alcohol content, the inconsistent classification of beverages, the deficient registration on a national level of the amount of alcohol used in the production of distilled liquors, and—especially in the estimation of annual consumption figures on the basis of production and foreign trade statistics—deficient information on changes in stocks, the industrial utilization of wine and pure alcohol, and waste consumption. Illicit, untaxed, and other unregistered consumption is not usually included in statistics. (For information about the errors possibly due to these factors, see ref. 58).

More surprising, perhaps, and also more restrictive from the standpoint of any investigation, however, is the fact that general international statistics cover alcoholic beverages very poorly. Thus for the following review, the required information about changes in consumption could be obtained from no more than 32 countries.

In many instances, the data at hand are inconsistent and incomplete. However, to make it possible to utilize in the trend analysis all the relevant information (random figures were not accepted for inclusion), the data from the early part of the observation period had to be rendered congruous. In Appendix 1, the methods used for this are explained in detail by countries. It should be pointed out here, however, that in the estimation of missing data it was not always sensible to apply any single consistent method—as, for instance, extrapolation on the basis of information available on the average annual change—but the more reliable procedure was to fall back on information not included in the material at hand, particularly for data relating to earlier years. In such cases, the value for the year 1950 was generally arrived at by applying to it the value for some proximate and probably corresponding year.

Figure 1, which represents the extent to which the WAP Data covers consumption, production, and international sales of beverages by the different types, shows, among other things, that, for the period prior to 1963, the sources of this kind include no data on distilled liquors and that the statistics on the beer trade starting backward from 1970 go back only to the year 1965. Regionally, it can be said that in the international system of statistics, alcohol is registered well wherever the official statistical system has been well developed. This means that information can be obtained best from developed capitalistic countries and from many socialist countries.

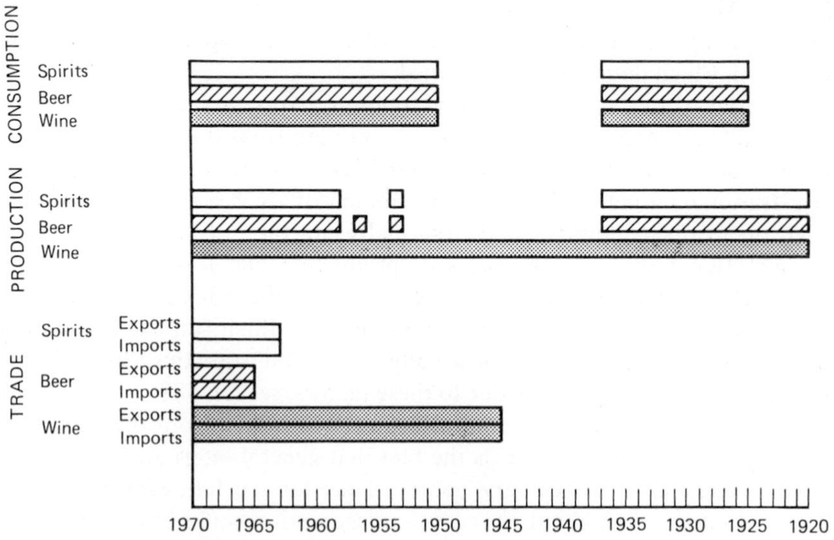

Fig. 1. Maximum information on the consumption, production, and international trade in WAP Data. The blanks in this diagram indicate that no information was available in the sources cited in WAP Data (57).

The data available from the socialist countries apply, to be sure, mostly to quite recent years. For the reasons mentioned in the introduction, this does not necessarily mean any fatal limitation. Alcohol conditions in developing countries are, at any rate, often hard to deal with in the framework of the kind of examination to be undertaken in the following sections.

3. STRUCTURE AND LEVEL OF ALCOHOL CONSUMPTION: TRADITIONS AND DRINKING PATTERNS

To gain an idea of the differences in alcohol consumption between various countries, we might start from the fact that the consumption is distributed very unevenly among the different regions of the world. For example, Europe, with its 455 million inhabitants, consumed at the end of the last decade about one-half of the alcoholic beverages covered by world statistics. The variation within the European continent, too, is great. The per capita consumption in terms of 100% alcohol ranged from France's 17 liters to Iceland's 3 liters. There are countries with a high level of alcohol consumption in other parts of the globe as well. Argentina, New Zealand, Chile, Canada, the United States, and Japan, together with the countries of Europe consumed roughly four-fifths of the alcohol used for drinking purposes throughout the world. The combined population of these countries, on the other hand, amounted in 1968 to about 800 million, or less than a quarter of the world total. Table 2 presents the combined share of the whole world's output in 1968 claimed by the five countries consuming the largest amount of each type of beverage, as calculated on the per capita basis. It can be noted that specifically wine consumption is most clearly

TABLE 2 CONSUMPTION SHARE OF TOP FIVE CONSUMING COUNTRIES OF TOTAL WORLD OUTPUT OF WINE, BEER, AND SPIRITS, 1968

Type of Alcohol	Consumption Share of Total World Output (%)	Share of Total World Population (%)
Beer[a]	30	4
Wine[b]	67	5
Spirits[c]	36	10

[a] Czechoslovakia, Belgium, Luxembourg, Australia, U.K.
[b] France, Italy, Spain, Argentina, Portugal
[c] Poland, Sweden, U.S.A., Yugoslavia, West Germany

TABLE 3 WINE CONSUMPTION AND PRODUCTION IN SELECTED COUNTRIES[a] IN 1970

Country	Consumption in Liters per Capita	Production in Millions of Hectoliters
EEC		
Belgium	13.9	—
France	112.0	74.4
Germany Fed. Rep.	16.9	9.1
Italy	114.6	68.9
Luxembourg	37.0	0.3
Netherlands	5.1	0.5
FINEFTA		
Austria	44.2	3.1
Denmark	5.9	—
Finland	4.1	—
Norway	2.3	—
Portugal	115.0	11.6
Sweden	6.4	—
Switzerland	40.8[b]	1.2
United Kingdom	2.9	—
U.S.A.	5.0	11.7
Canada	4.2	0.4
Japan	0.3	0.2
Bulgaria	21.7[c]	3.7
Greece	35.0	4.8
Hungary	39.0	4.4
Spain	61.5	25.0
Yugoslavia	28.3[b]	5.4
Algeria	1.5[b]	8.5
South Africa	9.3	4.2
Argentina	91.3	18.4
Chile	50.0	4.0

[a] EEC, FINEFTA, U.S.A., Canada, Japan, and a number of other countries, selected on the basis of a relatively high per capita consumption or total production.

[b] 1969.

[c] 1968.

concentrated in a few of the so-called wine countries of southern Europe and Latin America.

The national consumption of different alcoholic drinks is related to their production. The figures given in Table 3 show that, in all the countries where the consumption of wine per capita is heavy, wine is also produced in large quantities. An exception is Algerian wine production, which is nearly 10 million hl, although wine consumption remains at a very low level.

The ratio of foreign trade of alcoholic beverages to total world production is very low. For wines, it was about 10%, and for beer, about 5% in 1968. It is not possible to cite exact figures for distilled liquors, but since the exports of cognac exceed the domestic consumption of this liquor by about 400% and the exports of whisky from Britain exceed the domestic consumption by some 500%, the international markets in the sphere of distilled liquors must have greater relative significance (3).

On the other hand, in countries where the imports of any alcoholic beverage amount to a substantial proportion of its total consumption, that consumption is usually slight. With respect to wine, for instance, the fact is that in nearly all the countries where the share of imports is over 10% of the total consumption, that consumption is less than 5 liters a year per capita. The exceptions are West Germany and Switzerland, where the ratio of imports to consumption is 60% and 74% and the consumption 17 and 41 liters, respectively (statistics for 1970). In other words, in nearly all of the countries with heavy wine production, the average consumption per capita is also heavy; and, contrariwise, in nearly all the countries with a high level of consumption, the degree of self-sufficiency in the commodity is also high.

Compared with the volume of production, the export trade in beer is also relatively slight. Only Ireland (with about 40%) and Denmark (about 20%) export a substantial part of their production. On the other hand, only in Hungary does imported beer account for more than 10% of the consumption. Closest to this level comes Sweden, where foreign, mainly Danish, beer accounts for about 9% of the consumption—but this figure is falling.

In many countries, the production of alcoholic drinks has a long history. Even without a detailed study, it can be said that the development of the traditions in production has been affected by diverse social and environmental conditions. It has been pointed out that the production of wine and distilled liquors appears to depend—more than that of beer—on the availability of raw materials (57). Thus, the leading wine-producing countries are dependent on a favorable geographic location. In countries that produce distilled liquors, agricultural produce suitable for production of these liquors, such as grapes, fruits, grain, and potatoes—is generally abundant. By contrast, the production of beer appears to depend, to a lesser extent, on the domestic barley crop. Beer is largely the alcoholic drink of

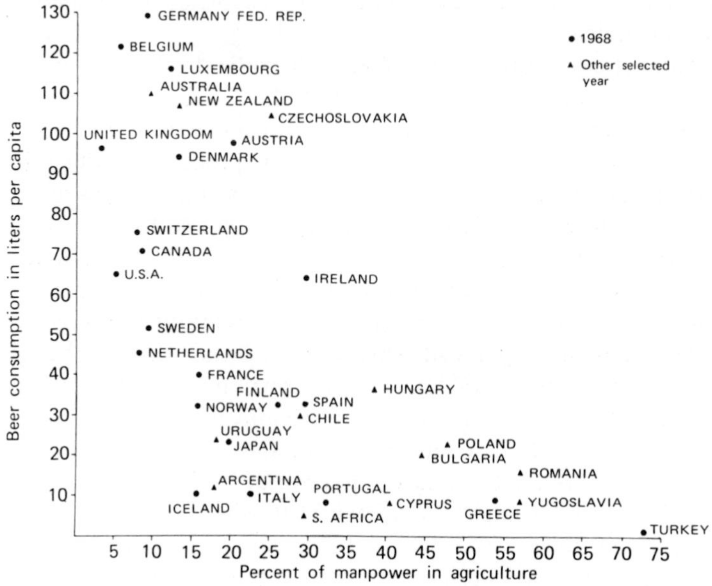

Fig. 2. Per capita consumption of beer and the percentage of manpower in agricultural occupations. *Notes*: The following list gives years for countries which have been marked with triangles: 1960: Argentina, Hungary, Chile, Poland, Cyprus, South Africa; 1961: Czechoslovakia, Yugoslavia; 1963: Urguay; 1965: Bulgaria; 1966: New Zealand, Australia, Romania. (Sources: "OECD Member Countries" in OECD Observer 38:1960. International Labour Yearbook 1970, Table 2A.)

industrial countries. Figure 2 shows that the consumption of beer per capita is heaviest where agricultural workers make up only a small proportion of the total labor force.

It is customary to distinguish between countries favoring beer, wine, or spirits. Often, conclusions concerning the typical drinking patterns in these different "alcohol cultures" are made (5a). The above remarks on the relationship between production of these different beverage types and their consumption encourage us to take a closer look at these cultural differences.

As we proceed in this task, the primary interest will be in the relation between drinking patterns and the overall level of alcohol consumption. It is hoped that the possibly divergent drinking patterns prevalent in these cultural constellations will reveal something of the use values of alcohol, i.e., the kinds of needs that alcoholic beverages are used to satisfy. As emphasized in Section 1, this is by no means equivalent, although highly relevant, to explaining adequately the quantitative differences in the consumption level. The point is, rather, to see if there is, in fact, a correlation between the consumption level, beverage preferences, and the typical drinking patterns; and whether the classification of countries on the basis of beverage preferences is justified from this point of view.

Since we are interested in traditional drinking habits, we are concerned here with historical trends. For the purposes of systematic analysis, this is of course problematic. We have to choose a certain point in time in which the possible traditions are to be seen as existent and observable. This is, to a certain extent, arbitrary, but the fact remains that as far as the use of alcohol is concerned, the period following World War II seems to mark a turning point in industrial countries, suitable to our purpose. As was observed in Section 1, it is during this period that the rising trends in alcohol consumption become established. Therefore we take the early 1950s as the base period and later analyze the trends from this period on.

Let us, first, attempt to carry out the classification of countries on the basis of the most favored beverages. This is given in Table 4, in which all countries for which the relevant information is available are grouped according to the percentages contributed to the total consumption of 100% alcohol by each beverage class. In the majority of cases, the classification can be done unambiguously. In some others (Luxembourg, Cyprus, German Democratic Republic) it was necessary to fall back on data relating to different periods to place the countries in the "right" categories, because the distribution of alcohol between the beverage classes was balanced between two competing beverages. Borderline cases are, moreover, Austria and Switzerland, where consumption in the early 1950s was distributed fairly evenly between all the beverage classes. With so few borderline cases, the classification seems to work rather well.

Also, the differences in the consumption level between these groups are strikingly obvious. In wine countries the total consumption of alcohol per capita is clearly the highest—it ranged from Switzerland's 7 liters to France's nearly 18 liters—unless one takes into account Rumania and Hungary, where, according to rather uncertain information, the figure was less than 5 liters.

In beer countries, the level of consumption varied closely between 3.5 and 6.5 liters. The sole exception was the German Democratic Republic, where it was under 2 liters.

Clearly, the lowest level of total consumption was measured in the spirits countries, where it was consistently at a maximum of about 2 liters. Exceptions were Sweden, with 4 liters, Poland, with 3 liters, and Yugoslavia, for which the 1955 figure was 2.7 liters.

Such distinct and consistent differences in the level of total consumption indicate that the classification of countries into traditional wine-, beer-, and

TABLE 4 BEVERAGE PREFERENCES AND TOTAL ALCOHOL CONSUMPTION PER CAPITA IN SELECTED COUNTRIES 1950–1952[a]

Countries	Percent of Total Alcohol Consumption			Total Consumption Per Capita
	Wine	Beer	Spirits	
Wine countries				
France	79.1	5.1	15.8	17.6
Hungary	78.5	6.0	15.5	4.8
Italy	90.8	1.7	7.5	9.4
Portugal[b]	95.8	0.4	3.8	12.9
Rumania[b]	60.8	6.0	33.2	4.7
Spain[b]	69.8	1.8	28.4	8.1
Switzerland[b]	51.7	29.6	18.6	6.6
Beer countries				
Australia[b]	13.4	73.8	12.7	6.4
Austria	32.7	43.5	23.8	5.4
Belgium	11.0	78.4	10.6	6.6
Canada	4.0	61.7	34.3	4.9
Czechoslovakia[b]	10.3	63.1	26.6	4.9
Denmark	9.8	78.3	11.9	4.0
Germany Fed. Rep.	20.0	50.2	29.8	3.6
Ireland	3.5	75.0	21.5	3.4
Luxembourg	42.8	43.1	14.1	6.8
New Zealand[b]	4.2	75.3	20.5	5.6
United Kingdom	2.1	87.1	10.8	4.9
U.S.A.	9.8	51.7	38.5	5.0
Spirits countries				
Bulgaria[b]	27.4	13.4	59.2	1.1
Cuba[b]	12.2	34.6	53.2	2.0
Cyprus[b]	43.7	13.0	43.3	3.1
Finland	6.6	33.9	59.5	2.2
Germany Dem. Rep.	3.6	47.0	49.5	1.9
Iceland[b]	15.9	37.9	46.1	1.1
Israel[b]	16.4	25.3	58.3	1.4
Netherlands	3.8	28.2	68.1	1.9
Norway	7.2	41.6	51.2	2.1
Peru[b]	10.2	24.0	65.8	1.3
Poland	4.6	24.2	71.2	3.1
South Africa	29.7	21.4	48.9	1.8
Sweden	4.5	31.8	63.7	4.0
Turkey[b]	27.5	17.3	55.2	0.3
Yugoslavia[b]	18.9	8.2	72.9	2.7

[a] Annual average.

[b] Figures are based on estimates for 1950 as shown in Appendix 1.

[d] Total Consumption per Capita given in Liters of 100% alcohol, per year.

spirits-drinking cultures is not merely a formal convention but actually has a substantial content from the standpoint of drinking patterns. The high consumption level prevailing in wine-drinking countries can be presumably related to the fact that wine is a relatively inexpensive nutriment and is used daily as a normal beverage with meals. It has been noted already in the foregoing (Section 2) that Italians at the beginning of the decade of the 1950s drank about 80% of all their alcohol in connection with meals (32). The French often take drinks also between meals (52).

On the other hand, in "hard-liquor countries", drinking alcohol with meals has not been very common, at least, it was not at the time following World War II. Kuusi's findings (23) indicate that in the rural districts of Finland, spirituous liquors were drunk invariably apart from meals (and meals eaten invariably without alcoholic beverages). Likewise in the Netherlands, which ranks clearly as a country leaning toward distilled liquors rather than wine or beer and with a low consumption level, alcohol is not ordinarily a concomitant of food. Of Gadourek's sample (18) representing the Dutch population, only 2% reported drinking some alcoholic beverage with meals.

The relatively high consumption level of beer-drinking nations is not based so much on the fact that beer is an everyday mealtime beverage but that its ingestion is connected with daily social contacts and, ordinarily, with conviviality outside the home—in pubs, taverns, and restaurants (37). In *Mass Observation's* excellent description of life in English pubs in the days before the war, it is noted that "the material . . . brought forward indicates that the pub is mainly sought as a social rather than an alcoholic environment. But it is a form of social environment that is only possible plus alcohol. And therefore a whole range of the social life of the ordinary pub-goer (who is one of the main sorts of 'ordinary man') is bound up with the idea of drink. The social and alcoholic aspects of pub-going cannot really be separated." Food, however, is not served—and seldom, if ever, eaten—in pubs (50).

The relation of alcohol to the taking of meals thus appears to be an essential feature distinguishing the drinking patterns of beer-, spirits- and wine-drinking nations. In wine countries, such a major part of the consumption of alcohol is connected with eating that it can be regarded as a natural component of a meal, and wine can, with good reason, be called a nutriment. In countries characterized by the consumption of beer and particularly spirituous liquors, the use of alcohol is confined to leisure time, and it has primarily other than nutritional use values, even if it is taken in the context of meals as appetizer or to highlight the meal as a social occasion.

In the light of the statistics so far set forth we can draw other conclusions too, about the prevailing differences in drinking patterns among these three traditional alcohol cultures. Comparing the liquid volumes, in liters, of the alcohol consumed in the respective countries, we might be able to make certain judgments about the prevalence on various levels of alcohol consumption. If, for example, 4 liters of alcohol a year per capita is consumed in some beer-drinking country and the alcoholic content of beer is estimated at an average of 4% by volume, we arrive at—if all alcohol is taken in the form of beer—100 liters of liquid per capita, which is by no means an uncommon quantity. This amounts to nearly a third of a liter of beer a day; and if children, the sick, and the elderly are taken into account as nondrinkers, well over a half a liter of beer a day is left for the potential consumers.

The same sort of estimates as to the drinking conditions prevailing in wine countries can be made. On this basis, we are obliged to conclude that a very high proportion of the population must join in the ingestion of liquor in the form and quantities statistically shown, no matter how skew and concentrated the distribution of consumption might be.

With respect to the nations favoring spirituous liquors, the situation is different. In Finland, for example, during the early 1950s, the amounts of alcoholic drinks consumed were: about 25 liters of beer, 0.5 liter of wine, and 3 liters of spirits, or together roughly 28 liters of liquor a year, which corresponded to slightly more than 2 liters of alcohol a person. Assuming that the consumption was concentrated to the extent that, for example, the heaviest drinking tenth of the population consumed one-half of the total amount, we arrive at the estimate that the share of the rest was on the average slightly over 1 liter of pure alcohol per person. Assuming, further, that the beverage preferences with respect to the three categories of beverages we are using are independent of whether any given consumer belonged to the 10% class of heavy consumers or not, the "normal drinker's" average quota of liquor yearly was about 15 liters, of which about 12 liters was beer and the rest spirituous liquors.

The purpose of this estimation is merely to show that, if Finnish drunkards did not have very much thirst quencher (of the legal kind, at least) 25 years ago, the rest of the Finns had to consider even more carefully how to make use of their meager liquor purchases. Per capita, only a liter of beer a month fits into these amounts, and the acquisition of a bottle of hard liquor was an even rarer incident. If, on the other hand, the whole quantity of alcohol were to be consumed in the form of, let us say, beer, the quota of the normal consumer would come to more than 25 liters of this beverage per annum—in other words, he would drink a liter of beer on the average every other week.

The assumption on which the estimation is based about the concentration of consumption is altogether realistic. Mäkelä, for instance, has observed that in 1968 10% of the adult Finnish males drank 53% of all the alcohol consumed by members of their sex, while 10% of the women drank as much as 72% of all the alcohol consumed by the female population (33). Actually, the distribution of consumption may be even more concentrated than indicated in the situation involved in our example. On the basis of a reanalysis of survey material concerning a number of different countries, Skog (9, 56) has observed that the concentration of consumption is all the greater, the lower the average level of consumption. A phenomenon like this seems intuitively natural, considering that the consumption of alcoholics has presumably a tendency to exceed, rather than fall short of 10 liters, although, to be sure, there occurs conspicuous variation according to the general level of consumption prevailing in a society (1, 8). It is reasonable to suppose that heavy consumers must stay above some minimum level to enable them as a rule to obtain the satisfaction and the pleasure they seek through the ingestion of alcohol.

Skog's finding is interesting from the standpoint of the argument set forth here in itself (56). If the concentration of alcohol consumption is, indeed, great in countries with a low consumption level, this sharpens the edge of the result arrived at by hypothetical calculations, as noted in the foregoing. The disparity between regular drinkers and "normal" consumers becomes conspicuous, for the latter presumably take enough to get drunk only on extremely rare occasions. The populations of spirits-drinking countries can therefore be expected to be polarized in two fairly distinct groups: regular users (a small minority) and abstainers or infrequent users (the great majority). The use of alcohol among the majority of the people is exceedingly rare—and all the rarer (*a*) the lower the average level of consumption is, (*b*) the higher the proportion of alcohol drunk in the form of spirits, and (*c*) the bigger the share of the total consumption claimed by alcoholics—in other words, the more concentrated the distribution of consumption.

The view of polarization in the alcohol consumption of spirits-drinking nations is reinforced by the fact that, in many cases, they have a strong temperance movement (47). Also the proportion of teetotalers and infrequent users represented in the population is generally higher in spirits-drinking than beer- and wine-drinking countries, as Table 5 shows clearly.

Although the figures given in the table are not mutually comparable, it can nevertheless be perceived, considering the effect of the research designs and methods, that in beer and wine countries there are usually fewer total abstainers than in countries favoring spirits.

In studying the table, one should bear in mind that the age, place of residence, and sex of the persons included in the sample influence the proportion of abstainers to a noticeable degree. Furthermore, it is important to pay attention to the definitions of temperance and infrequent consumption.

TABLE 5 PERCENTAGE OF ABSTAINERS AND INFREQUENT DRINKERS IN SELECTED POPULATIONS

			Abstainers		Infrequent drinkers			
Country	Population		Percent	Definition	Percent	Definition	Year	Reference
England	General population over 16 years	Total	32	Does not drink	—	—	1948	51a
Canada	General population over 20 years	Men	24	Abstainer	—	—	?	48a
		Women	36		—	—		
U.S.A.	General population over 20 years	Men	30	Abstainer	—	—	?	48a
		Women	54		—	—		
U.S.A.	General population over 20 years	Total	32	Drinks less than once a year	15	Drinks at least once a year but less than once a month	1964–1965	10
		Men	23		10			
		Women	40		18			
France	General population over 20 years	Men	—	—	10	Has not consumed alcoholic drinks in the last 24 hr	1956	52
		Women	—	—	44			
Italy	General population in Rome	Men	—	—	6	Has not consumed alcoholic drinks for a week	?	32
		Women	—	—	21			

Denmark	Men of 30–44 years in Copenhagen		2	Has not drunk for a year	—	—	1964	21
Sweden	Men of 30–44 years in Stockholm		4	Has not drunk for a year	—	—	1964	21
Finland	Men of 30–44 years in Helsinki		8	Has not drunk for a year	—	—	1964	21
Norway	Men of 30–44 years in Oslo		12	Has not drunk for a year	—	—	1964	21
Finland	General population over 20 years	Men	14	Has never drunk or considers himself a teetotaler	—	—	1946	24
		Women	72		—	—		
Finland	General population between 15 and 59 years in 7 villages in southern Finland	Men	20	Does not drink or has not drunk for a year	—	—	1951	23
		Women	53		—	—		
Finland	General population between 15 and 59 years	Men	20	Does not drink or has not drunk for a year	20	Has drunk at most twice during the past year	1968	35
		Women	76		55			
Norway	General population over 17 years	Men	25	Does not drink beer, wine, or spirits or has not drunk for a year	—	—	1956	7
		Women	37		—	—		
Norway	General population over 17 years	Men	21	Does not drink beer, wine, or spirits or has not drunk for a year	—	—	1962	7
		Women	37		—	—		
Norway	General population over 17 years	Men	12	Does not drink beer, wine, or spirits or has not drunk for a year	—	—	1966	7
		Women	22		—	—		
Sweden	General population over 15 years	Men	13	Does not drink	—	—	1955	6
		Women	26		—	—		
Netherlands	General population 20 years and over	Total	18	Does not drink	—	—	1958	18

The time any given survey was made is likewise important. As the level of consumption rises, the proportion of abstainers conversely decreases in the course of time.

When, for instance, age is taken into account, the observation may be made that the proportion of total abstainers is lower in England than in the United States or Canada. Although they are all clearly in the category of beer countries, and, although the average level of consumption in each is approximately the same (slightly under 5 liters), the share of beer in proportion to the total alcohol consumption is strikingly the greatest in England (nearly 90%).

The findings about adult males in the Nordic countries are mutually quite comparable, and they reveal that the proportion of abstainers is lower in Denmark than in Sweden, although the average level of consumption is roughly the same (about 4 liters in 1950 and about 5 liters in 1964). Denmark is unmistakably a beer country (the share of beer is 75% of the total alcohol consumption), and Sweden is a spirits-drinking country (63%). In the low consumption level, spirits-drinking countries of Norway and Finland (2 liters in 1950), the proportion of abstainers is the highest among the adult male residents of the respective Nordic (Finland and the other Scandinavian countries) capitals. Taking the total population, the proportion of abstainers is higher in Finland and Norway than in Sweden.

In spirits-drinking countries, the great differences in alcohol habits between regular users and infrequent users or abstainers highlights the conspicuous visibility of alcohol. Under such conditions, drinking as a general rule is always "deviant" behavior—especially when it leads to drunkenness. Finns tolerate liquor poorly—but how about the Norwegians, Poles or, for that matter, the Turks?

The visibility of drinking is intensified in countries favoring spirits by the fact that it is socially segregated there, constituting a separate activity, without its being linked to other aspects of social life in a kind of supplementary role (2, 8). This is brought out by the fact, for instance, that the catering institution in these countries is off limits to the great majority of the inhabitants. Restaurants are patronized mainly in these countries by members of the upper social classes and by heavy drinkers. Infrequent drinkers enjoy their liquor mostly at home or on special or random occasions in other places (2, 18, 21, 40, 46). In beer- and wine-drinking countries, on the other hand, restaurants attract a broader sector of the population, and drinking takes place less often in home surroundings (13, 37).

I have tried in the foregoing discussion to make the point that the classification of various nations into spirits, wine, and beer cultures is not merely a formal one, based on statistical averages. The admittedly few and crude facts that were brought up seemed to support the conventional idea that the typical drinking patterns prevailing in these countries are quite different.

Yet, I am not claiming unconditional validity for this grouping, of course. Further studies may show that drinking in context of meals is customary also in many beer countries and even in some spirits countries. Even less has it been possible to give detailed historical explanations as to why each country belongs to a certain group with its typical beverage structure, drinking patterns, and level of consumption (apart from the observations made on the relations between production and consumption of the traditional beverages). It is more important, however, that the similarities found within each group of countries have pointed to certain predominant use values of alcoholic beverages, that is, the needs which they are used to satisfy in these countries.

The wine countries are distinguished particularly by the fact that the ingestion of alcohol there is customarily done as an integral part of having a meal. Alcohol in these countries has a distinctly nutritional use value. The spirits-drinking countries can be differentiated from the others by the fact that the use of alcohol there is exceptional but, at the same time, conspicuous and segregated from other social activities; in these countries, the population is polarized into two groups, users and nonusers. The use value of alcohol in these countries is primarily that of an intoxicant. Beer countries form in this respect probably the least homogeneous group. In some, beer can only marginally be seen as food; in some others this is not so clear. Nevertheless, it seems that in these cultures beer has a distinct convivial function: it is an institution around which much of the everyday social life evolves.

It is possible and even likely that the different drinking patterns and use values are reflected in alcohol cultures of different types as typical attitudes. For instance, Pittman (47) classifies cultures according to the prevailing attitudes toward drinking into abstinent, ambivalent, permissive, and overpermissive groups. In line with such a classification the spirits countries might be characterized as abstinent or ambivalent, whereas the beer-drinking nations would be either ambivalent (England, Ireland) or permissive (Germany), and the wine-drinking nations permissive (Italy) or overpermissive (France). Or we might try to present the differences on the basis of Bales's classical typology (5). According to this classification, the attitudes toward alcohol may be wholly rejective (abstinent), or may accept it as a means of easing and livening human contacts on social occasions (convivial), or ritualistic, or exclusively aimed at releasing physical or mental pressure (utilitarian). The typical attitudes toward drinking in spirits-oriented countries could then perhaps be characterized as either abstinent or utilitarian, in beer-drinking countries as either convivial or utilitarian, and in wine-drinking countries as either convivial or utilitarian, depending on the aspect of consumption under consideration.

The problem of such classifications of attitudes, however, is that they apply to drinking as a general category, not accounting for differences in actual drinking patterns and the related use values. These attitudinal typologies seem to imply that the use of alcohol always involves a degree of intoxication and the moral concern for it as the *sole* or at least *most* relevant aspect of drinking. As such, they are more a mapping of public attitudes towards intoxication than the use of alcoholic beverages in all its complexity. Therefore, they may not always provide good characterizations of cultures where drinking for the most part is not a moral issue.

Such classifications are therefore best applicable in the conditions within spirits countries, where alcohol usually has scarcely any other use besides its value as an intoxicant. Therefore in these countries also the use of and attitudes towards alcohol can be described as one-dimensional. In international comparisons, attitudinal characterizations may best be used as supplementary and applied only as secondary criteria in differentiating alcohol cultures.

Although I have analyzed the use values of alcohol in the context of typical drinking patterns prevailing in different alcohol cultures, it is not being said that alcohol is food in one country and intoxicant in another. Certainly it is possible to get drunk from wine in Italy as well as in any other country, even independent of its combination with or action as food. Certainly, also, the caloric content of alcohol can be assimilated in the metabolic process independently of cultural norms regulating drinking behavior. Different use values can be and are coexistent. The foregoing analysis might rather be seen as further support for the hypotheses that some use values are more important than others, depending on social and cultural conditions. In fact, I have tried to stress that in wine countries alcohol does serve nutritional needs in addition to others; and the same is true probably even to a greater extent for beer countries. In this sense these alcohol cultures could perhaps be characterized as multidimensional in contrast to spirits countries where alcohol is more distinctly a drug.

Two reservations to this analysis should be added to those presented earlier. First, the methodologic procedure is apt to arouse confusion in that use values have been derived from descriptions of typical drinking patterns. This has been done for two reasons. (*a*) It is very difficult to study directly the needs which alcoholic beverages satisfy, and this is particularly true in a cross-cultural comparative study. For this reason, typical drinking patterns and situations in which drinking usually takes place may give us clues to conclusions concerning the use values. Therefore, an appetizer before the dinner does not necessarily involve a need to supplement the caloric content of the food, although it would be described as drinking with or at least in the context of a meal. (*b*) Although my conclusions on use values are derived from the analysis of drinking patterns, it is quite possible that changes in use values of alcohol in reality derive from changes in drinking patterns. The needs may be there as of old; but newly adopted drinking customs may induce the use of alcohol to satisfy them, thus replacing some other means of want satisfaction. However, they can also create new needs (addiction, for instance). Therefore it is useful to study drinking patterns as such.

Another problem arises with the geographic limits of the material presented over and above the consumption statistics. In this sense, the generalizations are far from conclusive. However, it is hoped that, as far as it goes, they can be used as a bench mark for closer historical studies. At least they seem to hold enough water, to the extent that the grouping of countries according to the dominant beverage type is not entirely arbitrary, and can be used in the following as a basis for investigating the developments in drinking patterns and the level of alcohol consumption since the 1950s.

4. DIFFUSION OF DRINKING PATTERNS AND THE RISING LEVEL OF CONSUMPTION

An idea can be gained about the magnitude of the growth of alcohol consumption on a global level by first examining Table 6, which gives figures indicating the increase in alcohol production in Europe and throughout the world. The figures for the world as a whole and for Europe in particular suggest that the world production of beer increased between 1960 and 1968 by about 41%, that of wine about 15% and that of distilled liquors about 40%. Assuming that equally large quantities were also consumed during the years covered by the table, we arrive at the result that total alcohol consumption, when the population growth is taken into account, increased throughout the world by about 9% and in Europe about 17%.

Table 7 presents the trends in consumption, calculated on a per capita basis, from the beginning of the 1950s to the end of the 1960s in detail for individual countries. Differences between the types of countries in the rate of growth of consumption can be perceived. For beer countries, the quantitative increase in alcohol consumption was on the order of about 25 or 30% between the annual averages of 1950 to 1952 and 1968 to 1970, so that, at the end of the 1960s, it most usually amounted to between 5.5 and 8.5 liters. Beer-drinking countries with an exceptionally high consumption level at the end of that decade were the Federal Republic of Germany (with an average figure of 9.8 liters for the years 1968–1970) and Austria (10.7 liters), whereas Ireland emerged as an exceptionally temperate beer-drinking country (with a

TABLE 6 THE DEVELOPMENT OF THE PRODUCTION OF ALCOHOLIC BEVERAGES IN EUROPE AND THE WORLD AS A WHOLE

	Wine		Beer		Distilled Alcoholic Liquors Converted into 100% Alcohol	
Year	Million Hectoliters	Liters per Capita	Million Hectoliters	Liters per Capita	Million Hectoliters	Liters per capita
Whole world						
1920	164	9.1	129	7.1		
1930	158	7.8	168	8.3		
1960	247	8.3	404	13.5	20.2	0.7
1962	285	9.2	444	14.3		
1968	283	8.1	568	16.3	28.2	0.8
Europe						
1920	147	44.7	118	35.9		
1930	130	36.5	156	43.8		
1960	187	44.0	191	44.9	6.1	1.4
1962	214	49.3	210	48.4		
1968	204	44.8	269	59.1	9.3	2.0

Populations of whole world and Europe (in millions)

	1920	1930	1960	1962	1968
World	1810	2013	2982	3100	3490
Europe	329	356	425	434	455

Soviet production is not included in the production figures for Europe for technical reasons. Data on the production of distilled liquors and wine in the U.S.S.R. in 1920 and 1930 are lacking.

It has been endeavored here to report the alcoholic liquors as converted to 100% alcohol, and for this reason the figures have been multiplied by 0.80. See also Table 9.

total consumption of only 4.4 liters). In certain beer countries, to be sure, the rate of increase in consumption was noticeably higher.

With the exception of Portugal and France, which fall into the category of countries with an exceptionally high level of alcohol consumption (the figures for Portugal are fairly uncertain), the increase in total consumption in the wine-drinking countries was generally more than 40% during this period, with Hungary topping the list (77%). The consumption level of these countries is nowadays in the neighborhood of 8.5–14 liters, though in France, it is true, the level is higher.

TABLE 7 TRENDS IN TOTAL PER CAPITA ALCOHOL CONSUMPTION IN SELECTED COUNTRIES (1950–1970)

Country	Consumption in Liters per Capita of 100% Alcohol 1950–1952	Consumption per Capita of 100% Alcohol in 1968–1970 (1950–1952 = 100)	Average Annual Increase	Number of Observed Years
Wine countries				
France	17.6	93.0	−0.3	20
Hungary	4.8	177.0	4.2	13
Italy	9.4	148.6	2.1	20
Portugal	12.9[a]	109.3	3.7	6
Rumania	4.7[a]	133.8	0.1	8
Spain	8.1[a]	144.4	1.8	8
Switzerland	6.6[a]	151.9	2.4	8
Beer countries				
Australia	6.4[a]	126.9	1.5	19
Austria	5.4	210.4	4.6	20
Belgium	6.6	126.0	1.5	20
Canada	4.9	133.2	1.8	20
Czechoslovakia	4.9[a]	163.0	3.4	16
Denmark	4.0	168.1	3.0	20
Germany Fed. Rep.	3.6	287.0	6.5	20
Ireland	3.4	132.8	1.8	19
Luxembourg	6.8	139.5	2.5	20
New Zealand	5.6[a]	126.4	1.8	17
United Kingdom	4.9	125.7	1.3	20
U.S.A.	5.0	115.5	0.9	20
Spirits countries				
Bulgaria	1.1[a]	498.4	7.7	5
Cuba	2.0[a]	89.2	−1.7	5
Cyprus	3.1[a]	106.1	−1.3	5
Finland	2.2	185.6	4.3	20
Germany Dem. Rep.	1.9	396.3	9.5	20
Iceland	1.1[a]	255.3	4.0	10
Israel	1.4[a]	131.9	−0.4	7
Netherlands	1.9	253.1	5.3	20
Norway	2.1	160.3	2.6	20
Peru	1.3[a]	208.4	5.7	9
Poland	3.1	178.4	3.0	20
South Africa	1.8	159.4	2.8	17
Sweden	4.0	143.2	2.0	20
Turkey	0.3[a]	135.6	5.4	8
Yugoslavia	2.7[a]	269.1	6.5	14

[a] Estimate. See Appendix 1.

The biggest changes occurred in the countries that, on the basis of the data for the years 1950–1952, could be classified as spirits drinking. A rise of over 100% in the average level of alcohol consumption in the 20-year period was by no means uncommon; according to certain estimates, the consumption of alcohol in Bulgaria increased fivefold. Sweden ranked second (5.7 liters), and Poland also held its place near the top (with 5.4 liters). The lowest level of consumption on the whole among the countries included in the table continued to be in Turkey (0.46 liters).

The more rapid than average rate of increase in consumption registered in the spirits-drinking countries, where the consumption level is usually very low, means that the level has risen more rapidly than the average in the countries where the level of consumption was low to begin with. This has had the effect of bringing closer together the consumption levels of the different groups of countries under consideration. This process of quantitative homogenization can be measured by, for example, a coefficient of variation. Table 8 shows that the value of the coefficient between countries diminishes systematically during the period under investigation in all the classes into which the countries have been divided.

The growth in the consumption of alcohol consumption has not taken place independently of the changes that have occurred in the structure of consumption. An overall picture of the trend of these changes is given by Table 9, in which an estimate has been made of the developments in the quantity of alcohol contained in the different classes of beverages during the 1960s on the basis of the figures representing total alcohol production in Europe and the world. Once more, it must be remarked that, on the basis of this table, only tentative observations can be made.

The most important of these observations is that wine appears to be unquestionably losing ground as a source of alcohol throughout the world,

TABLE 8 VARIATION COEFFICIENTS OF TOTAL PER CAPITA CONSUMPTION OF 100% ALCOHOL BETWEEN COUNTRIES

Group	1950	1960	1965	1969
1	0.77	0.63	0.61	0.55
2	0.75	0.60	0.53	0.45
3	0.70	0.64	0.55	0.48

Group 1, all countries listed in Table 7.
Group 2, all European countries.
Group 3, capitalist European countries, U.S.A. and Canada.

TABLE 9 ALCOHOLIC CONTENT OF INTOXICATING BEVERAGES PRODUCED IN THE WORLD AS A WHOLE AND IN EUROPE 1960 AND 1968

	Alcohol in Millions of Hectoliters Contained in				Rate of Increase in the production of 100% Alcohol in Relation to Population
	Wine	Beer	Distilled Liquors	Total	
World					
1960	24.7	20.2	20.2	65.1	100
1968	28.3	28.4	28.2	84.9	109
Europe					
1960	18.7	9.6	6.1	34.4	100
1968	20.4	13.5	9.3	43.2	117

Wines are assumed to contain 10% alcohol by volume, beer 5%, and distilled liquors an average of 80%. It is difficult to estimate, however, the strength of the different alcoholic beverages reported by different countries. Hence, averages of the kind used here are more or less arbitrary. As the production of distilled liquors has been reported by a number of countries in terms of 100% alcohol, whereas other countries have reported their production in terms of the consumption strength of the beverages, the assumption has been made here that the alcohol content of the totals average approximately 80% by volume.

especially in Europe, where it still rates as the most important class of alcoholic beverages. This is happening while the total amount of alcohol increases, particularly in countries not belonging to the European group. Among these the most notable in this respect is the U.S.S.R. (not included among the European countries in the present chapter for technical reasons).

The trends reflected by these total figures are based mainly on the fact that the increase in consumption that has taken place in wine countries has generally been slower than in spirits-drinking countries (Tables 6 and 7). They indicate further that important structural changes have also occurred within the countries.

An idea of the internal structural changes can be gained best by examining the distribution of the total alcohol consumption by classes of beverages, as has been done in Table 4. In Fig. 3, these percentages have been marked on an equilateral triangle, on which the position of a point representing a country denotes the percentage of the total amount of alcohol claimed by the classes of beverages. Thus, for example, in Finland in the years 1950–1952, hard liquor accounted for 60%, beer for 34%, and wine for 6% of the alcohol consumed on the average. The arrows drawn on

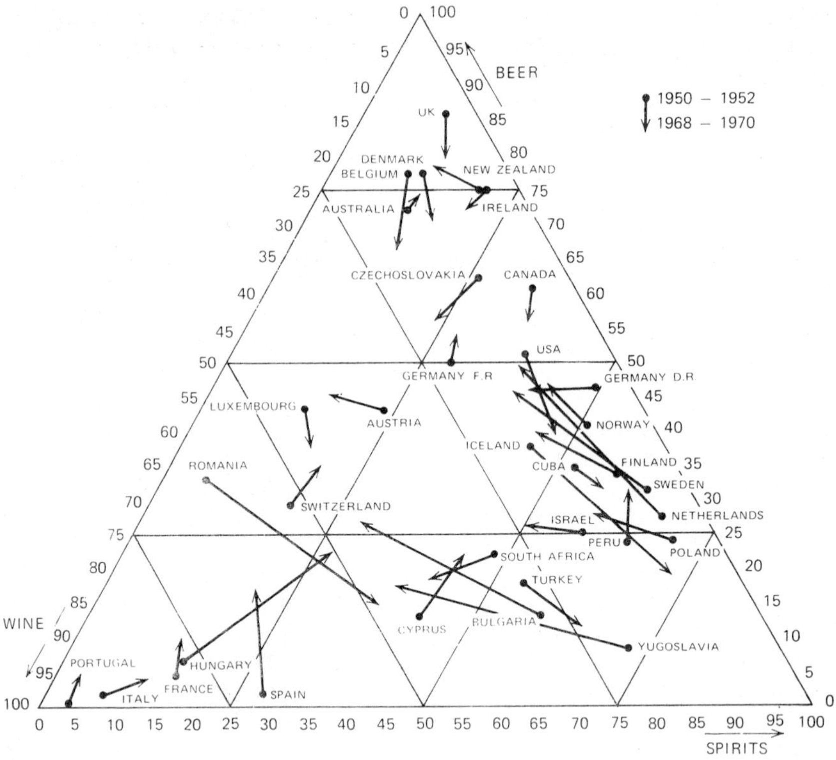

Fig. 3. Distribution of annual average alcohol consumption by beverage class in selected countries, 1968–1970 and 1950–1952.

the triangle indicate the changes in the structure of drinking from the 1950–1952 period (figure representing the average) to the 1968–1970 period (average).

The most important observation that can be made from Fig. 3 is that a general leveling process has occurred in the structure of drinking: the countries have shifted more or less straight toward the center of the triangle, which represents the distribution of alcohol evenly among all three classes of beverages.

We can measure the distance of each country from the midpoint by means of the equation

$$R = \sqrt{\sum_j \left(\frac{P_j - \frac{1}{3}}{3}\right)^2}; \quad j = 1, 2, 3 \tag{1}$$

where j = the type of beverage, Pj = the proportion of the type of beverage j of the total amount of alcohol, and R = the distance from the midpoint. The mean of this distance in the 1950–1952 period was 14.0, in 1959–1961 it was 13.0 and in 1968–1970, 11.9.

Let us assume in the manner set forth in the preceding section that the beverage structure reflects typical drinking patterns, which can be analyzed in terms of different use values. Then this triangle could be interpreted to indicate that between the 1950s and the 1970s, the drinking cultures systematically drew closer together, also qualitatively. The proportion of nontraditional beverages in the total alcohol consumption has risen.

In this respect too, the trend that has taken place in spirits-drinking countries has been the most drastic, judging by the length of the arrows (Figure 3, see also Tables 6 and 7). On the whole, the shift in these countries has taken place in the direction of an increase in the proportionate share of both beer and wine. The only exception is Peru, where the consumption of wine has also decreased.

The changes taking place in wine countries have been likewise conspicuous, mainly owing to the increase in the proportion of beer drunk. In Hungary and Rumania, also the proportion of hard liquor has risen noticeably. In beer-drinking countries, the changes have been structurally slighter on the whole; in them, the proportion of both wine and hard liquor consumed has risen.

Insofar as the assumption holds good that the beverage structure reveals something about the prevailing drinking pattens in wine-, spirits- and beer-drinking countries, the leveling out of the structure means that intercultural diffusion has taken place in drinking patterns. We shall here note a few developments that may have contributed to this trend, which can be called qualitative homogenization.

The explosive growth of foreign travel that took place during the 1960s, being directed largely from North America to Europe and from the beer- and spirits-drinking European countries (from Scandinavia, West Germany, and England) to the wine countries of the south (43), has made familiar the drinking habits and customs of the people living in the wine countries. The dominant place held in the global communications network by American films and television programs (64) increases the dissemination of the drinking culture adopted by the Americans; the cocktail hour is beginning to be a well-known custom even in Italy (31).

It is possible to point, however, to circumstances that influence the diffusion specifically of alcohol cultures. Although closer scrutiny of the matter is not feasible in this connection, it is impossible to ignore a phenomenon that, in capitalistic countries, has reached an unprecedented magnitude since World War II—namely, the concentration of economic activities. In the alcohol industry, this has meant, among other things, the fusion of brewing companies on a large scale, which is shown as it applies to the end of the 1960s in Table 10. In three years, the number of brewing companies in the EEC and FINEFTA countries (excepting Spain) has been reduced from 2556 to 2362, or by 7.6%. During the same period, production has increased about 10% (Combined Statistics, CBMC/EBIC 1970, Table 4). Mergers have been taking place at the fastest rate in Italy, where the number of brewing companies has fallen from 31 in 1968 to 16 in 1970. One result has been a doubling of the average production of Italian brewing firms, although the production per brewery plant has risen no more than 13.5%.

As a consequence of the many mergers in the brewing industry, the markets have taken on a monopolistic character. Table 11 represents the distribution of breweries by size in the EEC and FINEFTA countries. From these figures, it can be estimated that the 54 biggest brewhouses, excepting the ones located in Belgium, the Netherlands, and the United Kingdom, produce not less than 21% of the brewage consumed in these countries. If all the required information could be obtained from these countries, it could be demonstrated that the concentration of production is even greater than the available data indicate.

The mergers that have taken place in the brewing industry and the monopolization of the brewage markets have the effect of advancing in many ways (in Europe) the international diffusion of consumption patterns. In the first place, behind the mergers is the penetration of markets by foreign capital, facilitated especially by the legislation governing the EEC organization. For example, British brewers have made substantial investments of capital in continental Europe, notably Belgium, West Germany, and the Netherlands. A major Danish corporation recently established a large brewery in England. The second largest brewhouse in the Netherlands belongs to a British concern (36). Dutch brewers have notable interests in the beer markets of Italy. In the second place, as the brewing firms grow in size, their marketing power and competitive ability in bidding for customers increase. Beer advertising in the Federal Republic of Germany, for instance, underwent an investment rise from 30.6 million D-marks in 1967 to 94.4 million D-marks in 1972 (54). Owing to the influence of foreign investments, making foreign consumption models known is an important aspect of beer advertising.

The same processes are at work also in the marketing of spirituous liquors, but the situation is complicated by the fact that the production of many of the major brands requires both distilling and maturing as well as blending combined with effective marketing. The distilling is often done by small independent producers, who sell their output to big name-brand firms

TABLE 10 THE STRUCTURE OF BEER INDUSTRY IN EEC AND FINEFTA COUNTRIES IN 1968 AND 1970

Countries	Number of Active Breweries (Plants)		Number of Independent Brewing Companies		Production (1000 hl)[a]		Average Production per Plant (1000 hl)		Average Production per Company (1000 hl)	
	1968	1970	1968	1970	1968	1970	1968	1970	1968	1970
EEC										
Germany Fed. Rep.	1,908	1,815	1,840[b]	1,750[b]	79,016	86,952	41.4	47.9	42.9[b]	49.7[b]
Belgium	251	233	225	190	11,894	13,015	47.4	55.9	52.9	68.5
France	133	114	103	87	19,192	20,255	144.3	177.7	186.3	232.8
Italy	39	38	31	16	5,388	5,959	138.2	156.8	173.8	372.4
Luxembourg	10	8	9	8	512	541	51.2	67.6	56.9	67.6
Netherlands	28	23	18	16	6,854	8,724	244.8	379.3	380.8	545.3
FINEFTA										
Austria	82	77	72	67	7,151	7,231	87.2	93.9	99.3	107.9
Denmark	27	27	25	23	6,003	7,087	222.3	262.5	240.1	308.1
Finland	14	13	10	9	1,447	2,266	103.4	174.3	144.7	251.8
Norway	20	19	17	16	1,331	1,513	66.6	79.6	78.3	94.6
Portugal	5	5	4	4	830	1,353	166.0	270.6	207.5	338.3
Sweden	51	46	23	21	3,612	4,189	70.8	91.1	157.0	199.5
Switzerland	57	56	57	54	4,475	4,754	78.5	84.9	78.5	88.0
United Kingdom	220[b]	177	117[b]	96	51,418	55,147	233.7[b]	311.6	439.5[b]	574.4
Ireland	7	7	5	5	4,778	5,040	682.6	720.0	955.6	1,008.0
Spain	—	—	—	—	—	—	—	—	—	—

[a] There are some minor differences in these production figures as compared to those presented in table, due to different sources.
[b] Uncertain or estimated.
Source: Combined Statistics CBMC/EBIC 1968 and 1970.

TABLE 11 DIVISION OF BREWING PLANTS BY PRODUCTION 1970 IN EEC AND FINEFTA COUNTRIES

	Production in 1000 hl													
	0–10		10–60		60–120		120–500		500–1000		1000 and More		Total	
Countries	Plants	Output	Plants	Output	Plants	Output	Plants	Output	Plants	Output	Plants	Output	Plants	Output
EEC														
Germany Fed. Rep.	948	3,070	552	14,616	122	10,297	123	29,642	32[a]	29,327[a]	—	—	1,777[b]	86,952
Belgium	—	—	—	—	—	—	—	—	—	—	—	—	233	13,015
France	24	86	26	758	13[a]	1,223	38	8,527	13[a]	9,659[a]	—	—	114	20,255
Italy	1	2	6	194	12	1,152	18	3,974	1	637	—	—	38	5,959
Luxembourg	—	—	5	178	2	172	1	191	—	—	—	—	8	541
Netherlands	—	—	—	—	—	—	—	—	—	—	—	—	23	8,724
FINEFTA														
Austria	21	119	34	815	9	699	10	2,723	2	1.665	1	1,210	77	7,231
Denmark	11	—	9	—	2	—	3	—	—	—	2	—	27	7,087
Finland	1	4	4	183	3	283	4	1,196	1	600	—	—	13	2,266
Norway	—	—	12	295	2	145	5	1.073	—	—	—	—	19	1,513
Portugal	—	—	3	112	—	—	1	320	1	920	—	—	5	1,353
Sweden	2	19	25	746	11	931	7	1,538	1	955	—	—	46	4,189
Switzerland	11	65	28	759	4	319	12	2,751	1	860	—	—	56	4,754
United Kingdom	—	—	—	—	—	—	—	—	—	—	—	—	177	55,147
Ireland	—	—	—	—	4	—	2	—	—	—	1	—	7	5,040

[a] 500 and more.

[b] Excluding 38 breweries producing only for other account.

Source: Combined Statistics CBMC/EBIC 1970.

for the final stages of production. The size of such firms can be extremely large, like, for instance, the Distillers Co., Ltd., of Great Britain, which commands no less than 55% of the British whisky markets (3).

Another factor promoting the diffusion of cultures during the period under study has been the growth of international trade. Although what was said before (Section 4) about the relatively small significance of international trade in the world economy of alcoholic beverages—wine, and beer in particular—the quantitative growth of the global markets has, nevertheless, been noteworthy. This has signified an improvement in the availability of imported drinks. For example, the combined exports of beer increased from 1965 to 1970 by 40%. The total exports of the EEC countries increased during the same period by 33% and the exports of the FINEFTA countries about 50%. The trade in distilled beverages involving the EEC countries doubled from 1963 to 1970, while the combined exports from the FINEFTA countries rose 78%. This growth is due mostly to the expansion of the French and British export trades. Since these two countries rank among the world's biggest exporters, it is likely that the growth of trade in the world markets has been of remarkable proportions.

Table 12 gives an incomplete picture of the trends in the wine trade on world markets. This is due to the fact that Algerian wine dominates the statistical situation and because France has cut its purchases considerably after Algeria gained its independence, the growth of the total global export trade can be attributed to the substantial increase of wine shipments

TABLE 12 TOTAL EXPORTS OF ALCOHOLIC BEVERAGES IN MILLIONS OF HECTOLITERS AND AS PERCENTAGE OF TOTAL PRODUCTION FROM EEC AND FINEFTA COUNTRIES AND THE WORLD

	Wine		Beer		Spirits	
	1960	1970	1965	1970	1963	1970
Total EEC						
Million hl	5.5	10.6	3.2	4.2	1.0	2.0
Production (%)	4.4	7.0	2.9	3.3	32.0	53.4
Total FINEFTA						
Million hl	1.7	2.2	1.9	2.8	1.0	1.7
Production (%)	12.8	13.9	2.7	3.4	27.9	37.9
World						
Million hl	28.4	36.1	8.3	11.7	—	—
Production (%)	11.7	12.0	1.7	1.9	—	—

elsewhere. If Algeria is left out, total wine exports rose 50% from 1960 to 1970 and the proportion of total wine exports of total production rose from 3% in 1950 to 7.6% in 1970. The countries that increased their imports most were the U.S.S.R., the Netherlands, West Germany, England, and the United States. The countries mainly responsible for the growth of exports were Italy, France, Spain, and Hungary.

5. CUMULATIVE THEORY OF INCREASING ALCOHOL CONSUMPTION

In the foregoing sections, it was shown that the global growth of consumption involves two homogenizing tendencies: quantative and qualitative. By the former is meant that total average alcohol consumption is rising faster in (spirits-drinking) countries with a low starting level, and this was shown to have resulted in decreasing variation in the consumption level between countries. By the latter is meant that the differences between beverage structures are undergoing a process in which the traditional drink preferences in the three different types of countries are losing their significance through the increased acceptance of new beverages. This I have regarded as a result of intercultural diffusion of drinking patterns. In the following, I shall consider *the interconnections* between these homogenizing tendencies, with a view of the relationship of diffusing drinking patterns and increasing consumption level.

As noted in the foregoing, for many research purposes, drinking patterns are a focal concept. It can be thought that alcohol problems are related to the culturally accepted patterns of drinking, to attitudes and, above all, social norms controlling the use of alcohol. This emphasis has often been made at the expense of the overall level of consumption. As a matter of fact, this question has been one of the central themes of American and Scandinavian alcohol sociologists since the 1940s (34). In his classical article, which has already been referred to, Robert Bales observes that "high rates of consumption do not necessarily mean high rates of alcoholism" (5). In his view, the physical, psychological, and social complications induced by alcohol depend primarily on (*a*) the degree to which the culture produces "inner tensions and acute needs for adjustment in its members"; (*b*) the degree to which the culture provides "means other than the ingestion of alcohol to release tension"; (*c*) the sort of attitudes toward drinking the culture produces in its members. The implication of this theoretical approach, particularly of Bales's point (c) is that in the United States (and, it might be added, the Scandinavian countries) the attitudes and norms concerning drinking do not adequately regulate consumption. This is apt to cause difficulties that can only be remedied if the society "learns" the "healthy" attitudes and norms.

Such a theory is, of course, closely related to liberal programs of alcohol policy, and the whole approach is pointedly addressed against the temperance movement and its prohibitionist leanings. A compromise ought to be made between "asceticism" and "hedonism" (39) and alcohol should be dedramatized. In his influential and programmatic book on alcohol policy, Rupert Wilkinson, for example, goes so far as to call for "detoxification" of alcohol (66) by integrating it with society. The procedures usually recommended include attitude training, the teaching of civilized drinking habits to lower social classes and young people, associating the use of alcohol with various leisure pursuits, and so on. The drinking cultures of the Italians and the Jews are often held up as ideals, which explains the lively interest of researchers in the drinking habits and customs of these national and ethnic groups.

In fact, this program implies that harmful drinking might be substituted by learning to drink in moderation. Less harmful attitudes and less ambivalent norms could develop from new drinking patterns. The possible increase in total level of consumption is of less concern. Mäkelä calls this the "substitution hypothesis" (34).

This theory is applicable mainly to the drinking habits characteristic of spirits countries. We have already observed that, in spirits-drinking countries, the use of alcohol is dramatic (visible), segregated, concentrated within a particular group of consumers and aimed one-dimensionally at intoxication. The norms applying to the use of alcohol are often ambivalent, "utilitarian" or "abstinent" (see Section 3 above). In the light of Section 4, we could then think that the cultural diffusion of drinking patterns ought to promote in these countries the more normative drinking customs and habits characteristic of beer and wine cultures.

Certain research findings support the assumption that this has actually happened. In a consumer survey made in Finland in 1968–1969 by Klaus Mäkelä, the observation was made that as a consequence of the far-going liberalization of the liquor trade in the years 1968 and 1969, the frequency of occasions on which small quantities of alcohol were consumed increased noticeably. Beer of medium strength accounted for the main part of the increase. In the next few years, the consumption of hard liquors increased at the same rate as before. From this, Mäkelä drew the following conclusion:

> The liberalization of alcohol policy thus brought about, on the one hand, an increase in consumption and, on the other, created new drinking practices. But it did not moderate previously developed habits. The great increase in the number of times beer was drunk in small quantities reduced the average ingestion per time. If attention is paid only to such averages, the drinking habits would appear to have become more moderate. Any estimation of the situation based on averages would, however, be misleading, for the occasions on which heavy drinking, too, took place became more common. It thus appears that the

addition hypothesis is best applicable to representing the changes wrought by the beer reform in Finland." (34).

This controversy on alcohol policy is hard to carry over to conditions where the whole question of moderating drinking habits through the adoption of the new ones is not relevant. It nevertheless seems that also in these countries the changes in drinking habits and the consumption level have taken a course somewhat similar to that described by Mäkelä. The "addition hypothesis", according to which the adoption of new consumption practices does not lead to the rejection of old ones but only to an increase in consumption, seems to apply also to beer- and wine-drinking countries—Italy in particular.

This observation is reinforced by the fact that a leveling out in the structure of consumption is in most cases connected statistically with a rise in the level of average consumption. Operationally, this can be seen as extremely high time series correlations between the consumption level and the structure of consumption as depicted by index R (see Section 4). With few exceptions, they are negative and range from Australia's −0.33 to Yugoslavia's −0.99, the absolute value being usually well above −0.50 (Appendix 2). In Italy, this correlation is −0.82; in Spain, −0.76; in Portugal, −0.56 (deficient data); in Hungary, −0.68, etc. In France, the changes in both structure and level of consumption have been slight, so that the correlation is positive and as high as 0.90. As for the beer-drinking countries, it can be seen that in England, the correlation is −0.80, in Belgium −0.95, in Denmark −0.91, in the United States −0.65, and in Canada −0.96. In West Germany, the consumption structure has not leveled out, for the contribution of beer to the total consumption of alcohol has continued to increase (see Fig. 3), which renders a positive correlation (0.55).

As a general conclusion, it may be stated that diversification of consumption habits as reflected in the beverage structure has in most instances led primarily to a rise in the consumption level. When diversification has been supported by measures of alcohol policy, the result has by no means been the substitution of old drinking habits or traditional alcoholic drinks with new ones. Nontraditional consumption has simply laid a new layer over the traditional drinking patterns.

As a matter of fact, it is interesting to take a closer look at the contribution of traditional and novel beverages to the rise in the total consumption level. This may be done by breaking down the increase in the total alcohol consumption by the type of beverage. For this purpose, Mikko Pärnänen has developed the following simple model (45).

Let ΔA_i = the change in total consumption from the year *0* to the year *i* and B_{ij} = the amount of alcohol contained in beverage class *j* in the year *i*.

If this is so, then:

$$\Delta A_i{:}\ 100 = \frac{A_i - A_o}{A_o} = \frac{\sum_j B_{ij} - \sum_j B_{oj}}{A_o}$$
$$= \sum_j \left(\frac{B_{oi}}{A_{oj}} \cdot \frac{B_{ij} - B_{oj}}{B_{oj}}\right) = \sum_j c_j(\Delta B_{ij}). \qquad (2)$$

In this formula, c_j denotes the share contributed by beverage class j to the total alcohol consumption in the year *0* and ΔB_{ij}, the change in the consumption of beverage class j in terms of pure alcohol. The product $c_i\ (\Delta B_{ij})$ thus expresses the percentage of the increase in total consumption attributable to the increase in the beverage class j. If the consumption of other beverages had remained the same, this would be the total increase in the overall level of consumption. As can be seen from the formula, the model is completely additive, so that the additions caused by the respective classes of beverages are together equal to the increase in total consumption.

It is easy to observe from the formula that the relative increase in consumption caused by a class of beverage is directly proportional to its share of the total consumption in the base year. The consumption of the most important beverage class need increase relatively much less than that of other classes to have an effect of the same magnitude on total consumption. Therefore the biggest beverage class can (but does not have to) influence the rise in the total consumption level most at the same time as a leveling-out takes place in the beverage structure. The following sample calculation, which is close to France with respect to beverage structure, sheds light on the matter.

Let the total consumption in the year *0* be represented by the figure of 100 units—amounting to, for example, 10 million liters—, with the consumption of wine accounting for 80 units, beer 5 units, and spirits the rest, or 15 units. If the consumption of beer increases to the year *i* by 100%, that of spirits by 20%, and of wine 10%, we get the following tabulation:

	Consumption in Year *0* Million Liters	(%)	Consumption in Year *i* Million Liters	(%)	Effect on Total Increase (%)
Wine	80	80	88	75.9	8
Spirits	15	15	18	15.5	3
Beer	5	5	10	8.6	5
Total	100	100	116	100.0	16

In the year *0*, the value of R is 19.2 and in the year *i*, 17.5, which means that a leveling-out has occurred—this is obvious also directly from the percentages. At the same time, however, the biggest class of beverages,

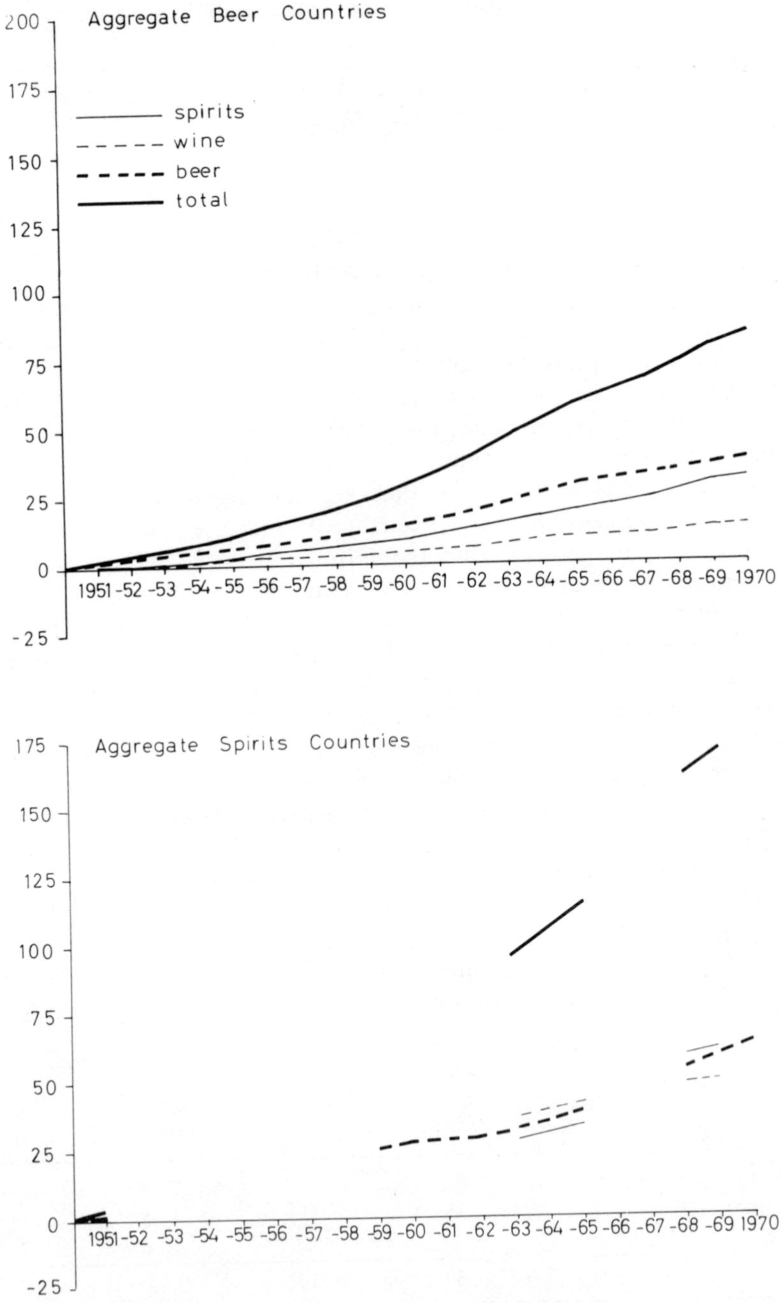

Fig. 4. Contributions of beverage types (in three-year annual averages) to total increase of alcohol consumption, 1950–1970 in aggregate wine, beer, and spirits countries.

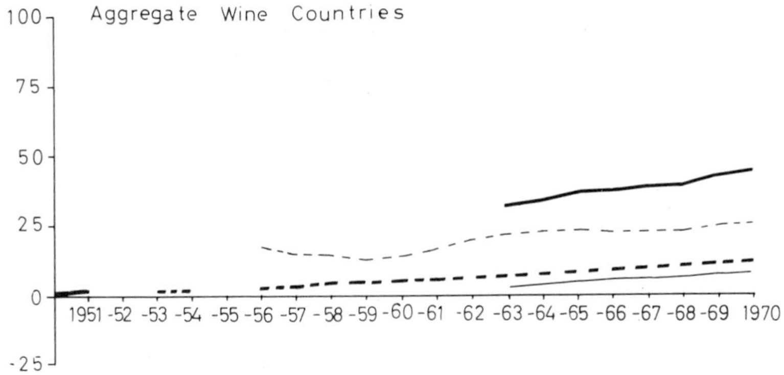

Fig. 4 *(Continued)*

wine, has influenced the growth of consumption by 8%, but beer only by 5% and distilled liquors by 3%.

The effects of this phenomenon can be presented graphically (Fig. 4). For the purpose of demonstration, we have calculated the combined consumption of all the wine-, beer-, and spirits-drinking countries by classes of beverages and, in this way, have formed three subtotals, which might be called, say, Aggregate Wine Country, Aggregate Beer Country, and Aggregate Spirits Country. For these "countries" the model was then calculated with three-year moving averages for the years 1950–1970, taking 1950–1951 as the base year. The curves indicate what percentage each class of drink contributed to the growth of total consumption up to 1969–1970. The years in between represent the averages for three-year periods—for instance, the figure given for 1960 represents the average value for the years 1959–1961.

The figures reveal that at the end of the 1960s, the total consumption in the Aggregate Wine Country was roughly 40%, in the Beer Country about 80%, and in the Spirits Country about 175% higher than in the year 1950. Of this growth, the share of wine was the biggest in the wine country, or about 25%. In the beer country, the increase in beer consumption caused the largest increase in the total result, or about 35%. In the spirits-drinking country, again, the biggest proportion of the total increase was accounted for by spirits, being about 65%.

Table 13 shows the distribution in detail in the increase of consumption among the classes of beverages in the different countries. This table makes it clear that, on the whole, the traditionally most popular type of drink actually induces the biggest rise in the level of average consumption. A typical case is that of Italy, where the increase in the consumption of wine has increased the level of total alcohol consumption by 51% and the

TABLE 13 DISTRIBUTION OF THE PERCENTAGE INCREASE IN TOTAL ALCOHOL CONSUMPTION 1969–1970/1950–1951 BY BEVERAGE GROUPS

Country	Beer	Wine	Spirits	Total
Wine countries				
France	6.62	5.67	−0.52	11.76
Hungary	38.74	23.05	41.00	102.79
Italy	5.38	51.39	12.70	69.47
Portugal[a]	4.64	23.60	0.39	28.63
Rumania[a]	19.90	17.06	26.21	63.17
Spain[a]	24.62	40.92	10.13	75.82
Switzerland[a]	43.33	35.50	22.12	105.73
Beer countries				
Australia[a]	69.87	11.15	10.98	92.00
Austria	61.56	60.10	4.76	126.42
Belgium	18.38	15.79	9.60	43.77
Canada	55.46	10.55	40.36	106.37
Czechoslovakia[a]	48.47	20.41	23.32	91.63
Denmark	66.18	12.23	21.81	100.22
Germany Fed. Rep.	146.65	41.54	69.63	257.81
Ireland	22.33	3.51	6.81	32.65
New Zealand[a]	68.76	10.91	5.42	85.09
United Kingdom	25.32	5.62	8.19	39.13
U.S.A.	11.95	8.61	35.65	56.21
Spirits countries				
Bulgaria[a]	177.39	246.57[b]	129.13[b]	507.48[b]
Cuba[a]	9.00	−0.98	26.05	34.07
Finland	85.25	24.87	28.98	139.10
Germany Dem. Rep.	121.03	40.02	120.72	281.76
Iceland[a]	32.91	11.07	229.90	273.87
Israel[a]	45.96	43.61	90.08	179.38
Netherlands	147.81	34.66	54.79	237.26
Norway	51.75	10.81	30.60	93.16
Peru[a]	85.18	4.73	133.28	221.20
Poland	41.54	24.16	65.80	131.50
South Africa	32.28	74.96	69.32	176.56
Sweden	37.52	18.60	10.77	66.88
Turkey[a]	10.24	24.00	82.25	116.48
Yugoslavia[a]	57.78	134.06	62.27	254.11

[a] Data for 1950–1951 is estimated as shown in Appendix 1.

[b] 1968–1969 average.

increase in beer and spirits consumption by only 18%, a total increase of 69%. (Note that in this calculation, we have not used consumption figures per capita as, for example, in Table 7. Therefore the percentages showing the increase are somewhat higher here, owing to population growth.) Among the beer-drinking countries, let us take England as our example. The total rise there has been 39%, the share of beer being 25%. The most exceptions from the rule occur in the spirits-drinking countries, where the rise in the level of total consumption has usually been quite steep and where also the structural changes have been the most conspicuous (Fig. 3).

Mäkelä's (34) "addition hypothesis" receives general support from these calculations. Nor has the adoption of new consumption habits in the beer- and wine-drinking countries been able to replace old habits. On the contrary, expressly in these countries, the traditional type of drink has lifted the consumption level most at the same time that the structure of consumption has become more nearly uniform. Also in the spirits-drinking countries, the consumption of hard liquor has caused a steep rise in the level of total consumption, although, on account of the very steepness in the rise of the consumption level and the sharpness of the change in structure, the increase in the consumption of beer in particular has, in many cases, had the biggest effect on the total consumption.

In the light of these empirical observations, therefore, there appear to be no grounds for any kind of substitution hypothesis. Rather, the development that has taken place resembles a cumulative process, in which new elements are piled up on top of old ones, forming new strata over the total constellation of drinking habits and customs and reinforcing the old traditions in the bargain. The strata of drinking patterns lying underneath absorb ingredients from the new ones without being undermined—at most, they might undergo a change in character. In this light, one would be tempted to see the nontraditional drinking patterns as complementary, rather than supplementary, to the traditional ones.

This is all very understandable if we keep in mind the differences in content that we analyzed in the various drinking cultures. There is no reason for supposing that the use of wine at mealtime would be cut down in wine-drinking countries because at house parties and in restaurants, as well as on quiet evenings spent at home, perhaps, it is becoming gradually customary to take drinks of beer or hard liquor in smaller or larger quantities.

Likewise in spirits-drinking and, in particular, beer countries, wine has become to some extent even a commonplace mealtime beverage (51). This does not, however, necessarily mean that the pub has lost its charm as a place to while away leisure hours, but, on the contrary, by bringing alcohol into the family circle it has the effect of diminishing the distance separating women and young people from drinking in general. Perhaps the extension of this practice into the home has a particularly great significance in spirits-drinking countries, where a large part of the population has traditionally remained quite out of touch with the use of alcohol or come into contact with it only in meeting inebriated people. On the other hand, the penetration of alcohol into normal social life in all kinds of situations opens up to heavy drinkers opportunities for socially acceptable imbibing, in addition to the fact that it can still be done within the protective confines of a restaurant.

The theory of cumulative growth has an important point of contact with the discussion on the so-called distribution theory, which in alcohol-political studies constitutes a direct antithesis to the views based on the substitution hypothesis. The distribution–theoretical approach is based on the empirical fact that the distribution of alcohol consumption is generally skew and so concentrated that a small part of the consuming public drinks the biggest part of the alcohol consumed by the population as a whole, regardless of the average level of consumption (56). Efforts have been made to explain this on the basis of the general assumption that the distribution of consumption adheres to some theoretical type of distribution, as if governed by a natural law, for example, like the log-normal so-called Ledermann distribution (26, 27, 56). To the extent that these generalizations are reliable, they are very valuable in explaining the fact that cirrhosis mortality has a high correlation with the average level of consumption whether considered in a time series or by comparing populations (countries) (9, 48, 55). This is because, insofar as the skew distribution of consumption can be represented by some one-parametric model, it is possible to estimate the number of people who consume more than a given amount, one that fundamentally adds to the health risk, simply on the basis of the average level of consumption in the population. Thus the prognosticative value of the consumption level with respect to the prevalence of alcohol-related problems is understandably high. Good results have been achieved in, for example, estimating the number of alcoholics by the use of the Ledermann model (48, 55).

An essential feature of the theories based on the skewness of the distribution of consumption is connected with the fact that in them the average level of consumption and the consumption level and number of heavy drinkers can be linked together mathematically. Since the average quantity is naturally also affected by every "normal consumer," this means that the number of heavy drinkers and the level of consumption are connected with the total consumption.

Not much has so far been done to explain this matter besides the

> general implication in the writings around the log-normal distribution in the alcohol field that there seems to be some kind of contagion effect. The more the randomly chosen individual consumes, the more the alcoholic consumes (and the larger the number of alcoholics—PS). Some cultures are supposed to have a 'wet' climate and others a 'dry' one and so on. We should then need a derivation of the log-normal distribution based on the contagion effect. (15).

Already Ledermann (27) has pointed to the possibility of explaining the regularity of the distribution of consumption in this way. Quite recently others also have paid attention to the contagion effect (9).

Dynamic conclusions are often drawn out of the theory of distribution, even though the empirical data on which it is founded are largely static. In only a few studies has information been obtained about changes in the form of the distribution accompanying a rise in the level of consumption. The cumulative growth process of alcohol consumption appears therefore to afford in an important way further dynamic support for the basic assumptions of the theory of distribution by offering an explanation of sorts for the "contagion effect" (applicable, it is true, only to the conditions of increasing consumption). As we were able to note in the foregoing discussion, the adoption of new models of consumption not only had no negative influence on traditional consumption but, in many instances, the traditional consumption itself has, in this process, affected the growth of consumption most. By adding to the number of social situations in which the use of alcohol is proper or permissible, the adoption of new consumption practices increases, above all, the chances of exposure to drink. It is therefore understandable that the moderate drinkers, forming the great majority, exercise an influence over the drinking behavior of heavy drinkers. Since every heavy drinker, for his part, usually has a manifold effect on total consumption in comparison with moderate drinkers, this process leads to a cumulative rise in the average level of alcohol consumption with all the greater effectiveness.

6. EMERGING DIMENSIONS OF DRINKING

The two processes connected with the rise of the level of alcohol consumption, the diffusion of drinking cultures, and the associated cumulative increase in consumption, cannot exist apart from changes in the use values of alcohol. Customs and habits are unlikely to be passed on from one culture to another without modification. They must become adapted to prevailing conditions and, correspondingly, they also influence old traditions by placing them into a new position and context. The Finns have not altogether assimilated the Italian custom of taking alcohol daily with meals, although the Finnish level of alcohol consumption is rapidly approaching that which prevailed in Italy a couple of decades ago. In Finland, the drinking of wine is always essentially an intoxicating experience, whether taken in the context of a meal or not. In other words, the trend is not towards "dry" alcohol but towards "wet" dinners.

This gives us grounds for going back to the concepts we have been applying and their position in the analysis of the changes taking place in drinking patterns and the level of consumption. The most important thing to note is that the attribute "traditional" is always relative and variable in content. It can be of value only if we are able to characterize traditions as historically determined and meaningful, as we have tried to do in the foregoing with respect to typical drinking patterns and use values of alcohol prevailing in wine-, beer-, and spirits-drinking countries. But when these typical phenomena blend into each other in the way we have described, we can no longer rest content with representing developments on the basis of these same concepts. On the contrary, it seems necessary to deal with new, evolving "traditions" and qualitatively new drinking practices characterizing them.

The shortcomings of the research material from the standpoint of analyzing new, emerging drinking patterns and use values are even greater than we could observe in a static analysis. This is due simply to the fact that the depiction of emerging drinking patterns requires dynamic data that are hard to acquire; in this, static international comparisons as such will not suffice. What we really need are the same sort of qualitative comparisons between internal changes undergone by cultures as were carried out quantitatively in the foregoing material.

Information of this kind is not actually available directly at all. The closest approach to an analysis of changes in consumption habits is made by market research, the chief task of which is to predict the market behavior of consumers, their taste preferences and susceptibility to advertising. Thereby we can reach some tentative conclusions—maybe of somewhat general validity—about changes taking place in three interesting countries, France, West Germany, and the United States.

All three countries tend both to prove in their own way the general rule emerging from the foregoing discussion and to constitute an exception to it. The level of consumption in France has not significantly risen during the past couple of decades, but the structure of consumption has become more uniform. In the United States, the level of consumption has risen and the structure of consumption has become somewhat more uniform, but beer, which we regard as the traditionally principal type of beverage there, has not affected the total increase in consumption very substantially. (About the spirits-consuming countries, to which the corresponding observation applies, we have spoken in the foregoing). And in West Germany, to the contrary, the traditionally principal type of drink has affected the rise in the level of consumption to the extent that the structure of the beverages consumed has not become more uniform but rather has taken on an increasingly heavy slant in favor of beer.

As, first of all, for the fact that the tendencies we have described are not everywhere uniform, it must be pointed out that there are many possible reasons for this. Among them, of course, is the possibility that we have seen regularities in phenomena where none exist, or then that we have formulated our observations erroneously. One *less* worrisome group of factors that tends to confound things, when the statistical unit is a state, consists of the internal geographical and cultural variations. In West Germany at present, this has presumably a very strong influence, particularly on the consumption of wine, which is concentrated in the wine-growing areas. The beer tradition in Germany is mainly upheld in the southern regions, which are Catholic by religion and the social conditions of which deviate otherwise too from those prevailing in the north. The German beer industry is, as is well known, the least concentrated in Europe (Table 10), and the many small breweries in rural districts can to a large extent be compared to the small family plantations in winegrowing countries. The increase in the consumption of beer involves primarily the products of vigorously expanding large enterprises; the rate of increase is the most rapid in the north, and young people are making a decisive contribution to this development (41). Alcohol is mainly used after working hours and "on social occasions" (45% of the respondents included in a representative sampling of the population at large) and while watching television (12%). Only 2% reported drinking because alcohol was supposed to be "healthful" and 6% to quench thirst.

With respect to Germany, we can observe the influence of two kinds of trends. On the one hand, the internal development of the country seems to correspond to the general diffusion tendencies that we have described already on the international level; on the other, drinking seems to be connected unmistakably with leisure-time recreational activities and as a counterbalance to work.

In France, geographical differences are, perhaps, of less consequence, though in the northern regions the drinking habits are less restrained and more cider and hard liquor are drunk than in the south. On the other hand, it is interesting from the standpoint of stability in the level of consumption to look into the evolution that has taken place inside the wine group. Figure 5 shows that the slight increase in the total consumption of alcohol is due mainly to a drop in the popularity of cider and the fact that the consumption of ordinary table wines (*vins courants*) has remained very close to the 1950 level, whereas that of dessert wines (VDN), champagne, and AOC wines has risen, even to a notable extent. Here, too, an exception in one respect thus seems to confirm the rule in another; within the wine group, a structural change is taking place in favor of more expensive luxury and prestige wines enjoyed in recreative hours.

In the United States, as in West Germany, geographic differences have to be taken into consideration. In the winegrowing region of California, the drinking of wine is considerably commoner than elsewhere in the country; and the drinking habits along the urbanized Eastern seaboard deviate from the beer-dominated consumption structure of the rural Middle West. Ethnic

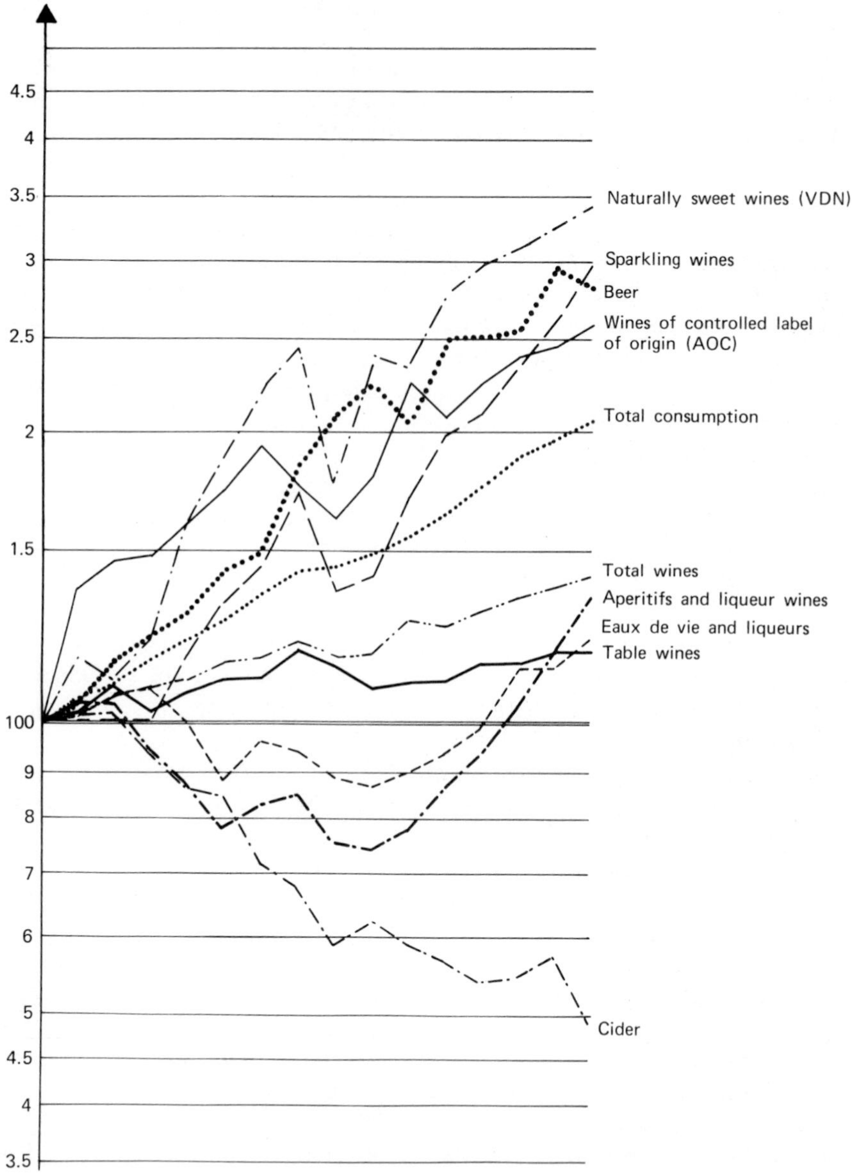

Fig. 5. Consumption of alcoholic beverages and total private consumption of households in France 1950–1965 (14).

and national factors in the United States further confuse ideas about a "traditional" drinking culture. At any rate, beer surged to the forefront following the repeal of the Volstead Act; after Prohibition, beer accounted for over half the total alcohol consumption in the country. Since then, the share of hard liquors has steadily increased at the expense of beer, and in the mid-1960s they rose to the top of the list of alcoholic beverages consumed. The share of wine has remained, for the whole time, around 10%, though, to be sure, it has shown signs of moving upward in recent years. In the United States too, therefore, the trend of consumption has been unmistakably in a direction marked by a leisure-time emphasis. Above all, young people have been adopting new habits of consumption (38).

Let us try to see what general conclusions concerning the emerging drinking habits and the related use values of alcohol might arise from our discussions so far.

The first thing to be said is that the differences between drinking cultures as characterized by beverage structures and drinking patterns seem to be—if not disappearing—at least losing ground. Here the question arises: which drinking patterns have gained favor and under what conditions, and what needs have the alcoholic beverages come to satisfy in this process?

To some extent, of course, the outcome could be described in terms of increasing "plurality" in drinking habits. But this is probably not all. From the above accounts, it seems that drinking in spirits countries has lost a degree of social isolation and instead impregnated wide segments of everyday life. Above all, it has meant the emergence of new consumer groups, particularly women and youth. At the same time, there have come to be very few situations in which alcohol is unthinkable; instead it is often a matter of course. There is no denying of the importance of the intoxicating value of drinking in these new situations and among these new consumer groups, whether played down or more prominently emphasized.

On the other hand, it is hard to see that the nutritional value of alcohol could be increasing, at least in the industrialized world. In most countries (with the important exceptions of wine in certain "wine economies") the prices of alcoholic beverages are kept relatively high by special taxation, and this fact alone makes alcohol an unsuitable supplement of the caloric content of food. With increasing incomes this is not economically out of the question, of course. But even if drinking with meals may have become more and more customary, it can be thought that usually other elements are involved than the nutritional value of alcohol: the believed digestive effects, appetizing qualities, symbols of celebration, and so on, including the pleasurable experience of intoxication.

In countries where alcohol traditionally is a food, the diversification of drinking patterns most clearly seems to be a development toward using alcohol for purposes other than nutrition. The increasing use of foreign type and expensive high quality beverages is rather involved in celebrations, recreational settings, and other leisure activities. It is likely that the intoxicating effects of alcohol are emphasized, at least to some extent, at the expense of nutritional ones.

So it seems that, with the intercultural diffusion of drinking patterns also, the use values of alcohol take on a broader range and they become less clearly demarcated; it is increasingly more difficult to differentiate drinking for intoxication from drinking for nourishment or from drinking as an element of recreation and conviviality. However, one is likely to get the impression that the use values of alcohol typical of beer and spirits countries play at least as dominant a role in the total constellations of emerging drinking patterns as does the drinking habits of the traditional wine cultures. In this sense, also, the substitution hypothesis developed in the course of debates on alcohol policies in some spirits countries appears to be untenable. Cumulative growth of alcohol consumption is immanently characterized by a greater or lesser emphasis on intoxication.

In the light of the theoretical considerations presented earlier in this chapter, it is not difficult to see how these kinds of new features in the use values of alcohol may come into existence. Alcohol, with its intoxicating qualities, is a ready means of recreation as such. According to Partanen (46a) for example, intoxication could be called a pseudoactivity. It is exempt from the tension between goals and their achievement, yet it enhances the feeling of activity, potency, and liveliness. Compared to many other forms of recreation, alcohol has a number of advantages. It is relatively inexpensive, it suits almost everybody, it is easily transported, and it can be combined with other kinds of recreation and leisure activities (television, sports, theater, music, dancing, etc.).

As a recreational practice, drinking could be seen, then, as replacing other similar activities. But even more important, it may have come to fill the increasing leisure hours and the accompanying proliferation of recreational needs. In this sense, alcohol might with increasing justification be called, following Edwards (12a), a recreational drug, a term often also applied to marijuana (19).

7. SUMMARY AND CONCLUSIONS

In the foregoing sections, I have made the following empirical observations about the trends in the level of alcohol consumption and in the beverage structure. (*a*) A rise in the consumption level is a global phenomenon insofar as it can be judged in the light of available statistical data. (*b*) The rise has been steepest in countries where the level of consumption was low to begin with and particularly in those countries where hard liquor has accounted for a high proportion of the total consumption of alcohol. (*c*) Differing rates of growth in consumption have brought the consumption levels closer together (quantitative homogenization). (*d*) A tendency toward uniformity has taken place in the structure of consumption in the sense that spirits-, beer-, and wine-drinking nations are beginning to resemble each other more and more in their typical consumption behavior (qualitative homogenization). (*e*) The qualitative homogenization of drinking patterns has resulted from the adoption of new consumption habits—not at the expense of but in addition to traditional habits. (*f*) In many cases, especially in wine and beer countries, the increase in the consumption of traditional types of beverages has had the greatest effect on the level of total consumption.

I have interpreted these statistical observations on the basis of the concepts use value and drinking patterns in such a way that the countries have been divided according to the structure of the beverages consumed into three groups representing different alcohol cultures—wine countries, beer countries, and spirits-consuming countries. Between them I found differences with respect to typical drinking patterns and use values. Changes taking place in the structure of consumption have signified, however, a diffusion of different drinking cultures. An important finding was the cumulative nature of the diversification of drinking patterns, by which is meant that new habits of consumption do not replace old ones but are complementary to them and even produce a so-called contagion effect, which stimulates the growth of traditional consumption too. The cultural diffusion of drinking patterns has led to a blending of use values to the extent of a qualitative change. In the present decade, it is increasingly difficult to distinguish the nutritional use of alcohol from its value as an intoxicant. Alcohol has become integrated with nearly all leisure activities, besides which it has an independent significance in giving pleasure on its own power. Its character might be described to be increasingly a recreational drug.

Many of the foregoing statements have a hypothetical character insofar as they are for the most part based only on data capable of systematic international comparisons. More detailed studies of the different national circumstances will probably supplement these propositions. A major implication of the conclusions drawn is that, in such studies, drinking can be profitably seen as part of general consumer behavior, reflecting the needs of the population and the means of satisfying these needs by alcohol use. This perspective is sensitive to the general social developments that may have a bearing on the need for drugs as a means of recreation and entertainment: working conditions, housing, opportunities for outdoor activities, competition for better living conditions, and so on. This aspect of drinking habits could also provide a useful link in historical causal explanations of the changes in the level of alcohol consumption by means of factors that contribute to the increasing facilities for satisfying various needs, such as consumption power, increasing leisure, prices of alcoholic beverages, and increasing physical availability among others.

My emphasis on the demand factors, consumer behavior, and use values is not intended to mislead to the devaluing of other types of processes that may be at work. Without doubt, for example, the recent WHO Expert Committee is correct in stating:

> While there is little in the scientific literature regarding the impact on alcohol consumption of various types and magnitudes of advertising, it is difficult to assume that the alcoholic beverage industry would continue to allocate large sums of money to advertising without evidence from its marketing studies that such expenditures were justified. That the pattern and sometimes the volume of sales of many consumer products may be favorably affected by advertising is well established, and there seems little reason to suppose that alcoholic beverages might differ in this regard. (65).

To name just two other important factors, government policies may be directed either favorably or restrictively toward the increasing use of alcoholic beverages, either by directly affecting the markets or by other means such as education campaigns. Or moral climates may be moving either towards a more favorable valuation of drinking and its pleasures or they may take a more critical appearance on such uses of time.

To a student of the trends in alcohol consumption these and other similar phenomena are by no means irrelevant. In the last concrete analysis, however, they also must be explained, and, in doing this, the question: what *is* drinking? may again come into sight.

ACKNOWLEDGMENTS

This chapter has been prepared with the financial support of the Finnish Foundation for Alcohol Studies. The necessary technical assistance has been provided by the staff of the Social Research Institute of Alcohol Studies of the State Alcohol Monopoly of Finland.

My work on international trends in alcohol consumption has been encouraged and inspired by Dr. Bruun of the Finnish Foundation and Dr. Mäkelä of the Social Research Institute. I am greatly indebted also to my other colleagues in these alcohol research units.

Dr. Schmidt and Dr. de Lint of the Addiction Research Foundation of Ontario and Professor Allardt of the Research Group of Comparative Sociology at the University of Helsinki have read the manuscript and given valuable suggestions for improvements. I wish to express my gratitude for their effort and help.

APPENDIX 1 METHODS OF ESTIMATING PER CAPITA CONSUMPTION FIGURES FOR 1950 IN COUNTRIES WITH INCOMPLETE DATA

	Spirits		Beer		Wine	
Country	Estimate for 1950 Liters 100% Alcohol	Method	Estimate for 1950 Liters	Method	Estimate for 1950 Liters	Method
Bulgaria	0.65	6% pa 1954[a]	2.94	13% pa 1957/aai	2.50	Year 1956
Czechoslovakia					5.14	6% pa 1953/aai[b]
Iceland	0.50	Year 1951[c]	8.05	1.6% pa 1954/aai	1.36	4% pa 1960/aai
Portugal	0.50	Year 1964	1.00	16% pa 1964/aai	103.83	Average 1955–1970
Rumania	1.58	Average 1954–1970[d]	5.75	7% pa 1954/aai	24.09	Year 1954
Spain	2.39	Average 1962–1970				
Switzerland	1.33	2% pa 1962/aai 1962–1968[e]				
Yugoslavia	2.00	Year 1955	4.50	Year 1955	4.32	Year 1955
Cuba	1.09	Year 1964	14.19	Year 1964	2.09	Year 1964
Peru	0.89	Year 1960				
Cyprus	1.37	Year 1964	8.19	Year 1960	11.50	Year 1960
Israel	0.98	Average 1963–1970	8.50	Year 1953	2.29	Year 1953
Turkey	0.19	Year 1954	1.19	Year 1954	0.79	Year 1954
Australia	0.84	Year 1951	93.00	Year 1951	7.00	Year 1951
New Zealand	1.16	Year 1951	85.39	Year 1951	2.00	Year 1951

[a] "6% pa 1954" means that the estimate has been arrived at on the assumption that the increase from 1950 to 1954 has been 6% per annum. Year 1954 is the earliest for which there is information in WAP Data.

[b] "6% pa 1953/aai" means the same, but the average annual increase has been estimated from the figures for 1953–1970.

[c] "year 1951" means that the figure for 1950 has been replaced by the figure for 1951.

[d] "average 1954–1970" means that the figure for 1950 has been replaced by the average of years 1954–1970.

[e] "2% pa 1962/aai 1962–1968" means that the annual average increase has been estimated from the figures for 1962–1968.

APPENDIX 2 CORRELATIONS BETWEEN THE MEASURE OF BEVERAGE STRUCTURE (R) AND CONSUMPTION LEVEL

Country	Consumption of 100% Alcohol in Liters per Capita 1950–1952	Increase of per Capita Alcohol Consumption 1968–1970/1950–1952	R 1950–1952	R 1968–1970 (1950–1952 = 100)	Correlation Between R and per Capita Consumption 1950–1970	Number of Observed Years
Austria	5.4	199.1	4.7	168.8	0.66	21
Belgium	6.6	125.6	18.4	76.3	−0.95	21
Bulgaria	1.1	498.6	11.1	35.9	−0.91	16
Czechoslovakia	4.9	163.8	12.7	79.1	−0.30	21
Denmark	4.0	168.9	18.4	87.5	−0.91	21
Finland	2.2	181.5	12.5	67.7	−0.56	21
France	17.6	92.0	18.8	92.6	0.90	21
Germany Dem. Rep.	1.9	310.7	12.2	75.6	−0.72	21
Germany Fed. Rep.	3.6	273.3	7.2	126.9	0.55	21
Hungary	4.8	177.7	18.6	38.4	−0.68	20
Iceland	1.1	254.2	7.4	225.0	0.83	14
Ireland	3.4	129.1	17.5	96.4	−0.92	21
Italy	9.4	145.2	23.5	87.7	−0.82	21
Luxembourg	6.8	139.1	7.9	87.4	−0.34	21
Netherlands	1.9	265.3	15.3	62.4	−0.68	21
Norway	2.1	159.5	10.9	91.4	−0.70	21

Poland	3.1	176.6	16.1	70.8	−0.67	19
Portugal	12.9	109.9	25.5	94.9	−0.56	10
Rumania	4.7	134.4	12.9	61.8	−0.57	20
Spain	8.1	144.9	16.1	77.1	−0.76	12
Sweden	4.0	141.8	14.0	58.8	−0.82	21
Switzerland	6.6	153.0	7.9	72.7	−0.95	13
United Kingdom	4.9	126.1	22.0	87.8	−0.80	21
Yugoslavia	2.7	270.5	16.4	40.7	−0.99	19
Canada	4.9	130.0	13.6	87.1	−0.96	21
Cuba	2.0	90.0	9.7	118.2	−0.81	10
U.S.A.	5.0	117.0	10.1	89.7	−0.65	1
Peru	1.3	210.2	13.6	98.2	0.24	14
Cyprus	3.1	105.8	8.3	66.6	=0.37	11
Israel	1.4	138.6	10.4	70.9	−0.41	11
Turkey	0.3	139.4	9.2	140.6	0.81	19
South Africa	1.8	161.2	6.7	91.6	−0.62	21
Australia	6.4	126.1	16.5	102.2	−0.33	21
New Zealand	5.6	127.6	17.6	104.6	−0.08	21
Aggregate beer countries	4.8	142.0	11.9	79.5	−0.99	21
Aggregate wine countries	10.7	119.7	19.5	85.5	−0.92	21
Aggregate spirits countries	2.0	195.5	12.8	45.5	−0.91	7
EEC	9.1	134.5	15.6	68.2	−0.94	21

REFERENCES

1. Ahlström-Laakso, S., *Drinking Habits Among Alcoholics,* The Finnish Foundation for Alcohol Studies, Helsinki, 1975, pp. 153–155.
2. Ahlström-Laakso, S., *European Drinking Habits: A Review and Some Suggestions for Conceptual Integration of Findings,* Reports from the Social Research Institute of Alcohol Studies No. 69 Helsinki, 1973. (Mimeograph).
3. *Alcohol in the EEC: Production and Marketing Structures of Alcohol in the EEC Countries,* European News Agency, Brussels, 1974.
4. Allardt, E., Drinking norms and drinking habits, in *Drinking and Drinkers,* Publication No. 6 of the Finnish Foundation for Alcohol Studies. Helsinki 1957.

4a. Balboni, C., Alcohol in relation to dietary patterns, in *Alcohol and Civilization,* S. P. Lucia (Ed.), McGraw-Hill, New York, 1963.

5. Bales, R. F., Cultural differences in rates of alcoholism, *Q. J. Stud. Alcohol,* **6,** 480 (1946).

5a. *Beer, Wine, and Spirits: Beverage Differences and Public Policy in Canada,* The Report of the Alcoholic Beverage Study Committee, Brewers Association of Canada, Ottawa, 1973, Chapters III and VI.

6. Boalt, G. and R. von Euler, *Alkoholproblem. Några Nyare Forskningsresultat,* Natur och Kultur, Uddevalla, 1959.
7. Brun-Gulbrandsen, S. and A. Amundsen, Spørsmål om alkohol, in *Tabellarisk Oversikt over Resultater fra Gallupundersøkelser 1956–1966,* Statens Institutt for Alkoholforskning, Oslo, 1967. (Mimeograph).
8. Bruun, K., *Alkoholi: Käyttö, Vaikutukset ja Kontrolli,* Tammi, Helsinki, 1972, pp. 90, 92–109.
9. Bruun, K., G. Edwards, M. Lumio, K. Mäkelä, E. Österberg, L. Pan, R. E. Popham, R. Room, W. Schmidt, O.-J. Skog, and P. Sulkunen, *Alcohol Control Policies in Public Health Perspective,* Publication No 25 of the Finnish Foundation for Alcohol Studies, Helsinki, 1975.
10. Cahalan, D., I. H. Cisin, and H. M. Crossley, *American Drinking Practices,* Monographs of the Rutgers Center of Alcohol Studies 6, New Brunswick, N.J., 1969.
11. Claudian, J., History of the usage of alcohol, in *International Encyclopedia of Pharmacology and Therapeutics,* Pergamon Press, Oxford, 1970.
12. *Combined Statistics CBMC/EBIC 1968 and 1970,* Communaute de Travail des Brasseurs du Marche Commun (CBMC) and EFTA Brewing Industry Council (EBIC).

12a. Edwards, G., Epidemiology applied to alcoholism, *Q. J. Stud. Alcohol,* **34,** 28 (1973).

13. Edwards, G., J. Chandler, and C. Hensman, Drinking in a London suburb I, Correlates of normal drinking, *Q. J. Stud. Alcohol,* Suppl. No. 6, 1972, pp. 69–93.
14. *Effets du Prix et du Revenu sur la Consommation des Boissons dans les Etats Membres des Communautés,* Etudes, Serie Concurrence—Rapprochement des legislations No. 19, 1972, Commission des Communautes Europeennes, Bruxelles.
15. Ekholm, A., The lognormal distribution of blood alcohol concentrations in drivers, *Q. J. Stud. Alcohol,* **33,** 508 (1972).
16. Food and Agriculture Organization of the United Nations, *Production Yearbook,* annual publication.

16a. Food and Agriculture Organization of the United Nations, *Energy and Protein Requirements*, Report of a Joint FAO/WHO Ad Hoc Expert Committee, Rome, 1973.

16b. Food and Agriculture Organization of the United Nations, *Trade Yearbook*, Rome, annual publication.

17. Gabrielson, J., *Consommation des Boissons Alcooliques dans les Différents Pays*, Paris, 1915.

18. Gadourek, I., *Riskante Gewoonten en Zorg voor Eigen Welzijn*, J. B. Wolters, Groningen, 1963, p. 114.

19. Goode, E., *The Marijuana Smokers*, Basic Books, New York, 1970, pp. 309–310.

20. *Hoeveel Alcoholhoudende Dranken Worden er in de Wereld Gedronken*? Produktschap voor Gedistilleerde Dranken, Schiedam, Nederland, 1962–1971.

21. Jonsson, E. and T. Nilsson, *Samnordisk Undersökning av Vuxna Mäns Alkoholvanor*, Centralförbundet för Alkohol–och Narkotikaupplysning (CAN), 1972.

22. Koller, A., *La production et la Consommation des Boissons Alcooliques dans les Différents Pays*, Lausanne, 1925.

23. Kuusi, P., *Alcohol Sales Experiment in Rural Finland*, Publication No. 3 of the Finnish Foundation for Alcohol Studies, Helsinki, 1957.

24. Kuusi, P., *Suomen Viinapulma Gallup-Tutkimuksen Valossa*, Otava, Helsinki, 1948.

25. Lau, H.-H., Cost of alcoholic beverages as a determinant of alcohol consumption, in *Research Advances in Alcohol & Drug Problems*, Vol. 2, R. J. Gibbins et al. (Eds.), Wiley, New York, 1975.

26. Ledermann, S., *Alcool—Alcoolisme—Alcoolisation. Données Scientifiques de Caractere Physiologique, Économique et Social*, Institut National d'Études Démographiques, Cahier No. 29, Presses Universitaires de France, 1956.

27. Ledermann, S., *Alcool—Alcoolisme—Alcoolisation. Mortalité, Morbidité, Accidents du Travail*, Institut National d'Études Démographiques, Cahier No. 41, Presses Universitaires de France, 1964.

28. De Lint, J. and W. Schmidt, Consumption averages and alcoholism prevalence: A brief review of epidemiological investigations, *Br. J. Addict.* **66,** 97 (1971).

29. De Lint, J. and W. Schmidt, The epidemiology of alcoholism, in *Biological Basis of Alcoholism*, J. Mardones and Y. Israel (Eds.), Wiley, New York, 1971.

30. De Lint, J. and W. Schmidt, Estimating the prevalence of alcoholism from alcohol consumption and mortality data, *Q. J. Stud. Alcohol*, **31,** 957 (1970).

31. Lolli, G., The cocktail hour: Physiological, psychological, and social aspects, in *Alcohol and Civilization*, P. S. Lucia (Ed.), McGraw-Hill, New York, 1963.

32. Lolli, G., E. Serianni, G. M. Golder, and P. Luzzatto-Fegiz, *Alcohol in Italian Culture*, Free Press & Yale Center of Alcohol Studies, Monographs No. 3, New Haven, 1958.

33. Mäkelä, K., Concentration of alcohol consumption, in *Scandinavian Studies in Criminology*, Vol. 3, Universitetsforlaget, Oslo, 1971, p. 80.

34. Mäkelä, K., Consumption level and cultural drinking patterns as determinants of alcohol problems, *J. Drug Issues*, **5,** 344, (1975).

35. Mäkelä, K., Raittiit. Kulutustutkimuksen ennakkoraportti, *Alkoholikysymys*, **37,** 45 (1969).

36. Mark, J., The British brewing industry, in *Lloyds Bank Review*, 1974.

37. Moser, J., *Problems and Programmes Related to Alcohol and Drug Dependence in 33 Countries*, WHO Offset Publication No. 6, World Health Organization, Geneva, 1974.

38. Moulton, K. S., *Changing Consumer Preferences in the American Wine Market*, International Wine and Cheese Symposium, New York, 1973.

39. Myerson, A., Alcohol: a study of social ambivalence, *Q. J. Stud. Alcohol*, **1**, 13 (1940).

40. Nilsson, T. and P.-G. Svensson, *Svenska Folkets Alkoholvanor och Alkoholattityder*, Statens Offentliga Utredningar, Stockholm, 1971:77.

41. Non-alcoholic and alcoholic beverages—Germany—Italy—Trade reviews. *Marketing in Europe (Brussels)*, **134**, 4 (1974), Economist Intelligence Unit, Brussels.

42. Nyberg, A., *Alkoholijuomien Kulutus ja Hinnat*, Publication No. 15 of the Finnish Foundation for Alcohol Studies, Helsinki, 1967.

42a. Organization for Economic Co-operation and Development, *Food Consumption Statistics 1960–1968*, Paris, 1970.

43. Organization for Economic Co-operation and Development, *International Tourism and Tourism Policy in OECD Member Countries*, 1972, Paris.

44. Österberg, E., The pricing of alcoholic beverages as an instrument of control policy, *Reports from the Social Research Institute of Alcohol Studies No. 83*, Helsinki, 1975.

45. Pärnänen, M., *Absoluuttialkoholin Vuosikulutusmuutoksen Kuvaus*, Manuscript, kept in the Social Research Institute of Alcohol Studies, State Alcohol Monopoly, Helsinki,

46. Partanen, J., Asiakastutkimus 1968. Ravintolakäyntien tiheyttä ja suhtautumista ravintoloihin kartoittavan tutkimuksen tulokset, *Alkoholipoliittisen Tutkimuslaitoksen Tutkimusseloste No. 53*, 1970, Helsinki. (Mimeograph).

46a. Partanen, J., *Intoxication: A Dialectical Approach*, International Research Group on Drug Legislations and Programs and the Finnish Foundation for Alcohol Studies: Symposium for directions for drug control, Helsinki, 13–15 June, 1973.

47. Pittman, D. J., International overview: Social and cultural factors in drinking patterns, pathological and nonpathological, in *Alcoholism*, D. J. Pittman (Ed.), Harper & Row, New York, 1967.

48. Popham, R. E., Indirect methods of alcoholism prevalence estimation: A critical evaluation, in *Alcohol and Alcoholism*, R. E. Popham (Ed.), University of Toronto Press, Toronto, 1970.

48a. Popham, R. E., Drinking practices in Canada, in *Drinking and Intoxication*, R. McCarthy (Ed.), The Free Press, Glencoe, Illinois, 1959.

49. Popham, R. E. and W. Schmidt, *Statistics of Alcohol Use and Alcoholism in Canada 1871–1956*, University of Toronto Press, Canada, 1958.

50. *The Pub and the People. A Worktown study*, Mass-Observation, Victor Gollancz, London, 1943, pp. 209, 251.

51. *Retail Business*, **191**, 21 (1974), (Table wines—special report), Economist Intelligence Unit, London.

51a. Rowntree, S. B. and G. R. Lavers, Drinking practices in England, in *Drinking and Intoxication*, R. McCarthy (Ed.), The Free Press, Glencoe, Illinois, 1959.

52. Sadoun, R., G. Lolli, and M. Silverman, *Drinking in French Culture*, Monographs of the Rutgers Center of Alcohol Studies No. 5, New Brunswick, N.J., 1965.

53. Sariola, S., *Drinking Patterns in Finnish Lapland*, Publication No. la of the Finnish Foundation for Alcohol Studies, Helsinki, 1956.

54. Schmidt W. and Pohlmann, *Werbeaufwendungen BSR Deutschland 1967–1972*.

55. Schmidt, W. and J. de Lint, Estimating the prevalence of alcoholism from alcohol consumption and mortality data, *Q. J. Stud. Alcohol,* **31,** 957 (1970).

56. Skog, O.-J., *Alkoholkonsumets Fødeling i Befolkningen,* Statens Institutt for Alkoholforskning, Oslo, 1971. (Mimeograph).

56a. Straus, R. and S. Bacon, *Drinking in College,* Yale University Press, New Haven, 1953.

57. Sulkunen, P., Alkoholijuomien tuotannosta ja kulutuksesta, *Alkoholipolitiikka* **38,** 111 (1973).

58. Sulkunen, P., *On International Alcohol Statistics. A Working Paper on WAP Data,* Reports from the Social Research Institute of Alcohol Studies No. 72, Helsinki, 1973. (Mimeograph).

59. Swiecicki, A., *Alcohol: Problems of Social Policy,* Warsaw, 1968.

60. United Nations, *The Growth of World Industry,* Vol. II, New York, annual publication.

61. United Nations, *Statistical Yearbook,* New York, annual publication.

62. United Nations, *World Trade Annual 1970,* Vol. I–V, New York, annual publication.

63. United Nations, *Yearbook of International Trade Statistics,* New York, annual publication.

64. Varis, T., *International Inventory of Television Programmes: Structure and the Flow of TV Programmes Between nations,* Research Reports, Series B, No. 20, Research Institute, University of Tampere, Finland 1973. (Mimeograph).

65. WHO Expert Committee on Drug Dependence, Twentieth Report, *WHO Technical Report Series No. 551,* World Health Organization, Geneva, 1974.

66. Wilkinson, R., *The Prevention of Drinking Problems: Alcohol Control & Cultural Influences,* Oxford University Press, New York, 1970.

67. Voionmaa, T., *An International Survey of Alcoholic Beverages,* Twenty-second International Congress against Alcoholism, Helsinki, 1939.

CHAPTER FIVE

CANNABIS AND EXPERIMENTAL STUDIES OF DRIVING SKILLS

HERBERT MOSKOWITZ, *University of California at Los Angeles and California State University, Los Angeles, California*

1. INTRODUCTION

Both epidemiologic and experimental studies are necessary to determine if and to what degree a drug increases driving accident rates. Unfortunately, epidemiologic studies of the relative appearance of marijuana in driving accidents are difficult to perform due to the lack of a simple technique for determining if marijuana is present in the accident participants. The difficulties are compounded by questions regarding the marijuana constituents and metabolites which are active in producing behavioral changes, their times of action, and their relative appearances in different body fluids. Also, attempts to correlate accident frequency with marijuana use face the problem that conclusions potentially are confounded by the many ways in which drug user populations may differ from control populations in dimensions other than marijuana use.

Currently, information regarding possible driving impairment by marijuana comes primarily from experimental studies of driving and driving-related tasks under administered marijuana. Unfortunately, these studies are limited in predicting the accident probabilities associated with various marijuana dose levels, since they do not take into account such interacting factors as age, driving experience, and drug-use experience. These have been shown to be important covariables for alcohol, the only drug for which we have extensive information about effects on driving. However, experimental studies do have the advantage of potentially going beyond a correlation between task impairment and drug treatment to an understanding of the nature of the impairment. In the long run, knowledge of how various drugs produce impairing effects on driving may lead to more adequate remedial measures than the frequently offered panacea of a law which proscribes use of the drug. The majority of studies on driving or driving-related skills under marijuana have attempted to determine if marijuana produces performance impairment. This review of experimental studies initially will examine studies which have addressed the issue of possible impairment of fairly complex functions and will then examine studies concerned with behavioral mechanisms involved in driving and possibly affected by marijuana.

2. PERFORMANCE IN AUTOMOBILES

Several investigators have attempted to obtain a gross estimate of possible marijuana-induced impairment by placing subjects who were under the influence of marijuana in cars and having them drive either in closed courses or in traffic. The earliest study, performed at the North Carolina Highway Safety Research Center, was described briefly in their monthly journal (1). In a cross-over design, subjects were tested both under an unstated oral dose of THC and under a placebo on performance in a closed course with seven traffic cone configurations. No differences were found between the two treatments in the number of cones struck, nor apparently on any car control measure. Interpretation of the reported findings is difficult since neither the course, the scores, nor the dose are described.

A more extensive examination of actual car handling was conducted by Hansteen et al. (9) for the Canadian Le Dain Commission. Unfortunately, a final report of the data obtained has never been published by the investigators and the only publicly available information is the summary in the Le Dain Commission report on cannabis (13). This experiment involved driving a vehicle six times around a 1.1 mile course set out on an airfield. The course had both curves and straight sections, as well as an area where subjects were required to perform forward and backward maneuvers in tightly constrained areas.

Sixteen subjects (12 male and 4 female) were examined under four treatments, using a double-blind Latin square design. Treatments were placebo, 21 and 88-μg delta-9 THC, and an alcohol dose designed to produce 0.07% BAC. At all sessions subjects drank a beverage, followed by smoking a cigarette. They were tested twice at each experimental session on the full six laps immediately after completing the cigarette, and then they were tested 3 hr later on a set of three laps.

Response measures were subjective judgments by observers in the cars and upon the course and the number of cones and poles delineating the course which were hit. The number of struck objects per lap increased from a mean of 13.2 under the placebo to 16.8 for the high marijuana dose and

17.4 for the alcohol test. The number struck under the lower marijuana dose did not differ from the placebo. Observers' reports showed no significant differences among the four treatments. Also, subjects were instructed to maintain specific speeds for various sections, and the only significant deviance occurred under the higher marijuana dose, where subjects drove 7% slower on the average.

A more extensive double-blind study was performed by Klonoff (12), with subjects driving both on closed courses and on the streets of Vancouver, B.C. Treatments administered by smoking were placebo, 4.9 and 8.4-mg delta-9 THC. The study reported findings for 64 subjects (43 males and 21 females), all of whom were examined on the closed course and 38 of whom were also tested on the streets.

Some details of the experimental design are unclear, but apparently the closed-course study used a random-group design with 13 males and 8 females receiving the low dose, 14 males and 8 females the high dose, and 16 males and 5 females the placebo. The street trials apparently involved a within-subject design in part, with each subject receiving both an active treatment and a placebo. Five males and four females received the low dose followed by the placebo; seven males and two females received the treatments in reverse order. Six males and two females received the high dose followed by the placebo, and seven males and four females received the reverse order.

The closed course consisted of eight tests, a slalom, two tunnels, a funnel, risk judgment, back-up, a corner, and an emergency braking. Response scores were number of cones struck, except for the risk-taking and the braking tests. Subjects received four blocks of five trials each. The first three blocks were considered learning trials and were used to establish an expected score by a regression curve for the fourth set. This expected score was compared with the actual achieved score on the fourth set of trials. Thus, the three treatment groups were not compared with each other. Rather, the score for each group was compared only with the expected score as calculated for that group.

This rather unusual data treatment appears to require some support for the assumption that the curves for the initial 15 trials (three sets of five trials) would in a linear manner continue to describe the next five trials. Scores under the placebo treatment, while not differing in a statistically significant fashion from the expected means, showed considerable variation.

Using the technique reported above, the author reports that two of the eight tests (tunnel one and the corner) were impaired under the low dose and five (slalom, two tunnels, and risk) under the high dose. There was a clear trend for lower performance under the drug treatments, although the mean size of the impairment was not large.

The city street driving sessions included a variety of different traffic conditions within the 16.8-mile course. Driving time averaged 46 min and was conducted during daylight hours. Subjects were scored by observers in the car, using 11 behavioral scales developed by the British Columbia Department of Motor Vehicles. Raw difference scores between the placebo and drug treatment on each behavioral dimension were converted to a transformed seven-point scale for statistical treatment. The high-dose group showed a significant decline, but the low-dose group, using a mean of scores based on all behavioral dimensions, did not. It is not clear from the discussion whether any single behavioral dimension alone showed statistically significant impairment under the treatments. Moreover, the behavioral scales treat deviations in two directions as decrements, so that the direction of any change is obscured. For example, both carelessness and extreme caution are on the same scale in the same direction, and a decrement cannot be meaningfully related to any hypothesis of possible drug action on behavioral mechanisms. Additionally, analysis of the deficits is limited by a lack of information about the reliability of the subjective observer judgments.

The study reports the strongest trend towards declines in performance in the categories of judgment and concentration. There was no evidence for a differential effect on performance under marijuana as a function of sex, driving experience, or previous driving experience under marijuana.

The results from the last two studies strongly suggest some degree of driving performance impairment. Both studies agree on objective measures of car handling or control deficits, and Klonoff (12) also reports evidence from observers' subjective ratings of impairment of attention and judgment.

It should be noted that none of these driving studies had the capability of measuring performance by the subject in the car. Although not yet widely used in drug studies, there have been experiments with instrumented cars which have measured responses such as steering amplitude, brake and accelerator control, speed variation, and lane position. In an interesting example of this type of research, Smiley (29) compared an alcohol treatment with an alcohol and marijuana treatment and found differences in the spectral distribution of frequency response of the steering wheel movements which was related to cue utilization in tracking. Had the study included a marijuana alone treatment, it would have contributed to a better understanding of the results of the two previously reported studies.

3. SIMULATOR STUDIES

Driving simulators are instruments for examining parts of the driving task in a laboratory situation. No simulator is capable of examining all aspects of driving; rather, the design of the instrument emphasizes aspects of performance in which the investigator is primarily interested. Although there is a loss of realism for the driver in comparison to actual car driving studies, simulators have the advantage of control and repeatability of stimulus presentation and tracking demands. They generally have more reliable and diverse methods for measuring performance variables than any currently available instrumented vehicle. The five simulator studies to be discussed below fall into two groups: those investigating perceptual and/or car control behavior and those investigating risk-taking behavior.

The earliest study of marijuana which used a simulator was performed by Crancer et al. (6). The performance of 36 subjects was measured at three sessions—once with a smoked 22-mg delta-9 THC dose, once with alcohol presumed to produce a 0.10%, BAC and once without any treatment administration.

The subject sat in a car mock-up with all the usual instruments and viewed a 23-min film. Although the subject was expected to manipulate the steering wheel and turn signals, and to brake and accelerate, these actions had no control effect. The accelerator did control the speedometer reading, and maintaining the speedometer reading within given limits was one of the response measures. Other measures were appropriate responses to the film when it appeared to require a stop, a turn, or some other maneuver. Although the alcohol treatment affected four of the five responses measures, the only marijuana effect was the speedometer measure.

It is difficult to evaluate this study since it is not obvious what the response scores, other than the speedometer, were measuring. Since there was no effect of the other responses upon the filmed drive, they cannot be described as measures of either car control or tracking. The speedometer measure clearly reflects monitoring of the speedometer, and the evidence that this was affected by marijuana agrees with other studies which indicate that marijuana affects perceptual processes.

It is necessary to restrict conclusions to this last finding, given the ambiguities in the study. Kalant (10) also has criticized the experimental design and drug treatments. Further questions have been raised regarding the quality of the marijuana, with the implication that the actual dose administered may have been less than reported (14).

The simulator in Rafaelsen et al. (22) used a car mock-up with a windshield on which was projected a moving landscape from a circular painting. The mock-up was equipped with a steering wheel, accelerator, brake, gear shift, and clutch. The accelerator controlled the speed of the circular landscape, and the steering wheel shifted the projected image on the windshield. Thus, the "car's" behavior was responsive to the driver's behavior. Red and green lamps were mounted just above the windshield. If the red light was lit, the subject was to stop the car and then start again only on the reappearance of the green light. The duration of the red light was always 10 sec, and it appeared 10 times at random intervals during the 10 min drive.

Response measures were brake time, start time, number of gear changes, and mean speed. The brake and start times were the latency in responding to the appearance of the red and green lights. The study compared marijuana treatments of 8, 12, and 16 mg of delta-9 THC with 70 g of alcohol. The marijuana was presented in a baked cake, an administration roughly one half to two-thirds as effective as smoking the same dose.

Both alcohol and marijuana produced increases in latency of responses to the lights, as measured in the brake and start times. The 8-mg marijuana dose had no effect, but the 12 and 16-mg doses produced large increases in latency with the alcohol dose effect about midway between the two higher marijuana doses. The number of gear changes was not affected by marijuana, but was affected to a small, statistically significant degree by alcohol. Neither drug affected the mean speed.

The third simulator study was performed by Moskowitz, McGlothlin, and Hulbert (17). They used a simulator which has a standard car mounted on a chassis dynamometer facing a 20-foot-wide screen subtended by a 160° view from the driver's eye. Subjects drive a 31-mile filmed route at their own speed, since the projector speed is controlled by the brake and accelerator. The subject must manipulate the steering wheel appropriately, as the projected scenes move laterally to follow the contours of the road. The car was also equipped with a visual subsidiary task which required subjects to respond appropriately to the appearance of four possible light signals. This task was introduced to increase the information-processing load and perceptual demands of the simulator to a level more typical of actual driving. Steering wheel, accelerator, and brake positions were recorded and used to derive 25 performance measures of speed, accelerator, brake, and steering wheel usage and tracking scores.

Twenty-three subjects were given four treatments in six replications of a 4 $\times$ 4 Latin square design. Treatments were smoked cigarettes containing 0, 50, 100, and 200-μg delta-9 THC/kg bodyweight. As in the Rafaelsen study (22), none of the measures of tracking or car control showed any significant decrements under the marijuana treatment. However, the subsidiary task was sensitive to drug effects. There was a significantly greater number of incorrect responses, showing misinterpretation of the light signals. Further, there was a dose-related linear increase in the reaction times to the light signals.

The simulators in the Rafaelsen et al. (22) and the Moskowitz et al. (17) studies are similar in that the driver has control of the speed of the drive and some lateral movement of the car relative to the road. Further, both studies included a visual task to represent the demands for monitoring aspects of the road environment other than those involved in lane positioning or tracking. Results from both studies are consistent in showing decrements in response measures associated with perceptual demands. In the study by Rafaelsen et al. there was increased delay in response to the signals for start and stop, and in that by Moskowitz et al. there was increased delay in response to the subsidiary task signals. Neither study reported difficulties in car control or tracking. Unfortunately, a negative finding in this regard is limited by the lack of a literature relating the tracking/car control demands of the simulator to those found on the road. Moreover, the findings regarding tracking are in contradiction to the two on-the-road studies by Hansteen et al. (9) and by Klonoff (12). It should be noted, however, that the tracking deficits found in these later studies were not large and required demanding course lay-outs to reveal a marijuana-related performance deficit. Although the simulators did not reveal the tracking errors found in the road studies, both simulators had tracking demands more characteristic of smooth curving roads with greater leeway for lane positions than were permitted in the two road studies. In a sense, the studies are complementary in that the road studies emphasized tracking measures and the simulator studies emphasized perceptual measures.

Two additional simulator studies have concentrated on measurement of risk-taking behavior. Dott (7) used a closed loop simulator which projected a scene from model cars moving on endless belts simulating two-car lanes. The subject was instructed that, under certain signals, he was permitted to pass a car in his lane, but he had to complete the passing maneuver before a car approached from the opposite direction in the passing lane.

Additional constraints were imposed by one signal which indicated the necessity for aborting the pass maneuver and another signal which indicated that a successful passing completion required very rapid movement. A repeated measures design examined 12 subjects under four conditions; three treatments of smoked marijuana containing 0, 11.25, and 22.5-mg delta-9 THC, and one nonsmoking condition. No differences in any measure occurred between the placebo treatment and the no-smoke condition which was a control for placebo effects. The prime effect of the marijuana treatment was to increase the frequency with which subjects aborted passing maneuvers when a warning signal was presented. Marijuana led to a general decrease in attempted passes but appeared to have no effect on performing the passing movement if attempted. There were no differences in the path length for the passing maneuver among the treatments. The only apparent evidence for a potential deficit was an increase in the time subjects under the influence of marijuana took to make a decision to attempt a pass when the opportunity for a pass occurred. Interestingly, this increased time for decisions occurred only in nonemergency situations. Decision times under the emergency warning signal remained at the same level for all treatments. Thus, under the marijuana treatments, subjects were able to change their behavior and respond when the situation required a faster response.

The author concluded that the study suggested a decreased willingness to take a risk when under the influence of marijuana. The increased time for nonemergency decisions conforms to the findings for increased reaction time in the studies by Rafaelsen et al. and Moskowitz et al. It should be noted that the signals for an emergency abort (for which there was no increase in response time under marijuana) was a very attention-commanding visual–auditory signal in contrast to the less startling purely visual signal for nonemergency information. The interaction of marijuana effects with these two types of signals may be due to their perceptual character, rather than to the nature of the information contained in the signal.

Another examination of risk taking under the influence of marijuana and alcohol was made by Ellingstad et al. (8) using six groups of 16 subjects each under the following conditions: 11.25 and 22.5-mg delta-9 THC, alcohol to produce 0.05% and 0.10% BAC, and two placebo groups composed of marijuana and nonmarijuana users. Two types of automobile-passing maneuvers were used as tasks. The first task trained subjects with a series of film presentations which demonstrated the minimum amount of time necessary to make an overtaking maneuver of a car traveling in front of the subject. This was followed by a series of test films in which the subject was to indicate the last point in time at which he felt a safe overtaking maneuver could be undertaken in the face of an approaching car in the other lane. No actual overtakings were attempted.

Both marijuana doses produced an earlier cutoff time for the passing maneuver. That is, subjects under marijuana reported at an earlier stage that any further delay would cause passing to be unsafe. Further, under marijuana, subjects less frequently would have performed an overtaking that would have been unsafe based on objective time differences between the two vehicles. Although this study apparently supports Dott's report (7) of decreased willingness to undertake risky maneuvers, the authors preferred to interpret the results as a deficit in time estimation, basing their interpretation upon a multiple discriminant analysis of various component measures of the task. They conceived the marijuana as producing a deficit in "judgmental accuracy" in contrast to the alcohol treatment, which produced a tendency to make "snap decisions." Whether one accepts the interpretation, clearly neither this study nor Dott's study supports any suggestion that marijuana increases the subjective tendency to perform risky maneuvers.

In summary, actual car driving studies suggest some impairment of tracking ability under marijuana, and simulator studies find strong evidence for perceptual performance impairment. Risk-taking appears to decrease. Laboratory studies, to be examined in the following section, investigate tracking and perceptual functions in an attempt to determine the nature of marijuana effects.

4. LABORATORY STUDIES

Tracking

Four types of tracking tasks have been studied under marijuana. Perhaps the simplest task is the pursuit rotor which was studied by Weil et al. (30) using treatments of smoked doses of 4.5 and 18-mg delta-9 THC with both naive and experienced users. There was a performance decrement for the naive users, but experienced smokers demonstrated no performance declines. Similar findings for the pursuit rotor task were cited in the Le Dain Commission report (13).

On the other hand, pursuit tracking studies have uniformly found performance declines at quite low dose levels. Manno et al. (14, 15) reported decrements at a dose of 5 mg of delta-9 THC for smoked marijuana on a rather complex tracking function. Using the same task, Kiplinger et al. (11) replicated the findings for treatments ranging from 6.25 to 50 μg delta-9 THC/kg bodyweight.

Roth et al. (24) compared 19 subjects who received placebo treatments with 18 subjects receiving a brownie containing 20 mg of delta-9 THC. They performed a 5-min paced contour tracking task. This type of task permits the subject to have preview information regarding the task demands so he can anticipate and organize responses over a longer time period than in pursuit tracking tasks. Both the size of the absolute error deviations and the within-subject variance of error increased significantly under the marijuana treatment.

Using a human operator tracking characteristics model, compensatory tracking was examined by Reid et al. (23) with a single axis compensatory tracking task. In comparison with placebo treatments, an 88-μg delta-9 THC/kg bodyweight dose produced a small increase in random output and a lower dose of 21 μg delta-9 THC/kg bodyweight had no effect at all. Neither the phase nor gain functions showed any deficit at the higher dose. Given the three preceding reports of tracking impairment under marijuana, this finding appears surprising, and it possibly may have occurred because the tracking-forcing function for the task did not push the operator to his maximum performance possibilities.

Moskowitz et al. (21) reexamined compensatory tracking, using a critical tracking test. This technique involves a compensatory tracking task which becomes increasingly difficult over time so that at some time point all subjects fail, establishing their maximum performance levels. In comparison with a placebo treatment, a dose of 200 μg delta-9 THC/kg bodyweight had a significant effect on performance. In this study subjects were tested at 15-min intervals for 4 h, and the statistically significant impairment remained for 3.5 hr after smoking was completed.

Clearly, the majority of studies substantiate the findings of the car handling studies in finding a tracking performance decrement. What remains to be clarified is which behavioral functions are affected so as to produce the tracking skills impairment. The variability in findings suggests that there may be different behavioral components in the various tracking studies.

Perceptual Functions

The deficits found in the simulator studies in response to visual signals have been described as perceptual, since there is little evidence that marijuana impairs sensory transduction or conduction functions. When simple sensory performance is examined with the sensory function in isolation, the subject attentive and the task requiring little information processing, no impairment is reported. Thus Caldwell et al. (2,3) reported visual brightness thresholds resistant to marijuana, while Clark et al. (5) failed to find any decrement in depth perception. Moskowitz et al. (19) examined 12 subjects on visual acuity, dark adaptation, and ocular motor control under three treatments: placebo, 0.69 g alcohol/kg bodyweight, and an oral dose of 310 μg delta-9 THC/kg bodyweight. The marijuana had no effect on visual acuity, dark adaptation, or binocular fusion. There was a slight decrement of lateral phoria under both the alcohol and marijuana treatments, but the change was so slight as to be of no importance in practical functioning.

Although there is considerable agreement that marijuana does not affect simple sensory functions, studies which require vigilance for unexpected sensory signals in space or time consistently report impairment of performance (20). Moskowitz and McGlothlin (16) reported that auditory signal detection was impaired in a dose-consistent manner under treatments of 0, 50, 100, and 200 μg delta-9 THC/kg bodyweight. Of interest was signal detection theory analysis of the data, indicating that the prime element in the marijuana deficit was a decrement in d', i.e., a decline in perceptual sensitivity independent of change in criterion. Using the same dose levels, Moskowitz et al. (18) examined detection of signal lights at various peripheral visual angles. Performance was again linearly dose-disrupted. Concurrently, performance of a central visual task with three levels of difficulty was required. The peripheral visual signal detection deficit occurred, regardless of the level of the central visual task. However, the performance on the central visual task also decreased under marijuana to a significant degree. Similar results were reported for visual central and peripheral light detection by Casswell et al. (4).

In a series of experiments, Sharma et al. (26, 27) examined marijuana effect on a visual vigilance or watch-taking task. The task was to watch an apparatus that presented lights successively about a round dial in a clock-like sequence. Occasionally, on a random and infrequent schedule, the light sequence made a double jump of lights that the subject was required to report. Performance was sharply impaired at doses ranging from 50 to 200 μg delta-9 THC/kg bodyweight. The study was conducted for 1-hr sessions, and the impairment increased over time with the lowest performance at the end of the sessions. This supports the previously mentioned study of tracking which found long-term impairment. Increasing the arousal of the subjects by increasing the frequency of appearance of the signals produced increased performance under all conditions, including the placebo treatment. The marijuana deficit, in reference to the placebo treatment did not decrease, although performance overall for all treatments was improved. In an as yet unpublished study by Moskowitz et al. (21), eye movements were examined while performing the task. It was found that eye movements correctly followed the movements of the lights even on the signals which were not reported. This suggests that the site of the deficit is in some behavioral mechanism for data processing, rather than in any peripheral failure to follow the signal.

Clearly, the laboratory examinations support the conclusions from the field car studies and the simulator studies that both tracking and perceptual functions are impaired by marijuana. The degree of impairment found for the perceptual functions appears greater proportionately than that found for the tracking functions.

The studies on perceptual and cognitive decrement under marijuana are currently being extended to determine precisely what behavioral and/or physiologic functions underlie the observed deficits. Similar work on the tracking functions decrement is required to understand the variation in marijuana effects among the differing tracking tasks and to generalize these to driving.

It is clear from the studies summarized above that marijuana impairs, to a greater or lesser extent, many of the performance skills required for driving. While it is impossible to derive from these studies an estimate of the increased probability of accidents as a function of dosage, the only prudent conclusion based on the available evidence is that marijuana will increase the probability of driving accidents.

REFERENCES

1. Anonymous, Pilot study of marihuana effects is conducted. *The Accident Reporter*, February (1972).
2. Caldwell, D. F., S. A. Myers, and E. F. Domino, Effects of marihuana smoking on sensory thresholds in man. *Chem. Abst.*, **72,** 109749 (1970).
3. Caldwell, D. F., S. A. Myers, E. F. Domino, and P. E. Mirriam, Auditory and visual threshold effects of marihuana in man, *Percept. Mot. Skills*, **29,** 755–759 (1969).
4. Casswell, S. and D. Marks, Cannabis induced impairment of performance of a divided attention task. *Nature*, **241,** 60–61 (1973).
5. Clark, L. D. and E. N. Nakashima, Experimental studies of marihuana, *Am. J. Psychiatry*, **125,** 379–384 (1968).
6. Crancer, A., J. M. Dille, J. C. Delay, J. E. Wallace, and M. D. Haykins, Comparison of the effects of marihuana and alcohol on simulated driving performance, *Science*, **164,** 851–854 (1969).
7. Dott, A. B., *Effect of Marihuana on Risk Acceptance in a Simulated Passing Task*, Public Health Service Report ICRL-RR-71-3, DHEW Publication No. HSM-72-10010, Washington, 1972.
8. Ellingstad, V. D., L. H. McFarling, and D. L. Struckman, *Alcohol, Marijuana and Risk Taking*, Report DOT-HS-191-2-301, Vermillion, S.D., University of South Dakota, Human Factors Laboratory, 1973.
9. Hansteen, R. W., L. Lonero, R. D. Miller, and B. Jones, *The Effects of Cannabis and Alcohol on Some Automobile Driving Tasks*, Unpublished Le Dain Commission Research Project, 1971. (Summarized in Le Dain Commission, 1972 [22]).
10. Kalant, H., Marihuana and simulated driving, *Science*, **166,** 640 (1969).
11. Kiplinger, G. F., J. E. Manno, B. E. Rodda, and R. B. Forney, Dose-response analysis of the effects of tetrahydrocannabinol in man, *Clin. Pharmacol. Ther.* **12,** 650–657 (1971).
12. Klonoff, H., Marijuana and driving in real-life situations, *Science*, **186,** 317–324 (1974).
13. Le Dain Commission, *Cannabis: A Report of the Commission of Inquiry into the Non-Medical Use of Drugs*, Ottawa, Information Canada, 1972.
14. Manno, J. E., G. F. Kiplinger, N. Scholz, and R. B. Forney, The influence of alcohol and marihuana on motor and mental performance, *Clin. Pharmacol. Ther.*, **12,** 202–211 (1971).
15. Manno, J. E., G. F. Kiplinger, I. F. Bennett, S. Haine, and R. B. Forney, Comparative effects of smoking marihuana and placebo on human motor and mental performance, *Clin. Pharmacol. Ther.* **11,** 808–815 (1970).
16. Moskowitz, H. and W. McGlothlin, Effects of marihuana on auditory signal detection. *Psychopharmacology*, **40,** 137–145 (1974).
17. Moskowitz, H., W. McGlothlin, and S. Hulbert, *The Effect of Marihuana Dosage on Driver Performance*, Institute of Transportation and Traffic Engineering Report UCLA-ENG-7341, Los Angeles, University of California at Los Angeles, 1973.
18. Moskowitz, H., S. Sharma, and W. McGlothlin, The effects of marihuana upon peripheral vision as a function of the information processing demands upon central vision. *Percept. Mot. Skills*, **35,** 875–882 (1972).
19. Moskowitz, H., S. Sharma, and M. Schapero, A comparison of the effects of

marihuana and alcohol on visual functions, in *Current Research in Marihuana,* M. F. Lewis (Ed.), New York, Academic Press, 1972.

20. Moskowitz, H., R. Shea, and M. Burns, Effect of marihuana on the psychological regractory period, *Percept. Mot. Skills,* **38,** 959–962 (1974).
21. Moskowitz, H., K. Ziedman, and S. Sharma, Marihuana effects on visual scanning patterns in the driving situation, Unpublished.
22. Rafaelsen, O., P. Bech, J. Christiansen, H. Christrup, J. Nyboe, and L. Rafaelsen, Cannabis and alcohol: Effects on simulated car driving, *Science,* **179,** 920–923 (1973).
23. Reid, L. D., M. K. F. Ibrahim, R. D. Miller, and H. W. Hansteen, *The Influence of Alcohol and Marijuana on a Manual Tracking Task,* Society of Automotive Engineers Congress, Technical Paper No. 730092, Detroit, Mich., January, 1973.
24. Roth, W. T., J. R. Tinklenberg, C. A. Whitaker, C. F. Darley, B. S. Kopell, and L. E. Hollister, The effect of marihuana on tracking task performance, *Psychopharmacology,* **33,** 259–265 (1973).
25. Secretary of Health, Education and Welfare, *Marijuana and Health,* Third Annual Report to the U.S. Congress, DHEW Publication No. ADM-74-50, Washington, 1974.
26. Sharma, S. and H. Moskowitz, Effect of two levels of attention demand on vigilance under marihuana, *Percept. Mot. Skills,* **38,** 967–970 (1974).
27. Sharma, S. and H. Moskowitz, Marihuana Dose Study of Vigilance Performance, Proceedings, 81st Annual Conference, American Psychological Association, 1035–1036 (1973).
28. Sharma, S. and H. Moskowitz, Effect of marijuana on the visual autokinetic phenomenon, *Percept. Mot. Skills,* **35,** 891–894 (1972).
29. Smiley, A. K., *The Combined Effects of Alcohol and Common Psychoactive Drugs: Field Studies with an Instrumented Automobile,* Laboratory Report No. LTR-ST-738, National Aeronautical Establishment, National Research Council Canada, Ottawa, 1974.
30. Weil, A. T., N. E. Zinberg, and J. M. Nelsen. Clinical and psychological effects of marijuana in man, *Science,* **162,** 1234–1242 (1968).

CHAPTER SIX

CURRENT TRENDS IN PRESCRIBED PSYCHOTROPIC DRUG USE

RUTH COOPERSTOCK, *Addiction Research Foundation, Toronto, Ontario, Canada*

1. GENERAL CONSIDERATIONS

> After all, if science and technology can produce a hydrogen bomb or propel a man to the moon, why cannot chemistry make us all happy, beautiful, sexually potent, brilliant and ageless?
>
> Dr. Gerald Klerman, Professor of Psychiatry,
> Harvard Medical School, in a speech to
> the American Psychiatric Association,
> Detroit, May 1974

> If prescribing were rational one-half to two-thirds of our patients would be treated with a placebo . . .
>
> Dr. Pierre Biron, in a paper presented
> at the Workshop/Symposium: Compliance
> with Therapeutic Regimens, McMaster
> University Medical Centre, Hamilton,
> Ontario, May 1974

The statements just quoted represent the extremes of the ideological spectrum on current attitudes toward drug prescribing in developed countries. Fifty years ago the concern in these nations was the adequate provision of medical services, while in Africa today many countries still cannot afford the 10¢ (United States) per head for the urgently needed mass preventive vaccination program against tuberculosis (29). In contrast, most industrialized nations have such a high proportion of their population on multiple medications that concern is increasing about compliance with a

Modification of a paper presented at the Vth International Congress of Social Psychiatry, Athens, Greece, September 1–7, 1974.

drug regimen and, particularly, about adverse reactions. In countries as far apart as Australia, the United States, and Ireland, studies have shown that about 5% of general hospital admissions result from illnesses caused by drugs (11).

While the primary focus of this paper is an examination of psychotropic drug use, in order to achieve some perspective on this class of drugs, it seems desirable first to consider the increase in the use of all pharmaceuticals. As the consumption of psychotropic substances has roughly paralleled that of other pharmaceuticals, they warrant particular attention because of the frequent nonspecific nature of the indications for their use.

The rate of growth of the pharmaceutical market in the Western nations was 11% per annum during the late 1960s at then current prices (inflation free currency). At these prices, and assuming an average rate of inflation similar to the 1960s, it is predicted that by 1980 the world market will be about two and a half times the size of the 1970 market (26). For example, Western Germany, one of the two largest manufacturers of pharmaceuticals, reports that the value of its pharmaceutical production increased by 55% between 1966 and 1970 (45), while in the United States pharmaceutical manufacturers have increased their domestic sales from $1 billion in 1950 to $4.3 billion in 1970 and $5 billion in 1972. Equally dramatic has been the latter's sales to foreign markets, an increase from $2.6 billion in 1970 to $3 billion in 1972 (46, p. 27). When we consider only psychotropics, we find an analogous situation. In 1971, Hoffmann–La Roche, whose products account for half of the world's sales of psychotropics, reported their sales had increased by 15% annually over the past few years (2).

Prior to the selection of countries for comparison of their use of psychotropics, it is first necessary to examine the relationship between pharmaceutical and health care expenditures and the implications of this relationship.

It is completely meaningless even to attempt a comparison between industrialized and developing nations of the world in a discussion of psychotropic drug consumption because of the vast differences in health care needs and expenditures. For example, in 1969, Great Britain spent about $100 per capita to provide for the National Health Service, and the United States spent closer to three times that figure for health care; whereas in many African nations the amount was less than 1 dollar per person per annum (20, p. 63). In many of the developing countries, the rural population has virtually no access to medical care, although they may have access to dispensaries for medications. Additionally, in countries without a chemical and pharmaceutical manufacturing industry, purchasing pharmaceuticals abroad poses such a drain on foreign exchange that large scale importing is virtually impossible. Because it lacks a pharmaceutical industry large enough to meet its own needs, even a country as industrially advanced as the U.S.S.R. is spending a large proportion of its pharmaceutical research budget on the development of galenicals (19).

For all the preceding reasons, this article will concentrate on drug use in the Western industrialized nations. In 1968 the World Health Organization conducted a preliminary survey of drug consumption in six European countries. A major finding of this study was the noncomparability of national data on drug consumption due to wide differences in the manner of collection and presentation of data (55). It was evident that drug consumption had increased markedly everywhere but, additionally, it was clear that comparisons between the various countries were not possible.

There are numerous factors militating against comparisons which need mention. Not the least of these is the ratio of physicians to patients which varies between countries. There is general agreement that this relationship affects the rate of drug prescriptions.* The WHO study (54) found that the two countries with the highest rate of drug consumption, Austria and Hungary, also had the highest ratio of physicians to population. More important than the overall physician/patient ratio is the geographical distribution of physicians within a country. For example, in the United States as a whole there were 159 physicians per 100,000 population in 1970. The variation between the lowest and highest ratio for individual states ranged from 75 physicians per 100,000 population in Alabama to 237 in New York State, a threefold advantage (12). A Norwegian study found a clear relationship between the physician/patient ratio and drug consumption in different regions of the country (23).

The ratio of general practitioners to specialists will influence prescribing rates as shown in a French study which reported that general practitioners wrote prescriptions at 77% of all consultations, while specialists wrote at only 57% (54). A Toronto study found that general practitioners constituted 62% of all physicians but wrote over 70% of the prescriptions for psychotropic drugs (14).

Similarly, a study in the United States found that general practitioners accounted for 31% of a national sample of physicians drawn from various medical specialties and wrote 40% of all psychotropic prescriptions (3). Since psychotropics are so commonly prescribed in response to a broad spectrum of symptoms, it is to be expected that the primary care physician will be the highest prescriber, and this is the case for all countries in which

* The ratio of physicians to patients has also been shown to affect elective surgical rates (51).

studies have been conducted. In the U.S.S.R., however, the primary care physician does not write prescriptions for tranquilizers or hypnotics; this is considered to be the role of the psychiatrist (42).

Another factor bearing on drug consumption has to do with the cost and the method of payment for medical services. There is general agreement that, in addition to the development of new drugs, the affluence which followed World War II, combined with the relatively new conception that medical services are a right and not a privilege, largely accounts for the enormity of the increase in drug consumption. Though the method of payment for pharmaceuticals does not bear a direct relationship to the amount consumed, on a national level it appears that the wealthiest nations tend to purchase the largest quantities of pharmaceuticals. Recent estimates place United States sales at approximately $3.8 billion at the manufacturers' level, that of Japan at $2 billion, with Germany, France, and Italy at about $1 billion each (24). Table 1 illustrates the relationship between the average cost of drugs per prescription, the number of prescriptions per person, and the total per capita cost for a number of countries.

These national differences reflect the variation in average cost of drugs, as well as the variation in utilization level. The data here indicate that the average prescription cost may be low, as in Italy and Germany, but the total per capita cost very high as a consequence of high utilization rates. Similarly, in the United States and Sweden, where high average prescription costs and lower utilization are found, the resultant yearly per capita cost is again high. Among the countries represented it is only in the United Kingdom that low cost combines with low consumption. It is of interest to note that drugs constitute a high proportion of total health expenditure in two countries, Italy and Germany, the two countries with high consumption.

Another factor of importance in any discussion of drug utilization is the range in the number of pharmaceutical preparations available. The Federal Republic of Germany has almost 60,000 pharmaceutical preparations on the market, while in Italy there are about 25,000, and in England, with the least costly drugs, only 2,500 (43).

Even in areas where health insurance has been instituted, other factors will affect the rate of utilization of medical services. As long as six years after the introduction of health insurance in Canada, working class individuals utilized physicians' services less than the higher income population (6). There are indications from research in France (54) and in Yugoslavia (7) that with morbidity held constant, rural people use medical services to a lesser extent than urban populations. Additionally, at least in New Zealand, physicians with practices in rural areas write fewer prescriptions for hypnotics and tranquilizers than their nonrural counterparts (48).

TABLE 1 NUMBER AND PER CAPITA COST OF PRESCRIBED DRUGS IN SELECTED COUNTRIES

Country and Year	Average Cost per Prescription (in U.S. dollars)	No. of Prescribed Drugs per Person per Year	Total per Capita Cost per Year (in U.S. dollars)	Drugs as Proportion of Total Health Expenditure (%)
Italy (INAM) 1970	1.43	15.4	22.04	22
Federal Republic of Germany (Bavaria) 1970	1.57	11.2	17.62	21
England and Wales (NHS) 1970	1.62	5.6	9.12	10
United States 1970	4.02	4.9	19.62	12
Sweden 1971	3.69	4.8	17.75	10

Sources: Reference 43; Nordic Statistical Secretariat. *Yearbook of Nordic Statistics, 1973*. Nordic Council and the Nordic Statistical Secretariat, Stockholm, Sweden, 1974, Table 156, p. 207; McInnes, N., What happens when Pharmacy is Nationalized, *Drug Topics*, **116,** 44 (1972).

There are also national preferences regarding the form of medications—the French seem to set great store by suppositories, Italians favor injectables, and so forth. The variety of national customs, fads, and fashions are shown by some striking contrasts. In a damp and chilly climate the people of Sweden spend approximately 1 dollar per capita on vitamins and tonics, while the English, in a similarly damp and chilly climate, spend less than one-sixth that sum per capita on the same substances (17). Even a drug with seemingly clear indications for use such as phenylbutazone is used with three times the frequency per capita in Switzerland than in neighboring France (17).

These national variations are partially the result of differences in medical philosophy, training in therapeutics, and differential perceptions of patients on the part of prescribing physicians.

Prior to the involvement of any physician, however, there are national differences in the availability of drugs to the public. A hypnotic available over-the-counter in Japan will require a prescription in the United Kingdom. A prescription may be refilled almost ad infinitum in one country but will require an additional visit to the physician in another. Clearly the ease of availability of a drug is reflected in consumption patterns and, hence, in consumption rates, playing havoc with the task of making international comparisons of drug consumption.

The multitude of controls on manufacture, import, export, and sale of pharmaceutical products will affect prescribing even more than variations in prescribing patterns. An examination of the consumption of amphetamines in Japan, Sweden, Canada, and other countries before and after the introduction of some form of control legislation, demonstrates the effect of legislative change. In Canada, for example, consumption of amphetamines dropped 90% within the first year after the introduction of new legislation (32).

The symposium on drug consumption convened by the World Health Organization dealt with many of the salient issues hindering comparability of data (53). The most basic issue was perhaps the definition of terms, (i.e., What is a drug?). Following this were problems of drug classification; initially, agreement must be established on whether drugs should be classified according to therapeutic effect, chemical structure, condition treated, and so forth.* A third major problem was finding basic common units of measurement of consumption. Neither monetary units nor physical quantities were deemed adequate. Monetary units were inadequate because of variations and fluctuations in price, and physical measurements were

* For an excellent discussion on this topic see Blum, R. H., D. Bovet, J. Moore, et al., *Controlling Drugs*, Jossey-Bass, San Francisco, 1974 (8).

wanting because comparisons were only possible between individual products, not between drug classes. It was generally felt that average daily dose would be the most meaningful unit for comparison.*

In the face of these problems, a few brave researchers have recently attempted comparative studies in drug consumption. Following is a brief description of three of these which were singled out because their data are of interest and, more importantly, they indicate some of the conflicting findings that can occur in cross-national studies.

Utilizing marketing data, Helfand contrasts drug use in the United States with that in 27 other countries, finding that psychotropics constituted the second most popular class of drugs in the United States but, combining the other countries, only the fifth most popular elsewhere (24). Figure 1, from the same source, shows the therapeutic class of the three best-selling products in 1968 in a number of countries.

The second study, a comprehensive comparison of medical care utilization in seven countries (39), was only incidentally concerned with drug consumption. It took the form of a survey of 1000–2000 households in each of 12 communities within the seven countries. The investigators inquired about the use of prescribed and nonprescribed medicines within the 48 hours prior to the interview. The age–sex standardized rates for all individuals taking medicines, prescribed and nonprescribed, tended to be high in North America (both United States and Canadian centers), low in Poland and Yugoslavia, and intermediate elsewhere.† For prescribed drugs alone, the two study communities in the United States had individual consumption rates considerably higher than those of any other area; more than twice as high as the lowest rates.

The last study, also utilizing survey techniques, but conducted by market research organizations in nine European countries in 1971, asked about consumption of antianxiety agents and sedatives during the entire previous year (4). A range of from 10% of respondents in Spain to 17% of respondents in Belgium and France claimed to have used antianxiety or sedative drugs in the past 12 months.‡ The investigators contrasted these findings with the results of the United States national survey and found that, on the basis of self-reports of consumption, the United States population fell just slightly above the mid-point of the European countries in their

* Out of these meetings plans were laid for the first careful cross-national study of drug consumption, which involved comparisons of prescriptions in Sweden, Norway, and Northern Ireland.

† The other communities represented were located in Argentina, Finland, and the United Kingdom.

‡ The other countries involved were Denmark, Germany, Italy, The Netherlands, Sweden, and the United Kingdom.

United States	British Isles	France	Japan	Germany	Spain
Tranquilizer	Antibiotic	Cardiovascular	Vitamin	Tranquilizer	Antibiotic
Tranquilizer	Antiarthritic	Cardiovascular	Vitamin	Oral Contraceptive	Analgesic
Analgesic NN	Tranquilizer	Tranquilizer	Lipotropic and hematinic	Antidiabetic	Antibiotic

Fig. 1. Therapeutic class of top three products (1968) (27).

use of antianxiety drugs and sedatives. In view of the sales figures for psychotropics presented in the first study and the rate differences in consumption of prescribed medicines shown in the second, this last finding is difficult to understand except as a possible artifact of memory distortion.

Thus sales figures indicate that psychotropics as a drug class are more popular in the United States than in other countries, a second study reports that North Americans, particularly those in the United States, consume more prescribed drugs than do other nationals, and finally, that in the use of antianxiety agents and sedatives, the United States population consumes no more than Europeans. In view of such discrepant conclusions from international studies, the remainder of this paper will concentrate on presenting consumption figures in individual countries.

Psychotropics are generally defined as including all tranquilizing agents, antidepressants, other sedatives and hypnotics (primarily the barbiturates and the nonbarbiturate sedatives), and stimulants (largely amphetamines and other amphetamine-like anorexiants) although analgesics affect the central nervous system, they are not usually classed as psychotropic drugs. The prescribing of mixed drugs or preparations containing a psychotropic substance has been largely ignored in the research literature, leading to a marked underreporting of consumption. As an illustration of the extent of such consumption, a recent Finnish study found that one prescription for a psychotropic drug was written for every tenth diagnosis by a physician, and one "hidden" psychotropic was prescribed for every 14th diagnosis (25). Hidden psychotropics can be defined as those mixed drugs marketed for treatment of somatic conditions but containing a psychotropic component as well as other active ingredients, e.g., Librax and Stelabid, both antianxiety and anticholinergic combinations.

Analysis of a year's prescriptions dispensed to 40,000 families by an insuring agency in southern Ontario found 17.8% of all prescriptions were pure psychotropics, another 6.4% were hidden psychotropics, and an additional 19.1% were other CNS drugs.* The pure and hidden psychotropics

* These included analgesics, antihistamines, and narcotics. The prescription totals do not include oral contraceptives and insulin.

totaled 24.2% of all prescriptions and, adding to these the other CNS drugs, it was found that 43.3% of the prescriptions dispensed contained a mood-altering substance.

2. CANADA

There are new developments in Canada that will no doubt influence future consumption patterns. Two provinces are in the process of introducing comprehensive insuring schemes that will include controlled formularies, encourage generic prescribing, purchase drugs in volume and, hence, generally reduce costs. The absolute cost per prescription is slightly higher in the United States than in Canada, but when wage rates are adjusted, Canadians now pay more for their drugs (30).

By 1970 the ethical drug industry had sales of over $300 million in Canada with approximately 82 million prescriptions dispensed from retail pharmacies, yielding a utilization rate of 3.8 prescriptions per capita* (49). By 1972 there were 91 million prescriptions sold, translating to a rate of 4.1 prescriptions per capita (10). Table 2, giving the numbers of oral analgesic prescriptions for Canada from 1964 to 1973, illustrates the increase. There is a steady progression in the prescriptions for analgesics from just over 2 million in 1964 to more than 5 million nine years later. The second column demonstrates the market share of propoxyphene (Darvon) over the same time period. Prescriptions for this drug increased four and a half times. Examining the last column on this table, it becomes obvious that number of

TABLE 2 ORAL ANALGESIC PRESCRIPTIONS IN CANADA, 1964–1973 (SHOWN IN THOUSANDS)

	No. of Analgesic Prescriptions	No. of Propoxyphene Prescriptions	Most Common Size of Propoxyphene Prescriptions
1964	2079.0	199.8	12 or 24
1966	2715.9	361.3	12 or 24
1968	3215.5	507.8	12 or 24
1970	4014.5	770.8	24 or 30
1972	4827.5	900.1	30 or 50
1973	5133.0	910.4	30 or 50

Source: Data provided through personal communication.

* This figure underrepresents consumption, as it omits all hospital-dispensed prescriptions and those issued to institutionalized populations.

prescriptions alone is an inadequate measure of volume consumed. The most common number of units contained in each prescription has more than doubled in the nine years, thus indicating that propoxyphene consumption has increased eightfold rather than fourfold, as would appear if only numbers of prescriptions were shown. The proportion of narcotic analgesics to all analgesics has remained fairly stable over the same nine-year period, consistently accounting for well over 60% (37).

Table 3 reveals a number of clear trends in patterns of prescribing.* First, it demonstrates the relative stability of the major tranquilizers and antidepressants, the two psychotropic drug classes with the most clearly defined indications for use. The sedative and hypnotic drugs show a slight decline over the four years, a decline largely accounted for by the barbiturates since the nonbarbiturates have shown a steady increase from 6.4% in 1970 to 11.1% in 1973; most of the increase in the nonbarbiturates can be attributed to methaqualone. Although amphetamine-like anorexiants have remained popular, the amphetamines have virtually disappeared. The decrease was initially a result of a voluntary cut-back in prescribing, while the decline between 1972 and 1973 was the result of the introduction of federal legislation.

The minor tranquilizers, particularly the benzodiazepines, represent the current most commonly prescribed class of drugs. The rise in their proportion of all psychotropics from 30.5% in 1970 to 43.6% in 1973 has been dramatic. As important as this increase may appear however, the actual consumption of the minor tranquilizers is masked by these figures. As mentioned earlier, a large proportion of psychotropics are hidden and, therefore, never caught in the statistician's net. For example, almost half the drugs classed as antispasmodics sold in Canada last year were in fact mixtures of an anticholinergic and an ataractic. Similarly, in 1973, Stelabid (a mixture of trifluoperazine and isopropamide) was prescribed with approximately the same frequency as Stelazine (trifluoperazine) (37). Returning to Table 3, an examination of the bottom row of figures showing the proportion of psychotropics to all prescriptions with the decline from 22.7% in 1970 to 17.4% in 1973, assumes a somewhat different meaning. (By 1974 this figure had climbed again to 18.4% of all drugs.) At least in Canada, it appears that the usual statistics relating to these drug classes are inadequate as a means of indicating actual consumption patterns of agents containing psychotropes. It would appear that the "hidden psychotropes" or combination drugs containing psychotropes introduced to the Canadian

* The studies from which the information in Table 3 is taken have been conducted yearly from 1970 to the present covering prescriptions dispensed over two days in a carefully selected sample of retail pharmacies located throughout the Province of Ontario. The author is grateful to the Ontario Ministry of Health for making these data available.

TABLE 3 DISTRIBUTION OF PSYCHOTROPIC PRESCRIPTIONS IN ONTARIO 1970–1973

	Prescriptions							
	1970 (%)		1971 (%)		1972 (%)		1973 (%)	
Major tranquilizers	6.9		6.2		5.8		6.2	
Minor tranquilizers	30.5		38.0		40.0		43.6	
Benzodiazepines		25.7		33.1		36.6		39.6
All others		4.8		4.9		3.4		4.0
Antidepressants	10.7		10.9		12.1		12.0	
MAO inhibitors		0.5		0.3		0.2		0.1
Tricyclics		9.4		9.5		10.8		10.9
Others		0.8		1.1		1.1		1.0
Sedatives and hypnotics	39.5		34.3		34.9		33.2	
Barbiturates:								
Phenobarbital and methylphenobarbital		9.0		5.8		7.2		5.7
Other		24.1		20.5		19.4		16.4
Nonbarbiturate		6.4		8.0		8.3		11.1
Amphetamines and anorexiants	12.4		10.6		7.2		5.0	
Amphetamines		7.3		6.1		3.5		0.3
Anorexiants		5.1		4.5		3.7		4.7
Total percent	100		100		100		100	
Total all psychotropics (N)		1,977		2,551		2,229		2.522
Total all prescriptions (N)		8,709		11,872		11,276		14,516
Psychotropics as percent of total		22.7		21.5		19.8		17.4

Source: Annual Ontario Prescription Survey, Ontario Ministry of Health.

market after the pure psychotropes, and so heavily advertised in the past few years, may be taking up a larger share of the market. However, these drugs are not defined by the prescribing physicians, the formularies, or the patients in ways that make them easily identifiable. It would appear that the only means of gathering completely accurate information lies in a more detailed analysis of individual drug sales.

3. THE UNITED KINGDOM

Data from the United Kingdom could afford this opportunity since all prescriptions written under the National Health Service are available for analysis. In contrast to the Canadian situation, the medical services and drug costs of about 97% of the population of the United Kingdom are covered by the National Health Service. Prescription charges are set at 20 pence, regardless of quantity per prescription, though even this minimal fee is dispensed with in approximately 59% of all prescriptions (18).

In 1970 the National Health Service spent £170 million on pharmaceuticals at manufacturers' prices. The NHS market for pharmaceuticals has been growing at about 10.5% per year, and it is estimated that the growth of the industry from 1970 to 1980 will be between 55 and 70% (26). It is of interest that, in 1973, the industry's advertising expenditure (£33 million) exceeded the money spent on research in the United Kingdom (£30 million) (16).

Table 4 shows the total number of prescriptions dispensed through the NHS in England and Wales from 1961 to 1971, as well as the number of psychotropic drug prescriptions and the proportion of all drugs represented by the various psychotropic drug classes. Of interest here is the 30% increase in total prescriptions over the 10 years, from 205.0 million to 266.5 million. Over the same time the number of psychotropics dispensed rose from 32.2 to 47.8 million prescriptions, thus increasing even faster at 48% (34). By 1973 total prescriptions climbed to 284.1 million, a 39% increase from 1961, and psychotropics had reached 49.6 million prescriptions, a 54% rise (35).

There are numerous similarities between the United Kingdom and Canadian figures, such as the slow but steady decline over the years in the proportion of barbiturates, and the concurrent growth in the share taken by the nonbarbiturate hypnotics. Again, there is a relative drop in the use of stimulant and appetite suppressant drugs. Although the tranquilizers appear to follow the same pattern as in Canada, the classification systems in the two countries differ and therefore render such comparisons difficult. From other sources, however, it is possible to contrast benzodiazepine consumption. As seen in Table 3, these drugs represented 39.6% of all psychotropics in Canada in 1973. For the same year the figure in the United Kingdom was over 33%.* In the course of that year, 12% of the population of the United Kingdom over 15 years of age received treatment with a tranquilizer or hypnosedative (35).

4. THE SCANDINAVIAN COUNTRIES

Drug consumption can be measured more accurately and easily in Sweden and Norway than elsewhere in Scandinavia because purchasing, distribution, and sales are centralized under government agencies, and the data are

* In a recent paper on this subject, Parish suggests that there is evidence indicating an increase in the number of "standard doses" per prescription for the benzodiazepines (35).

TABLE 4 PSYCHOTROPIC DRUGS: PERCENTAGE OF PRESCRIPTIONS IN ENGLAND AND WALES 1961–1971

Year	Barbiturates	Non-barbiturate Hypnotics	Tranquilizers	Anti-depressants	Stimulant and Appetite Suppressants	No. of Psychotropic Prescriptions (millions)	Total No. of Prescriptions (millions)	Percent of Psychotropic Drugs
1961	7.4	1.7	3.0	0.6	2.9	32.2	205.0	15.7
1962	8.0	1.3	3.4	1.0	2.7	32.3	196.6	16.4
1963	7.7	1.2	3.5	1.2	2.4	32.8	205.5	16.0
1964	7.7	1.2	4.3	1.3	2.4	35.5	209.4	17.0
1965	6.6	1.1	4.5	1.4	2.2	39.7	244.3	16.3
1966	6.4	1.1	4.6	1.5	2.0	42.1	262.0	16.1
1967	5.9	1.8	5.4	1.8	1.8	45.3	271.2	16.7
1968	5.7	2.2	6.0	2.0	1.5	46.3	267.4	17.3
1969	5.3	2.4	6.2	2.2	1.4	46.4	246.2	18.9
1970	4.9	2.7	6.5	2.4	1.3	47.1	266.6	17.7
1971	4.4	2.9	6.9	2.7	1.1	47.8	266.5	17.9

Source: Department of Health and Social Security, U.K.

fully recorded and computerized. Although there are minor differences in methods of data collection and classification between Sweden, Norway, and Denmark, the close cooperation among them permits reasonable accuracy in the presentation of comparative figures.*

Over the past few years the use of ethical drugs has increased by 10–15% a year in these countries when estimated on a cost basis. Because a number of new, more expensive drugs have recently been substituted for cheaper ones, e.g., the benzodiazepines replacing barbiturates as hypnotics, and because prices have generally risen, the real increase in yearly consumption is estimated at about half the amount suggested above, or between 5 and 7½% (22).

Data for 1972 on the per capita consumption of psychotropics in Norway, Sweden, and Denmark, show Norway to have the lowest consumption, followed by Sweden, with Denmark the highest. Using an index of 100% for Sweden, the Norwegians consumed only 81% as much while the Danish figure stood at 123% of the Swedish consumption (22).

Based on sales statistics, Table 5 shows the number of daily doses consumed per 1000 inhabitants per day in Sweden and Norway from 1970 to 1973. The Norwegians consumed more minor tranquilizers than their neighbors but less of all other psychotropics. This table is of special interest because it shows a gradual decline in the consumption of psychotropics. Except for the Finnish study mentioned earlier, there are no data readily available for these countries on hidden psychotropic drug consumption, thus making it impossible to assess the reality of this decline. In both Norway and Sweden, there have been public health campaigns directed at physicians as well as the general public regarding psychotropics (52).

An examination of data on the benzodiazepines, reveals marked differences among these countries. In 1972, 1.9% of the Swedish population used a benzodiazepine on any one day, in contrast to 2.4% of the Finnish population, 2.5% cent of Norwegian, and 5% of the Danish (22).

5. THE UNITED STATES

Unlike the countries already discussed, the United States has no national computer system, as in some of the Scandinavian countries, no national recording of prescriptions, as in the United Kingdom, and not even any published longitudinal studies of prescriptions dispensed to a large, geographically dispersed population as reported for Canada. As a senior United States government representative commented, "Data on the number of . . . prescriptions for these drugs dispensed in hospitals and pharmacies

* While information for Finland is more limited, some comparable Finnish data are available.

TABLE 5 YEARLY SALE OF PSYCHOTROPIC DRUGS IN SWEDEN AND NORWAY 1970–1972 (No. of Daily Doses/1000 Inhabitants per Day) (52)

	1970		1971		1972		1972-ratio
Group of Drugs	Norway	Sweden	Norway	Sweden	Norway	Sweden	Norway/ Sweden (%)
Sedatives and hypnotics	26	40	23	38	23	32	73
Minor tranquilizers	41	32	39	32	36	32	113
Major tranquilizers	6	8	6	8	6	9	62
Antidepressants	5	8	5	8	5	8	67
	78	88	73	87	70	81	87

would be available only from commercial market research sources . . ." (38). There are, however, a number of disparate types of studies reported from which the following has been culled.

The average number of new or refill prescriptions obtained per capita has risen from 2.4 in 1950 to 3.5 in 1960, and jumped to 5.5 in 1972 (46, p. 18). During 1972, 1443 million prescriptions were filled in retail outlets (roughly one for every physician visit) and, additionally, 938 million were filled in hospital pharmacies (46, p. 16). While the consumption of prescription drugs has almost doubled in the 10 years prior to 1973, the proportion of the public who constitute these consumers has remained relatively stable at approximately 60 to 66% of the total population (40). Careful epidemiologic studies of prescriptions dispensed through various health insurance plans in the United States have been published (5, 9, 31, 41, 44). These, however, represent a select and usually a local population, and thus are not equivalent as national data to that for the countries already discussed.

A 1968 study of prescriptions dispensed in a mid-Atlantic state found that almost 17% of all prescriptions were written for psychotropics (47). On the basis of a national prescription audit by a marketing agency, Parry et al. report the same 17% figure for psychotropics in 1970 (36), while three years later in New York State these same drugs accounted for 15.4% of all prescriptions, with analgesics constituting another 9.1% (15).

Figure 2 illustrates a pattern of prescribing similar to that of other countries. The only drug class showing a marked decrease in both absolute numbers of prescriptions written as well as proportion of prescriptions relative to other psychotropics were the stimulant drugs while the total number of psychotropes has not markedly changed. However, in the three year period shown, the antianxiety agents increased from 38.8% of all psychotropic prescriptions to 44.3%. More than four-fifths of these antianxiety agents were accounted for by benzodiazepines. The actual number of prescriptions

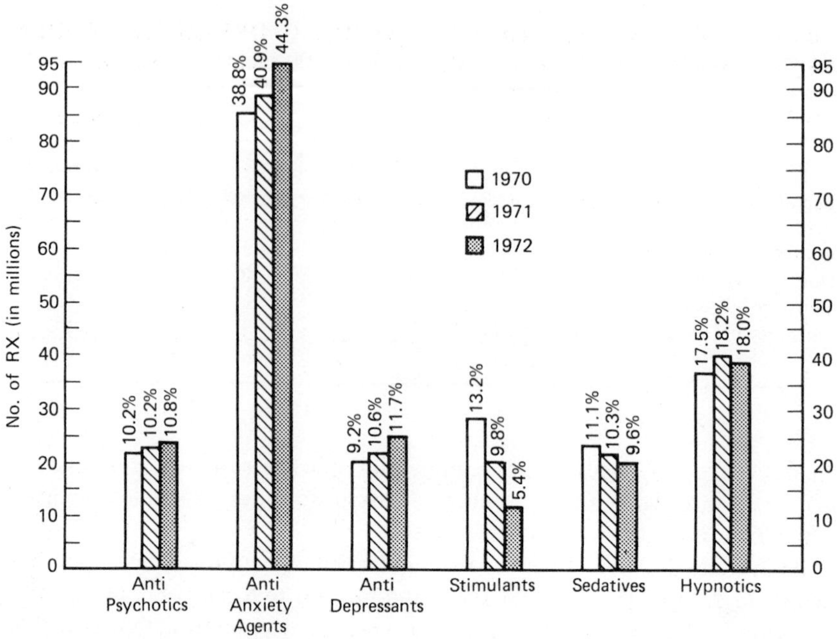

Fig. 2. Number and percentage of psychotropic drug prescriptions filled in United States retail pharmacies 1970–1972 (24).

for benzodiazepines filled in United States outpatient pharmacies and used as antianxiety agents* rose from 61 million in 1970 to 77 million in 1972 (21, p. 267).

According to a 1973 National Prescription Audit of drugs dispensed by community pharmacies, Valium is the most popular individual drug in the United States, followed by the analgesic Darvon Compound-65, and then by Librium (40). According to drug industry sources, 1 in 10 Americans 18 years of age and over was given a prescription for Valium during 1973 (1). Evidence is also accumulating that Valium is increasingly being used for "nonmedical" purposes in the United States (33).

6. CONTROL LEGISLATION

This paper has attempted to indicate the magnitude of the increase in the use of ethical drugs and particularly in the use of psychotropics.

* These include chlordiazepoxide, diazepam, oxazepam, chlorazepate.

Various nations have implemented control legislation which has profoundly affected consumption of psychotropics (27, 32). Without data on manufacturing, and on imports and exports from pharmaceutical manufacturers, however, there is no way to assess the international movement and therefore the consumption of these drugs. Some nations are concerned enough to have established commissions or agencies to study or implement new control methods for the licensing, manufacture, and distribution of pharmaceuticals. Nine member states of the European Free Trade Association have agreed on a mutual recognition of their comparable methods of inspection and standards of manufacture (13). Other national agreements regarding standards are coming into force as well.*

It would appear, however, that until the Convention on Psychotropic Substances, written in Vienna in 1971, is finally signed by enough member states to allow its implementation, adequate measuring instruments will be deficient. The Convention provides for international reporting on manufacture, import, export, and stocks on hand by manufacturers for Schedules I and II drugs (those with the greatest abuse potential) and the same information, omitting stocks on hand, for Schedules III and IV drugs.

In view of the increasing use of mixed psychotropics it is unfortunate that no preparations containing psychotropics are to be included in the Convention and, more important today, neither chlordiazepoxide nor diazepam come under any of the Schedules, although both were originally included by the Expert Committee (50). Implementation of the Convention requires 40 countries as signatories; as of February, 1974, only 16 nations had signed. It comes as no surprise that none of the 16 signatories is a major manufacturer of pharmaceuticals.

REFERENCES

1. Altman, L. K., Valium, most prescribed drug, is center of a medical dispute, *New York Times*, May 9, 1974.
2. Ball, R., The secret life of Hoffmann–La Roche, *Fortune*, **84**, 130 (1971).
3. Balter, M. B. and J. Levine, Character and extent of psychotherapeutic drug usage in the United States, *Excerpta Medica International Congress Series No. 274*, 80 (1971).
4. Balter, M. B., J. Levine, and D. I. Manheimer, Cross-national study of the extent of anti-anxiety/sedative drug use, *N. Engl. J. Med.*, **290**, 769 (1974).
5. Baron, S. H. and S. Fisher, Use of psychotropic drug prescriptions in a prepaid group practice plan, *Public Health Rep.*, **77**, 871 (1962).

* Canada has recently signed bilateral Letters of Agreement with the United States, the United Kingdom, Sweden, and Switzerland on the exchange of information concerning manufacturing standards and control regulations (28).

6. Beck, R. G., Economic class and access to physician services under public medical care insurance, *Int. J. Health Serv.*, **3,** 341 (1973).
7. Bice, T. W. and K. L. White, Factors related to the use of health services: An international comparative study, *Med. Care*, **7,** 124 (1969).
8. Blum, R. H., D. Bovet, J. Moore, et al., *Controlling Drugs*, Jossey-Bass, San Francisco, 1974.
9. Brewster, A. W., S. I. Allen, and A. Holen, Patterns of drug use by type in a prepaid medical plan, *Public Health Rep.*, **79,** 403 (1964).
10. Canadian Pharmaceutical Association Survey, Reported in the *Toronto Star*, August 20, 1974.
11. Cluff, L. E., Iatrogenic disease, *Prevent*, **1,** 11 (1972/3).
12. Confrey, E. A., The logic of a "shortage of health manpower." *Int. J. Health Serv.*, **3,** 253 (1973).
13. Convention for the Mutual Recognition of Inspections in Respect of the Manufacture of Pharmaceutical Products, EFTA Secretariat, 9–11 rue de Varembre, CH-1211, Geneva 27, Switzerland, 1971.
14. Cooperstock, R. and M. Sims, Mood-modifying drugs prescribed in a Canadian city: hidden problems, *Am. J. Public Health*, **61,** 1007 (1971).
15. DeNuzzo, R. V., 18th Annual Prescription Survey by the Albany College of Pharmacy, *Med. Market. Media*, **9,** 13 (1974).
16. Drug promotion "excesses," *Pharmaceut. J.*, **212,** 411 (1974).
17. Dunlop, D. and R. S. Inch, Variations in pharmaceutical and medical practice in Europe, *Br. Med. J.*, **3,** 749 (1972).
18. England: cost of prescriptions 10 per cent in 1973, *Pharmaceut. J.*, **213,** 119 (1974).
19. Fayle, R. C., Pharmacy in the Soviet Union and the Soviet state pharmacopeia, *J. Am. Pharmaceut. Assoc.*, **NS11,** 652 (1971).
20. Gish, O., *Doctor Migration and World Health*, G. Bell, London, 1971.
21. Greenblatt, D. J. and R. I. Shader, *Benzodiazepines in Clinical Practice*, Raven Press, New York, 1974.
22. Halse, M., Comparison of medicinal drug consumption in the Nordic countries, in *Control Policy and Narcotics*, Report from the Second Nordic Symposium on Narcotics, September 30–October 3, 1973, Nordic Investigation Series, Finland, (9) 1974, pp. 81–87.
23. Halse, M. and O. M. Samseth, Drug consumption and statistics, Paper presented at the Second Nordic Research Symposium on Narcotics, September 30–October 3, 1973.
24. Helfand, W. H., The United States and the international pharmaceutical market, *J. Am. Pharmaceut. Assoc.*, **NS10,** 658 (1970).
25. Hemminki, E., The effect of a doctor's personal characteristics and working circumstances on the prescribing of psychotropic drugs, *Med. Care*, **12,** 351 (1974).
26. Keeping the pharmaceutical industry healthy, *Pharmaceut. J.*, **209,** 299 (1972).
27. Khan, I. and B. Westerholm, The Swedish Drug Control and Drug Market, Manuscript prepared for the World Health Organization, DEM/73.5.
28. Lalonde, M., Address to the Canadian Pharmaceutical Association Annual Meeting and Pharmaceutical Conference, May, 1974, Ottawa, Canada.
29. Lambo, T. A., Pressing needs in many lands, *World Health*, 12, April, (1974).

30. Levasseur, R., Special Advisor for the Drug Quality Assurance Program of the Federal Health Protection Branch. Quoted in the *Globe and Mail*, October 26, 1972.

31. McCaffree, K. and H. F. Newman, Prepayment of drug costs under a group practice prepayment plan, *Am. J. Public Health*, **58**, 1212 (1968).

32. Morrison, A. B., Regulatory control of the Canadian government over the manufacturing, distribution and prescribing of psychotropic drugs, in *Social Aspects of the Medical Use of Psychotropic Drugs*, R. Cooperstock (Ed.), Addiction Research Foundation, Toronto, 1974, pp. 9–19.

33. National Commission on Marihuana and Drug Abuse. *Drug Use in America: Problem in Perspective*, U.S. Government Printing Office, Washington, 1973.

34. Parish, P. A., The prescribing of psychotropic drugs in general practice, *J. R. Coll. Gen. Pract.*, **21**, Supplement No. 4, 1 (1971).

35. Parish, P. A., Perspective from England and Wales, Paper presented at the Conference on Prescribing and Use of Anti-Anxiety Agents in Out-Patients, Clinical, Pharmacological and Social Considerations, May, 1974, Maryland, U.S.A.

36. Parry, H. J., M. B. Balter, G. D. Mellinger, I. H. Cisin, and D. I. Manheimer, National patterns of psychotherapeutic drug use, *Arch. Gen. Psychiatry*, **28**, 769 (1973).

37. Personal Communication.

38. Personal Communication.

39. Rabin, D. L. (Ed.), International comparisons of medical care, *Milbank Mem. Fund Q.*, **50**, Part 2: 1 (1972).

40. Rucker, T. D., Drug use: Data, sources, and limitations, *J.A.M.A.*, **230**, 888 (1974).

41. Rosenberg, S. N., L. B. Berenson, F. Kavaler, E. R. Gorelik, and B. Levine, Prescribing patterns in the New York City medicaid program, *Med. Care*, **12**, 138 (1974).

42. Personal Communication.

43. Schicke, R. K., The pharmaceutical market and prescription drugs in the Federal Republic of Germany: cross-national comparisons, *Int. J. Health Serv.*, **3**, 223 (1973).

44. Shapiro, S. and S. H. Baron, Prescriptions for psychotropic drugs in a noninstitutional population, *Public Health Rep.*, **76**, 481 (1961).

45. Siegel, O., Five years of pharmaceutical production in Germany, *Pharma Int.*, **6**, 24 (1971).

46. Silverman, M. and P. R. Lee, *Pills, Profits and Politics*, University of California Press, Berkeley, 1974.

47. Stolley, P. D., M. H. Becker, J. D. McEvilla, L. Lasagna, M. Gainor, and L. M. Sloane, Drug prescribing and use in an American community, *Ann. Intern. Med.*, **76**, 537 (1972).

48. Thompson, A. W. S., Prescribing of hypnotics and tranquilizers in New Zealand, *Pharmaceut. J. N. Zealand*, **35**, 15 (1973).

49. Torrance, G. M., The influence of the drug industry in Canada's health system, A commissioned paper for the Community Health Center Project, Canadian Public Health Association, 1973.

50. *United Nations Conference for the Adoption of a Protocol on Psychotropic Substances, Vienna, 1971.* (Vol. II, Summary Records of Plenary Meetings), United Nations, New York, 1973.

51. Vayda, E., A comparison of surgical rates in Canada and in England and Wales, *N. Engl. J. Med.*, **289**, 1224 (1973).

52. Westerholm, B., Prescribing of psychotropic drugs in Sweden, Paper presented at the Conference on Prescribing and Use of Anti-Anxiety Agents in Out-Patients: Clinical, Pharmacological and Social Considerations, May, 1974, Maryland, U.S.A.

53. World Health Organization, Consumption of Drugs, Report on a Symposium convened by the Regional Office for Europe of the WHO, Copenhagen, 1970, EURO 3102.

54. World Health Organization, The consumption of drugs, *WHO Chronicle,* **24,** 68 (1970).

55. World Health Organization, Drug consumption in Europe, *WHO Chronicle,* **25,** 458 (1971).

CHAPTER SEVEN

DEATH IN AMPHETAMINE USERS: CAUSES AND ESTIMATES OF MORTALITY*

ORIANA JOSSEAU KALANT, *Addiction Research Foundation, Toronto, Canada*

AND

HAROLD KALANT, *Addiction Research Foundation and University of Toronto, Toronto, Canada*

1. INTRODUCTION

During the decades in which the amphetamines were used primarily for medical purposes, they were considered remarkably safe drugs which were only rarely responsible for death. With the advent of widespread nonmedical use, however, especially the intravenous use of illicit methamphetamine, or "speed," this view was replaced by alarming claims of high mortality risk. Following the apparent subsidence of the speed epidemic, the view is again being advanced that there is very little mortality attributable to the drug, especially in relation to the direct effect of overdoses.

Yet these changes of opinion have not been based on thoroughly documented evidence. A survey of the medical literature up to 1963 (58) yielded only nine reported cases of death attributed to amphetamine toxicity. The same nine cases were found in an independent survey three years later (31). Since then, no systematic survey of the literature appears to have been conducted until 1974 (32). The present paper contains a detailed examination of the fatalities reported to date and a comparison with available medicolegal data from the Province of Ontario, which permits some inferences about the nature and frequency of amphetamine-related deaths,

* A preliminary version of this study was published in the *Canadian Medical Association Journal*, **112**, 299 (1975). Literature was reviewed to the end of 1974.

and which indicates the type of investigation which is needed for reliable answers.

For the purposes of this paper, the term amphetamines is applied to racemic (*d, l*) amphetamine, *d*-amphetamine, methamphetamine, phenmetrazine, methylphenidate, diethylpropion, and propylhexedrine, which is the ring-saturated analog of methamphetamine. All these drugs share roughly the same spectrum of sympathomimetic, central stimulant and anorexiant effects which underlie both their medical and nonmedical uses. Hallucinogenic derivatives of amphetamine, such as mescaline, methylenedioxyamphetamine (MDA), and *p*-methoxy-amphetamine (PMA), are not included because their spectrum of pharmacologic actions has led to a different pattern of nonmedical use, and they have never had any recognized medical application.

2. REVIEW OF PUBLISHED CASE REPORTS

This review is based on an intensive search of the world literature. It is impossible to be certain that every published case, particularly during the past two years, has been located, but this has been the objective. For the sake of completeness, we have included cases in which some role of amphetamines in the fatal outcome has been stated or implied, even where there are strong grounds to question the association. These cases will be commented upon below.

Table 1 lists the 47 cases found, with the principal data on drug exposure, clinical and pathologic findings, and causes of death suggested by the respective authors. It is evident that the causes of death fall into two major categories, those directly attributable to the pharmacologic actions of the drugs and those attributable to secondary complications related to the route of administration.

Deaths Directly Attributable to Amphetamine Action

It is generally accepted that the pharmacologic actions of the amphetamines are produced through a combination of displacement of stored transmitter substances from catecholaminergic nerve endings, direct postsynaptic adrenergic action, and varying degrees of monoamine oxidase (MAO) inhibitor activity. Therefore, it can be anticipated that the mechanisms of death would be those typical of excessive catecholamine activity. This is borne out by the case histories. In the text which follows, italicized numbers refer to case numbers (Table 1) and *not* to the list of references.

TABLE 1 REPORTS OF AMPHETAMINE-RELATED DEATHS PUBLISHED IN THE WORLD MEDICAL LITERATURE UP TO 1974

Case No.	Ref. No.	Sex	Age	Chronic Drug Use	Drug Use Related to Death: Drug[a]	Estimated Dose (mg)	Route	Other Drugs	Clinical Findings	Duration of Fatal Illness	Autopsy Findings	Suggested Cause of Death
1	52	M	25	A before examinations	A	30 in 3 days	Oral	None	Sudden loss of consciousness, stertorous breathing	Minutes	Intense congestion of liver, gastric mucosa, meningeal vessels.	Cardiovascular collapse due to A, heavy meal and fatigue.
2	42	M	25	N.S.	*dl*-A	45+	Oral	None	Vague malaise, profuse sweating, weakness, fever; sudden dyspnea, intense sweating, tonic-clonic seizures, collapse. Very rapid onset of rigor mortis.	14 hr	Lungs, liver, kidneys and meninges congested. Pleural ecchymoses.	Cardiovascular collapse in hypersensitive individual.
3	25	F	1	None	A	40	Oral	$FeSO_4$	Found in collapse, pallor. Admitted in semicomatose state, cyanotic. Vomited brown material. Rapid weak pulse. Shallow breathing, respiratory arrest.	21 hr	Lungs edematous, mottled hemorrhage. Gastric and duodenal mucosa discolored, gave strong stain for iron pigment. Adrenals hemorrhagic.	Amphetamine poisoning, with gastric hemorrhage and pulmonary edema.

[a] Abbreviations for drugs: A, amphetamine; d-A, dextroamphetamine; dl-A, racemic amphetamine; meth-A, methamphetamine; meth-P, methylphenidate; PM, phenmetrazine; P-hex, propylhexedrine.

[b] This case appears to be the same as that described by Smith (51).

[c] The same patient was described independently by Jaffe and Koschmann (27).

TABLE 1 (CONTINUED)

Case No.	Ref. No.	Sex	Age	Chronic Drug Use	Drug Use Related to Death: Drug[a]	Estimated Dose (mg)	Route	Other Drugs	Clinical Findings	Duration of Fatal Illness	Autopsy Findings	Suggested Cause of Death
4	19	M	36	Intermittent alcohol binges	A	120	Oral	none	Admitted in confused state, with intense headache, bradycardia. Developed hemiplegia, respiratory difficulty. Heart rate increased to over 100, temp. 104°, vomiting. Death by respiratory failure.	7+ hr	Massive subdural and subarachnoid hemorrhage, hemorrhage in pons, multiple petechiae in cerebrum and cerebellum.	Intracranial hemorrhage.
5	24	M	35	Known alcoholic	*dl*-A	500	Oral	alcohol	Abdominal pain, auditory and visual hallucinations. Irritable, nervous; tachycardia, fever. Very thirsty, but vomited frequently. Sudden jaundice, cyanosis, irrationality, collapse.	1.5 days	Central necrosis, fatty infiltration of liver. Petechiae on all peritoneal, pleural, pericardial surfaces. Brain and lungs edematous.	Hepatic failure due to alcohol and amphetamine intoxication.
6	38	F	21	*dl*-A, ca 50 mg daily, for 9–12 mo; barbiturates, amount?	d-A	?	Oral	?	Tiredness, sore throat, fever, enlarged lymph nodes. No response to antibiotics. Panhemocytopenia. Epistaxis, vaginal bleeding, hematemesis, melena, with progressive	24 days	Not done.	Toxic bone marrow depression.

									exsanguination despite massive transfusions.			
7	5	F	56	N.S.	A	100	i.v.	Nikethamide 11 g, caffeine and Na benzoate 11.5 g	Admitted in coma after ingestion of unknown dose of barbiturate. Given A and analeptics, with no benefit. Sudden hypotension. EEG showed depressed ST segments, V waves. Ventricular fibrillation, no response to procainamide.	8 hr	Not done.	Ventricular fibrillation.
8	43	M	3	None	d-A	40	Oral	None	Agitated, violently hyperactive, no response to barbiturates. Severe tachycardia, respiration rapid and irregular. Cardiovascular collapse.	10.5 hr	Marked edema of brain, internal hydrocephalus, pressure conus. Fatty liver, edema of spleen, kidneys and glottis.	Cardiovascular collapse, exhaustion.
9	6	M	25	N.S.	*dl*-A Meth-A	81 24	Oral	Caffeine	Collapsed during bicycle race in hot weather; spasms, coma. Cyanosis, hyperthermia (109.4°F), pulmonary edema. No response to cooling, analeptics, i.v. fluid, tracheostomy. Death of cardiac and respiratory failure.	13 hr	Cardiac dilatation, lungs edematous and hemorrhagic, petechial hemorrhages on all serosal surfaces. Necrotic foci in heart, liver, spleen, kidney, etc. Cerebral petechiae.	Heat stroke due to A, strenuous exercise, and hot weather.

TABLE 1 (CONTINUED)

Case No.	Ref. No.	Sex	Age	Chronic Drug Use	Drug Use Related to Death: Drug[a]	Estimated Dose (mg)	Route	Other Drugs	Clinical Findings	Duration of Fatal Illness	Autopsy Findings	Suggested Cause of Death
10	30	F	25	N.S.	A	310+	Oral	A.S.A.	Had been unusually energetic for 2 days. Sudden severe headache, coma, fever rising to 109°F, increased intracranial pressure. After chlorpromazine and sponging, temperature fell, sensorium cleared. Sudden collapse, death.	4 hr	Cerebral edema.	Hyperpyrexia due to A.
11	59	F	54	N.S.	d-A	?	Oral	Tranylcypromine 20 mg and chlordiazepoxide 40 mg daily	Depressed patient receiving tranylcypromine, chlordiazepoxide and shock therapy. Given A to relieve drowsiness. Soon developed severe headache, vomiting, collapse, hemiplegia, hypertension, coma.	3 days	Not done.	Intracranial hemorrhage, due to interaction between A and tranylcypromine.
12	37	M	39	N.S.	Meth-A	25	i.v.	Tranylcypromine 30 mg/day	Meth-A given for abreactive therapy. Tranylcypromine given for 2 wk before last session. Immediate severe headache, followed by hemiparesis, blood in CSF.	2.5 days	Massive hemorrhage in basal nuclei and internal capsule; small pontine hemorrhage. Left ventricular hypertrophy. Cerebral atheroma.	Intracranial hemorrhage due to A + tranylcypromine in hypertensive with atherosclerosis.

13	18	F	39	d-A, 6–8 tablets daily for several years	d-A?	?	Oral?	Tranylcypromine 20 mg/day	Known d-A addict, given tranylcypromine for depression. Took 8 times prescribed dose, developed headache, coma, stertorous breathing. BP 170/110, temp. rose to 107.4°F, apnea developed.	5 days	Large frontoparietal cerebral hemorrhage. No aneurysm or atheroma.	Intracranial hemorrhage due to tranylcypromine, presumably interacting with d-A.
14	58	M	22	N.S.	Meth-A	140	Oral	None	Found unconscious and in shock; rectal temp. 108°F, respirations 50/min. Maintained with i.v. fluid, norepinephrine, cortisone, but renal failure and jaundice developed. Despite peritoneal dialysis and cooling, developed ventricular fibrillation.	5 days	Petechial hemorrhages in all viscera. Cerebral edema. Lungs congested and hemorrhagic. Liver congested, centrilobular necrosis. Focal necrosis of renal tubules.	Ventricular fibrillation, resulting from shock and hyperthermia.
15	3	?	49	N.S.	A	?	Oral	MAO inhibitor	Not described	n.s.	Subarachnoid hemorrhage.	Subarachnoid hemorrhage due to combination of A plus MAO inhibitor.
16	23	F	2.5	None	Meth-P	100	Oral	Tripelennamine 500 mg	Nausea, convulsions, admitted in moribund state. No response to intracardiac coramine.	75 min	Edema and intense congestion of brain, lungs. Microscopic edema of brain and degeneration of vascular endothelium. Enlargement of lymph nodes and thymus.	Poisoning by tripelennamine aggravated by meth-P; implied mechanism, cerebral edema.

TABLE 1 (CONTINUED)

Case No.	Ref. No.	Sex	Age	Chronic Drug Use	Drug Use Related to Death: Drug[a]	Estimated Dose (mg)	Route	Other Drugs	Clinical Findings	Duration of Fatal Illness	Autopsy Findings	Suggested Cause of Death
17	36	F	30	Phenelzine 45 mg and trifluoperazine 2 mg daily for 5 wk	d-A	20	Oral	As stated	Rapid onset of intense head pain, BP 150/100. After sedatives, became comatose, BP 170/100.	3+ hr	Hemorrhage in left internal capsule and basal ganglia. No aneurysm or signs of hypertension.	Intracranial hemorrhage due to combination of d-A plus MAO inhibitor.
18	7	M	24	*dl*-A, 8–16 tablets daily for 2.5 yr	*dl*-A	N.A.	Oral	N.S.	Progressive weakness, dyspnea, sweating, muscular pains, fever. Hematologic diagnosis of acute myeloblastic leukemia. No response to 6-mercaptopurine, prednisone, antibiotics, transfusions.	4 mo	Leukemic infiltration of all viscera. Multiple hemorrhages throughout cerebrum, cerebellum, and pons.	Intracranial hemorrhage due to leukemia.
19	2	M	16	N.S.	A	29 tablets (200 mg?)	Oral	N.S.	Sudden collapse and death after taking drugs at nightclub.	N.S.	Cerebral hemorrhage.	Intracranial hemorrhage due to amphetamine.
20[b]	16	M	19	N.S.	Meth-A	2 bags (amount?)	Oral	None	Swallowed drug to evade police search. Rapid onset of delusions and auditory hallucinations. Temp. 104°F, hypotension, severe acidosis.	5.5 hr	Lungs congested and hemorrhagic. Liver congested, focal hepatitis. Bleeding into pericardial sac.	Not stated, but hyperthermia and acidosis implicated.
21	21	M	30	Meth-P for 4 mo, dosage N.S.	Meth-P	?	i.v.	N.S.	Previous hospitalization for cutaneous lesions resulting from i.v. injection of suspen-	?	Hemorrhagic pneumonia, with foreign body granulomata throughout lungs.	Overdose. Mechanism of death not stated.

									sions of meth-P tablets. Sudden collapse after overdose. Dead on arrival.		Talc crystals in liver and spleen R.E. cells.
22[c]	21	F	28	Meth-P or heroin i.v. Duration, dose, frequency?	Meth-P	N.A.	i.v.	As described	Progressive congestive heart failure with fever and aortic regurgitation. Blood cultures grew enterococcus. Given penicillin and streptomycin. While awaiting surgery, died of myocardial infarction.	N.S.	Bacterial endocarditis of aortic and mitral valves; left coronary occluded by embolus (vegetation ?). Pulmonary edema, multiple foreign body granulomata. Mild cirrhosis of liver, multiple small infarcts, talc crystals.	Subactue bacterial endocarditis due to i.v. drug use.
23	28	M	19	8 mo treatment with thyroxin, digitalis, meth-A, trichlormethiazide and K^+ gluconate for obesity	Meth-A	25 daily	Oral	As described	Developed severe weakness in legs, anorexia, temp. 102.4°F, pulse 102, flaccid quadriparesis, serum K^+ 2 mEq/liter. Artificial respiration and i.v. KCl started. EEG showed ventricular extrasystoles progressing to fibrillation, resistant to cardioversion or lidocaine.	2.5 days	Congestion and focal hemorrhages in heart, lungs, brain.	Ventricular fibrillation due to combined effects of thyroxin, meth-A, digitalis and K^+ deficiency.
24	44	F	37	Alcohol	PM	?	i.v.	none	Steady drug use for a week. Hospitalized 9 days later with high fever, unconscious.	4 days	Bacterial inflammation of cardiac valves, lungs, bronchi, bladder. General septicemia. Numerous recent injection marks.	Septicemia, acute bacterial endocarditis.

TABLE 1 (CONTINUED)

Case No.	Ref. No.	Sex	Age	Chronic Drug Use	Drug Use Related to Death: Drug[a]	Estimated Dose (mg)	Route	Other Drugs	Clinical Findings	Duration of Fatal Illness	Autopsy Findings	Suggested Cause of Death
25	13	M	19	Meth-A daily i.v. for 2 yr (dose?)	Meth-A	N.A.	i.v.	N.S.	Nausea, vomiting, headache, impaired vision and urinary frequency for 2 days. Lethargic, BP 195/135, bilateral retinal detachments. Progressive renal failure. Angiography showed multiple microaneurysms in kidney. No response to peritoneal dialysis.	1+ mo	Cardiac hypertrophy. Organizing patchy bronchopneumonia. Kidneys atrophied, multiple infarcts. Necrotizing angiitis with multiple aneurysms in all organs.	Renal failure due to necrotizing angiitis, attributed to meth-A.
26	13	F	21	Heroin addict and alcoholic; marihuana; meth-A suspected	Meth-A	n.a.	i.v.	As described	Intense pain in calves, epigastric cramps, and nausea. Fever, weight loss, leukocytosis. Raised serum amylase; pancreatitis diagnosed. Peripheral neuropathy developed. Angiograms showed necrotizing angiitis in viscera. Steroid therapy led to hypertension.	6 mo	Jaundice. Cardiac hypertrophy and dilatation. Recent pulmonary infarct. Hepatic congestion and centrilobular necrosis. Kidneys very atrophic, nodular. Angiitis and aneurysms in all viscera.	Renal failure and pancreatitis due to necrotizing angiitis, attributed to i.v. drug use.
27	13	F	21	Meth-A, d-A, heroin and barbiturates i.v. 3 years	Meth-A	n.a.	i.v.	As described	Sore throat, fever, myalgia, anorexia, weight loss. Emaciated, peripheral neuropathy, anemia,	4+ mo	Cachexia. Left ventricular hypertrophy. Kidneys atrophic, numerous infarcts. Severe cerebellar	Intracranial hemorrhage due to necrotizing angiitis and hypertension.

									leukocytosis. Spiking fever to 105°F, ceased after steroid therapy, but BP rose to 180/120. Mental dulling, progressive deterioration.		hemorrhage, smaller ones in cerebrum and pons. Destructive arterial lesions in all viscera. Left pulmonary hemorrhage.	
28	13	F	47	History of drug abuse	Meth-A	n.a.	i.v. ?	N.S.	Admitted in confused, disoriented state, with muscular weakness, pain and burning in legs; temp. 105°F, BP 140/110, leukocytosis. Diagnosed acute appendicitis, chronic pyelonephritis. Given antibiotics, surgery. Angiography showed renal aneurysms. Developed pneumonia, G.I. hemorrhage.	40+ days	Severe atherosclerosis, cardiac dilatation and hypertrophy. Duodenal ulcer penetrating into pancreas. Pulmonary edema and multiple thromboemboli. Kidneys coarsely granular. Arterial necrosis in all viscera and skeletal muscle.	Renal failure and pancreatitis secondary to necrotizing angiitis, attributed to i.v. drug use.
29	17	M	20	N.S.	Meth-A	?	i.v.	None	Checked into motel, found dead next morning.	<12 hr	Lungs distended, markedly congested.	N.S.
30	17	M	21	Occasional alcohol, barbiturates	Meth-A	?	i.v.	None	After use at party, felt unable to drive. Appeared drunk, put to bed. Found dead next morning.	<12 hr	Moderate pulmonary and cerebral edema. Congestive changes in myocardium.	N.S.
31	17	M	21	Regular use of Meth-A, and heroin to "come down"	Meth-A	?	i.v.	N.S.	Unaccounted for overnight. Found in coma next morning. Died shortly after admission.	<24 hr	Lungs distended and congested.	N.S.

TABLE 1 (CONTINUED)

Case No.	Ref. No.	Sex	Age	Chronic Drug Use	Drug Use Related to Death: Drug[a]	Estimated Dose (mg)	Route	Other Drugs	Clinical Findings	Duration of Fatal Illness	Autopsy Findings	Suggested Cause of Death
32	41	F	18	Regular use of A, MP, meth-P, i.v. for 2 yrs	A	750–1500	i.v.	None	Found dead in hotel room.	<24 hr	Lungs moderately congested, hemorrhagic. Gastric mucosal hemorrhages. Marked congestion in liver, kidney, spleen. Focal hepatitis.	N.S.
33	41	M	49	Previous suicide attempts with barbiturates	A	?	N.S.	None	Found dead.	?	Lungs, liver, kidneys and spleen congested. Fatty degeneration in liver.	N.S.
34	41	M	59	i.v. stimulants, regular use 6–7 yr	A	?	i.v.	None	Found unconscious in bath. Admitted in coma, cyanotic, temp. 105.8°F. Pulse 120, BP 80/60, profuse sweating. Acidosis increasingly severe.	38 hr	Lungs, liver, kidneys and spleen congested. Subpleural hemorrhages. Focal hepatitis and fatty degeneration.	N.S.
35	57	M	18	N.S.	A	?	N.S.	None	Football player complained of marked fatigability for 1 mo. Few days before death showed surpris-	Minutes	Marked venous congestion, lungs heavy and congested, heart showed focal lesions of myotonic type.	Acute heart failure due to effect of A on diseased heart.

									ing energy and speed. Suddenly collapsed during game, gasped, died.			
36	57	M	23	Regular use of meth-A in bicycle races	Meth-A	?	Subcut.	Alcohol	Injected meth-A into thigh through trousers during bicycle race. Next day had full normal activity, went to bed 10:30 p.m. Next morning, found groaning, gasped, died.	<12 hr	Lungs congested, serosanguinous pleural effusion. Liver dark, partly necrotic, containing gas bubbles. Gram-positive spore-bearing bacilli in portal venules.	Septicemia due to unsterile injection. [Autopsy done 48 hr after death].
37	8	M	22	?	A	?	?	None	Behaving strangely; suddenly threw self in front of truck, killed.	Instant	N.S.	Trauma (suicide)
38	8	M	26	PM?	PM, A	?	i.v.	Alcohol	Taking drugs with a companion. Injected a dose, shortly afterwards took a gun and shot self.	Instant	N.S.	Trauma (gunshot, suicide)
39	1	M	24	i.v. Meth-A use, up to several "spoons" a day for 2 yr	Meth-A	10,000–15,000	Oral	None	Patient with previous history of amphetamine psychosis. Swallowed huge amount to destroy evidence in police raid. Became wildly agitated, delirious. Admitted in shock, respiratory failure. No recovery after 7.5 hr in respirator.	14 hr	N.S.	N.S.

TABLE 1 (CONTINUED)

Case No.	Ref. No.	Sex	Age	Chronic Drug Use	Drug Use Related to Death: Drug[a]	Estimated Dose (mg)	Route	Other Drugs	Clinical Findings	Duration of Fatal Illness	Autopsy Findings	Suggested Cause of Death
40	35	M	30	7 yr use of barbiturates, A, LSD, marijuana; i.v. heroin 4 yr; methadone maintenance, 8 mo; meth-P i.v., 6 mo.	Meth-P	N.A.	i.v.	As described	Increasing dyspnea on exertion. Right heart failure. Punctate hemorrhages in retina, with white nodules along arteries. Diffuse reduction in pulmonary perfusion. Diagnosis: pulmonary hypertension, tricuspid insufficiency. Sudden collapse, death.	5 mo	Lungs edematous, consolidated. Multiple granulomata throughout lungs and retina, with talc crystals inside. Ventricular hypertrophy. Hepatic portal lymphadenopathy and inflammation.	Heart failure due to cor pulmonale (caused by foreign body granulomata).
41	22	M	26	Marijuana and hallucinogens, 2 yr; heroin twice	Meth-A	125–150	i.v.	None	Rapid onset of excruciating head pain, ataxia, disorientation. On admission, agitated and aggressive, hallucinating. BP 170/100. Hyperreflexia. Despite i.m. chlorpromazine, progressed to spastic hemiplegia. Arteriogram showed large intracranial mass. Despite i.v. mannitol and steroids, died.	8.5 hr	Massive left cerebral hemorrhage and uncal herniation. No evidence of cerebral atheroma or arteriovenous anomaly. Microemboli in lungs, consistent with i.v. foreign body reaction.	Intracranial hemorrhage

42	33	M	24	Meth-A and heroin user (duration, amounts?)	Meth-A	N.A.	i.v.	As described	Recurrent abdominal pain and tenderness, fever, chills, muscle pains. Clinical and lab test, HB–Ag + and biopsy indicated viral hepatitis. Treated with prednisone. Several months later, retroperitoneal hemorrhage, hypotension and renal failure; bleeding artery ligated, but patient died.	6+ mo	Necrotizing angiitis, with widespread lesions in viscera, extensive infarction of liver and kidneys.	N.S.
43	45	F	21	Denied	A	100+	?	None	Asthmatic with no known drug use, heard retching, fell to floor, gasping for breath, died.	Minutes	Brain moderately edematous, arteries normal. Passive congestion of liver, kidneys, spleen. Patchy interstitial hemorrhages in myocardium, with apparent spasm of arterioles. Lymphocytic thyroiditis.	Hypertension and cardiac arrhythmia, in asthmatic with thyroiditis.
44	40	M	17	PM? known drug user	PM	?	i.v.	None	Found dead in bed in the morning.	Hours	Numerous fresh and old needle marks on arms. Lungs markedly edematous, aspirated material in bronchi and bronchioles.	Acute drug overdose.

TABLE 1 (CONTINUED)

Case No.	Ref. No.	Sex	Age	Chronic Drug Use	Drug Use Related to Death: Drug[a]	Estimated Dose (mg)	Route	Other Drugs	Clinical Findings	Duration of Fatal Illness	Autopsy Findings	Suggested Cause of Death
45	55	F	19	Drank heavily	P-hex	?	Oral	Alcohol	After a period of drinking, became nauseated. Went out for fresh air, suddenly collapsed and died.	Minutes	Acute pulmonary edema. Focal consolidation due to pulmonary sarcoidosis.	N.S.
46	55	M	29	Known i.v. drug user	P-hex	?	?	None	Collapsed after working in garden; taken to hospital but could not be resuscitated.	· 1 hr?	Bullous emphysema, pulmonary fibrosis secondary to sickle cell disease. Foreign body granulomata in lungs and subcutaneous nodules. Cor pulmonale and pulmonary congestion and edema.	Aggravation of cardiorespiratory disease by drug-induced hypertension.
47	56	M	22	Known drug user meth-A?	A	?	i.v.	None	Steady drug use for 6 days, without eating. Intermittent periods of violent irrational behavior. Went outdoors in midwinter, running wildly. Found dead next morning, tangled in barbed wire fence.	Hours	Lungs markedly congested. Numerous skin lacerations, many old venipuncture marks and fibrosed veins.	Acute drug overdose.

Cerebrovascular Accidents

The group contains seven clear-cut cases of death due to intracranial hemorrhage: *4, 11, 12, 15, 17, 19,* and *41*. The diagnosis was proven by autopsy in all except No. *11*, in which the clinical picture leaves little room for doubt. It is reasonable to attribute these hemorrhages to acute hypertensive crises, both because this would be expected from catecholamine overdose, and because specific mention of elevated blood pressure is made in the histories of cases *11, 17,* and *41*. Three patients (*11, 12,* and *15*) are in an age group in which vascular degenerative changes could have been an important factor in the rupture of the vessel. In fact, specific mention of cerebral atheroma is made in connection with case *12*. However, three patients (*17, 19,* and *41*) were under 30 years, and, in two cases, there is specific mention of the *absence* of vascular abnormality.

Four of the seven cases illustrate the now well-recognized danger of combining amphetamines with MAO inhibitors, such as tranylcypromine and phenelzine. The inhibition of monoamine oxidase leads to a much greater discharge of catecholamine in response to even a small dose of amphetamine. Cases *11, 12,* and *15* received the combination from their physicians before this hazard was generally recognized. Patient *17* took *d*-amphetamine on her own initiative while under treatment with phenelzine. In the remaining three cases, the hemorrhage appears to have resulted from the action of amphetamine or methamphetamine alone, but in much larger doses than were taken in combination with the MAO inhibitors. Case *13* should probably also be included here, although it cannot be regarded as clear-cut. The patient was a known heavy user of *d*-amphetamine, who was then given tranylcypromine by her physician. On the eighth day of treatment, she took eight times the prescribed dose and died of an intracranial hemorrhage that occurred later that day. Conceivably, this might have been due to the massive dose of tranylcypromine alone. However, the possibility of self-administration of *d*-amphetamine as well cannot be ruled out because of her history of addiction.

Acute Cardiac Failure

One of the known effects of catecholamines is sensitization of the myocardium to ectopic stimuli, increasing the risk of ventricular arrhythmias. Indeed, part of the antiarrhythmic effect of propranolol is based on its β-blocking action. It is of interest, therefore, that six cases (*1, 7, 23, 35, 43,* and *45*) died suddenly with either electrocardiographic (*7* and *23*), pathologic (*43*), or circumstantial (*1, 35,* and *45*) evidence of ventricular fibrillation. Another (*46*) died of acute cardiac failure superimposed on chronic cor pulmonale. Two individuals (*29* and *33*) were found dead, but the pathologic findings are suggestive of acute left ventricular failure, even though the authors did not specify the cause of death.

As in the group with cerebrovascular accidents, other factors may contribute to the production of the fatal dysfunction. For example, in case *7*, the amphetamine was administered with nikethamide, and caffeine and sodium benzoate; these drugs may well have contributed to myocardial hyperirritability. Similarly, in case *23*, the patient also received large doses of thyroxine and digitalis, and had hypokalemia due to overzealous administration of trichlormethiazide, all of which would be expected to increase the risk of ventricular fibrillation. In cases *35* and *43*, pathologic examination revealed focal myocardial lesions, which might have served as ectopic foci under the influence of the amphetamine. All but two were aged 25 years or younger, and none had evidence of rheumatic fever or other illness severe enough to explain the sudden deaths.

Hyperthermia

In three cases (*9*, *10*, and *14*) death was clearly associated with hyperpyrexia, with temperatures of the order of 109°F. Neither the clinical nor the pathologic findings provide any recognizable cause of hyperthermia. Since the catecholamines are known to play a major role in central thermoregulatory processes, it seems reasonable to attribute the disturbance to a direct pharmacologic effect of the amphetamines. This suggestion, first emphasized by Jordan and Hampson (30) and by Zalis and Parmley (58), is strengthened by recent accounts of hyperthermia in several cases of death following overdose of the hallucinogenic amphetamine derivative PMA (12). A more detailed examination of the pharmacologic mechanism operant in these cases is being prepared by Sellers and Robinson (48).

In one of the three cases mentioned (No. *14*) the immediate cause of death was ventricular fibrillation. In view of the rest of the history, however, it seems reasonable to attribute this to the hyperpyrexia rather than to the direct effect of amphetamine on the myocardium. Two patients (*20* and *34*) had recorded temperatures of 104 and 105.8°F, respectively, which would not ordinarily be expected to have a fatal outcome. However, the other clinical features suggest that the temperature may well have been higher at other times during the fatal illness. In case *2* only a mild fever was recorded on admission, but the profuse sweating and thirst that preceded the collapse also raise the possibility of a progressively developing hyperthermia.

Trauma

Two deaths by suicide seem directly related to behavior precipitated by the taking of drugs. One (case *37*) involved amphetamine, the other (*38*) phenmetrazine. The blood levels, together with the observed behavior of one of the victims, suggest that paranoid or confused mental states led to the suicide.

Mechanism of Death Uncertain

In a group of 10 patients there appears to be a definite connection between the intake of amphetamines and death, but the mechanism is unclear.

Two of these (*8* and *16*) were small children who swallowed large amounts of preparations containing *d*-amphetamine and methylphenidate, respectively. At autopsy both were found to have severe cerebral congestion and edema, and No. *8* had internal hydrocephalus and brain stem compression. In case *16*, the edema may have been a reflection of repeated tonic–clonic convulsions that occurred shortly before death, but it is specifically stated that convulsions did not occur in the other case. Tripelennamine was also involved in case *16*, and the authors attribute a major share of the toxicity to it.

In one instance (case *44*), the autopsy revealed aspirated material throughout the bronchial tree, so that asphyxia may have been the immediate cause of death. However, one cannot be certain that vomiting or regurgitation was not a terminal event resulting from some other effect of overdose.

In the remaining seven cases (*21, 30, 31, 32, 36, 39,* and *47*), virtually no history is available because the patients were found dead, or died within minutes of being found, and one case (*39*) is mentioned in another context with only scanty details. The pathologic findings are not sufficiently specific to permit these cases to be assigned to any of the major groups discussed above. In case *36* death was attributed to septicemia resulting from unsterile parenteral administration through the subject's clothing. However, the patient was obviously well on the day before death, died suddenly the following morning, and was not submitted to autopsy until 48 hr later. Moreover, bacteria were found only in the liver and not in other organs, so that the diagnosis seems most improbable.

Deaths Due to Complications of Intravenous Administration

It is now well recognized that intravenous self-administration of drugs for nonmedical purposes is often done with unsterile equipment and bad technique. Consequently, there have been many reports of morbidity due to viral hepatitis, septicemia, foreign body reactions, and other pathologic processes not related to the specific pharmacologic actions of the drugs.

The present series includes one death from subacute bacterial endocarditis (*22*), one from septicemia with acute bacterial endocarditis (*24*), one from cor pulmonale due to foreign body granulomata in the lungs with consequent pulmonary hypertension (*40*), and four cases of necrotizing angiitis (*25, 26, 27,* and *42*). Foreign body granulomata in the lungs were also found at autopsy in cases *21* and *46*, but the history does not permit any decision as to whether the sudden death was in any way related to this finding. Of the four patients with necrotizing angiitis, three died of renal failure (*25, 26,* and *42*), and one of cerebral hemorrhage (*27*). The latter patient is not listed under cerebrovascular accidents attributable to amphetamine because she died in hospital after a long illness, during which she presumably had no further access to the drug.

When necrotizing angiitis was first described as a complication of intravenous drug use, methamphetamine was suggested as the common causal factor (13). However, no cases have ever been reported in exclusively oral users of amphetamines, so that the importance of the intravenous route must be emphasized. Koff et al. (33) have recently suggested that the disease may be due to hepatitis B virus rather than to the drug. It is worth noting that one patient (*28*), who died of necrotizing angiitis with renal failure and pancreatitis, is not really known to have taken methamphetamine at all. She was included in the series described by Citron et al. (13) in which methamphetamine was suggested as the common etiologic factor, but the case record describes her only as having "a history of drug abuse." This issue requires further investigation.

Deaths of Uncertain Etiology

Table 1 contains four cases in which the authors attributed an etiologic role to amphetamine, but in which there is reason to doubt the connection. In case *3*, a one-year-old child swallowed large amounts of amphetamine and ferrous sulfate tablets. Though the authors (25) ascribed primary importance to the amphetamine, the description of her clinical course and the pathologic findings are quite compatible with acute iron poisoning. Case *5* is that of a known alcoholic whose death in hepatic failure could well be attributed to alcoholic hepatitis alone. He evidently took a large amount of amphetamine (together with a large amount of alcohol) to which the authors ascribed a contributory role. However, there is no independent evidence of amphetamine hepatotoxicity that would lend credence to this suggestion.

The third case (*6*) is that of a young woman who died of panhemocytopenia attributed to a toxic depression of the bone marrow. She was found to be a regular heavy user of *d*-amphetamine even while she was in hospital.

Since this is the only case of its kind ever reported, despite the wide use of amphetamines, the possible role of other toxic factors must be considered. She apparently used barbiturates also, and the possible use of other drugs cannot be ruled out.

The last case (*18*) is that of a man who died of acute myeloblastic leukemia, and who was also known to have been a regular user of amphetamine for 2.5 years. Present day views on the etiology of leukemias do not lend support to any causal role of amphetamine in this case. Prior use of *d*-amphetamine was recently reported to be associated with a significantly increased risk of Hodgkin's disease (39), although this association has since been challenged (29).

Comment

Considering the extremely wide medical use of amphetamines in the past, there are remarkably few fatalities reported in patients receiving the drugs under supervision. There were only five such cases described, and three of these involved the simultaneous administration of MAO inhibitors. Most of the deaths listed in Table 1 occurred in people using the drugs nonmedically or without the knowledge of their physicians. However, among those for which the history permits a reasonable conclusion, nearly half (13 cases) were individuals who could not be considered regular users or "addicts," and all of them died of acute overdose effects. In contrast, of the 16 deaths among known regular users, 8 were due to complications of intravenous use, and only 8 were due to overdose, in 2 of which the simultaneous use of MAO inhibitors was the main factor.

It is of some interest that only three reports were found of deaths attributed to use of phenmetrazine, and none to diethylpropion, despite their pharmacologic similarities and widespread nonmedical use in some parts of the world.

3. AMPHETAMINE-RELATED DEATHS IN ONTARIO IN 1972–1973

The cases in Table 1 cover a span of 35 years and have been gathered from a number of different countries and different types of populations. It is therefore of interest to see how the pattern of death reflected in them corresponds to that occurring within a single population which includes substantial numbers of amphetamine users. For this purpose, the records of the Chief Coroner of the Province of Ontario for 1972 and 1973 were searched for all deaths in which amphetamines were involved in any way.

The following brief case histories represent the total gathered from this source. The first 14 deaths occurred during 1972, and the remainder were during 1973.

Case 1

A male, aged 44, known to be an amphetamine user and trafficker, died of a bullet wound in the head inflicted while he was under the influence of drugs.

Case 2

A male, aged 25, also a known user and trafficker, was killed by bullet wounds in the head while under the influence of amphetamines. The accused murderer was also said to be "high on speed" at the time of the shooting. Bags of methamphetamine and syringes were found at the scene, and the fight was believed related to the drugs.

Case 3

A female, aged 18, with a previous history of depression and suicide attempts, committed suicide by jumping from a bridge. Traces of methamphetamine were found in the urine and stomach contents.

Case 4

A male, aged 35, who was a known drug user with a criminal record, was found dead of carbon monoxide poisoning in his car. A syringe was found with the body, and chemical analysis revealed amphetamines in the blood and urine. Talc and starch granules were found in the lungs and liver along with microscopic signs of pericholangitis.

Case 5

A female, aged 18, was a known multiple drug user, mainly of amphetamines, LSD, and mescaline. Death was due to massive hepatic necrosis as a result of serum hepatitis.

Case 6

A male, aged 25, was known to be a very heavy user of amphetamine as well as a trafficker. Death was caused by a massive gastrointestinal hemorrhage due to posthepatitic cirrhosis with continuing active serum hepatitis attributed to intravenous use of amphetamine.

Case 7

A female, aged 55, and a known *d*-amphetamine addict, was found dead in bed. The autopsy revealed pulmonary edema and myocardial hypertrophy. "Significant levels" of amphetamines were found in the body.

Case 8

A male, aged 28, died of carbon monoxide poisoning. He had left his car running inside a garage, so that the noise of the motor would cover the alarm signal on a cigarette vending machine he was trying to burgle. Syringes were found in the car. Toxicologic examination revealed high levels of amphetamines in the blood and urine.

Case 9

A male, aged 24, took speed intravenously, and also at least one capsule of Tuinal by mouth. He was seen by witnesses to be under distinct drug effects. He wandered out on to the roof of the building without his glasses, even though he was very myopic, and fell to his death.

Case 10

A male, aged 26, who was a known drug user and trafficker, spent the evening drinking and then attended an all-night party. According to witnesses, he took several "spoons" of MDA. When the party broke up he suddenly collapsed, went into convulsions, and talked irrationally. He was taken to hospital, but died while being transferred to another. Autopsy findings included pulmonary congestion, substantial amounts of mucus and vomitus in the bronchi, and petechiae over the lungs, pericardium, and brain. Death was attributed to asphyxia due to aspiration of vomitus.

Case 11

A female, aged 41, with a previous history of attempted suicides by drugs, was found dead in bed. Tablets of barbiturates, amphetamine and primidone were missing from bottles at the bedside. The autopsy revealed nothing of significance, except for the toxicologic findings.

Case 12

A male, aged 22, who was believed to have made earlier suicide attempts by slashing his wrists, shot himself in the head while under the influence of drugs. A witness to the shooting could add no further information because he was also very "high" on drugs at the time.

Case 13

A female, aged 26, who was a known drug user with a police record of drug offenses, spent the night with a man, drinking and taking drugs. She was found unconscious in the morning, but was left to sleep it off. Several hours later she was found dead. The autopsy showed recent venipuncture marks, congestion of the liver and lungs, multiple foreign body granulomata in the lungs, and a low grade subacute hepatitis.

Case 14

A male, aged 26, well known to the police as a speed user, had been drinking beer and using speed most of the day. He was known to go "mentally blank" when "coming down" from the effects of speed. In this condition he wandered on to a major highway late at night, with his back to the traffic, and was struck and killed by a car.

Case 15

A female, aged 40, was found dead in bed with a large amount of prescription drugs by her bedside, including two preparations with *d*-amphetamine. The lungs were intensely congested, yet the myocardium and coronary vessels were normal, and the heart was normal in size. Death was attributed to acute cardiac failure due to the drug combination.

Case 16

A male, aged 19, was a known heavy amphetamine user who, after a quarrel with his parents about his speed use, committed suicide by gunshot to his chest. He survived for 1 hr in hospital, during which time almost his entire blood volume was replaced by transfusion during unsuccessful attempts to stop the bleeding. No drug was found in the blood at autopsy, but, in view of the massive transfusion, no conclusion can be drawn about recent use.

Case 17

A male, aged 22, who was a known "speed freak," shot and killed a police officer while under the influence of the drug. He was traced by the police to a house which was surrounded. He refused to surrender and shot himself in the head. Incidental findings at autopsy included numerous sclerosed veins in the forearms, multiple foreign body granulomata in the lungs, and foci of chronic inflammatory cells in the portal areas.

Case 18

A male, aged 25, and also a known speed user, was involved in the same shooting as case *17*. He also committed suicide by shooting himself in the head. Autopsy showed multiple sclerosed veins, many foreign body granulomata in the lungs and in the skin of the forearms, chronic inflammatory lesions in the portal areas, and hyperplasia of the portal lymph nodes and hepatic reticuloendothelial cells.

Case 19

A male, aged 18, was a known drug user and heavy drinker. At a party in which he consumed a large amount of alcohol, he was said to have injected heroin twice. He became faint and nauseated, and vomited. In order to avoid trouble with the police, his companions decided not to call an ambulance, but put him to bed instead. Shortly afterwards he went into convulsions, and a friend attempted to treat him by giving an intravenous injection said to be speed. Within seconds, he turned white and died. The autopsy showed hemorrhagic congestion in the lungs, and gastric contents in the larynx and treachea. The liver showed heavy lymphocytic infiltration in the portal tracts. Toxicologic examination confirmed the presence of alcohol and methamphetamine, but not of opiate.

Case 20

A male, aged 22, had been under psychiatric treatment for depression for several months. He was found dead in the barn, having shot himself in the chest with a rifle. Toxicologic examination showed the presence of amphetamine in the blood.

Case 21

A male, aged 18, was known to be an intravenous speed user. He was found dead in a laneway in winter time, frozen into the ice, and covered with snow. Autopsy revealed a linear fracture of the left side of the skull extending from the frontal bone posteriorly to the occiput. He is believed to have fallen while under the influence of drugs, struck his head, lost consciousness, and frozen to death.

Case 22

A male, aged 19, lost his driving license on conviction for impaired driving. While still under suspension of his license, he again drove while under the influence of drugs and alcohol and crashed into a building, killing himself and seriously injuring his three companions. An incidental finding at autopsy was mild periportal inflammation in the liver. A tinfoil package containing methamphetamine powder was found in his pocket.

Case 23

A male, aged 24, was a known drug user and trafficker with a police record, who had dropped out of a treatment program for drug dependence. At a party at which heroin, diazepam, and Mandrax (methaqualone and diphenhydramine) were said to have been taken, the subject and his friends all fell asleep. Next morning the friends awoke but could not rouse him and called an ambulance. He was dead on arrival. The autopsy showed fresh needle marks over the forearm and numerous thrombosed veins. The lungs and glottis were edematous and congested, the pericardium was covered with petechiae, and traces of stomach contents were found in the trachea. Death was attributed to suffocation. Toxicologic examination showed the presence of methaqualone, amphetamine, and methamphetamine, but no opiates.

Case 24

A female, aged 22, who was a drug addict and well known to the police, was found dead in the apartment of two chance acquaintances. Both of them were also under the influence of drugs at the time. One of them later said that the victim had taken a large dose of methadone by mouth during the evening, and she had become stuporous and incoordinated, with constant back and forth rocking movements. After vomiting she fell asleep and was later found dead. Autopsy showed sclerosed veins and foreign body granulomata in the forearms. The lungs were congested, edematous, and hemorrhagic, and they also contained numerous foreign body granulomata. The blood, urine, and liver contained methamphetamine and amphetamine, but no methadone, alcohol, or other drugs. Death was attributed to methamphetamine poisoning.

Case 25

A male, aged 27, was a known drug user who was "high on speed" at the time of death. There was a domestic quarrel, and a policeman was called to intervene. The subject seized a kitchen knife, and he attacked the policeman, who shot him in self-defense. Autopsy showed only findings attributable to bullet wound.

Case 26

A male, aged 23, was a known amphetamine addict who had been taken to the hospital the previous evening in an irrational state. He was treated for an overdose of amphetamine and later released. He waded into a river, and his body was found later in the water. The autopsy findings were consistent with death by drowning. Toxicologic analysis confirmed the presence of amphetamines.

Comment

The pattern of causes of death among this series is strikingly different from that revealed in Table 1. The most marked difference is that two-thirds of the deaths were of a violent nature: seven were due to accidental violence, seven to suicide, and three to homicide.* One of the accidental deaths (case *4*) may perhaps be questioned on the grounds of insufficient evidence to connect the amphetamines with the behavior leading to death. The same may be said of three of the suicides (cases *3, 11,* and *20*). Case *22* may be excluded because of the major role of a very high blood alcohol level. In the remaining 12 cases, however, the behavior leading to death is wholly consistent with the state of amphetamine intoxication and with the toxicologic evidence. Erratic behavior, paranoid ideas, overt aggression, feelings of omnipotence, and in some cases confusion, are all well documented manifestations of amphetamine intoxication (31). Depression is both a symptom of amphetamine withdrawal and a predisposing cause of amphetamine use. Suicide among amphetamine users is therefore not surprising. A further possibility is that amphetamines, when taken by depressed persons, may mobilize them sufficiently to enable them to commit suicide; cases *3* and *20,* which were excluded above, may possibly belong in this category.

The remaining nine cases are attributable to medical causes. Two of them appeared to be cardiac deaths of the type described above, which may be considered the result of primary amphetamine toxicity. Two were fatalities resulting from viral hepatitis or posthepatitic cirrhosis. Although they belong in the category of complications of intravenous administration, this particular complication was not encountered in the literature series (Table 1), despite the many references to the frequency of its occurrence among intravenous drug users (46). The remaining five cases may be classed as drug overdoses (though not necessarily of amphetamines), three of them

* For comparison, one may note a recent study by Haberman and Baden (20b) in which 29% of deaths among 297 alcoholics were attributable to accident, suicide, or homicide.

resulting from asphyxia by aspiration of vomitus, and two by unknown mechanisms.

Another important feature is the frequency of multiple drug use. This should come as no surprise since there are very few chronic amphetamine users who are not also multiple drug users. The classification of users by single drugs is rather arbitrary. In 18 of the 26 cases, the toxicologic examination revealed the presence of other drugs in addition to the amphetamines. Indeed, in nine cases, other drugs or toxic materials were present in such large amounts that they were probably primarily responsible for the death. They included carbon monoxide (cases *4* and *8*), MDA (case *10*), alcohol (cases *15, 19,* and *22*), methaqualone (case *23*), and barbiturates and minor tranquilizers (cases *11* and *13*). However, even in these cases it is not possible to exclude a significant contribution of the amphetamines to the fatal outcome. For example, in case *8* the death was due to carbon monoxide poisoning, but this resulted from behavior which was most probably provoked by the amphetamine. In case *15,* the blood alcohol level alone is too low to have caused death, but the addition of amphetamine might well have contributed to a ventricular arrhythmia. In case *19,* the testimony of the witnesses relates the death almost immediately to the injection of speed, even though the main drug found was alcohol. The motor vehicle accident in case *22* could be attributed to the alcohol alone, yet the amphetamine probably contributed to the reckless and overconfident behavior.

It is perhaps not surprising that the medical literature revealed only two reports of violent deaths in amphetamine users. Such cases are much more likely to be found in the popular press or the legal or criminological literature. It is rather more surprising that the psychiatric literature does not appear to contain any documented reports of suicides during the amphetamine withdrawal depression. The lack of clinical reports of deaths from hepatitis may be in a sense artifactual, such cases being designated as drug users instead of amphetamine users.

4. TOXICOLOGIC FINDINGS

Toxicologic examinations of various degrees of completeness were carried out in 21 of the 42 cases described in the literature, and in 24 of the 26 Ontario Coroner's cases. Those with positive findings are presented in Tables 2 and 3. Several points can be deduced from the data. The first is that the wide range of values found in any given tissue, or in the blood, does not necessarily reflect an extremely wide variation in lethal dose. The times between last intake of drug and performance of the analysis were widely different and in many cases unknown. It is therefore probable that quite different amounts of drug had been excreted or metabolized, and to this must be added the wide range of doses taken. Unfortunately, there is also no consistent pattern of sampling of tissues and body fluids in the different cases. Where no value is shown, this means, in most instances, that no analysis was done, rather than that no drug was found.

Nevertheless, of those cases in which numerical values for the blood level are given, all but two in each of Tables 2 and 3 exceed the values found after therapeutic dosage of amphetamine, which are up to 0.01 mg/100 ml according to the Centre of Forensic Science (Toronto), or up to 0.005 mg/100 ml according to Campbell (11). This tends not only to confirm the connection of amphetamine with the fatalities, but also to emphasize that most of the decedents had taken high doses. Indeed, the observed levels are in the same range as those measured in known heavy drug users taking doses of up to 200 mg at a time by intravenous injection (9, 10).

5. EPIDEMIOLOGIC INFERENCES

The data presented above are too limited and unsystematic to permit any firm conclusions. Nevertheless, the comparison of the literature reports with the Coroner's data provides some valuable clues from which we may infer that mortality in amphetamine users is neither as high as was believed a few years ago ("speed kills"), nor as low as is now frequently stated.

The first point to emphasize about medical case reporting is that it tends to be qualitative rather than quantitative. When a new phenomenon is recognized, there is usually a cluster of case reports confirming it, but once it has become a part of medical knowledge publication of reports ceases. The groups of reports concerning amphetamine–MAO inhibitor interactions, necrotizing angiitis, and pulmonary granulomata after intravenous methylphenidate, illustrate this point. Obviously, therefore, the number of published reports provides no valid estimate of the actual incidence of the conditions.

This conclusion is fully justified by the comparison between Table 1 and the Coroner's data. Table 1 lists only 6 amphetamine-related deaths described in the world medical literature during 1972–1973, while there were at least 16 during that period in Ontario alone, in addition to 10 others in which amphetamine may have played a role. There were approximately 60,000 deaths a year in Ontario from all causes during that time, of which about 40% were reviewed by Coroners. Of the total of 26 cases in the Coroner's series, 17 were violent deaths, and 2 were sequelae of viral hepatitis, yet only 2 cases in the first category, and none in the second were

TABLE 2 TOXICOLOGIC DATA IN PUBLISHED CASES OF AMPHETAMINE-RELATED DEATHS

Case No.[a]	Ref.	Drug[a]	Blood	Urine	Stomach Contents	Liver	Kidney	Brain	Other	Injection Site	Other Drugs
			Concentrations found (mg/100 ml or /100 g)								
1	52	*dl*-A	–	–	1.04	–	–	–	–	–	–
2	42	*dl*-A	–	0.25	–	–	Pooled viscera 0.32		–	–	–
4	19	*dl*-A	–	–	0.00	–	–	–	–	–	–
5	24	*dl*-A	–	–	–	0.30	–	0.30	Heart 0.3	–	–
9	6	*dl*-A	0.02	2.04	0.32	–	–	–	Muscle 0.053	–	–
		Meth-A	0.053	0.70	0.12	–	–	–	0.036	–	–
10	30	*dl*-A SO_4	–	–	Total 310 mg	–	–	–	–	–	–
14	58	Meth-A	0.133[b] 0.097[c]	–	–	–	–	–	Peritoneal dialysate, total 24.8 mg[d]	–	–
16	23	Meth-P	–	–	Total 400 mg	0.03	–	0.04	–	–	Tripelennamine in all tissues at 5 times the concentration of Meth-P
20	16	Meth-A	4.0	–	+	20.6	8.7	14.4	–	–	–
23	28	Meth-A	–	–	–	0.1	–	–	–	–	Digitalis alkaloids in myocardium
29	17	Meth-A	0.01	–	–	0.07	–	0.03	–	Injection site 10.0 total	–
30	17	A	0.05	–	–	0.03	0.02	0.08	–	Injection site 16.9 total	–
		Meth-A	0.06	–	–	0.04	0.02	0.08	–	–	–

31	17	A	0.01	0.04	–	0.02	0.08	0.02	–	Injection site 0.00	Morphine, 0.002 mg in bile
		Meth-A	0.00	0.10	–	0.06	0.10	0.02	–	0.00	
32	41	A	0.70	–	–	1.20	0.80	–	–	–	–
33	41	A	0.60	70.0	–	3.50	–	–	–	–	–
34	41	A	<0.05	–	–	4.50	0.40	–	–	–	–
35	57	A	0	+	0	–	–	–	–	–	–
36	57	A	+++	–	–	Pooled viscera +++		–	–	–	Alcohol, 46 mg/100 ml in blood and 30 mg/100 g in viscera
37	8	A	0.017	–	–	–	–	–	–	–	–
38	8	PM	0.80	5.0	–	0.70	–	–	–	–	Alcohol 40 mg/100 ml in blood
43	45	A	1.10	–	–	4.00	–	–	–	–	–
44	40	PM	0.40	2.4	–	0.50	–	–	Bile 0.70	–	–
45	55	P-hex	0.27	–	0.54 (Total, 1.15 mg)	1.18	0.95	–	–	–	Alcohol, 122 mg/100 ml in blood
46	55	P-hex	0.18	1.6	–	0.28	0.15	–	Vitreous humor, 0.17	–	–
47	56	A	0.70	24.2	2.1	1.2	1.9	0.30	Lung 1.7, Muscle 0.4	–	–

[a] Case Nos. and abbreviations of drug names as in Table 1.

[b] Blood level of A on second day after admission.

[c] Blood level of A on fourth day after admission.

[d] Dialysis performed on fifth day after admission.

TABLE 3 TOXICOLOGIC DATA IN AMPHETAMINE-RELATED DEATHS IN ONTARIO, 1972–1973

		Concentrations Found (mg/100 ml or /100 g)			
Case No.	Drug	Blood	Urine	Liver	Other Observations
1	Meth-A	0.02	–	0.76	Meth-A traces in skin
2	Meth-A	0.09	46	–	Salicylates in urine
	d-A		+	–	
3	Meth-A	–	+	–	Meth-A present in stomach contents
4	Meth-A	+	+	–	CO 58% saturation in blood
	d-A	+	+	–	
5	*d*-A	–	–	+	–
7	Meth-A	+	–	–	Barbiturates in blood
	A	+	–	–	
8	Meth-A	0.18	+	–	CO 46% saturation in blood
	A	0.08	+	–	
9	Meth-A	–	0.3	–	Barbiturate level in blood 0.7
	A	–	0.2	–	
10	Meth-A	0.05	+	–	MDA 1.0 in blood, and + in urine
	A	0.05	+	–	Alcohol 100 in urine
11	A	+	0.3	–	Blood: amobarbital 0.8, secobarbital 0.7; phenobarbital 4.5; salicylate 8.0. Stomach contents: barbiturates +; salicylates +.
12	Meth-A	–	0.006	+	Alcohol in urine 20.
	A	–	0.003	+	
13	Meth-A	0.023	+	–	Blood: barbiturates, 3.5; diazepam, 0.07. Stomach contents: barbiturates +, diazepam +
	A	0.005	+	–	

found in the medical literature. A similar predominance of violence and of complications of intravenous injection, as the major cases of death in amphetamine users, is noted in the 1969–1971 findings in the Final Report of the Le Dain Commission in Canada (14) and in those of Inghe (26) in Sweden. It is noteworthy that there were over twice as many amphetamine-related deaths recorded in Ontario in 1972–1973, as in all Canada during 1969–1971. This may not reflect a true increase in incidence so much as a more complete retrieval of the cases on record. This should be further facilitated by a computer-based indexing system which has just been instituted in the office of the Chief Coroner of Ontario.

As already noted, most of the acute overdose fatalities in Table 1 occurred in individuals who were not regular heavy users, while a majority of

TABLE 3 (CONTINUED)

		Concentrations Found (mg/100 ml or /100 g)			
Case No.	Drug	Blood	Urine	Liver	Other Observations
14	Meth-A	–	+	–	Blood: alcohol, 70; urine, alcohol 110.
	A	–	+	–	
15	d-A	0.03	–	–	Blood: alcohol 100.
17	Meth-A	0.002	+	–	Blood: barbiturates 1.
	A	+	+	–	
18	Meth-A	+	+	–	Blood: barbiturates 0.75
	A	+	+	–	
19	Meth-A	–	+	–	Blood: Alcohol 100; Urine: alcohol 180
20	A	+	–	–	–
21	Meth-A	0.70	+	+	Blood: salicylates +; Liver: salicylate +; propoxyphene +; diazepam +. Urine: salicylates +
22	Meth-A	+	+	–	Blood: Alcohol, 160; Urine: Alcohol, 220
	A	+	+	–	
23	Meth-A	–	0.012	–	Methaqualone: in blood 0.2; in liver +; bile +; stomach contents +
	A	–	0.007	–	
24	Meth-A	0.08	+	+	–
	A	+	+	–	
25	Meth-A	0.02	+	+	Blood: barbiturate 0.75
	A	–	+	+	Liver: secobarbital +
26	Meth-A	0.12	+	–	–
	A	+	+	–	

deaths in the latter group were due to complications of intravenous injection. This is compatible with the observation that regular use, either oral (31) or intravenous (34, 51), may lead to the development of high levels of tolerance, so that death by overdose occurs only after a sudden massive increase in dose (e.g., cases *20* and *39* in Table 1). The Le Dain Report (14) indicates that during 1972 there were approximately 3000 regular and 4000 occasional users of intravenous methamphetamine in Canada versus approximately 353,000 regular and occasional users of oral preparations. At the same time there were about 600 reported poisonings, of which 296 were attributed to speed, 115 to phenmetrazine, 51 to amphetamine, 38 to *d*-amphetamine, 20 to methamphetamine, and the rest unstated. If one assumes that the term "speed" refers to illicit methamphetamine for intravenous use, there would appear to be approximately 50 times as great a chance of poisoning with intravenous as with oral use. This does not really contradict the preceding remarks about tolerance in regular users because there is no way of knowing how many of the poisonings occurred in experimenters as opposed to regular users. Moreover, very few of these poisonings were fatal.

In contrast, there is clearly a greater risk of death from all other causes in the regular intravenous users. Among the Ontario Coroner's cases, 16 of the deaths were in known regular intravenous methamphetamine users versus only three in oral users. There is insufficient information concerning the route of administration in the other cases; though intravenous and oral routes are the most common, sniffing or "snorting" is also practiced (15). The best current estimates (14, 49) suggest that the population of regular intravenous users in Ontario during 1972–1973 numbered about 1500. On the assumption that all the 16 fatalities were in males, and that the frequency distribution of amphetamine users in the age range of 15–34 years was the same as in the total male population of the same age range in Ontario, the expected number of deaths among users was calculated on two bases: (*a*) that the mortality rates would be the same as those of the same age groups in the general population according to the Ontario Vital Statistics for 1971, and (*b*) that it would be the same as that among treated alcoholics (47). The results in Table 4 show that the observed death rate in the users is at least four times as high as would be predicted on the basis of the death rate in the general population. This difference is highly significant ($p < 0.001$). Though the rate also appears higher than in treated alcoholics, the difference is not statistically significant ($p > 0.05$).

It should further be noted that the excess mortality in amphetamine users (i.e., observed death rate minus predicted death rate) is actually underestimated here because of the assumptions made above; if the absolute numbers had been large enough to permit separate computations for males and females, the lower death rates in the female general population would have given a lower predicted mortality in the user group. In addition, the age distribution of the fatal cases suggests a disproportionately large representation of the younger age groups (15–19 years) among the using population than among the general population. If it had been possible to take this into account accurately it would also have reduced the expected mortality. In addition, 10 of the Coroner's cases were excluded from the calculation because of inadequate information, but some of these possibly belonged in the group of regular users.

From the foregoing considerations it is fair to conclude that the numbers of amphetamine-related deaths reported, both in the medical literature and in Coroner's reports from various parts of the world, represent a rock-bottom minimum. In the city of Philadelphia alone, for example, during 1969

TABLE 4 COMPARISON OF MORTALITY RATES IN REGULAR INTRAVENOUS AMPHETAMINE USERS AND IN AGE-MATCHED GROUPS OF GENERAL POPULATION AND TREATED ALCOHOLICS

Age	Ontario Male Population 1971	% of Total	Assumed Age Distribution of Amphetamine Users[a]	Rate of Death per 1,000 Ontario Males	Expected Deaths in Amphetamine Users Based on Ontario Male Mortality Rates	Rate of Death per 1,000 Male Alcoholics[b]	Expected Deaths in Amphetamine Users Based on Mortality of Alcoholics	Observed Deaths in Amphetamine Users
15–19	362,100	29.5	886	1.2	1.063	0.0	0.000	4
20–24	334,900	27.3	820	1.5	1.230	10.3	8.446	4
25–29	286,700	23.4	703	1.2	0.843	2.2	1.546	6
30–34	242,000	19.7	591	1.5	0.887	3.6	2.130	2
Totals	1,225,700	100.0	3,000		4.023		12.122	16

[a] It is assumed that amphetamine users have the same age distribution as the Ontario Male Population. Estimated number of amphetamine users = 1,500; period of observation = 2 years. Number of man years of exposure to the risk of death = 3,000.
[b] Based on the mortality experience of alcoholic patients in in-patient and out-patient facilities of the Addiction Research Foundation.

there were 37 instances of death associated with the presence of amphetamine and other stimulants in the body as detected by toxicologic analysis (54). In Ontario, Coroners must review deaths in a number of different categories, including those caused by violence or misadventure; sudden or unexpected deaths, including those of individuals declared dead on arrival at hospital; those due to natural causes in people not under the care of a licensed physician; and all unexplained or mysterious deaths, or those which, in the physician's opinion, warrant further investigation. These categories would cover most amphetamine-related deaths, but one type which might be missed rather easily would be death due to some medical complication such as hepatitis or pulmonary fibrosis, occurring after a lengthy illness and possibly some time after the last drug use.

It is now recognized that there is a relatively high turnover rate in the population of regular intravenous methamphetamine users. Many of them give up amphetamines and change to heroin or other drugs after two or three years (14, 20, 53). Consequently, deaths from complications of intravenous use beginning during the amphetamine period may well be recorded eventually as due to the use of other drugs. Among the Ontario Coroner's cases, incidental findings at autopsy included multiple foreign body granulomata in the lungs in five (cases *4, 13, 17, 18,* and *24*), and hepatic inflammatory lesions in six (cases *4, 13, 17, 18, 19,* and *22*). If they had not died of other causes, these lesions would probably have contributed to morbidity and premature mortality at a later stage. Further, since many of the fatalities of this type occur after prolonged hospitalization or illness, there may be no toxicologic evidence to tie them to specific drug use. One may wonder, for example, how many intracranial hemorrhages may occur as a consequence of an unrecognized necrotizing angiitis, so that the role of drug use goes unrecorded.

A truly valid answer must await the completion of longitudinal studies in groups of known amphetamine users. Such studies are in progress in Sweden (4, 26), and possibly elsewhere. Preliminary results (26) indicated a mortality rate of 3.6% in a three-year follow-up of 83 cases of viral hepatitis in stimulant users in Stockholm, compared with 0.1% in a comparable age group of the general population. It should be noted that these cases were selected on the basis of an already diagnosed liver disease, so that their mortality rate would be expected to exceed that of the overall population of stimulant users. Another study showed 5.8% mortality in two years among 156 central stimulant users on a drug maintenance program, most of them due, once more, to accidental deaths and complications of drug use. Such studies are needed in Canadian and American populations if we are ever to have accurate knowledge of the situation in North America, rather than clinical impressions or slogans.

With due allowance for the qualifications that have already been made, it is clear that regular heavy amphetamine use, especially by intravenous injection, is associated with a significantly higher mortality rate than that of the general population. However, it is not strikingly different from that found among alcoholics of the same age, and is comparable to that reported in several studies of heroin addicts (50). The alarm with which the public, the press, and the relevant professions have reacted to the speed and heroin problems is in sharp contrast to the relative apathy towards the continuing and vastly larger alcohol problem. There are presently about 300,000 alcoholics in Ontario, of whom about 60,000 are in the same age range as the amphetamine users covered in this study, i.e., about 40 times as many. Deaths among these young alcoholics numbered about 480 during the same two-year period in which the 16 deaths occurred among regular amphetamine users. Moreover, it should be noted that excess mortality among alcoholics begins to rise steeply above the age of 35 (47). Such comparison should help to provide needed perspective for an appropriate social response.

6. SUMMARY

The world medical literature contains 47 reports of fatalities associated with amphetamines in a 35-year period. These included 7 cerebrovascular accidents, 6 sudden cardiac deaths, 3 cases of hyperpyrexia, 10 fatal poisonings of uncertain mechanism, 7 cases of medical complications of intravenous injection, 2 deaths by violence, and the remainder of uncertain etiology. In contrast, in Ontario alone, during 1972–1973, there were 26 deaths in amphetamine users, of which 16 were due to accident, suicide, or homicide. Of the remaining cases, two were cardiac, two hepatic, and the rest were mixed drug overdose. Pulmonary granulomata, subacute hepatitis, and other lesions resulting from intravenous drug use were common findings at autopsy. On the basis of the estimated number of regular intravenous amphetamine users in Ontario, the mortality rate in such users is at least four times as high as in the general population of the same age, and is comparable to that in alcoholics and heroin addicts. However, the absolute number of alcohol-related deaths is far greater than in amphetamine or heroin users.

ADDENDUM

At the 30th International Congress on Alcoholism & Drug Dependence, held in Amsterdam in September, 1972, Gunne (20a) reported on amphetamine-related deaths in Sweden, The published proceedings of this Congress did not become available to us until after completion of this review.

During a six-year period (1966–1971) there were 15 deaths attributed to amphetamne or phenmetrazine alone and 9 to amphetamine in association with other drugs. These deaths occurred in the Stockholm and Uppsala area with a population of two million people. All but one of the victims were known intravenous users of central stimulants. There were 18 men and 6 women. Their mean age of 36.4 years is considerably higher than that of the Ontario cases; this may reflect the fact that intravenous use of stimulants appeared much earlier in Sweden.

Most of the fatalities mentioned by Gunne were of uncertain mechanism because the victims were found dead. In two cases, however, brief clinical summaries are available. One had moderate hyperthermia, and both died of acute cardiac failure attributed to extreme tachycardia or ventricular fibrillation. Toxicologic examination confirmed the presence of phenmetrazine in one case (liver, 5 μg/g; urine, 50 μg/ml), and amphetamine in the other (plasma, 14 μg/ml; liver, 12 μg/g; urine, 500 μg/ml). Obviously these cases belong in the category of acute overdose.

ACKNOWLEDGMENTS

We are greatly indebted to Dr. H. B. Cotnam, Chief Coroner of Ontario; Dr. R. C. Bennett, Deputy Chief Coroner; and Mr. G. Cimbura, Chief Chemist, Centre for Forensic Science, Toronto, for their kindness in making available to us the records of amphetamine-related deaths in Ontario. We are specially grateful to our colleagues, Dr. W. Schmidt and Mrs. J. Moreau, for the calculations which form the basis of Table 4, and Mrs. L. Vegers for her valuable bibliographic assistance.

REFERENCES

1. Angrist, B. and S. Gershon, Possible dose-response relationships in amphetamine psychosis, in *Drug Abuse, Proceedings of the International Conference*, C. J. D. Zarafonetis (Ed.), Lea & Febiger, Philadelphia, 1972, p. 263.
2. Anonymous, Amphetamine overdose kills boy, *Pharm. J.*, **198,** 172 (1967).
3. Bartlet, J. E. A., The side-effects of modern psychiatric drugs, *Anglo-German Med. Rev.*, **3,** 67 (1965).
4. Bejerot, N., *Addiction—An Artificially Induced Drive*, Charles C Thomas, Springfield, Ill., 1972.
5. Bennett, I. L. and W. F. Walker, Cardiac arrhythmias following the use of large doses of central nervous system stimulants, *Am. Heart J.*, **44,** 428 (1952).

6. Bernheim, J. and J. N. Cox, Coup de chaleur et intoxication amphétaminique chez un sportif, *Schweiz. Med. Wschr.*, **90,** 322 (1960).

7. Berry, J. N., Acute myeloblastic leukemia in a Benzedrine addict, *South. Med. J.*, **59,** 1169 (1966).

8. Blomquist, M., R. Bonnichsen, C.-G. Fri, Y. Mårde, and R. Ryhage, Gas chromatography–mass spectrometry in forensic chemistry for identification of substances isolated from tissue, *Z. Rechtsmed.*, **69,** 52 (1971).

9. Bonnichsen, R., A. C. Maehly, and S. Åqvist, Arzneimittel und Fahrtüchtigkeit. II. Zentralstimulierende Amine und aromatische Kohlenwasserstoffe, *Blutalkohol*, **6,** 245 (1969).

10. Bonnichsen, R., A. C. Maehly, Y. Mårde, R. Ryhage, and B. Schubert, Determination and identification of sympathomimetic amines in blood samples from drivers by a combination of gas chromatography and mass spectrometry, *Z. Rechtsmed.*,**67,** 19 (1970).

11. Campbell, D. B., A method for the measurement of therapeutic levels of (+)-amphetamine in human plasma, *J. Pharm. Pharmacol.*, **21,** 129 (1969).

12. Cimbura, G., PMA deaths in Ontario, *Can. Med. Assoc. J.*, **110,** 1263 (1974).

13. Citron, B. P., M. Halpern, M. McCarron, G. D. Lundberg, R. McCormick, I. J. Pincus, D. Tatter, and B. J. Haverback, Necrotizing angiitis associated with drug abuse, *N. Engl. J. Med.*, **283,** 1003 (1970).

14. Commission of Inquiry into the Non-Medical Use of Drugs, *Final Report*, Information Canada, Ottawa, 1973.

15. Cox, C. and R. G. Smart, Social and psychological aspects of speed use, A study of types of speed users in Toronto, *Int. J. Addict.*, **7,** 201 (1972).

16. Cravey, R. H. and R. C. Baselt, Methamphetamine poisoning, *J. Forensic Sci. Soc.*, **8,** 118 (1968).

17. Cravey, R. H. and D. Reed, Intravenous amphetamine poisoning. Report of three cases, *J. Forensic Sci. Soc.*, **10,** 109 (1970).

18. Ehtishamuddin, M., Tranylcypromine, *Lancet*, **2,** 1015 (1963).

19. Gericke, O. L., Suicide by ingestion of amphetamine sulfate, *J.A.M.A.*, **128,** 1098 (1945).

20. Gunne, L.-M., Personal communication.

20a. Gunne, L.-M., High dose amphetamine effects in man, *Proc. 30th Int. Congr. Alcoholism & Drug Dependence, Amsterdam, 1972.* A. Tongue and E. Tongue (Eds.), I.C.A.A., Lausanne, p. 56.

20b. Haberman, P.W., and M. M. Baden, Alcoholism and violent death, *Q. J. Stud. Alcohol*, **35,** 221 (1974).

21. Hahn, H. H., A. I. Schweid, and H. N. Beaty, Complications of injecting dissolved methylphenidate tablets, *Arch. Intern. Med.*, **123,** 656 (1969).

22. Hall, C. D., D. E. Blanton, J. H. Scatliff, and C. E. Morris, Speed kills: Fatality from the self-administration of methamphetamine intravenously, *South. Med. J.*, **66,** 650 (1973).

23. Hardmeier, E., and J. Schmidlin-Meszaros, Todliche Vergiftung eines Kleinkindes mit dem Antiallergicum Plimasin, *Arch. Toxikol.*, **21,** 131 (1965).

24. Harvey, J. K., C. W. Todd, and J. W. Howard, Fatality associated with Benzedrine ingestion: A case report, *Del. Med. J.*, **21,** 111 (1949).

25. Hertzog, A. J., A. E. Karlstrom, and M. J. Bechtel, Accidental amphetamine sulfate poisoning, *J.A.M.A.*, **121,** 256 (1943).

26. Inghe, G., The present state of abuse and addiction to stimulant drugs in Sweden, in *Abuse of Central Stimulants*, F. Sjöqvist and M. Tottie (Eds.), Raven Press, New York, 1969, p. 187.

27. Jaffe, R. B., and E. B. Koschmann, Intravenous drug abuse. Pulmonary, cardiac, and vascular complications, *Am. J. Roentgenol. Radium Ther. Nucl. Med.*, **109,** 107 (1970).

28. Jelliffe, R. W., D. Hill, D. Tatter, and E. Lewis, Jr., Death from weight-control pills. A case report with objective postmortem confirmation, *J.A.M.A.*, **208,** 1843 (1969).

29. Jick, H., Amphetamines and malignant lymphoma, *J.A.M.A.*, **229,** 1462 (1974).

30. Jordan, S. C. and F. Hampson, Amphetamine poisoning associated with hyperpyrexia, *Br. Med. J.*, **2,** 844 (1960).

31. Kalant, O. J., *The Amphetamines—Toxicity and Addiction,* second ed., University of Toronto Press, Toronto, and Charles C Thomas, Springfield, Ill., 1973.

32. Kalant, O. J. and H. Kalant, *Amphetamines and Related Drugs—Clinical Toxicity and Dependence. A Comprehensive Bibliography of the International Literature,* Addiction Research Foundation, Toronto, 1974.

33. Koff, R. S., W. C. Widrich, and A. H. Robbins, Necrotizing angiitis in a methamphetamine user with hepatitis B—Angiographic diagnosis, five-month follow-up results and localization of bleeding site, *N. Engl. J. Med.*, **288,** 946 (1973).

34. Kramer, J. C., V. S. Fischman, and D. C. Littlefield, Amphetamine abuse. Pattern and effects of high doses taken intravenously, *J.A.M.A.*, **201,** 305 (1967).

35. Lewman, L. V., Fatal pulmonary hypertension from intravenous injection of methylphenidate (Ritalin) tablets, *Hum. Pathol.*, **3,** 67 (1972).

36. Lloyd, J. T. A. and D. R. H. Walker, Death after combined dexamphetamine and phenelzine, *Br. Med. J.*, **2,** 168 (1965).

37. Mason, A., Fatal reaction associated with tranylcypromine and methylamphetamine, *Lancet* **1,** 1073 (1962).

38. Mitchell, H. S., and R. L. Denton, Overdosage with Dexedrine, *Can. Med. Assoc. J.* **62,** 594 (1950).

39. Newell, G. R., W. Rawlings, B. K. Kinnear, P. Correa, B. E. Henderson, R. Dworsky, H. Menck, R. Thompson, and W. W. Sheehan, Case-control study of Hodgkin's disease. I. Results of the interview questionnaire, *J. Natl. Cancer Inst.*, **51,** 1437 (1973).

40. Norheim, G., A fatal case of phenmetrazine poisoning, *J. Forensic Sci. Soc.*, **13,** 287 (1973).

41. Orrenius, S. and A. C. Maehly, Lethal amphetamine intoxication, *Z. Rechtsmed.*, **67,** 184 (1970).

42. Pontrelli, E., Sopra un caso di avvelenamento mortale da sulfato di betafenilisopropilamina (Simpamina), *G. Clin. Med.*, **23,** 591 (1942).

43. Pretorius, H. P. J., Dexedrine vergiftiging. Twee gevalle waarvan een noodlottig, *S. Afr. Med. J.*, **27,** 945 (1953).

44. Rexed, I., (Ed.), *Narkotikaproblemet* (*The narcotic problem*), Chapter 3, (Abuse of stimulants). Official reports of the Swedish Commission on Treatment of Drug Addiction, Part III (Coordinated Actions). Statens Offentliga Utredningar (SOU) **52,** 445 pp., Stockholm, 1969.

45. Richards, H. G. H. and A. Stephens, Sudden death associated with the taking of amphetamines by an asthmatic, *Med. Sci. Law,* **13,** 35 (1973).

46. Rutherdale, J. A., A. Medline, J. C. Sinclair, B. Buchner, and J. S. Olin, Hepatitis in drug users, *Am. J. Gastroenterol.*, **58,** 275 (1972).

47. Schmidt, W. and J. de Lint, Causes of death of alcoholics, *Q. J. Stud. Alcohol*, **33**, 171 (1972).

48. Sellers, E. M. and D. W. Robinson, Hyperthermia and rigidity after amphetamine intoxication (in preparation).

49. Smart, R. G., Personal communication.

50. Smart, R. G., The probable value of heroin maintenance for Canadian narcotic addicts, *Can. Ment. Health*, **22**, 3 (1974).

51. Smith, D. E., The characteristics of dependence in high-dose methamphetamine abuse, *Int. J. Addict.*, **4**, 453 (1969).

52. Smith, L. C., Collapse with death following the use of amphetamine sulfate, *J.A.M.A.*, **113**, 1022 (1939).

53. Smith, R. C., Compulsive methamphetamine abuse and violence in the Haight-Ashbury district, in *Current Concepts on Amphetamine Abuse*, E. H. Ellinwood and S. Cohen (Eds.), U.S. Government Printing Office, Washington, D.C., 1972, p. 205.

54. Speaker, J. H., Death as related to drug abuse, *Am. J. Pharm.*, **141**, 175 (1970).

55. Sturner, W. Q., F. G. Spruill, and J. C. Garriott, Two propylhexedrine-associated fatalities: Benzedrine revisited, *J. Forensic Sci.*, **19**, 572 (1974).

56. Van Hoof, F., A. Heyndrickx, and J. Timperman, Report of a human fatality due to amphetamine, *Arch. Toxicol.*, **32**, 307 (1974).

57. Yacoub, M., J. Faure, M. Marka, and G. Cau, La mort du jeune sportif: Role éventuel du doping, *Med. Leg. Dommage Corpor.*, **3**, 275 (1970).

58. Zalis, E. G. and L. E. Parmley, Fatal amphetamine poisoning, *Arch. Intern. Med.*, **112**, 822 (1963).

59. Zeck, P., The dangers of some antidepressant drugs, *Med. J. Aust.*, **2**, 607 (1961).

CHAPTER EIGHT

BEHAVIORAL MODIFICATION TECHNIQUES IN THE TREATMENT OF ALCOHOLISM: A REVIEW AND CRITIQUE

GLORIA K. LITMAN, *Addiction Research Unit, Institute of Psychiatry, London, England.*

1. INTRODUCTION

The systematic use of behavioral modification as a method of therapeutic intervention in the treatment of alcoholism is a fairly recent innovation, although some of the basic techniques were in fact used as far back as Roman times when Pliny suggested drowning eels in the wine of excessive drinkers. Simplistically defined, behavior modification is the systematic application of principles derived from learning theory to the rational modification of undesirable behavior (27). Therefore, the application of the learning model concentrates on behavior itself, i.e., the observable activity of the individual in relation to his environment, and attempts to attack deviant behaviors directly, focusing primarily on current behavior patterns rather than underlying dynamics or past history. Basic to the approach is that *all* behaviors, no matter how diverse, are subject to the same psychological principles of learning. Inherent in the application of the techniques is that appropriate and objective measures be taken and that the results be open to scientific scrutiny.

Within the context of the behavioral approach, excessive drinking is seen as a learned response, which is acquired according to the same principles as any other instrumental response and which is shaped and maintained because of its reinforcing consequences. The emphasis is on current behaviors rather than historical causes. Therefore, regardless of *why* the excessive drinking behavior originated, the therapeutic intervention is concentrated primarily on those behaviors currently in the repetoire of the patient when he is presented for treatment.

The behavioral model of alcoholism as an acquired habit is in sharp contrast to the conceptualization of alcoholism as an irreversible disease. The disease concept of alcoholism has been challenged by many workers (36, 65, 71, 83), and the implications of such a model have been elaborated by Robinson (71). Germane to this discussion is the fact that if alcoholism is seen as an irreversible disease with the assumption of underlying biochemical pathology and susceptibility, then the treatment dictum is based on the notion "once an alcoholic, always an alcoholic." Therefore total abstinence must be the *sole* criterion and goal of treatment (24, 80). In fact, there is now a respectable body of evidence to cast doubt on the "once an alcoholic, always an alcoholic" precept (50).

It has recently been the contention of some workers that the requirement of abstinence as the sole condition and goal of treatment may, in fact, be dysfunctional because it may often mitigate *against* successful treatment (11, 12, 29, 65, 67, 83). Furthermore, this belief may not only be antitherapeutic in its consequences but, even to some extent, covertly punitive in that it may be based on hidden moral judgments long discarded in other areas of treatment intervention. One of the fundamental requisites of any therapeutic endeavor, the therapist's acceptance and respect for the patient's autonomous freedom of choice is implicitly denied in requiring abstinence as the sole condition and goal of treatment regardless of the patient's physical condition, degree of dependence and social milieu.

On the other hand, if alcoholism is seen as undesirable behavior acquired and maintained in the same way as other behaviors, the assumption may be made that this behavior may be subject to modification, so that alternative goals of treatment, e.g., controlled or modified drinking, rather than abstinence may be seen as acceptable outcomes.

The purpose of this chapter is to discuss briefly learning theory principles underlying various behavioral techniques, review in some depth the results of treatment trials utilizing such techniques, and then attempt to evaluate the efficacy of the various approaches used in modifying excessive drinking behavior. For the sake of convenience, treatment trials will be reviewed under the particular form of behavior therapy employed. In those instances where a variety of techniques were used, these will be classified under the most central form of treatment.

2. AVERSION THERAPY

The models underlying the use of aversion therapy may be based on the Pavlovian or classical conditioning paradigm in which a conditioned stimulus (CS) is paired with an unconditioned stimulus (UCS) until a conditioned response (CR) follows administration of the conditioned stimulus alone. In this sense, classical conditioning is *not* contingent upon the behavior of the organism being conditioned. The temporal contiguity of the UCS and the CS is thought to be sufficient to produce changes in the organism which are presumably beyond the organism's cognitive control. The two-factor theory (63) goes on to postulate that, during this process, a conditioned anxiety response is developed. If there is concomitant development of avoidance behavior, this is followed by a reduction in anxiety. This reduction in anxiety is presumed to serve as a reinforcer for the avoidance behavior.

However, the Pavlovian model may not be the only conceptual basis for the utilization of electrical aversion procedures. A fuller description of procedures based on other theoretical formulations will be given below in the discussion of relevant investigations.

Electrical Aversion Conditioning

This review will first consider the use of electric shock as the unconditioned stimulus. Among the advantages of electric shock as the noxious stimulus are said to be the fact that greater precision can be obtained in terms of the subjective pain threshold of the subject and that the temporal contiguity of the application of shock and the particular behaviors involved can be better controlled (70). The use of chemical agents as the UCS present special problems and will be dealt with in a separate section.

One of the first contemporary applications of the use of electrical aversion in the treatment of alcoholism was reported by Kantorovich (44). The basic assumption was that the sight, thoughts, smell, and taste of alcohol were the eliciting stimuli for the drinking response. Using the Pavlovian model, he attempted to condition these stimuli to the aversive stimulus of electric shock.

Twenty alcoholics participated in 5 to 18 sessions in which cards containing names of drinks, the actual sight of bottles of spirits, wine, and beer and the smell and taste of these alcoholic beverages were successively paired with electric shocks. A control group of 10 patients received hypnotic suggestion and medication. Of the 20 experimental patients, 14 were reported as totally abstinent when evaluated from three weeks to 20 months following treatment. All the controls were reported as having relapsed within a brief period following discharge from hospital. Despite these results, Kantorovich's methods aroused little interest until fairly recently.

McGuire and Vallance (57) presented a brief case history of a 40-year-old male alcoholic treated with electrical aversion. The subject was presented with slides of alcoholic beverages and also with the actual beverages themselves. These presentations were followed by electric shock. Neutral stimuli were interspersed with alcoholic stimuli. On six months follow-up, the patient was reported to be completely abstinent.

Using the actual ingestion of alcohol as the conditioned stimulus, Hsu (39) utilized electric shock contingent on the drinking of beer, wine, and spirits rather than milk, water, or fruit juice. The treatment was given daily for five days. Two-day booster treatment was given for four weeks and then six months after completion of the initial series. To eliminate the therapist as an influencing factor in the conditioning process, a semiautomatic device, which was activated when an alcoholic beverage was selected, was introduced in the latter part of the study.

The subjects were "40 voluntary male patients admitted to an alcoholic unit of a state hospital." Of these 40, 24 completed the initial sessions, and only 16 completed both the initial and first "booster" sessions. Four additional patients did not complete the initial treatment but did undergo the first "booster" treatment. Of these 20 patients (i.e., those who had "booster" sessions) 13 were discharged from hospital and were either working or seeking employment. Seven of the 20 patients were known to have been drinking after treatment. Therefore, of the 40 original patients 13 or 32% were considered successes after the initial "booster" session.

Although the author concedes that a few years of careful follow-up are necessary to assess accurately the results of this program, he concludes that electrical aversion seems a useful adjunct in the rehabilitation of this group of alcoholic patients, since they represented a group for whom many other attempts at rehabilitation had failed and especially for those patients who would benefit from educational or insight procedures.

In his report, Hsu noted that most of his patients generally complained that the intensity of the unpleasantness of the treatment was associated with their favorite drinks, although in fact the amount and duration of current was held constant for each individual. After treatment, many patients reported that the sight of alcohol or the idea of drinking gave rise to unpleasant responses such as dread or nausea, but managed to "overcome the conditioned response" particularly when overwhelmed by stressful situations.

It would seem that Hsu's interpretation of the results may be overly optimistic, particularly in view of his high dropout rate, which may be accounted for by the inordinate intensity of the shock levels used and the reported emotional and physical reactions to the treatment situation. Because of the intensity of reaction to the treatment and, in particular, the perceived relationship on the part of the subjects between the intensity of the shock and their preferred beverage, one might suspect that other factors, such as heightened suggestibility, may have been operative in this group of patients. Post-treatment reports of dread and nausea would also appear to be at variance with results of other aversion trial results where the most common response to the stimulus after aversion therapy is "indifference" rather than fear of aversion (70).

In the introduction to this section, it was noted that electrical aversion procedures may have conceptual bases other than the classical conditioning paradigm. "Escape" procedures which are based on what Skinner has termed "negative reinforcement" may also be used. "Negative reinforcement" involves setting up conditions under which the subject may obtain *relief* from the aversive stimulus. The use of escape procedures involves the requirement of an instrumental response on the part of the subject which is followed by the termination of shock. The escape paradigm then involves relief from aversive stimuli made contingent on some behavior on the part of the subject.

Blake (9) utilized an escape paradigm in his procedures. Subjects were supplied with a glass, water, and alcoholic beverage. The subjects were instructed to sip the drink but not to swallow. Contiguous with the sipping of the drink, shocks of increasing intensity were delivered. The subjects were then instructed to spit out the alcohol in order to terminate the shock.

However, theoretically, the effectiveness of punishment in controlling the emission of a tension-reducing response is unpredictable in that it may vary from response suppression to response enhancement. The latter may occur in those instances where the anxiety generated by the punishment is of sufficient magnitude to increase the probability of tension-reducing behavior. If we accept the fact that one of the properties of alcohol is its tension-reduction function, then punishment of the consumption of alcohol may result in sufficient anxiety to cause the alcoholic to drink in order to reduce this anxiety. In order to counteract this paradoxical "vicious circle" behavior, Blake (9) attempted to combine relaxation procedures with his electrical aversion treatment. The combination of progressive relaxation and aversion conditioning seems incompatible on theoretical grounds. If relaxation reduces drive or arousal, the subject approaches the conditioning situation in a state of low drive or arousal which should obviate the establishment of a strong conditioned response to the aversive procedures. In an attempt to counteract this, an arousal stage intermediate between relaxation and aversion was incorporated into the therapeutic procedure.

The description of patient parameters in this study is reasonably detailed. There were 37 middle-class fee-paying patients (27 male, 10 female). The mean duration of alcoholic drinking as self-reported was 4.65 years for the men and 2.7 years for the women, although the psychiatrist's assessment, based on case histories and reports from physicians and relatives, put the mean at 8.84 years for the men and 9.5 for the women. Subjects were requested to return to hospital for interviews at 1, 3, 6, 9, and 12 months following completion of treatment. These interviews appeared to serve a therapeutic "after-care" function.

In a further report (10) the 12-month follow-up data for the 37 patients treated with relaxation–aversion and for 22 patients treated by electrical aversion alone are detailed.

In the relaxation–aversion group, 17 subjects (46% of the group) were found to be abstinent on the basis of self-report and corroboration by spouse, relative, G.P. and/or employer; 5 (or 13%) were found to be improved. "Improvement" was defined either as persons whose drinking was now of a "social" order and appeared to be in no danger of pathologic escalation (one case) or those whose drinking throughout the period of follow-up had been substantially reduced compared with their former level of drinking, concurrent with an improvement in general level of adjustment. Such improvement was evaluated against defined criteria. Eleven subjects were reported as relapsed, and four were reported as having been lost to follow-up. Only one subject in the group refused to complete treatment. In the group receiving electrical aversion only, five patients (23%) were found to be abstinent, six (27%) improved, six (27%) relapsed, and five (23%) were lost to follow-up.

While other reports (85) of Blake's relaxation procedures are highly enthusiastic, on the theoretical grounds that he manipulated more learning variables accompanying the drinking of alcohol (i.e., suppressing the response, relaxation to reduce anxiety, and the development of a "new" response of rejecting alcohol), in fact, the results that Blake (10) actually reported indicated that 59% of his relaxation–aversion group were abstinent or improved, whereas 50% of his aversion-only group were abstinent or improved—a difference which was not statistically significant. It would appear that the addition of relaxation training did not significantly enhance the effects of aversion. However, Blake contends that these results do not necessarily refute the hypothesis that it is necessary to extinguish the fear or anxiety drive motivating the drinking of alcohol, while simultaneously attempting to suppress the "habit" by means of aversion conditioning. He suggests that a more rigorous procedure must include the selection of subjects on the basis of the presence or absence of "neurotic anxiety."

Some points arising from this work appear to merit discussion. The first, and probably the most obvious point is that Blake's results, both in his relaxation–aversion and aversion-only groups, cannot be said to be negligible; although, as he says, they do not invite complacency when compared to Glatt's (31) report of one-third recovered, one-third improved, or to Davies et al. (22) 36% abstinent, 42% "improved" using similar samples of well-motivated middle-class patients. In particular, the fact that Blake's patients were also paying fees for treatment would lead to the expectation that the results would in general be more satisfactory than if his groups were comprised of more socially unstable, non–fee-paying subjects (45).

Another point is the nature of effectiveness of the intervening motivation arousal stage which followed the achievement of competence at relaxation and preceded the first session of aversive training. While in a relaxed state, the patient was instructed to think about drinking and related problems. The patient was then brought out of relaxation and the problems were fed back. Observations were made of agitation, loss of calm, tears and expressions of shame, guilt and loss of self-esteem during this phase.

The concept of arousal or activation has been reviewed by Malmo (56). Stated briefly, the theory conceptualizes a continuum from deep sleep at the lowest levels of arousal to hyperactive states at the other extreme. The relationship between arousal level and behavioral efficiency in terms of cue function or level of performance is said to be an inverted "U" in that it is presumed to rise monotonically with increasing activation level until an optimum point is reached. Beyond this optimum point, further increases in activation produce a fall in performance level, this fall being directly related to the amount of increase in level of arousal. It would appear, in terms of the model postulated by Blake, arousal to an *optimal* point for subsequent conditioning was not sufficiently controlled during the treatment trials.

While it may seem arbitrary to focus upon this, given the fact that there are many possible explanations for the failure to find significant differences between the two groups, investigations of refinements of Blake's techniques seem to be warranted in view of the results reported by Blake. However, there is also the question of suitable alternative behaviors to excessive drinking. Blake's "new" response of spitting out the drink could hardly be considered a socially acceptable or satisfactory alternative behavior.

Bhakata (7) attempted to replicate Blake's techniques with an "unselected" group of 20 patients referred from various sources. From his account, there is no explicit record of his having trained his patients in progressive relaxation, although imaginal procedures are mentioned. A one-year follow-up indicated that, of the 20 patients, 1 remained abstinent, 7 were drinking in controlled fashion (this was not defined), and 12 remained uncontrolled drinkers. Bhakata concludes that realistic goal may be controlled drinking. He also notes that booster therapy seems to have positive therapeutic advantages.

MacCulloch et al. (54) reported on four patients who were treated with electrical aversion in an anticipatory avoidance situation. An anticipatory avoidance situation involves instrumental conditioning in which avoidance of the punishing stimulus is contingent on the performance of a specific operant response—in this case, the avoidance of the previously attractive stimulus. It differs conceptually from a pure escape situation that the subject may avoid the aversive stimulus completely if his reaction is sufficiently rapid. However, in actual practice, many of the trials conducted involved both avoidance and escape procedures. Although this procedure had been found previously to be successful with homosexuals, the work with alcoholics was presented as a "record of therapeutic failure." In an attempt to explain their results they hypothesize that the presence of a "pathological biochemical necessity for alcohol" could not be subject to psychological methods of control. This does not seem to be an adequate explanation in terms of Blake's (9, 10) results, and one would suspect that conditioning only to the sight of alcohol is too specific and does not take into account other sensory modalities such as smell and taste. The "biological pathology" has not been demonstrated and, as mentioned in the introduction, there is an ample body of evidence to cast doubt on this concept.

Vogler et al. (84) attempted to evaluate the degree of effectiveness of conditioning treatment by using control groups. Subjects were 73 male alcoholics who volunteered for the program and who evidenced chronic alcoholism of at least three years duration prior to the study.

Subjects were assigned randomly to four groups—booster or reconditioning; conditioning only; pseudoconditioning (subjects were shocked on a random basis to control for treatment effect of associated environmental stimuli); or sham conditioning (subjects received same treatment as booster or conditioning group, but without shock). A group of subjects receiving routine hospital treatment was later added. Appointments for follow-up interview and/or booster conditioning sessions were rarely kept. Because of this difficulty, subsequent subjects assigned to the conditioning-only group were also requested to return for booster sessions.

Median follow-up was eight months. The results indicated that 3 of the 10 remaining patients in the booster group and 8 of the 15 remaining patients in the conditioning-only group relapsed—about 44% of these two groups combined, as compared with 50% (3 out of 6) in the pseudoconditioning group and 87% (7 out of 8) in the "sham" group, and 58% (7 out of 12) of the ward controls. The investigators concluded that electrical aversion method of conditioning significantly reduced excessive drinking behavior when compared with pseudoconditioning, sham conditioning, and ward controls.

However, of the total of 38 subjects originally assigned to the booster and conditioning groups, approximately one-third (13) dropped out of treatment and were not included in the final analysis. This is a high proportion of the total groups, as compared with pseudoconditioning group where only one patient refused to continue. Since all three groups received electrical aversion, the dropout rate cannot be explained by the use of shock alone. Unfortunately, no explanation is given in the report.

The use of patients given hospital treatment only is also open to question. Although the initial duration of treatment was two weeks for all groups, including the ward controls, the selection of this latter group is not sufficiently detailed to enable the evaluation of this group as a proper control group—proper in the sense that they may have been selected on the basis of criteria similar to that of the experimental groups.

The nonrandom assignment of patients to the booster group should also be taken into account. While this seems perfectly warranted in terms of therapeutic expedience, the conclusion that booster treatment significantly added to the efficacy of the treatment is somewhat attenuated by the fact that motivational factors cannot be separated from the administration of the reconditioning procedure per se.

Deveniyi and Sereny (23) reported on electroconditioning with 21 male alcoholics who were randomly assigned to four groups. The first group (N = 5) received electric shock when they tasted alcohol beverages but were not shocked when sipping milk, orange juice, or ginger ale. The second group (N = 6) received "backward" conditioning, i.e., shock before drinking on the presentation of alcoholic stimuli. The third group (N = 5) received shock only after consumption of the third drink. The fourth group (N = 5) were shocked before the third drink. Each patient received 10 daily sessions and was instructed to return for booster treatment at specified intervals.

At one year follow-up after completion of treatment, 11 patients were known to be drinking and 7 patients were lost to follow-up. Only one patient in the first group and one in the second were abstinent and still in treatment following six booster sessions, but neither showed a clear aversion to alcohol. The authors conclude that the ineffectiveness of treatment may have been due either to an insufficiently strong aversive stimulus or to the lack of a positive reinforcement program in which patients are rewarded for sobriety, as well as punished for drinking.

Using an operant model (see Contingency Management in a subsequent section) Mills et al. (62) attempted to train social drinking as an acceptable alternative response to excessive drinking. Previous research (75) had indicated that alcoholics differ from social drinkers in four measurable ways: (*a*) there is a significant preference for straight rather than mixed drinks; (*b*) there is a significant tendency to gulp rather than sip drinks; (*c*) there is a tendency to drink continuously rather than to space drinks; (*d*) the alcoholic continues to drink well beyond the point at which an ordinary social drinker would have stopped. Based on this evidence, the treatment program was designed to use electrical aversion to "shape in" appropriate behaviors of diluting drinks, sipping, spacing, and stopping when a certain limit was reached.

The subjects in this investigation were 13 male voluntary patients, with a mean of six previous hospitalizations for alcoholism. Each subject had experienced withdrawal symptoms in the process of "drying out," ranging from shakes and convulsions to delirium tremens.

The treatment trials took place in a day room that had been converted into a rather elaborate cocktail lounge and bar. Socially acceptable drinking was defined as ordering diluted drinks, sipping the drinks, spacing, and drinking a maximum of 3 fl oz of 86 proof liquor. During the first three drinks of a session, the intensity of a given shock was a function of the kind of drink ordered (i.e., diluted or straight) and whether it was sipped or gulped. When a subject exhibited two inappropriate drinking behaviors, he received a high intensity shock immediately. If he emitted only one inappropriate behavior, he received a low shock. After the first three drinks were consumed, if the subject ordered an additional drink, he received a 100% intensity shock from the time his hand touched the glass until the time he released the glass. There were a total of 14 experimental sessions, each having a maximum duration of 2 hr.

Twelve-month follow-up data on the experimental group and a control group comprised of 13 patients who had volunteered for the study and who came from the same population as the experimental group but had not received social drinking training were reported by Schaefer (73). The patients were contacted either by telephone or in person by a social worker. In addition at least one other person was contacted to verify the information obtained. Of the nine patients who completed treatment, eight were located for the entire 12 months. Of these, three were reported as abstinent, two were reported as drinking excessively, and one was imprisoned. Controlled drinking was defined as the consumption of less than 6 oz of 42% alcohol on any given day and less than 10 oz on any 2 consecutive days. Of the 13 patients who served as controls, 11 were located. Two were reported as abstinent, none were controlled drinkers, six were reported as excessive drinkers, and three were imprisoned. The difference between the two groups were reported as being statistically significant.

The results of this present investigation, when examined closely, do not in fact demonstrate at all that the experimental treatment was significantly more effective in maintaining abstinence or moderation, since two patients who were reported as "controlled drinkers" in the follow-up had been reported previously as having been part of a group that had absconded from hospital in the early sessions of the treatment trials and "consequently had no opportunity for shaping in subsequent sessions" (62, p. 23).

Hallam et al. (35) present an account of 11 patients treated with electrical aversion. Two procedures were used. The first consisted of projecting slides of a bar or bottles of alcohol and shocking the patient when he signalled a fantasy of drinking in that situation. The second involved administering shocks during the tasting, smelling, and seeing several preferred alcoholic beverages. Their follow-up period of 4 months was too brief to evaluate their results. However, they report that five out of six middle-class patients were substantially improved while only two of five working class patients showed improvement.

In a second experiment, an aversion therapy group was compared to a control group receiving conventional hospital therapy, including group psychotherapy, A. A. meetings, drug therapy and rehabilitation. All subjects were drawn from higher socioeconomic range. Again, their follow-up period of 4 months is too brief to evaluate the results. However, they report that 6 of the 10 aversion subjects and 2 of the 8 controls were categorized as "successes" in that they were either completely abstinent or had no "serious" bouts of drinking.

Claesȯn and Malm (16) used electrical aversion therapy with 26 male patients who were "severe chronic alcoholics" and who had been admitted to hospital several times a year prior to the treatment trials.

The conditioning procedure was aimed at conditioning as wide a spectrum of behaviors as possible including proprioceptive stimuli such as movements of the arm and tongue; perceptive modalities of vision, hearing, smell, and taste; and associative stimuli in the form of imagination of different situations. During the first four sessions, shocks were given with 100% reinforcement in order to accelerate the conditioning. During the remaining sessions, which ranged from 16 to 50 sessions of approximately 25 minutes each, 50% shocks were used on a random interval basis in an attempt to prevent extinction of the conditioned response.

The results were evaluated in terms of readmission to hospital during the follow-up period. This evaluation was based on the rationale that reports by patients and their cohorts had proved to be unreliable and that these subjects were so chronically addicted that, once they resumed drinking excessively, readmission to hospital would be almost inevitable. These criteria do not seem unreasonable in view of the fact that each of this particular group of patients was reported to have had at least three hospital admissions during the 12 months prior to treatment.

Based on the criterion of readmission to hospital, the overall one year follow-up results indicate that 24% remained sober, 64% relapsed, and 12% were lost to follow-up. If the results are scrutinized more carefully, two interesting factors emerge. Those subjects who were exposed to maximal imaginal stimulation seemed to do better than those whose conditioning to imaginal stimulation was minimal.

The number of treatment sessions seemed to be related to outcome but not in any clear-cut linear fashion. Patients who had undergone between 16 and 35 sessions had a higher relapse rate than those who had undergone 21–

44 sessions. However, in both groups, the subjects who subsequently relapsed had actually undergone more conditioning sessions than those who were considered "successes." This was particularly evident in the maximal imaginal stimulation group. While the authors content that overlearning is desirable, the results they present would actually suggest that, beyond a certain point, increasing the number of sessions does not enhance the success rate. In the maximal imaginal conditioning group who had undergone an average of 31 conditioning trials, the "success" rate was 44%, whereas the group who were exposed to minimal imaginal stimulation and had experienced an average of 25 conditioning trials achieved a "success" rate of 13%. Although the actual difference in terms of number of patients in the two groups was small, the findings of imaginal stimuli as a factor would seem to warrant further investigation, particularly in view of Bandura's (6) concept of "cognitive rehearsal." Bandura emphasizes the fact that cognitive events can mediate adverse physiologic reactions. A symbolic association between the aversive stimulus (i.e., alcohol) and the UCS may be strengthened when thoughts of the treatment are precipitated by external stimuli or when the patient voluntarily recalls treatment in order to control his attraction to the undesirable stimulus.

Miller et al. (61) conducted an analogous study of 30 chronic alcoholic patients. The patients, matched on age, education, and length of drinking problem, were assigned to three groups. The first group received high shock paired with alcohol sips; the second group received very low shock paired with alcohol sips; and the third group received group therapy based on the confrontation model. Subjects in each group were given instructions designed to produce high expectancy for therapeutic success. The results indicated that there were no significant differences among the three groups in terms of reduced alcohol consumption or attitudes towards alcohol.

Summary and Discussion of Electrical Aversion Trials

Given the fact that so few studies reported have used control group designs and given the fact that follow-up data in most of these studies are neither convincing nor of sufficient duration (30), it is difficult to evaluate properly electrical aversion as an efficient and effective means of therapeutic intervention in the treatment of alcoholism.

The interesting theoretical question that arises from these studies is *why* aversion therapy is successful in those cases where it does work. There is certainly evidence to indicate that when aversion therapy is effective, neither the Pavlovian model nor the two-factor avoidance model is sufficient to account for the results.

For example, the two-factor model states that conditioned anxiety is developed in aversive procedures. The hypothesis that conditioned anxiety to alcohol would develop after treatment by electrical aversion was tested by Hallam et al. (35). Their results failed to produce evidence of psychophysiologic changes in alcoholic patients following electrical aversion therapy. However, when this data was reanalyzed on the basis of clinical outcome, it was found that successful patients did maintain an increased cardiac response to imaginal alcoholic stimuli. This effect was found to be independent of the type of treatment, i.e., successes in their aversion therapy group *and* those in the group receiving standard hospital procedures, including psychotherapy, manifested the response.

Some investigators (27, 35, 39, 68) have reported that patients perceive differences in the qualities of the alcoholic stimulus during or after aversion, although there has been no change in the physical attributes of the stimulus itself. The role that subjective devaluation of alcohol plays in successful treatment by aversion would not be predicted by conditioning theory. The finding too that social class was related to successful outcome (27, 35) is certainly at variance with the purely theoretical models, in which the emphasis is either placed on the temporal contiguity of the UCS and CS or in the reinforcement subsequent to the instrumental response.

In the description of aversive procedures given in this section, it should be apparent that the theoretical models underlying these procedures do differ. However, whatever the conceptual basis may be, the actual applications of these models in either laboratory or clinical settings may not be as clear-cut as the theories would imply. Kanfer and Phillips (43) have pointed out the fictional purity of a classical conditioning paradigm in the aversive treatment of alcoholism and other behaviors. The UCS usually has reinforcing characteristics not only for the CR and UCR, but also for other behaviors that occur immediately prior to the CS and during the CS-UCS interval. Operant or instrumental conditioning may thus intrude. The conditioned stimulus of alcohol behaviors usually consists of a series of S-R chains, such as lifting the glass, putting it to the lips, taking a sip, tasting it, etc. Thus the punishment (UCR) actually follows a set of *instrumental* acts, and the occurrence of punishment is thus contingent not only upon the temporal contiguity of CS and UCS but upon these *operant* chains.

However, in this regard, the theoretically unalloyed operant conditioning paradigm is also fiction. Under conditions where there are fairly stable situational cues, these cues may function as a CS, thus permitting classical conditioning to occur on the basis of the contiguity of a more complex CS and subsequent reinforcing stimulus. As Kanfer and Phillips (43) note "the mixture of respondents and operants, the concurrent social setting for drinking, the multiplicity of cues associated with the entire sequence make it quite obvious that a simple laboratory analogue, be it of classical conditioning to the sight of alcohol or an operant punishment for sipping, only deals with a small sample of behaviors involved."

Lovibond (51) has suggested the need for thorough experimental investigation of the possibility that response to contingent aversive stimulation produces motivational changes that are *centrally* mediated, rather than peripheral suppression of behavior by competing anxiety responses. Miller et al. (61) reported that trends in the data from their analogous study indicate that the effects of electrical aversion may be more related to therapeutic instructions, expectancies, and the demand characteristics of the treatment situation than to conditioning factors.

It might be well to pause here and note that the term "behavioral" modification is misleading and a misnomer. In order to produce changes outside the treatment situation, attitudinal and motivational modification is also required. Taking all of the above considerations into account, it would appear that the role of aversion therapy in the treatment of alcoholism may possibly serve an initial function in suppressing the deviant behavior (59, 60). However, it must be emphasized that this is a mere precursor to the more positive aspects of therapy, i.e., the initiation and maintenance of adaptive behaviors which are satisfactory competing alternative responses to excessive drinking behavior.

Chemical Agents as the Unconditioned Stimulus

As was noted previously, chemical agents present particular problems in aversive control of behavior. Disulfiram, a drug that leads to nausea and vomiting if followed by the ingestion of alcohol, is widely used as a treatment agent. Strictly speaking, this is not a conditioning procedure in the usual sense since its action is directly physical in relation to alcohol. Some mild conditioned aversion to alcohol consequent on disulfiram therapy has been reported. However, the process involved is not a matter of established associations between stimuli and response where none existed before, but it results as a direct pharmacologic action of the drug upon alcohol metabolism (28). The processes involving Emetine and Apomorphine as aversive stimuli can be considered conditioning procedures since they do involve the attempt to establish a new connection between stimulus and response. Emetine and Apomorphine as aversive stimuli are generally unsatisfactory. Because of variable and fluctuating individual differences in response, there is considerable difficulty in controlling the temporal contiguity of the presentation of the drug and the onset of nausea. Franks (28) has also pointed out that these drugs may produce a central depressant effect which could interfere with conditioning. Because of the difficulty in controlling time factors, spurious conditioning may result. Bhakata (7) has also highlighted the considerable subjective distress in using these drugs, and Hsu (39), among others, has cited the risk of such undesirable side effects as cardiac arrest and myocardial failure.

A comprehensive review of chemical aversion trials may be found in Franks' (28) paper. Therefore, this section will concentrate primarily on studies because they highlight certain important features of chemical aversion procedures.

Successful use of chemical aversion techniques were reported by Lemere and Voegtlin (49). They used Emetine as the UCS. In their procedure, the patient was given drugs to control serious side effects, oral saline to provide easily vomited stomach contents, and both injected and oral emetine. Just prior to the expected onset of nausea and vomiting, various forms of alcohol were smelled and tasted by the patients. They also gave large quantities of nonalcoholic beverages to the patients between sessions to maximize differentiation between the conditioned response to alcohol and the response to other liquids. Booster treatment was given at the patients's request and routinely at the end of six months and then after a year of treatment. "Accurate" follow-up data was available on 4096 patients; of these 44% remained totally abstinent since their first course of treatment. Of the patients who relapsed, 878 were treated. Of these 39% were reported as sober since their last conditioning treatment, giving an overall rate of 51%. Sixty percent remained abstinent for one year, 51% for at least 2 years, 38% for at least 5 years, and 23% for at least 10 years after their first treatment. However, it is of special interest that the *suggestive* effects of the conditioning sessions, the therapeutic attitude of the staff and vocational, social and recreational rehabilitation procedures were noted as important adjuncts to the aversive treatment. Since no control group was used, the relative effect of aversive conditioning and other procedures cannot be evaluated. Miller et al. (60) used the Voegtlin technique in a group procedure and reported 50% total abstinence on an eight-month follow-up.

A more drastic procedure has employed scoline, a curarizing drug that momentarily produces complete paralysis, including cessation of the patient's respiratory function, without affecting his state of consciousness. Bhakata (7) maintains that he has been unable to find an anesthetist who could be persuaded to undertake the administration of this procedure.

When this method was compared (17) with a pseudoconditioning group receiving only the UCS that was not paired with the sight, taste, and smell of alcohol, and a placebo group receiving only the CS but not the aversive stimulus, no significant difference in terms of days of abstinence was found among the three groups on a three-month follow-up. Of the 12 patients treated, only two remained abstinent after one year.

Laverty (48) found that two-thirds of patients treated by contingent scoline reported a changed reaction to alcohol, whereas one-fifth of a control group which received no aversive stimulus, but were given heightened expectations of trauma, reported this change. The majority of patients experimented with alcohol again, even when the symptoms of conditioned aversion were severe. The reports of therapeutic outcome of this study and of others which have compared contingent scoline to control methods (17, 55, 72) have indicated that this conditioning procedure was not more effective than control procedures in producing abstinence at one-year follow-up. Some subjects developed an aversive reaction to the entire treatment situation. They absconded from hospital or assiduosly avoided that part of the hospital in which treatment was carried out.

In view of the terrifying and traumatic nature of this procedure and because of the disappointing results reported, one must conclude that ethically and practically, the use of contingent scoline as an aversive procedure is neither justified nor warranted.

Verbal Aversion Techniques: Covert Sensitization

The method of covert sensitization was introduced by Cautela (13–15). In this procedure, the noxious stimulus is aversive verbal imagery rather than electrical or chemical. The patient is first taught relaxation usually in accordance with Jacobsen's (41) procedure and then asked to visualize very clearly the stimulus and specific scenes involving this stimulus. As each scene is visualized, the patient is instructed in very graphic and explicit terms to imagine step by step the onset of violent nausea and vomiting, so that scenes involving that stimulus and nausea become strongly associated. The patient is usually instructed to practice these sequences between treatment sessions, a form of "cognitive rehearsal" (6) mentioned previously.

Cautela (14) reported on results using this technique on seven alcoholic patients. The patients were given a total of nine treatment sessions. In addition the patients were instructed to rehearse the imaginary sequence, from handling to touching the glass with the lips at least 10 to 20 times daily upon return home from the therapy center. The patients were trained to imagine that they vomited into their drinks, whenever either one was ordered or when there was temptation to do so. At the end of a six-months follow-up, two of the seven treatment patients had resumed drinking, compared to one of four nontreated controls.

Anant (3) reported on the use of this technique on 26 alcoholics. He claimed that 96% of his patients remained abstinent based on 8–15 months follow-up. However in a further report (4) the results are not quite as impressive. Patients who were treated on an individual basis seemed to be more successful than those treated in groups, since only 3 of the 15 patients who received group treatment remained sober on a 6–23-month follow-up. Periodic "booster" sessions were suggested to prevent extinction of the negative response to alcohol.

Ashem and Donner (5) investigated the relative efficacy of covert sensitization, backward conditioning, and no treatment on a group of 23 male alcoholics whose average drinking history was 18 years and each of whom had been in some kind of treatment for alcoholism previously. The results indicated that the backward conditioning group (N = 7) were not receiving pseudoconditioning as originally thought, but quickly made an association between alcohol and nausea as did the systematic covert sensitization group (N = 8).

Because of this, the two conditioning groups were combined for comparison with the control group (N = 8). At six months follow-up, 6 of the 15 treated patients, but none of the controls had stopped drinking.

Bhakata (7) mentioned briefly two cases treated with covert sensitization. He noted that, in both cases, nausea become strongly associated with thoughts, sights, and s ıell of drink, but did not detail any follow-up results.

An investigation by Fleiger and Zingle (26) attempted to test the efficacy of covert sensitization in the treatment of alcohol as against a "problem-solving" approach.

The sample consisted of 32 patients, 15 of whom were assigned to covert sensitization treatment and the remaining 17 to problem-solving treatment which was the standard form of therapy used at that institution. Eight staff counselers, intensively trained in covert sensitization, conducted the verbal aversion treatment. Covert sensitization was administered on an individual basis, while problem-solving was conducted in small groups. Treatment for both groups consisted of 40 one-hour sessions over a 20-day period. The goal of treatment in both groups was total abstinence.

The results indicated no differences between the two groups on three months follow-up in terms of abstinence. However the authors noted that no provision was made for rehearsal for the covert sensitization patients after release from treatment. There was also some indication from the results that female therapists may tend to more effective in covert sensitization than males, a trend which seemed also to appear in the Ashem and Donner (5) results.

There are advantages to using covert sensitization as a form of treatment in that it does not require elaborate equipment, is less traumatic than electrical aversion, and does not involve the possible serious consequences to the health of the patient as do chemical aversion techniques. Since covert sensitization involves imaginal stimuli for both the conditioned and unconditioned stimuli, no external stimuli are present. In addition, the locus of control of the treatment is eventually given over to the patient, so that, at least theoretically, he is taught a technique which he may practice and use outside of the treatment situation itself and thus may be self-administered.

However, there are limitations to the technique as well. The powerful visual imagery which is required may be difficult for some patients to create at will and even greater difficulty may be experienced in achieving the appropriate intensity of the emotional response required. At this point, more research is required as to the type of patient for whom this technique may be appropriate. The point needs to be reiterated here that, with any technique utilizing aversive procedures, these techniques can only be thought of as initial procedures which may be useful in initially suppressing the deviant behavior. However, the goal of therapy should be the training of appropriate and *positive* alternative responses to excessive drinking behavior.

3. PROGRESSIVE RELAXATION AND SYSTEMATIC DESENSITIZATION

This technique is based on Wolpe's (86) principle of reciprocal inhibition. The formal statement of this principle is: "If a response inhibitory of anxiety can be made to occur in the presence of anxiety-evoking stimuli it will weaken the bond between these stimuli and the anxiety." The response incompatible with anxiety is relaxation. In practice, therefore, the patient is first taught deep relaxation techniques. A hierarchy of anxiety-provoking scenes is constructed from least to most distressing. In a state of relaxation, the patient is asked to imagine these scenes, going slowly and systematically through the hierarchy, until the anxiety associated with these scenes is no longer present.

Kraft (46, 47) has developed a relaxation and systematic desensitization program for alcohol patients in whom social anxiety seemed to be the chief motivation for excessive drinking. Kraft maintained that detailed history-taking in the primary alcoholic may reveal that social anxiety is present, although the patient may be unable to make the connection between the anxiety and his drinking behavior.

The method used included deep relaxation by hypnosis or intravenous methohexitone sodium in subanesthetic doses. A standardized stimulus hierarchy was used in the desensitization procedure. Despite the usual protestations of many behavior therapists that transference and dependency relationships do not occur with behavioral techniques as opposed to psychotherapeutic techniques, Kraft found that an additional procedure had to be incorporated as a second phase of treatment to counteract the patient's dependence on the therapist. A hierarchy was developed for the patient to cope on his own without the therapist for increasing periods of time. This second phase of treatment appeared to be more difficult for patients than the first. For example, one patient had 23 desensitizing treatments for social anxiety but required a further 27 sessions for his dependence on the therapist.

Four cases are detailed in this report. Two were diagnosed as "primary alcoholism and psychopathic disorder." For one of these patients, his daily alcohol consumption was two bottles of whiskey plus wine, brandy, and beer; for the other one bottle of brandy plus an average of 12 pints of beer a day. On a two-year and one-year follow-up, respectively, both drank the occasional pint of beer but were no longer excessive drinkers, nor did they become compulsive teetotalers.

The other two cases described in this report were females who were given a diagnosis of "secondary alcoholism." One drank six measures of gin in order to cope with social situations, but did not consider herself an alcoholic. After completing treatment, she would drink two light ales occasionally but no longer had the desire to drink gin. Her improvement was maintained on a one-year follow-up. The second was referred for treatment because of excessive blushing and gin drinking. She had found that after four measures of gin she no longer blushed, and after seven measures she felt "very well indeed." Since completing treatment, she indulges only in an occasional glass of cherry brandy. An 18-month follow-up indicated her improvement was maintained.

The results of the four cases reported seem promising. However, it can be a time-consuming treatment. For these four patients, the total treatment time was 50, 76, 71, and 25 hours, respectively, on a daily basis. Since a standardized hierarchy was used, it might be possible to conduct this therapy on a very small group basis. Treating more than one patient simultaneously might also serve to diminish dependency on the therapist. A procedure that might merit investigation would be to treat several patients, two in a group, then concurrently and very gradually merge the groups. This may further serve as an in vivo desensitization process. Cheek (private communication) has adapted these techniques to group therapy situations with good results.

An experimental trial comparing systematic desensitization with standard hospital treatment was conducted by Storm and Cutler (81). Fifty patients treated by Wolpe's method of desensitization were compared with 55 patients treated by standard hospital methods. Sixty-two percent of each group dropped out of treatment before the fifth session. Of those contacted at six months follow-up, marked improvement was noted in 53% of the patients in the desensitization group and in 29% of the dropouts in that group. In the group treated by standard hospital methods, 35% showed improvement in the treatment group and 29% in the dropout group. The investigators encountered difficulties in the desensitization group because of their relatively low level of anxiety and the foci of anxiety were not readily identified.

An individual case (69) details the treatment of a young woman alcoholic with psychopathic and self-destructive tendencies. Treatment consisted of Wolpe's desensitization procedures and standard ward care. During the two years since her discharge, the patient was reported to drink socially and to have remained "well-adjusted." Reference was also made to the case of another alcoholic who had stopped drinking but was fearful of being addicted if he took one drink. After treatment by Wolpe's technique, the patient was able to take an occasional social drink without anxiety or the compulsion to continue drinking.

My own clinical experience has indicated that, where phobic states, such as social anxiety, agoraphobia, etc., are concurrent with alcoholism, relaxation and desensitization procedures can be extremely effective. While these procedures can hardly be considered a panacea for all forms of alcoholism, they can be a useful adjunct to other forms of treatment, particularly where the locus or loci of anxiety can be identified and relevant hierarchies constructed, followed by in vivo desensitization.

4. CONTINGENCY MANAGEMENT

Contingency management techniques refer to the application of laboratory findings of operant behavior and instrumental conditioning to clinical problems. They are predicated on the assumption that the consequences of any given behavior govern the probability of emission of behavior. The frequency of emitted behavior is the prime operational definition of reinforcing stimuli, although latency and amplitude may sometimes be used.

There are two prerequisites for the application of these techniques. The first is to identify the target behavior to be controlled. The second is to find effective reinforcers that are sufficiently powerful, not only to modify the target behavior, but also to diminish the value of those reinforcers which are maintaining the behavior. It may also be desirable to isolate the latter reinforcers.

Applications of Contingency Management

A single case investigation (82) reports on the use of these principles with an individual patient referred because of a long history of frequent alcoholic intoxication. The primary goal of therapy was a marked reduction or cessation of alcohol drinking. The patient's concern about losing the friendship of two men who were now avoiding his company because they found his frequent drunken states so objectionable suggested the creation of a situation in which social reinforcement for nonalcoholic behavior might be developed. A plan was formulated and agreed upon whereby the patient and his friends would meet daily in a tavern. If the patient ordered or drank hard liquor, the friends were instructed to leave immediately. An agreement was also made that social interaction would also take place in the homes of the three, contingent upon the patient's not drinking. The treatment program appeared to be successful with this particular patient. Within a month he had stopped drinking completely, despite the fact that his job necessitated frequent visits to taverns and bars. No further follow-up data have been reported.

A series of investigations into the application or reinforcement contingencies with chronic alcoholics have been detailed by Cohen and her colleagues in Baltimore (8, 18–21).

The first of these investigations (18) details the intensive study of an individual patient in order to determine if conditions could be specified under which drinking could be controlled in a setting where environmental variables could be systematically manipulated and drinking behavior precisely defined. The subject was a 39-year-old male who had been hospitalized at least 20 times for alcoholism and whose alcohol consumption was about 2 quarts of gin per day. The duration of his drinking problem was about 10 years.

His history for the five years prior to the investigation suggested that the only attention he received was from the police, his father, or hospital personnel and this only at the end-stage of a drinking episode. The analysis suggested that reinforcement in the form of increased interpersonal interactions that *followed* drinking contributed to the maintenance of his drinking behavior.

Experiments were designed to determine if reversing contingencies for drinking would alter his drinking behavior. Instead of being reinforced with attention for excessive drinking, moderate drinking would be reinforced with a variety of social and environmental privileges, while excessive drinking would result in the removal of these reinforcers.

During the investigations, contingent weeks were alternated with noncontingent weeks. During contingent weeks, if the subject drank 5 oz of 95 proof ethanol or less per day he was placed in an enriched environment, which included the opportunity to work and earn money, recreation, group therapy, work privilege, and a telephone. If he drank 6–10 oz he was placed in an impoverished environment where these privileges were not made available. During noncontingent weeks he remained in the impoverished environment regardless of how much he drank. An upper limit of 10 oz was set. It was found at the end of four weeks that the subject consumed his maximum of 10 oz every day, during both contingent and noncontingent weeks. The conditions were *not* sufficient to maintain moderate drinking.

Therefore, a second experiment involved instituting a greater contrast between the enriched and impoverished environments. Reading material and a bedside chair were added to the enriched environment while a pureed diet became part of the impoverished environment. The length of stay in the impoverished environment was increased by 24 hr during the contingent weeks. The results indicated that under these conditions the subject consumed 5 oz each day during the contingent weeks and 10 oz per day during noncontingent weeks. Increasing the maximum amount of alcohol to 24 oz did not serve to alter his drinking behavior during contingent weeks, i.e., he drank only 5 oz per day. During noncontingent weeks, he exceeded the 5 oz every day. The findings also indicated that it was not the aversiveness of the impoverished environment that was causing the excessive drinking and that moderation was due to the contingency conditions of differential reinforcement.

The hypothesis was also tested that excessive drinking during noncontingent weeks may have resulted from the opportunity of a five-day binge as well as the absence of contingencies. In order to eliminate the opportunity for binge drinking, the subject was allowed to drink only every other day during noncontingent weeks. The results indicated that the subject drank excessively five times during the contingent weeks and six times during noncontingent weeks. In other words, where there was no opportunity for binges as there had been on the previous experiments, the subject drank excessively throughout. The implication was that the moderation of drinking during contingent weeks may have been related to drinking opportunities in the previous week.

Finally, an attempt to determine if the subject could drink moderately for more than a week at a time was made. Reinforcement contingencies were in effect for five weeks during which the subject drank moderately for all but two days.

The examinations of the interaction between a target behavior, abstinence, and delay of reinforcement (a monetary reward) has also been explored (21). The effect of a priming dose of alcohol on subsequent abstinence was also investigated. The subjects were four alcoholics who had lost their jobs and required hospitalization because of excessive drinking.

The effect of delay of monetary payment as a reinforcement disrupted abstinence behavior. The actual time delay necessary to cause this disruption was a function of the individual, ranging from 3 days in one case to 14 days. In order to reinstate abstinence, it was found that an increase in the magnitude of the reward was required. The effect of a priming dose of alcohol was also to disrupt subsequent abstinence. In this sequence, the subjects were required to drink for 0–300 ml between 7 a.m. and 10 a.m. and received payment if they did not drink any alcohol beyond the required dose for that day. If they drank, the payment for stopping after the primary dose was increased. If they elected to abstain, the priming dose was increased. Again an increase in the magnitude of the monetary reward was required to reinstate abstinence.

The authors interpret the results as indicating that the consequences of moderate drinking or abstinence play an important part in maintaining these behaviors. However, the real point at issue here seems the question of what was actually being reinforced. In the first sequence, when abstinence was presumably being reinforced, drinking was followed by an increase in payment for abstinence, while abstinence was followed by a decrease in payment. In the delay of reinforcement trials, if they drank, again payment for abstinence was increased, while if they abstained delay in reinforcement was increased. In the third manipulation where moderation was presumably being reinforced if they drank the optional alcohol, payment for stopping after the priming dose was increased. If they abstained, the priming dose was increased. It would appear from this account that abstinence was, in fact, being punished throughout while drinking brought an increase in reward. It would have been of great interest to interview the subjects at the end of the trials to determine whether the experimental strategy had been grasped and to what extent this may have influenced their behavior.

Replication of the single case study mentioned previously (18), using as subjects five "gamma" alcoholics who had been admitted via the emergency department in varying stages has also been detailed (20).

The target behavior was the maintenance of moderate drinking which was defined as the consumption of 5 oz or less of 95 proof ethanol per day. Participation in an enriched environment was used as the reinforcer. Subjects were given a written account of the experiment before it began. Subjects had the option to drink up to 24 oz 95 proof ethanol on week-days for five consecutive weeks. On alternate weeks, contingency conditions were in effect, i.e., if more than 5 oz per day were consumed, the subject was impoverished for an additional 24 hours. During the noncontingent weeks, the subjects remained in the impoverished environment, and moderate drinking was not differentially enforced.

The results seem quite clear. When contingency conditions were in effect, subjects seldom exceeded their 5 oz a day. Under noncontingent conditions, the subjects invariably exceeded this amount. The contingency conditions were maintaining moderation.

Four of the five subjects participated in a further experiment to determine if the excessive drinking during noncontingent weeks was due to aversive environment. Subjects remained in the enriched environment during noncontingent weeks. Again, the results were similar. Moderation was almost invariable during the contingent weeks, and consumption of alcohol increased markedly during the noncontingent weeks.

A further paper (19) describes an investigation again using an enriched environment as a reinforcer for moderate drinking. The patients were five chronic "gamma" alcoholics, each of whom had manifested severe withdrawal symptoms on admission. The procedures were identical to those in the investigation described above (20): contingent versus noncontingent weeks, impoverished environment during noncontingent weeks, etc. The results, too, were very similar. When contingency conditions were in effect, all five patients moderated their drinking (i.e., consumed 5 oz or less per day). During noncontingency weeks, four of the five drank the maximum alcohol available (10 oz in this investigation).

Discussion

Contingency management procedures as described by the Baltimore group seem remarkably effective in moderating drinking behavior within an institutional setting, and the application of these procedures to a hostel situation for example would appear to be promising.

However, there would appear to be some important practical and theoretical considerations to be taken into account if one were to attempt to adopt these techniques. The first concerns the feasibility of maintaining attendance in such a program. In the various investigations conducted, the participants were paid generously to participate in the program for a specified time. In a hostel or other institutional type of situation, continuous payment over an indefinite period of time to insure attendance may not be a viable proposition.

Then too, the results do not demonstrate that contingency procedures will maintain moderation for an indefinite time period. The longest amount of time moderation was practiced, without intervening binge drinking, was noted in the single case study as five weeks.

The successful extrapolation of these procedures to noninstitutional settings has not as yet been established. The results have demonstrated effectively that the external constraints of contingencies of reinforcement were maintaining the behavior. Once the external constraints were removed, during the noncontingent weeks, excessive drinking was resumed. To apply these reinforcement procedures to excessive drinking behavior as it occurs to the world outside the institution or therapist's office seems a difficult task. Contingencies which are not applied consistently and repeatedly tend to be ineffective. In an extrainstitutional setting such consistency could seldom be maintained over a sufficiently wide range of activities. However, as Cohen et al. (20) point out, some of the agencies controlling reinforcers relevant to alcoholism in the outside world—family, employer, medical, welfare and rehabilitation services—dispense reinforcements such as money, shelter, medical care, attention, and sympathy, contingent only upon excessive drinking and its end-stage consequences. While sobriety may be reinforced, moderation seldom is. They suggest that the reinforcers cited above may be also manipulated as contingencies for moderation.

The possibilities of such a community reinforcement approach has been reported by Hunt and Azrin (40). Their approach was designed specifically to rearrange the vocational, family, and social reinforcers for a group of hospitalized alcoholics, where abstinence was the goal of treatment. A single case study (58) reported the successful use of contingency management procedures in a marital setting where the aim was to reduce the patient's alcohol consumption within limits acceptable to his spouse.

Token Economy Techniques

Token economy methods of behavior therapy can also be subsumed under contingency management techniques. Relatively tight control of social and environmental rewards and punishments were used by Narroll (64) in his pilot project. Subjects were required to work for points or tokens which could then be exchanged for every possible purchase in the hospital, including such basics as room and board, clothing, maintenance, Alcoholics Anonymous meetings, treatment, etc.

The subjects were originally assigned to a deprivation status in a closed ward of low status and substandard conditions. The patient's task was then to work his way through a five-level hierarchy in order to improve his material and social status. Many patients rebelled at being assigned to the project, but only 3 of 17 failed to remain less than nine weeks. The work output of project members averaged 8 hr/day compared with an average of 4 hr/day of nonproject workers. However, it was also noted that work performance in the project group deteriorated when contingencies controlling work output were relaxed.

The main aim of the project was an attempt to retrain chronic alcoholics in regular, systematic work habits which they could utilize in the "real" world. Follow-up data on the subsequent outcome of the subjects after their release from hospital are being collected.

The central objection to contingency management as used at the present time seems to be the failure to demonstrate that the actual learning of appropriate alternative behaviors to excessive drinking has been instituted.

On the contrary, the results would appear to indicate that moderate drinking was not learned, although it would be controlled effectively under contingency conditions for specified periods of time.

The principles of contingency management were originally developed in circumscribed laboratory situations mainly using animal subjects with precise control of all conditions. Control was seen as the specifications of the relevant antecedents and the consequences of a given behavior. Skinner (76) has contended that "when all relevant variables have been arranged, an organism will or will not respond. If it does not, it cannot, if it can, it will."

However, the applications of contingency management procedures in the treatment of alcoholism highlight the fact that, in such highly complex situations, we are still far from being able to specify and arrange "all the relevant variables" and to control precisely the consequences of behavior so that, at the present time, change in behavior instituted by these procedures is a limited one. The most appropriate conclusion would seem to be that the shaping and control of behavior cannot necessarily be equated with the learning of new behaviors or the restitution of behaviors which may have been, at an earlier point in time, part of the behavioral repertoire of the individual. The "automatic" response due to the strengthening effect of reinforcing consequences inherent in the underlying principles simply does not take into account cognitive, attitudinal, and motivational factors. This will be discussed more fully in a subsequent session.

5. DISCRIMINATED ELECTRICAL AVERSION AND SELF-REINFORCEMENT

Lovibond et al. (52, 53) introduced a treatment program whereby individuals were trained, with the use of electrical aversion, to discriminate their own blood alcohol levels.

Discrimination training consisted of providing the subject with a very general scale of behavioral effects which typically accompany various blood alcohol concentration (BAC). The subject was then given pure alcohol in fruit juice and asked to analyze his own subjective responses and behaviors as a basis for estimating his own BAC. Breathalyser readings were taken every 15–20 min, and the subject was required to make an estimate of his own BAC. As soon as this estimate was made, immediate feedback in the form of readings on a large meter was given. Each time a BAC was given to the subject, he was encouraged to make associations between his present subjective experience and the actual meter readings. Essentially, each subject constructed his own subjective BAC symptom scale.

During the actual conditioning procedure, electrodes were applied to various parts of the subject's neck and face. The subject was required to drink the alcoholic beverage of his choice at a steady rate such that BAC's of 0.065% were raised within 1½ hr. In order to insure conditioning, the subject was required to drink after BAC's of 0.065% were reached. The subject was shocked on 80% of the trials, the duration of shock was varied from 1 to 6 sec, and shock intensity varied from 4 to 7 mA (intense to very intense). The point in the drinking sequences at which shock occurred varied from trial to trial—from the subject's picking up his glass to the actual swallowing of the alcohol.

Also incorporated in the treatment regime were self-control and self monitoring procedures. Self-control procedures (42, 43) are based on the assumption that purposefulness, self-actualization, morality, etc., are not innate characteristics, but are learned behaviors maintained because of their adaptive function in the relationship between the individual and his social environment. In particular, it is proposed that self-control involving behaviors that have conflicting outcomes can be analyzed as a function of both current environmental variables and self-generated variables initiated into the repertoire by previous training.

A conceptual model is postulated based on what have been termed "alpha" and "beta" variables. Alpha variables refer to multiple sources of behavior regulation that emanate directly from the external environment. Beta variables refer to moderating psychological processes that mediate the "input–output" relationship. It is assumed that beta variables are the product of past history, biologic constitution, sensory and proprioceptive feedbacks, discrimination, and response-produced situations. The extent to which internal stimulation and self-generated reinforcing events operate is dependent upon the magnitude and specificity of these variables and the variety and complexity of the individual's available covert behaviors in their perception of an interaction with the effects of his external environment. "Private" events, such as verbal and imaginal forms of internal behavior are presumed to be subject to the same rules of acquisition, maintenance, and extinction as overt behavior. The assumption is also made that these internal behaviors can be trained by systematic external regulation.

Self-regulation is concerned with the processes whereby an individual alters or maintains his behavior in the absence of environmental supports. Internal control procedures would attempt to decrease the probability of approaching an immediately rewarding situation in order to avoid long-term negative outcomes (2, 32, 33, 34). When the response to be controlled loses its pleasurable or aversive consequences, then internal control is no longer a relevant explanatory mechanism. If the external situation compels a change in the probability of a particular response, internal control is not involved. The critical element in internal control is the individual's own actions toward altering a strong pattern of behavior to meet a criterion he has set.

Self-regulation procedures used in the work by Lovibond et al. included the monitoring and recording of drinking behavior by the subject and by at least one other confederate, usually a family member. The initiation of self-regulation and self-control was dependent upon the patient's acceptance of the view that his drinking behavior could be brought within his own control. The patients were encouraged to recognize the fact that, although they had lost control of this drinking behavior, the aim of the treatment program was to reinstate self-control. Any attempt by the patient to deny his own ultimate responsibility or to deny his ability to learn to control drinking was firmly negatively reinforced. In other words, "learned helplessness" was challenged consistently. Specific training in self-control procedures was given. The patient was trained to recognize the degree to which excessive drinking was under stimulus control and instructed how to change his own environment to reduce the extent to which drinking behavior was triggered and maintained, for example how to cope with social pressures to continue drinking after maximum BAC's had been reached. Outside the experimental situation, patients were encouraged to substitute an alternate response with reinforcing consequences as the limit of acceptable BAC was approached. The patients were also taught to self-administer rewards and punishments for maintaining or failure to maintain the requirements of the program—a procedure similar to that of the "contingency management" of Homme (38).

There were three experimental groups used. The first received aversion plus self-regulation (AV + SR). The second group received self-regulation (SR) treatment. They were treated with the same procedures as the AV + SR group, except that no shock was used. When patients in the SR group reached a BAC of 0.065%, it was emphasized to them that they were at their limit and that further drinking would almost certainly result in intoxication and loss of control. The third group was given aversion training (AV) only. No emphasis was placed on self-control of drinking behavior in the latter procedure. Implicit in the procedure was the contention that the conditioning process would act automatically on the regulation of alcohol consumption.

Seventy-eight applications for treatment were received. Of these 12 patients were refused because they required immediate hospitalization and 6 failed to begin treatment after being accepted. The remaining 60 subjects included 49 males and 11 females, with an age range of 21 to 68 years. Thirty-one were psychiatric referrals, 6 were referred by general practitioners, and 23 were self-referred. The majority of patients were described as having a history of alcoholism over 10 years duration. Most had required several hospitalizations for alcoholism.

Follow-up interviews were conducted 6 months and 12 months after completion of treatment (12-month follow-up data were available for 37 patients at the time of writing). Patients and significant other either attended for assessment or were visited in their homes. Five subjects in the AV + SR groups, four in the SR group, and seven in the AV group failed to complete treatment. Their results were included in the follow-up data. Three categories were used. A "complete success" was defined as drinking in controlled fashion, exceeding 0.07% "rarely." "Considerable improvement" implied the patient was drinking less but exceeding 0.07% once or twice a week. "Slight or no improvement" indicated the patient was drinking as much as pretreatment levels.

On 12-month follow-up, there were data for 13 subjects in the AV + SR group. Of these 13, 5 were "complete successes," 5 were "considerably improved," and 3 showed no improvement. Data available for 14 patients in the SR group indicate the 12-month figures as 4, 5, and 5, respectively, while for 10 patients in the AV group, the results were 1, 4, and 5, respectively.

Because the 12-month follow-up data is incomplete, only very tentative conclusions can be made about the efficacy of the program. These should be regarded as hypotheses to be tested against more complete results. The first hypothesis is the discriminated aversion training (AV) alone produces very poor results in terms of "complete success," with only one patient (10% of the follow-up group) included in this category. If we collapse the "complete success" and "considerably improved" categories, five patients (50% of the follow-up group) would be included. The second hypothesis is that aversion training does not add sufficiently to the effectiveness of the program to warrant the discomfort and distress which must be endured by the patient because of the high intensity of shock used. This hypothesis is based on comparison of the 12-month follow-up results of the self-regulation plus aversion group (SR + AV) and self-regulation only (SR) group. Even if we collapse the "complete success" and "considerably improved" categories, the actual difference is only one patient, the percentage difference about 7%.

Ewing and Rouse (25) attempted to replicate the techniques of Lovibond et al. with a group of alcoholics on an outpatient basis. The treatment goal was moderation of drinking.

The 21 subjects who participated were diverse as far as age, education, and occupation. Except for one student who was clearly not an alcoholic but was concerned because his part-time job as bartender was leading to the daily consumption of a large amount of drink, Ewing and Rouse describe the remaining 26 patients as "fulfilling the criteria of gamma alcoholism."

The principal treatment modality was that of Lovibond et al. although other behaviors were taught, such as diluting drinks, spacing drinks, sipping rather than gulping, etc. Self-monitoring also took the form of having patients keep a weekly detailed drinking diary which was discussed at each meeting. Modeling of behaviors was also demonstrated by the therapist's participation in drinking in a limited, socially acceptable fashion. In an average 3-hr session, about one-third of the time would be spent in discussing acceptable and unacceptable drinking behavior, putative reasons for drinking, alternatives for drinking behavior, etc.

Of the 21 patients who participated, only 6 completed the required minimum of 12 sessions. Of these six, three showed significant controlled drinking behavior during the four-month (one patient) to 15-month follow-up period. One patient who completed all sessions was also found to be successfully controlling his drinking. No other patient who failed to complete the program was found to be abstinent or drinking in moderation on follow-up.

Although the authors conclude that more effective treatment may result from increased emphasis on self-regulation and decision making and less emphasis on aversion therapy, a suggestion that seems to concur well with the results of Lovibond et al. (52, 53), there is no indication that this was based on any empirical evidence. Since no control group procedures were used at all by Ewing and Rouse, the results of their investigation cannot be evaluated properly, and any conclusions must be considered speculative.

6. INDIVIDUAL BEHAVIOR THERAPY: ALCOHOLISM AS A DISCRIMINATED OPERANT RESPONSE

Sobell and Sobell (77–79) have evolved an individualized treatment program for moderation of drinking based on the rationale that excessive drinking could be considered as a discriminated operant response which occurs in selective and definable situations and which is acquired and maintained as a result of its consequences.

Forty male "blue collar" patients were selected for controlled drinking trials from a group of alcoholics who had been voluntarily hospitalized and who had volunteered for the study. The patients were assigned at random to a controlled drinking experimental or to a controlled drinking group.

In addition, 30 patients were selected for abstinence trials and were randomly assigned to two groups: a nondrinker experimental group (N = 15) or a nondrinker control group (N = 15). Subjects who could socially identify with Alcoholics Anonymous, had requested abstinence as a treatment goal and/or were evaluated as lacking sufficient social support to maintain a controlled drinking pattern were always assigned to the nondrinker goal.

The actual treatment program consisted of 17, 90-min daily sessions. Central emphasis was placed upon defining prior setting events for excessive drinking and training the individual in alternative socially acceptable responses to those situations. Stimulus-control variables, setting events for drinking were defined as those which had either immediately preceded or accompanied the onset of heavy drinking in the past. Holloway (37) noted that excessive drinking in in vivo situations did not conform to the stereotyped patterns reported in the literature, but it seems to be a fairly stable individual phenomenon. After these stimulus control variables were delineated, the subject was asked to generate a universe of possible alternative responses to each event. Once an array of alternatives had been elicited, the subjects were asked to evaluate each in terms of long-term consequences and whether they would be effective or self-destructive. Efforts were also made to construct situations in which the subject could actually practice various alternative responses to provide discrimination training in effective versus noneffective responses.

During each treatment session, except for five "probe" days, the experimental subjects were also given aversion training contingent on appropriate drinking behaviors, i.e., diluting, sipping, spacing, and stopping after three drinks. In addition there were three noncontingent sessions consisting of two videotape confrontations, one while drunk and one while sober, and two "stimulus control" sessions when shock contingencies were not in effect. An education session was included early in the program to inform the patient of the treatment program, to advise him of the contingencies under which shock would be administered and to give him an explanation of the treatment rationale—that excessive drinking is a *learned* behavior, occurring under certain stimulus conditions and not in others and controlled by its consequences. Training in certain responses was also given during this session such as resisting social pressures to continue drinking. One session consisting of an "artificial failure" experience was also included. Control subjects received conventional hospital treatment which included group therapy, AA meetings, chemotherapy, physiotherapy, etc.

Follow-up was conducted for subjects and their cohorts every three to four weeks. Subjects were classified as (*a*) abstinent, (*b*) controlled drinking, defined as the daily consumption of 6 oz or less of 86 proof liquor or equivalent, or any one-day isolated sequence when between 7 and 9 oz were consumed, (*c*) drunk, any day on which more than 10 oz were consumed or any sequence longer than two consecutive days when between 7 and 9 oz were consumed each day.

The two-year follow-up data (79) indicate that of the 19 experimental controlled drinking subjects located, approximately 92% were abstinent and/or controlled drinkers, 7% were drunk, and the remainder incarcerated in hospital or prison. The figures for the controlled drinking control group were, respectively, 47%, 43%, and 10%.

The two-year follow-up data on the nondrinker groups indicate that of the 13 experimental subjects located, approximately 63% were abstinent, approximately 3% were controlled drinkers, approximately 20% were drunk, and the remaining 14% were either in hospital or prison. The results for the nondrinker control group (N = 14) were, respectively, 46%, 2%, 36%, and 16%.

While the results of this investigation are impressive, particularly with the controlled drinking experimental group, and the procedures warrant detailed attention, so many procedures were involved that it is difficult to sort out the relative efficacy of each, but "educated" guesses can be made from the results reported in the monograph (77) and from other reports from this group.

First of all, it is quite unlikely that a gradually accumulated conditioned aversion to shock was controlling the subjects' drinking behavior. Seven of the subjects never received shock; 14 of the 20 patients received two or less total shocks during the 10 sessions when shock contingencies were in effect. The results indicate that response contingent aversive stimulation suppressed drinking behavior rather than shaped it, since alcohol consumption increased during the "probe" (nonshock) sessions.

The relative contribution of video tape confrontation cannot be assessed accurately. However, previous reports from this group (74) indicated that experimental subjects given videotape confrontations showed an "alarming but not significant" trend toward greater degrees of drunkenness.

It is the contention of the investigators that the stimulus control sessions not only constituted the majority of the treatment sessions, but also were the primary factors responsible for satisfactory results. Specifically, those subjects who learned to generalize from rehearsed situations to more generalized situations were found to be those who were functioning most successfully on discharge. They recommended that there should be a decreasing emphasis on specifying stimulus control variables and increasing importance given to the developing alternative response to situations. They also suggested such self-monitoring procedures as having the subject write down stimulus control variables for his drinking, evaluating alternative responses, and recording the frequency of behaviors he wishes to increase or decrease.

The difference between the "stimulus control" procedures in the present investigation and the "contingency management" of Cohen et al. (18–21) should be apparent. While both are based on operant conditioning formulations, greater emphasis in the present investigations was placed on internal control and self-regulation while the procedures of Cohen et al. primarily manipulated external or environmental variables only.

7. CONCLUSIONS

Learning theory principles are based on the assumption that behavior is malleable and can be modified. The implications of these principles are that appropriate alternative behaviors to excessive drinking can be trained and, with sufficient ingenuity on the part of the investigators, crucial strengths in the behavioral repertoire of the alcoholic may be reinforced and crucial weaknesses identified so that more adaptive behaviors may be instated.

Applications of behavioral techniques to the treatment of alcoholism highlight the fact that there is a gap between theory and clinical application.

Both Hullian and Skinnerian (76) theory are strongly dependent on the role of reinforcement in either maintaining or modifying behaviors. However, when reinforcement principles are applied, either in aversive conditioning or contingency management procedures, while excessive drinking behavior may be *shaped* and *controlled,* this cannot necessarily be equated with the *learning* of new, more adaptive behaviors. The conceptual formulation assumes that, given a set of environmental cues, these stimuli are followed by a given response. However, in actual practice, the same stimulus may be followed by differing responses within the same individual over time. In addition, dissimilar stimuli may produce identical or widely discrepant responses dependent on certain moderating conditions. Deviations such as these present a serious challenge to a simple input, output reinforcement model. Theory developed in tightly controlled laboratory situations cannot be extrapolated directly to such highly complex and intricate in vivo situations as the treatment of alcoholism with all its complicated social, interpersonal, emotional, and physiologic ramifications. Then too, cognitive factors have largely been ignored.

It is not within the scope of this chapter to consider the wide implications and ramifications of cognitive factors in behavioral modification, and, for detailed analysis, the reader is referred to the work of Mahoney (55a), Miller and Dallard (57a) and Bandura and Walters (6a). However, it should be pointed out that Skinnerian operant formulations have concentrated on contingency-governed rather than rule-governed behavior and thus have been particularly remiss in incorporating the extensive body of work on perception, awareness, vicarious and incidental learning, motivation, expectations, and higher mental processes which have been generated from other areas of psychology.

Basic to the work on perception is that the organism responds not to some "pure" external stimulus (or stimuli) but to the stimulus as perceived. Therefore accurate predictions of subsequent behavior cannot be made without taking into account the individual's perception of the experimental stimuli. Mahoney (55a) cites several examples of stimulus transformation through mediational processes which indicate that the simple assumption cannot even be made that any given stimulus or set of stimuli is either reinforcing or aversive on the basis of the experimenter's standards. In clinical situations, as we know, the patient's report or even behavior may indeed coincide with the clinician's, but this may be more related to the patient's desire to meet the clinician's expectations within that particular context rather than the individual's private perceptions (1). The work of Hsu (39) cited earlier, where subjects manifested what would appear to be inordinate reactions in the treatment trials may illustrate this point. Thus, the consequences of any given response sequence may or may not have the experimentally desired effect outside the constraints of the treatment situation.

The role of awareness in human learning has also been largely ignored by what Mahoney (55a) has termed the "nonmediational" theorists who view response consequences as automatic habit stampers rather than informative cues. If performance contingencies are informative cues, then highly complex mental operations, such as information processing, reasoning, covert verbal mediation, and strategy planning are brought into play. Awareness represents rule-governed behavior in which the subject responds to a *symbolic* representation or labeling of performance contingencies. In the Cohen et al. (21) study described previously, the role of awareness in terms of the subjects' grasping the nuances of the experimental strategies may have been a factor.

The role of attribution in determining outcome cannot be overlooked, since perceived causality may dramatically influence behavior. The behavioral model stresses excessive drinking as learned behavior. However, if alcoholism is still seen by the patient as caused by heredity, addiction, or disease, active participation in a self-improvement program may be less likely, although empty verbalizations may be rampant.

Expectations may be categorized as a complex of mediational processes which influence selective attention, response utilizations, and anticipated consequences. Despite the inferred power of behavioral techniques, a subject who does not anticipate improvement from a procedure is less likely to attend to, retain, or implement its features. For alcoholics, particularly those who have been subjected to various treatment regimes with little apparent success, expectations may be important mediators in determining outcome.

Mahoney (55a) has pointed out that researchers in behavior modification have often taken a defensive stance regarding expectancy factors and have tended to minimize or deny them. However, if expectations are viewed as significant elements in behavior change, rather than as annoying artifacts, it is within the scope of the behavioral scientist to develop systematic techniques to modify and change expectations in their subjects.

The residual drive strength factor, even when withdrawal from alcohol has been accomplished, has probably been underestimated. Neither classical conditioning nor operant reinforcers present appropriate alternatives for the response of drinking alcohol. The "new" response of either rejecting alcohol completely or even moderation of drinking may leave the patient still unable to cope with social, interpersonal, and emotional situations, for which the alcoholic may have no adaptive skills other than excessive drinking.

Overall, the use of many behavioral techniques thus far has proved to be at least as successful as conventional treatment and, in some cases (e.g., 9, 10, 49, 77–79), outstanding results have been reported. However, interpretation of the results of many of investigations using behavioral techniques have been hampered by inadequate designs, unsatisfactory control group procedures, the selectivity of intake, ill-defined measures of outcome, and unconvincing follow-up procedures. Therefore, evaluation of the precise efficacy of various techniques cannot be made at the present time.

It is unrealistic, in fact, to attempt to evaluate the efficacy of a given technique or techniques without taking into account the interaction of patient and therapist variables as well.

To my knowledge, there has been no systematic investigation made of this interaction, since the assumption is usually made that therapist variables are irrelevant in the application of behavioral techniques. However, there is some evidence, admittedly scattered, that this might not be so. For example, Kraft's (46) results, mentioned previously, in which an additional procedure had to be incorporated to desensitize patients to their dependence on the therapist, after relaxation and a standardized hierarchy had been used, and the covert sensitization trials (5, 26) in which female therapists were found to be more effective, suggest that behavioral techniques are not immune to therapist–patient interaction. Koenig and Masters also found therapist–patient interaction effects in the application of behavioral techniques to smoking.

Certainly it does seem apparent that no single treatment modality can be the optimal procedure for all alcoholisms. More systematic application of a variety of techniques require investigation so that not only may more appropriate treatment programs be developed, but also that the most appropriate and effective *sequences* of treatment regimes be formulated in terms of the individual patient.

Included in such a program could be behavioral techniques to reduce tension, particularly deep relaxation techniques (41) and where appropriate, systematic desensitization could be incorporated. Stimulus flooding, i.e., response prevention techniques to reduce craving, may be of value and are being investigated at the present time (Hodgson, private communication). From the theoretical and empirical evidence cited (and from this author's own predilictions), the main therapeutic investment should be made in the development and training of broad coping skills to provide suitable alternative responses to excessive drinking behavior, with the client placed in the role of an active and responsible agent in his own adjustment.

A multiplicity of techniques, in fact the entire spectrum of behavioral techniques, may require incorporation of the following into such a program orientation: systematic and continuous self-monitoring, instruction, modeling, coverant control procedures, graduated performance assignments, assertive training, social skills training, the generation of multiple solutions to particular problems and situations, solution testing, the evaluation of feedback, etc. Mahoney (55a) maintains there are no therapeutic "failures"—only inefficient solutions. In such a program, all the therapist's training, experience, skill, and ingenuity must be brought in to insure that there is ample scope for alternative solutions and correction at every step.

Individually tailored treatments on an intensive basis may, in fact, prove to be more efficient than brief intervention, followed by relapse, followed by brief intervention, ad infinitum. Although cost-effectiveness analyses of various approaches have not been made, the possibility remains that a greater initial investment of time and systematic therapeutic effort tailored to the needs of the patient and requirements may prove in the long run to be more economical. The results from some studies (e.g., 9, 10, 49, 77–79) also indicate that frequent and regular follow-up procedures may serve as a therapeutic after-care function.

The evidence also seems to indicate that there is a high dropout rate in those trials where aversion therapy only is used, i.e., without the adjunct of more positive treatments. The ethical question of using aversive techniques per se is still under debate, but the fact remains that some of these treatments do cause great discomfort and distress to the patients involved. At this point in time, the results of aversion trials cannot be stated with certainty to be so effective that they can be used indiscriminately without the strictest of safeguards being applied.

Pattison (66) has emphasized the fact that the goal of treatment should be seen as rehabilitation in its broadest sense. Abstinence need not be the sole criterion and goal of treatment. Modified, controlled, and social drinking are also viable alternatives. Treatment should be visualized as multidimensional, so that therapeutic efforts should also be concentrated on enhancement of interpersonal relationships, vocational rehabilitation, and emotional health.

The real point at-issue is that evaluation of outcome in terms of "dry" or "drunk" is no longer realistic nor tenable. There exists a range of outcome possibilities not only in terms of alcohol consumption but in terms of individual functioning. The focus of treatment intervention only on the achievement and maintenance of abstinence may be detrimental to the extent that such a unidimensional approach leaves a wide range of other feasible and suitable possibilities of rehabilitation relatively unexplored.

ACKNOWLEDGMENT

Grateful acknowledgment is due to Dr. Griffith Edwards for his support, encouragement, and invaluable comments on this chapter.

REFERENCES

1. Allport, G. W., *Personality: A Psychological Interpretation*, Holt, New York, 1957.
2. Alterman, A. I., E. Gottheil, T. E. Skoloda, and J. C. Grasberger, Social modification of drinking by alcoholics, *Q. J. Stud. Alcohol*, **35,** 917 (1974).
3. Anant, S. S., A note on the treatment of alcoholics by a verbal aversion technique, *Can. J. Psychol.*, **8,** 19 (1967).
4. Anant, S. S., Treatment of alcoholics and drug addicts by verbal aversion techniques, *Int. J. Addict.*, **3,** 381 (1968).
5. Ashem, B. and L. Donner, Covert sensitization with alcoholics: A controlled replication. *Behav. Res. Ther.*, **6,** 7 (1968).
6. Bandura, A., *Principles of Behavior Modification*, Holt, Rinehart and Winston, Inc., New York, 1969.
6a. Bandura, A. and E. H. Walters, The development of self-control, in *Behaviour Change through Self-Control.*, M. R. Goldfried and M. Merbaum (Eds.), Holt, Rinehart and Winston, New York, 1973.
7. Bhakata, M., Clinical application of behavior therapy in the treatment of alcoholism, *J. Alcohol*, **6,** 75 (1971).
8. Bigelow, G., M. Cohen, I. Liebson, and L. A. Faillace, Abstinence or moderation? Choice by alcoholics. *Behav. Res. Ther.*, **10,** 209 (1972).
9. Blake, B. G., The application of behavior therapy to the treatment of alcoholism, *Behav. Res. Ther.*, **3,** 75 (1965).
10. Blake, B. G., A follow-up of alcoholics treated by behavior therapy, *Behav. Res. Ther.*, **5,** 89 (1967).
11. Bolman, W. M., Abstinence versus permissiveness of the psychotherapy of alcoholism, *Arch. Gen. Psychiat.*, **12,** 456 (1965).
12. Canter, F. M., The problem of abstinence as a problem in institutional treatment of alcoholics, *J. Alcohol.*, **5,** 48 (1970).
13. Cautela, J. R., Treatment of compulsive behavior by covert desensitization, *Psychol. Rep.*, **16,** 33 (1966).
14. Cautela, J. R., Covert sensitization, *Psychol. Rep.*, **20,** 459 (1967).
15. Cautela, J. R., Covert reinforcement, *Behav. Ther.*, **1,** 33 (1970).
16. Claeson, L. E. and U. Malm, Electro-aversion therapy of chronic alcoholism, *Behav. Res. Ther.*, **11,** 663 (1973).

17. Clancy, J., E. Vanderhoof, and D. Campbell, Evaluation of an aversive technique as a treatment of alcoholism, *Q. J. Stud. Alcohol*, **28,** 746 (1967).

18. Cohen, M., I. A. Liebson, and L. A. Faillace, The role of reinforcement contingencies in chronic alcoholism: An experimental analysis of one case, *Behav. Res. Ther.*, **9,** 375 (1971).

19. Cohen, M., I. A. Liebson, and L. A. Faillace, A technique for establishing controlled drinking in chronic alcoholics, *Dis. Nerv. Sys.*, **33,** 46 (1972).

20. Cohen, M., I. A. Liebson, L. A. Faillace, and R. P. Allen, Moderate drinking by chronic alcoholics, *J. Nerv. Ment. Dis.*, **153,** 434 (1971).

21. Cohen, M., I. A. Liebson, L. A. Faillace, and W. Speers, Alcoholism: Controlled drinking and incentives for abstinence, *Psychol. Rep.*, **28,** 575 (1971).

22. Davies, D. L., M. Shepherd, and E. Myers, The two year prognosis of 50 alcohol addicts after treatment in hospital, *Q. J. Stud. Alcohol*, **17,** 485 (1955).

23. Devenyi, P. and G. Sereny, Aversion treatment with electroconditioning for alcoholism, *Br. J. Addict.*, **65,** 289 (1970).

24. Evans, M, Modification of drinking, *J. Alcohol*, **8,** 111 (1973).

25. Ewing, J. A. and B. A. Rouse, *Outpatient Group Treatment to Inculcate Controlled Drinking in Alcoholics*, Presented at the 30th International Congress on Alcoholism and Drug Dependence, Amsterdam, 1972.

26. Fleiger, D. L. and H. W. Zingle, Covert sensitization treatment with alcoholics, *Can. Counsel.*, **7,** 269 (1973).

27. Franks, C. M., Behavior therapy, the principles of conditioning and the treatment of the alcoholic, *Q. J. Stud. Alcohol*, **24,** 511 (1963).

28. Franks, C. M., Conditioning and conditioned aversion therapies in the treatment of the alcoholic, *Int. J. Addict.*, **1,** 61 (1966).

29. Freed, E. X., Abstinence for alcoholics reconsidered, *J. Alcohol*, **8,** 106 (1973).

30. Gerard, D. L. and G. Saenger, *Outpatient Treatment of Alcoholics: A Study of Outcome and Determinants*, University of Toronto Press, Toronto, 1966.

31. Glatt, M. M., Treatment results in an English mental hospital alcoholic unit, *Acta. Psychiatr. Scand.*, **37,** 143 (1961).

32. Gottheil, E., L. O. Corbett, J. C. Grasberger, and F. S. Cornelison, Jr., Treating the alcoholic in the presence of alcohol, *Am. J. Psychiatry*, **128,** 475 (1971).

33. Gottheil, E., L. O. Corbett, J. C. Grasberger, and F. S. Cornelison, Jr. Fixed interval drinking decisions. I. A research and treatment model, *Q. J. Stud. Alcohol*, **33,** 311 (1972).

34. Gottheil, E., B. F. Murphy, T. E. Skoloda, and L. O. Corbett, Fixed interval drinking decisions. II. Drinking and discomfort in 25 alcoholics, *Q. J. Stud. Alcohol*, **33,** 325 (1972).

35. Hallam, R., S. Rachman, and W. Falkowski, Subjective, attitudinal and physiological effects of electrical aversion therapy, *Behav. Res. Ther.*, **10,** 1 (1972).

36. Hershon, H., Alcoholism and the concept of disease, *Br. J. Addict.*, **69,** 123 (1974).

37. Holloway, I., *Behavioral Modification of Excessive Drinking in the Environmental Setting*, Presented at the 30th International Congress on Alcoholism and Drug Dependence, Amsterdam, 1972.

38. Homme, L. E., Contiguity theory and contingency management, *Psychol. Rep.*, **16,** 233 (1966).

39. Hsu, J. J., Electroconditioning therapy of alcoholics, *Q. J. Stud. Alcohol*, **26,** 449 (1965).

40. Hunt, G. M. and N. H. Azrin, A community reinforcement approach to alcoholism, *Behav. Res. Ther.*, **11,** 91 (1973).

41. Jacobson, E., *Progressive Relaxation*. University of Chicago Press, Chicago, 1938.

42. Kanfer, F. H. and P. Karoly, Self-control: A behavioristic excursion into the lion's den, *Behav. Ther.*, **3,** 398 (1972).

43. Kanfer, F. H. and J. S. Phillips, *Learning Foundation of Behavior Therapy*. Wiley, New York, 1970.

44. Kantorovich, N. V., An attempt at associated-reflex therapy in alcoholism, (*Nov. Reflexol. Fixiol. Nerv. Sist.*, **3,** 436 [1929]), *Psychol. Abstr.*, **4,** 493 (1930).

45. Kessel, N. and H. Walton, *Alcoholism*, MacGibbon and Kee, London, 1966.

46. Kraft, T., Alcoholism treated by systematic desensitization: A follow-up of eight cases, *J. R. Coll. Gen. Pract.*, **18,** 336 (1968).

47. Kraft, T., and I. Al-Lssa, Alcoholism treated by desensitization: A case study, *Behav. Res. Ther.*, **5,** 69 (1967).

48. Laverty, S. G., Aversion therapies in the treatment of alcoholics, *Psychosom. Med.*, **28,** 651 (1966).

49. Lemere, F. and W. L. Voegtlin, An evaluation of the aversion treatment of alcoholism, *Q. J. Stud. Alcohol*, **11,** 199 (1950).

50. Litman, G. K., "Once an alcoholic, always an alcoholic." I. Experimental studies of intoxication and moderation as a by-product of treatment, *Q. J. Stud. Alcohol* (in press).

51. Lovibond, S. H., Aversive control of Behavior. *Behav. Ther.* **1,** 80 (1970).

52. Lovibond, S. H. and G. Caddy, Discriminated aversive control in the moderation of alcoholic drinking behavior, *Behav. Ther.*, **3,** 234 (1970).

53. Lovibond, S. H., G. Caddy, and M. Cross, Self-regulation and discriminated aversive conditioning in the modification of alcoholics' drinking behavior, *Behav. Ther.*, **3,** 234 (1972).

54. MacCulloch, M. J., M. P. Feldman, J. F. Orford, and M. L. MacCulloch, Anticipatory avoidance learning in the treatment of alcoholism: A record of therapeutic failure, *Behav. Res. Ther.*, **4,** 187 (1966).

55. Madell, M. F., D. Campbell, S. G. Laverty, R. E. Sanderson, and S. L. Vanderwater, Aversion treatment of alcoholics by succinyl choline-induced apreic paralysis, *Q. J. Stud. Alcohol*, **27,** 483 (1966).

55a. Mahoney, M. J., *Cognitive and Behavior Modification.*, Ballinger, Cambridge, Mass., 1974.

56. Malmo, R. B., Anxiety and behavioral arousal, *Psychol. Rev.*, **64,** 276 (1957).

57. McGuire, R. J. and M. Vallance, Aversion therapy by electric shock: A simple technique, *Br. Med. J.*, **1,** 151 (1964).

57a. Miller, N. and J. Dallard, Higher mental processes, in *Behavior Change through Self-Control.*, M. R. Goldfried and M. Merbaum (Eds.), Holt, Rinehart and Winston, New York, 1973.

58. Miller, P. M., The use of behavioral contracting in the treatment of alcoholism, *Behav. Ther.*, **3,** 593 (1972).

59. Miller, P. M., and D. H. Barlow, Behavioral approaches to the treatment of alcoholism, *J. Nerv. Ment. Dis.*, **157,** 10 (1973).

60. Miller, P. M., B. A. Dvorak, and D. W. Turner, A method of creating aversion to alcohol by reflex conditioning in a group setting, *Q. J. Stud. Alcohol*, **21,** 424 (1960).

61. Miller, P. M., M. Hersen, R. M. Eisler, and D. Hemphill, Electrical aversion with alcoholics: An analogue study, *Behav. Res. Ther.*, **11,** 491 (1973).

62. Mills, K. C., M. B. Sobell, and H. H. Schaefer, Training social drinking as an alternative to abstinence for alcoholics, *Behav. Ther.*, **2,** 18 (1971).

63. Mowrer, O. H., On the dual nature of learning—A reinterpretation of "conditioning" and "problem solving," *Harvard Educ. Rev.*, **17,** 102 (1947).

64. Narroll, H. G., Experimental application of reinforcement principles to the analysis and treatment of hospitalized alcoholics, *Q. J. Stud. Alcohol*, **28,** 105 (1967).

65. Pattison, E. M., A critique of alcoholism treatment concepts with special reference to abstinence, *Q. J. Stud. Alcohol*, **27,** 49 (1966).

66. Pattison, E. M., *Drinking Outcomes of Alcoholism Treatment: Abstinence, Social, Modified, Controlled, and Normal Drinking*, Presented at First International Medical Conference on Alcoholism, London, 1973.

67. Pattison, E. M., E. C. Headley, G. C. Gleser, and L. A. Gottschalk, Abstinence and normal drinking: An assessment of changes in drinking patterns in alcoholics after treatment, *Q. J. Stud. Alcohol*, **29,** 610 (1968).

68. Quinn, J. T., and R. Henbest, Partial failure of generalization in alcoholics following aversion therapy, *Q. J. Stud. Alcohol*, **28,** 70, 1967.

69. Quirk, D. A., Former alcoholics and social drinking: An additional observation, *Can. Psychol.*, **9,** 35 (1968).

70. Rachman, S. and J. Teasdale, *Aversion Therapy and Behavior Disorders*, Routledge, London, 1969.

71. Robinson, D., The alcohologist's addiction, *Q. J. Stud. Alcohol*, **33,** 1028 (1972).

72. Sanderson, R. E., D. Campbell, and S. G. Laverty, An investigation of a new aversive conditioning treatment for alcoholism, *Q. J. Stud. Alcohol*, **24,** 261 (1963).

73. Schaefer, H. H., Twelve month follow-up of behaviorally trained ex-alcoholic social drinkers, *Behav. Ther.*, **3,** 286 (1972).

74. Schaefer, H. H., M. B. Sobell, K. C. Mills, Some sobering data on the use of self-confrontation with alcoholics, *Behav. Ther.*, **2,** 28 (1971).

75. Schaefer, H. H., M. B. Sobell, and K. C. Mills, Baseline drinking behavior in alcoholics and social drinkers: Kinds of drink and sip magnitudes, *Behav. Res. Ther.*, **9,** 23–27, (1971).

76. Skinner, B. F., *Science and Human Behavior*, MacMillan, New York, 1953.

77. Sobell, M. B. and L. C. Sobell, *Individualized Behavior Therapy for Alcoholics: Rationale, Procedures and Preliminary Results*, California Department of Mental Hygiene, Research Monograph, 13, 1972.

78. Sobell, M. B. and L. C. Sobell, Individualized behavior therapy for alcoholics, *Behav. Therapy*, **4,** 49 (1973).

79. Sobell, M. B. and L. C. Sobell, *Evidence of Controlled Drinking by Former Alcoholics:*

A Second Year Evaluation of Individualized Behavior Therapy, Presented at 81st Annual Convention of the American Psychological Association, Montreal, 1973.

80. Soren, P. V. and E. J. Thomas, An experiment in group after-care for alcoholics, *J. Alcohol,* **5,** 48 (1970).

81. Storm, T. and R. E. Cutler, *Systematic Desensitization in the Treatment of Alcoholics: An Experimental Trial,* Alcoholism Foundation of British Columbia, Vancouver, 1968.

82. Sulzer, E. S., Behavioral modification in adult psychiatric patients, in *Case Studies in Behavior Modification,* L. P. Ullman and Krasner L. (Eds)., Holt, Rinehart and Winston, New York, 1965.

83. Verden, P. and D. Shatterly, Alcoholism research and resistance to understanding the compulsive drinker, *Ment. Hyg.,* **55,** 331 (1971).

84. Vogler, R. E., S. E. Lunde, G. R. Johnson, and P. L. Martin, Electrical aversion conditioning with chronic alcoholics, *J. Con. Clin. Psychol.,* **34,** 302 (1970).

85. Vogel-Sprott, M, Alcoholism and learning, in *The Biology of Alcoholism,* Vol. II, B. Kissin and H. Begleiter (Eds)., Plenum Press, New York, 1970.

86. Wolpe, J., *Psychotherapy by Reciprocal Inhibition,* Stanford University Press, Stanford, 1958.

CHAPTER NINE

NONABSTINENT DRINKING GOALS IN THE TREATMENT OF ALCOHOLICS

E. MANSELL PATTISON, *Department of Psychiatry and Human Behavior, University of California, Irvine; Training Division Orange County Department of Mental Health, Irvine, California*

1. INTRODUCTION

During the past decade a fundamental assumption in the field of alcoholism has been severely challenged. It has long been held that alcoholics must attain abstinence in order to achieve rehabilitation, and that abstinence is the necessary treatment goal insofar as use of alcohol is concerned. Although there were passing references to nonabstinent methods of treatment and nonabstinent drinking goals in the earlier literature, such observations were not systematic, were inbedded in other data, and generally such data were ignored or dismissed.

The watershed of new data commenced in 1962 when Davies, (41) reported that 7 of 93 alcohol addicts whom he had treated and followed for a period of years had returned to normal drinking after a period of abstinence. Subsequent theoretical analyses by Krystal (118) and Bolman (20) supported the reasonable basis for consideration of nonabstinence. In 1966 Pattison (183) published a review of treatment literature that revealed that alcoholics who had not achieved abstinence had attained a successful rehabilitation, that alcoholics who had achieved abstinence had successfully returned to some degree of moderate drinking, and that some alcoholics who had achieved abstinence did not attain rehabilitation or had undergone deterioration of their life adjustment. Interest in these issues has crescendoed, as reflected in a variety of commentaries (48, 50, 58, 72, 79, 106, 182, 186, 204, 206, 247). In addition to scientific discussions, these issues have attracted publicity in the public press and in lay organizations in the field of alcoholism. Consequently, in alcoholism circles people have come to the point of labeling this the "abstinence–moderate drinking controversy."

However, the issue of nonabstinent drinking goals is far broader. For the assumptions of abstinence are intimately entwined with a series of concepts about the nature of alcoholism. These include the concept of craving, the concept of loss of control, the concept of progression, the concept of irreversibility, the concept of arrest but no cure for alcoholism. Taken as a whole, these concepts were woven together into a model paradigm of alcoholism, the so-called "disease model," which was formulated with some rigor and elegance in 1960 by Jellinek (101) in his book *The Disease Concept of Alcoholism*.

Although Jellinek was modest, circumspect, and even tentative in his formulations, the model of alcoholism which he presented exerted a profound effect upon the field. It organized and synthesized the scientific observations of his day into a model or paradigm of alcoholism that had both clinical utility and theoretical coherence. This model became the general accepted paradigm.

Now it is important to recognize the role of paradigms in the development of science. The traditional view of scientific progress is that change results from the gradual accretion of new data resulting in sequential modification and extension of concepts and theories. However, revisionist historians of science over the past 20 years have promulgated a major reformulation (21). In this new view, scientific theory does not change with new data, for new data is interpreted in accord with the established theory. Only when a new theoretical model is proposed and adopted, does the data assume relevance. This has been termed the "paradigm" concept of scientific change by the philosopher of science, Thomas Kuhn (19). Kuhn demonstrates that new data that do not fit the current theoretical paradigm will be rejected. A new paradigm is not adopted primarily on the basis of new data. Rather a new paradigm is adopted on the basis of logic, persuasiveness, elegance, and utility. Ultimately, the fit between data and paradigm is always loose, and it is linked by logic and conviction.

The process of "paradigmatic change" is exemplified in the issues under consideration here. For the issue of nonabstinent drinking goals, which developed out of clinical observations, presented a new data base that did not accord with the traditional model of alcoholism. In turn, further systematic clinical observations led to clinical and laboratory experimentation, not only on nonabstinent drinking, but also to investigations of other concepts involved in the traditional model.

As a result, over the past decade a variety of challenges have been presented to the traditional paradigm. Therefore it is not possible to appropriately evaluate the current data on nonabstinent drinking goals without due consideration of the fundamental theoretical and conceptual basis for the traditional model of alcoholism. This involves an analysis of the traditional model of alcoholism, a review of data on the concepts inherent in the model, and an examination of proposals for a new paradigm of alcoholism.

2. SOURCES OF CONTROVERSY

The challenge to the traditional paradigm of alcoholism is not just based on scientific data, but upon a variety of factors that have begun to coalesce. These I shall list briefly. Many of these factors may be ultimately more important in paradigmatic change than is apparent at this time, although I shall explore in detail the portent of these sources of controversy.

Reported Social Drinking

The first source of controversy was the report of alcoholics who had returned to normal drinking. Although there are now close to 100 papers that report this type of drinking outcome, the interpretation of these observations has been rendered difficult because of lack of uniform criteria as to what constitutes an alcoholic in the population sample, and what constitutes normal, controlled, social, or moderate drinking. Such definitional problems have been the basis of the arguments to discount the relevance of the data. On the other hand, there is a broad consistency to these reports which contravene the predictions of the traditional model (7–9, 13, 20, 22, 34, 41–45, 47, 49, 65, 66, 69, 75, 78, 81, 83, 92, 108–110, 120, 123, 136, 140, 152, 163, 164, 171, 190, 191, 195, 197, 199, 204, 208, 209, 213, 215, 221, 223, 224, 241, 243, 246, 253, 254).

Training Alcoholics to Drink

A more direct test of the assumption that alcoholics cannot ever drink in a moderate fashion has been the development of experimental clinical programs that have demonstrated that alcoholics can be trained to modify their drinking (35–38, 61, 84–88, 125, 131, 160, 161, 169, 174, 179, 180, 205, 215). Although these programs do not have long-term follow-up, the fact that moderate drinking outcomes can be demonstrated supports the prior clinical observations.

The Experience of Craving

A key concept in the traditional model is the notion of craving, i.e., the alcoholic, in contradistinction to the normal drinker, acquires a "craving" for alcohol which leads the alcoholic to inexorably seek alcohol. The traditional model concept of craving is based on the commonplace clinical observation that alcoholics do report an experience of craving. However, that description is not an explanation. The traditional model, however, provides an explanation, namely, that some undefined change has occurred in the alcoholic so that a craving has been irreversibly established.

The experience of craving is amenable to direct experimental test. A variety of recent experimental studies have shown that when alcoholics are provided alcohol under different test situations, they do not always crave alcohol nor do they exhibit craving behavior to acquire alcohol (40, 56, 134, 135, 139, 151, 178–180, 230, 231). Such data do not challenge the observation that alcoholics experience craving. However, it does challenge the explanation that craving is an undefined change in the alcoholic that cannot be modified.

The Inability to Stop Drinking

While craving is related to the initiation of drinking, inability to stop is related to termination of drinking. In the traditional model, the alcoholic is said to be unable to terminate drinking. Again, this inability to terminate is said to be present in the alcoholic while not present in the nonalcoholic. Like craving, inability to stop is assumed to be an irreversible acquired trait. Again, clinical observation readily discloses that alcoholics do manifest behavior that would show an inability to stop drinking (130, 132, 142–144, 149, 168, 173, 240).

The clinical observation of return to moderate or controlled drinking, and the experimental clinical training of alcoholics to control drinking controvert the traditional model assumption of an irreversible trait. A more direct test of this concept comes from the numerous laboratory experiments in which alcoholics are provided with alcohol under various experimental contingencies. These experiments show that alcoholics do exhibit the ability to stop drinking under many different types of experimental contingencies (104, 105). Taken as a whole, the new data describe patterns of inability to stop which the traditional model dismisses. The two models also differ in their explanation. The traditional model explains inability to stop as an undefined basic change in the alcoholic. The new data explains this inability on the basis of contingency reinforcements for either continuation or termination of drinking. The traditional model asserts this inability is irreversible, while the new data suggest that inability is both modifiable and reversible.

The Loss of Control Phenomenon

The two concepts of craving and inability to stop can be subsumed, then, under a more general concept of loss of control. The traditional model assumes an essential *discontinuity* between moderate and even excessive drinkers who retain control over drinking. Whereas, at some undefined point, the drinker loses control, and at that point becomes alcoholic, that is, a person who has no control over his drinking. Thus, there is a major qualitative change in the control behavior of the alcoholic.

Although all of the new evidence accumulated in regard to the preceding concepts bear inferential significance, it does not directly test loss of control. The major experimental test of loss of control, however, comes from clinical laboratory experiments in which the behavior of the alcoholic while drinking is analyzed. These observations demonstrate that drinking behavior is neither random nor indiscriminate. Rather, the alcoholic drinks in predictable and purposeful manners (6, 15, 91, 121, 141). These data do not controvert the observation of seeming loss of control, but the explanation is different. The new data suggest that the alcoholic changes the contingencies for control of alcohol intake. The alcoholic controls his drinking, but uses different definitions of desirable drinking patterns. Further, these data suggest a continuity of drinking controls, so that the loss of control phenomenon does not represent a unique quality of the alcoholic that is irreversible, but that it is a continuum of behavioral contingencies that control all drinking behavior.

The Progression of Alcoholism

According to the traditional model, once a person has acquired the condition of alcoholism, there is an inexorable progression of the disease. This concept of progression is based upon a one-time sample conducted by Jellinek that resulted in a prototypic chart of the progressive deterioration of the alcoholic. More recent clinical studies and epidemiologic surveys reveal that certain classes of alcoholics do not demonstrate progressive deterioration and, furthermore, that alcoholics may move in and out of symptomatic alcoholism (47, 51, 52, 166, 188). These data controvert the traditional model assumption of a universal progressive deterioration in the disease of alcoholism.

Irreversibility, Arrest, and Cure

If we assume, with the traditional model, that alcoholism is a qualitative discontinuous state that is a disease, characterized by craving, inability to stop, loss of control, and progressive deterioration, then one may conclude that the process is irreversible, that the disease process can be arrested, but cannot be cured. This conclusion is based on the assumption of an irreversible disease process such as cancer. The conclusion is not tenable if based on the assumption of a reversible disease process such as tuberculosis (202, 203). The traditional model assumes an irreversible disease model. The new data suggest a reversible disease model.

New Treatment Goals and Abstinence

In the traditional model, abstinence was the primary goal of treatment and the criterion of successful treatment. Two corollaries followed: (*a*) if an alcoholic was abstinent it was assumed that rehabilitation was the consequence; (*b*) if an alcoholic was not abstinent that there was no rehabilitation. Against these assumptions, a multitude of follow-up studies have examined alcoholics from a multivariate set of outcome criteria, such as emotional adjustment, interpersonal relations, social adaptation, vocational stability, and physical health (111–113, 186, 188–190, 244, 245, 251). These follow-up studies demonstrate that abstinent alcoholics may show no rehabilitation or even deteriorate in their life adjustment despite abstinence. Conversely, nonabstinent alcoholics may show partial or total rehabilitation in terms of these other life variables. Thus, these data demonstrate the inadequacy of abstinence taken in isolation as a criterion for treatment goals or rehabilitation.

New Alcoholic Populations

The traditional model was formulated at a time when there was severe social stigma attached to alcoholism and few treatment resources. The general acceptance of the model may well be related to a good "fit" between the model and the observed behavior of the alcoholic population, as well as the context of the observations. However, in the past two decades the range of alcoholic populations has been expanded, so that we now observe alcoholics in executive positions, in industry, in schools, and churches, as well as on skid row (57, 111–113, 188, 189, 243–245). Likewise, the clinical contexts range widely from intramural programs in business and industry, to outpatient clinics, to hospitals and sanatoriums. Thus, it is not surprising that discrepant observations are now reported in which different alcoholism patterns do not follow the predictions of the traditional model (186).

New Methods

In the era of 1940–1960 the methods of treatment focused primarily on the individual. Treatment conducted within a model of individual pathology was consonant with a traditional model of alcoholism that presented a picture of individual disease. However, system-oriented treatment—starting with marital and family psychotherapy and involving social and vocational rehabilitation and the sophisticated technique of behavioral interaction/analysis and behavioral contingency modification—present clinical opportunities to observe behavior in a systems framework rather than an individualistic framework. The traditional model of alcoholism is based on an individualistic theory of behavior, whereas the new behavioral treatment is based on a human systems theory of behavior (91).

New Personnel

The field of alcoholism was long neglected in professional and scientific circles. Hence the traditional model of alcoholism was not subject to intense scrutiny in terms of either its clinical utility or its theoretical coherence (25). With the increasing influx of both clinical and experimental personnel, there is an increasing level of clinical and theoretical sophistication in the field of alcoholism. Perhaps of great significance is that many such personnel do not enter the field of alcoholism with scientific or professional commitments to the pervading ideologies of the field. Hence, these personnel are less reticent to challenge accepted methods or theories.

New Sociology of Roles

Along with the psychological emphasis on behavior as a system transaction, during the last decade sociologists have been studying the effect of social roles on behavior. In essence, role theory ascribes the behavior of the actor to the lines and plot given him by his family, community, and society. In this view, deviant behavior is not the product of the internal processes of the actor, but the product of the ascribed social role (10, 210, 211, 217, 232). Alcoholism, viewed as social deviant role behavior, is the product of social reinforcement of alcoholismic behavior. Alcoholism is not a state or disease that one acquires. Rather, alcoholism is a role behavior that is consistently reinforced. In addition, such sociological analysis applied to alcoholism has led to the conclusion that people are forced into extreme role definitions of being alcoholic which are both unnecessary and which may be destructive. According to this view, abstinence is not a biologic or psychological necessity, but it is merely a social role requirement unnecessarily maintained by the traditional model.

Social-Political-Legal Changes

Although there has been much stress on the broad social advantages that have accrued from the traditional model under the rubric of "alcoholism as disease," there has been resistance to the continuing extension of this model (114, 115). Physicians, for example, resist the concrete analogy of alcoholism as a disease of the same genre of measles, cancer, or diabetes (207). Mental health professionals resist the concept of alcoholism as a biologic state rather than a psychological development (39). Judges and lawyers resist the concept of alcoholism as determined by immutable forces which exculpate the alcoholic from legal responsibility. Politicians resist the extension of alcoholism as a disease for which the state must assume treatment, compensation, and liability responsibilities (255). These objections to the so-called disease model appear not to be against labeling alcoholism as a disease but seem to be objections to assumptions, inherent in this model, about the alcoholic. These assumptions are then used in the attempt to force social, legal, and political actions.

3. REACTIONS TO THE CONTROVERSY

Resistance to change may be seen at various levels. At the cultural level, it has been observed that American culture is strongly ambivalent about the use of alcohol. Thus the culture does not give open sanction to alcohol use, nor provide specific positive and negative sanctions for the use of alcohol. The traditional model places responsibility for alcoholism on the alcoholic and fails to define cultural responsibility for norms and mores (62, 129). Thus, cultural ambivalence continues to support the traditional model. At a social level, the same pattern of social ambivalence obtains, so that the alcoholic becomes the social scapegoat for social group guilt over drinking excesses. Sociologists have termed this the social need for the perpetuation of deviant behavior (10).

Reactions of Professionals

Surveys, such as by Cahn (25), reveal that many of the professional staff in alcoholism treatment facilities are often marginal to their professions. Alcohol programs attract those who fail to achieve better status professional positions. These professional personnel maintain and perpetuate a model of alcoholism congruent with their current styles of clinical operation. A new paradigm provides a challenge to their accustomed clinical modes of operation.

In another way, the traditional model reinforces the power and sanction of the professional. In the traditional model, the alcoholic is sick, weak, and helpless. The professional is strong, powerful, and controlling. The new paradigm shifts the power balance between the helper and the helped (232).

Reactions of Paraprofessionals

The field of treating alcoholism has long been manned by paraprofessional personnel. It is not surprising that paraprofessionals look upon the influx of scientific professional personnel with some concern. In fact, if the paraprofessionals were to desert this field, most alcohol programs would quickly cease to function. If the professional manpower left the field, however, the impact would be modest. Thus, the alcoholism treatment field is supported by paraprofessional values, attitudes, and concepts (184).

There is marked difference in the personal approach to concepts of alcoholism. The professional is trained in an analytical–objective–inductive–cognitive style. The paraprofessional usually lacks training and uses an intuitive–subjective–deductive style. Empirical data is often seen as obscure or irrelevant in contrast to their own personal experiential understanding.

In the field of alcoholism, then, we have two groups who approach a model of alcoholism from divergent points of view. The professional approaches a model on the basis of academic science, whereas the paraprofessional uses the basis of folk science. Ravetz (200) analyzes the consequences in his book on social problems of science:

> A folk science is a body of accepted knowledge whose function is not to provide the basis for further advance, but to offer comfort and reassurance to some body of believers . . . in an immature field of scientific development there is inevitable conflict which occurs when the results of disciplined scientific inquiry contradict the beliefs of a folk science, usually a popular one which is also adopted by the established cultural organs of society.

In summary, the new data emanating from academic science meet major resistance from the folk science views of the paraprofessional manpower.

Reactions of Lay and Self-Help Groups

The traditional model of alcoholism grew out of the experiences and ideology of the self-help movement in alcoholism (1). The traditional model is consonant with views of the self-help movement.

Yet what is overlooked is the fact that one characteristic of self-help groups is an antiprofessional bias. In his classic study of self-help groups, Hans Toch found a loyalty to the group concepts that had an antiprofessional bias; i.e., "either the professionals have tried and can't help us, or they are not interested in us." This bias is not necessarily detrimental. Pattison (184) has observed:

> an inherent anti-professional bias, contains a self-fulfilling prophecy of success, and the validation of its theories is ideological rather than scientific. However, these elements of a self-help group are the "social glue" that holds a self-help group together, promotes cohesion and integration, validates hope and commitment and in short makes it work.

Thus, the sources of controversy meet with ideological conflict with lay and self-help groups, not based on reactions to the data, but on the perceived challenge to the ideology.

4. DEFINITION OF THE TRADITIONAL MODEL OF ALCOHOLISM

The definition of the traditional model is by no means easy. When Jellinek published his influential monograph, *The Disease Concept of Alcoholism,* he made clear he had no intent of casting a rigid model into place, and even noted that his concepts were already being misused. Keller (106, 107) has recently pointed out the many misuses and misinterpretations that have been made of the Jellinek formulations. Keller suggests that the major source of misinterpretation was Alcoholics Anonymous, which had already formulated a theory of alcoholism, parallel to but not identical with the Jellinek formulas. Thus, it is not particularly helpful to conduct a reanalysis of Jellinek, for the traditional model is just that—an accretion of beliefs, values, and ideologies that form a model based on "conventional wisdom." However, this conventional wisdom does support the "folk science" traditional model of alcoholism. Here I shall state a series of propositions that comprise a traditional model of alcoholism, without appeal to published authority, with the caution that everyone in the field of alcoholism might not agree with this exact formulation.

Proposition 1. The alcoholic is essentially different from the nonalcoholic.

Corollary a. There are inborn genetic differences or developmental genetic differences.

Corollary b. These genetic differences lead to fundamental changes in the biochemical, endocrine, or physiologic systems of the alcoholic.

Proposition 2. Because of an organic difference, the alcoholic experiences a different reaction to alcohol than does the nonalcoholic.

Corollary a. The alcoholic develops an allergy to alcohol.

Corollary b. The allergic reaction creates untoward responses to alcohol, including a craving for alcohol, an inability to stop drinking, and a loss of control over the use of alcohol.

Proposition 3. The alcoholic has no control over these inexorable processes which is a disease process.

Corollary a. The disease process will proceed in inexorable progression to ultimate deterioration and death.

Corollary b. The disease process is irreversible.

Corollary c. The disease process can be arrested but not cured.

Proposition 4. The alcoholic is not personally responsible for his alcoholism, since the disease process is an impersonal illness with which the alcoholic is afflicted.

Corollary a. The alcoholic is relieved of social stigma for moral failure.

Corollary b. The alcoholic is relieved of personal guilt for his alcoholism.

Corollary c. The alcoholic is not to be blamed and punished for his alcoholism.

Corollary d. Society has a responsibility to rehabilitate sick members of society, including the sick alcoholic.

It is noteworthy that these propositions and corollaries are not mutually dependent. In fact, the key proposition is the fourth, which establishes a series of personal and social goals for rehabilitation. The prior three propositions justify and explain the claims of the fourth. In turn, one may achieve the personal and social goals of rehabilitation without invoking the first three propositions (186).

5. UTILITY OF THE TRADITIONAL MODEL

There are several ways in which the traditional model has proved most useful: (*a*) it removed social stigma from alcoholics; (*b*) it moved alcohol rehabilitation from blame and punishment to concern and treatment; (*c*) it provided a coherent organization to the field of alcoholism; (*d*) it established viable treatment goals; (*e*) it supported reasonable treatment methods; (*f*) it achieved general social, legal, and political support for the rehabilitation of alcoholics.

6. PROBLEMS WITH THE TRADITIONAL MODEL

Shortly we shall examine the research data that is at variance with the traditional model. However, it is also important to review the general conceptual problems involved in this model.

Reification of the Disease Concept

Robinson (206) recently published a trenchant critique of the disease concept. He points out that, in the field of alcoholism, the concept of disease has been taken in the most concrete sense, i.e., an organic disorder of the body. This literalistic usage is both unnecessary and inappropriate. The definition of disease is based on three variables: body dysfunction, personal discomfort, and social relevance. Body dysfunction may occur without labeling a person as diseased—such as wearing eyeglasses. Personal discomfort may occur without body dysfunction—such as the hypochondriac. Social relevance involves the social utility of placing a person in a sick role. All three variables optimally combine only in instances of acute trauma or manifest metabolic or infectious states.

Ultimately the labeling process of calling a state a disease is a social process, where it is both useful to the person and the society to consider a person sick and afflicted with a disease. With disorders of human behavior, our society has used the label of disease to sanction certain behavioral or life condition states as situations where the person and the society concur to consider this a disease.

Therefore, it is unnecessary to infer some organic process in order to invoke the social process of labeling alcoholism a disease. Contrariwise, the inference of an organic process in the disease concept of alcoholism has led to oversimplified rhetoric and unjustifiable assumptions that are not supportable by the available scientific knowledge. Writing from a legislative point of view, Fingarette (64) expresses similar caution: "one tempting road to reform—the building of a new constitutional doctrine on the basis of purported medical knowledge—is also a very dangerous one."

Reification of Discontinuity

A key assumption is that the alcoholic state is discontinuous with antecedent drinking states; which infers a basic discrete difference between the alcoholic and the nonalcoholic. Thus Jellinek (101) states:

> The disease concept of alcohol addiction does not apply to excessive drinking, but solely to the "loss of control" which occurs in only one group of alcoholics and then only after many years of drinking.

The conceptual problem here is that Jellinek built a case for a disease definition of alcoholism using the extreme instance of a behavioral syndrome. If one postulates a continuum of alcohol abuse, then one indeed is faced with the clinical and social dilemma of where to draw the line between accepted alcohol use and deviant alcohol use. However, the resolution of the dilemma by artificially labeling one end of the continuum alcoholic by virtue of a deus ex machina explanation seems unjustified. In similar fashion, the species of alcoholism—alpha, beta, delta, gamma, epsilon—created by Jellinek appear as heuristic devices without rational justification other than as a phenomenologic nomenclature.

In a recent critique, Edwards (50) concludes that there is no utility to the division of alcoholismic behavior into discrete and discontinuous species, but rather to view alcoholismic behavior as a continuity of multidimensional variables that produce different syndromes of drinking behavior.

Therefore, it is logically plausible to define behavioral alcoholism syndrome that vary in terms of craving, inability to stop, and loss of control. These are not due to a qualitative characteristic of alcoholics, in general, but they represent the establishment of certain relatively invariant behavior patterns which are subject to either maintenance or modification.

Reification of the Sick Role

When alcoholism is taken as a disease, in the concrete sense, then certain role expectations derived from the cultural expectancies of sick or ill behavior apply to the alcoholic (9, 217). Roman and Trice (211) point out that such a sick role assignment may result in legitimizing deviant drinking patterns for individuals labeled as alcoholics. They conclude that the disease model: "has resulted in a labelling process that may in itself set the stage for the development of true alcohol addiction." Yet, in another way, the use of the disease model may acculturate and induce people into a role definition of themselves as alcoholics, which may not necessarily be the case, and which may preclude appropriate analysis of their alcohol problem. Or it may serve as a blockade toward definition of an alcohol problem because people refuse to accept the extreme definition of alcoholic behavior that is necessary for entering the role of alcoholic (28).

Finally, the traditional model of alcoholism has a built-in set of role expectations. The rehabilitated alcoholic must behave in accord with the model definition. This, of course, precludes treatment programs and treatment goals at variance with the traditional model.

Reification of Etiology

The traditional model posits a linear model of cause and effect, that is, there is a specific defect (whether biologic, psychological, social, or cultural) which leads to a specific set of behavioral consequences that result in a specific disease—alcoholism.

The most widespread popular folk-science concept of linear etiology is the "allergy" theory, that is, certain persons have a genetic inborn trait that makes them allergic to alcohol, so that when exposed to alcohol (the allergen) they will develop alcoholismic symptoms and become alcoholic. The origin of this theory is obscure in the body of conventional wisdom. So far as I can personally determine, this folk-science theory developed out of the medical milieu of the 1930s. At that time, allergy theories were in their heyday in medicine. Physicians ascribed an allergic etiology to a wide range of common illnesses, and employed many therapies to rid the person of his allergies, such as tonsillectomies, enemas, purgatives, skin balms, and desensitization shots. So it was consonant to ascribe an allergic theory to alcoholism which fit with the medical wisdom of the day. In addition, one of the earlier friends and supporters of Alcoholics Anonymous was a Dr. Silkworth, a New York internist and allergist. From A. A. testimonials it would appear that Dr. Silkworth supported the allergic theory of alcoholism and lent medical credence and influence to the adoption of this theory.

Similar theories based on vitamin, endocrine, or genetic abnormalities posit a unitary biologic/physiologic defect common to all alcoholics. These theories are generally subsumed under the rubric of "genotropic theories." The genotropic theory has long been sharply criticized (124, 196). (*a*) No such unitary biologic/physiologic abnormalities have been demonstrated in a broad population sample of alcoholics. (*b*) Abnormalities that are identified only involve subjects who are already alcoholic. Thus, studies of metabolic variation in alcoholics do not demonstrate the preexistence of such defects before the subjects became alcoholic. (*c*) If such a theory were valid, one would predict comparable rates of presence and severity of alcoholism across social and cultural boundries. However, a critical review of the socioanthropological data reveal just the opposite, which contradicts the theory. (*d*) Even if one were to grant the presence of such factors, the genotropic theory affirms an extremely simplistic model of alcoholism. To assert that complex behavior, such as alcoholism, can be determined solely by a simple biologic/physical defect goes far beyond the available data on genetic determinants of behavior. This is not to say that biologic and physiologic variables may not play a role, but rather that even should such factors be demonstrated, they would most likely only be partial determinants. Their influence would covary with other determinants of alcoholismic behavior. (5) The clinical evidence that alcoholics can develop appropriate drinking behavior, and the experimental evidence pertinent thereto, controvert the theoretical prediction.

The fact that genotropic theories continue to enjoy popularity despite their dubious scientific validity leads us to examine other factors. The genotropic theory is used to support the contention that alcoholism is a disease. It allows the alcoholic to proclaim his dignity and reject the definition of alcoholism as an immoral condition. The theory is attractive to scientists who seek a "hard science" approach to behavioral problems.

The obverse side of the genotropic theory is the contention that all alcoholics develop unitary biologic/physiologic defects as a result of drinking. Such postdrinking changes in the body then may perpetuate and reinforce alcoholismic behavior. The experimental work of Mendelson and others (144, 149) and the theoretical formulations of Ludwig et al. (134, 135) suggest that there may be some relatively uniform biologic and physiologic patterns that do develop. Similar patterns established by drinking, in terms of conditioned psychological responses, have been postulated for alcoholism behavior as "state-dependent" learning (30, 175).

Such postdrinking changes, both biologic and psychological, may play a role in alcoholismic behavior. However, several cautious caveats must be raised. (*a*) The alcoholism-related factors have been demonstrated only with chronic severe alcoholics. There is no data to show whether such states are present or absent, or to what degree, in other drinking behavior along a continuum. (*b*) Scientists who describe these changes do not assert that these changes initiate alcoholism behavior, but rather it maintains and reinforces alcoholism behavior. (*c*) The same scientists do not assert that such changes are the only factors in alcoholism, but only one variable in a total set of variables responsible for alcoholism. Thus, this latter formulation avoids a genotropic reductionism.

The linear etiology concept has also had adherents who posit a unitary psychological, sociological, or anthropological explanation for alcoholism. However, the attempt to define and predict alcoholism on the basis of a single factor has proved fruitless, whether one uses psychological parameters (16, 27, 162, 239), sociological parameters (17, 218), or anthropological parameters (137, 138). The fact that adherents of each approach continue to propound unitary theories may reflect the linear etiology built into the traditional model.

Reification of Responsibility

Alcoholism, in common with drug addiction, homosexuality, promiscuity, and other socially deviant behavior, has undergone a change in social perception. Pattison et al. (187) and Linsky (126, 127) among others have documented the change in public images of social deviants, including alcoholics. Briefly, there has been a shift from viewing such deviancy as a reflection of personal immoral choice to a view of deviancy as a nonmoral situation resulting from biologic and social forces beyond the person's control. In other words, there has been a shift from a view of alcoholism as sinful behavior to a view of alcoholism as sick behavior.

However, many people, both lay and professional, do not accept this shift because it is incongruent with their perceptions of alcoholismic behavior. Therefore, they reject the concept of sick behavior and the sickness or disease model as presented in the traditional model.

TABLE 1 MODELS OF ILLNESS

The Sin Model of Illness	The Sickness Model of Illness
1. Person chooses behavior.	1. Person does not choose behavior.
2. Person's status reflects prior good or bad choice.	2. Person's status does not reflect choice.
3. Physical or mental malfunction reflects prior bad choice.	3. Malfunction does not reflect bad choice.
4. Person is to blame for his or her status.	4. Person is not to blame for his or her status.
5. Person should be punished for bad choice.	5. Person is not punished but helped.
6. Punishment will "heal" person by propitiation, making up, and justice.	6. Punishment will not heal person.
7. Person should be more responsible for himself or herself; he or she has been negligent.	7. Person should be less responsible for himself or herself.
8. Person has increased social responsibility.	8. Person has less social responsibility.
9. Person should help himself or herself.	9. Person cannot help himself or herself.
10. Society (others) have no responsibility to help person; it is his or her problem.	10. Society (others) have responsibility to help the person; he or she cannot do it.

The problem lies in the basic assumptions concerning the social meanings of sin and sickness (185). Table 1 summarizes the assumptions of sinful behavior and sick behavior. The crux of the transition from sin to sickness is this. If personal behavior is labeled sinful, then the person is blamed and punished. To avert blame and punishment, behavior can be labeled sickness. Now whether socially deviant behavior is labeled as sin or sickness revolves around the degree of perceived personal choice (67).

Because the alcoholic, the addict, and other people with "character disorders" do exhibit appropriate social behavior in many contexts, the public, in general, and professionals, as well, tend to ascribe a high degree of "choice" to the alcoholic. What is lacking is a thorough understanding of the basic ego qualities of the impulsive addictive character style. Shapiro (222) describes these qualities:

> The individual characterized in extreme by this style is neither accustomed to nor equipped for the general self-critical thought that is one of the essential bases for conscience . . . I refer to the impairment in these people of a subjective sense of deliberateness and intention and to the general attentuation of

> phases preparatory to action . . . moral responsibility seems to require a sense of actual responsibility, that is, intentionality, deliberateness, and choice among alternatives . . . there is an absence of a sense of having chosen to act in this particular way.

It is paradoxical, yet understandable, that the alcoholic is perceived to act with intention and choice, when he experiences within himself a lack of a sense of intention and choice. But the clinical part of this paradox is that the community, friends, relatives, and, indeed, professional treatment staff do not see this paradox. Hence, most people find it hard to accept the concept of the alcoholic as "sick," for he does not appear to be suffering from a "determined" condition but a "chosen" condition. Thus surveys of community attitudes toward alcoholics consistently demonstrate that laymen and professionals alike do not fully accept the notion that the alcoholic is "sick."

A second aspect of this problem is that although the sick model eliminates blame and punishment, it also eliminates *personal responsibility*. If one is not to blame, then one is not responsible. Obviously this is not a necessary conclusion. But it is a conclusion that determines staff behavior in many treatment settings (236). Critics of the disease model, such as Steiner (232) and Scheff (217), allege that alcoholics are responsible for their behavior and that alcoholics are not sick; treatment can only proceed effectively when the alcoholic stops playing sick and assumes responsibility for his alcoholismic behavior.

At issue here is the interpretation of the sick role. In its most concrete form, the sick role states that a person is neither blamable nor responsible. In certain acute disease states that situation obtains. But it does not obtain for chronic illness, for the recuperative stages of illness, or for conditions where the person is not socially labeled as sick despite defects. However, the fact is that the traditional model has sustained a concrete interpretation of the sick role. And in the attempt to enforce personal responsibility for alcoholics, there has been a polarized rejection of a disease model of alcoholism. What is lacking is an appreciation of varied states of personal responsibility, while avoiding a blame and punishment attribution.

A third aspect is the public response to the sin and sickness models. If a person is sinful, then the community has no responsibility, whereas if a person is sick there is a general social sanction to help rehabilitate him. Again there is polarization of responsibility. Either the alcoholic is totally responsible for himself or society is totally responsible. In neither case do we have a conceptual basis for shared responsibility (185).

What we have not devised is a third alternative to the sick model or the sin model for deviant behavior. A learning theory model with the associated behavioral analyses and behavioral training methodologies perhaps comes closest on a conceptual basis, but it is still far removed from the public conceptual domain where public policy is formulated.

This third alternative might be summarized as follows: (*a*) human behavior is both chosen and determined; (*b*) blame and punishment are not remedial; (*c*) it is irrelevant to impute blame; (*d*) the community has a responsibility to the deviant; (*e*) the deviant must be responsible for his behavior.

To sum up, the traditional model did succeed in transforming alcoholism from the sin model to the sick model. It accomplished the goal of eliminating blame and punishment, but it confused and distorted the concept of responsibility.

7. THE RELATION BETWEEN DATA AND THEORY

Data itself does not make a theory. To this point we have examined the general sets of data which are discrepant with the postulates or predictions of the traditional model of alcoholism. We then examined some of the logical problems presented by the data for which the traditional model does not provide a theoretical fit. We shall next examine several sets of data in more detail, in which each set of data often has multiple implications for a theoretical model of alcoholism.

8. DATA ON ALCOHOLICS WITH CONTROLLED DRINKING

Up to this point there has been no clear definition in the literature of what criteria and definitions shall be used to classify alcoholics who no longer abuse alcohol but do drink in some type of fashion. Various authors have used the terms *normal, controlled, stabilized, attenuated, moderate,* or *social.* Other authors merely note that alcoholics are no longer in trouble in various life areas despite some degree of drinking. Later I shall offer a proposed nomenclature. At this point, we shall note the types of observations that have been made in regard to the general phenomenon of alcoholics who drink without deleterious consequence.

Follow-up Studies

The first follow-up to specifically focus on normal drinkers was in 1962 by Davies (41). He found 7 of 93 addicts, who after a period of abstinence, had returned to a nonpathologic pattern of drinking, which he termed normal drinking. In 1966 Pattison (183) published a review of a dozen prior follow-up studies which reported the same phenomenon, ranging from 5 to 15%. Numerous other follow-up studies have been unearthed or have been published subsequently that report a cohort of controlled drinkers, as cited in the introduction. In a recent review of 261 follow-up studies of psychological treatment programs, Emrick (55) reports 40 studies that include data on controlled drinkers, who comprise 10% of the drinking outcomes. In almost all of these studies, the finding of controlled drinking was serendipitous, that is, the research did not specifically include controlled drinking as an outcome, yet that outcome was noted nonetheless. Two exceptions are the 1968 report by Pattison et al. (190) who reported 11 of the 34 alcoholics as normal drinkers; and the second is a major long-term follow-up program by Sobell and Sobell (226–228) who are following a matched group of alcoholics trained for controlled drinking versus a control group trained for abstainence. The Sobell data demonstrates that the controlled drinking group are maintaining their controlled drinking and also maintaining a much higher level of life adaptation than the control group treated by conventional psychological methods.

Random Observations

Several single case reports have been published of controlled drinking that was observed during other treatment, such as aversion conditioning, psychoanalysis, or other treatment (3, 73, 197, 223). The significance of these observations may be that alcoholics may acquire a controlled drinking pattern regardless of a specific treatment methodology.

Survey Observations of Untreated Alcoholics

In a community survey of alcoholism, Bailey and Stewart (7) found that, of 91 subjects, there were 12 who reported prior alcoholism who were now moderate drinkers. They reinterviewed them and classed six as normal drinkers and six as controlled drinkers. Kendall (108, 109) also reported a small group of social drinkers in a community survey. Others have reported on small samples of alcoholics who, without treatment, changed their patterns of alcoholism to nonpathologic drinking patterns, (199).

Controlled Drinking Groups

In a clinic in France, the goal of social drinking was defined as a specific treatment outcome. De Morsier and Feldman (45) prospectively followed 500 patients, some of whom sought abstinence, some who sought social drinking. Out of 500 patients, 72 (15%) were classed as social cures, while

155 (31%) were abstinent. They comment that the social cures were noticeably superior in their adjustment, did not want to present themselves socially as abstainers, and so learned to avoid the bad psychological effects of alcohol and now drank only in a family and social context. Similarly, Bruun (22) has reported on a self-help group in Finland, called the Polar Bears, whose goal is moderate drinking. In 1969, Davies (42) conducted a study of this group. He reports that 68% were normal drinkers with certainty and that 86% were probably normal drinkers. He found only 3% with drinking problems. In another study, Gerard, Saenger, and Wile (76) found that one-third of the patients became social controlled drinkers in an outpatient clinic in the United States, where controlled drinking was an acceptable treatment outcome. (75)

Treatment Programs for Controlled Drinking

The advent of rehabilitation programs, based on the principles of behavioral analysis and broad-spectrum behavioral retraining, have defined controlled drinking as their goal. There are several reports in the literature of short-term follow-up, in which the majority of the alcoholics in these programs do maintain controlled drinking (35–38, 61, 84–88, 125, 131, 160, 169, 174, 179, 180, 205, 215). Long-term follow-up data is not yet available, except for the Sobell studies. The major conceptual problem here is the definition of what constitutes controlled drinking, which has varied with each of the research programs. Yet they do offer at least preliminary data that alcoholics can be trained to participate in controlled drinking.

Data Limitations

In summary, these several types of clinical data offer a substantial body of about 100 published papers, indicating that with or without treatment, and under various treatment conditions, some proportion of alcoholics do change their drinking behavior from a pathologic alcoholismic pattern to some type of nonpathological drinking.

Although this is a rather impressive body of data, it does not provide a sound data base per se for a reformulation of a theory of alcoholism.

1. The reports do not systematically define the population of alcoholics under observation. Critics who allege that the alcoholics who become controlled drinkers were not "true" alcoholics or were "pseudoalcoholics" engage in specious and tautological reasoning. This line of argument merely says that, if people meet all the criteria of an alcoholic, but do not meet the theoretical prediction, they must not be alcoholic. It is just as plausible to argue that the theoretical prediction is wrong. In general, the clinical

reports cited above do not give a precise definition of the alcoholic—but such precise definitions are already lacking in all the alcoholism literature. It is a fair generalization, however, that the reports do describe the controlled drinkers as previously chronic severe alcoholics that would generally fit the "gamma" type of Anglo-Saxon alcoholic described by Jellinek.

2. The definition of a controlled drinker is neither uniform, nor precise. Therefore, it is not possible to state precisely what types of changes in alcoholismic drinking has occured.

3. Because the reports come from widely different contexts and treatment settings, one cannot draw any firm conclusions as to what types of alcoholismic patterns may predispose to a controlled drinking outcome, to what degree controlled drinking is a reasonable outcome with which populations, or which treatment methodologies might be most efficacious.

Miller et al. (159) have reviewed the deficiencies in most evaluation methodologies for assessment of alcoholism treatment. These confounding variables are: (*a*) the definition of alcoholism used by a program; (*b*) the precise specification of the population enrolled; (*c*) the reputation of the program, (*d*) refusal of referral, (*e*) rejection of applicants, (*f*) failure to report after acceptance, (*g*) exclusions from study protocol, (*h*) dropouts, (*i*) partial participation in treatment regimen, (*j*) deaths, (*k*) untraceables, (*l*) uncooperative with follow-up.

To these factors we may add some very specific factors in assessing controlled drinking: (*a*) the investigator may not include this type of outcome and hence not gather the appropriate data; (*b*) the study protocol may be constructed to not count such an outcome because of investigator bias; (*c*) subjects may distort their responses in order to meet the expectational set that controlled drinking is not feasible, hence not reportable; (*d*) controlled drinking subjects may avoid participation in studies to avoid anticipated skepticism, criticism, or attempts to enroll them again in treatment.

A modest generalization can be made however. The dictum that an alcoholic can never drink again is controverted by the above data. Further, we may infer that alcoholismic drinking behavior is reversible, and that an alcoholic cannot just arrest his drinking, but can be cured of his alcoholismic drinking behavior.

9. DATA ON CRAVING FOR ALCOHOL

Behavioral Observation

The first major experimental research on craving behavior came out of the laboratory work of Mendelson and Mello (144–150), during the 1960s. Mello (144) summarized their work recently with the conclusion that the construct of a symbolic craving for alcohol had little clinical or scientific utility. She argued that the concept of craving was a logical tautology in that it merely states that a behavior is craving because craving is by definition that behavior. Thus, craving has no explanatory power. Mello based her conclusions on the following evidence:

1. No alcoholic subjects allowed to freely program their ethanol intake showed loss of control or drank to oblivion.
2. No alcoholic subjects drank all alcohol available, even when freely offered.
3. Alcoholics allowed to drink 30–60 days continuously often started and stopped during this experimental period.
4. Amount of alcohol consumed by alcoholics was shown to be a function of amount of work or effort required to obtain alcohol.
5. With sufficient money or other social rewards, alcoholics will abstain even though alcohol is freely available.
6. Alcoholics demonstrate the ability to taper their drinking to avoid severe consequences of abrupt withdrawal.
7. Alcoholics display social drinking and periods of abstinence during the course of a drinking career.
8. Priming doses of alcohol do not lead to increased reported craving.

Disguised Experiments

In addition to this early work, which discounted craving, several recent studies by Engle and Williams (56), Merry (151), Marlatt et al. (139), Cutter et al. (40), Ludwig et al. (132–135), and Paredes et al. (178–180) have provided alcoholics with alcohol under disguised forms, with placebos, and at different alcohol strengths. These studies demonstrate that single or even multiple doses of alcohol do not in themselves precipitate craving feelings in the alcoholic or craving responses.

Traditional Explanations

Some people conclude that such studies clearly eliminate the concept of craving. However such studies do not demonstrate the craving does not exist. Rather they demonstrate that the traditional model of craving is incorrect. The traditional model states that craving "makes" the alcoholic drink, and that once he takes one drink he will inexorably continue drinking. Thus the dictum that the alcoholic is "one drink away from a drunk."

Jellinek (101) defined craving as part of the loss of control phenomenon:

> Loss of control means that as soon as a small quantity of alcohol enters the organism a demand for more alcohol is set up which is felt as a physical demand by the drinker, but could possibly be a conversion reaction.

It is noteworthy that Jellinek here defines craving as a cognitive–emotional experience. He equivocates as to whether it is a biologic or psychological phenomenon.

In the traditional folk-science model of alcoholism craving is the manifestation of "cell hunger" when cells are deprived of alcohol. This is metaphysical speculation at best.

Craving as Experience

Shall we discount craving altogether then? We cannot do so, without taking into account other relevant data. To begin with, alcoholics do report an experience of craving, even when sober, as in the "dry drunk" syndrome (66, 253). Reports by Sobell (230), Hore (96), and Litman (128) all describe craving responses in alcoholics. However, an analysis of the responses reveal that craving is described in *emotional terms*, such as depression, anxiety, tenseness, fear, worry, etc. It is not surprising that the alcoholic *interprets* these feelings as physical states. At issue is the fact that feelings are experiences. Feelings are not thoughts. A feeling state is a bodily experience. You do not experience love or hate in the center of your brain. You experience the feeling of hate or love in bodily terms, and there are biophysiologic concomitants to feeling states. The more intense the feeling, the more intense the bodily experience. Ludwig and Wikler (135) state the issue clearly:

> Alcoholics . . . may express the same feeling state in a variety of ways. Some translate their experience into socially desirable terms (e.g. I want to drink to be sociable), some will psychologize (e.g. I want to drink to relieve my tension or depression), some will translate their desire into a compulsion (i.e. I just need a drink), some will deny their feelings (i.e. I don't want a drink), some will distort their feelings (e.g. I took a drink because it was available), and others may be unable to find any appropriate reason for their behavior (e.g. I don't know why I drank—I just drank.)

A Conditioning Paradigm

In two very perceptive articles, Ludwig has reformulated the concept of craving to take into account the craving experimental data, as well as relevant data on the addiction process from other drug research. I shall state the Ludwig (135) formulation since it is so explicit:

> craving for alcohol (during periods of no physical dependence), similar to "narcotic hunger," represents the cognitive-symbolic correlate of a subclinical conditioned withdrawal syndrome that can be produced by appropriate interoceptive and exteroceptive stimuli.

Let us consider exteroceptive stimuli. In the craving experiments cited above, alcoholics experienced more craving when they were told they were given alcohol, when the dose of alcohol was higher, when there were associated cues for drinking, such as friends, environment, stress, etc. It is suggested that the alcoholic has become conditioned to these external symbols that convey the message that the alcoholic should drink. The various studies on drinking situations strongly support the postulate that craving experience is related to the ambient social environment that provides the symbolic triggering cues that initiate a psychological response which is experienced as a craving (29, 175).

The major contribution of the Ludwig group, however, is the elucidation of the interoceptive cues, that likewise trigger a cognitive-symbolic response. Contrary to prior belief that the visceral organs had no psychic representation, Miller (153) has shown that operant conditioning of visceral organs can be accomplished. Further work on clinical syndromes, such as on obesity by Stunkard (237) has shown that a person may pursue conditioned behavior such as eating without regard to hunger or satiety. The obese person responds to lack of food as an internal conditioned response, which itself becomes a conditioned stimuli for food craving response. In similar fashion, Ludwig has shown how the alcoholic acquires internal biophysiologic conditioned responses to alcohol acquisition. The absence of alcohol in the internal visceral systems then become conditioned stimuli which produce an internal sense of craving.

Vulnerability Due to Multiple Cue Response

Ludwig, however, overlooks an interesting paradox, namely, that, although the alcoholic experiences craving in response to external and internal cues which are conditioned stimuli, the alcoholic is also more vulnerable to such cues because the alcoholic does not utilize good cue discrimination. What I have in mind is similar to the phenomenon of obesity. The obese person does not eat at the cue of hunger and stop eating at the cue of satiety. Rather, the obese person eats in response to multiple symbolic cues, both external and internal, regardless of hunger per se. Studies on alcoholic drinking perceptions reveal similar symbolic cue responses (95, 225, 228).

In his review of state-dependent learning, Overton (175) presents evidence that the alcoholic learns behavior in an alcoholic state, but cannot transfer that learning to a sober state. Thus, the initiation of drinking evokes a set of learning responses not contingent on sober internal and external cues. But further, there is evidence that alcoholics do not discriminate accurately. That is, their ego discriminative functions are much like a young child. The young child does not discriminate accurately between anger, frustration, irritation, and pain as internal cue states. While the young child entering a strange room may notice only the familiar face of the parent and fail to perceptually peruse the rest of the room. For example, studies on internal-external locus of control in alcoholics shows that alcoholics tend to have a high external locus of control, that is, feel that events control them instead of controlling events, (46, 122, 176, 177). Studies on cognitive style of alcoholics using the field dependence methods of Witkin, show that alcoholics are generally field dependent reflecting an immature level of cognitive development (103, 214, 238). Other studies infer that alcoholics are less able to discriminate blood levels of alcohol, that is, they are less aware of alcohol intake than normals (19, 248). Similarly, the work of the Sobells and others show that alcoholics are less aware of differences in drinks, of how fast they are drinking, how large a sip they take, etc., (216, 219, 225, 229), and alcoholics are not able to define their emotional states as clearly as normals (96, 194, 242).

To conclude, the data do not substantiate the "one drink then drunk" postulate. However, craving is an experience of the alcoholic. The data support the interpretation of craving as a cognitive-emotional experience that is the product of response to both internal and external symbolic cues that convey an alerting signal to the alcoholic that he is in danger and should seek protective relief through alcohol. Thus, the alcoholic may indeed trigger off an alcoholic binge after he takes one drink. At issue is the explanation of the phenomenon and its occurrence and nonoccurrence.

10. DATA ON LOSS OF CONTROL

Repeated reference has been already made to the various studies on loss of control. There are several sets of observations that bear directly on loss of control.

Control Drinking among Alcoholics

This data has been summarized above, save to indicate that alcoholics who have lost control, have with or without treatment gained control of their drinking.

Behavioral Analysis of Alcoholic Drinking

The major set of observations under this category come from the work of Mello and Mendelson and their colleagues. Their observations have been outlined above. In addition, other research projects have described how alcoholismic drinking is a response to group variables that sustain or restrain drinking behavior (2, 82, 89, 157, 240, 256). Some studies demonstrate the influence of social status factors, or family interactions (23, 165, 218, 233–235). In brief, these studies show that alcoholismic drinking is not random, purposeless, or uncontrolled. Rather such drinking is clearly conditioned by a complex set of social and psychological interaction variables (130, 132, 142–144, 149, 168, 173, 240, 252).

Observations from Behavioral Training Programs

Perhaps the largest set of observations come from researchers who have established experimental training programs to teach alcoholics controlled drinking. The prior studies analyzed alcoholics in varied drinking contexts or manipulated the drinking opportunities or work requirements. This might be termed naturalistic variation of drinking. However, the training programs do not stop at just that, but have attempted to use a variety of experimental techniques to achieve controlled drinking with the alcoholic subjects (14). Three types of observations have been made: (*a*) that in such treatment programs one can define variables that influence the alcoholic's control of his drinking; (*b*) that one can experimentally manipulate the variable so that the alcoholic will measurably increase his control; (*c*) that the alcoholic can acquire control over his drinking under these conditions and will continue to utilize such control after discharge (173, 174).

Variables of Control

The basic theoretical foundation for the above observations and experiments with control modification is learning theory. A variety of recent reviews have set out the animal and laboratory foundations for such clinical experimentation (29, 77). In essence, drinking behavior is viewed as a multidimensional behavior based upon environmental conditioning (104, 105).

The earliest clinical experiments were unidimensional, based upon simple avoidance conditioning. Thus, the first era of behavioral modification was simply some type of aversive conditioning (4, 5, 13, 30, 33, 70, 71, 98, 116, 117, 156, 201).

More recent theoretical experimental and clinical work has been termed "broad-spectrum" conditioning (15, 32, 59, 60, 74, 91, 94, 103, 104, 121, 141, 142, 154, 155, 192, 198, 205). In a recent review, Hamburg (91) questions whether simple aversion conditioning even has a place in his modern repertoire. In broad-spectrum conditioning, there is an analysis of cognitive functioning, emotional response, drinking behavior per se, and social and family interaction (6, 15, 121, 141). This approach combines the clinical and theoretical methods of both learning theory and psychodynamic theory into a broad based intervention program utilizing both operant conditioning techniques and more conventional psychological interventions (32, 60, 99, 121). The intent of such programs is (*a*) to define the internal and external cues that initiate and perpetuate drinking; (*b*) to specify to the alcoholic the cues and responsive behavior; (*c*) to interject specific modifiers of the cues and the responses. The specific methodologies are beyond the scope of this chapter. However it should be emphasized that such programs assert that through a careful analysis of alcoholismic drinking behavior, one can provide appropriate modification interventions that result in a modification of drinking to a controlled pattern.

Explanation of Loss of Control

The phenomenon of loss of control, like craving, is an observable event. Keller has pointed out that any experienced clinician can observe many occasions when the alcoholic drinks in a controlled fashion. So it is not necessarily striking to read reports of alcoholics engaging in controlled drinking. Keller (106) restates the loss of control hypothesis rather neatly:

> He (the alcoholic) has become disabled from choosing invariably whether he will drink. That is the essential loss of control over drinking.

However, Keller does not give up the traditional model of alcoholism which posits that loss of control is a qualitative, and perhaps irreversible attribute of the alleged "alcoholic." Serial quotes from the same Keller article will illustrate the conceptual impasse:

> there is no room for an alcoholism without loss of control. Without loss of control there is only a prealcoholismic phase . . . Is drug addiction a disease? I assume that it is. And if we are talking about alcohol addiction, and if, being an addiction, it is a disease, I find it unbelievable that the alcohol addict can indeed control whether he will drink on any given occasion.

Thus we see that loss of control is conceptualized in terms of supporting a theoretical model which posits the presence of a "disease" which produces an "alcoholic" who is qualitatively different, and irreversibly so from the nonalcoholic. For Keller, as for Jellinek, there is a wide conceptual gap between drinkers and alcoholics.

Just following the above quotes, Keller recognizes the importance of the data under discussion for he states:

> But the fact that he sometimes can choose not to drink, or that he sometimes can drink moderately, does not alter the fact that he is an alcohol addict; that

> has the disease we can conveniently call alcoholism. If and when a critical cue or signal impinges, he will drink and, given that he is not prevented by external circumstances, such as unavailability of enough alcohol, he will get drunk.

This passage is critical, for it recognizes that control of drinking is related to cues and signals. What Keller does not accept is that the alcoholic can be retrained to recognize the cues and signals, and develop a different response reportoire to those cues and signals. He accepts the theory, rejects its practicality.

The problem can be put simply. Loss of control has been postulated in the traditional model as discontinuous, that is, the prealcoholic is losing control but still retains critical control. Then at some mysterious point, the prealcoholic crosses an invisible line and loses control and has become an alcoholic who has the disease alcoholism. In contrast, the controlled drinking experiments suggest a model of continuity. As a person engages in repetitive drinking he acquires a larger repertoire of internal and external conditioned stimuli that evoke a more consistent pattern of alcoholismic drinking. Thus, there is no such "thing" as an alcoholic. There are degrees of severity of conditioned alcoholismic drinking patterns. Therefore, loss of control is a relative phenomenon. Loss of control is not mysterious, but is related to the particular complex of drinking versus nondrinking reinforcements in action at any given point in time. Thus loss of control covaries with the reinforcement contingencies.

Abstinence and Control

A commonplace observation made by rehabilitated alcoholics is that they can never take a drink—that they are still alcoholic. From a learning theory perspective, this is true. The abstinent alcoholic cannot control drinking, so maintains total control of abstinence. The abstinent alcoholic is indeed vulnerable to alcohol, and, as Keller observed, the abstinent alcoholic might with impunity take one drink, but he *does not know* what might happen. The abstinent alcoholic has learned nothing about the internal and external cues to his drinking behavior, so he is just as vulnerable to alcohol after 20 years of sobriety as he was as a drinking drunk. As alcoholics sometimes say, he is indeed a dry drunk. An analogy may illustrate. Imagine an adolescent who tries to drive a car and smashes it into a tree. He sees the damage wrought by trying to drive so he vows never to drive again. After 20 years of nondriving, he is still afraid to drive a car—and, with good reason, because he has taken no driving lessons, and knows no more about driving than when he was an adolescent. Even so, the abstinent alcoholic has acquired no skill in drinking. The abstinent alcoholic retains a loss of control over alcohol. The only avenue open to him is to avoid the situation (alcohol) over which he has no control.

11. DATA ON PROGRESSION

The concept of inexorable progression of alcoholism is based again on the work of Jellinek. His paper on the phases of alcoholism proved to be immensely influential in the formulation of a disease theory (102). In brief, Jellinek proposed that the drinker began to develop prodromal symptoms that led to a prealcoholismic phase, and then if the alcoholic passed that invisible line he became alcoholic.

The data was a self-report questionnaire that Jellinek sent out to successful Alcoholics Anonymous members, which was distributed by the A.A. Grapevine, an in-house newsletter. The questionnaire was an open-ended instrument, from which Jellinek extracted material for a secondary statistical analysis which produced the phases of symptoms Jellinek extrapolated into a proposed progression.

The Jellinek Data Base

The initial data base is open to serious methodological question. It was a self-report. The data was open-ended. The distribution was not random. The sample was biased in that it involved alcoholics who were self-identified as successful A. A. members, and who were willing to return a questionnaire. And finally, as Seiden (220) points out, A. A. members are atypical of the general population of alcoholics (53), while the sample itself had only 98 respondents.

Data Reanalysis

A second serious problem is with the Jellinek analysis of the data. A recent sophisticated statistical analysis of the Jellinek data published by Park fails to support the original sequence or weighting of symptoms proposed by Jellinek. Park concludes that the data does not support the phase and progression thesis (181).

Data on Nonprogression

Of more recent and direct import are reports by Drew (47) and by Pattison (188) of alcoholics who never show progressive deterioration, and finally, community epidemology surveys by Cahalan (24), Edwards (51, 52), and Mulford (166) reveal nonprogressive patterns of alcohol abuse. Cahalan, in particular, reported that 15% of his community sample of alcoholics moved in and out of symptomatic alcoholism.

This data is consistent with the loss of control data in that this naturalistic data supports the notion that control over alcoholismic drinking patterns varies over time. When controls diminish, a person may exhibit symptoms, whereas when controls are increased, the person may become asymptomatic. These observations suggest that much alcoholismic drinking may be more cyclic, rather than progressive, in pattern.

12. DATA ON THE UNIFORMITY OF ALCOHOLICS

There has long been a search for the alcoholic personality. The traditional model posits that there is a disease state of alcoholism. Thus, one would expect to find some congruence of variables associated with the disease state of alcoholism. Yet just the opposite is found. Keller (107) has recently summarized the many published studies, modestly proclaimed as "Keller's Law": "The investigation of any trait in alcoholics will show that they have either more or less of it. . . . Alcoholics are different in so many ways that it makes no difference."

One would assume that such a nihilistic conclusion would controvert the traditional prediction of a specific alcoholic syndrome. Yet, conventional wisdom has held that such evidence just proves that one drunk is just like another drunk, and that they all have in common the same drunk problem; so, in the end, this confirms the theoretical prediction that there *is* such a thing as an alcoholic.

Against this viewpoint are studies that do define specific alcoholism subpopulations. These studies show that groups of alcoholics can be clustered according to variables such as definitions of alcoholism, attitudes, role ascriptions, treatment goals, and degrees of dysfunction in different areas of life such as social, vocational, interpersonal, emotional, and physical adjustment (100). Whereas the severity of drinking may be identical, the degree of dysfunction among these "alcoholics" varies widely from the "high-bottom" alcoholic with little life dysfunction to the "low-bottom" alcoholic who has never had much competence in life in any area. The work by Trice (244, 245) and by Kissin et al. (111–113) have shown that meaningful differences in sociopsychological variables can be demonstrated in terms of response to different treatment modalities. Pattison et al. (186, 188, 189) have demonstrated that different alcoholism populations have distinctly different characteristics. That work has been replicated in independent studies by Tomsovic (243) and by English and Curtin (57).

Thus, all alcoholics are not the same, nor does just the definition of a person as alcoholic predict treatment response or the pattern of alcoholism. Rather, this data suggests that there are discriminable patterns of alcoholismic drinking. In fact, to assert that a person is an alcoholic who has a disease obscures clinically meaningful differences. Furthermore, these studies suggest that, for some alcoholic populations, nonabstinent drinking goals may be feasible and appropriate, whereas abstinence may be the appropriate drinking goal in other populations.

13. CRITICISMS OF NONABSTINENT DRINKING GOALS

The following criticisms are often voiced in the discussion of nonabstinent drinking goals: (*a*) that controlled drinkers are not true alcoholics; (*b*) that controlled drinkers are pseudoalcoholics; (*c*) that personal experience is more important than scientific experiments and personal experience demonstrates that alcoholics cannot drink; (*d*) that if an alcoholic has a slip or binge he is just an alcoholic and has no control; (*e*) that the discussion of controlled drinking will encourage alcoholics to avoid treatment and engage in dangerous attempts to continue drinking; (*f*) that nonabstinent goals undercuts the hard-fought battle to obtain social recognition of alcoholism as a disease; (*g*) that nonabstinent goals will undermine the morale and effort of Alcoholics Anonymous. Overall it must be noted that such criticism appears to be based on fear, concern, and anxiety. It is understandable that such alarms be raised. However, the issue is whether the traditional model is adequate for the present data, or whether a new model is required which is not only scientifically credible, but which may also be of value to the field of alcoholism.

14. DISADVANTAGES OF THE ABSTINENCE CRITERION

Although problems with the abstinence criterion have been noted for some time, there has been no clear formulation of the problems. The following list summarizes the questions that have been raised: (*a*) abstinence sets up a rehabilitation goal that may be difficult or impossible for many alcoholics to attain; (*b*) abstinence may be an inappropriate goal for patients with moderate or minimal degrees of alcoholism problems; (*c*) the requirement of abstinence may lead alcoholics to avoid treatment or refuse treatment, or fail to participate fully in treatment; (*d*) abstinence may be an inferior goal for treatment than a nonabstinent goal; (*e*) a requirement of abstinence often leads to punishment or rejection of the alcoholic who is not abstinent; (*f*) the goal of abstinence per se often obscures the real improvement that an alcoholic can attain in modifying his drinking behavior, (*g*) the goal of abstinence does not focus on meaning, values, and cues that produce alcoholismic behavior and therefore leaves the abstinent alcoholic vulnerable to alcohol; (*h*) the abstinent alcoholic may experience continuing dysfunctional anxiety about his vulnerability to alcohol; (*i*) the goal of abstinence obscures other treatment goals that are critical to recovery such as social, emotional, vocational, and interpersonal rehabilitation; (*j*) the goal of abstinence places all the responsibility on the alcoholic, while condemning him if he fails, (*k*) the goal of abstinence does not help the alcoholic work at other goals beyond abstinence per se, it may short-circuit rehabilitation; (*l*) the requirement of abstinence obstructs the development of other treatment methods and goals that are nonabstinent.

15. TOWARD A REVISED MODEL OF ALCOHOLISM

Although it is premature to propose a formal revised model of alcoholism, the concepts and data reviewed here lead to some tentative proposals. A revised model might have the following characteristics.

1. Alcoholism is a behavioral syndrome characterized by various degrees of use of alcohol that lead to varying degrees of physical, personal, and social harm.
2. Vulnerability to the abuse of alcohol may be defined in terms of a system matrix of variables including biologic, psychological, social, and cultural variables, no one of which in itself produces alcoholismic behavior.
3. The development of abusive patterns of alcohol use may occur along physical, psychological, or social dimensions or combinations thereof.
4. Alcoholism syndromes vary along a continuum, from nonpathologic to severely pathologic.
5. Increasing severity of alcoholismic behavior is generated through both internal and external conditioning processes that lead to the establishment of internal and external conditioned stimuli that perpetuate and extend the behavior.
6. Drinking behavior in a given person is variably plastic. In some persons, such behavior may remain relatively immutable. Yet for others, their drinking behavior may be modified or reversed through naturalistic processes or through treatment processes.
7. Dependent upon the individual alcoholic, it may or may not be

appropriate in different phases or contexts for an alcoholic to assume a sick role, or some modification thereof.

8. As a general social position, it is appropriate to consider alcoholism as a disease, although the social implications will vary with special social requirements.

16. OPERATIONAL DEFINITION OF DRINKING GOALS

For many years only one drinking goal was considered—total abstinence. Although Emrick (55) points out in his massive review of follow-up studies that other variables and other drinking outcomes have been considered, he fails to recognize the conceptual gap between the researcher and the practitioner. For although scientific research personnel have recognized and utilized many of the concepts and data presented in this chapter, the same cannot be said for the professional and paraprofessional personnel who conduct treatment, formulate policy, and command the tenor of conventional wisdom in the field of alcoholism. Thus the abstinence criterion has had a "halo effect" that at the operational level of alcoholism programs had confounded the development of more rigorous and specific treatment and evaluation concepts.

If we consider rehabilitation in terms of total "life health," then we may consider subsets of rehabilitation outcome in terms of the following: (*a*) drinking health; (*b*) emotional health; (*c*) vocational health; (*d*) interpersonal health, (*e*) physical health.

Now it is important to note that not all alcoholics are impaired in each area of life health, nor do all alcoholics require rehabilitation in each area of life health. Neither does impairment in one area necessarily bear a high correlation with impairment in other areas.

If we consider rehabilitation in terms of specific areas of life health, then we can define the specific areas of impairment for a specific population, we can define the probability for improvement in an area of impairment for a specific population, and we can define specific rehabilitation methods that address the specific impairment. In a series of comparative studies, Pattison et al. (186, 188–190) and others (31, 45, 46, 55, 88, 97, 111–113, 244, 245, 251) have shown that such discriminations can be made in clinically relevant terms.

The use of the total abstinence criterion implies that if the alcoholic achieves abstinence he will also demonstrate improvement in the other four areas of life health. However empirical data do not support this assumption. Pattison et al. (186, 188–190) presented empirical and clinical data to illustrate that abstinent alcoholics often did not exhibit improvement in these other areas of life health, and, in fact, some abstinent alcoholics showed *deterioration* in these other four areas. Similar instances of life deterioration as a concomitant of abstinence have been reported by Rossi et al. (213), Wilby and Jones (252), and Flaherty et al. (66). The most illuminating study has been that by Gerard et al. (76). In their evaluation of a group of totally abstinent "successes" they found 43% overtly disturbed, 24% inconspicuously inadequate, 12% "A.A. addict" successes, and only 10% independent successes. Thus abstinence does *not* necessarily indicate *rehabilitation*.

Case Study

This 56-year-old white salesman had been a compulsive drinker since age 18. He had asthma and stuttered. He was plagued with guilt feelings and inability to express himself in social situations. He was in treatment for five years. He had been abstinent for two years, yet he continually feared a relapse. He felt psychotherapy helped him understand his conflicts, but he ascribed his sobriety to intensive participation in A. A. Although he enjoyed his sobriety, he had multiple neurotic complaints that interfered with social function, so that he stayed mostly at home where his wife sheltered him. He could not work effectively because of his inhibitions, and he was so dependent upon his wife, that he could not assume any assertive role with her. Any anxiety or frustration would precipitate psychosomatic symptoms.

In this case we see a man who is abstinent but who has major dysfunctions in the emotional area, vocational area, interpersonal area, and physical area.

On the other side of the abstinence coin, it has been assumed that alcoholics who did drink were not successfully treated. This assumption was not examined in most of the earlier evaluation studies which did not examine other life health areas. It was merely assumed that, if an alcoholic was not abstinent, he was not rehabilitated. The reports on normal drinking, beginning with Davies (41) in 1962, have shown that alcoholics do develop the capacity to change their drinking patterns and attain a successful life adjustment.

In summary, the use of total abstinence as the outcome criterion of alcoholism treatment is misleading. It may be associated with improvement, no change, or deterioration in other critical areas of total life health.

The focus on abstinence tends to obscure attention that needs to be given to treatment methods aimed at rehabilitation in other areas of life health, and abstinence may neither be a necessary nor desirable goal in terms of a drinking outcome.

Therefore, we shall turn to consideration of several subsets of the drinking variable that can be considered.

The Abstinence Subset

Although we have challenged the use of abstinence as the sole or primary criterion for evaluation of treatment outcome, abstinence may be a feasible outcome goal (245). However, two caveats must be made: (*a*) abstinence should only be considered as a subset goal for the drinking variable, and not be used as an inferential indication of change in any of the other areas of life health; (*b*) abstinence is only one of several possible subsets in drinking variable outcome. There is no logical justification for assuming that abstinence is a more desirable or superior drinking outcome than any other drinking outcome per se. Rather, it may be more appropriate to determine the circumstances under which abstinence is the necessary or desirable drinking outcome, and the circumstances where it may be a less desirable outcome or where it may be desirable but not achievable. In the latter case, one would accept a different drinking outcome as an acceptable and successful drinking outcome.

The Social Drinking Subset

"Social drinking" is a vague and ambiguous term, for it merely states that one drinks among other people. It does not specify the meaning, function, amount, or result of drinking. Hayman (93) calls this "the myth of social drinking," for the rubric of social drinking may only obscure, justify, and rationalize many dysfunctional, dyssocial, and psychopathological forms of alcoholismic drinking in social settings. This does not seem to be an appropriate nor useful concept. Therefore, I suggest we discard the term "social drinking."

The Attenuated Drinking Subset

Recognition that continued drinking might not indicate a poor rehabilitation has occasioned research that differentiates between the drinking variable and other life health variables.

One of the best studies, from a methodological point of view, was conducted by Ludwig et al. (133). They found that, although 80–90% of patients returned to their previous patterns of pathological drinking, there was sustained improvement in all other areas of life health. They conclude: "return to drink need not be automatically equated with return to all the maladaptive behavior which led to mental hospitalization in the first place . . . most patients are able to carry on most of their other social tasks at least at a higher level than that noted on hospital admission."

Other recent studies support the concept that following treatment the alcoholic may show no change in his drinking pattern or only modest improvement, and yet profit from treatment as evidenced by better adjustment in the other four areas of life health. For example, Mayer and Myerson (140) report on alcoholics who achieved stability and drank less, even though still experiencing episodes of insobriety. Gillis and Keet (78) report that 58% of their sample showed significant improvement in life adjustment although still drinking. At the same time the *extent* of pathologic drinking was reduced from 70% of drinking episodes to 20% of drinking episodes. In this same sample some 47% had improved drinking without deterioration, while 23% improved in drinking but showed some deterioration of overall function. Fitzgerald et al. (65) found that of their alcoholic sample, 22% with good adjustment were abstinent, 19% with good adjustment were drinking, while 18% with poor adjustment were drinking. Kish and Hermann (110) report 22% of improved alcoholics were abstinent, while 26% of improved alcoholics were occasionally or regularly engaged in alcoholismic drinking. In a recent review, Belasco (11) sums up the issue quite simply: behavioral and social adjustment does not have a high correlation with indices of drinking.

In these studies, there is suggestive evidence that some moderation in the amount of alcohol taken, the frequency of drinking, the degree of intoxication, all measures of increased control, do have a correlation with improvement in other areas of life health. We do not know which particular measures or modification of pathologic drinking may be more significant for overall adaptation. But the evidence is beginning to accumulate that continued pathologic drinking may not be a dire indicant of treatment failure. Further, the goal of modification or attenuation of the *degree* of pathologic drinking may be an acceptable goal in conjunction with improvement in other areas of life health. It may not be an ideal goal, but it may suffice to return an alcoholic to a degree of successful life function. On the other hand, if we ignore these facts, we may fail to help an alcoholic achieve at least some degree of improvement or fail to help him see and utilize the real gains he may have made in several areas. And finally, it may avert our attention from the fact that successful treatment does not have to be black or white. Degrees of improvement are realistic goals.

Another aspect of attenuated drinking as a goal is reflected in recent research on the progression of alcoholism, which has been discussed above. Surveys of nontreated alcoholics in the community indicate that "progression" is by no means uniform or inexorable. In fact, alcoholics vary over time in the degree of severity of alcoholism, and may even "move in and out" of symptomatic alcoholism.

Thus, it is possible to set as a treatment goal the modification of the severity of the drinking pattern, so that the alcoholic continues to drink in an alcoholic fashion, but in an attenuated fashion. The result may be a shift from an incapacitating alcoholic state to a pattern of successful adaptation despite ongoing alcoholismic drinking.

In summary, the subset of attenuated drinking defines a drinking goal in which pathologic drinking is not eliminated but is attenuated.

Case Study

This 46-year-old single male lives with his widowed mother. For five years his drinking increased until he had no control over his drinking intensity. He drank daily usually to intoxication, often until he passed out. His job as a warehouseman was in jeopardy. He was fed up with his drinking, while his mother urged he seek treatment. He had several interviews at an Alcoholism Information Center, but he refused any further treatment. His drinking subsequently subsided. He stated that the few interviews were enough for him to see his problems and alter his behavior. Now four years later he drinks only on specific occasions, usually alone. He will usually drink to intoxication on those occasions, but he does not pass out any more. He is no longer absent from work and has no problems in job performance.

The Controlled Drinking Subset

The development of behavior modification programs for alcoholics has stimulated attention in regard to a drinking goal that is defined, not by attenuation, but by the establishment of control over the drinking situation, the frequency of drinking, or the amount of alcohol drunk. This does not mean that the meaning or functional use of alcohol has necessarily been changed, but rather that the alcoholic is able to control his drinking within limits that are not dysfunctional. Davies (42) has recently described this pattern as "stabilized" drinking.

Various behavioral modification protocols attempt to produce behavioral control through a variety of methods. In external locus of control methods, the alcoholic is taught to avoid situations where he would have difficulty controlling drinking, such as at bars or when nervous or angry. In internal locus of control methods, the alcoholic is taught to examine his response to situations and either devise other forms of response other than drinking, or he is taught to limit his drinking in terms of type of drink, or how fast he drinks, or how much he drinks.

Many behavior modification programs also build learning procedures for other areas of life health. But, in all, there is an attempt to analyze the pattern of drinking with the alcoholic, specify the changes to be made, and program a reinforcement schedule to achieve the desired behavioral goals. Usually there is no attempt made to change the internal motivation, meaning, or function of drinking alcohol.

Perhaps an illustration by analogy will help here. Suppose that we have a voyeur who peeps into a neighbor's windows every night. Eventually he is caught and enters a treatment program. The voyeur might be taught to control his "Peeping Tom" impulses so that he no longer prowls the neighborhood. His basic sexual problems are not changed, but he has increased his control over his impulse to peep. Still further, he might be taught to satisfy his voyeuristic impulses by going to a cheap strip-tease show, rather than peering into the neighbor's window. Again, his sexual problem remains unchanged, but he learns a more socially adaptive means of gratifying his sexual impulses.

In similar fashion, behavior modification may not change the basic psychological problems that lead to impulsive alcoholismic drinking. However, the behavior modification program may increase the control over the impulse or provide alternative means of gratifying the impulse. (The defense mechanism of displacement can be seen elsewhere. For example, many abstinent alcoholics have displaced their addiction to alcohol with an addiction to food, candy, coffee, and cigarettes.)

Since alcoholismic drinking results in manifold disruptions in a person's capacity to function, it may be only necessary to control the alcoholismic behavior in some instances in order to affect substantial rehabilitation. Also in this case, even if the basic conflicts and impulses remain unchallenged and untouched, the achievement of controlled drinking may be possible. The alcoholic can and does control his drinking, and can be taught to modify that control. However, it should be noted that control of drinking per se, just like abstinence or moderation of drinking per se, does not necessarily imply that there will be improvement in other areas of life health.

Case Study

A 36-year-old machinist had drunk heavily since adolescence. Drinking became a compulsive daily routine that threatened to disrupt job and marriage. He was in therapy for two years during which he noticed a change in his pattern of drinking. He now drinks about once a week and does not experience a compulsion to drink more. However, when he feels depressed he feels the urge to go and get drunk, and he avoids drinking at bars because he would drink more with buddies than he would at home.

Case Study

A 45-year-old musician had drunk compulsively for 20 years. He had been in psychoanalysis for five years, which improved his emotional adaptation, but his drinking worsened to the point he could not perform in public. During the course of two years of therapy focused on drinking behavior change, he learned to limit himself to one drink before a performance and to avoid drinking at parties. He occasionally would drink to intoxication at home when severely depressed.

In both the above cases the alcoholic changed his overt pattern of drinking. To the casual observer, neither now drank in an alcoholic fashion. However, in both cases, they were aware of their continued impulse to use alcohol in order to cope with life, and both had to maintain specific conscious limits on where and how much they drank. The meaning of drinking was not changed, but the actual drinking was changed.

The Normal Drinking Subset

Many reports have now been published that indicate that a certain proportion of alcoholics, perhaps 10–15% develop normal drinking either after treatment, or with changes in life circumstances. However, many of these reports do not provide enough clinical data to determine whether the change in drinking pattern was attenuated, controlled, or normal. There are few specific reports that provide case details so that one can state that the meaning and functional use of alcohol has changed with these alcoholics (7, 41–44, 190).

In both the "attenuated" drinking outcome and the "controlled" drinking outcome, the alcoholic continues to use alcohol as a functional drug, although he is able to increase his control over the use of alcohol. In other words, the alcohol has not changed his symbolic perception of the meaning of drinking. The same is true for the typical abstinent alcoholic, who differs from the above two categories only in that he maintains total control over drinking. So, for example, many abstinent alcoholics respond to my discussion of drinking outcomes somewhat as follows: "What? Stop with one drink. Who would want to do that. That would spoil drinking. If I could only take one drink I wouldn't need to learn that. It's all or nothing. So it's better to be abstinent."

In contrast, normal drinking involves a change in the symbolic meaning of drinking. In this sense the abstinent alcoholic has not changed the meaning of drinking, and although the abstinent alcoholic may not have taken a drink for 10 or 20 years, he is still vulnerable to abuse alcohol should he even drink small amounts. The one drink breaks the defensive control barrier, and there are no stopping places beyond—thus the commonplace observation that the abstinent alcoholic cannot take a drink without risking loss of control and start alcoholismic drinking again.

The concept of normal drinking has been colorfully described by Berne (12) in terms of the game of alcoholism: "The criterion of a true game cure is that former alcoholics should be able to drink socially without putting himself into jeopardy . . . the psychological cure of an alcoholic also lies in getting him to stop playing the game altogether . . . the usual total abstinence cure will not satisfy the game analyst." Berne goes on to note that the abstinent alcoholic can continue the alcoholism game as "dry alcoholic." In similar vein Cain (26) observes that the recovered alcoholic does not drink primarily because he does not want to drink, whereas the arrested alcoholic still has the desire to drink but knows that he cannot and avoids doing so. Cain states: "The recovered alcoholic, by definition, does not care whether he can drink normally, and he definitely does not want to become intoxicated again." Cain goes on: "most alcoholics do not want to return to normal drinking: rather by normal drinking they (the alcoholics) mean the intoxication they were once able to control—which is nothing like our definition of normal drinking . . . the arrested alcoholic never really loses his desire to become intoxicated with alcohol. He learns to control his desire (he learns to live with his disease) but he never learns to transcend his desire . . . The fact that normal drinking has been achieved is a dramatic indication of one's successful effort to attain social, intellectual and religious maturity."

It is worth noting that many alcoholics have never been normal drinkers. In the past five years, I have interviewed several hundred alcoholics in regard to this specific point. I have not yet found one alcoholic who originally drank in a normal fashion. They report that they drank in alcoholismic fashion from the time of their first drink, even though they exercised control over their alcoholismic behavior. Thus, they did not perceive of themselves, nor did others perceive them as drinking in alcoholismic fashion because their drinking pattern was "appropriate social drinking."

Parenthetically, I might add that much American social drinking is actually psychopathologic. That is, drinking in the service of conflict reduction, affect change, etc., in a word instrumental drinking—drinking to achieve an effect. Further, American drinking practices exist without clear boundaries and limit constraints. Thus the novice drinker is introduced to drinking practices that are potentially alcoholismic. The majority of drinkers control what is essentially alcoholismic drinking. The alcoholic differs only in that he is unable to maintain those controls as well as the majority.

We commonly observe that alcoholics will report 20 years of "social drinking" after which they "suddenly" become alcoholic. Careful analysis of their social drinking behavior reveals that actually they engaged in controlled alcoholismic drinking for 20 years, conducted in social settings where the drinking was not defined as aberrant. So in actuality we have a 20-year history of prodromal alcoholism with gradual development of secondary effects that reach such a manifest level that the person is suddenly labeled an overt alcoholic.

The import for treatment is that the alcoholic does not return to normal drinking, for he has never been a normal drinker. Rather, he must learn normal drinking for the first time in his life, and he must change the symbolic meaning of alcohol and change his use of alcohol. Most treatment programs have not made such goals explicit. Thus the number of alcoholics who develop attenuated, controlled or normal drinking may not reflect what can be achieved in treatment. There are some indications, however. Gerard and Saenger (75) report that the normal drinking outcome appears to vary with treatment philosophy and whether normal drinking is made a specific goal. De Morsier and Feldmann (45) followed 500 cases in which 15% achieved a social cure as a deliberate goal. A social cure was defined as avoiding the psychological bad effects of drinking, changing their attitude toward drinking, and drinking only in a family and social context. And final mention should be made of the Scandinavian Polar Bear Clubs, whose aim is to teach their members how to drink normally (22, 42).

Case Study

This 30-year-old mechanic had drunk heavily for 10 years. For six years he had been unable to work steadily because of his drinking. His marriage had been stormy and his wife had left him at the time he entered treatment. At that point, he was depressed and suicidal. Individual and conjoint marital therapy resulted in resolution of marital conflict. He stopped drinking and obtained a steady job. He resumed drinking only at family gatherings with his wife's full acceptance. He experienced no compulsion to drink. He had no desire to get drunk, and he felt no need to drink as a way of coping with his life.

17. DRINKING AND OTHER TREATMENT GOALS

The final issue which must be briefly touched upon, is the relationship between drinking goals and the related goals in rehabilitation or change in social, vocational, interpersonal, emotional, and physical adjustment. A variety of studies have shown that changes in drinking status is not highly predictive of changes in these other areas of life adjustment. There is a positive association between improvement in drinking and improvement in other life areas, but I would estimate the correlation as around 0.20–0.30. There may be several reasons for the low correlation. (*a*) The so-called "high-bottom" alcoholic has little dysfunction in other life areas save for his alcoholism drinking pattern, hence little room for improvement (188, 189); (*b*) the "low-bottom" or skid-row alcoholic has major dysfunctions as part of his total life-style, hence little potential for major life adaptation even if sober (18, 63, 158, 167); (*c*) treatment programs have often focused their efforts primarily on drinking behavior and have not sought to directly intervene in specific ways to modify other life area functions (170); (*d*) changes in drinking behavior may simply not have a high correlation with changes in other areas of life function for many alcoholics (31).

In addition, one cannot necessarily ascribe a causal relationship between changes in drinking producing changes in other areas of life function or vice versa. Improvement in drinking may not cause improvement in other areas or vice versa. It is a reasonable clinical assumption that a person will be in a better position to achieve improvement in other areas of his life as his drinking behavior improves. Conversely, positive changes in other areas of life may enhance the opportunity to change drinking behavior. However, there are two confounding sets of observations we have noted: (*a*) is that drinking may not improve, while there may be improvement in other life areas; (*b*) is that drinking may improve, but there may be no change or deterioration in other areas of life.

The most important issue, however, for treatment is to develop specified treatment criteria, as Belasco (11), Einstein (54) and others (9, 68, 97, 161, 193) have spelled out. By this, I mean a specification of several parameters of the alcoholic's behavior: (*a*) the degree of dysfunction in each life area; (*b*) the behavioral parameters that operationalize the dysfunctions; (*c*) an assessment of the extent to which interventions can be made in that operational analysis, (*d*) an assessment of how much change can be reasonably expected through intervention; (*e*) the establishment of reasonable treatment goals and treatment priorities; (*f*) a specific monitor and assessment process that provides an ongoing criterion measure of the effectiveness of the intervention methods in attaining stated goals.

Thus, we end up with a differential assessment process that provides an individualized treatment schedule for each alcoholic, with individualized treatment goals. Since alcoholics will vary in their initial status, degree of dysfunction, and degree of possible change, we would expect to have different patterns of improvement toward different treatment goals.

In this light, the specification of drinking goals would include both abstinent and nonabstinent drinking goals. Further, one would like to define the drinking goal that is both desirable and attainable with a specific alcoholic. The specification of such drinking goals may depend on severable variables: (*a*) the choice of the alcoholic himself; (*b*) the attitudes, values, and choices offered by a treatment facility, (*c*) the specific pattern of alcoholismic drinking that may indicate the feasibility of a specific drinking goal; (*d*) the staff potential to offer specific interventions to achieve different drinking goals; (*e*) the life context of the alcoholic which militates against or supports different drinking goals. Thus, the choice of different drinking goals does not lie solely with the desire of the alcoholic, nor with the propensity of the treatment staff. From a scientific point of view, one would define drinking goals in terms of the specific set of circumstances that define the system matrix of a given alcoholic.

18. SUMMARY

This chapter reviews the development of nonabstinent drinking goals in the treatment of alcoholics. The proposal to establish nonabstinent goals is contradictory to the established traditional model of alcoholism and its treatment. Therefore, it has been necessary to review a broad range of clinical and experimental data which demonstrate the conceptual and clinical inadequacy of the traditional model of alcoholism. Revisions are suggested for the interpretation and explanation of the phenomena of craving, loss of control, and progression of alcoholism, as well as revisions of the concepts of alcoholism as a disease, alcoholism as an entity, and the alcoholic as a sick person. Preliminary postulates for a revised model of alcoholism are presented based upon learning theory that incorporates both biophysiological and sociopsychological conditioning paradigms. Alcoholism is presented as continuum of behavioral syndromes that vary from nonpathologic to pathologic in the extreme. The use of a disease concept of alcoholism has social and clinical utility within modifiable boundaries, so long as we avoid reification of certain conventional notions. A conceptual classification of drinking goals is presented, along with case examples. Finally, the relationship between drinking goals and other treatment goals is noted.

Three major conclusions may be drawn from this analysis. (*a*) there will continue to be tensions in the field of alcoholism between a folk-science approach to alcoholism and an academic-science approach. This provides a major challenge to those who would seek a rapprochement. (*b*) Clinical research on nonabstinent treatment methodologies and assessment of long-term efficacy is still in an early stage of development. Many of the propositions presented here are in need of more extensive documentation and evaluation. (*c*) The most positive gain to this point has been an emphasis on careful analysis of alcoholic behavior, which promises to lead to more specific and precise broad-spectrum treatment programs.

REFERENCES

1. Alcoholics Anonymous, *Alcoholics Anonymous: The Story of How Thousands of Men and Women Have Recovered from Alcoholism*, 2nd Ed., New York, 1955.
2. Allman, L. R., H. A. Taylor, and P. E. Nathan, Group drinking during stress: Effects on drinking behavior, affect, and psychopathology, *Am. J. Psychiatry*, **129,** 669 (1972).
3. Anant, S. S., Former alcoholics and social drinking: An unexpected finding, *Can. Psychol.*, **9,** 35 (1968).
4. Anant, S. S., Treatment of alcoholics and drug addicts by verbal aversion techniques, *Int. J. Addict.*, **3,** 381 (1968).
5. Anant, S. S., The use of verbal aversion (negative conditioning) with an alcoholic; A case report, *Behav. Res. Ther.*, **6,** 395 (1968).
6. Azrin, N. H., B. J. Naster, and R. Jones, Reciprocity counseling: A rapid learning-based procedure for marital counseling, *Behav. Res. Ther.*, **11,** 365 (1973).
7. Bailey, M. B., and J. Stewart, Normal drinking by persons reporting previous problem drinking, *Q. J. Stud. Alcohol*, **28,** 305 (1967).
8. Barchha, R., M. A. Stewart, and S. B. Guze, The prevalence of alcoholism among general hospital ward patients, *Am. J. Psychiatry*, **125,** 681 (1968).
9. Bateman, N. I., and D. M. Peterson, Variables related to outcome of treatment for hospitalized alcoholics, *Int. J. Addict.*, **6,** 215 (1971).
10. Becker, H. C., *Outsiders: The Sociology of Deviance*, Free Press, New York, 1963.
11. Belasco, J. A., The criterion question revisited, *Br. J. Addict.*, **66,** 39 (1971).
12. Berne, E., *Games People Play*, Grove Press, New York, 1964.
13. Bhakata, M., Clinical application of behavior therapy in the treatment of alcoholism, *J. Alcohol*, **6,** 75 (1971).
14. Bigelow, G., M. Cohen, I. Liebson, and L. Faillace, Abstinence or moderation? Choice by alcoholics, *Behav. Res. Ther.*, **10,** 209 (1972).
15. Blake, B. G., The application of behavior therapy to the treatment of alcoholism, *Behav. Res. Ther.*, **3,** 74 (1965).
16. Blane, H. T., *The Personality of the Alcoholic: Guises of Dependency*, Harper & Row, New York, 1968.
17. Blane, H. T. and W. R. Meyers, Social class and the establishment of treatment relations by alcoholics, *J. Clin. Psychol.*, **20,** 287 (1964).
18. Blumberg, L. U., T. E. Shipley, Jr., and J. O. Moor, Jr., The skid row man and the skid row status community: With perspectives for their future, *Q. J. Stud. Alcohol*, **32,** 909 (1971).
19. Boise, C., and M. Vogel-Sprott, Discrimination of low blood alcohol levels and self-titration skills in social drinkers, *Q. J. Stud. Alcohol*, **35,** 86 (1974).
20. Bolman, W. M., Abstinence versus permissiveness in the psychotherapy of alcoholism, *Arch. Gen. Psychiatry*, **12,** 456 (1965).
21. Brush, S. G., Should the history of science be rated X? *Science*, **183,** 1164 (1974).

22. Bruun, K., *The Polar Bear Approach to Alcoholism.* Proceedings, 12th International Institute on the Prevention and Treatment of Alcoholism, Prague, 1966.

23. Burton, G. and H. M. Kaplan, Marriage counseling with alcoholics and their spouses. II. The consolation of excessive drinking with family pathology and social deterioration, *Br. J. Addict.*, **63,** 161 (1968).

24. Cahalan, D., *Problem Drinkers; a National Survey,* Jossey-Bass, San Francisco, 1970.

25. Cahn, S., *The Treatment of Alcoholics: An Evaluation Study,* Oxford University Press, New York, 1970.

26. Cain, A. H., *The Cured Alcoholic,* John Day Press, New York, 1964.

27. Canter, F. M., Personality factors related to participation in treatment of hospitalized male alcoholics, *J. Clin. Psychol.*, **22,** 114 (1966).

28. Canter, F. M., The requirement of abstinence as a problem in institutional treatment of alcoholics, *Psychiat. Q.*, **42,** 217 (1968).

29. Cappell, H., and C. P. Herman, Alcohol and tension reduction: A review, *Q. J. Stud. Alcohol,* **33,** 33 (1972).

30. Cautela, J. R., The treatment of alcoholism by covert sensitization, *Psychother. Ther. Res. Practice,* **7,** 81 (1970).

31. Chandler, J., C. Hensman, and G. Edwards, Determinants of what happens to alcoholics, *Q. J. Stud. Alcohol,* **32,** 349 (1971).

32. Cheek, F. E., Broad spectrum behavioral training in self-control for drug addicts and alcoholics, *Behav. Res. Ther.*, **3,** 515 (1972).

33. Clancy, J. E., E. Vanderhoof, and P. Campbell, Evaluation of an aversive technique as a treatment for alcoholism: Controlled trial with succinylcholine-induced apnea, *Q. J. Stud. Alcohol,* **28,** 476 (1967).

34. Clancy, J., R. Vornbrock, and E. Vanderhoof, Treatment of alcoholics: A follow-up study, *Dis. Nerv. Syst.*, **26,** 555 (1965).

35. Cohen, M., I. A. Liebson, and L. A. Faillace, Controlled drinking by chronic alcoholics over extended periods of free access, *Psychol. Rep.*, **32,** 1180 (1973).

36. Cohen, M., I. A. Liebson, and L. A. Faillace, A technique for establishing controlled drinking in chronic alcoholics, *Dis. Nerv. Syst.*, **33,** 46 (1972).

37. Cohen, M., I. A. Liebson, L. A. Faillace, and R. P. Allen, Moderate drinking by chronic alcoholics; A schedule dependent phenomenon, *J. Nerv. Ment. Dis.*, **153,** 434 (1971).

38. Cohen, M., I. A. Liebson, L. A. Faillace, and W. Speers, Alcoholism: Controlled drinking and incentives for abstinence, *Psychol. Rep.*, **28,** 575 (1971).

39. Curlee, J., Attitudes that facilitate or hinder the treatment of alcoholism, *Psychother. Theor. Res. Prac.*, **8,** 68 (1971).

40. Cutter, H. S. G., E. L. Schwaab, Jr., and P. E. Nathan, Effects of alcohol on its utility for alcoholics and non-alcoholics. *Q. J. Stud. Alcohol,* **31,** 368 (1970).

41. Davies, D. L., Normal drinking in recovered alcohol addicts, *Q. J. Stud. Alcohol,* **23,** 94 (1962).

42. Davies, D. L., Stabilized addiction and normal drinking in recovered alcohol addicts, in *Scientific Basis of Drug Dependence,* H. Steinberg, (Ed.), Churchill, London, 1969.

43. Davies, D. L., D. F. Scott, and M. E. L. Malherbe, Resumed normal drinking in recovered psychotic alcoholics, *Int. J. Addict.*, **4,** 187 (1969).

44. Davies, D. L., M. Shepard, and E. Myers, The two-year's prognosis of 50 alcohol addicts after treatment in hospital, *Q. J. Stud. Alcohol,* **17,** 485 (1956).

45. De Morsier, G. and H. Feldman, Le traitment de l'alcoolisme par l'apomorphine: etude 500 Cas., *Schweiz. Arch. Neurol. Psychiatr.*, **70,** 434 (1952).

46. Distefano, M. K., M. W. Pryer, and J. L. Garrison, Internal-external control among alcoholics, *J. Clin. Psychol.*, **28,** 36 (1972).

47. Drew, L., Alcoholism as a self-limiting disease, *Q. J. Stud. Alcohol,* **29,** 956 (1968).

48. Drewery, J., Social drinking as a therapeutic goal in the treatment of alcohol, *J. Alcohol,* **9,** 43 (1974).

49. Dubourg, G. O., After-Care for alcoholics—A follow-up study, *Br. J. Addict.*, **64,** 155 (1969).

50. Edwards, G., Drugs: Drug dependence and the concept of plasticity, *Q. J. Stud. Alcohol,* **35,** 176 (1974).

51. Edwards, G., J. Chandler, and C. Hensman, Drinking in a London suburb. I. Correlates of normal drinking, *Q. J. Stud. Alcohol,* Suppl. 6 (May 1962).

52. Edwards, G., J. Chandler, C. Hensman, and J. Peto, Drinking in a London suburb. II. Correlates of trouble with drinking among men, *Q. J. Stud. Alcohol,* Suppl. 6 (May 1972).

53. Edwards, G., C. Hensman, A. Howker, and V. Williamson, Who goes to Alcoholics Anonymous? *Lancet,* **2,** 382 (1966).

54. Einstein, S., E. Wolfson, and P. Gecht, What matters in treatment: Relevant variables in alcoholism, *Int. J. Addict.*, **5,** 43 (1970).

55. Emrick, C. D., A review of psychologically oriented treatment of alcoholism. I. The use and interrelationships of outcome criteria and drinking behavior following treatment, *Q. J. Stud. Alcohol,* **35,** 523 (1974).

56. Engle, K. A. and T. K. Williams, Effect of an ounce of vodka on alcoholics' desire for alcohol, *Q. J. Stud. Alcohol,* **33,** 1099 (1972).

57. English, G. E. and M. E. Curtin, Personality differences in patients at three alcoholism treatment agencies, *J. Stud. Alcohol,* **36,** 52 (1975).

58. Evans, M., Modification of drinking, *J. Alcohol,* **8,** 111 (1973).

59. Everett, P. B. and R. A. King, Schedule-induced alcohol ingestion, *Psychonom. Sci.*, **18,** 278 (1970).

60. Ewing, J. A., Behavioral approaches for problems with alcohol, *Int. J. Addict.*, **9,** 389 (1974).

61. Faillace, L. A., R. N. Flamer, S. D. Imber, and R. F. Ward, Giving alcohol to alcoholics: An evaluation, *Q. J. Stud. Alcohol,* **33,** 85 (1972).

62. Fallding, H., The source and burden of civilization illustrated in the use of alcohol, *Q. J. Stud. Alcohol,* **25,** 714 (1964).

63. Feeney, F. E., D. F. Mindlin, V. H. Minear, and E. E. Short, The challenge of the skid-row alcoholic: A social psychological and psychiatric comparison of chronically jailed alcoholics and cooperative alcohol clinic patients, *Q. J. Stud. Alcohol,* **16,** 645 (1955).

64. Fingarette, H., The perils of Powell: In search of a factual foundation for the "disease" concept of alcoholism, *Harvard Law Rev.*, **83,** 793 (1970).

65. Fitzgerald, B. J., R. A. Pasework, and R. Clark, Four-Year follow-up of alcoholics treated in a rural state hospital, *Q. J. Stud. Alcohol,* **32,** 636 (1971).

66. Flaherty, J. A., H. T. McGuire, and R. L. Gatski, The psychodynamics of the "dry drunk," *Am. J. Psychiatry,* **112,** 460 (1955).

67. Fletcher, C. R., Perceived personal causation as a predictor of punitive vs. psychiatric recommendations for deviants, *Criminologica,* **4,** 12 (1966).

68. Foster, M. F., J. L. Horn, and W. Wanberg, Dimensions of treatment outcome: A factor analytic study of alcoholics' responses to a follow-up questionnaire, *Q. J. Stud. Alcohol,* **33,** 1079 (1972).

69. Fox, V. and M. A. Smith, Evaluation of a chemopsychotherapeutic program for the rehabilitation of alcoholics: Observations over a two-year period, *Q. J. Stud. Alcohol,* **20,** 767 (1959).

70. Franks, C. M., Behavior therapy, the principles of conditioning and the treatment of the alcoholic, *Q. J. Stud. Alcohol,* **24,** 511 (1963).

71. Franks, C. M., Conditioning and conditioned aversion therapies in the treatment of the alcoholic, *Int. J. Addict.,* **I,** 61 (1966).

72. Freed, E. X., Abstinence for alcoholics reconsidered, *J. Alcohol,* **8,** 106 (1973).

73. Freed, E. X. and Hymoiwetz, A fortuitous observation regarding 'psychogenic' polydypsia, *Psychol. Rep.,* **24,** 224 (1969).

74. Freed, E. X. and D. Lester, Schedule-induced consumption of ethanol: Calories or Chemotherapy, *Physiol. Behav.,* **5,** 555 (1970).

75. Gerard, D. L. and G. Saenger, *Outpatient Treatment of Alcoholism,* University of Toronto Press, Toronto, 1966.

76. Gerard, D. L., G. Saenger, and R. Wile, The abstinent alcoholic, *Arch. Gen. Psychiatry,* **6,** 83 (1962).

77. Gilbert, R. M. and J. D. Kuhn, (Eds.), *Schedule Effects: Drugs, Drinking and Agression,* University of Toronto Press, Toronto, 1972.

78. Gillis, L. S. and M. Keet, Prognostic factors and treatment results in hospitalized alcoholics, *Q. J. Stud. Alcohol,* **30,** 426 (1967).

79. Glatt, M. M., The question of moderate drinking despite "loss of control," *Br. J. Addict.,* **62,** 267 (1967).

80. Glock, C. Y., Images of man and public opinion, *Pub. Opinion Q.,* **28,** 539 (1964).

81. Goldfried, M. R., Prediction of improvement in an alcoholism Clinic, *Q. J. Stud. Alcohol,* **30,** 129 (1969).

82. Goldman, M. S., To drink or not to drink: An experimental analysis of group drinking decisions by four alcoholics, *Am. J. Psychiatry,* **131,** 10 (1974).

83. Goodwin, D. W., J. B. Crane, and S. B. Guze, Felons who drink; an 8-year follow-up, *Q. J. Stud. Alcohol,* **32,** 136 (1971).

84. Gottheil, E., A. I. Alterman, T. E. Skoloda, and B. F. Murphy, Alcoholics' patterns of controlled drinking, *Am. J. Psychiatry,* **130,** 418 (1973).

85. Gottheil, E., L. O. Corbett, J. C. Grasberger, and F. C. Cornelison, Jr., Fixed interval drinking decisions. I. A research and treatment model, *Q. J. Stud. Alcohol,* **33,** 311 (1972).

86. Gottheil, E., L. O. Corbett, J. C. Grasberger, and F. S. Cornelison, Jr., Treating the alcoholic in the presence of alcohol, *Am. J. Psychiatry,* **128,** 475 (1971).

87. Gottheil, E., H. D. Crawford, and F. S. Cornelison, The Alcoholic's ability to resist available alcohol, *Dis. Nerv. Syst.,* **34,** 80 (1973).

88. Gottheil, E., B. F. Murphy, T. E. Skoloda, and L. D. Corbett, Fixed interval drinking decisions. II. Drinking and discomfort in 25 alcoholics, *Q. J. Stud. Alcohol,* **33,** 325 (1972).

89. Griffiths, R., G. Bigelow, and I. Liebson, Assessments of effects of ethanol self-administration on social interactions in alcoholics, *Psychopharmacologia,* **38,** 105 (1974).

90. Hacquard, M., M. Beaudoin, G. Derby, and H. Berger, Contribution a l'etude des

resultats eloignes des cures de deintoxication ethylique, *Rev. Hyg. Med. Soc.*, **8,** 686 (1960).

91. Hamburg, S., Behavior therapy in alcoholism: A critical review of broad-spectrum approaches, *J. Stud. Alcohol,* **36,** 69 (1971).

92. Harper, J. and B. Hickson, The results of hospital treatment of chronic alcoholism, *Lancet,* **261,** 1057 (1951).

93. Hayman, M., The myth of social drinking, *Am. J. Psychiatry,* **124,** 585 (1967).

94. Hersen, M., R. M. Eisler, and P. M. Miller, Development of assertive responses: Clinical, measurement and research considerations, *Behav. Res. Ther.*, **11,** 505 (1973).

95. Holman, R. B. and R. D. Myers, Ethanol consumption under conditions of psychogenic polydypsia, *Physiol. Behav.*, **3,** 369 (1968).

96. Hore, B. D., Craving for alcohol, *Br. J. Addict.*, **69,** 137 (1974).

97. Horn, J. L. and K. W. Wanberg, Symptom patterns of alcoholics, *Q. J. Stud. Alcohol,* **30,** 45 (1969).

98. Hsu, J. J., Electroconditioning therapy of alcoholics: A preliminary report, *Q. J. Stud. Alcohol.*, **26,** 449 (1965).

99. Hunt, G. M. and N. H. Azrin, A community-reinforcement approach to alcoholism, *Behav. Res. Ther.*, **11,** 91 (1973).

100. Hurwitz, J. I. and D. Lelos, A Multilevel interpersonal profile of employed alcoholics, *Q. J. Stud. Alcohol.*, **29,** 74 (1968).

101. Jellinek, E. M., *The Disease Concept of Alcoholism,* Hillhouse Press, Highland Park, N. J., 1960.

102. Jellinek, E. M., Phases in the drinking history of alcoholics, *Q. J. Stud. Alcohol.*, **7,** 1 (1946).

103. Karp, S. A., B. Kissin, and F. E. Hustmyer, Field dependence as a predictor of alcoholic therapy dropouts, *J. Nerv. Ment. Dis.*, **150,** 77 (1970).

104. Keehn, J. D., Reinforcement of alcoholism: Schedule control of solitary drinking, *Q. J. Stud. Alcohol.*, **31,** 28 (1970).

105. Keehn, J. D., Translating behavioral research into practical terms for alcoholism, *Can. Psychol.*, **10,** 438 (1969).

106. Keller, M., On the loss-of-control phenomenon in alcoholism, *Br. J. Addict.*, **67,** 153 (1972).

107. Keller, M., The oddities of alcoholics, *Q. J. Stud. Alcohol.*, **33,** 1147 (1972).

108. Kendall, R. E., Normal drinking by former alcohol addicts, *Q. J. Stud. Alcohol.*, **26,** 247 (1965).

109. Kendall, R. E. and M. C. Staton, The Fate of untreated alcoholics, *Q. J. Stud. Alcohol.*, **27,** 30 (1966).

110. Kish, G. B. and H. T. Hermann, The Fort Meade Alcohol Treatment Program: A follow-up study, *Q. J. Stud. Alcohol.*, **32,** 628 (1971).

111. Kissin, B., A. Platz, and W. H. Su, Social and psychological factors in the treatment of chronic alcoholism, *J. Psychiatr. Res.*, **8,** 13 (1970).

112. Kissin, B., S. M. Rosenblatt, and S. Machover, Prognostic factors in alcoholism. Part I. *Psychiatr. Res. Rep.*, **24,** 22 (1968).

113. Kissin, B., S. M. Rosenblatt, and S. Machover, Prognostic factors in alcoholism. Part II. *Psychiat. Res. Rep.*, **24,** 44 (1968).

114. Knox, W. J., Attitudes of psychiatrists and psychologists toward alcoholism, *Am. J. Psychiatry*, **127,** 1675 (1971).

115. Knox, W. J., Attitudes of social workers and other professional groups toward alcoholism, *Q. J. Stud. Alcohol.*, **34,** 1270 (1973).

116. Kraft, T. and I. Al-Issa, Alcoholism treated by desensitization: A case report, *Behav. Res. Ther.*, **5,** 69 (1967).

117. Kraft, T. and I. Al-Issa, Desensitization and the treatment of alcohol addiction, *Br. J. Addict.*, **63,** 19 (1968).

118. Krystal, H., The problem of abstinence by the patient as a requisite for the psychotherapy of alcoholism. II. The evaluation of the meaning of drinking in determining the requirement of abstinence by alcoholics during treatment, *Q. J. Stud. Alcohol.*, **23,** 112 (1962).

119. Kuhn, T. S., *The Structure of Scientific Revolutions*, 2nd Ed, University of Chicago Press, Chicago, 1970.

120. Lambert, B. E. U., "Social" drinking by the alcohol-damaged, *Svenska Labartidn.*, **61,** 315 (1964).

121. Lazarus, A. A., *Behavioral Therapy and Beyond*, McGraw Hill, New York, 1968.

122. Lazarus, A. A., Towards the understanding and effective treatment of alcoholism, *S. Afr. Med. J.*, **39,** 736 (1965).

123. Lemere, F., What happens to alcoholics?, *Am. J. Psychiatry* **109,** 674 (1953).

124. Lester, D., Self-Selection of alcohol by animals, human variation and the etiology of alcoholism: A critical review, *Q. J. Stud. Alcohol.*, **27,** 395 (1966).

125. Liebson, I. A., M. Cohen, L. A. Faillace, and R. F. Ward, The token economy as a research method in alcoholism, *Psychiatr. Q.*, **45,** 574 (1971).

126. Linsky, A. S., Changing public views in alcoholism, *Q. J. Stud. Alcohol.*, **31,** 692 (1970).

127. Linsky, A. S., Theories of behavior and the social control of alcoholism, *Soc. Psychiatry*, **7,** 47 (1972).

128. Litman, G. K., Stress, affect and craving in alcoholics: the single case as a research strategy, *Q. J. Stud. Alcohol.*, **35,** 131 (1974).

129. Lolli, G., *Social Drinking*, Collier, New York, 1960.

130. Lovald, K., and G. Neuwirth, Exposed and shielded drinking: Drinking as role behavior and some consequences for social control and self-concept, *Arch. Gen. Psychiatry*, **19,** 95 (1968).

131. Lovibond, S. H. and G. Caddy, Descriminated aversive control in the moderation of alcoholics' drinking behavior, *Behav. Ther.*, **1,** 437 (1970).

132. Ludwig, A. M., On and off the wagon: Reasons for drinking and abstaining by alcoholics, *Q. J. Stud. Alcohol.*, **23,** 91 (1972).

133. Ludwig, A. M., J. Levine, and L. H. Stark, *LSD and Alcoholism: A Clinical Study of Treatment Efficacy*, Charles C Thomas, Springfield, Ill., 1970.

134. Ludwig, A. M. and A. Wikler, "Craving" and a relapse to drink, *Q. J. Stud. Alcohol.*, **35,** 108 (1974).

135. Ludwig, A. M., A. Wikler, and L. H. Stark, The first drink: Psychobiological aspects of craving, *Arch. Gen Psychiatr.* **30,** 539 (1974).

136. Lundquist, G. A. R., Alcohol dependence, *Acta Psychiatr. Scand.*, **49,** 332 (1973).

137. Mac Andew, C. and R. B. Edgerton, *Drunken Comportment: A Social Explanation*, Aldine, Chicago, 1969.

138. Madsen, W., The alcoholic agringado, *Am. Anthropol.*, **66,** 355 (1966).

139. Marlatt, G. A., B. Demming, and J. B. Reid, Loss of control drinking in alcoholics; an experimental analogue, *J. Abnorm. Psychol.*, **81,** 233 (1973).

140. Mayer, J. and D. J. Myerson, Outpatient treatment of alcoholics: Effects of status stability and nature of treatment, *Q. J. Stud. Alcohol.*, **32,** 620 (1971).

141. McBrearty, J. F., M. Dichter, Z. Garfield, and G. A. Heath, Behaviorally oriented treatment program for alcoholism, *Psychol. Rep.*, **22,** 287 (1968).

142. McCelland, P. C., W. M. Davies, R. Kalin, and E. Vanner, *The Drinking Man: Alcohol and Human Motivation,* Free Press, New York, 1972.

143. McNamee, H. B., N. K. Mello, and J. H. Mendelson, Experimental analysis of drinking patterns of alcoholics: Concurrent psychiatric observations, *Am. J. Psychiatr.*, **124,** 1063 (1968).

144. Mello, N. K., Behavioral studies of alcoholism, in *The Biology of Alcoholism. Vol. II. Physiology and Behavior,* B. Kissith, and H. Begleiter, (Eds.), Plenum Press, New York, 1972.

145. Mello, N. K., H. B. McNamee, and J. H. Mendelson, Drinking patterns of chronic alcoholics: Gambling and motivations for alcohol, *Psychiatr. Res. Rep.*, **24,** 83 (1968).

146. Mello, N. K. and J. H. Mendelson, Drinking patterns during work—Contingent and noncontingent alcohol acquisition, *Psychosom. Med.*, **34,** 139 (1972).

147. Mello, N. K. and J. H. Mendelson, Experimentally induced intoxication in alcoholics: A comparison between programmed and spontaneous drinking, *J. Pharmacol. Exp. Ther.*, **173,** 101 (1970).

148. Mello, N. K., and J. H. Mendelson, Operant analysis of drinking patterns of chronic alcoholics, *Nature,* **201,** 43 (1965).

149. Mendelson, J. H. (Ed.), *Alcoholism,* Little Brown, Boston, 1966.

150. Mendelson, J. H., J. LaDou, and P. Solomon, Experimentally induced chronic intoxication and withdrawal in alcoholics. III. Psychiatric findings, *Q. J. Stud. Alcohol.*, **Suppl. 2,** 40 (1964).

151. Merry, J., The "loss of control" myth, *Lancet,* **1,** 1257 (1966).

152. Miller, M. M., Prognosis in periodic and daily inebriates, *Q. J. Stud. Alcohol.*, **5,** 430 (1944).

153. Miller, N. E., Learning of visceral and glandular responses, *Science,* **163,** 434 (1969).

154. Miller, P. M., The use of behavioral contracting in the treatment of alcoholism: A case report, *Behav. Res. Ther.*, **3,** 593 (1972).

155. Miller, P. M. and D. H. Barlow, Behavioral approaches to the treatment of alcoholism, *J. Nerv. Ment. Dis.*, **157,** 10 (1973).

156. Miller, P. M., M. Hersen, R. M. Eisler, and D. P. Hemphill, Electrical aversion therapy with alcoholics; an analogue study, *Behav. Res. Ther.*, **11,** 491 (1973).

157. Miller, P. M., M. Hersen, R. M. Eisler, and G. Hilsman, Effects of social stress on operant drinking of alcoholics and social drinkers, *Behav. Res. Ther.*, **12,** 67 (1974).

158. Miller, B. A., A. D. Pokorny, and T. E. Kanas, Problems in treating homeless, jobless alcoholics, *Hosp. Community Psychiatry,* **21,** 98 (1970).

159. Miller, B. A., A. D. Pokorny, J. Valles, and S. E. Cleveland, Biased sampling in alcoholism treatment research, *Q. J. Stud. Alcohol.*, **31,** 97 (1970).

160. Mills, K. C., M. B. Sobell, and H. H. Schaefer, Training social drinking as an alternative to abstinence for alcoholics, *Behav. Res. Ther.*, **2,** 18 (1971).

161. Mindlin, D. F., The characteristics of alcoholics as related to prediction outcome, *Q. J. Stud. Alcohol.*, **20,** 604 (1959).

162. Mogar, R. E., U. M. Wilson, and S. T. Helm, Personality subtypes of male and female alcoholic patients, *Int. J. Addict.*, **5,** 99 (1970).

163. Monnerot, E., Cure hospitaliere psychiatrique de l'alcoolomonie; Reflexions therapeutiques sur un bilan, une enquète, U n essai particulier, *Rev. Alcoolisme*, **9,** 114 (1963).

164. Moore, R. A. and F. Ramseur, Effects of psychotherapy in an open-ward hospital on patients with alcoholism, *Q. J. Stud. Alcohol.*, **21,** 233 (1960).

165. Mowrer, H. R. and E. R. Mowrer, Ecological and familial factors associated with inebriety, *Q. J. Stud. Alcohol.*, **6,** 36 (1945).

166. Mulford, H. A., *Identifying Problem Drinkers*, USPHS Publication 1000, Washington, 1966.

167. Myerson, D. J. and J. Mayer, Origins, treatment and destiny of skid row alcoholic men, *N. Engl. J. Med.*, **275,** 419 (1966).

168. Nathan, P. E. and J. S. O'Brien, An experimental analysis of the behavior of alcoholics and nonalcoholics during prolonged experimental drinking: A necessary precursor of behavior therapy, *Behav. Res. Ther.*, **2,** 455 (1971).

169. Nathan, P. E., N. A. Titler, L. U. Lowenstein, P. Solomon, and A. M. Rossi, Behavioral analysis of chronic alcoholism: Interaction of alcohol and human contact, *Arch. Gen. Psychiatry*, **22,** 419 (1970).

170. Negrete, J. C., A. S. MacPherson, and T. E. Dancey, A comparative study on the emotional and social problems of active and arrested alcoholics, *Lav. Med.*, **27,** 162 (1966).

171. Norvig, J. and B. Nielsen, A follow-up study of 221 alcohol addicts in denmark, *Q. J. Stud. Alcohol*, **17,** 633 (1956).

172. O'Leary, M. R., D. M. Donovan, and W. H. Hague, Relationships between locus of control and MMPI scales among alcoholics: A replication and extension, *J. Clin. Psychol.*, July (1974).

173. Orford, J., A comparison of alcoholics whose drinking is totally uncontrolled and those whose drinking is mainly controlled, *Behav. Res. Ther.*, **11,** 565 (1973).

174. Orford, J., Controlled drinking in the existing behavior repertoires of alcohol dependent men, *J. Alcohol.*, London, **9,** 56 (1974).

175. Overton, D. A., State-Dependent learning produced by alcohol and its relevance to alcohol, in *Biology of Alcoholism, Vol. II*, B. Kissin and H. Begleiter (Eds.), Plenum, New York, 1970.

176. Oziel, L. J. and F. W. Obitz, Control orientation in alcoholics related to extension of treatment, *J. Stud. Alcohol.*, **36,** 158 (1975).

177. Oziel, L. J., F. W. Obitz, and M. Keyson, General and specific perceived locus of control in alcoholics, *Psychol. Rep.*, **30,** 957 (1972).

178. Paredes, A., Denial, deceptive maneuvers and consistency in the behavior of alcoholics, *Am. N.Y. Acad. Sci.*, **233,** 23 (1974).

179. Paredes, A., D. Gregory, and B. M. Jones, Induced drinking and social adjustment in alcoholics: Development of a therapeutic model, *Q. J. Stud. Alcohol*, **35,** 1279 (1974).

180. Paredes, A., W. R. Hood, H. Seymour, and M. Gollob, Loss of control in alcoholism: An investigation of the hypothesis, with experimental findings, *Q. J. Stud. Alcohol*, **34,** 1146 (1973).

181. Park, P., Developmental ordering of experiences in alcoholism, *Q. J. Stud. Alcohol.*, **34,** 473 (1973).

182. Pattison, E. M., Abstinence criteria: A critique of abstinence criteria in the treatment of alcoholism, *Int. J. Soc. Psychiatry,* **14,** 268 (1968).

183. Pattison, E. M., A critique of alcoholism treatment concepts with special reference to abstinence, *Q. J. Stud. Alcohol,* **27,** 49 (1966).

184. Pattison, E. M., The differential utilization of manpower, in *The Paraprofessional in the Treatment of Alcoholism: A New Profession,* G. E. Staub and L. Kent, (Eds.), Charles C Thomas, Springfield, Ill., 1973.

185. Pattison, E. M., Morality and the treatment of character disorders, *J. Relig. Health,* **4,** 290 (1967).

186. Pattison, E. M., The rehabilitation of the chronic alcoholic, in *The Biology of Alcoholism. Vol. III. Clinical Pathology,* B. Kissin and H. Begleiter, (Eds.), Plenum Press, New York, 1974.

187. Pattison, E. M., L. A. Bishop, and A. S. Linsky, Changes in public attitudes on narcotic addiction, *Am. J. Psychiatry,* **125,** 160 (1968).

188. Pattison, E. M., R. Coe, and H. D. Doerr, Population variation between alcoholism treatment facilities, *Int. J. Addict.,* **8,** 199 (1973).

189. Pattison, E. M., R. Coe, and R. A. Rhodes, Evaluation of alcoholism treatment: Comparison of three facilities, *Arch. Gen Psychiatry,* **20,** 478 (1969).

190. Pattison, E. M., E. B. Headley, G. C. Gleser, and L. A. Gottschalk, Abstinence and normal drinking: An assessment of changes in drinking patterns in alcoholics after treatment, *Q. J. Stud. Alcohol,* **29,** 610 (1968).

191. Pfeffer, A. Z. and S. Berger, A follow-up study of treated alcoholics. *Q. J. Stud. Alcohol,* **18,** 624 (1957).

192. Pickens, R., G. Bigelow, and R. Griffiths, An experimental approach to treating chronic alcoholism: A case study and one-year follow-up, *Behav. Res. Ther.,* **11,** 321 (1973).

193. Pisani, V. D. and G. U. Motanby, Prediction of premature termination of outpatient follow-up group psychotherapy among male alcoholics, *Int. J. Addict.,* **5,** 731 (1970).

194. Pliner, P. and H. Cappell, Modification of affective consequences of alcohol: A comparison of social and solitary drinking, *J. Abnorm. Soc. Psychol.,* **83,** 418 (1974).

195. Pokorny, A. D., B. A. Miller, and S. E. Cleveland, Response to treatment of alcoholism; a follow-up study, *Q. J. Stud. Alcohol,* **29,** 364 (1968).

196. Popham, R., A critique of the genotropic theory of the etiology of alcohoism, *Q. J. Stud. Alcohol,* **14,** 228 (1953).

197. Quirk, P. A., Former alcoholics and social drinking: An additional observation, *Can. Psychol.,* **9,** 498 (1968).

198. Rachman, S. and J. Teasdale, *Aversion Therapy and Behavior Disorders: An Analysis,* University of Miami Press, Coral Gables, Fla., 1969.

199. Rakkolainen, V. and S. Turunen, From unrestrained to moderate drinking, *Acta Psychiatr. Scand.,* **45,** 47 (1969).

200. Ravetz, J., *Scientific Knowledge and Its Social Problems,* Oxford, New York, 1971.

201. Raymond, M. J., The treatment of addiction by aversion conditioning with apomorphine, *Behav. Res. Ther.,* **1,** 287 (1964).

202. Reinert, R. E., The concept of alcoholism as a bad habit, *Bull. Menninger Clin.,* **32,** 35 (1968).

203. Reinert, R. E., The concept of alcoholism as a disease, *Bull. Menninger Clin.,* **32,** 21 (1968).

204. Reinert, R. E. and W. T. Bowen, Social drinking following treatment for alcoholism, *Bull. Menninger Clin.*, **32,** 280 (1968).

205. Ritson B., The prognosis of alcohol addicts treated by a specialized unit, *Br. J. Psychiatry*, **114,** 1019 (1968).

206. Robinson, D., The alcohologist addiction: Some implications of having lost control over the disease concept of alcoholism, *Q. J. Stud. Alcohol*, **33,** 1028 (1972).

207. Robinson, L. and B. Podnoe, Resistance of psychiatrists in treatment of alcoholism, *J. Nerv. Ment. Dis.*, **143,** 220 (1966).

208. Robson, R. A. H., I. Paulus, and G. G. Clark, An evaluation of the effect of a clinic treatment program on the rehabilitation of alcoholic patients, *Q. J. Stud. Alcohol*, **26,** 264 (1965).

209. Rohan, W. P., A follow-up study of hospitalized problem drinkers, *Dis. Nerv. Syst.*, **31,** 259 (1970).

210. Roman, P. M. and H. M. Trice, The development of deviant drinking behavior, *Arch. Environ. Health*, **20,** 424 (1970).

211. Roman, P. M. and H. M. Trice, The sick role, labelling theory and the deviant drinker, *Int. J. Soc. Psychiatry*, **14,** 245 (1968).

212. Rosengren, E., Behandling an alkoholister med amituptylin, *Labartigningen*, **63,** 231 (1966).

213. Rossi, J. J., A. Stach, and N. J. Bradley, Effect of treatment of male alcoholics in a mental hospital: A follow-up study, *Q. J. Stud. Alcohol*, **24,** 99 (1963).

214. Rudic, R. E. and L. S. McGaughran, Differences in developmental experiences, defensiveness and personality organization between two classes of problem drinkers, *J. Abnorm. Soc. Psychol.*, **62,** 659 (1961).

215. Schaefer, H. H., Twelve-month follow-up of behaviorally trained ex-alcoholic social drinkers, *Behav. Res. Ther.*, **3,** 286 (1972).

216. Schaefer H. H., M. B. Sobell, and K. C. Mills, Baseline drinking behaviors in alcoholics and social drinkers: Kinds of drinks and sip magnitude, *Behav. Res. Ther.*, **9,** 23 (1971).

217. Scheff, T. J., *On Being Mentally Ill*, Aldine, Chicago 1966.

218. Schmidt, W. G., R. G. Smart, and M. K. Moss, *Social Class and the Treatment of Alcoholism*, University of Toronto Press, Toronto, 1968.

219. Schuster, C. R. and T. Thompson, Self administration of the behavioral dependence on drugs, *Annu. Rev. Pharmacol.*, **9,** 483 (1969).

220. Seiden, R. H., The use of alcoholics anonymous members in research on alcoholism, *Q. J. Stud. Alcohol* **21,** 506 (1960).

221. Selzer, M. L. and W. H. Holloway, A follow-up of alcoholics committed to a state hospital, *Q. J. Stud. Alcohol*, **18,** 98 (1957).

222. Shapiro, D., *Neurotic Styles*, Basic Books, New York, 1965.

223. Shea, J. E., Psychoanalytic therapy and alcoholism. *Q. J. Stud. Alcohol*, **15,** 595 (1954).

224. Sikes, M. P., G. Faibish, and J. Valles, Evaluation of an intensive alcoholic treatment program, *Am. Psychol.*, **20,** 574 (1965).

225. Sobell, M. B., H. H. Schaefer, and K. C. Mills, Differences in baseline drinking behavior between alcoholics and normal drinkers, *Behav. Res. Ther.*, **10,** 257 (1972).

226. Sobell, M. B. and L. Sobell, Alcoholics treated by individualized behavior therapy; One-year treatment outcome, *Behav. Res. Ther.*, **11,** 599 (1973).

227. Sobell, M. and L. Sobell, Individualized behavior therapy for alcoholics, *Behav. Res. Ther.*, **4,** 49 (1973).

228. Sobell, M. and L. Sobell, *Individualized Behavior Therapy for Alcoholics: Rationale Procedures,* Preliminary Results and Appendix. California Mental Health Res. Monogr. No. 13. California Department of Mental Hygiene, Sacramento, 1972.

229. Sobell, L. C. and M. B. Sobell, A self-feedback technique to monitor drinking behavior in alcoholics, *Behav. Res. Ther.*, **11,** 237 (1973).

230. Sobell, L. C., M. B. Sobell, and W. C. Christelman, The myth of one drink, *Behav. Res. Ther.*, **10,** 119 (1972).

231. Stein, L. I., D. Niles, and A. M. Ludwig, The loss of control phenomenon in alcoholics, *Q. J. Stud. Alcohol,* **29,** 598 (1968).

232. Steiner, C. M., *Games Alcoholics Play; the Analysis of Self Scripts,* Grove Press, New York, 1971.

233. Steinglass, P., S. Weiner, and J. H. Mendelson, Interactional issues as determinants of alcoholism, *Am. J. Psychiatry,* **128,** 275 (1971).

234. Steinglass, P., S. Weiner, and J. H. Mendelson, A systems approach to alcoholism: A model and its clinical application, *Arch. Gen. Psychiatry,* **24,** 401 (1971).

235. Steinglass, P. and S. Wolin, Explorations of a systems approach to alcoholism: Clinical observations of a simulated drinking gang, *Arch. Gen. Psychiatry,* **31** (Oct. 1974).

236. Sterne, M. W. and D. J. Pittman, The concept of motivation; A source of institutional and professional blockage in the treatment of alcoholism, *Q. J. Stud. Alcohol,* **26,** 41 (1965).

237. Stunkard, A. J., Hunger and satiety, *Am. J. Psychiatry,* **118,** 212 (1961).

238. Sugerman, A. A., D. Reilly, and R. S. Albahary, Social competence and the essential-reactive distinction in alcoholism, *Arch. Gen. Psychiatry,* **12,** 552 (1965).

239. Sutherland, E. H., H. G. Schroeder, and O. L. Tordella, Personality traits and the alcoholic: Critique of existing studies, *Q. J. Stud. Alcohol,* **11,** 547 (1950).

240. Tamerin, J. and J. H. Mendelson, The Psychodynamics of chronic inebriation: Observations of alcoholics during the process of drinking in an experimental group setting, *Am. J. Psychiatry,* **125,** 886 (1969).

241. Thomas, R. E., L. H. Gliedman, J. Freund, S. D. Imber, and A. R. Stone, Favorable response in the clinical treatment of chronic alcoholism, *J.A.M.A.*, **169,** 1994 (1959).

242. Tokar, J. T., A. J. Brunse, V. J. Stefflre, D. A. Napior, and J. A. Sodergren, Emotional states and behavioral patterns in alcoholics and nonalcoholics, *Q. J. Stud. Alcohol,* **34,** 133 (1973).

243. Tomsovic, M., A follow-up study of discharged alcoholics, *Hosp. Community Psychiatry,* **21,** 38 (1970).

244. Trice, H. M. and P. M. Roman, Sociopsychological predictors of affiliation with alcoholics anonymous: A longitudinal study of "treatment success." *Soc. Psychiatry,* **5,** 51 (1970).

245. Trice, H. M., P. M. Roman, and J. T. Belasco, Selection for treatment: A predictive evaluation of an alcoholism treatment regimen, *Int. J. Addict.*, **4,** 303 (1969).

246. vanDijk, W. K., vanDijk and A. Koffeman, A follow-up study of 211 treated male alcohol addicts, *Br. J. Addict.*, **68,** 3 (1973).

247. Verden, P. and D. Shatterly, Alcoholism research and resistence to understanding the compulsive drinker, *Ment. Hyg.*, **55,** 331 (1971).

248. Vogel-Sprott, M., Self-Evaluation of performance and the ability to discriminate blood alcohol concentrations, *J. Stud. Alcohol*, **36,** 1 (1975).

249. Wanberg, K. W. and J. Knapp, A multidimensional model for the research and treatment of alcoholism, *Int. J. Addict.*, **5,** 69 (1968).

250. Ward, F. F. and G. A. Faillace, The alcoholic and his helpers, *Q. J. Stud. Alcohol*, **31,** 684 (1970).

251. Wellman, M., Fatigue during the second six months of abstinence, *Can. Med. Assoc. J.*, **72,** 338 (1955).

252. Wilby, W. E. and R. W. Jones, Assessing patient response following treatment, *Q. J. Stud. Alcohol*, **23,** 325 (1962).

253. Wilkinson, R., *Prevention of Drinking Problems; Alcohol Control and Cultural Influences*, Oxford University Press, New York, 1970.

254. Wolin, S. and P. Steinglass, Interactional behavior in an alcoholic community, *Med. Ann. D.C.*, **43,** 183 (1974).

CHAPTER TEN

SEX DIFFERENCES IN CRIMINALITY AMONG DRUG ABUSE PATIENTS IN THE UNITED STATES

JOHN C. BALL, *Department of Psychiatry, Temple University Medical Center, Philadelphia, Pennsylvania*

1. INTRODUCTION

The relationship of drug abuse to criminal behavior has been the subject of considerable attention by criminologists, physicians, academicians, and rehabilitation practitioners in recent years (8, 10). Although there is general agreement that drug users are more involved in various criminal offenses than the base population, the etiology of such behavior patterns is inadequately understood. Closely related to these etiologic concerns are unresolved questions regarding the concentration of persistent drug abuse and crime in metropolitan minority group slum neighborhoods, and the sex differences which exist with respect to both types of deviant behavior. The present research addresses itself to one aspect of this last subject—differences in criminal behavior among male and female drug abuse patients.

It is relevant to comment briefly about the appropriateness of utilizing data obtained from a patient population to investigate the issue of sex differences in criminality among drug users. Fundamentally, there are three sources of data available in pursuing this research question (10): school and household surveys (8), arrest records (13), and information concerning patients in treatment. Although each of these sources has definite methodological advantages and limitations, the available national data pertaining to drug abuse patients provide the most comprehensive information directly related to the issue of sex differences in criminality. Furthermore, in investigating this criminological topic, it seemed convenient to focus upon persistent drug users (i.e., patients who had been involved in the daily consumption of illicitly procured drugs over a period of years; in the present case, the predominant drug was heroin), rather than occasional users, in order to analyze sex differences within a population already committed to a deviant lifestyle.

2. THE RESEARCH PROCEDURE

In order to ascertain the extent and nature of sex differences in criminality among drug abuse patients, it was decided to employ a national data bank of treatment data available at the Institute of Behavioral Research in Fort Worth, Texas. This Drug Abuse Reporting Program (DARP) was established in 1968 by the National Institute of Mental Health at Texas Christian University to provide standardized admission data and progress reports on drug abuse patients in federally funded programs throughout the United States.

The DARP data bank contains over 200,000 records on some 43,000 drug abuse patients who entered treatment programs between 1968 and 1973. The data amassed during this period has served as a basis for numerous technical reports, scientific papers, and special governmental analyses of the drug abuse problem (13). The scientific and programmatic usefulness of the DARP data bank is based upon the standardized data collection procedure (10), the comprehensiveness and continuity of the information obtained (8), the national scope of the file (13), and the consistent editing, checking, and computerization of data obtained (5).

In the present criminological analyses, use is made only of the admission

TABLE 1 AGE OF 42,293 DARP PATIENTS AT TIME OF ADMISSION FOR TREATMENT OF DRUG ABUSE

Age at Admission (Years)	Male Patients		Female Patients		Total Patients	
	No.	Percent	No.	Percent	No.	Percent
17 or less	2,233	6.9	1,200	12.2	3,433	8.1
18–20	5,566	17.2	1,995	20.2	7,561	17.9
21–25	11,742	36.2	3,479	35.2	15,221	36.0
26–30	5,690	17.5	1,599	16.2	7,289	17.2
31 and over	7,187	22.2	1,602	16.2	8,789	20.8
Total	32,418	100.0	9,875	100.0	42,293	100.0

Difference in age by sex: $p < 0.001$.

Note: In Tables 1–6, the total number varies due to missing or invalid entries on particular items.

data provided to the DARP data bank, although subsequent progress reports and collateral material have methodological relevance in ascertaining the reliability and validity of the DARP file. In this regard, a number of technical reports provide detailed information on the validity and representativeness of the DARP data (5, 9).

The admission data were obtained directly from the patient by personal interview at each of the 50 treatment programs. A standard admission form was employed; it consisted of 94 questions pertaining to the patient's drug abuse history, demographic characteristics, family background, employment experience, and criminality. With respect to the patient's criminal history and experiences, two items refer to present legal status, two refer to juvenile delinquency, and the remaining five items refer to arrest history, convictions, history of incarceration, and illegal means of support. These last five items provide the principal data for the present study.

3. THE PATIENT POPULATION

The patient population selected for study consisted of the entire cohort of 42,293 drug abusers who were admitted to 50 treatment programs during a four-year period, 1969–1973. These 50 programs are located in 38 cities within 23 states and the Commonwealth of Peurto Rico, and they include most, if not all, of the major modalities of treatment currently available in the United States.

The present DARP patient population is generally representative of the young adults and adolescents found in drug treatment programs throughout the United States (6). With respect to age, 80% are 30 years of age or younger, and 26% are under 21 (Table 1). Although the age difference by sex is statistically significant—the female drug abusers are slightly younger—the overall similarity of the two age distributions is the more fundamental point in describing the two populations. In this regard, it is pertinent to note that onset of drug abuse typically occurred several years prior to admission for treatment, and this age distribution (of onset) is even more skewed toward the early years.

Of the 42,293 drug abuse patients, some two-thirds are either black, Puerto Rican or Mexican American (Table 2). This concentration of the drug abuse problem within specific race and ethnic groups is similar to that reported generally for the United States since World War II (2). With respect to sex differences, a higher proportion of the female patients were white and a lower proportion were from minority groups than among the male patients.

With respect to sex, 44 of the 50 programs reported that their patients

TABLE 2 RACE AND ETHNIC DISTRIBUTION OF DARP PATIENTS BY SEX

Race or Ethnic Group	Male Patients		Female Patients		Total Patients	
	No.	Percent	No.	Percent	No.	Percent
Black	15,325	47.3	4,515	45.7	19,840	46.9
White	10,917	33.7	4,120	41.7	15,037	35.6
Puerto Rican	3,046	9.4	569	5.8	3,615	8.5
Mexican-Amer.	2,745	8.4	499	5.1	3,244	7.7
Other	385	1.2	172	1.7	557	1.3
Total	32,418	100.0	9,875	100.0	42,293	100.0

Difference in race–ethnic distributions by sex: $p < 0.001$.

were from 67 to 86% male; in all 50 programs, at least 14% of the patients were female. The proportion of females in the DARP population is somewhat higher than that reported from the Lexington and Fort Worth hospitals in the 1960s (1), but similar to the 25% reported from the New York City Narcotics Register for 1973 (11).

4. THE RESEARCH FINDINGS

Regional differences in criminality among 41,530 DARP patients are depicted in Table 3. Inasmuch as drug abuse patients are concentrated in the nation's metropolitan centers, some city tabulations have been added to the regional classifications.

Over four-fifths of the 41,530 drug abuse patients had been arrested prior to treatment. This overall figure (81.7%) somewhat obscures the higher arrest rates on the East and West Coasts, and the appreciably lower rates in the Midwest and South. The regional differences are statistically significant, with 88% of the Pacific Coast patients reporting prior arrests; only 71% of those in the Southeast part of the nation had been arrested before treatment.

A further analysis of arrest rates within each of the 50 treatment programs revealed a surprising similarity in prior criminality rates; a majority of the programs reported that 80–89% of their patients had been arrested. Although the range was from 44 to 94%, only four programs reported less than 66% with prior arrests.

The research findings reveal marked differences in prior criminality between male and female drug abuse patients. The male patients were more likely to have been arrested prior to treatment, more likely to have had repeated arrests, more often convicted, and more frequently incarcerated than the female patients. Thus, of the 31,850 male drug abuse patients, 86% were arrested prior to treatment, and most of these had been arrested at least four times (Table 4). Conversely, 67% of the 9746 females had been arrested, but only 27% of these had more than four arrests. Thus, the data are consistent in showing a lesser involvement in criminality among the female drug abusers.

In addition to the differential arrest rates by sex, it is worth noting that the drug abuse patients of both sexes include quite distinct patterns of criminal involvement. Almost a fifth of the patients have never been arrested, while some 15% have been arrested over 10 times. Clearly, there are markedly different degrees and types of criminal involvement, apprehension, and judicial disposition among drug abuse patients.

Within this drug abuse population, the lesser number of criminal convictions compared with arrests indicates the general attrition within the criminal justice system due to plea bargaining, extent of cooperation with authorities, seriousness of offense, extent of guilt, socioeconomic status of offender, and prior criminal record. A comparison of the convictions among male and female patients reveals a similar pattern of attrition in that both sexes had markedly fewer convictions than arrests (Table 5). The modal number of convictions for both sexes was one, and less than 4% of the patients had over 10 convictions.

The length of time that offenders spend in jail or prison is a significant social fact in that it indicates the extent of prior officially recognized criminality. Thus, the more serious offenders and recidivists are those who tend to be incarcerated for appreciable periods. From the DARP data, it can be seen that approximately half of the patients had a history of penal incarceration. As in the previous analyses, the females were less likely than the males to be involved in criminal behavior which leads to such official penalties (Table 6). Thus, only 30% of the female patients had been in jail or prison for a month or longer, and only 6% had been incarcerated for three years or longer. By contrast, 54% of the male patients had been confined for more than a month at some period prior to treatment, and 20% of these had been incarcerated for at least three years. The finding that one-fifth of the males had been in prison for three years or longer before their treatment for drug abuse seems especially significant, as it indicates that a sizable proportion of the male patients are deeply enmeshed in a criminal life-style. This is notably less evident among the female patients.

TABLE 3 REGIONAL DISTRIBUTION OF 41,530 DRUG ABUSE PATIENTS BY PERCENT ARRESTED PRIOR TO TREATMENT AND SEX

City, State, or Region of Treatment Program	No. of Programs	No. of Patients	Percent in Region	No. Arrested	Percent Arrested	Percent Male	Percent Female
(1) New England	6	4994	12.0	4195	84.0	80.0	20.0
(2) New York City	6	4036	9.7	3369	83.5	83.6	16.4
(3) New Jersey	3	5125	12.3	4303	84.0	82.2	17.8
(4) Philadelphia	3	5168	12.5	4319	83.6	82.9	17.1
(5) Southeast	8	5982	14.4	4265	71.3	82.0	18.0
(6) Pacific Coast	8	4844	11.7	4253	87.8	74.9	25.1
(7) Southwest	4	3517	8.5	2963	84.2	83.2	16.8
(8) Midwest–Central	12	7864	18.9	6270	79.7	79.3	20.7
Total	50	41,530	100.0	33,937	81.7	80.8	19.2

TABLE 4 NUMBER OF ARRESTS PRIOR TO TREATMENT FOR DARP PATIENTS BY SEX

No. of Arrests	Male Patients		Female Patients		Total Patients	
	No.	Percent	No.	Percent	No.	Percent
None	4378	13.7	3215	33.0	7593	18.3
1	4550	14.3	1873	19.2	6423	15.4
2–3	6882	21.6	1987	20.4	8869	21.3
4–5	4564	14.3	988	10.1	5552	13.3
6–10	5690	17.9	983	10.1	6673	16.0
11 and over	5786	18.2	700	7.2	6486	15.6
Total	31,850	100.0	9,746	100.0	41,596	100.0

Differences in number of arrests by sex: $p < 0.001$.

5. SEX DIFFERENCES IN PATTERNS OF CRIMINALITY AT ONE DARP TREATMENT FACILITY

In considering the greater criminality of the male drug abuse patients as contrasted with the females, it is pertinent to emphasize that both populations include patients with quite diverse patterns of criminality. Some are deeply involved in a criminal lifestyle, while others are only partially committed to illegal activities, and still others are relatively uninvolved in crime, apart from their drug abuse.

In order to delineate more fully the diverse patterns of criminality among

TABLE 5 NUMBER OF CRIMINAL CONVICTIONS PRIOR TO TREATMENT FOR DARP PATIENTS BY SEX

No. of Convictions	Male Patients		Female Patients		Total Patients	
	No.	Percent	No.	Percent	No.	Percent
None	11,148	34.9	5,615	57.6	16,763	40.2
1	11,105	34.8	2,693	27.6	13,798	33.1
2–3	2,794	8.8	507	5.2	3,301	7.9
4–5	3,027	9.5	450	4.6	3.477	8.3
6–10	2,620	8.2	331	3.4	2,951	7.1
11 and over	1,229	3.8	161	1.7	1,390	3.3
Total	31,923	100.0	9,757	100.0	41,680	100.0

Difference in number of convictions by sex: $p < 0.001$.

TABLE 6 LENGTH OF INCARCERATION PRIOR TO TREATMENT FOR DARP PATIENTS BY SEX

No. of Months in Jail or Prison	Male Patients		Female Patients		Total Patients	
	No.	Percent	No.	Percent	No.	Percent
None	14,811	45.7	6,872	69.6	21,683	51.3
1	1,238	3.8	429	4.3	1,667	3.9
2–6	3,620	11.2	888	9.0	4,508	10.7
7–12	2,210	6.8	392	4.0	2,602	6.2
13–37	4,173	12.9	667	6.8	4,840	11.4
37 and over	6,365	19.6	627	6.3	6,992	16.6
Total	32,417	100.0	9,875	100.0	42,292	100.0

Difference in incarceration by sex: $p < 0.001$.

male and female DARP patients, a reanalysis of criminological data from one of the largest DARP methadone treatment facilities was undertaken. The treatment program and its addict population have previously been described (3); for the purposes of this paper, the detailed criminological findings have been reexamined to substantiate and elucidate the findings from the national data base.

From a population of 924 patients in methadone maintenance treatment, a sample of 224 was systematically selected and interviewed; these patients were generally similar to the DARP population with respect to such demographic characteristics as sex, age, and race. With respect to criminality, these 224 patients were also quite similar to the national sample; 87% of the males and 64% of the females had been arrested prior to treatment.

Four quite different patterns of association between crime and drug abuse were found to exist among these 224 drug abuse patients (Table 7). First, there were those patients who had only been arrested for drug-related offenses; this group constituted some one-third of the sample. Second, there were those who had only been arrested for non–drug-related offenses; this group comprised less than one-fifth of the patients. Third, there were those patients who had been arrested for both types of offenses (drug-related as well as non–drug-related); this group consisted of two-fifth of the patients. And fourth, there were those who had never been arrested constituting some 16 percent of the sample.

As might be expected, the female drug abuse patients were less involved in criminality than the males. Almost three times as many females as males had not been arrested (36% versus 13%); of those arrested, fewer of the

TABLE 7 CRIMINAL HISTORY OF 224 METHADONE MAINTENANCE PATIENTS PRIOR TO TREATMENT BY SEX, NUMBER OF ARRESTS, TYPE OF ARRESTS, AND ONSET SEQUENCE OF DRUG USE AND ARREST

	Male Patients (N = 196)					Female Patients (N = 28)				
Arrest History Typology	No.	Type (%)	Total Arrests (No.)	Drug Arrests (No.)	Drug Use before Arrests (%)	No.	Type (%)	Total Arrests (No.)	Drug Arrests (No.)	Drug Use before Arrests (%)
Drug arrests only	54	27.6	454	454	87	9	32.1	54	54	89
Other arrests only	32	16.3	229	—	41	5	17.9	40	—	60
Both types of arrest	85	43.4	1040	546	38	4	14.3	62	11	67
No arrests	25	12.8	—	—	100	10	35.7	—		100
Total	196	100.0	1723	1000	54[a]	28	100.0	156	64	72[a]

[a] Percent of those arrested.

females were involved in non-drug-related arrests. In addition, the mean number of arrests for the females was less than that for the males (8.7 versus 10.1 arrests).

Although the number of arrests among both male and female patients tends to increase with age (Table 8), it is significant that the four patterns of association between drug abuse and criminality persist. Thus, the pattern of drug arrests only, of nondrug arrests only, of mixed types of arrests, and of no arrests are not merely a correlate of age. Rather, these diverse patterns of criminality reflect quite different life-styles among the male and female drug abuse patients which persist over the years. As a consequence, male and female patterns of criminality prior to treatment seem clearly related to post-treatment criminality and the different "natural histories" which have been so carefully traced in follow-up studies of opiate addict patients (4, 12, 15).

6. INTERPRETATION OF THE RESEARCH FINDINGS

The present national research findings indicate that a majority of drug abuse patients are consistently involved in criminal behavior prior to treatment. Over 80% of the drug abusers had been arrested at least once, 66% had two or more arrests, 60% had one or more criminal conviction, and 28% had been in prison for one or more years.

This considerable involvement in criminal behavior leading to arrest, conviction, and imprisonment actually underestimates the extent of the subjects' criminality, as it is known that only a small proportion of criminal behavior results in apprehension and arrest. The President's Commission on Law Enforcement and Administration of Justice reported that only 25% of reported crimes resulted in arrests (14). With regard to drug abusers specifically, Chambers (2, p. 137) reported that less than 1% of their offenses (both drug offenses and non-drug-related offenses) resulted in arrests. In this context, officially recorded crime may be viewed as an index of involvement in criminal behavior, rather than as a catalog of the number and type of offenses committed (7).

Although the present analysis has relied primarily upon data pertaining to official records of criminality, it is relevant to note that 43% of the 32,418 male drug abusers and 34% of the 9,875 female drug abusers stated that they had a steady illegal source of income (numbers, drug selling, theft, prostitution). These data, even more than that of arrest, delineate the continual involvement in criminal behavior patterns among the majority of these narcotic addicts.

TABLE 8 MEAN PRETREATMENT ARRESTS OF MALE AND FEMALE PATIENTS BY AGE AT TIME OF TREATMENT

Age of Patient	Male Patients: Arrest History Yes	Male Patients: Arrest History No	Male Patients: Mean Arrests[a]	Male Patients: Percent Drug Arrests[a]	Female Patients: Arrest History Yes	Female Patients: Arrest History No	Female Patients: Mean Arrests[a]	Female Patients: Percent Drug Arrests[a]
17–19	14	2	5.1	56.9	1	2	2.0	50.0
20–24	68	16	8.7	49.7	5	2	4.2	90.5
25–29	32	1	6.7	40.8	3	1	5.0	80.0
30–39	29	3	11.1	35.3	8	3	11.4	36.3
40–49	22	3	20.7	66.9	1	2	27.0	0.0
50 and over	6	0	13.3	93.8	—	—	—	—
Total	171	25	10.1	52.8	18	10	8.7	41.7

[a] Percent of those arrested.

7. CONCLUSION

The present study was undertaken in order to delineate the extent and type of criminal behavior pursued by male and female drug abusers in the United States prior to their seeking treatment. It was found that there are definite patterns of criminality associated with persistent drug abuse; four major patterns of association between drug abuse and crime were delineated. These patterns of pretreatment criminality were found to be related to sex differences; the male patients were more frequently and seriously involved in criminal behavior than the female patients.

REFERENCES

1. Ball, J. C. and W. M. Bates, Nativity, parentage, and mobility of opiate addicts, in *The Epidemiology of Opiate Addiction in the United States,* p. 101.
2. Ball, J. C. and C. D. Chambers, *The Epidemiology of Opiate Addiction in the United States,* Charles C Thomas, Springfield, Ill., 1970.
3. Ball, J. C., H. Graff, and J. J. Sheehan, Jr., The heroin addicts' view of methadone maintenance, *Br. J. Addict.,* **69,** 87 (1974).
4. Ball, J. C. and R. W. Snarr, A test of the maturation hypothesis with respect to opiate addiction, *Bull. Narc.,* **12,** 9 (1969).
5. Butler, M. C., *DARP Population Description: A Description of Certain Characteristics of the Patients Admitted to the Joint NIDA–TCU Drug Abuse Reporting Program from December 1971 through March 1973,* Fort Worth, Texas, Texas Christian University, IBR Report No. 74-10, 1974.
6. Glasscote, R., J. N. Sussex, J. H. Jaffe, J. Ball, and L. Brill, *The Treatment of Drug Abuse,* American Psychiatric Association, Washington, D.C. (1972).
7. Inciardi, J. A., The villification of euphoria: Some perspectives on an elusive issue, *Addict. Dis.,* **1,** 3, 241 (1974).
8. Inciardi, J. A. and C. D. Chambers, *Drugs and the Criminal Justice System,* Sage Publications, Beverly Hills, Calif. (1974).
9. Long, G. L. and R. G. Demaree, *Indicators of Criminality during Treatment for Drug Abuse,* Texas Christian University, Fort Worth, Texas, IBR Report No. 74-27, 1974.
10. National Commission on Marihuana and Drug Abuse, Technical Papers of the Second Report. *Vol. 1: Patterns and Consequences of Drug Use, Part Two, Drugs and Anti-social Behavior,* U.S. Government Printing Office, Washington, 1973, pp. 240.
11. Newman, R. G., M. Cates, A. Tytun, and B. Werbell, Narcotic addiction in New York City: Trends from 1968 to mid-1973, *Am. J. Drug Alcohol Abuse,* **1,** 58 (1974).
12. O'Donnell, J. A., *Narcotic Addicts in Kentucky,* U.S. Government Printing Office, Washington, 1969.
13. Sells, S. B. (Ed.), *Studies of the Effectiveness of Treatment of Drug Abuse, Vol. 1, Evaluation of Treatments.* Ballinger, Cambridge, Mass., 1974.

14. Task Force Report: *Science and Technology*, A Report to the President's Commission on Law Enforcement and Administration of Justice, U.S. Government Printing Office, Washington, p. 8, 1967.

15. Vaillant, G. E., The natural history of a chronic disease, *N. Engl. J. Med.*, **275,** 1282, (1966).

INDEX